HISTORY AND RELATED DISCIPLINES
SELECT BIBLIOGRAPHIES
GENERAL EDITOR: R. C. RICHARDSON

SOCIETY AND ECONOMY
IN EARLY MODERN EUROPE,
1450–1789

HISTORY AND RELATED DISCIPLINES
SELECTED BIBLIOGRAPHIES
GENERAL EDITOR: R. C. RICHARDSON

Bibliographical guides designed to meet the needs of undergraduates, postgraduates and their teachers in universities, polytechnics, and colleges of higher education. All volumes in the series share a number of common characteristics. They are selective, manageable in size, and include those books and articles which are most important and useful. All volumes are edited by practising teachers of the subject and are based on their experience of the needs of students. The arrangement combines chronological with thematic divisions. Most of the items listed receive some descriptive comment.

Uniform with this volume
THE STUDY OF HISTORY
RUSSIA AND EASTERN EUROPE, 1789 – 1985

In preparation:
ANCIENT GREECE AND ROME
BRITISH ARCHAEOLOGY
NORTH AMERICAN HISTORY, 1492 – 1980
AFRICA, ASIA AND SOUTH AMERICA, 1800 – 1980
JAPANESE STUDIES
WOMEN'S HISTORY IN BRITAIN

SOCIETY AND ECONOMY IN EARLY MODERN EUROPE, 1450–1789

A BIBLIOGRAPHY OF POST-WAR RESEARCH

COMPILED BY

BARRY TAYLOR

MANCHESTER UNIVERSITY PRESS
Manchester and New York
Distributed exclusively in the USA and Canada by
St. Martin's Press

Published by
MANCHESTER UNIVERSITY PRESS
Oxford Road, Manchester M13 9PL, UK
and Room 400, 175 Fifth Avenue, New York, NY 10010, USA
Distributed exclusively in the USA and Canada
by St. Martin's Press, Inc., 175 Fifth Avenue, New York,
NY 10010, USA

Reprinted in 1990

British Library cataloguing in publication data
Taylor, Barry
    Society and economy in early modern Europe, 1450–1789. —
    (History and related disciplines select bibliographies).
    1. Europe. Social conditions, 1450–1789. Bibliographies
    I. Title.
    016.9402'1

Library of Congress cataloging in publication data
Taylor, Barry.
    Society and economy in early modern Europe, 1450–1789
    / compiled by Barry Taylor.
    p.   cm. — (History and related disciplines select bibliographies)
    1. Europe—Economic conditions. 2. Europe—Social conditions.
    I. Title. II. Series.
    HC240.T356 1989
    330.94'02—dc19
            ISBN 0 7190 1948 6 *hardback*

Photoset in Linotron Plantin
by Northern Phototypesetting Company, Bolton
Printed in Great Britain
at The Camelot Press, Trowbridge, Wiltshire.

CONTENTS

General editor's preface—ix
Preface—x
Abbreviations—xii

1 HISTORIOGRAPHY AND METHODOLOGY

General works	1
The Annales school	2
Biography and assessment of individual historians	3

2 GENERAL SURVEYS

Works covering long time-span	6
Bibliographies	6
Source material	6
Monographs and articles	7
Fifteenth and sixteenth centuries	10
c.1550-1700	10
c.1660-1789	11
The debate on capitalism	12

3 NATIONAL, REGIONAL, AND LOCAL HISTORY

France	15
Historiography and sources	15
National surveys: general	15
c.1450-1700	16
Eighteenth century	16
Provincial and local studies	17
The Low Countries	18
Spain and Portugal	19
Historiography and sources	19
Spain: works covering long time-span	20
Spain: to c.1650	21
Spain: 1650-1800	21
Spanish regions and provinces	22
Portugal	23
Italy	23
Historiography and sources	23
National history	23
Individual states and regions	24
Germany and Switzerland	26
Historiography and sources	26
Germany: works covering long time-span	26
Germany: to 1648	27
Thirty Years' War	27
1648-1800	28
German states and regions	28
Switzerland	28
Habsburg territories and East Central Europe	28
Historiography and sources	28
General surveys	29
Hungary	29
Poland	30
Other regions	30
Turkey and the Balkans	30
Historiography and sources	30
General surveys	31
Individual countries and regions	32
Scandinavia and the Baltic region	32
Historiography and sources	32
General surveys	33
Sweden: works covering long time-span	33
Sweden: special periods	33
Other Scandinavian countries	33
Russia and the Baltic Duchies	34
Historiography and sources	34
Works covering long time-span	34

Pre-Petrine Russia 35
Russia after 1689 35
Regional and local history 36

4 GEOGRAPHY AND ENVIRONMENT

General works 37
Climate 38
Natural resources 39
Transport and communications 40
Settlement patterns 42
Regions and regional disparities 42
Europe and the wider world. Expansion and its effects 43

5 DEMOGRAPHY

Methods and models. Population levels and rates 46
France 50
Low Countries 52
Spain and Portugal 53
Italy 54
Germany, Switzerland and Austria 55
East Central Europe 56
Turkey and the Balkans 56
Scandinavia 57
Russia and the Baltic provinces 58
Sexual behaviour 59
France 60
Other regions 61
Family, kinship, and household. Marriage and inheritance 61
Bibliographies 61
General 61
France 63
Low Countries 65
Spain and Italy 66
Germany, Switzerland, and Austria 66
Eastern and Northern Europe 67
Life cycle: childhood, youth, old age 69
Infancy, childhood and adolescence 69
Old age 71
Women in family and society 72
Migration, settlement, and colonisation 75
Ethnic groups. Minorities 76
Racial-religious intolerance in Spain
1. General works, antisemitism 76
2. The Moriscos 77
Jews in other European countries 78
Other groups 81

6 SOCIAL STRATIFICATION ESTATES AND ORDERS

General works. Status, wealth, and social mobility 83

France 84
Other states and regions 85
Elites. Nobility, patricians, and upper bourgeoisie 86
France 86
Low Countries 89
Spain 90
Italy 91
Germany, Switzerland, and Austria 93
Eastern Europe: general 94
Bohemia, Hungary, and Poland 94
Balkans 95
Scandinavia 95
Russia and the Baltic provinces 95
Middling and lower classes 97
Servants 98
Slaves 98

7 RURAL SOCIETY

General works. Peasant economy and tenure. Estate management 99
France 101
French village studies 103
Low Countries 104
Spain and Portugal 104
Italy 106
Germany, Switzerland, and Austria 107
Eastern Europe: general 110
Bohemia, Hungary, and Poland 110
Turkey and the Balkans 111
Scandinavia 112
Russia and the Baltic provinces 113
Agricultural productivity, crops, and techniques 114
General productivity. Cereals cultivation and yields 114
Farming methods and innovations. New crops 116
Viticulture 117
Animal husbandry 118

8 CITIES AND TOWNS

General works 119
Historiography and methodology 119
General history 119
Regional surveys and history of individual cities 121
France 121
Low Countries 122
Spain and Portugal 123
Italy 124
Germany, Switzerland, and Austria 125
East Central Europe 126
Turkey and the Balkans 127
Scandinavia 127

Russia 128
Urban morphology and design 129

9 COMMERCE AND INDUSTRY

Trade, enterprise, and investment. General
works 131
  France 132
  Low Countries 133
    Netherlands ports and trading centres 134
  Spain and Portugal 135
  Italy 135
  Switzerland and Germany 136
  East Central Europe and the Balkans 137
  Northern Europe 138
Aristocracy and business enterprise 139
Regional and colonial trade. Routes and ports 140
  Baltic and North Sea trade: general 140
  Baltic and North Sea trade: ports and
  trading centres 142
  Mediterranean and Levant trade: general 143
  Mediterranean and Levant trade: ports and
  trading centres 144
  Colonial trade: general 145
  Atlantic and Transatlantic trade: general 145
  Atlantic ports 147
  Trade with the Orient 148
Commodities traded 149
  Agricultural produce: general works 149
  Grain trade 149
  Other crops and comestibles 150
  Salt 151
  Fisheries 151
  Timber 151
  Wool and textile raw materials 151
  Slave trade 152
Banking and insurance 152
Industry. General works. The proto-
industrialisation debate 155
  France and the Low Countries 156
  Spain and Italy 156
  Germany, Switzerland, Austria 157
  Bohemia, Hungary, Poland 158
  Scandinavia 158
  Russia 158
Technology and engineering 158
Labour organisation and conditions 160
Particular industries 161
  Textiles 161
  Mining and metallurgy 164
  Building 166
  Glassmaking 166
  Shipbuilding and seafaring 166
  Other industries and crafts 167

10 STATE AND SOCIETY

Political sociology. State formation. Courts and
clientage 168
  France 170
  Low Countries 171
  Spain and Italy 171
  Holy Roman Empire and Switzerland 171
  Eastern and Northern Europe 172
Economic thought and policy 173
  France and the Low Countries 174
  Spain and Portugal 175
  Italy 176
  Holy Roman Empire 176
  Eastern and Northern Europe 177
Taxation and public finance 178
  France 178
  Low Countries 180
  Spain and Portugal 181
  Italy 181
  Holy Roman Empire and Switzerland 182
  Eastern and Northern Europe 183
Bureaucrats and lawyers. The administrative
elite 183
  France 184
  Other states and principalities 186
Police. Crime and punishment. Litigation 189
  France 190
  Low Countries 192
  Spain 193
  Italy 193
  Germany and Switzerland 194
  Eastern and Northern Europe 194
Armed forces and the impact of war 194
  France 196
  Low Countries 197
  Spain 197
  Italy 197
  Holy Roman Empire and Switzerland 197
  Eastern and Northern Europe 198

11 LIVING STANDARDS, HEALTH, AND WELFARE

Money, prices, and wages 200
  France 201
  Low Countries 202
  Spain and Portugal 203
  Italy 204
  Central, Eastern, and Northern Europe 204
Metrology 205
Food supplies and diet 206
  France 207
  Other regions 208
Housing and clothing 209
Poverty and charity 210
  France and the Low Countries 210

Spain 212
Italy 212
Germany, Switzerland, and Austria 213
Disease and medical services 214
France 215
Low Countries 216
Spain 217
Italy 218
Germany and Switzerland 219
•Eastern and Northern Europe 219
Mental illness 220

12 SOCIAL CONFLICT. PROTEST, REBELLION, CIVIL WAR

General surveys 221
France: general 223
The Wars of Religion in France 224
The Fronde 225
Low Countries 225
Spain: general 226
The Comunero Revolt 226
Italy 226
Germany, Switzerland, and Austria: general 227
The German Peasant War of 1525 228
Eastern and Northern Europe 229
Pugachev's Revolt 230

13 RELIGION AND SOCIETY

General works. Church and community. Popular piety 231
France 233
Low Countries 234
Spain and Portugal 235
Italy 235
Germany 236
Eastern Europe 237
The clergy. Recruitment, finances, and institutions 237
France 237
Spain and Italy 238

Germany and Switzerland 239
Turkey and the Balkans 240
Russia 240
The impact of the Reformation 240
The German Reformation 241
Calvinism. Huguenots. The French and Dutch Reformations 244
Movements and sects 247
The radical Reformation. Anabaptism 247
Jansenism 248
Other movements 249
The Inquisition 249
Witchcraft and the occult 250
France, Switzerland, and the Low Countries 252
Spain and Italy 252
Germany and Austria 253
Eastern Europe 253

14 CULTURAL AND MENTAL HORIZONS

General works. Values; beliefs; customs and recreations 254
France and the Low Countries 256
Spain and Italy 258
Central, Northern, and Eastern Europe 259
Attitudes to death 260
Education and literacy 261
France and the Low Countries 262
Spain and Italy 264
Germany 265
Eastern and Northern Europe 266
Learning and the arts 267
Elite culture. Courts, academies, and the learned community 267
Printing. Books and their readers 269
Science 273
Theatres and entertainments 275
The visual arts 276
Music 277

Topographical index—279
Index of authors and editors—284

GENERAL EDITOR'S PREFACE

History, to an even greater extent than most other academic disciplines, has developed at a prodigious pace in the twentieth century. Its scope has extended and diversified, its methodologies have been revolutionized, its philosophy has changed, and its relations with other disciplines have been transformed. The number of students and teachers of the subject in the different branches of higher education has vastly increased, and there is an ever-growing army of amateurs, many of them taking adult education courses. Academic and commercial publishers have produced a swelling stream of publications – both specialist and general – to cater for this large and expanding audience. Scholarly journals have proliferated. It is no easy matter even for the specialist to keep abreast of the flow of publications in his particular field. For those with more general academic interests the task of finding what has been written on different subject areas can be time-consuming, perplexing, and often frustrating.

It is primarily to meet the needs of undergraduates, postgraduates and their teachers in universities, polytechnics, and colleges of higher education, that this series of bibliographies is designed. It will be a no less valuable resource, however, to the reference collection of any public library, school or college.

Though common sense demands that each volume will be structured in the way which is most appropriate for the particular field in question, nonetheless all volumes in the series share a number of important common characteristics. First – quite deliberately – all are *select* bibliographies, manageable in size, and include those books and articles which in the editor's judgement are most important and useful. To attempt an uncritically comprehensive listing would needlessly dictate the inclusion of items which were frankly ephemeral, antiquarian, or discredited and result only in the production of a bulky and unwieldy volume. Like any select bibliography, however, this series will direct the reader where appropriate to other, more specialised and detailed sources of bibliographical information. That would be one of its functions. Second, all the volumes are edited not simply by specialists in the different fields but by practising teachers of the subject, and are based on their experience of the needs of students in higher education. Third, there are common features of arrangement and presentation. All volumes begin with listings of general works of a methodological or historiographical nature, and proceed within broad chronological divisions to arrange their material thematically. Most items will receive some descriptive comment. Each volume, for ease of reference, has an index of authors and editors.

R. C. RICHARDSON

ix

PREFACE

Until very recently it was impossible to refer students to any convenient retrospective bibliographies which attempted broad coverage of the post-medieval economic and social history of continental Europe, and took adequate account of the new directions that have come to dominate research since the 1950s. The appearance of D. H. Aldcroft and R. Rodger's *Bibliography of European Economic and Social History* (also published by Manchester University Press) brought welcome relief to this situation for the period of the Industrial Revolution and after, though regrettably, if understandably, its coverage is restricted to English-language material.

The present work aims to provide a comparable guide for the early modern period. Since the literature is not so overwhelming in bulk, it is conceived in rather more ambitious terms linguistically, and my hope is that it will prove useful in the early stages of research work as well as to teachers, undergraduates, and sixth-formers. Even so, it remains highly selective, of course, as any single-volume bibliography must, and all the more so given the shifting and ill-defined frontiers of social history. As the title indicates, I have concentrated essentially on material published since the Second World War, because of the great changes in method, range, and volume of writing that have

marked these decades; but in notes and occasional entries I have also indicated a few of the many valuable older works on which research has built. No publications later in date than 1987 are included, and scrutiny for the two or three years before that has inevitably been somewhat patchy in nature.

Within these terms, I have tried to be as comprehensive as possible as far as literature in English is concerned – the principal disclaimer here being a reluctance to venture very far into the historiography of economic theory (especially that concerning individual thinkers) or that of colonial activity. Foreign language publications called for a much finer sieve. It seemed essential to include a fair sprinkling of untranslated work by French historians, whose innovative spirit has been particularly directed towards the *ancien régime*; and to call attention to the productivity and range of such outstanding historians as Hermann Kellenbenz, Peter Blickle, or Antonio Domínguez Ortiz. On the other hand to extend that philosophy to contributions in Norwegian, Greek, or the Slav languages would impose unrealistic ambitions on both bibliographer and the majority of potential users. The languages most accessible to an Anglo-Saxon audience, it seemed clear, are French, German, Italian, and Spanish; and beyond these, except for occasional bibliographical items, I have not ventured, in the hope that the utility of this decision would outweigh the undoubted skew which it gives to the bibliography's geographical coverage. Only a few principal national journals have been drawn on for foreign-language articles, and only where such articles approach monograph length or provide useful literature reviews.

The French Revolution marks the obvious termination, chronologically, for a bibliography of early modern Europe; a convenient starting place is a more debateable matter. Turning points in economic and social history are not so easily discerned as in the realms of war, politics, and ideas. The plagues of the mid-fourteenth century could certainly be regarded as one such decisive break in continuity, but I have preferred to begin more traditionally with the commercial revival and consequent geographical discoveries of the later fifteenth. Only from this period onwards does the abundant documentation already discernible for the Mediterranean region and the South German cities begin to colour the historiographical record for Europe as a whole.

The classification scheme is designed primarily to foster topical and comparative study, though I have tried by extensive cross-referencing to avoid repetition of items which straddle two or more subjects. Bibliographies have generally been given first place under any particular topic; and to aid students needing to take a national or local approach general works are then followed by a set geographical sequence, sometimes explicitly signalled, sometimes – to avoid a multiplicity of headings – simply indicated through departures from the prevailing alphabetic arrangement by author or editor. This sequence runs as follows: France – the Low Countries – Spain and Portugal – Italy – Germany, Switzerland, and Austria –Bohemia, Hungary, and Poland (these last two goups sometimes rearranged to allow for political boundaries) – Turkey and the Balkans – Scandinavia – Russia and the Baltic

duchies. (For working purposes Europe's eastern boundary has been taken to follow a line running roughly from the Urals to the Syrian coast, thus bringing Anatolia and Asia Minor into the coverage.) Geography rather than authorship has also been allowed to dictate the order of entries at numerous other points, for example where it seemed convenient to cluster material relating to a particular city or minor state. A topographical index of smaller units (provinces, towns, etc.) provides further help for the local approach.

Book citations refer generally to the first edition, and to British imprints in preference to any other; only substantially revised subsequent editions are noted. First place of publication only is given where publishers have multiple offices. Where foreign works have been translated, the English-language version has usually been cited, with a brief indication of when and in what language the original appeared.

The explanatory notes are in the main designed to place entries in their scholarly context, or to provide further information on scope, length, documentary basis, review articles provoked, etc. Needless to say, they reflect also the fact that I have drawn heavily on the specialist expertise of others, both published and informally garnered (I have looked at the great majority of items noted, but often, of course, only in a superficial way). Many entries originated in suggestions and recommendations of colleagues and former colleagues at the University of East Anglia: notably Jim Casey and Oliver Logan (Spanish and Italian history respectively), David Sabean (Germany), and Vic Morgan (general aims and methodology of social history). Ann Wood's speedy inter-library loan service was invaluable in cutting down the amount of travel required to check citations. I owe a special debt of gratitude to my wife, Ann, for much patient and unrewarding labour in checking the cross-references, and her skill in assembling the indexes.

ABBREVIATIONS

Acad. Academy, académie, etc.
Agric. Agriculture, agricultural
Am. American
Ann. Annales
Annales Used in full to represent *Annales.*
Économies, Sociétés, Civilisations
Arch. Archiv, archives, etc.
Assoc. Association
Bibl. Bibliothèque
Bibliog. Bibliographical
Bijd. Bijdragen
Boll. Bolletino
Bull. Bulletin
Bus. Business
Cah. Cahiers
Can. Canadian
Cath. Catholic
Cent. Century
Comp. Comparative
Contemp. Contemporary, contemporaine
Dev. Development
Dt. Deutsch(e)
Ec. Economic
Eccles. Ecclesiastical
Educ. Education
Entrepren. Entrepreneurial
Estud. Estudios
Ét. Études
Ethnol. Ethnology/ist
Eur. European
Explor. Explorations
Forsch. Forschungen
Fr. French, Français
Geog. Geography/ical
Ger. German
Gesch. Geschichte
Geschied. Geschiedenis
Hisp. Hispanic

Hist. History, histoire, etc; historical
Inst. Institute
Int. International
Interdisc. Interdisciplinary
Ital. Italy, Italian(o)
J. Journal
Jb. Jahrbuch
Lib. Library
Med. Medieval
Meded. Mededelingen
Mediterr. Mediterranean
Mél. Mélanges
Mid.E. Middle East
Mitteil. Mitteilungen
Mod. Modern(e)
n.s. New series
Nat. National
Newsl. Newsletter
Österr. Österreichisch
Osteur. Osteuropa/äisch
P.& P. *Past and Present*
Pap. Papers
Phil. Philosophy/ical
Pol. Politics, political
Pop. Population
Proc. Proceedings
Q. Quarterly
Relig. Religion, religious
Renaiss. Renaissance
Res. Research
Rev. Review, revue
Revol. Revolution
Riv. Rivista
Roy. Royal
Russ. Russian
Scan. Scandinavian
Sci. Science, scientific
Soc. Society, social

Sociol. Sociology/ical
Sov. Soviet, soviétique
Stor. Storico
Stud. Studies
Tech. Technology/ical
Tijd. Tijdschrift

Trans. Transactions
Univ. University/ies
VSWG *Vierteljahrschrift für Sozial- und Wirtschaftsgeschichte*
Yrbk. Yearbook
Zeitschr. Zeitschrift

1

HISTORIOGRAPHY
AND METHODOLOGY

GENERAL WORKS

*See also 2.16; and entries under particular topics
– e.g. for historiography of debate on origins of capitalism see 2.108-43.*

1.1 **Braudel**, F., 'History and the social sciences', in P. Burke, ed., *Economy and Society in Early Modern Europe. Essays from Annales*, 1972, 11-42. Transl. from *Annales*, 13, 1958, 723-53. Expounds his concept of different temporal perspectives, and its relevance to methodology of social science.

1.2 —— *On History*, Chicago, 1980. Transl. from French ed. of 1969. Collection of occasional pieces and reviews, incl. previous entry. Review article (of original): J. H. M. Salmon, *Hist.& Theory*, 10, 1971, 347-55.

1.3 **Burke**, P., *Sociology and History*, 1980. Clear and balanced discussion by scholar of early modern popular culture.

1.4 **Chaunu**, P., *Histoire Quantitative, Histoire Sérielle*, Paris, 1978. Essay collection, mainly on compilation and use of time series, by leading proponent of their application to analysis of early modern economy and society.

1.5 **Clubb**, J. M., and Scheuch, E. K., eds., *Historical Social Research. The Use of Historical and Process-Produced Data*, Stuttgart, 1980. Mainly on general aspects of data processing, but contains some relevant case-studies.

1.6 'Economic history. Retrospect and prospect', *J.Ec.Hist.*, 31, 1971, 3-258. Conference papers. Note D. Herlihy and H. Miskimin on developments in early

modern field (153-64, 172-83).

1.7 **Febvre**, L., (ed. P. Burke), *A New Kind of History. From the Writings of [Lucien] Febvre*, 1973. Illustrates, in methodological articles and case studies, Febvre's stress on studying *mentalités*. Transl. from his collections *Combats Pour l'Histoire* (1953); *Au Coeur Religieux du 16e Siècle* (1957); *Pour une Histoire à Part Entière* (1962).

1.8 **Gaunt**, D., *Memoir on History and Anthropology*, Stockholm, 1982. Short monograph which surveys work in progress in Europe and the U.S., much of which has early modern focus. For two views on use of anthropological insights by historians of this period, see K. Thomas, 'History and anthropology', *P.& P.*, 24, 1963, 3-24; and H. Medick, ' "Missionaries in the row boat"? Ethnological ways of knowing as a challenge to social history', *Comp.Stud.Soc.& Hist.*, 29, 1987, 76-98.

1.9 **Gilbert**, F., and Graubard, S. R., eds., *Historical Studies Today*, New York, 1972. Originally publ. in *Daedalus*, 100, 1971. Note L. Stone on 'Prosopography' (107-40) and P. Goubert on 'Local history' (300-14); some other contributions separately listed below.

1.10 *Histoire Sociale: Sources et Méthodes. Colloque de l'École Normale Supérieure de Saint-Cloud*, Paris, 1967. Includes discussion of early modern source

1.11 **Iggers**, G. G., *New Directions in European Historiography*, Middletown, Conn., 1975. 2nd ed., 1985. Useful for its treatment of *Annales* school and Marxist approach to social history. Review article: P. L. Ward, *Hist.& Theory*, 15, 1976, 202-12.

1.12 **Irsigler**, F., ed., *Quantitative Methoden in der Wirtschafts- und Sozialgeschichte der Neuzeit*, Stuttgart, 1978. Ten case-studies (in German), incl. J.-P. Bardet and Ingrid Bátori on computers in early modern urban history research; and Micheline Baulant on inventories.

1.13 **Kammen**, M. L., ed., *The Past Before Us. Contemporary Historical Writing in the U.S.*, Ithaca, N.Y., 1980. Note W. Bouwsma on historians of early modern Europe (78-94).

1.14 **Le Goff**, J., and others, eds., *La Nouvelle Histoire (Les Encyclopédies du Savoir Moderne)*, Paris, 1978. Dictionary-encyclopedia, carrying some quite lengthy articles, and esp. useful on approaches to, concepts in, and some leading practitioners of, early modern history.

1.15 —— and Nora, P., eds., *Faire de l'Histoire*, 3 vols., Paris, 1974. Collection of papers on new problems, approaches, and aims, several by early modern specialists (P. Chaunu, E. Le Roy Ladurie, A. Burguière, etc.). Selection publ. in English as *Constructing the Past*, Cambridge, 1985.

1.16 **Le Roy Ladurie**, E., *Le Territoire de l'Historien*, 2 vols., Paris, 1973-78. Collected essays and reviews, partially transl. as *The Territory of the Historian*, 1979 (vol.1); and *The Mind and Method of the Historian*, 1981 (vol.2). Note also his collection of shorter (mostly newspaper) reviews, *Parmi les Historiens*, Paris, 1983.

1.17 **Mousnier**, R., and Pillorget, R., 'Contemporary history and historians of the sixteenth and seventeenth centuries', *J.Contemp.Hist.*, 3 (ii), 1968, 93-109. Alleges that modern preoccupations and dogmas, particularly Marxism, have coloured approach to early modern history.

1.18 **Rabb**, T. K., and Rotberg, R. I., eds., *The New History. The 1980s and Beyond*, Princeton, N.J., 1982. Symposium first publ. in *J.Interdisc.Hist.*, 12, 1981, 1-332. Among contributors drawing to a considerable extent on early modern examples note L. Stone on family history (51-87); D. Herlihy on quantification (115-35); E. A. Wrigley on demography (207-26); B. S. Cohn, J. W. Adams, Natalie Z. Davis, and C. Ginzburg on anthropology and history (227-78).

1.19 **Stone**, L., *The Past and the Present*, 1981. Though primarily a historian of early modern England, Stone's collected essays and reviews have broad historiographical interest. Includes well-known expression of disillusion with quantitative history, 'The revival of narrative' (first publ. in *P.& P.*, 85, 1979; cf. criticisms of E. Hobsbawm, *ib.*, 86, 1980, 3-8; and of C. Tilly, *Review*, 7, 1984, 363-406). Revised ed., *The Past and the Present Revisited*, 1987, reprints sharp exchanges with Michel Foucault on latter's historical competence.

1.20 **Tilly**, C., *As Sociology Meets History*, New York, 1981. Essay collection, partly methodological, partly exemplary, by important contributor to debate on pre-industrial social conflict.

1.21 **Topolski**, J., 'The model method in economic history', *J.Eur.Ec.Hist.*, 1, 1972, 713-26. Uses several early modern examples, for example Mauro's on implications of overseas expansion (4.113).

1.22 **Wilson**, C. H., 'The historical study of economic growth and decline in early modern history', in *Cambridge Economic History of Europe*, 5, (2.15), 1-41. Methodological considerations.

THE ANNALES SCHOOL
See also 1.11,63; 4.1; 14.4,16,69,114

1.23 **Aymard**, M., '*Annales* and French historiography (1929-72)', *J.Eur.Ec.Hist.*, 1, 1972, 491-511.

1.24 **Forster**, R., 'The achievements of the *Annales* school', *J.Ec.Hist.*, 38, 1978, 58-75. Argues that these historians, perhaps because of early modern period orientation, have been happier to draw on sociology and anthropology than on economic theory and statistical methods.

1.25 **Furet**, F., 'Beyond the *Annales*', *J.Mod.Hist.*, 55, 1983, 389-410. Also appears as introduction to his *In the Workshop of History*, Chicago, 1984 (transl. from French ed. of 1982). Indicates variety of approaches masked by lumping *Annalistes* together as one historical school.

1.26 'The impact of the *Annales* school on the social sciences', *Review*, 1 (iii-iv), 1978, whole issue. Proceedings of inaugural conference of Fernand Braudel Center at State University of New York (Binghampton), attended by Braudel. Among those giving papers: T. Stoianovich, P. Burke, C. Tilly, M.

Aymard (impact in Italy), H. Inalcik (impact on Ottoman studies), and K. Pomian (impact in Eastern Europe).

1.27 **Pomian**, K., 'L'heure des *Annales*', in P. Nora, ed., *Les Lieux de Mémoire. La Nation*, Paris, 1986, 1, 378-429. Essay which forms part of survey of French historical tradition.

1.28 **Stoianovich**, T., *French Historical Method. The* Annales *Paradigm*, Ithaca, N. Y., 1976. Rather portentous in tone. Review articles: B. Bailyn, *J.Ec.Hist.*, 37, 1977, 1028-34; S. Wilson, *Hist.J.*, 21, 1978, 721-35.

BIOGRAPHY AND ASSESSMENT
OF INDIVIDUAL HISTORIANS
On P. Francastel see 14.400; on E. Le Roy Ladurie, 14.16,23; on R. Mousnier, 6.10.

1.29 **Fulbrook**, Mary, and Skocpol, Theda, 'Destined pathways. The historical sociology of Perry Anderson', in Skocpol, ed., *Vision and Method in Historical Sociology*, 1985, 170-210. On long-serving editor of *New Left Review* and author of *Lineages of the Absolutist State* (10.1).

1.30 **Ariès**, P., *Un Historien du Dimanche*, Paris, 1980. Entertaining autobiography by veteran (and non-professional) social historian of great influence. Review article: P. G. Spagnoli, *J.Family Hist.*, 6, 1981, 434-41. See also 14.116.

1.31 **Braudel**, F., 'Personal testimony', *J.Mod.Hist.*, 44, 1972, 448-67. Recounts his early career and associations, with customary charm. In addition to following entries on Braudel, see 1.1,2,79.

1.32 **Bulhof**, Ilse N., 'The cosmopolitan orientation to history and Fernand Braudel', *Clio*, 11, 1981, 49-63.

1.33 **Burke**, P., 'Fernand Braudel', in J. Cannon, *The Historian at Work*, 1980, 188-201.

1.34 **Hexter**, J. H., 'Fernand Braudel and the *monde Braudellien*', *J.Mod.Hist.*, 44, 1972, 480-539. Repr. in his *On Historians*, Cambridge, Mass., 1979, 61-148. Masterly essay combining analysis of institutional structure of French academic history during Braudel's ascendancy and detailed critique of his *The Mediterranean* (2.57).

1.35 **Kinser**, S., '*Annaliste* paradigm? The

geohistorical structuralism of Fernand Braudel', *Am.Hist.Rev.*, 86, 1981, 63-105.

1.36 *Une Leçon d'Histoire de Fernand Braudel. Châteauvallon, Octobre, 1985*, Paris, 1986. Transcript of conference held shortly before his death to honour Braudel's work. Braudel, in excellent form, comments on papers by many of his old colleagues and disciples.

1.37 **Trevor-Roper**, H. R., 'Fernand Braudel, the *Annales*, and the Mediterranean', *J.Mod.Hist.*, 44, 1972, 466-79. Another assessment primarily concerned with 2.57.

1.38 **Nicholas**, D. M., 'New paths of social history and old paths of historical romanticism. Essay review on the work and thought of Otto Brunner', *J.Soc.Hist.*, 3, 1970, 277-94. German historian (b.1898) who imparted unusually marked social dimension to his speciality of constitutional and administrative history. Prompted by issue of his collected papers *Neue Wege der Verfassungs- und Sozialgeschichte*, 2nd ed., Göttingen, 1968. See also, O. G. Oexle, 'Sozialgeschichte–Begriffsgeschichte–Wirtschaftsgeschichte. Anmerkungen zum Werk Otto Brunners', *VSWG*, 71, 1984, 305-41.

1.39 **Cipolla**, C. M., 'Fortuna plus homini quam consilium valet', in L. P. Curtis, ed., *The Historian's Workshop. Original Essays by Sixteen Historians*, New York, 1970, 65-76. Brief autobiography.

1.40 'Natalie Zemon Davis', in *Visions of History. Interviews with...MARHO, the Radical Historians' Organization*, 1984, 97-122. Influential historian of sixteenth-century France discusses her career.

1.41 **Blomquist**, T. W., 'De Roover on business, banking, and economic thought', *J.Ec.Hist.*, 35, 1975, 821-30. Assessment of Raymond De Roover, leading authority on late medieval and early modern business.

1.42 **Herlihy**, D., 'Raymond de Roover, historian of mercantile capitalism', *J.Eur.Ec.Hist.*, 1, 1972, 755-62.

1.43 **Lapeyre**, H., 'L'oeuvre de Raymond de Roover', *Rev.Hist.Ec.et Soc.*, 53, 1975, 413-24.

1.44 **Bakewell**, P., 'An interview with Antonio Domínguez Ortiz', *Hisp.Am.Hist.Rev.*, 65, 1985, 189-202. Gives brief account of career and modern developments in Spanish historiography.

1.45 **Smith**, D., 'Norbert Elias – established or outsider?', *Sociol.Rev.*, 32, 1984, 367-89. See also Z. Bauman, *Sociology*, 13, 1979, 117-25.

1.46 **Mann**, H. D., *Lucien Febvre. La Pensée Vivante d'un Historien*, Paris, 1971.

1.47 **Mansfield**, B. E., 'Lucien Febvre and the study of religious history', *J.Relig.Hist.*, 1, 1960, 102-11.

1.48 **Throop**, P. A., 'Lucien Febvre', in S. W. Halperin, ed., *Some Twentieth-Century Historians*, Chicago, 1961, 277-98.

1.49 **Major-Poetzl**, Pamela, *Michel Foucault's Archaeology of Western Culture. Towards a New Science of History*, Chapel Hill, N.C., 1983. Commentary on Foucault's arcane philosophy of history and knowledge is very considerable. This work and following items seem most useful for assessment of his contribution to early modern historiography. See also 1.19, 10.371, 11.370, 14.19.

1.50 **Kent**, C. A., 'Michel Foucault: doing history, or undoing it?', *Can.J.Hist.*, 21, 1986, 371-95. Sympathetic view.

1.51 **Megill**, A., 'Foucault, structuralism, and the ends of history', *J.Mod.Hist.*, 51, 1979, 451-503. Strongly critical.

1.52 —— 'Recent writing on Michel Foucault', *ib.*, 56, 1984, 499-511. Review article.

1.53 **Weeks**, J., 'Foucault for historians', *Hist.Workshop*, 14, 1982, 106-19. Helpful.

1.54 **White**, H. V., 'Foucault decoded. Notes from underground', *Hist.& Theory*, 12, 1973, 23-54. Itself takes some decoding.

1.55 **Schutte**, Anne J., 'Carlo Ginzburg', *J.Mod.Hist.*, 48, 1976, 296-315. Notable Italian historian of early modern popular mentality.

1.56 **Zambelli**, Paola, 'From Menocchio to Piero della Francesca. The work of Carlo Ginzburg', *Hist.J.*, 28, 1985, 983-99.

1.57 **Montgomery**, A., 'Eli F. Heckscher', in J. T. Lambie, ed., *Architects and Craftsmen in History. Festschrift for A. P. Usher*, Tübingen, 1956, 119-46. Eminent historian of Swedish economy and mercantilism.

1.58 **Uhr**, C. G., 'Eli F. Heckscher, 1879-1952, and his treatise on mercantilism revisited', *Ec.& Hist.*, 23, 1980, 3-39. Comprises both brief biography, and historiographical review of his most influential work. See also 10.82,100,153.

1.59 'Eric Hobsbawm' in *Visions of History* (1.40), 27-46. Interview with prominent Marxist historian (initiator of "seventeenth-century crisis" debate).

1.60 **Anchor**, R., 'History and play. Johan Huizinga and his critics', *Hist.& Theory*, 17, 1978, 63-93. See also Ilse N. Bulhof, 'Johan Huizinga, ethnographer of the past', *Clio*, 4, 1975, 201-24.

1.61 **Hahn**, F., 'From darkness to revolution in Bohemia. The historical writings of Arnošt Klima', *East-Central Eur.*, 9, 1982, 49-83. See also briefer assessment of this veteran Czech economic historian by R. L. Rudolph, *ib.*, 39-48.

1.62 **Renouvin**, P., 'Ernest Labrousse', in H. A. Schmitt, ed., *Historians of Modern Europe*, Baton Rouge, La., 1971, 235-54.

1.63 **Burrows**, T., ' "Their patron saint and eponymous hero". Jules Michelet and the *Annales* school', *Clio*, 12, 1982, 67-81. Considers how far Michelet has been inspiration for certain preoccupations of modern French historians.

1.64 **Senécal**, Yoland, 'Pour une anthropologie historique du quotidien. Entretien avec Robert Muchembled', *Hist.Sociale/Social Hist.*, 17, 1984, 175-86. Talks about his conception of popular culture. See also 14.23.

1.65 **Kellenbenz**, H., 'Fritz Redlich (1892-1978)', *J.Eur.Ec.Hist.*, 11, 1982, 447-72. Indefatigable scholar and pioneer of entrepreneurial history, who published several studies of early modern businessmen in addition to work on modern era and on theory and methodology.

1.66 **Krantz**, F., ed., *History from below. Studies in Popular Protest and Popular Ideology in Honour of George Rudé*, Montreal, 1985. Contains biography and assessment of Rudé, chiefly by Krantz and H. Stretton, 3-59.

1.67 **Rudé**, G., 'The changing face of the crowd', in Curtis (1.39), 189-204. Rudé's own account of his development as historian.

1.68 **Anderson**, Pauline R., 'Gustav von Schmoller (1838-1917)', in S. W. Halperin, ed., *Essays in Modern European Historiography*, Chicago, 1970, 289-317. See also F. C. Lane's paper dealing with Schmoller's influence on Sombart, Schumpeter, and others, in Lambie (1.57), 9-39 (repr. in his *Venice and History* (9.86), 462-95).

1.69 **Parker**, H. T., 'Henri Sée (1864-1936)', in Halperin (1.68), 318-51. Leading economic historian in inter-war France. See also M. M. Knight in Lambie (1.57), 107-18.

1.70 **Petrovich**, M. B., 'V. I. Semevskii (1848-1916), Russian social historian', in J. S. Curtiss, ed., *Essays in Russian and Soviet History in Honor of G. T. Robinson*, Leiden, 1963, 63-84. Pioneer historian of eighteenth-century peasantry.

1.71 **Carosso**, V. P., 'Werner Sombart's contribution to business history', *Bus.Hist.Rev.*, 26, 1952, 27-49. Sombart did much to shape terms of debate about rise of capitalism (see 2.108-43, esp. 129 and 131). See also E. Salin, 'Sombart and the German approach', in Lambie (1.57), 41-51; and 2.129, 5.600.

1.72 **Hunt**, L., 'Charles Tilly's collective action', in Skocpol (1.29), 244-75. After much-praised study of Vendée during French Revolution, Tilly's main preoccupation has been statistics of violence and protest from sixteenth century onwards.

1.73 **Parker**, W. N., 'Abbot Payson Usher', in Lambie (1.57), 157-66. Versatile economic historian whose principal contribution to early modern history dealt with grain trade in France (see 9.345).

1.74 **Halperin**, C. J., 'Russia and the steppe. George Vernadsky and Eurasianism', *Forsch.Osteur.Gesch.*, 36, 1985, 55-194. Monograph-length account of Vernadsky's career, concentrating on his handling of "Eurasianism", i.e. view that Russian history has been shaped by openness of steppe lands to east (see 3.378).

1.75 **Payne**, S. G., 'Jaime Vicens Vives and the writing of Spanish history', *J.Mod.Hist.*, 34, 1962, 119-34.

1.76 **Kaye**, H. J., 'Totality. Its application to historical and social analysis by Wallerstein and Genovese', *Hist.Reflections*, 6, 1979, 405-19. Examination of two leading Marxist historians; in this context it is Wallerstein who is of interest.

1.77 **Ragin**, C., and Chirot, D., 'The world system of Immanuel Wallerstein. Sociology and politics as history', in Skocpol (1.29), 276-312. See also 2.112 and 2.117.

1.78 **Gilbert**, F., 'From art history to the history of civilization. Aby Warburg', *J.Mod.Hist.*, 44, 1972, 381-9. Repr. in his *History: Choice and Commitment*, Cambridge, Mass., 1977, 423-39. On Warburg's part in broadening art history to take in general intellectual and social factors.

1.79 **Roth**, G., and Schluchter, W., *Max Weber's Vision of History. Ethics and Methods*, Berkeley, Calif., 1979. Commentary on Weber almost rivals that on Karl Marx; this work is singled out mainly for its comparison, in chap. 5, of Braudel and Weber. For discussion of "Weber thesis" on Protestantism and capitalism, see 2.108-43 *passim*.

2

GENERAL SURVEYS

WORKS COVERING LONG TIME-SPAN

BIBLIOGRAPHIES

2.1 **Albion**, R. G., *Naval and Maritime History. An annotated Bibliography*, 4th ed., Mystic, Conn., 1972. All aspects of maritime history covered; most useful in this context for material on commerce. Journal articles not included, but does note many unpubl. theses.

2.2 **Aldcroft**, D. H., and Rodger, R., *Bibliography of European Economic and Social History*, 1984. Concentrates on Industrial Revolution and after, but includes a good deal on eighteenth century. English-language material only. Not annotated.

2.3 **Comité Français des Sciences Historiques,** *La Recherche Historique en France de 1940 à 1965*, Paris, 1965. Account of general tendencies in French historiography, lists of research organisations, and comprehensive bibliography of books. Supplement (1980) less ambitious bibliographically, though gives useful list of theses completed.

2.4 **Dunthorne**, H., and Scott, H. M., *Early Modern European History, c.1492-1788. A Select Bibliography*, 1984. Brief but surprisingly inclusive work sponsored by Historical Association. Entries not numbered but embedded in running commentary. Roughly equal sections devoted to general topics and to national/regional history.

2.5 Historical Association, *Annual Bulletin of Historical Literature*, 1911–. Since about 1970 has become very much more ambitious, not to say occasionally esoteric, in coverage.

2.6 **Roach**, J. P. C., *A Bibliography of Modern History*, 1968. Produced in conjunction with contributors to the *New Cambridge Modern History* (2.39). Erratic and difficult to use, but occasionally useful as guide to older material

2.7 *Trends in History. A Review of Current Periodical Literature in History*, New York, 1979- . Bibliographical journal in which recent articles are grouped and dealt with in broad thematic reviews. Many leading historians contribute.

SOURCE MATERIAL
See also 1.10; 4.62.

2.8 **Brezzi**, P., and Lee, E., eds., *Sources of Social History. Private Acts of the Late Middle Ages*, Toronto, 1984. Essays (many Italian and French) on uses to be made of notarial documents; several extend coverage well into sixteenth century. See also 2.11.

2.9 **Jeannin**, P., 'Les comptes du Sund comme source pour la construction d'indices généraux de l'activité économique en Europe (16e-18e siècle)', *Rev.Hist.*, 231, 1964, 55-102, 307-40. Attempt to use Sound toll registers not for evidence simply on Baltic trade but as indicator of general

6

economic cycles. Registers publ. by Nina E. Bang and K. Korst, 4 vols. in 5, Copenhagen, 1906-53.

2.10 **Van der Woude**, A., and Schuurman, A., eds., *Probate Inventories (A.A.G. Bijdragen, 23)*, Wageningen, 1980. Multilingual symposium on vital source of evidence for wealth levels, standard of living, household arrangements, etc. See also 1.12 and 3.333.

2.11 **Vogler**, B., ed., *Les Actes Notariés: Source de l'Histoire Sociale, 16e-19e Siècles*, Strasbourg, 1979. 22 conference papers. Heavily French in emphasis, but includes contributions on Amsterdam, Württemberg, and Austria.

2.12 **Wilson**, C., and Parker, G., eds., *Introduction to the Sources of European Economic History, 1500-1800, vol.1*, 1977. Sources here means statistical material; this vol. presents data for Mediterranean region, Britain, France, Netherlands, and Germany.

MONOGRAPHS AND ARTICLES
See also 4.4.

2.13 **Anderson**, R. T., *Traditional Europe. A Study in Anthropology and History*, Belmont, Calif., 1971. Anthropologist's view of European culture from tenth to eighteenth centuries.

2.14 **Braudel**, F., *Civilization and Capitalism, Fifteenth to Eighteenth Century*, 3 vols., 1981-84. Transl. from French ed. of 1979. Loosely organised but very stimulating economic and social history of early modern world. Volumes deal in turn with basic production and consumption; development and political context of markets and finance; and changes in loci of economic importance. Review articles: S. Kinser, *J.Mod.Hist.*, 53, 1981, 281-303; Olwen Hufton, *Ec.Hist.Rev.*, 2nd ser., 35, 1982, 140-5; A. W. Lovett, *Hist.J.*, 26, 1983, 747-53; L. Makkai, *Review*, 6, 1983, 435-53; M. Morineau, *Rev.Hist.Mod.et Contemp.*, 28, 1981, 624-68. For review of earlier version of vol.1 (1967), transl. as *Capitalism and Material Life, 1400-1800*, 1973, see T. Stoianovich, *J.Mod.Hist.*, 41, 1969, 68-81. See also foretaste given in lecture series at Johns Hopkins Univ., *Afterthoughts on Material Civilization and Capitalism*, Baltimore, Md., 1977.

2.15 *Cambridge Economic History of Europe*, 7 vols. in 9, 1941-78. Relevant vols., from which articles will be cited as appropriate, are E. E. Rich and C. H. Wilson, eds., *The Economy of Expanding Europe in the Sixteenth and Seventeenth Centuries*, 1967 (vol.4); and *The Economic Organization of Early Modern Europe*, 1977 (vol.5).

2.16 **Chaunu**, P., *Histoire, Science Sociale. La Durée, l'Espace, et l'Homme à l'Époque Moderne*, Paris, 1974. Tries to discern long-term trends and constrictions affecting early modern history. Strong committment to methods of *Annales* school.

2.17 **Cipolla**, C. M., *Before the Industrial Revolution. European Society and Economy, 1000-1700*, 1976. 2nd ed., 1981. Written with dash (and sometimes with slapdash).

2.18 **Clough**, S. B., and Cole, C. W., *Economic History of Europe*, Boston, Mass., 1941. 3rd ed., 1952. For long, with 2.28, a basic student textbook.

2.19 **Clough**, S. B., and Rapp, R. T., *European Economic History. The Economic Development of Western Civilization*, New York, 1975. 3rd ed. of work publ. in 1959 under subtitle. Part 3 covers early modern period. See also Clough's *The Rise and Fall of Civilization. An Inquiry into the Relationship between Economic Development and Civilization*, New York, 1951, which seeks to link major achievements in art and science with periods of relative prosperity.

2.20 **Davis**, R., *The Rise of the Atlantic Economies*, 1973. Valuable survey, covering West Europe and colonies in relevant period.

2.21 **Dülmen**, R. van, 'Formierung der europäischen Gesellschaft in der frühen Neuzeit', *Gesch.und Gesellschaft*, 7, 1981, 5-41. Some bold generalisations about shape of early modern society, notably emergence of partly aristocratic, partly bourgeois elite as arbiter of state and economy.

2.22 **Durand**, Y., *Les Républiques au Temps des Monarchies*, Paris, 1973. Looks at common factors in political situation and social structures of non-monarchic states, i.e. United Provinces, Swiss cantons, Italian and German city-states.

2.23 **Eyre**, E., ed., *European Civilization. Vol.5: Economic History of Europe since the Reformation*, 1937. Some essays in this detailed survey still repay consultation, e.g. A. V. Judges on early modern finance and banking (401-99).

2.24 *Fontana Economic History of Europe*, 6 vols. in 9, 1972-76. Under general editorship of C. Cipolla. Some chapters of this invaluable pocket series appeared earlier as separate pamphlets. Vol.2, *The Sixteenth and Seventeenth Centuries* (1974) is most central; relevant material also appears in vols.3-4 which in different ways both cover period 1700-1914.

2.25 **Frank**, A. G., *World Accumulation, 1492-1789*, New York, 1978. Cruder version of thesis propounded in better known work of Wallerstein (2.49).

2.26 **Gerhard**, D., *Old Europe. A Study of Continuity, 1000-1800*, New York, 1981. Extended essay stressing continuities in pre-industrial Europe, especially in terms of corporate and regional loyalties.

2.27 **Gould**, J. D., *Economic Growth in History. Survey and Analysis*, 1972. Examines recent historiography of growth and offers interpretation of major factors. Not confined to particular period.

2.28 **Heaton**, H., *Economic History of Europe*, New York, 1936. Revised ed., 1948. Pioneer textbook.

2.29 **Hicks**, Sir J. R., *A Theory of Economic History*, 1969. Brilliant essay, surmising how stages of economic history emerge in accordance with principles of classical theory (as would be expected, conflicts of interest do not feature largely). Review articles: P. T. Bauer, *Economica*, n.s., 38, 1971, 163-79; J. R. T. Hughes, *J.Interdisc.Hist.*, 2, 1972, 479-96 (misnumbered).

2.30 *Histoire Générale des Civilisations, 4-5*, Paris, 1953-54. Relevant vols. of durable French series which give particular attention to European expansion and relations with other cultures. Vol.4 is by R. Mousnier, *Les 16e et 17e Siècles*, 5th ed., 1967; vol.5 by Mousnier, E. Labrousse, and M. Bouloiseau, *Le 18e Siècle*, latest ed., 1985.

2.31 **Huppert**, G., *After the Black Death. A Social History of Early Modern Europe*, Bloomington, Ind., 1986. Well-written brief survey. Concentrates on Western Europe and concrete case-studies. Topical approach (rural society, cities, rebellion, etc.) makes for somewhat static picture.

2.32 **Imhof**, A. E., *Die Verlorenen Welten. Alltagsbewältigung durch unsere Vorfahren...*, Munich, 1984. Recreates material life of late seventeenth-century German peasant and moves outward to general popular history of "world we have lost", displaying some nostalgia for its fixed moral values.

2.33 **Jones**, E. L., *The European Miracle. Environment, Economies, and Geopolitics in the History of Europe and Asia*, 1981. Sweeping comparative study attempting to isolate factors which favoured long-term economic growth in Europe rather than Asia up to about 1850.

2.34 **Kamen**, H., *European Society, 1500-1700*, 1984. Brave attempt at comprehensive survey. Review article: D. Nicholls, *J.Eur.Stud.*, 15, 1985, 209-19. See also his more chronologically restricted *Iron Century* (2.73).

2.35 **Kellenbenz**, H., *The Rise of the European Economy. An Economic History of Continental Europe from the Fifteenth to the Eighteenth Century*, 1976. Focusses largely on Central and Eastern Europe. Best on agrarian aspects.

2.36 **Kriedte**, P., *Peasants, Landlords, and Merchant Capitalists. Europe and the World Economy, 1500-1800*, 1983. Transl. from German ed. of 1980. Excellent textbook, focussing on genesis of industrialisation.

2.37 **Léon**, P., ed., *Histoire Économique et Sociale du Monde*, 6 vols., Paris, 1977-78. Collaborative monument to *Annales* school of history, with emphasis on social structure and little technical economic theory. Valiant attempt to avoid Eurocentric bias. Vol.1 covers fourteenth–sixteenth centuries; vol.2, 1580-1730; vol.3, 1730-1840.

2.38 **McNeill**, W. H., *The Shape of European History*, 1974. By leading protagonist of macro-historical approach. Here posits cultural interchange rather than ecological determinism as main driving force in European history.

2.39 *New Cambridge Modern History*, 13 vols. and atlas, 1957-79. Collaborative work, generally criticised for emphasis on traditional Euro-centric political history. Vols.1-8 cover period 1493 to 1793. Occasional articles useful. Some interesting longitudinal studies, topically arranged, in vol.13, *Companion Volume*, ed. P. Burke (E. L. Jones on environment and economy; J. Dupâquier on demography; E. Le Roy Ladurie on peasants; articles on bureaucracy, secularisation, etc.).

2.40 **North**, D. C., *Structure and Change in Economic History*, New York, 1981. Similar in aim, though not in details of model, to 2.29.

2.41 —— and Thomas, R. P., *The Rise of the Western World. A New Economic History*, 1973. Seeks to determine how preconditions for European economic growth were laid down in medieval and early modern periods, notably in strength of property rights. For criticism of views on France see 3.34.

2.42 —— 'An economic theory of the growth of the western world', *Ec.Hist.Rev.*, 2nd ser., 23, 1970, 1-17. Useful potted summary of previous entry. See also debate with D. R. Ringrose, *ib.*, 26, 1973, 285-94.

2.43 **Parker**, W. N., 'European development in millennial perspective', in C. P. Kindleberger and G. Di Tella, eds., *Economics in the Long View. Essays in Honor of W. W. Rostow*, 1982, 2, 1-24. View of European economic history since High Middle Ages based on insights of Malthus, Smith, and Schumpeter.

2.44 **Rabb**, T. K., *The Struggle for Stability in Early Modern Europe*, New York, 1975. Tries to account for gradual subsidence of conflicts over religion and centralisation that convulsed Europe in period 1500-1650.

2.45 **Rosenberg**, N., and Birdzell, L. E., *How the West Grew Rich. The Economic Transformation of the Industrial World*, 1986. Another "growth model" approach (cf. 2.27,39,46), this one strongly emphasising freeing of markets from church-state control as recipe for advance.

2.46 **Rostow**, W. W., *Stages of Economic Growth. A Non-Communist Manifesto*, Cambridge, Mass., 1960. Gave currency to concept of "take-off into self-sustaining growth". Review articles: A. K. Cairncross, *Ec.Hist.Rev.*, 2nd ser., 13, 1961, 450-8; P. Baran and E. J. Hobsbawm, *Kyklos*, 14, 1961, 234-42; G.

Myrdal, *Scan.Ec.Hist.Rev.*, 15, 1967, 1-12.

2.47 —— *The World Economy. History and Prospect*, 1978. Ambitious effort at unified interpretation of past, present, and future of world economy.

2.48 —— *How It All Began. Origins of the Modern Economy*, 1975. Material on early modern developments in 2.47 appeared in preliminary form in this work. See also 2.102

2.49 **Wallerstein**, I., *The Modern World System*, 2 vols. to date, New York, 1974-80. Expounds theory of "core-periphery" relations (unequal terms of trade, chronic indebtedness of raw materials suppliers, etc.) as central to capitalist world-economy developing from sixteenth century onwards. First 2 vols. cover roughly 1500-1750. Review articles: F. C. Lane, *Comp.Stud.Soc.& Hist.*, 18, 1976, 517-32; symposium in *Peasant Stud.*, 6, 1977, 2-40; P. O'Brien, *Ec.Hist.Rev.*, 2nd ser., 35, 1982, 1-18 (with further debate, *ib.*, 36, 1983, 580-5). See also 2.83,112,117.

2.50 —— 'The rise and future demise of the world capitalist system. Concepts for comparative analysis', *Comp.Stud.Soc.& Hist.*, 16, 1974, 387-415. Amplifies aspects of previous entry.

2.51 **Watts**, S. J., *A Social History of Western Europe, 1450-1720*, 1984. Stimulating, though often scanty in evidence furnished. Review article: D. Nicholls, *J.Eur.Stud.*, 15, 1985, 209-19.

2.52 **Weber**, E., *Modern History of Europe. Men, Cultures, and Societies from the Renaissance to the Present*, New York, 1971. Textbook with strong emphasis on social background.

2.53 **Zschocke**, A., 'Kondratieff cycles in the pre-industrial period. A statistical investigation', *Hist.Soc.Res.*, 31, 1984, 63-84. Analyses various non-price time series, finding some evidence for cycles of 40-45 years in period 1550-1800. On Kondratieff cycles see also 11.11.

FIFTEENTH AND SIXTEENTH CENTURIES

2.54　**Ferguson**, W. K., 'Recent trends in the economic historiography of the Renaissance', *Stud.in Renaiss.*, 7, 1960, 7-26. Useful survey, reaching back to work of 1930s and '40s. For coverage of earlier material see F. L. Nussbaum, 'The economic history of Renaissance Europe', *J.Mod.Hist.*, 13, 1941, 527-45.

2.55　**Ozment**, S. E., ed., *Reformation Europe. A Guide to Research*, St. Louis, Mo., 1982. Collection of bibliographical essays on Reformation and Reformation society. Strongest on Germany. Chaps. on Peasants' War (R. W. Scribner); witchcraft (H. C. E. Midelfort); religious culture (Natalie Z. Davis); and sexual questions (Joyce Irwin).

2.56　**Aston**, Margaret, *The Fifteenth Century. The Prospect of Europe*, 1968. Good popularisation, well-illustrated. Main emphasis on intellectual change.

2.57　**Braudel**, F., *The Mediterranean and the Mediterranean World in the Age of Philip II*, 2 vols., 1972. First French ed. 1949, several later revisions. (Should be read in original, preferably, style being the man in this case). Most influential historical work of last fifty years thanks to its concepts of "total history" and of differing time-scales of change. See round-up of reviews by H. Kellner, *Hist.& Theory*, 18, 1979, 197-222. For general articles on Braudel see 1.31-7.

2.58　**Chamberlin**, E. R., *Everyday Life in Renaissance Times*, 1965. Enjoyable popular work, covering c.1450-1600.

2.59　**Delumeau**, J., *La Civilisation de la Renaissance*, 1967. Sumptuously illustrated, but much more than a coffee-table book.

2.60　**Hale**, J. R., *Renaissance Europe, 1480-1520*, 1971. Volume in trusty *Fontana History of Europe* series. Fair attention to social history.

2.61　**Koenigsberger**, H. G., and Mosse, G. L., *Europe in the Sixteenth Century*, 1968. Chapters 3-5 most useful.

2.62　**Margolin**, J.-C., ed., *L'Avènement des Temps Modernes*, 1977. New sixteenth-century vol. for well-established series *Peuples et Civilisations*, with good chapters by Margolin on popular culture and J. F. Bergier on economic history.

2.63　**Mauro**, F., *Le 16e Siècle Européen. Aspects Économiques*, Paris, 1966. Textbook much enamoured of quantitative approach.

2.64　**Miskimin**, H. A., *The Economy of Later Renaissance Europe, 1460-1600*, 1977. Good, though brief.

2.65　**Powell**, J. M., 'Crisis and culture in Renaissance Europe', *Medievalia et Humanistica*, n.s., 12, 1984, 201-24. On shift of wealth and power to lay elite following plagues of fourteenth century.

2.66　**Rice**, E. F., *The Foundations of Early Modern Europe, 1460-1559*, 1971. Reasonable attention to social and economic matters.

CIRCA 1550-1700

2.67　**Clark**, P., ed., *The European Crisis of the 1590s*, 1985. Conference papers on decade heralded as onset of seventeenth-century "general crisis". 11 papers take area approach (P. Burke on S. Italy, J. Casey on Spain, etc. – Eastern Europe not covered); 5 deal with general questions such as demography, popular disorder, and war.

2.68　**Coveney**, P. J., 'An early modern European crisis?', *Renaiss.& Mod.Stud.*, 26, 1982, 1-26. Review of long controversy about reality of seventeenth-century crisis.

2.69　**De Vries**, J., *The Economy of Europe in an Age of Crisis, 1600-1750*, 1976. Excellent survey, concentrating on economic consequences of levelling-off in population growth. Review article: Joan Thirsk, *Comp.Stud.Soc.& Hist.*, 22, 1980, 626-38.

2.70　**Dunn**, R. S., *The Age of Religious Wars, 1559-1689*, 1971. See notably Chapter 3, 'The psychology of limited wealth'.

2.71　**Elliott**, J. H., *Europe Divided, 1559-98*, 1968. Another vol. in *Fontana History of Europe* series. Chapter 2 most useful.

2.72　**Hobsbawm**, E. J., 'The general crisis of the European economy in the seventeenth century', *P.& P.*, 5, 1954, 33-53; 6, 1954, 44-65. Repr. in T. Aston, ed., *Crisis in Europe, 1560-1660. Essays from Past & Present*, 1965, 5-58. Seminal article which provoked spate of discussion, as evidenced by this section. Argues that limitations of mainly luxury market led to depression, which eventually generated its own solution in rise of rural industry and colonial trade.

2.73 **Kamen**, H., *The Iron Century. Social Change in Europe, 1550-1660*, 1971, 2nd ed., 1976. Review article: T. K. Rabb, *J.Mod.Hist.*, 45, 1973, 456-62.

2.74 **Kiernan**, V. G., *State and Society in Europe, 1550-1650*, 1980. Stimulating. Takes form of region by region survey.

2.75 **Koenigsberger**, H. G., 'The crisis of the seventeenth century. A farewell?', in his *Politicians and Virtuosi*, 1986, 149-68. Argues that concept of crisis implies departure from normal equilibrium; whereas in fact political structures were inherently unstable.

2.76 **Nef**, J. U., *La Naissance de la Civilisation Industrielle et le Monde Contemporain*, Paris, 1954. Lectures given at Collège de France, with theme that period 1570-1640 saw turn from quality to quantity production that marks beginning of industrial era.

2.77 **Parker**, G., *Europe in Crisis, 1598-1648*, 1979. Textbook in *Fontana History of Europe* series. Note that "crisis" concept is embodied in title.

2.78 —— and Smith, Lesley M., eds., *The General Crisis of the Seventeenth Century*, 1978. Collection of reprints and translations, with useful introduction.

Note general survey by N. Steensgaard (26-56); and article by R. Romano on economic crisis of 1619-22, seen as critical transition between periods of growth and stagnation (165-225).

2.79 **Pennington**, D. H., *Seventeenth-Century Europe*, 1970. Chapters 3, 4, and 10 of most interest.

2.80 **Reed**, C. G., 'Transaction costs and differential growth in seventeenth-century Western Europe', *J.Ec.Hist.*, 33, 1973, 177-90. Hypothesises that states with relatively unrestricted market systems forged ahead because of economies of scale.

2.81 **Trevor-Roper**, H., ed., *The Age of Expansion. Europe and the World, 1559-1660*, 1968. Of interest mainly for illustrations. Chapters organised on area basis, mixing social and political analysis.

2.82 —— 'The general crisis of the seventeenth century', *P.& P.*, 16, 1959, 31-64. Repr. in his *Religion, the Reformation, and Social Change, and Other Essays*, 1967, 46-89; and in Aston (2.72), 59-116. Celebrated article which sees revolutions of mid-century as provoked by exorbitant demands of extravagant courts and their swelling bureaucracies; see also discussion by E. J. Hobsbawm, J. H. Hexter, and others, *ib.*, 18, 1960, 8-42.

2.83 **Wallerstein**, I., 'The "crisis of the seventeenth century" ', *New Left Rev.*, 110, 1978, 65-73. Contends that stagnation increased regional differentiation.

2.84 **Wilson**, C. H., *The Transformation of Europe, 1558-1648*, 1976. Chaps. 1 and 2 of most interest.

CIRCA 1660-1789
See also 2.30

2.85 *The Eighteenth Century. A Current Bibliography. N.s., 1, 1975-*, Philadelphia, 1978- . Annual bibliography with substantial section on 'historical, social, and economic studies'. Entries annotated, sometimes at length. Continues series with similar format which appeared as part of *Philological Q.*, 1970-74.

2.86 **Anderson**, M. S., *Europe in the Eighteenth Century, 1713-83*, 1961. 2nd ed., 1976. Balanced general history.

2.87 —— *Historians and Eighteenth-Century*

Europe, 1715-89, 1979. Particular attention to modern French historiography.

2.88 **Behrens**, C. Betty A., *The Ancien Régime*, 1967. Illustrated work aimed at general reader.

2.89 **Chaunu**, P., *La Civilisation de l'Europe Classique*, Paris, 1966. Richly illustrated popularising work which summarises much distinguished research.

2.90 —— *La Civilisation de l'Europe des Lumières*, Paris, 1971. Work in same series as previous entry. Review article: J.

Meyer, *Annales*, 29, 1974, 888-902.

2.91 **Cobban**, A., ed., *The Eighteenth Century. Europe in the Age of Enlightenment*, 1969. Coffee-table work, but includes some distinguished contributors on socio-economic themes (e.g. D. C. Coleman, K. G. Davies, Olwen Hufton).

2.92 **Doyle**, W., *The Old European Order, 1660-1800*, 1978. Valuable.

2.93 **Forster**, R., and Forster, Elborg, *European Society in the Eighteenth Century*, New York, 1969. Readings from contemporary sources.

2.94 **Godechot**, J., *France and the Atlantic Revolution of the Eighteenth Century, 1770-99*, New York, 1965. Not direct transl., but rather similar to his *Les Révolutions, 1770-99*, Paris, 1963. Finds common causes of revolution and class conflict throughout "Atlantic world". See also 2.100-1.

2.95 **Hatton**, Ragnhild, *Europe in the Age of Louis XIV*, 1969. Popular illustrated work with good coverage of social aspects.

2.96 **Hufton**, Olwen H., *Europe, Privilege and Protest, 1730-89*, 1980. Volume of *Fontana History of Europe* series by versatile social historian.

2.97 **Jeannin**, P., *L'Europe du Nord-Ouest et du Nord aux 17e et 18e Siècles*, Paris, 1969. Deals principally with Britain, Netherlands, and Scandinavia. Quite strong on social and economic topics.

2.98 **Léon**, P., *Économies et Sociétés Pré-Industrielles, 2. 1650-1780*, Paris, 1970. Subtitled 'origins of an acceleration in history' – but opening section deals with continuing recession of "long seventeenth century". Vol.1, scheduled to be by R. Gascon, appears not to have been publ.

2.99 **Mandrou**, R., *L'Europe Absolutiste. Raison et Raison d'État, 1649-1775*, Paris, 1977. First publ. in German, 1976. Good text-

book, organised round what are taken to be competing models of French and British government and economic system.

2.100 **Palmer**, R. R., *The Age of the Democratic Revolution. A Political History of Europe and America, 1760-1800*, 2 vols., Princeton, N.J., 1959-64. Like Godechot (2.94) portrays American and French revolutions as part of irrepressible change in western society and mentalities.

2.101 **Amann**, P., ed., *The Eighteenth-Century Revolution: French or Western?*, Boston, Mass., 1963. Selection of readings mainly revolving around "Palmer thesis" as developed in previous entry. Includes Palmer's early exposition, 'The world revolution of the west', from *Pol.Sci.Q.*, 69, 1954, 1-14.

2.102 **Rostow**, W. W., 'The beginnings of modern growth in Europe', *J.Ec.Hist.*, 33, 1973, 547-80. Seeks to isolate factors leading to Britain's outstripping of continental Europe in eighteenth century.

2.103 **Rudé**, G., *Europe in the Eighteenth Century. Aristocracy and the Bourgeois Challenge*, 1972.

2.104 **Soboul**, A., and others, *Le Siècle des Lumières, 1. L'Essor (1715-50)*, 2 vols., Paris, 1977. Major synthesis, not yet completed.

2.105 **Treasure**, G., *The Making of Modern Europe, 1648-1780*, 1985. Sixth-form level. Early chapters relevant.

2.106 **Treue**, W., *Wirtschaftsgeschichte der Neuzeit. Im Zeitalter der Industriellen Revolution, 1700 bis 1960*, Stuttgart, 1962. Textbook on grand scale. Contains c.300 pages on eighteenth century, surveyed regionally.

2.107 **Woloch**, I., *Eighteenth-Century Europe. Tradition and Progress, 1715-89*, New York, 1982. Considerable attention to economy and society.

THE DEBATE ON CAPITALISM

See also 3.153,357; 4.118; 5.586,600; 6.251; 7.2,23,70; 8.15,19; 9.38,52,635,647;10.90,97,159; 13.183

2.108 **Baechler**, J., *The Origins of Capitalism*, 1975. Transl. from French ed. of 1971. Extended essay. Unlike most works in this section, not concerned with "Weber thesis".

2.109 **Baron**, S. H., 'The Weber thesis and the failure of capitalist development in early

modern Russia', *Jb.Gesch.Osteur.*, 18, 1970, 321-36. Repr. in Baron (9.130). Finds major hindrance to be government restrictions on private economic activity.

2.110 **Beaud**, M., *A History of Capitalism, 1500-1980*, 1984. Transl. from French ed. of 1981. Schematic work by political economist. Left-wing in tone.

2.111 **Besnard**, P., *Protestantisme et Capitalisme. La Controverse Post-Weberienne*, Paris, 1970. Useful introduction of some 100 pages. Remainder devoted to extracts and articles of well-known commentators on Weber thesis (Tawney, Robertson, etc.).

2.112 **Brenner**, R., 'Origins of capitalist development. A critique of neo-Smithian Marxism', *New Left Rev.*, 104, 1977, 25-92. Long critique of core-periphery analysis of Frank and Wallerstein (2.25,49) as mechanical and insufficiently analytic of class formation. See also *ib.*, 108, 1978, 94-6; 109, 1978, 88-95, for further discussion.

2.113 **Burrell**, S. A., 'Calvinism, capitalism, and the middle class. Afterthoughts on an old problem', *J.Mod.Hist.*, 32, 1960, 129-41. Reviews literature on Weber thesis, and puts forward Scotland as Calvinist society which does not conform to model.

2.114 **Cox**, O. C., *The Foundations of Capitalism*, New York, 1959. Work by sociologist on mercantilist era, virtually equating capitalism and mercantilism.

2.115 **Dobb**, M. H., *Studies in the Development of Capitalism*, 1946. 2nd ed., 1963. Influential source of debate, though conducted mainly in terms of English history. Stresses pressures on feudal landlords to maximise income. Review article: R. H. Tawney, *Ec.Hist.Rev.*, 2nd ser., 2, 1950, 307-16 (repr. in his *History and Society*, ed. J. M. Winter, 1978, 202-14). See also 2.120.

2.116 **Eisenstadt**, S. N., ed., *The Protestant Ethic and Modernization. A Comparative View*, New York, 1968. Essays (mostly reprints) on Weber thesis. Case studies take British and non-European examples, but general papers of some interest.

2.117 **Gottlieb**, R. S., 'Feudalism and historical materialism. A critique and a synthesis', *Sci.& Soc.*, 48, 1984, 1-37. Reviews Brenner debate (see 2.112 and 7.2) and work of Perry Anderson and Immanuel Wallerstein. Note riposte of D. Laibman, *ib.*, 257-94, reasserting primacy of forces of production.

2.118 **Green**, R. W., ed., *Protestantism, Capitalism, and Social Science. The Weber Thesis Controversy*, Lexington, Mass., 1973. Readings.

2.119 **Hayek**, F. A. von, ed., *Capitalism and the Historians*, 1954. Collection of essays deploring anti-capitalist bias in historians.

2.120 **Hilton**, R. H., ed., *The Transition from Feudalism to Capitalism*, 1976. Collects together various contributions to famous debate between Paul Sweezy and Maurice Dobb arising out of 2.115, from Hilton, K. Takahashi, and C. Hill in *Science & Society*, 1950-53, to J. Merrington (8.19).

2.121 **Hirschmann**, A. O., *The Passions and the Interests. Political Arguments for Capitalism before its Triumph*, Princeton, N.J., 1977. Looks at seventeenth- and eighteenth-century origins of argument for giving individual acquisitiveness free rein.

2.122 **Hobsbawm**, E., 'The seventeenth century in the development of capitalism', *Sci.& Soc.*, 24, 1960, 97-112. Argues that discontinuities of seventeenth-century economic crisis opened way for industrial capitalism to take over from commercial capitalism of feudal society.

2.123 **Holton**, R. J., *The Transition from Feudalism to Capitalism*, 1985. Provides useful summary of previous historiography (Marxist and neo-classical explanatory models), and advocates "greater measure of causal pluralism".

2.124 **Hudson**, W. S., 'The Weber thesis reexamined', *Church Hist.*, 30, 1961, 88-99.

2.125 **Kamenka**, E., and Neale, R. S., eds., *Feudalism, Capitalism, and Beyond*, Canberra, 1975. Stimulating symposium on Marxist model of historical change, concentrating esp. on property law; however, British experience tends to dominate discussion.

2.126 **Landes**, D. S., ed., *The Rise of Capitalism*, New York, 1966. Reader. Valuable introductory article by Landes.

2.127 **Marshall**, G., *In Search of the Spirit of Capitalism. An Essay on Max Weber's Protestant Ethic Thesis*, 1982. Best introduction.

2.128 **Medick**, H., 'The transition from feudalism to capitalism. Renewal of the debate', in R. Samuel, ed., *People's History and Socialist Theory*, 1981, 120-30.

2.129 **Mendes-Flohr**, P. R., 'Werner Sombart's *The Jews and Modern Capitalism*. An analysis of its ideological premises', *Yrbk.Leo Baeck Inst.*, 21, 1976, 86-107. Sees Sombart's premises as both anti-capitalist and anti-semitic. See also 2.131. For wider view of Sombart's contribution see 1.71; Nussbaum's article mentioned in

2.54; and 5.600.

2.130 **Meyer**, J., *Les Capitalismes*, Paris, 1981. Concentrates on medieval and early modern emergence of mercantile capital.

2.131 **Mosse**, W. E., 'Judaism, Jews, and capitalism. Weber, Sombart, and beyond', *Yrbk.Leo Baeck Inst.*, 24, 1979, 3-15.

2.132 **Otsuka**, H., *The Spirit of Capitalism. The Max Weber Thesis in an Economic Historical Perspective*, Tokyo, 1982. Essays reflecting view that capitalism is more product of enterprising artisans and yeomen than putting-out merchants. Review article (in German): E. Schremmer, *VSWG*, 70, 1983, 363-78.

2.133 **Poggi**, G., *Calvinism and the Capitalist Spirit. Max Weber's Protestant Ethic*, 1983. Close textual study rather than historical assessment.

2.134 **Riemersma**, J. C., *Religious Factors in Early Dutch Capitalism, 1550-1650*, The Hague, 1967. Weber thesis considered in Dutch context.

2.135 **Roos**, H.-E., 'The origin of Swedish capitalism', *Ec.& Hist.*, 19, 1976, 49-65. Schematic essay on new elements in financing trade and production in sixteenth and seventeenth centuries taken to constitute initial stages of capitalism.

2.136 **Samuelsson**, K., *Religion and Economic Action*, Stockholm, 1957. Transl. from Swedish ed. of 1957. One of most influential criticisms of Weber thesis. Long extract in Green (2.118), 106-49 (including review article by N. M. Hansen, originally publ. in *Zeitschr.f.Nationalökonomie*, 24,

1964).

2.137 **Schorsch**, L. L., 'Direct producers and the rise of the factory system', *Sci.& Soc.*, 44, 1981, 401-42. Argues that definitive transition to capitalism – mode of production rather than relations of production – only occurs with factory.

2.138 **Sprinzak**, E., 'Weber's thesis as an historical explanation', *Hist.& Theory*, 11, 1972, 294-320. Defence of Weber's insights.

2.139 **Stuijvenberg**, J. H. van, 'The Weber thesis. An attempt at interpretation', *Acta Hist.Neerlandica*, 8, 1975, 50-66.

2.140 **Trevor-Roper**, H. R., 'Religion, the Reformation, and social change', in *Historical Studies. Papers Read before the Irish Conference of Historians, 4*, 1963, 18-44. Repr. in Trevor-Roper (2.82), 1-45. Sceptical examination of Weber thesis.

2.141 **Tribe**, K., *Genealogies of Capitalism*, 1981. Useful for theoretical discussion, though mainly illustrated from British developments.

2.142 **Vilar**, P., 'Problems of the formation of capitalism', *P.& P.*, 10, 1956, 15-38. Partly repr. in Landes (2.126), 26-40. Disputes primacy of monetary factors and "profit inflation" (as advanced by Earl Hamilton and popularised by Keynes) in rise of capitalism.

2.143 **Yamey**, B. S., 'Scientific bookkeeping and the rise of capitalism', *Ec.Hist.Rev.*, 2nd ser., 1, 1949, 99-113. Examines arguments for double-entry system in accounting manuals of early modern period.

3

NATIONAL, REGIONAL, AND LOCAL HISTORY

The distinction between local history which is general in nature, and hence included in this section, and that more appropriately placed under particular subjects, has obviously had to be somewhat arbitrary at times. The topographical index should overcome most of these problems. Cities and towns are mainly dealt with in Sections 8 and 9, and village studies in Section 7.
For national historical bibliographies of a general or comprehensive nature see A. J. Walford, ed., Guide to Reference Material. Vol.2: Social and Historical Sciences, Philosophy, and Religion, 4th ed., 1982, 645 ff.

FRANCE

HISTORIOGRAPHY AND SOURCES
See also 1.10; 2.3,11.

3.1 **Bédarida**, F., and others, *Pour une Histoire de la Statistique*, Paris, 1977. Conference papers chiefly devoted to availability of sources for French socio-economic history.

3.2 **Corvisier**, A., *Sources et Méthodes en Histoire Sociale*, Paris, 1980. Essentially for students of French history, offering guidance on archival sources.

3.3 **Gille**, B., *Les Sources Statistiques de l'Histoire de France. Des Enquêtes du 17e Siècle à 1870*, Paris, 1964. Important guide to sources and reliability of statistical material.

3.4 **Richet**, D., 'Economic growth and its setbacks in France from the fifteenth to the eighteenth century', in *Social Historians in Contemporary France. Essays from* Annales, New York, 1972, 180-211. Transl. from *Annales*, 23, 1968, 759-87. Review of historiography presented to Franco-Hungarian symposium.

NATIONAL SURVEYS: GENERAL

3.5 **Braudel**, F., *L'Identité de la France*, 3 vols., Paris, 1986. Braudel's last major work. French history in triptych form – geography, demography, and economy form its panels.

3.6 —— and Labrousse, E., eds., *Histoire Économique et Sociale de la France*, 4 vols. in 8, Paris, 1970-82. Collaborative work involving many of France's most distinguished historians of post-war generation. Vol.1 covers 1450-1660; vol.2, 1660-1789. Review articles: vol.1: R. Descimon, *Annales*, 28, 1973, 572-82; vol.2: D. Ligou, *Rev.Hist.Éc.et Soc.*, 50, 1972, 551-64; I. Woloch, *J.Interdisc.Hist.*, 4, 1974, 435-57.

3.7 **Duby**, G., and Mandrou, R., *A History of French Civilization*, New York, 1964. Transl. from French ed. of 1958. Excellent popular social history, covering origins to present day.

3.8 **Esmonin**, E., *Études sur la France des 17e et 18e Siècles*, Paris, 1964. Most useful for its essays on demography (239-328), and those on Grenoble (429-94).

3.9 **François**, M., *La France et les Français*, Paris, 1972. Part of *Pléiade* encyclopedia series. Chapters on many aspects of social history; contributors incl. A. Armengaud, R. Mandrou, A. Soboul, etc.

3.10 **Goubert**, P., *Clio parmi les Hommes*.

Recueil d'Articles, The Hague, 1976. Reprints of occasional pieces on early modern France.

3.11 —— *L'Ancien Régime*, 2 vols., Paris, 1969-73. Masterly but deterministic account of society (vol.1) and institutions (vol.2), which he sees as shaped by demographic pressures and coercive structures. Vol.1 transl. as *The Ancien Régime. French Society, 1600-1750*, 1973.

3.12 —— and Roche, D., *Les Français et l'Ancien Régime*, 2 vols., Paris, 1984. Handsomely illustrated synthesis. Vol.1 reworks previous entry; vol.2 deals particularly with religion, culture, and life cycle.

3.13 **Mandrou**, R., *La France au 17e et 18e Siècles*, Paris, 1967. Textbook with strong emphasis on social history.

3.14 **Méthivier**, H., *L'Ancien Régime en France: 16e, 17e. 18e Siècles*, 6th ed., Paris, 1974. Collates and augments his well-tried guides to early modern France publ. in *Que Sais-Je* series.

3.15 **Mousnier**, R., *The Institutions of France under the Absolute Monarchy*, 2 vols., Chicago, 1979-84. Transl. from French ed. of 1974-80. Interesting to compare with 3.11. Mousnier attaches much more importance to value system which sustained hierarchy, and which began to be challenged in eighteenth century. Review article: R. Mettam, *History*, 66, 1981, 221-32.

CIRCA 1450-1700
See also 10.498.

3.16 'Aspects de l'économie française au 17e siècle', *Dix-Septième Siècle*, 70-71, 1966, whole issue. Useful symposium, consisting of surveys by J. Meuvret (economic thought), J. Jacquart (agriculture), J.-Y. Tirat (transport and internal trade), J. Delumeau (external trade), R. Pillorget (monetary problems). P. Deyon on manufactures is transl. in Ragnhild Hatton, ed., *Louis XIV and Absolutism*, 1976, 226-42.

3.17 **Bluche**, F., *La Vie Quotidienne au Temps de Louis XIV*, Paris, 1984. Popular but scholarly. Works down social pyramid from Court and Parisian society to provinces.

3.18 **Briggs**, R., *Early Modern France, 1560-1715*, 1977. Competent introductory survey.

3.19 **Carr**, J. L., *Life in France under Louis XIV*, 1966. Fairly superficial. Illustrated.

3.20 **Chaunu**, P., and others, 'Les éléments de longue durée dans la France du 17e siècle', *Dix-Septième Siècle*, 106-7, 1975, whole issue. Five papers which examine static or very slowly changing aspects of demography, institutions, and intellectual or emotional life.

3.21 **Coveney**, P. J., ed., *France in Crisis, 1620-75*, 1977. Transl. readings, with lengthy introduction.

3.22 **Febvre**, L., *Life in Renaissance France*, Cambridge, Mass., 1977. Lecture series on sixteenth-century life and culture, rather obscurely publ. in 1925, and here transl. from selection of Febvre's essays which appeared in 1962 (*Pour une Histoire à Part Entière*).

3.23 **Goubert**, P., *Louis XIV and Twenty Million Frenchmen*, 1970. Transl. from French ed. of 1966. Sets diplomatic and cultural achivements of reign against grimmer social realities.

3.24 **Greengrass**, M., *France in the Age of Henri IV*, 1984. Competent general history, with chapters on economic conditions and upper echelons of society.

3.25 **Lough**, J., *An Introduction to Seventeenth Century France*, 1954. Designed as background for literature students. See also his parallel work on eighteenth century (3.35).

3.26 **Mandrou**, R., *Introduction to Modern France, 1500-1640*, 1975. Transl. from French ed. of 1961. Sensitive attempt to reconstruct mental and physical world of early modern French – what was general and what was specific to particular classes.

3.27 **Mettam**, R., ed., *Government and Society in Louis XIV's France*, 1977. Student sources (in transl.).

3.28 **Mongrédien**, G., *La Vie Quotidienne sous Louis XIV*, Paris, 1948. Early vol. of popular and prolific series; now seems rather thin.

3.29 **Salmon**, J. H. M., *Society in Crisis. France in the Sixteenth Century*, 1975. Good account of society and economy presented as background to study of Religious Wars.

EIGHTEENTH CENTURY
See also 10.113

3.30 **Bluche**, F., *La Vie Quotidienne au Temps de*

Louis XVI, Paris, 1980.

3.31 **Crouzet**, F., 'England and France in the eighteenth century. A comparative analysis of two economic growths', in R. M. Hartwell, ed., *Causes of the Industrial Revolution in England*, 1967, 139-74; and in *Social Historians in Contemporary France* (3.4), 59-86. Transl. from *Annales*, 21, 1966, 254-91. Suggests that French economy was no less dynamic than British, despite lagging in technology. Non-quantitative. Cf. similar argument in longer-term perspective in 3.34.

3.32 **Gossman**, L., *French Society and Culture. Background for Eighteenth-Century Literature*, Englewood Cliffs, N.J., 1972. Chapters 1 and 2 deal with general social history; 3 and 4 with sociology of literature and Enlightenment.

3.33 **Landes**, D. S., 'The statistical study of French crises', *J.Ec.Hist.*, 10, 1950, 195-211. Questions some aspects of E. Labrousse's thesis (in *La Crise de l'Économie Française à la Fin de l'Ancien Régime et au Début de la Révolution*, Paris, 1944) that under eighteenth-century conditions poor harvests triggered off general business slumps.

3.34 **Leet**, D. R., and Shaw, J. A., 'French economic stagnation, 1700-1960. Old economic history revisited', *J.Interdisc.Hist.*, 8, 1978, 531-44. Claims alleged stagnation is a myth, and that French institutions did not constitute barrier alleged by North and Thomas (2.41).

3.35 **Lough**, J., *An Introduction to Eighteenth-Century France*, 1960. Similar background vol. for seventeenth century, 3.25.

3.36 **Meyer**, J., *La Vie Quotidienne en France au Temps de la Régence*, Paris, 1979. Popular work by distinguished historian.

3.37 **Morineau**, M., *Les Faux-Semblants d'un Démarrage Économique. Agriculture et Démographie en France au 18e Siècle*, Paris, 1971. Contends (in two essays and long documentary appendix) that neither agricultural nor population statistics provide evidence of significant improvement in economic performance. Review article: A. Armengaud, *Rev.Hist.Éc.et Soc.*, 49, 1971, 406-15.

3.38 **Riley**, J. C., *The Seven Years War and the Old Regime. The Economic and Financial Toll*, Princeton, N.J., 1986. Finds that economic repercussions have been exaggerated, but financial ones if anything underestimated.

3.39 **Sagnac**, P., *La Formation de la Société Française Moderne*, 2 vols., Paris, 1945-46. Covers 1660-1789. Now rather dated. Review article: L. Gottschalk, *J.Mod.Hist.*, 20, 1948, 137-48.

3.40 **Schaeper**, T. J., *The Economy of France in the Second Half of the Reign of Louis XIV*, Montreal, 1980. Short research report publ. by Interuniversity Centre for European Studies.

3.41 **Shennan**, J. H., *France Before the Revolution*, 1983. Handy introductory pamphlet on eighteenth-century France.

3.42 **Soboul**, A., *La France à la Veille de la Révolution*, 2 vols., Paris, 1966. Sorbonne lecture course. Similar course publ. in stencilled form as *La Société Française dans la Seconde Moitié du 18e Siècle*, 1969.

3.43 —— *La Civilisation et la Révolution Française. Vol.1: La Crise de l'Ancien Régime*, Paris, 1970. Copiously illustrated dissection of pre-Revolutionary social fabric. First vol. of work that can be regarded as Soboul's summing-up. Review article: G. Lemarchand, *Rev.Hist.Mod.et Contemp.*, 19, 1972, 73-91.

PROVINCIAL AND LOCAL STUDIES

Note also substantial studies, though with mainly rural emphasis, on Auvergne (7.64); Beauce (8.41); Beauvaisis (8.36); Brittany (8.60); Burgundy (7.68, 10.39); Ile de France (7.49,71); Languedoc (7.56); Lorraine (7.32); Lyonnais (7.53); Massif-Central (7.50-1); Normandy (7.30); Provence (7.27).

3.44 *Univers de la France et des Pays Francophones*, Toulouse, 1967-. Excellent collection of collaborative histories of major provinces and cities, publ. by firm of Privat under general editorship of P. Wolff, to which most of France's leading historians contributed. No scholarly apparatus. Additional documentary vols. for certain provinces.

3.45 *Pays et Villes de France*, Toulouse, 1980- . Related series, also ed. by Wolff, covering lesser provinces and towns.

3.46 **Le Roy Ladurie**, E., *Love, Death, and Money in the Pays d'Oc*, 1982. Transl. from French ed. of 1980. Seeks to establish social context of Occitan novella *Jean-l'Ont-Pris* by Abbé Fabre (1756). Review article: Hope Glidden, *Hist.& Theory*, 23,

3.47 **Bendjebbar**, A., *La Vie Quotidienne en Anjou au 18e Siècle*, Paris, 1983.

1984, 267-72.

3.48 **Bercé**, Y. M., *La Vie Quotidienne dans l'Aquitaine du 17e Siècle*, 1978. Two fairly scholarly contributions to this popular series.

3.49 **Croix**, A., *La Bretagne aux 16e et 17e Siècles. La Vie, La Mort, La Foi*, 2 vols., Paris, 1981. Huge doctoral thesis, concerned particularly with mortality – both its demographic context and its pervasiveness in mental and cultural terms.

3.50 **Mireaux**, E., *Une Province Française au Temps du Grand Roi: La Brie*, Paris, 1958.

3.51 **Souriac**, R., *Le Comté de Comminges au Milieu du 16e Siècle*, Paris, 1977. Comprehensive account of political, social, and economic structures.

3.52 **Roupnel**, G., *La Ville et la Campagne au 17e Siècle. Étude sur les Populations du Pays Dijonnais*, Paris, 1922. Not surprisingly this work which prefigures so many themes of contemporary social history was repr. in 1955.

3.53 **Claverie**, Élisabeth, and Lamaison, P., *L'Impossible Mariage. Violence et Parenté en Gévaudan, 17e, 18e, et 19e Siècles*, Paris, 1982. Court records illustrating everyday nature of violence in poor, upland region, and its relation to village social and family structures.

3.54 **Lemaître**, Nicole, *Un Horizon Bloqué. Ussel et la Montagne Limousine aux 17e et 18e Siècles*, Ussel, 1978. Area bypassed by general demographic and economic progress of eighteenth century.

3.55 **Cabourdin**, G., *La Vie Quotidienne en Lorraine aux 17e et 18e Siècles*, Paris, 1984. For Cabourdin's more academic work on rural Lorraine see 7.32.

3.56 **Bouton**, A., *Le Maine. Histoire Économique et Sociale, 14e, 15e, et 16e Siècles*, Le Mans, 1970. Further vol., *...17e et 18e Siècles*, 1973. Local *érudit's* work – piles up data without much shaping.

3.57 **Bouvet**, M., and Bourdin, P. M., *A Travers la Normandie des 17e et 18e Siècles*, Caen, 1968. Two independent monographs on demography and social history of groups of parishes, one group near Caen, other near Alençon.

3.58 **Dehergne**, J., *Le Bas Poitou à la Veille de la Révolution*, Paris, 1963. Interesting region for study in view of its later role in Vendée rebellion.

3.59 **Collier**, R., *La Vie en Haute-Provence de 1600 à 1850*, Digne, 1973. Substantial work by director of *département* archives.

3.60 **Vovelle**, M., *De la Cave au Grenier. Un Itinéraire en Provence au 18e Siècle*, Quebec, 1980. General picture of society and culture.

3.61 **Faure-Soulet**, J. F., *La Vie Quotidienne dans les Pyrénées sous l'Ancien Régime, du 16e au 18e Siècle*, Paris, 1974.

3.62 **Lartigaut**, J., *Les Campagnes du Quercy après la Guerre de Cent Ans, vers 1440 vers 1500*, Toulouse, 1978. Based on notarial acts. Deals esp. with resettlement of Cahors and hinterland, and background of in-migrants.

3.63 **Sol**, E., *La Vie Économique et Sociale en Quercy aux 16e et 17e Siècles*, Paris, 1950. Rather antiquarian approach.

3.64 **Nicolas**, J., and Nicolas, Renée, *La Vie Quotidienne en Savoie aux 17e et 18e Siècles*, Paris, 1979.

3.65 **Frêche**, G., *Toulouse et la Région Midi-Pyrénées au Siècle des Lumières, vers 1670-1789*, Paris, 1974. Large-scale thesis with primary emphasis on economic structures, esp. increase in cereals production. See also article on uses of *compoix* for social history of this region, *Rev.Hist.Mod.et Contemp.*, 18, 1971, 321-53.

3.66 **Molinier**, A., *Stagnations et Croissance. Le Vivarais aux 17e-18e Siècles*, Paris, 1985. Comprehensive study of small, mountainous province on eastern side of Massif Central (present-day Ardèche).

THE LOW COUNTRIES
See also 2.97,134; 4.128; 10.119,504,506; 14.74,256.

3.67 '[Netherlands historiography]', *Riv. Stor. Ital.*, 95, 1983, 591-978. Valuable bibliography contained in series of articles contributed to this Italian journal by Dutch historians (G. de Bruijn, D. J. Roorda, etc.), surveying historical writing in

Netherlands since 1945.

3.68 **Aymard**, M., ed., *Dutch Capitalism and World Capitalism*, 1982. Essays in French and English. Contains general appraisals of Dutch economy (principally in seventeenth century) by, among others, B. Slicher van Bath, I. Wallerstein, P. Jeannin, and M. Morineau.

3.69 **De Vries**, J., 'The decline and rise of the Dutch economy, 1675-1900', *Res.in Ec.Hist.*, suppl.3, 1984, 149-89. Experiment in estimating national income and related economic indicators.

3.70 —— 'On the modernity of the Dutch Republic', *J.Ec.Hist.*, 33, 1973, 191-202. On absence of feudal encumbrances in land system, and well-developed public credit.

3.71 **Dillen**, J. G. van, 'Economic fluctuations and trade in the Netherlands, 1650-1750', in P. Earle, ed., *Essays in European Economic History, 1500-1800*, 1974, 199-211.

3.72 **Geyl**, P., *The Netherlands in the Seventeenth Century*, 2 vols., 1961-64. Standard general history with emphasis on essential cultural unity of Dutch-speaking areas in both Republic and Spanish-ruled provinces. Vol.1 is revision of work first publ. in 1936 as *The Netherlands Divided*.

3.73 **Haley**, K. H. D., *The Dutch in the Seventeenth Century*, 1972. Popular illustrated work.

3.74 **Houtte**, J. A. van, *An Economic History of the Low Countries, 800-1800*, 1977. Informative survey, descriptive rather than analytic.

3.75 **Huizinga**, J., *Dutch Civilisation in the Seventeenth Century, and Other Essays*, 1968. Celebrated title essay (9-104) first publ. in Dutch, 1941.

3.76 **Riley**, J. C., 'The Dutch economy after 1650. Decline or growth?', *J.Eur.Ec.Hist.*, 13, 1984, 521-69. Suggests that economy may in fact have reached prosperous plateau.

3.77 **Schilling**, H., 'Die Geschichte der nördlichen Niederlande und die Modernisierungstheorie', *Gesch.und Gesellschaft*, 8, 1982, 475-517. Assessment of "progressive" elements in Dutch society in two centuries following emancipation from Spain.

3.78 **Schöffer**, I., 'Did Holland's golden age coincide with a period of crisis?', *Acta Hist.Neerlandica*, 1, 1966, 82-107. Repr. in Parker and Smith (2.78), 83-109.

3.79 **Uytven**, R. van, 'What is new socially and economically in the sixteenth-century Netherlands', *ib.*, 7, 1974, 18-53.

3.80 **Van der Wee**, H., 'The economy as a factor in the start of the revolt in the Southern Netherlands', *ib.*, 5, 1971, 52-67.

3.81 —— 'Das Phänomen des Wachstums und der Stagnation im Lichte der Antwerpener und südniederländischen Wirtschaft des 16. Jahrhunderts', *VSWG*, 54, 1967, 203-49.

3.82 **Wilson**, C. H., 'The decline of the Netherlands', in his *Economic History and the Historian. Collected Essays*, 1969, 22-47. Revised version of paper first publ. in 1939, dealing with eighteenth-century economy.

3.83 —— *The Dutch Republic and the Civilisation of the Seventeenth Century*, 1968. Lively account for general reader.

3.84 **Zumthor**, P., *Daily Life in Rembrandt's Holland*, 1962. Transl. from French ed. of 1959. Another popularisation.

SPAIN AND PORTUGAL

HISTORIOGRAPHY AND SOURCES

3.85 **Bishko**, C. J., 'The Iberian background of Latin American history. Recent progress and continuing problems', *Hisp. Am. Hist. Rev.*, 36, 1956, 50-80. Historiographical article on Spanish and Portuguese society in colonial period.

3.86 **Linz**, J. J., 'Five centuries of Spanish history. Quantification and comparison', in V. R. Lorwin and J. M. Price, eds., *The Dimensions of the Past. Materials, Problems, and Opportunities for Quantitative Work in History*, New Haven, Conn., 1972, 177-261.

3.87 **Mackay**, A., 'Recent literature on Spanish economic history', *Ec.Hist.Rev.*, 2nd ser., 31, 1978, 129-45. To c.1850. Excludes English-language material.

3.88 **Molas Ribalta**, P., 'La economía
española en la epoca preindustrial.
Balance bibliografico, 1950-83', *VSWG*,
71, 1984, 384-95.

3.89 **Pérez Moreda**, V., 'The journal *Moneda y
Crédito* and its contribution to Spanish
historiography', *J.Eur.Ec.Hist.*, 4, 1975,
753-88. Includes index of articles and
reviews from journal over these years.

3.90 **Vicens Vives**, J., and others, 'L'Espagne
aux 16e et 17e siècles. Tendances,
problèmes, et perspectives de travail de la
recherche historique en Espagne',
Rev.Hist., 220, 1958, 1-42. Useful for
some lesser-known works of 1950s.

SPAIN: WORKS COVERING LONG TIME-SPAN
See also 4.136

3.91 **Amalric**, J.-P., and others, *Aux Origines du
Retard Économique de l'Espagne, 16e-19e
Siècles*, Paris, 1983. Collective work, in
which Parts 1 (dealing with eighteenth-
century agriculture and its investment
potential) and 3 (dealing with cultural
obstacles to growth) are relevant.

3.92 **Atkinson**, W. C., *A History of Spain and
Portugal*, 1960. Short work, interpretative
rather than narrative.

3.93 **Castro**, A., *The Spaniards. An Introduction
to their History*, Berkeley, Calif., 1971.
Later version of thesis first expounded in
España en Su Historia (1948) that Spanish
society was shaped by interaction and
tensions between Old Christians, *conversos*,
and *moriscos*.

3.94 **Domínguez Ortiz**, A., *El Antiguo
Régimen. Los Reyes Católicos y los
Austrias*, Madrid, 1973. Textbook by
distinguished and prolific historian of early
modern Spain.

3.95 **Elliott**, J. H., *Imperial Spain, 1469-1716*,
1963. Standard introductory work.

3.96 **Herr**, R., *An Historical Essay on Modern
Spain*, Berkeley, Calif., 1974. By specialist
on eighteenth-century Spain. Chapters 3-4
cover early modern period.

3.97 **Kamen**, H., 'The decline of Spain. A
historical myth?', *P.&P.*, 81, 1978, 24-50.
Argues that despite Spain's imperial role its
economy was always underdeveloped and
dependent. See also debate with J. I. Israel,
ib., 91, 1981, 170-85.

3.98 —— *Spain, 1469-1714. A Society of
Conflict*, 1983. Stronger on social and

economic history than 3.95 and 100.

3.99 **Klaveren**, J. van, *Europäische
Wirtschaftsgeschichte Spaniens im 16. und
17. Jahrhundert*, Stuttgart, 1960. Early
chaps. concentrate on Castile and America;
survey of industry and agriculture by
regions follows.

3.100 **Lynch**, J., *Spain under the Hapsburgs*, 2
vols., 1964-69. 2nd ed., 1982. Most
substantial English-language synthesis.

3.101 **Menéndez Pidal**, R., and Jover Zamora,
J. M., eds., *Historia de España*, 40 vols. in
50 (projected), Madrid, 1935- .
Monumental, sumptuously produced
collaborative history, founded by leading
cultural historian of inter-war period
(Menéndez), and still some way from
completion. Vols.17-31 will cover late
fifteenth century to accession of Joseph
Bonaparte; but those most specifically
directed to social and economic themes (19,
23, 28, and 30) have still to appear.

3.102 **Payne**, S. G., *A History of Spain and
Portugal*, 2 vols., Madison, Wis., 1973.
Bulky general history. Portugal receives
relatively little space.

3.103 **Phillips**, Carla R., 'Time and duration. A
model for the economy of early modern
Spain', *Am.Hist.Rev.*, 92, 1987, 531-62.
Argues squarely for Malthusian model
down to late seventeenth century.

3.104 **Silva**, J. G. da, *En Espagne.
Développement Économique, Subsistance,
Déclin*, Paris, 1965. Deals mainly with
sixteenth and seventeenth centuries.

3.105 **Schwarzmann**, M., 'Background factors
in Spanish economic decline', *Explor.
Entrepren. Hist.*, 3, 1951, 221-47. Tries to
isolate factors which hindered emergence
of entrepreneurial class.

3.106 **Vázquez de Prada**, V., *Historia
Económica y Social de España. Vol.3: Los
Siglos 16 y 17*, Madrid, 1978. First vol. to
appear of major new series, of which author
is also general editor. Well-illustrated.
Review article: A. Eiras Roel, *Hispania*,
148, 1981, 433-51.

3.107 **Vicens Vives**, J., *Approaches to the History
of Spain*, Berkeley, Calif., 1970. Transl.
from second Spanish ed. of 1960 (first
appeared, 1952). Along with A.
Domínguez Ortiz, Vicens turned Spanish
historiography decisively towards
economic and social themes neglected by
nationalist tradition.

3.108 —— *An Economic History of Spain*,

Princeton, N.J., 1969. Transl. from third
Spanish ed. of 1964 (first appeared 1955).
Chapters 29-30 publ. as 'The decline of
Spain in the seventeenth century' in C. M.
Cipolla, ed., *The Economic Decline of
Empires*, 1970, 121-67.

.109 ──, ed., *Historia Social y Económica de
España y América*, 5 vols., Barcelona,
1957-59. Pioneering collaborative work
whose contributors incl. J. Nadal, J.
Reglá, and A. Domínguez Ortiz.
Vols.2-4 have material on relevant period.

.110 **Young**, G. F. W., 'The trajectory of
Castile, 1492-1700', *Hist. Reflections* 6,
1979, 353-65. Sketch of Castile's rise and
decline as European power considered in
relation to its social base.

SPAIN: TO CIRCA 1650
See also 10.212.

.111 **Bennassar**, B., *Un Siècle d'Or Espagnol
(Vers 1525-Vers 1648)*, Paris, 1982.
Strongly recommended.

.112 **Castillo**, A., 'Population et "richesse" en
Castille durant la seconde moitié du 16e
siècle', *Annales*, 20, 1965, 719-33.
Observations based on assessments for tax
called "milliones".

.113 **Chaunu**, P., *L'Espagne de Charles Quint*, 2
vols., Paris, 1973. University lectures.

.114 **Defourneaux**, M., *Daily Life in Spain in
the Golden Age*, 1970. Transl. from Spanish
ed. of 1965. Tends to rely on literary
evidence.

.115 **Devèze**, M., *L'Espagne de Philippe IV,
1621-65. Siècle d'Or et de Misère*, 2 vols.,
Paris, 1970-71. Vol.2 contains most of
relevant material.

.116 **Domínguez Ortiz**, A., *The Golden Age of
Spain, 1516-1659*, 1971. Composed for
Anglo-Saxon audience.

.117 ── *La Sociedad Española en el Siglo 17*, 2
vols., Madrid, 1963. Contains sections on
demography, nobility, and Church.

.118 **Elliott**, J. H., 'The decline of Spain', *P.&
P.*, 20, 1961, 52-75. Repr. in Aston (2.72),
167-94; and Cipolla (3.108), 168-95.
Concentrates on social and economic
problems besetting Castile in period
1590-1620.

.119 ── 'Self-perception and decline in early
seventeenth-century Spain', *P.& P.*, 74,
1977, 41-61. Prescriptions for perceived
political and economic crisis as reflected in
writings of *arbitristas* (publicists on fringes

of government). On *arbitristas* see also
10.127.

3.120 **Kellenbez**, H., 'The impact of growth on
government. The example of Spain',
J.Ec.Hist., 27, 1967, 340-62. Questions
how adequate Spanish resources were for
coping with world power in sixteenth
century.

3.121 **Lovett**, A. W., *Early Habsburg Spain,
1517-98*, 1986. Note esp. chap.15 on
financial system, and chaps.16-19 on
economic and social questions.

3.122 **Ladero Quesada**, M. A., *España en 1492*,
Madrid, 1978. Authoritative portrait of
country on eve of imperial acquisitions
(forms vol.1 of *Historia de América
Latina*).

3.123 **Stradling**, R. A., 'Seventeenth-century
Spain. Decline or survival?', *Eur. Stud.
Rev.*, 9, 1979, 157-94. Debates whether
Spain's political and economic decline can
be considered simultaneous. But see 3.97.

3.124 **Vilar**, P., 'The age of *Don Quixote*', in
Earle (3.71), 100-12. Transl. from *Europe*,
34, 1956, 3-16. Also publ. in *New Left
Rev.*, 68, 1971, 59-71. Impressionistic
account of early seventeenth-century
Spanish society.

SPAIN: 1650-1800

3.125 **Anes Alvarez**, G., *El Antiguo Régimen.
Los Borbones*, Madrid, 1976. Good
textbook, with strong emphasis on social
history.

3.126 **Artola**, M., *Antiguo Régimen y Revolución
Liberal*, Barcelona, 1978. Charts economic
changes which eventually led Cortes of
1810 to embark on dismantling of
corporate structures.

3.127 **Callahan**, W. J., *Church, Politics, and
Society in Spain, 1750-1874*, Cambridge,
Mass., 1984. Two useful introductory
chapters on period 1750-90.

3.128 **Domínguez Ortiz**, A., *Sociedad y Estado
en el Siglo 18 Español*, Barcelona, 1976.
Much revised version of work first publ. in
1955.

3.129 *La Economía del Antiguo Régimen. La
Renta Nacional de la Corona de Castilla*,
Madrid, 1977. Collaborative work which
attempts to assess Spanish national income
and its distribution in mid-eighteenth
century.

3.130 *La Economía Española al Final del
Antiguo Régimen*, 4 vols., Madrid, 1982.

Not a connected history, but essays fashioned from research in progress and organised round themes of agriculture (vol.1); manufactures (vol.2); commerce and colonies (vol.3); institutions (vol.4). Deals mainly with second half of eighteenth century.

3.131 **Fernández**, R., ed., *España en el Siglo 18. Homenaje a Pierre Vilar*, Barcelona, 1985. Collection organised on regional lines. Contributors incl. A. García Baquero (Andalusia), G. Anes (Asturias), A. García Sanz (central provinces and Extremadura), etc.

3.132 **González Enciso**, A., and Patricio Merino, J., 'The public sector and economic growth in eighteenth-century Spain', *J.Eur.Ec.Hist.*, 8, 1979, 553-92. Looks at government-run estates and factories, their poor management and somewhat contradictory objectives.

3.133 **Herr**, R., *The Eighteenth-Century Revolution in Spain*, Princeton, N.J., 1958. Principally a study of origins of liberalism, but contains chapters on economic and social conditions.

3.134 **Kamen**, H., 'The decline of Castile. The last crisis', *Ec.Hist.Rev.*, 2nd ser., 17, 1964, 63-76. Economic and demographic problems of period 1677-86.

3.135 —— *Spain in the Later Seventeenth Century*, 1980. Global portrait of society in neglected era of Carlos II, emphasising signs of economic renewal.

3.136 **Plaza Prieto**, J., *Estructura Economica de España en el Siglo 18*, Madrid, 1975. Substantial work.

3.137 **Sarrailh**, J., *L'Espagne Éclairée de la Seconde Moitié du 18e Siècle*, Paris, 1954. Large-scale work of intellectual history, which also contains much on social background.

SPANISH REGIONS AND PROVINCES

See also 3.131. Note also semi-general studies on Alicante region (9.241); Andalusia (9.313); Aragon (10.432); Galicia (7.106, 9.469); Granada (8.76); Murcia (8.80, 12.86).

3.138 **Domínguez Ortiz**, A., ed., *Historia de Andalucía. Vols.4-5*, Madrid, 1980-83. Valuable collective history. These vols. cover late fifteenth to late eighteenth centuries.

3.139 **Ladero Quesada**, M. A., ed., *Andalucía,*

de la Edad Media a la Moderna, Madrid, 1977. Miscellany on late medieval and early modern region.

3.140 *Historia de Asturias, 6-7. Edad Moderna*, Vitoria, 1977-80. Vol.6 on sixteenth century is by M. Fernández Alvarez and others; vol.7 on seventeenth and eighteenth centuries by G. Anes.

3.141 **García Cárcel**, R., *Historia de Cataluña, Siglos 16-17*, 2 vols., Barcelona, 1985. Vol.1, the more substantial, deals with general culture and social structure; vol.2 with "histoire événementielle".

3.142 **Vilar**, P., *La Catalogne dans l'Espagne Moderne. Recherches sur les Fondements Économiques des Structures Nationales*, 3 vols., Paris, 1962. Huge work that deals particularly with origins of industrialisation in eighteenth century, after sketching province's economic and political evolution up to this point. Unfinished (Vilar intended to deal with economic roots of modern Catalan nationalism). Condensed ed., 2 vols., 1977. Review articles: P. Chaunu, *Rev.Hist.Éc.et Soc.*, 41, 1962, 145-82; F. Braudel, *Annales*, 23, 1968, 375-89.

3.143 —— 'Le déclin catalan du bas moyen-âge. Hypothèses sur sa chronologie', *Estud.de Hist.Mod.*, 6, 1956-59, 1-68. Looks at reasons for collapse of Catalan prosperity during fifteenth century.

3.144 **García Sanz**, A., *Desarrollo y Crisis del Antiguo Régimen en Castilla la Vieja. Economía y Sociedad en Tierras de Segovia de 1500 a 1814*, Madrid, 1977. Substantial work, mainly, but not exclusively, on rural sector of region.

3.145 **Meijide Pardo**, A., *Economía Marítima de la Galicia Cantábrica en el Siglo 18*, Valladolid, 1971. Fishery trade looms large.

3.146 **Casey**, J., *The Kingdom of Valencia in the Seventeenth Century*, 1979. Rich study embracing society, politics, economic weakness, and demographic repercussions of Morisco expulsion.

3.147 **Fernández de Pinedo**, E., *Crecimiento Economico y Transformaciones Sociales del País Vasco, 1100-1850*, Madrid, 1974. Major emphasis on period from late fifteenth century onwards.

3.148 **García de Cortazar**, J. A., *Vizcaya en el Siglo 15. Aspectos Económicos y Sociales*, Bilbao, 1966.

PORTUGAL
See also 4.130; 7.116.

3.149 **Descamps**, P., *Histoire Sociale du Portugal*, Paris, 1959. Pioneering work, completed in 1939 and published posthumously.

3.150 **Hanson**, C. A., *Economy and Society in Baroque Portugal, 1668-1703*, Minneapolis, Minn., 1981. Commerce and public finance loom largest.

3.151 **Oliveira Marques**, A. H. R. de, *History of Portugal*, 2 vols., New York, 1972. 2nd ed., 1976.

ITALY

HISTORIOGRAPHY AND SOURCES
See also 3.180,182,190-1.

3.152 **Cipolla**, C. M., 'List of books and articles on Italian economic history published in Italy, 1939-49', *Ec.Hist.Rev.*, 2nd ser., 4, 1951, 271-80.

NATIONAL HISTORY

3.153 **Aymard**, M., 'From feudalism to capitalism in Italy. The case that doesn't fit', *Review*, 6, 1982, 131-208. Transl. from *Storia d'Italia: Annali*, vol.1 (see 3.168) Contends that feudal relations, even in Southern Italy, had already given way to freer structures by 1500.

3.154 **Braudel**, F., 'A model for the analysis of the decline of Italy', *Review*, 2, 1979, 647-62. Transl. from *Storia d'Italia*, 2, ii (item 3.168). Discusses graph of Italy's high and low economic points between 1100 and 1650.

3.155 **Carpanetto**, D., and Ricuperati, G., *Italy in the Age of Reason, 1685-1789*, 1987. Part of *Longman History of Italy* series, welcome because syntheses (as opposed to local studies) are scanty in Italian history. Vols. covering Renaissance and early seventeenth century not yet available. This work gives rather disproportionate attention to reform movements highlighted by work of Franco Venturi (see 10.95,130; 11.155).

3.156 **Cipolla**, C. M., 'The decline of Italy', in B. Pullan, ed., *Crisis and Change in the Venetian Economy in the Sixteenth and Seventeenth Centuries*, 1968, 127-45; and Cipolla (3.108), 196-214. Expanded version of article first publ. in *Ec.Hist.Rev.*, 2nd ser., 5, 1952, 178-87. Attributes seventeenth-century stagnation to high labour costs and growing competition of other areas in textiles and financial services.

3.157 **Delumeau**, J., *L'Italie de Botticelli à Bonaparte*, Paris, 1974. Useful textbook.

3.158 **Fasano Guarini**, Elena, ed., *Potere e Società negli Stati Regionali Italiani del '500 e '600*, Bologna, 1978. Collection of studies on government and society in principal states; note R. B. Litchfield on Florentine bureaucracy, M. Berengo on aristocracy of Verona, G. Galasso and R. Villari on Neapolitan feudalism.

3.159 **Gage**, J. S., *Life in Italy at the time of the Medici*, 1968. Well illustrated popular work.

3.160 **Laven**, P., *Renaissance Italy, 1464-1534*, 1966. Sound general history with introductory chapters on economic background.

3.161 **Lopez**, R. S., *The Three Ages of the Italian Renaissance*, Charlottesville, Va., 1970. Short but erudite lecture series providing background to cultural achievements for period 1450-1560.

3.162 **Martines**, L., *Power and Imagination. City-States in Renaissance Italy*, New York, 1979. Complex account of society, politics, and culture from eleventh to sixteenth centuries.

3.163 **Mazzei**, Rita, 'Decline of the city economies of Central and Northern Italy in the seventeenth century', *J.Ital.Hist.*, 2, 1979, 197-208. Rather disjointed essay, mainly based on research into trade relations with Poland.

3.164 **Molho**, A., ed., *Social and Economic Foundations of the Italian Renaissance*, New York, 1969. Reader drawn from sources and secondary works covering thirteenth to fifteenth centuries.

3.165 **Procacci**, G., *History of the Italian People*, 1970. Transl. from French ed. of 1968.

Broad social and cultural history, eleventh
century to present day.

3.166 **Romano**, R., 'Italy in the crisis of the
seventeenth century', in Earle (3.71),
185-98. Transl. from *Studi Stor.*, 9, 1968,
723-41. Pessimistic view of economic
performance.

3.167 —— *Tra Due Crisi. L'Italia del
Rinascimento*, 1971. Collection of
previously publ. articles covering general
aspects of society and economy.

3.168 —— and Vivanti, C., eds., *Storia d'Italia*,
Turin, 1972- . Complex series, generally
known, from publisher, as "Einaudi"
history. Inspired by French models
(Braudel was contributor, see 3.154), and
undoubtedly most interesting general
survey of Italian history. Main narrative in
vols.1-4 (in 7), followed by supplementary
volumes (*Documenti, Annali*, etc.) dealing
with special topics such as language,
folklore, medicine, landscape (see items
4.18; 13.71; 14.265,374).

3.169 **Santosuosso**, A., 'The Italian crisis at
mid-sixteenth century. A matter of shift
and decadence', *Can.J.Hist.*, 10, 1975,
147-64. General survey of social, political,
and cultural developments, starting from
Koenigsberger's article 'decadence or shift'
(14.242).

3.170 [U.T.E.T.] *Storia d'Italia*, Turin, 1978- .
Another multi-volume history (cf.3.168),
most useful for its regional sections, e.g. C.
Costantini, *La Repubblica di Genova
nell'Età Moderna* (vol.9, 1978); D. Sella
and C. Capra, *Il Ducato di Milano dal 1535
al 1796* (vol.11, 1984); M. Caravale and A.
Caracciolo, *Lo Stato Pontificio da Martino V
a Pio IX* (vol.14, 1978).

3.171 **Vaussard**, M., *Daily Life in Eighteenth-
Century Italy*, 1962. Transl. from French
ed. of 1959. Lightweight, mainly relying
on travel accounts.

3.172 **Woolf**, S., *A History of Italy, 1700-1860.
The Social Constraints of Political Change*,
1979. Excellent synthesis, much of which
first appeared in Italian in vol.3 of 3.168.

INDIVIDUAL STATES
AND REGIONS
See also 3.158,170.

3.173 **Caizzi**, B., *Il Comasco sotto il Dominio
Spagnolo [e] Austriaco*, 2 vols., Como, 1955.
Special attention to fiscal burdens of
foreign rule.

3.174 **De Maddalena**, A., *Dalla Città al Borgo.
Avvio di una Metamorfosi Economica e
Sociale nella Lombardia Spagnola*, Milan,
1982. Miscellany spanning early modern
period: studies of firms and agricultural
enterprises, with some concluding general
essays.

3.175 —— and others, eds., *Economia,
Istituzioni, Cultura in Lombardia nell'Età
di Maria Teresa*, 3 vols., Milan, 1982.
Collects papers from three conferences;
great diversity of topics covered.

3.176 **Sella**, D., *Crisis and Continuity. The
Economy of Spanish Lombardy in the
Seventeenth Century*, Cambridge, Mass.,
1979. Argues that countryside fared less
badly than Milan and other towns during
recession. Note series of review articles in
Società e Storia, 5, 1982, 351-99.

3.177 **Berner**, S., 'Florentine society in the late
sixteenth and early seventeenth centuries',
Stud.in Renaiss., 18, 1971, 203-46.
Examines both state and society under
Ferdinand I (1587-1609).

3.178 **Brucker**, G. A., *Florence, 1138-1737*,
1984. Coffee-table book, but text by
distinguished historian of Renaissance
state.

3.179 **D'Addario**, A., 'Burocrazia, economia e
finanze dello stato fiorentino alla metà del
Cinquecento', *Arch.Stor.Ital.*, 121, 1963,
362-456.

3.180 **Diaz**, F., 'Recent studies on Medicean
Tuscany', *J.Ital.Hist.*, 1, 1978, 95-110.
Bibliographical review.

3.181 **Malanima**, P., 'Industria e agricoltura in
Toscana tra Cinque e Seicento', *Studi Stor.*,
21, 1980, 281-309. Useful survey.

3.182 **Najemy**, J. M., 'Linguaggi storiografici
sulla Firenze rinascimentale', *Riv. Stor.
Ital.*, 97, 1985, 102-59. Discusses several
recent works, incl. 6.148,248; 9.640;
10.45.

3.183 **Heers**, J., *Gênes au 15e Siècle. Activité
Économique et Problèmes Sociaux*, Paris,
1961. Large-scale cross-sectional study of
Genoa in 1450s and '60s. For analysis of
social forces behind resistance to French
domination in succeeding period, see P.
Coles, 'The crisis of Renaissance society.
Genoa, 1488-1507', *P.& P.*, 11, 1957,
17-47. For further material on Genoa as
financial and mercantile centre see Section
9.

3.184 **Bulferetti**, L., *Agricoltura, Industria e
Commercio in Piemonte nel Secolo 18*, Turin,

1963.

3.185 **De Felice**, R., *Aspetti e Momenti della Vita Economica di Roma e del Lazio nei Secoli 18 e 19*, Rome, 1965. Collection of related studies, strongest on agrarian conditions.

3.186 *Aspetti e Cause della Decadenza Economica Veneziana nel Secolo 17*, Venice, 1961. Influential in establishing "seventeenth-century decline" as orthodoxy; contributors incl. F. Braudel, R. Romano, H. Kellenbenz. See further D. Sella's book (9.88).

3.187 **Berengo**, M., *La Società Veneta alla Fine del '700*, Florence, 1955. Substantial study of conditions which led to rise of Jacobinism.

3.188 **Chambers**, D. S., *The Imperial Age of Venice, 1380-1580*, 1970. Well-illustrated popular work.

3.189 **Georgelin**, J., *Venise au Siècle des Lumières*, Paris, 1978. Mine of information, though detail and statistics tend to overwhelm interpretation. For much lighter work on Enlightenment Venice see N. Jonard, *La Vie Quotidienne à Venise au 18e Siècle*, Paris, 1965.

3.190 **Grubb**, J. S., 'When myths lose power. Four decades of Venetian history', *J.Mod.Hist.*, 58, 1986, 43-94. Convenient literature review built round theme that historians have gradually displaced picture of balanced society and polity.

3.191 **Lane**, F. C., 'Recent studies on the economic history of Venice', *J.Ec.Hist.*, 23, 1963, 312-34. Second half of review essay deals with early modern period.

3.192 —— *Venice. A Maritime Republic*, Baltimore, Md., 1973. General history of Venetian state and economy. Review article: E. Cochrane and J. Kirshner, *J.Mod.Hist.*, 47, 1975, 321-34.

3.193 **McNeill**, W. H., *Venice, the Hinge of Europe, 1081-1797*, Chicago, 1974. On Venetian role as intermediary between Western and Eastern Europe.

3.194 **Pullan**, B., 'The significance of Venice', *Bull.John Rylands Lib.*, 56, 1974, 443-62. Attempt to explain relative social and political stability of seventeenth-century Venice.

3.195 **Tenenti**, A., *Piracy and the Decline of Venice, 1580-1615*, Berkeley, Calif., 1967. Transl. from Italian ed. of 1961. Explains problems in defending shipping against incursions of English as well as Barbary and Uskok corsairs. See also earlier work on insurance aspects of problem, *Naufrages, Corsaires, et Assurances Maritimes à Venise, 1592-1609*, Paris, 1959.

3.196 **Caracciolo**, F., *Il Regno di Napoli nei Secoli 16 e 17. Vol.1: Economia e Società*, Rome, 1966. Strongly critical of Spanish administration's deleterious effects on Neapolitan economy.

3.197 **Chorley**, P., *Oil, Silk, and Enlightenment. Economic Problems in Eighteenth-Century Naples*, Naples, 1965. Useful, though rather narrowly focussed. Wider, less academic work is R. Bouvier and A. Laffargue, *La Vie Napolitaine au 18e Siècle*, Paris, 1957.

3.198 **Coniglio**, G., *Aspetti della Società Meridionale nel Secolo 16*, Naples, 1978. Concentrates esp. on poverty and criminality in Naples. See also his earlier work, written more from perspective of government, *Il Regno di Napoli al Tempo di Carlo V. Amministrazione e Vita Economico-Sociale*, Naples, 1951.

3.199 **De Rosa**, G., and Cestaro, A., *Territorio e Società nella Storia del Mezzogiorno*, Naples, 1973. Substantial reader on southern society from sixteenth century onwards, incorporating documents, contemporary sources, and modern historiography.

3.200 **Galasso**, G., *Economia e Società nella Calabria del Cinquecento*, Naples, 1967. Explores factors which defeated promising economic diversification of earlier sixteenth century.

3.201 **Lepre**, A., *Storia del Mezzogiorno, 1. La Longa Durata e la Crisi (1500-1656)*, Naples, 1986. On Kingdom of Naples only, and its economic and power structures. Chap. on revolt of 1647 and aftermath.

3.202 **Marino**, J. A., 'Economic idylls and pastoral realities. The "trickster economy" in the Kingdom of Naples', *Comp. Stud. Soc. & Hist.*, 24, 1982, 211-34. Somwhat diffuse essay on cultural values of Neapolitans as manifested in economic behaviour.

3.203 **Villani**, P., *Mezzogiorno tra Riforme e Rivoluzione*, Bari, 1973. Essays on social issues of late eighteenth and early nineteenth centuries. See also earlier collection on this period, concentrating on agrarian issues, *Feudalità, Riforme, Capitalismo Agrario...*, Bari, 1968.

3.204 **Villari**, R., ed., *Il Sud nella Storia d'Italia. Antologia della Questione Meridionale*, Bari, 1966. Anthology of writings on "Southern problem" beginning with substantial section from eighteenth century.

3.205 **Koenigsberger**, H. G., *The Government of Sicily under Philip II of Spain*, 1951. Revised ed., under title *The Practice of Empire*, Ithaca, N.Y., 1969. Primarily study of Spanish administration, but provides good deal of information on general conditions.

3.206 **Smith**, D. M., *A History of Sicily. Vols.2-3*, 1968. General history of medieval and modern Sicily.

3.207 **Titone**, V., *La Società Siciliana sotto gli Spagnoli e le Origini della Questione Meridionale*, Palermo, 1978. More substantial, but also more diffuse, is his *La Sicilia dalla Dominazione Spagnola all'Unità d'Italia*, Bologna, 1955.

GERMANY AND SWITZERLAND

HISTORIOGRAPHY AND SOURCES
See also 3.227.

3.208 **Conze**, W., 'Writings on social and economic history in Germany, 1939-49', *Ec.Hist.Rev.*, 2nd ser., 3, 1950, 126-32.

3.209 **Dorpalen**, A., *German History in Marxist Perspective. The East German Approach*, 1985. Two chapters devoted to East German treatment of early modern period.

3.210 —— 'Post-mortem on Prussia. The East German position', *Central Eur.Hist.*, 4, 1971, 332-45. Strengths and weaknesses of East German historians' general model of Prussia's development and role in German society from Great Elector to 1871.

3.211 **Wehler**, H.-U., *Bibliographie zur Modernen Deutschen Sozialgeschichte, 18.-20. Jahrhundert*; and *Bibliographie zur Modernen Deutschen Wirtschaftsgeschichte, 18.-20. Jahrhundert*, Göttingen, 1976. Two short selective guides; topical arrangement makes eighteenth-century material difficult to extract

3.212 ——, ed., *Die Moderne Deutsche Geschichte in der Internationalen Forschung, 1945-75*, Göttingen, 1978. Ten review articles on foreign contributions to German historiography. Main emphasis outside our period.

3.213 **Zophy**, J. W., *An Annotated Bibliography of the Holy Roman Empire*, Westport, Conn., 1986. Excellent range, though comments too often merely paraphrase title.

GERMANY: WORKS COVERING LONG TIME-SPAN
See also 2.35.

3.214 **Aubin**, H., and Zorn, W., eds., *Handbuch der Deutschen Wirtschafts- und Sozialgeschichte*, 2 vols., Stuttgart, 1971-76. Best available synthesis; collective work with contributions from leading historians such as W. Abel, H. Kellenbenz, W. Conze, etc. Vol.1 covers to 1800.

3.215 **Bechtel**, H., *Wirtschaftsgeschichte Deutschlands*, 3 vols., 1951-56. Condensed single vol. ed., 1967. Vol.2 covers sixteenth to eighteenth centuries. Now rather dated in preoccupation with economic thought and policy.

3.216 **Engelsing**, R., *Sozial- und Wirtschaftsgeschichte Deutschlands*, Göttingen, 1973. 2nd ed., 1976. Handy textbook.

3.217 **Kellenbenz**, H., *Deutsche Wirtschaftsgeschichte*, 2 vols., Munich, 1977-81. Researcher of remarkable application and industry, but not at his best in synthesis.

3.218 **Kuczynski**, J., *Geschichte des Alltags des Deutschen Volkes. Studien*, 5 vols., Berlin, 1980-82. Late work by veteran E. German historian of working class. Vols.1-2 deal with period 1600-1810, but are avowedly a mosaic of other historians' writings.

3.219 **Lütge**, F., *Deutsche Sozial- und Wirtschaftsgeschichte. Ein Überblick*, Berlin, 1952. 3rd ed., 1966. Another now somewhat old-fashioned textbook.

3.220 **Mottek**, H., and others, *Wirtschaftsgeschichte Deutschlands. Ein Grundriss*, 3 vols., 1957-74. East German textbook which has gone through several editions. Dogmatic but informative. Vol.1 extends to late eighteenth century.

GERMANY: TO 1648

3.221 **Abel**, W., 'Zur Entwicklung des Sozialprodukts in Deutschland im 16. Jahrhundert', *Jb.Nationalökonomie*, 173, 1961, 448-89. Intended as follow-up to 3.225, with emphasis on development of agricultural production.

3.222 **Bog**, I., 'Wachstumsprobleme der oberdeutschen Wirtschaft, 1540-1618', *ib.*, 179, 1966, 493-537. Draws mainly on evidence of German and Swiss cities, esp. Nuremberg.

3.223 **Carsten**, F. L., 'Was there an economic decline in Germany before the Thirty Years War?', *Eng.Hist.Rev.*, 71, 1956, 240-7. Uses rather slender evidence of buoyancy in Bavarian duties on drink to argue against decline.

3.224 **Holborn**, H., *A History of Modern Germany. The Reformation*, New York, 1959. Part of classic trilogy of liberal historiography. See also 3.241.

3.225 **Lutge**, F., 'The fourteenth and fifteenth centuries in social and economic history', in G. Strauss, ed., *Pre-Reformation Germany*, 1972. Transl. from *Jb.Nationalökonomie*, 162, 1950, 161-213. Argues that Black Death originated great changes in German social structure.

3.226 —— 'Die wirtschaftliche Lage Deutschlands vor Ausbruch des Dreissigjährigen Kriegs', *Jb.Nationalökonomie*, 170, 1958, 43-99. Repr. in his *Studien zur Sozial- und Wirtschaftsgeschichte*, Stuttgart, 1963, 336-95.

3.227 **Rowan**, S. W., 'The Common Penny (1495-99) as a source of German social and demographic history', *Central Eur.Hist.*, 10, 1977, 148-64. Poll tax; usefulness illustrated by analysis of returns for Freiburg-im-Breisgau.

3.228 **Steinmetz**, M., *Deutschland von 1476 bis 1648*, Berlin, 1965. 2nd ed., 1978. By veteran E. German exponent of "early bourgeois revolution" interpretation of Reformation era. Range impressive, subtlety less so.

3.229 **Strauss**, G., ed., *Manifestations of Discontent in Germany on the Eve of the Reformation. A Collection of Documents*,

Bloomington, Ind., 1971. Useful student source-book.

THIRTY YEARS' WAR

3.230 **Benecke**, G., *Germany in the Thirty Years' War*, 1978. Documentary extracts.

3.231 —— 'The problem of death and destruction in Germany during the Thirty Years' War. New evidence from the Middle Weser front', *Eur.Stud.Rev.*, 2, 1972, 239-53. Examines conditions in principality of Lippe (see also 3.246), and suggests that claims of war damage were exaggerated to keep down occupation costs.

3.232 **Ergang**, R. R., *The Myth of the All-Destructive Fury of the Thirty Years' War*, Pocono Pines, Pa., 1956. Short study. With 3.239, one of earliest essays to challenge old orthodoxy of devastating effects.

3.233 **Franz**, G., *Der Dreissigjährige Krieg und das Deutsche Volk. Untersuchungen zur Bevölkerungs- und Agrargeschichte*, 3rd ed., Stuttgart, 1961. Reworking of important book first publ. in 1940.

3.234 **Haan**, H., 'Prosperität und dreissigjähriger Krieg', *Gesch.und Gesellschaft*, 7, 1981, 91-118.

3.235 **Kamen**, H., 'The economic and social consequences of the Thirty Years' War', *P.& P.*, 39, 1968, 44-61. Argues that German economies (east and west) followed general European trends, only marginally aggravated by effects of war.

3.236 **Langer**, H., *The Thirty Years' War*, 1980. Transl. from E. German ed. of 1978. Well-illustrated work directed at wide audience, emphasising social and cultural impact of war in Germany.

3.237 **Rabb**, T. K., 'Effects of the Thirty Years' War on the German economy', *J.Mod.Hist.*, 34, 1962, 40-51. Review of literature on question, concluding that areas of prosperity certainly shrank.

3.238 **Schröer**, F., *Das Havelland im Dreissigjährigen Krieg. Ein Beitrag zur Geschichte der Mark Brandenburg*, Köln, 1966. Posthumous publ. of work researched in 1930s.

3.239 **Steinberg**, S. H., 'The Thirty Years' War. A new interpretation', *History*, 32, 1947, 89-102. Brief exposition of view that catastrophic effects on Germany have been exaggerated.

GERMANY: 1648-1800
See also 3.211 (bibliography).

3.240 **Bruford**, W. H., *Germany in the Eighteenth Century. The Social Background of the Literary Revival*, 1935. Remains useful general work, somewhat akin to Lough's on France (3.25,35).

3.241 **Holborn**, H., *A History of Modern Germany, 1648-1840*, New York, 1964.

3.242 **Sagarra**, Eda, *A Social History of Germany, 1648-1914*, 1977. Useful introduction, but lacks quantitative data.

3.243 **Vierhaus**, R., *Deutschland im Zeitalter des Absolutismus, 1648-1763*, Göttingen, 1978. Brief survey, but good coverage of social history.

GERMAN STATES AND REGIONS
See also semi-general studies on Bavaria (5.194; 9.484); Brandenburg (3.238); Hannover (7.149); Prussia (10.145,517); Upper Rhineland (4.93; 8.122); Württemberg (10.148).

3.244 *Handbuch der Bayerischen Geschichte. Vols.2-3*, Munich, 1969-71. Valuable collaborative work. Vol.2 covers old Bavaria; vol.3 regions of Franconia, Swabia, and Upper Palatinate; both down to end of eighteenth century.

3.245 **Ingrao**, C., ' "Barbarous strangers". Hessian state and society during the American Revolution', *Am.Hist.Rev.*, 87, 1982, 954-76. Background of state which provided largest contingent of mercenaries to British forces in America. See also Ingrao's book on government of Hesse, 10.139.

3.246 **Benecke**, G., *Society and Politics in Germany, 1500-1750*, 1974. Treats principality of Lippe as microcosm of social and administrative structures of

Empire. Review article: J. A. Vann, *Central Eur.Hist.*, 14, 1981, 79-86.

3.247 —— 'Labour relations and peasant society in Northwest Germany, c.1600', *History*, 58, 1973, 350-9. Rather haphazard catalogue of economic and moral regulations in force in Lippe.

3.248 **Büsch**, O., and Neugebauer, W., eds., *Moderne Preussische Geschichte, 1648-1947*, 3 vols., Berlin, 1981. Anthology reprinting notable essays publ. between 1877 and 1980, incl. several on social and economic history before 1800.

3.249 **Treue**, W., *Wirtschafts- und Technikgeschichte Preussens*, Berlin, 1984. Comprehensive economic history of Prussian kingdom in pre-unification period (1701-1871), emphasising role of bureaucrats and entrepreneurs.

3.250 **Blickle**, P., and Blickle, Renate, *Schwaben von 1268 bis 1803*, Munich, 1979. Excellent documentary history.

SWITZERLAND

3.251 **Bergier**, J.-F., *Histoire Économique de la Suisse*, Lausanne, 1983. Popular illustrated work by leading historian; follows tripartite schema, dealing in turn with population and land; industry; and infrastructure (communications and finance). Preliminary version publ. as *Problèmes de l'Histoire Économique de la Suisse*, Bern, 1968 – its last section (on commercial routes) transl. in R. Cameron and others, eds., *Essays in French Economic History*, Homewood, Ill., 1970, 110-22.

3.252 **Braun**, R., *Das Ausgehende Ancien Régime in der Schweiz. Aufriss einer Sozial- und Wirtschaftsgeschichte des 18. Jahrhunderts*, Göttingen, 1984. Major synthesis.

HABSBURG TERRITORIES
AND EAST CENTRAL EUROPE

HISTORIOGRAPHY AND SOURCES
See also 3.270,277-8,285.

3.253 **Di Vittorio**, A., 'Economic history in Austria over the last 25 years as represented in national and local historical reviews', *J.Eur.Ec.Hist.*, 1, 1972, 763-87.

3.254 **Jelavich**, C., ed., *Language and Area

Studies. East Central and Southeastern Europe, a Survey*, Chicago, 1969. Includes chapter on historiography. Covers Balkans and Central Europe (not incl. Poland and Russia).

3.255 **Petrovich**, M. B., 'American work on East European history, 1966-76', *Balkanistica*,

4, 1977-78, 89-122. Supplements above.

GENERAL SURVEYS
See also 2.35.

3.256 **Benecke**, G., *Maximilian I (1459-1519). An Analytical Biography*, 1982. In fact deals rather more with social history of Emperor's Austrian environs than high politics or administration.

3.257 **Bruckmüller**, E., *Sozialgeschichte Österreichs*, Vienna, 1985. Deals mainly, but not exclusively, with German-speaking provinces. Some 150 pages on early modern period.

3.258 **Dvornik**, F., *The Slavs in European History and Civilization*, New Brunswick, N.J., 1962. Covers late medieval and early modern history, and aims to show relatively unitary development of Slav nations.

3.259 **Evans**, R. J. W., *The Making of the Habsburg Monarchy, 1550-1700. An Interpretation*, 1979. Synthesis by leading historian of Central European culture.

3.260 **Kann**, R. A., *A History of the Habsburg Empire, 1526-1918*, Berkeley, Calif., 1974. Substantial basic introduction. See also Kann and Z. V. David, *The Peoples of the Eastern Habsburg Lands, 1526-1918*, Seattle, Wash., 1984 (similar work, with rather more concentration on Slavs and Magyars).

3.261 **Maczak**, A., and others, eds., *East-Central Europe in Transition. From the Fourteenth to the Seventeenth Century*, 1985. 12 essays, covering social and economic evolution of Bohemia, Hungary, and Poland. Contributors incl. I. Kiss, Maria Bogucka, M. Malowist, and J. Topolski.

3.262 **Matis**, H., ed., *Von der Glückseligkeit des Staates. Staat, Wirtschaft, und Gesellschaft in Österreich im Zeitalter des Aufgeklärten Absolutismus*, Berlin, 1981. Bulky collection on many aspects of social history and policy under Maria Theresa and Josef II.

3.263 *Österreich im Europa der Aufklärung. Kontinuität und Zäsur in Europa zur Zeit Maria Theresas und Josephs II*, 2 vols., Vienna, 1985. Another large-scale conference symposium; over 50 papers, tackling virtually every aspect of eighteenth-century Austro-Hungary.

3.264 **Portal**, R., *The Slavs*, 1969. Transl. from French ed. of 1965. Survey spanning origins to twentieth century. Economy and society well covered.

3.265 **Tapié**, V.-L., *L'Europe de Marie-Thérèse*, Paris, 1973. Somewhat misleading title. General history of Habsburg states during reign.

3.266 —— *The Rise and Fall of the Habsburg Monarchy*, 1971. Transl. from French ed. of 1969. Substantial proportion devoted to early modern period, in which Tapié is most at home.

3.267 **Tremel**, F., *Wirtschafts- und Sozialgeschichte Österreichs*, Vienna, 1969. Pioneering history, covering territory of present-day Austria. Somewhat feeble in social history area, where there was then little research to draw on.

3.268 **Wangermann**, E., *The Austrian Achievement, 1700-1800*, 1973. Popular illustrated work, very well done.

3.269 **Zimányi**, Vera, ed., *La Pologne et la Hongrie aux 16e-18e Siècles*, Budapest, 1981. Miscellany of socio-economic themes presented at bi-national symposium.

HUNGARY
See also 3.253-69 passim.

3.270 **Hanak**, P., 'Short survey of recent literature on Hungarian economic history', *Ec.Hist.Rev.*, 24, 1971, 667-81. Useful bibliography appended; goes back to c.1945.

3.271 **Benda**, K., 'Hungary in turmoil, 1580-1620', *Eur.Stud.Rev.*, 8, 1978, 281-304. Social and political conditions in non-Turkish Hungary and Transylvania.

3.272 **Den Hollander**, A. N. J., 'The great Hungarian plain. A European frontier area', *Comp.Stud.Soc.& Hist.*, 3, 1960-61, 74-88, 155-69. Historical anthropology.

3.273 **Király**, B.-K., *Hungary in the Late Eighteenth Century. The Decline of Enlightened Despotism*, New York, 1969. Principally study of political crisis at end of Joseph II's reign, but background information is valuable.

3.274 **Kiss**, I. N., 'Die demographische und wirtschaftliche Lage in Ungarn vom 16.-18. Jahrhundert', *Südost-Forsch.*, 42, 1983, 183-222.

3.275 **Pamlényi**, E., ed., *A History of Hungary*, 1975. Collaborative work. Medieval and early modern periods dealt with by L. Makkai (29-206).

3.276 **Wessely**, K., 'The development of the Hungarian military frontier until the middle of the eighteenth century', *Austrian Hist.Yrbk.*, 9-10, 1973-74, 55-110. Further debate with G. E. Rothenberg and W. S. Vucinich, *ib.*, 111-20.

POLAND
See also 3.253-69 passim; and 7.217.

3.277 **Davies**, N., *Poland, Past and Present. A Select Bibliography of Works in English*, Newtonville, Mass., 1977. Despite title includes a good deal in French, and occasional titles in German and Italian. Topical arrangement scatters early modern subjects.

3.278 **Rostworowski**, E., 'La Pologne pendant la seconde moitié du 18e siècle. Bilan de recherches, 1945-56', *Annales*, 13, 1958, 123-35. Virtually all Polish-language material.

3.279 **Davies**, N., *God's Playground. A History of Poland*, 2 vols., 1982. Remarkable single-handed history, over 1,300 pages long, concentrating on period since late sixteenth century. Interweaves thematic social history with narrative.

3.280 **Gieysztor**, A., and others, *History of Poland*, Warsaw, 1968. Substantial semi-official collaborative work; relevant section is J. Tazbir and E. Rostworowski, 'The commonwealth of the gentry', 169-398.

3.281 **Gieysztorowa**, Irena, 'Guerre et régression en Masovie aux 16e et 17e siècles', *Annales*, 13, 1958, 651-68. Contends that economic decline of Central Poland was independent of damage caused by Swedish invasion of 1655-60.

3.282 **Topolski**, J., 'La régression économique en Pologne du 16e au 18e siècle', *Acta Poloniae Hist.*, 7, 1962, 28-49.

3.283 —— 'Sixteenth-century Poland and the turning point in European economic development', in J. K. Fedorowicz and others, eds., *A Republic of Nobles. Studies in Polish History to 1864*, 1982, 70-90. Considers esp. key questions of east-west trade and profitability of manorial system.

3.284 **Wojcik**, Z., 'Poland and Russia in the seventeenth century. Problems of internal development', in B. Geremek and A. Maczak, eds., *Poland at the Fourteenth International Congress of Historical Sciences*, Wroclaw, 1975, 113-33. Examines economic and social factors behind loss of Polish power and rise of Russia.

OTHER REGIONS

3.285 **Seibt**, F., *Bohemica. Probleme und Literatur seit 1945*, Munich, 1970. Historiographical review. Chapters 7-8 cover early modern period.

3.286 **Bradley**, J. F. N., *Czechoslovakia. A Short History*, 1971. Outline history, without bibliography. Early modern period gets balanced treatment.

3.287 **Thomson**, S. H., *Czechoslovakia in European History*, 2nd ed., Princeton, N.J., 1953.

3.288 **Pascu**, S., *A History of Transylvania*, Detroit, 1982. Transl. from Rumanian ed. of 1972-79. Rumanian nationalist standpoint. Pages 96-149 cover early modern period.

TURKEY AND THE BALKANS

HISTORIOGRAPHY AND SOURCES
See also 3.311.

3.289 **Grozdanova**, Elena, 'Contemporary Bulgarian historiography (1971-80) on the impact of Ottoman rule...', *Bulgarian Hist.Rev.*, 9, 1981, 68-85. Useful summaries.

3.290 **Inalcik**, H., 'The impact of the *Annales* school on Ottoman studies and new findings', *Review*, 1 (iii-iv), 1978, 69-96. Repr. in his *Studies in Ottoman Social and Economic History*, 1985. Careful study of recent historiography of sixteenth and early seventeenth centuries.

3.291 **Islamoğlu**, H., and Keyder, Ç., 'Agenda for Ottoman history', *ib.*, 1 (i), 1977, 31-55. Suggests framework for research might be transition from world-empire to peripheral area of capitalist world system. See also I. Wallerstein's comments, *ib.*, 2, 1979, 389-98.

3.292 **Topping**, P., 'Greek historical writing on

the period 1453-1914', *J.Mod.Hist.*, 33, 1961, 157-73. Indicates some relevant material on *Tourkokratia* for those with knowledge of Greek.

3.293 **Vucinich**, W. S., 'The Yugoslav lands in the Ottoman period. Postwar Marxist interpretations of indigenous and Ottoman institutions', *J.Mod.Hist.*, 27, 1955, 287-305.

GENERAL SURVEYS
See also 8.159.

3.294 **Beldiceanu**, N., *Le Monde Ottom.in des Balkans (1402-1566)*, 1976. Collected papers (all French) on variety of economic and social topics, with emphasis on Rumanian principalities.

3.295 **Çizakça**, M., 'Incorporation of the Middle East into the European world-economy', *Review*, 8, 1985, 353-77. Sees two-stage process (1550-1650 and 1830-1900) by which Ottoman economy became dominated by European capitalism, with partial recovery of autonomy and prosperity between.

3.296 **Cook**, M. A., ed., *History of the Ottoman Empire to 1730*, 1976. Comprises chapters from *Cambridge History of Islam* and *New Cambridge Modern History*.

3.297 **Ergil**, D., and Rhodes, R. I., 'Western capitalism and the disintegration of the Ottoman Empire', *Ec.& Hist.*, 18, 1975, 41-60. Highly schematic presentation of Turkish history since sixteenth century.

3.298 **Inalcik**, H., *The Ottoman Empire. The Classical Age, 1300-1600*, 1973. Standard work on early Turkish history.

3.299 —— *The Ottoman Empire. Conquest, Organization, and Economy*, 1978. Collected papers on variety of topics, some separately noted.

3.300 **Jelavich**, C., and Jelavich, Barbara, eds., *The Balkans in Transition*, Berkeley, Calif., 1963. Useful essays on effects of Ottoman rule by S. J. Shaw and W. S. Vucinich, 56-114.

3.301 **Lampe**, J. R., and Jackson, M. R., *Balkan Economic History, 1550-1950. From Imperial Borderlands to Developing Nations*, Bloomington, Ind., 1982. Though concentrating on last century, has lengthy introduction on Ottoman period. Review article: I. T. Berend, *Ec.Hist.Rev.*, 2nd ser., 37, 1984, 268-73.

3.302 **Lewis**, B., 'Some reflections on the decline of the Ottoman Empire', in his *Emergence of Modern Turkey*, 1961, chapter 2; repr. in Cipolla (3.108), 215-34.

3.303 **Lewis**, Raphaela, *Everyday Life in Ottoman Turkey*, 1971. Popular work; chronology often vague as no sources are cited.

3.304 **McGowan**, B., *Economic Life in Ottoman Europe. Taxation, Trade, and the Struggle for Land, 1600-1800*, 1982. Not sustained history, but separate essays on aspects mentioned in title.

3.305 **McNeill**, W. H., *Europe's Steppe Frontier, 1500-1800*, Chicago, 1964. Deals with frontier region between Habsburg, Russian, and Ottoman empires.

3.306 **Mantran**, R., *L'Empire Ottoman du 16e au 18e Siècle. Administration, Économie, Société*, 1984. Collected papers (all French), many arising from research for his masterly work on Istanbul (8.160).

3.307 **Mardin**, S., 'Power, civil society, and culture in the Ottoman Empire', *Comp.Stud.Soc.& Hist.*, 11, 1969, 258-81. Characterises Turkish society as lacking autonomous groups with institutionalised privileges and immunities.

3.308 **Naff**, T., and Owen, R., eds., *Studies in Eighteenth-Century Islamic History*, Carbondale, Ill., 1977. Note esp. section 'Resources, population, and wealth', with papers (in English and French) by Owen, C. Issawi, Bistra Cvetkova, and R. Mantran.

3.309 **Pantazopoulos**, N. J., *Church and Law in the Balkan Peninsula during the Ottoman Rule*, Salonica, 1967. Very much a lawyer's approach, but interesting for light it throws on family structures, inheritance, etc.

3.310 **Ristelhueber**, R., *History of the Balkan Peoples*, New York, 1971. Transl. and slight updating (by S. D. Spector) of French ed. of 1950, a classic general history.

3.311 **Shaw**, S. J., *History of the Ottoman Empire and Modern Turkey*, 2 vols., 1976-77. Work that has provoked criticism for reliance on government perspectives and neglect of social movements. Vol.1 extends to 1808. Useful annotated bibliography.

3.312 **Stavrianos**, L. S., *The Balkans since 1453*, New York, 1958. Basic introduction, with about 200 pages on pre-nineteenth century history.

3.313 **Stoianovich**, T., 'Material foundations of preindustrial civilization in the Balkans', *J.Soc.Hist.*, 4, 1971, 205-62. Detailed survey of technological lag, and mental attitudes responsible for this.

3.314 —— *A Study in Balkan Civilization*, New York, 1967. Short introduction to millennium of social history, inevitably rather static presentation.

3.315 **Sugar**, P., 'Some thoughts on the pre-conditions of modernization and their applicability to the European provinces of the Ottoman Empire in the eighteenth century', *Ét.Balkaniques*, 13 (ii), 1977, 42-55. Finds that on any broadly agreed definition Balkan society shows no symptoms of modernisation during eighteenth century.

3.316 —— *Southeastern Europe under Ottoman Rule, 1354-1804*, Seattle, Wash., 1977. Excellent survey, part of series on history of East Central Europe.

3.317 **Vryonis**, S., 'Byzantine legacy and Ottoman forms', *Dumbarton Oaks Pap.*, 23-24, 1969-70, 253-308. General survey, with emphasis on culture, of effects of Turkish rule on former Byzantine Empire.

3.318 **Vucinich**, W. S., 'The nature of Balkan society under Ottoman rule', *Slavic Rev.*, 21, 1962, 597-616. Further comment by S. J. Shaw, T. Stoianovich, and author, *ib.*, 617-38.

INDIVIDUAL COUNTRIES AND REGIONS

3.319 **Hill**, Sir George, *History of Cyprus. Vol.4: The Ottoman Province, the British Colony, 1571-1948*, 1952.

3.320 **Jenness**, D., *The Economics of Cyprus. A Survey to 1914*, Montreal, 1962. Begins with prehistoric times.

3.321 **Carter**, F. W., *Dubrovnik (Ragusa). A Classic City State*, New York, 1972. Lengthy general history, with main emphasis on commercial position from Venetian period to Napoleonic annexation.

3.322 **Topping**, P., 'Premodern Peloponnesus. The land and the people under Venetian rule (1685-1715)', *Ann.New York Acad.Sci.*, 268, 1976, 92-108. Repr. in his *Studies on Latin Greece, 1205-1715*, 1977, together with report of 1691 to Venetian Senate.

3.323 **Vacalopoulos**, A. E., *The Greek Nation, 1453-1669. The Cultural and Economic Background of Modern Greek Society*, New Brunswick, N.J., 1976. Detailed and informative, but basically anachronistic in concept of "Greek nation" in this period.

3.324 **Wagstaff**, J. M., 'The economy of the Máni peninsula in the eighteenth century', *Balkan Stud.*, 6, 1965, 293-304. Reconstructed from travel accounts.

3.325 **Zakythinos**, D. A., *The Making of Modern Greece. From Byzantium to Independence*, 1976. Compiled and transl. from lectures and articles. Useful introduction to Turkish period.

3.326 **Chirot**, D., *Social Change in a Peripheral Society. The Creation of a Balkan Colony*, New York, 1976. Study of Wallachia from about 1250 to 1917, strongly permeated by terminology of Wallerstein thesis.

3.327 **Clissold**, S., ed., *A Short History of Yugoslavia from Early Times to 1966*, 1966. Most valuable for H. C. Darby's province by province survey of pre-1918 region.

3.328 **Dedijer**, V., and others, *History of Yugoslavia*, New York, 1974. Valuable introductory work, though transl. from text that, to some extent, had to toe party line.

3.329 **Gestrin**, F., 'Économie et société en Slovénie au 16e siècle', *Annales*, 17, 1962, 663-90.

3.330 **Longworth**, P., 'The Senj Uskoks reconsidered', *Slavonic & E.Eur.Rev.*, 57, 1979, 348-68. Piratical frontier society in maritime Croatia of sixteenth and seventeenth centuries.

SCANDINAVIA AND THE BALTIC REGION

HISTORIOGRAPHY AND SOURCES

3.331 *Excerpta Historica Nordica*, Copenhagen, 1955- . Periodical bibliography giving summaries in English, French, and German of works in Scandinavian languages.

3.332 **Hornby**, O., and Mogensen, G. V., 'The study of economic history in Denmark. Recent trends and problems', *Scan. Ec. Hist. Rev.*, 22, 1974, 61-87.

3.333 **Kuuse**, J., 'The probate inventory as a source for economic and social history', *ib.*, 22-31. Discussed in Swedish context (where inventories were compulsory after 1734).

3.334 **Oakley**, S. P., *Scandinavian History, 1520-1970. A List of Books and Articles in English*, 1984. Invaluable. Handily arranged by topic within centuries.

3.335 **Oden**, Birgitta, 'Historical statistics in the Nordic countries', in Lorwin and Price (3.86), 263-99. Substantial attention to pre-1800 material.

GENERAL SURVEYS
See also 2.97,135.

3.336 **Derry**, T. K., *A History of Scandinavia. Norway, Sweden, Denmark, Finland, and Iceland*, 1979. Extremely useful for regional approach and generous coverage of economic and social matters.

3.337 **Hovde**, B. J., *The Scandinavian Countries, 1720-1865*, 2 vols., Boston, Mass., 1943. Valuable material in vol.1.

3.338 **Malowist**, M., 'The economic and social development of the Baltic countries from the fifteenth to the seventeenth centuries', *Ec.Hist.Rev.*, 2nd ser., 12, 1959, 177-89. Emphasises shaping influence of expanding grain and timber exports.

3.339 **Samsonowicz**, H., 'Changes in the Baltic zone in the 13th to 16th centuries', *J.Eur.Ec.Hist.*, 4, 1975, 655-72. Attempts rough measure of degree of economic development over this period.

SWEDEN: WORKS COVERING LONG TIME-SPAN

3.340 **Heckscher**, E. F., *An Economic History of Sweden*, Cambridge, Mass., 1954. Transl. from Swedish ed. of 1941. Capable survey by pioneer historian. His more detailed history of seventeenth- and eighteenth-century Swedish economy remains untranslated – see extensive review by B. Boëthius, *Scan.Ec.Hist.Rev.*, 1, 1953, 143-77.

3.341 **Moberg**, V., *A History of the Swedish People*, 2 vols., 1971. Transl. from Swedish ed. of 1970. Novelist's view of "history of the common man in Sweden".

3.342 **Oakley**, S., *The Story of Sweden*, 1966. Relatively brief general history, chronologically well-balanced. Similarly

brief is I. Andersson, *A History of Sweden*, 1956. 2nd ed., 1970.

3.343 **Samuelsson**, K., *From Great Power to Welfare State. Three Hundred Years of Swedish Social Development*, 1968. First two chapters have some useful observations.

3.344 **Scott**, F. D., *Sweden. The Nation's History*, Minneapolis, Minn., 1977. More generously proportioned than items in 3.342, with correspondingly more space for social and economic material.

SWEDEN: SPECIAL PERIODS

3.345 **Ågren**, K., 'The *reduktion*', in M. Roberts, ed., *Sweden's Age of Greatness, 1632-1718*, 1973, 237-64. Social effects of Crown resumptions of alienated land after 1680.

3.346 **Åström**, S.-E., 'The Swedish economy and Sweden's role as a great power, 1632-97', *ib.*, 58-101. Important essay on material foundations of Swedish imperialism.

3.347 **Nordmann**, C. J., *Grandeur et Liberté de la Suède, 1660-1792*, Louvain, 1971. Very good on socio-economic conditions.

3.348 **Roberts**, M., *Gustavus Adolphus. A History of Sweden, 1611-32*, 2 vols., 1953-58. Masterly work, with considerable attention to economic, social, and educational history. Its chronological predecessor, *The Early Vasas. A History of Sweden, 1523-1611*, 1968, is more purely political and administrative.

3.349 —— 'Queen Christina and the general crisis of the seventeenth century', *P.&P.*, 22, 1962, 36-59. Repr. in Aston (2.72), 195-222; and in his own *Essays in Swedish History*, 1967, 111-37. Analyses social and constitutional unrest in Sweden around 1650 in light of "general crisis" concept.

3.350 —— *The Swedish Imperial Experience, 1560-1718*, 1979. Lecture series summarising effects of expansion both on domestic society and in conquered territories. Review article: S.-E. Åström, *Scan.Ec.Hist.Rev.*, 30, 1982, 227-33.

3.351 ——, ed., *Sweden as a Great Power, 1611-97*, 1968. Short collection of documentary extracts.

OTHER SCANDINAVIAN COUNTRIES

3.352 **Oakley**, S., *The Story of Denmark*, 1972.

Brief survey for general reader.

3.353 **West**, J. F., *Faroe. The Emergence of a Nation*, 1972. Two chapters deal with pre-nineteenth century society.

3.354 **Åström**, S.-E., 'The role of Finland in the Swedish national and war economies during Sweden's period as a great power', *Scan.J.Hist.*, 11, 1986, 135-47. Tries to assess demands made on Finland via taxation and conscription.

3.355 **Jutikkala**, E., and Pirinen, K., *A History of Finland*, 1962. 2nd ed., 1979. Post-medieval Finland covered by Jutikkala, an eminent and prolific economic historian.

3.356 **Larsen**, Karen, *A History of Norway*, Princeton, N.J., 1948. Substantial section on social developments under Danish rule (roughly corresponding with early modern period).

RUSSIA AND BALTIC DUCHIES

HISTORIOGRAPHY AND SOURCES

3.357 **Baron**, S. H., 'The transition from feudalism to capitalism in Russia. A major Soviet historical controversy', *Am. Hist. Rev.*, 77, 1972, 715-29. Review of Russian-language symposium of this title (ed. V. I. Shunkov and others, Moscow, 1969), where Lenin's views on development of market economy in seventeenth century came under strong criticism.

3.358 **Clendenning**, P. H., and Bartlett, R. P., *Eighteenth-Century Russia. A Select Bibliography of Works Published since 1955*, Newtonville, Mass., 1981. Good selection of material in Russian and English (plus sprinkling of French and German).

3.359 **Crowther**, P. A., *A Bibliography of Works in English on Early Russian History to 1800*, 1969. Update would be useful.

3.360 **Eaton**, H. L., 'Cadasters and censuses of Muscovy', *Slavic Rev.*, 26, 1967, 54-69. Guide to these records as sources for Russian social and economic history from Mongol period to eighteenth century.

3.361 **Kazmer**, D. R., and Kazmer, Y., *Russian Economic History. A Guide to Information Sources*, Detroit, Mich., 1977. By no means exhaustive, even for English-language material it is confined to. Arranged by topic, each having section covering period up to 1860.

WORKS COVERING LONG TIME-SPAN
See also 10.71.

3.362 **Baykov**, A., 'The economic development of Russia', *Ec.Hist.Rev.*, 2nd ser., 7, 1954, 137-49. Repr. in B. E. Supple, ed., *The Experience of Economic Growth*, New York, 1963, 413-25; and W. L. Blackwell, ed., *Russian Economic Development from Peter the Great to Stalin*, New York, 1974, 5-20. Argues that long-term Russian backwardness can be attributed more to resource and transport deficiencies than to social and institutional factors.

3.363 **Clarkson**, J. D., *History of Russia*, New York, 1961. Stimulating survey, with emphasis on socio-economic determinants.

3.364 **Cross**, A. G., ed., *Russia under Western Eyes, 1517-1825*, 1971. Anthology of travellers' accounts. See also 3.375.

3.365 **Florinsky**, M. T., *Russia. A History and an Interpretation*, 2 vols., New York, 1947-53. Valuable textbook despite its age. Devotes considerable space in vol.1 to early modern social and economic history.

3.366 **Gerschenkron**, A., *Europe in the Russian Mirror. Four Lectures in Economic History*, 1970. Note particularly views on role of Old Believers in development of textile industry (test of Weber thesis); and on Petrine reforms as type of mercantilism.

3.367 **Gille**, B., *Histoire Économique et Sociale de la Russie du Moyen Age au 20e Siècle*, Paris, 1949. Review article: A. Gerschenkron, *J.Ec.Hist.*, 13, 1953, 344-7.

3.368 **Hellie**, R., 'The structure of modern Russian history. Toward a dynamic model', *Russ.Hist.*, 4, 1977, 1-41. Vigorous statement of "continuity" thesis of Russian history, i.e. that lack of frontiers and hostile climate have perpetuated repressive society and institutions. With comments by Ann Kleimola and others.

3.369 **Lyashchenko**, P. I., *History of the National Economy of Russia to the 1917 Revolution*, New York, 1949. Transl. from 3rd Russian ed of 1939. Standard interpretation laid down in Stalin period, but useful for its detailed research. Review article: A. Gerschenkron, *J.Ec.Hist.*, 12, 1952, 146-59.

3.370 **Nolte**, H.-H., 'The position of Eastern Europe in the international system in early modern times', *Review*, 6, 1982, 25-84. Transl. from *Jb.Gesch.Osteur.*, 28, 1980, 161-97. Deals predominantly with Russia's market role and social system.

3.371 **Pipes**, R. E., *Russia under the Old Regime*, 1974. Trenchant and controversial survey from origins of state to nineteenth century, emphasising social context of despotism. Review article: M. Szeftel, *Can.-Am.Slavic Stud.*, 14, 1980, 74-87.

3.372 **Riasonovsky**, N. V., *A History of Russia*, New York, 1963. 3rd ed., 1977. Well-established textbook.

.373 **Riha**, T., ed., *Readings in Russian Civilization*, 3 vols. in 1, Chicago, 1964. Mixture of sources and extracts. Relevant material in vols.1-2.

.374 **Vernadsky**, G., and others, eds., *A Source Book for Russian History from Early Times to 1917*, 3 vols., New Haven, Conn., 1972. Sources (in transl.). Vols.1-2 cover early modern period.

.375 **Wilson**, Francesca, *Muscovy. Russia through Foreign Eyes, 1553-1900*, 1970. Some overlap with 3.364.

PRE-PETRINE RUSSIA
See also 3.284.

.376 **Crummey**, R. O., *The Formation of Muscovy, 1304-1613*, 1987. Likely to be standard textbook, though social and economic history mainly concentrated in opening chapter.

.377 **Hellie**, R., ed., *Readings for an Introduction to Russian Civilization. Muscovite Society*, Chicago, 1967. Documents in transl., with commentary, on variety of social topics (serfdom, towns, crime, etc.). Another useful documentary reader (though in French transl.) is M. Laran and J. Saussay, eds., *La Russie Ancienne, 9e-17e Siècles*, Paris, 1975.

.378 **Vernadsky**, G., *Russia at the Dawn of the Modern Age*, New Haven, Conn., 1959; and *The Tsardom of Moscow, 1547-1682*, 2 vols., New Haven, Conn., 1969. These works form vols.4-5 of an uncompleted *History of Russia* (later sections were to have been written by M. M. Karpovich).

Magisterial work. Review article: J. Keep, *Slavonic & E.Eur.Rev.*, 49, 1971, 607-10; and see Halperin's long discussion in 1.74.

RUSSIA AFTER 1689
See also 3.358 (bibliography).

3.379 **Black**, C. E., 'The nature of Imperial Russian society', *Slavic Rev.*, 20, 1961, 565-600. Discussion, with H. Seton-Watson and N. V. Riasonovsky, of distinctive features of Russian society in eighteenth and nineteenth centuries, and dynamics of change.

3.380 **Crisp**, Olga, 'The Russian economy under serfdom', in her *Studies in the Russian Economy before 1914*, 1976, 55-72. Article cobbled together from book reviews, covering various aspects of eighteenth-century economy.

3.381 **Dmytryshyn**, B., ed., *The Modernization of Russia under Peter I and Catherine II*, New York, 1974. Student reader, with extracts from contemporary sources and subsequent historiography.

3.382 **Dukes**, P., 'Russia and the eighteenth-century revolution', *History*, 56, 1971, 371-86. Argues that Russia was not so backward as to be immune to general revolutionary current discerned by Godechot and Palmer (2.94,100).

3.383 —— , ed., *Russia under Catherine the Great*, 2 vols., Newtonville, Mass., 1977-78. Vol.1 consists of select documents on government and society; vol.2 is a transl. of *nakaz* to Legislative Commission of 1767.

3.384 **Kahan**, A., *The Plow, the Hammer, and the Knout. An Economic History of Eighteenth-Century Russia*, Chicago, 1985. Impressive synthesis, though somewhat disproportionate in space given to industrial enterprises. Review article: M. Confino, *Peasant Stud.*, 13, 1986, 149-70.

3.385 **Lentin**, A., *Russia in the Eighteenth Century from Peter the Great to Catherine the Great, 1696-1796*, 1973. Short introductory work.

3.386 **Madariaga**, Isabel de, *Russia in the Age of Catherine the Great*, 1981. Major work. Though author claims to have emphasised political history at expense of economic, to redress historiographical balance, there remains plenty to interest social historians.

3.387 **Oliva**, L. J., *Russia in the Era of Peter the Great*, Englewood Cliffs, N.J., 1969. Reasonable coverage of social history.

3.388 **Raeff**, M., *Imperial Russia, 1682-1825*.

The Coming of Age of Modern Russia, New York, 1971. Useful thematic treatment.

3.389 —— 'Seventeenth-century Europe in eighteenth-century Russia?', *Slavic Rev.*, 41, 1982, 611-38. Debates his thesis that eighteenth-century Russian state and society were catching up with seventeenth-century models further west, with E. L. Keenan, Isabel de Madariaga, and J. Cracraft.

3.390 **Wren**, M. C., *The Western Impact on Tsarist Russia*, New York, 1971. Brief survey, about half devoted to eighteenth century.

REGIONAL AND LOCAL HISTORY
See also 5.549 and 9.639 on Urals region in eighteenth century.

3.391 **Berkis**, A. V., *History of the Duchy of Courland (1561-1795)*, Towson, Md., 1969. Some useful material, esp. on Latvian peasantry.

3.392 **Lang**, D. M., *The Last Years of the Georgian Monarchy, 1658-1832*, New York, 1957.

3.393 **Portal**, R., *Russes et Ukrainiens*, Paris, 1970. Useful brief introduction to Ukrainian history.

3.394 **Ukrainian National Association**, *Ukraine. A Concise Encyclopedia*, 2 vols., Toronto, 1963-71. Based on Ukrainian publ. of 1949. Hardly concise, but useful, as data is presented in broad sections – law, economic history, folklore, etc. – rather than dictionary fashion.

4

GEOGRAPHY AND ENVIRONMENT

GENERAL WORKS

Note also 8.9. On France see also 3.5; on Balkan frontier region 3.272,276,305,327; on Sweden 7.326. For convenience material on Russian frontier and eastward expansion has been grouped in section on migration, 5.544-52 (see also 1.74).

1 **Baker**, A. R. H., 'Reflections on the relations of historical geography and the *Annales* school of history', in Baker and D. Gregory, eds., *Explorations in Historical Geography*, 1984, 1-27. See also P. Claval, 'The historical dimension of French geography', *J.Hist.Geog.*, 10, 1984, 229-45 (brief view of interaction between geographers and historians from work of Vidal de la Blache onwards).

2 ——, ed., *Progress in Historical Geography*, 1972. Historiographical essays, including accounts of work in France, Scandinavia, Central Europe, and the U.S.S.R.

3 **McNeill**, W. H., *The Human Condition. An Ecological and Historical View*, Princeton, N.J., 1980. Lecture series in which history is seen as determined by parasites – micro-organic and human.

4 **Pounds**, N. J. G., *An Historical Geography of Europe, 1500-1840*, 1979. Might equally well have featured in Section 2 as it is hard to distinguish from straight economic history; as such, lucid and valuable.

5 **Smith**, C. T., *An Historical Geography of Western Europe before 1800*, 1967. Provides only broad outline, as coverage begins with prehistoric Europe.

6 **Whittlesey**, D., *Environmental Foundations of European History*, New York, 1949. Very brief overview.

4.7 **Clout**, H. D., ed., *Themes in the Historical Geography of France*, 1977. Collective work that forms a more or less continuous and comprehensive work. Particularly strong on agricultural themes. For briefer and more unified treatment see A. Fierro-Domenech, *Le Pré Carré. Géographie Historique de la France*, Paris, 1986.

4.8 **Fox**, E. W., *History in Geographic Perspective. The Other France*, New York, 1971. Views social and political conflicts as shaped from earliest times by differing outlooks of agricultural and mercantile communities.

4.9 **Pitte**, J.-R., *Histoire du Paysage Français*, 2 vols., Paris, 1983. Most comprehensive work on French landscape. Volumes split at late fifteenth century. Pioneer earlier work is R. Dion, *Essai sur la Formation du Paysage Rural Français*, Tours, 1934.

4.10 **Lambert**, Audrey M., *The Making of the Dutch Landscape. An Historical Geography of the Netherlands*, 1971. Chronological treatment, starting from earliest times.

4.11 **Smith**, Catherine D., *Western Mediterranean Europe. A Historical Geography of Italy, Spain, and Southern France since the Neolithic*, 1979.

4.12 **Cabo**, A., *Condicionamientos Geográficos (Historia de España Alfaguara, 1)*, 2nd ed., Madrid, 1975. Serves as preface to series.

4.13 **García Fernández**, J., *Sociedad y Organización Tradicional del Espacio en Asturias*, Oviedo, 1976. Concentrates on early modern evolution of land use in this province.

4.14 **Gomez-Ibañez**, D. A., *The Western Pyrenees. Differential Evolution of the French and Spanish Borderland*, 1975. Historical geography of Catalan Pyrenees, especially as affected by partition of mid-seventeenth century.

4.15 **Hess**, A. C., *The Forgotten Frontier. A History of the Sixteenth-Century Ibero-African Frontier*, Chicago, 1978. Mainly concerned with formation of Muslim society in North Africa under continued pressure of Spanish crusading spirit.

4.16 **Humbert**, A., 'L'empreinte castillane sur les paysages des hauts plateaux Grenadins', *Mél.Casa de Velazquez*, 16, 1980, 5-38. Questions how far Spaniards altered agararian landscape taken over from Moors.

4.17 **Stanislawski**, D., *The Individuality of Portugal. A Study in Historical-Political Geography*, Austin, Tex., 1959. Centres on factors that have fostered resistance to union with Spain.

4.18 **De Seta**, C., ed., *Il Paesaggio*, Turin, 1982. Forms vol.5 of *Annali* section of Einaudi *Storia d'Italia* (see 3.168). Vol.8, *Insediamenti e Territorio* (also ed. by De Seta, 1985), offers further miscellany on man and landscape in Italy.

4.19 **Munk**, Judith, and Munk, W., 'Venice hologram', *Proc.Am.Phil.Soc.*, 116, 1972, 415-42. Retrospect of Venetian impact on marine environment from origins to present.

4.20 **Lawless**, R. I., 'The economy and landscapes of Thessaly during Ottoman rule', in F. W. Carter, ed., *An Historical Geography of the Balkans*, 1977, 501-33.

4.21 **Pitcher**, D. E., *An Historical Geography of the Ottoman Empire, from Earliest Times to the End of the Sixteenth Century*, Leiden, 1972. Carries detailed maps.

4.22 **Mead**, W. R., *An Historical Geography of Scandinavia*, 1981. Chronological treatment; chapters 4-7 relevant.

4.23 **Oakley**, S. P., 'The geography of peasant ecotypes in pre-industrial Scandinavia', *Scandia*, 47, 1981, 199-223. Maps contrasting regions of peasant society and economy in eighteenth and early nineteenth centuries.

4.24 **Jones**, M., *Finland, Daughter of the Sea*, Hamden, Conn., 1977. Concerned with reactions to land emergence along western coast of Finland.

4.25 **Bater**, J. H., and French, R. A., eds., *Studies in Russian Historical Geography*, 2 vols., 1983. See section in vol.1, 'Man and the land', containing studies on forests, soil erosion, and the 3-field system; and D. J. B. Shaw, 'Southern frontiers of Muscovy, 1550-1700'.

4.26 **Kerner**, R. J., *The Urge to the Sea: the Course of Russian History. The Role of Rivers, Portages, Ostrogs, Monasteries, and Furs*, Berkeley, Calif., 1942. Basic work; particular emphasis on river navigation as key to Russian expansion.

4.27 **Parker**, W. H., *An Historical Geography of Russia*, 1968. Ranges from earliest times to Soviet period.

CLIMATE
See also 11.118.

4.28 **Anderson**, J. L., 'Climatic change in European economic history', *Research in Ec.Hist.*, 6, 1981, 1-34. Takes sceptical view of thesis that climatic fluctuations have markedly affected economic performance.

4.29 **Eddy**, J. A., 'The "Maunder minimum". Sunspots and climate in the reign of Louis XIV', *Science*, 92, 1976, 1189-1202. Repr. in Parker and Smith (2.78), 226-68. Investigates possible links between European "Little Ice Age" and absence of sunspot activity.

4.30 **Rotberg**, R. I., and Rabb, T. K., eds., *Climate and History. Studies in Interdisciplinary History*, Princeton, N.J., 1981. Essays of most interest are J. De Vries on effects in early modern Netherlands (19-50); A. B. Appleby on epidemics and famine, chiefly in France and Britain, during Little Ice Age (63-84); C. Pfister on thermal and wetness indices in Central Europe in this period (85-116); and E. Le Roy Ladurie and Micheline Baulant on northern grape harvests from fifteenth to nineteenth centuries as climatic index (259-70). Previously publ. in *J.Interdisc.Hist.*, 10, 1980, 583-858.

.31 **Lamb**, H. H., *Climate. Present, Past, and Future*, 2 vols., 1972-77. Parts of vol.2 relevant. Review article: J. D. Post, *J.Interdisc.Hist.*, 10, 1979, 291-301. See also Lamb's more condensed *Climate, History, and the Modern World*, 1982 (historical section, pp.101-309).

.32 **Le Roy Ladurie**, E., *Times of Feast, Times of Famine. A History of Climate since the Year 1000*, 1972. Transl. from French ed. of 1967. Stimulating and richly documented; covers methods of reconstructing past weather patterns and works back from precise records of modern era to scattered clues of medieval chronicles. Review article: J. D. Post, *J.Interdisc.Hist.*, 3, 1973, 721-32; P. Chaunu, *Rev.Hist.*, 238, 1967, 365-76.

.33 —— 'Climat et récoltes aux 17e et 18e siècles', *Annales*, 15, 1960, 434-65. Looks esp. at glacier activity in correlation with harvests.

.34 —— 'History and climate', in Burke (1.1), 134-69. Transl. from *Annales*, 14, 1959, 3-34.

.35 —— 'History without people. The climate as a new province of research', in his *The Territory of the Historian*, 1979, 287-319. Transl. from French ed. of 1973.

.36 **Parry**, M. L., *Climatic Change, Agriculture, and Settlement*, 1978. Ranges widely in time; concentrates territorially on North-West Europe.

.37 **Post**, J. D., 'Climatic variability and the European mortality wave of the early 1740s', *J.Interdisc.Hist.*, 15, 1984, 1-30. Points to links between extreme weather conditions of 1739-42 and epidemics of typhus and dysentery in same period. See also 11.118 for wider context of this article.

4.38 **Utterström**, G., 'Climatic fluctuations and population problems in early modern history', *Scan.Ec.Hist.Rev.*, 3, 1955, 3-47. Pioneering article on effects of Little Ice Age.

4.39 **Wigley**, T. M. L., and others, eds., *Climate and History*, 1981. Apart from methodological articles, note C. Pfister on "Little Ice Age" effects on Swiss agriculture (214-48); A. Mackay on climate and popular unrest in late medieval Castile (356-76); and D. Sutherland on weather and the Breton peasantry in the 1780s.

4.40 **Desplat**, C., 'The climate of eighteenth-century Béarn', *Fr.Hist.*, 1, 1987, 27-48.

4.41 **Pfister**, C., *Agrarkonjunktur und Witterungsverlauf im Westlichen Schweizer Mittelland, 1755-97*, Bern, 1975. Unusually detailed weather records of Bern Economic Society provide basis for examination of effects on agriculture and agricultural prices.

4.42 —— 'Climate and economy in eighteenth-century Switzerland', *J.Interdisc.Hist.*, 9, 1978, 223-43. Based on findings of previous entry. See also his contributions to 4.30 and 4.39.

4.43 **Goldenberg**, S., 'Le climat et l'histoire. Contributions à une histoire du climat dans les pays roumains aux 16e-17e siècles', *Rev.Roumaine d'Hist.*, 13, 1974, 305-21. Calendar of weather reports over these centuries. Further material in *ib.*, 19, 1980, 267-75.

NATURAL RESOURCES
See also 9.168,609 (general); 10.318 (France); 7.236 (Sweden).

4.44 **Maczak**, A., and Parker, W. N., eds., *Natural Resources in European History*, Washington, D.C., 1978. Section 1 (9-136) deals with early modern Europe, comprising papers by Maria Bogucka and S.-E. Åström on resource implications of Baltic trade; A. Wyrobisz on construction industry; I. Blanchard on mining and metallurgy; and E. L. Jones on administrative measures to alleviate famine and disease.

4.45 —— 'Natural resources and economic development', in *Proc. Seventh International Economic History Congress*, 1978, 1, 5-20. Maczak surveys early modern period.

4.46 **Romano**, R., 'Landscape and society', *Diogenes*, 61, 1968, 1-16. Considers reciprocal influences by example of demand for wood in early modern societies.

4.47 **Allen**, E. A., 'Deforestation and fuel crisis

in pre-Revolutionary Languedoc, 1720-89', *Fr.Hist.Stud.*, 13, 1984, 455-73. Concludes that failure to enforce conservation policies led to real shortages.

4.48 **Bamford**, P. W., 'French forest legislation and administration, 1660-1789', *Agric.Hist.*, 29, 1955, 97-107.

4.49 **Corvol**, Andrée, 'Forêt et communautés en Basse-Bourgogne au 18e siècle', *Rev.Hist.*, 256, 1976, 15-36; followed by 'Les déliquances forestières en Basse-Bourgogne depuis la réformation de 1711-18', *ib.*, 259, 1978, 345-88. Covers both individual and commercial plundering of woodland.

4.50 **Devèze**, M., *La Vie de la Forêt Française au 16e Siècle*, 2 vols., 1961. Emphasises importance of woodland in sixteenth-century economy, for both landlords and peasants.

4.51 **Fruhauf**, C., *Forêt et Société. De la Forêt Paysanne à la Forêt Capitaliste en Pays de Sault sous l'Ancien Régime, vers 1670-1791*, Paris, 1980. Intensive micro-study of forest exploitation in area of some 600 sq.km. on borders of Aude and Ariège departments.

4.52 **Young**, D. B., 'Forests, mines, and fuel. The question of wood and coal in eighteenth-century France', *Proc.Western Soc.Fr.Hist.*, 3, 1975, 328-36. Factors militating against any major change from wood to coal as domestic or industrial fuel.

4.53 **Unger**, R. W., 'Energy sources for the Dutch golden age. Peat, wind, and coal', *Res.inEc.Hist.*, 9, 1984, 221-53. Maintains that importance of imported coal to Dutch economy of seventeenth century has been underestimated.

4.54 **Zeeuw**, J. W. de, 'Peat and the Dutch golden age. The historical meaning of energy-attainability', *A.A.G.Bijd.*, 21, 1978, 3-31. Emphasises importance of this fuel in circumstances of deforestation.

4.55 **Cuvillier**, J.-P., 'L'irrigation dans la Catalogne mediévale et moderne', *Mél.Casa de Velazquez*, 20, 1984, 145-87. Most attention given to medieval origins of system.

4.56 **Maluquer de Motes**, J., 'El agua en el crecimiento catalán de los siglos 17 y 18', *Review*, 10, 1986, 315-47. Sees exploitation of water power as basis of Catalan industrial growth.

4.57 **Mager**, F., *Der Wald in Altpreussen als Wirtschaftsraum*, 2 vols., Köln, 1960. Forests of Polish Prussia from thirteen to nineteenth centuries and their exploitation.

4.58 **Radkau**, J., 'Holzverknappung und Krisenbewusstsein im 18. Jahrhundert', *Gesch.und Gesellschaft*, 9, 1983, 513-43. Argues that perception of wood shortage in Germany was exaggerated. See similar 'Zur angeblichen Energiekrise des 18. Jahrhunderts', *VSWG*, 73, 1986, 1-37.

4.59 **Sporhan**, L., and Stromer, W. von, 'Die Nadelholz-Saat in den Nürnberger Reichswaldern zwischen 1469 und 1600', *Zeitschr.Agrargesch.*, 17, 1969, 79-106. City's development of conifer plantations.

4.60 **Lindqvist**, S., 'Natural resources and technology. The debate about energy technology in eighteenth-century Sweden', *Scan.J.Hist.*, 8, 1983, 83-107. Charts concern about depletion of timber resources.

TRANSPORT AND COMMUNICATIONS
See also 9.178,649-64 passim.

4.61 **Lane**, F. C., 'Progrès technologiques et productivité dans les transports maritimes de la fin du Moyen Age au début des temps modernes', *Rev.Hist.*, 251, 1974, 277-302. Looks at various ways in which cargoes may have been increased and passages speeded up. See also later chaps. of R. W. Unger, *The Ship in the Medieval Economy, 600-1600*, 1980.

4.62 **Mollat**, M., and others, eds., *Actes des Colloques Internationaux d'Histoire Maritime*, Paris, Brussels, 1957-74. Ten

conferences noted. Papers on great variety of naval and commercial themes. Second conf. (publ.1959) concentrated on Mediterranean; Third (1960) on Northern Europe; Fourth (1962) on sources; Fifth (1966) on geographical discoveries; Eighth (1970) on Asian commerce; Ninth (1969) on Atlantic routes.

4.63 **Parry**, J. H., 'Transport and trade routes', in *Cambridge Economic History of Europe,4* (2.15), 155-219.

4.64 **Scammell**, G. V., 'European seamanship

in the great age of discovery', *Mariner's Mirror*, 68, 1982, 357-76. Scholarly account of sailing techniques and hazards of period 1400-1600.

4.65 **Arbellot**, G., 'La grande mutation des routes de France au milieu du 18e siècle', *Annales*, 28, 1973, 765-91. Emphasises increased speed of communications and cartography of network.

4.66 **Buisseret**, D. J., 'The communications of France during the reconstruction of Henri IV', *Ec.Hist.Rev.*, 2nd ser., 18, 1965, 267-77. On Sully's public works programme in this area.

4.67 **Cocula-Vaillières**, Anne M., *Les Gens de la Rivière de Dordogne, 1750 à 1850*, 2 vols., Paris, 1979. Centres on importance of river to economic life of region. Portions later reworked as *Un Fleuve et des Hommes. Les Gens de la Dordogne au 18e Siècle*, Paris, 1981.

4.68 **Cavailles**, H., *La Route Française. Son Histoire, sa Fonction*, Paris, 1946. Standard work on network and upkeep of roads from seventeenth century onwards.

4.69 **Lepetit**, B., *Chemins de Terre et Voies d'Eau. Réseaux de Transports et Organisation de l'Espace en France, 1740-1840*, Paris, 1984. Valuable.

4.70 **Roubert**, Jacqueline, 'Essai sur les transporteurs de marchandises en relation avec le commerce Lyonnais au 18e siècle', *Actes Congrès Nat.Soc.Savantes*, 92 (ii), 1967, 99-177. Case-study of transport options available to major commercial centre.

4.71 **Tirat**, J.-Y., 'Les voituriers par eau Parisiens au milieu du 17e siècle', *Dix-Septième Siècle*, 57, 1962, 43-66. Study from notarial sources.

4.72 'Les transports de 1610 à nos jours', *Actes Congrès Nat.Soc.Savantes*, 104 (i), 1979, 19-229. Symposium with several relevant papers on French road and water networks and postal services.

4.73 **Vaillé**, E., *Histoire Générale des Postes Françaises*, 6 vols. in 7, Paris, 1947-55. Whole work from vol.2 onwards is devoted to period from Louis XI to Revolution. See also his single-vol. condensation, *Histoire des Postes Françaises jusqu'à la Révolution*, Paris, 1948.

4.74 **De Vries**, J., *Barges and Capitalism. Passenger Transportation in the Dutch Economy, 1632-1839 (A.A.G. Bijdragen, 21)*, Wageningen, 1978. Volume of traffic taken as indicator of general state of economy (marked recession, 1680-1750).

4.75 **Roebroeck**, E., 'How did navigation and commerce on the Meuse develop from the Middle Ages until the end of the eighteenth century?', in *Studies Concerning the Social-Economic History of Limburg*, Assen, 1970, 50-74.

4.76 **Wilson**, C., 'Transport as a factor in the history of economic development', *J.Eur.Ec.Hist.*, 2, 1973, 320-37. Transport facilities of seventeenth-century Netherlands discussed as contribution to debate on whether railways were necessary instrument of economic growth.

4.77 **Molénat**, J.-P., 'Chemins et ponts du Nord de la Castille au temps des Rois Catholiques', *Mél.Casa de Velazquez*, 7, 1971, 115-62. Studies road network around Burgos. Good maps.

4.78 **Ringrose**, D. R., *Transportation and Economic Stagnation in Spain, 1750-1850*, Durham, N.C., 1970. Failure to modernise transport patterns seen as primary cause of Castilian economic retardation. See also following associated articles.

4.79 —— 'Transportation and economic stagnation in eighteenth-century Castile', *J.Ec.Hist.*, 28, 1968, 51-79.

4.80 —— 'The government and the carters in Spain, 1476-1700', *Ec.Hist.Rev.*, 2nd ser., 22, 1969, 45-57. Traces long interest of Crown in transport facilities, esp. as regards provisioning of Madrid.

4.81 **Berov**, L., 'Transport costs and their role in trade in the Balkan lands in the sixteenth-nineteenth centuries', *Bulgarian Hist.Rev.*, 3, 1975, 74-98. Shows high costs of both overland and water transport.

4.82 **Faroqhi**, Suraiya, 'Camels, waggons, and the Ottoman state in the sixteenth and seventeenth centuries', *Int. J. Mid. E. Stud.*, 14, 1982, 523-39. Repr. in her *Peasants, Dervishes, and Traders in the Ottoman Empire*, 1986. Pioneering study of transport system in Anatolia.

4.83 **Wittendorff**, A., 'Public roads and royal privilege. The development of the road system in Denmark and the King's private roads', *Scan.J.Hist.*, 1, 1976, 243-64. Deals particularly with *kongeveje*, roads built exclusively for royal use in Zealand (sixteenth-seventeenth centuries).

4.84 **Alef**, G., 'Origin and early development of the Muscovite postal service', *Jb. Gesch.*

Osteuropas, 15, 1967, 1-15. Repr. in Alef (6.217).

4.85 **Jones**, R. E., 'Getting the goods to St. Petersburg. Water transport from the interior, 1703-1811', *Slavic Rev.*, 43, 1984, 413-33. On problems of Petersburg's geographical position up to opening of Mariinsk and Tikhvin canals.

SETTLEMENT PATTERNS

See also 4.36. Also 5.114 (Jura region); 7.179 (Germany); 7.245 (Finland); 8.93 (Italy); 8.156 (Turkey).

4.86 **Pesez**, J.-M., and Le Roy Ladurie, E., 'The deserted villages of France. An overview', in R. Forster and O. Ranum, eds., *Rural Society in France. Selections from the* Annales, Baltimore, Md., 1977, 72-106. Transl. from *Annales*, 20, 1965, 257-90 (note also associated essay by M. Roncayolo, *ib.*, 218-42). Looks at whole span of late medieval and ancien régime abandonment of settlements.

4.87 **Roessingh**, H. K., 'Village and hamlet in a sandy region of the Netherlands in the middle of the eighteenth century', *Acta Hist.Neerlandica*, 4, 1970, 105-29. Deals with settlement patterns and economic geography of Veluwe area of Guelderland.

4.88 **Wagstaff**, J. M., 'Settlements in the South-Central Peloponnisos, c.1618', in Carter (4.20), 197-238. Attempts to reconstruct pattern and rationale of settlements in the Máni from documentary evidence.

4.89 **Goehrke**, C., *Die Wüstungen in der Moskauer Rus'*, Wiesbaden, 1968. Discusses social evidence provided by geography of wasteland and deserted villages.

REGIONS AND REGIONAL DISPARITIES

Additional material will be found in 9.439-99 on development of rural industry; see also 8.63 (Netherlands) and 9.587 (Germany).

4.90 **De Vries**, J., 'Regional economic inequality in the Netherlands since 1600', in P. Bairoch and M. Levy-Leboyer, eds., *Disparities in Economic Development*, 1981, 189-98.

4.91 **Klaassen**, L. H., and others, 'Very long term evolution of a system of regions', in *Sixth International Congress on Economic History. Themes*, Copenhagen, 1974, 93-108. Theoretical model, illustrated by example of Netherlands. See further discussion in *ib. Proceedings*, Copenhagen, 1978, 149-63.

4.92 **Mendels**, F. F., 'Seasons and regions in agriculture and industry during the process of industrialisation', in S. Pollard, ed., *Region and Industrialisation*, Göttingen, 1980, 177-90. Argues that regions and their particular agricultural rhythms are proper framework for studying proto-industrialisation.

4.93 **Scott**, T., 'Economic conflict and co-operation on the Upper Rhine, 1450-1600', in E. I. Kouri and Scott, eds., *Politics and Society in Reformation Europe*, 1987, 210-31. Traces emergence of regional economy based on Basel, Colmar, and Freiburg.

4.94 **Freudenberger**, H., and Mensch, G., *Von der Provinzstadt zur Industrieregion*, Göttingen, 1975. Case study of Brno in Moravia. See following entry for English resumé.

4.95 —— 'Regional differences, differential development, and generative regional growth', in Bairoch and Levy-Leboyer (4.90), 199-209.

4.96 **Söderberg**, J., 'A long-term perspective on regional economic development in Sweden, c.1550-1914', *Scan.Ec.Hist.Rev.*, 32, 1984, 1-16. About half devoted to period up to 1750.

EUROPE AND THE WIDER WORLD.
EXPANSION AND ITS EFFECTS

See also 2.20,30; 4.62; 5.526,531-5,538; 7.300; 9.258-339,357-60,362,369-72,387-400; 10.328,465; 11.273.

4.97 **Canny**, N., and Pagden, A., eds., *Colonial Identity in the Atlantic World*, Princeton, N.J., 1987. Interesting essay collection on weakening (or otherwise) of colonial identification with metropolitan society and culture.

4.98 **Chaudhuri**, K. N., 'The world-system east of longitude 20: the European role in Asia, 1500-1750', *Review*, 5, 1981, 219-45. Historiographical article which looks at research from both Asian and European economic perspectives.

4.99 **Chaunu**, P., *Conquête et Exploitation des Nouveaux Mondes (16e Siècle)*, Paris, 1969. Text in *Nouvelle Clio* series, following common three-part arrangement: sources, general account, problems needing particular interpretation or research.

4.100 **Chiapelli**, F., and others, eds., *First Images of America. The Impact of the New World on the Old*, 2 vols., Berkeley, Calif., 1976. Over fifty essays, some splendidly illustrated. Mostly on intellectual impact of discoveries – apart from rather desultory paper by E. J. Hamilton, economic aspects are neglected.

4.101 **Cole**, R. G., 'Sixteenth-century travel books as a source of European attitudes toward non-white and non-western culture', *Proc.Am.Phil.Soc.*, 116, 1972, 59-67.

4.102 **Crone**, G. R., *Maps and their Makers*, 1953. 5th ed., 1978. Best short account. Latest ed. carries more illustrations. Another excellently-illustrated survey is L. Bagrow, *History of Cartography*, 1964 (ed. revised and enlarged by R. A. Skelton).

4.103 **Crosby**, A. W., *The Columbian Exchange. Biological and Cultural Consequences of 1492*, Westport, Conn., 1972. Deals with impact of new diseases, crops, and livestock introduced to Europe or to America as a result of colonisation.

4.104 —— *Ecological Imperialism. The Biological Expansion of Europe, 900-1900*, 1986. Related theme, emphasising that temperate zones most suited European settlement and flora and fauna that came in their train.

4.105 **Davies**, K. G., *The North Atlantic World in the Seventeenth Century*, Minneapolis, Ma., 1974. Relations of Europe and North America. Organised by topic, e.g. nature of colonists, colonial products, impact on Amerindians.

4.106 **Devèze**, M., *L'Europe et le Monde à la Fin du 18e Siècle*, Paris, 1970.

4.107 **Duncan**, T. B., *Atlantic Islands. Madeira, the Azores, and the Cape Verdes in Seventeenth-Century Commerce and Navigation*, Chicago, 1972. Good treatment of both insular economies and general strategic importance.

4.108 **Elliott**, J. H., *The Old World and the New, 1492-1650*, 1970. Explores variety of impacts of New World on European culture and society.

4.109 **Lach**, D., *Asia in the Making of Europe*, 2 vols. in 5, Chicago, 1965-77. Ambitious work begun with intention of describing Asian influences on European civilisation between 1500 and 1800, but in practice only sixteenth century was covered. Some treatment of commerce, but chief concern is intellectual and artistic impact.

4.110 **Liss**, Peggy K., *Atlantic Empires. The Network of Trade and Revolution, 1713-1826*, Baltimore, Md., 1983. Looks at downfall of European empires from variety of viewpoints. Review articles: J. P. Greene and others, *Int.Hist.Rev.*, 6, 1984, 507-69.

4.111 **McNeill**, W. H., *The Great Frontier. Freedom and Hierarchy in Modern Times*, Princeton, N.J., 1983. Two lectures, suggesting that, esp. in early colonial empires, forced labour and slavery were more characteristic of frontier than freedom and equality of "Turner thesis" (see 4.123).

4.112 **Mauro**, F., *L'Expansion Européenne (1600-1870)*, Paris, 1964. Another *Nouvelle Clio* volume (see 4.99).

4.113 —— 'Towards an "intercontinental model". European overseas expansion between 1500 and 1800', *Ec.Hist.Rev.*, 2nd ser., 14, 1961, 1-17. Designed as theoretical framework in which to consider early modern international trade.

4.114 **Parry**, J. H., *The Age of Reconnaissance*, 1963. Good all-round account of maritime discoveries and growth of colonisation down to end of seventeenth century.

4.115 —— *Europe and a Wider World*, 1949. 3rd ed., 1966. Briefer, more introductory work.

4.116 —— *Trade and Dominion. The European Oversea Empires in the Eighteenth Century*, 1971. Continuation of 4.114.

4.117 **Penrose**, B., *Travel and Discovery in the Renaissance, 1420-1620*, Cambridge, Mass., 1952. Similar scope to Parry (4.114).

4.118 **Rabb**, T. K., 'The expansion of Europe and the spirit of capitalism', *Hist.J.*, 17, 1974, 675-89. Argues that imperialism was inherent product of qualities of early modern capitalism.

4.119 **Scammell**, G. V., 'The New Worlds and Europe in the sixteenth century', *ib.*, 12, 1969, 389-412.

4.120 —— *The World Encompassed. The First European Maritime Empires, c.800-1650*, Berkeley, Calif., 1981. Useful, but Eurocentric account, concentrating on national or quasi-national motives for expansion.

4.121 **Taylor**, Eva G. R., *The Haven-Finding Art. A History of Navigation from Odysseus to Captain Cook*, 1956. 2nd ed., 1971. Standard history of navigational science. About half devoted to period from Portuguese voyages to solution of longitudinal problem.

4.122 **Verlinden**, C., *The Beginnings of Modern Colonization*, Ithaca, N.Y., 1970. Collection of essays not previously available in English. Rather miscellaneous in nature, but primarily concerned with Iberian expansion and Italian influences on it. Cf. 9.286.

4.123 **Webb**, W. P., *The Great Frontier*, Boston, Mass., 1952. Classic general application of Turner's American frontier thesis, linking rise of western individualism to colonial opportunities. But see McNeill, 4.111.

4.124 **Williams**, G., *The Expansion of Europe in the Eighteenth Century. Overseas Rivalry, Discovery, and Exploitation*, 1966. Textbook with main emphasis on warfare generated by competition for commerce and settlement.

4.125 **Wolf**, E. R., *Europe and the People without History*, Berkeley, Calif., 1982. Studies mutual impact of European and non-European cultures since 1500, esp. its economic context.

4.126 **Atkinson**, G., *Les Nouveaux Horizons de la Renaissance Française*, Paris, 1935. Looks at accounts of discoveries and geographical works publ. before 1610, and their influence on general culture. See also his *The Extraordinary Voyage in French Literature before 1700*, New York, 1920; with supplement to 1720, Paris, 1922.

4.127 **Priestley**, H. I., *France Overseas through the Old Regime*, New York, 1939. Still useful as basic outline, but new look at French seaborne empire along lines of 4.128,130,136 would be useful.

4.128 **Boxer**, C. R., *The Dutch Seaborne Empire, 1600-1800*, 1965. Chap.10 publ. as 'The Dutch economic decline' in Cipolla (3.108), 235-63.

4.129 **Masselman**, G., *The Cradle of Colonialism*, New Haven, Conn., 1963. Emphasises profits as driving force in early Dutch colonialism (East Asia, c.1580-1620).

4.130 **Boxer**, C. R., *The Portuguese Seaborne Empire, 1415-1825*, 1969. By remarkable expert on both Dutch and Portuguese maritime history.

4.131 **Diffie**, B. W., and Winius, G. D., *Foundations of the Portuguese Empire, 1415-1580*, Minneapolis, Ma., 1977. Most up-to-date account of exploration and commercial exploitation.

4.132 **Law**, J., 'On the social explanation of technical change. The case of the Portuguese maritime expansion', *Tech.& Culture*, 28, 1987, 227-52. Looks at interaction of technical and social forces in light of systems theory; rather hard going.

4.133 **Newitt**, M., ed., *The First Portuguese Colonial Empire*, 1986. Collection of four essays which briefly sketch impulse behind Portuguese maritime enterprise, and structure of their Asian trade empire in sixteenth century.

4.134 **Kellenbenz**, H., 'Die Finanzierung der spanischen Entdeckungen', *VSWG*, 69, 1982, 153-81. Valuable new approach.

4.135 **McAlister**, L. N., *Spain and Portugal in the New World, 1492-1700*, Minneapolis, Ma., 1984. Topically organised, within 3 broad chronological periods: Old World antecedents; conquest, 1492-1570; empire, 1570-1700.

4.136 **Parry**, J. H., *The Spanish Seaborne Empire*, 1966.

4.137 **Romeo**, R., *Le Scoperte Americane nella*

Coscienza Italiana del Cinquecento, Milan, 1954. Note also more minutely researched F. Ambrosini, *Paesi e Mari Ignoti. America e Colonialismo Europeo nella Cultura Veneziana (Secoli 16-17)*, Venice, 1982.

5

DEMOGRAPHY

METHODS AND MODELS.
POPULATION LEVELS AND RATES

See following sub-section (5.248-92) for material on bastardy and some aspects of contraception; 11.262-364 on epidemic mortality; and 1.18; 4.37-8; 5.254,435; 8.23; 9.168,449. For bibliography and historiography note esp. 5.13,30,35,42,62,85,96,154,219,228,247,294.

5.1 **Åkerman**, S., 'Evaluation of family reconstitution technique', *Scan. Ec. Hist. Rev.*, 25, 1977, l60-70. Recapitulates some drawbacks of technique.

5.2 **Alter**, G., 'Estimating mortality from annuities, insurance, and other life contingent contracts', *Hist.Methods*, 16, 1983, 45-58.

5.3 —— and Riley, J. C., 'How to bet on lives. A guide to life contingent contracts in early modern Europe', *Res.in Ec.Hist.*, 10, 1986, 1-53. This and previous entry look at demographic models developed by providers of pensions, annuities, tontines, etc., esp. in Netherlands.

5.4 **Armengaud**, A., 'Population in Europe, l700-l914', in *Fontana Economic History of Europe*, 3 (2.24), 22-76.

5.5 **Bardet**, J.-P., La démographie des villes de la modernité (16e-18e siècles). Mythes et réalités', *Ann.Démographie Hist.*, 1974, 101-26. Considers, mainly with French examples, how far it is appropriate to assume cities had demographic rhythms different from remainder of population.

5.6 **Braudel**, F., 'Demography and the scope of the human sciences', in Braudel (1.2), 132-61. Transl. from *Annales*, 15, 1960, 493-523.

5.7 **Cabourdin**, G., and others, 'La

démographie avant les démographes (1500-1670)', *Ann.Démographie Hist.*, 1980, 13-153. Looks at methods for dealing with period where sources are weakest – various countries and regions examined in this context.

5.8 **Charbonneau**, H., and Larose, A., eds., *The Great Mortalities. Methodological Studies of Demographic Crises in the Past*, Liège, 1979. As well as methodology, includes general papers on Italy, Northern Europe, and Spain in early modern period; short studies of particular epidemics; and good bibliography.

5.9 **Cipolla**, C. M., 'The plague and the pre-Malthus Malthusians', *J.Eur.Ec.Hist.*, 3, 1974, 277-84. Early seventeenth-century expressions of view that disease acts as population regulator for poor.

5.10 **Cohen**, J. E., 'Childhood mortality, family size, and birth order in pre-industrial Europe', *Demography*, 12, 1975, 35-55. Mainly on France and Switzerland, spanning sixteenth to late nineteenth centuries.

5.11 **Drake**, M., 'Age at marriage in the pre-industrial West', in F. Bechhofer, ed., *Population Growth and the Brain Drain*, Edinburgh, 1969, l96-208.

5.12 **Dupâquier**, J., *Pour la Démographie*

Historique, Paris, 1984. Recognises repetitiveness of many studies based on parish reconstitution methods, and suggests new goals and approaches.

5.13 **Easterlin**, R. A., 'Economics and sociology of fertility: a synthesis', in C. Tilly, ed., *Historical Studies of Changing Fertility*, Princeton, N.J., 1978, 57-133. Offers method of graphing fertility constraints. Note that Tilly's collection contains extremely useful bibliography.

5.14 **Fischer**, W., 'Rural industrialization and population change', *Comp.Stud.Soc.& Hist.*, 15, 1973, 158-70. Summarises recent research on population factors involved in "proto-industrialisation" (subject treated mainly in Section 9).

5.15 **Flinn**, M. W., *The European Demographic System, 1500-1820*, 1981. Valuable summary of intensive research of last few decades.

5.16 —— 'The stabilisation of mortality in pre-industrial Western Europe', *J. Eur. Ec. Hist.*, 3, 1974, 285-318. Seeks to explain diminution of mortality crises in seventeenth and eighteenth centuries.

5.17 **Gaskin**, Katharine, 'Age at first marriage in Europe before 1850. A summary of family reconstitution data', *J.Family Hist.*, 3, 1978, 23-33. Throws doubt on existence of uniform European trends, particularly alleged earlier marriage in period 1750-1850.

5.18 **Glass**, D. V., and Revelle, R., eds., *Population and Social Change*, 1972. Contains important methodological articles by J. A. Banks, L. Henry, T. H. Hollingsworth, and others, as well as national surveys or case-studies noted separately infra. Previously publ. in *Daedalus*, 97, 1968.

5.19 **Grigg**, D., *Population Growth and Agrarian Change. An Historical Perspective*, 1980. Considers how far European and Third World demography has been constrained by available food resources.

5.20 **Guillaume**, P., and Poussu, J.-P., *Démographie Historique*, Paris, 1970. Substantial textbook.

5.21 **Habakkuk**, H. J., *Population Growth and Economic Development*, 1971. Short, breezy lectures, mainly dealing with pre-industrial England, but offering some comparative perspective.

5.22 **Hajnal**, J., 'European marriage patterns in perspective', in D. V. Glass and D. E. C. Eversley, eds., *Population in History*, Chicago, 1965, 101-46. Classic article postulating distinctive West European pattern of high age at marriage and high proportion of persons not marrying at all.

5.23 **Harsin**, P., and Helin, E., eds., *Problèmes de Mortalité. Méthodes, Sources, et Bibliographie en Démographie Historique*, Liège, 1965. International conference proceedings; papers mainly report national research in progress; also several on mortality crises of early modern period.

5.24 **Helleiner**, K. F., 'Population of Europe from the Black Death to the eve of the vital revolution', in *Cambridge Economic History of Europe*, 4 (2.15), 1-95.

5.25 —— 'The vital revolution reconsidered', *Can.J.Ec.& Pol.Sci.*, 23, 1957, 1-9. Repr. in Glass and Eversley (5.22), 79-86. Ascribes population turning point of early eighteenth century to reduction in mortality crises.

5.26 **Henry**, L., 'The verification of data in historical demography', *Pop.Stud.*, 22, 1968, 61-81. On methods of checking and compensating for non-registration of births, deaths, etc. See also his article in 5.18.

5.27 **Hollingsworth**, T. H., *Historical Demography*, 1969. On methods and sources. See also his article on quality of data in 5.18.

5.28 **Imhof**, A. E., 'From the old mortality pattern to the new', *Bull.Hist.Medicine*, 59, 1985, 1-29. Describes some findings of major University of Berlin research project on mortality decline over last four hundred years.

5.29 **Knodel**, J., 'Family limitation and the fertility transition. Evidence from the age patterns of fertility in Europe and Asia', *Pop.Stud.*, 31, 1977, 219-49. Argues that innovative behaviour rather than simply adjustment to economic change is important factor.

5.30 **Krause**, J. T., 'Some implications of recent work in historical demography', *Comp.Stud.Soc.& Hist.*, 1, 1959, 164-88. Repr. in M. Drake, ed., *Applied Historical Studies*, 1973, 155-83. Supports view that birth control and age of marriage, rather than mortality, were main limiters of population growth before 1800.

5.31 **Kunitz**, S. J., 'Speculations on the European mortality decline', *Ec.Hist.Rev.*, 2nd ser. 36, 1983, 349-64.

Views changes in disease patterns, beginning in seventeenth century, as main cause of decline.

5.32 **Langer**, W. L., 'Europe's initial population explosion', Am.Hist.Rev., 69, 1963, 1-17. Repr. in his *Explorations in Crisis*, Cambridge, Mass., 1969, 433-51. Suggests potato may have been important factor in mortality decline.

5.33 **Laslett**, P., 'Age of menarche in Europe since the eighteenth century', *J.Interdisc.Hist.*, 2, 1971, 221-36. Repr. in his *Family Life and Illicit Love in Earlier Generations*, 1977, 214-32; also in R. I. Rotberg and T. K. Rabb, eds., *The Family in History*, New York, 1973, 28-47; and same editors' *Marriage and Fertility: Studies in Interdisciplinary History*, Princeton, N.J., 1980, 285-300. Evidence from Belgrade in 1730s suggests that menarche occurred earlier than had been supposed.

5.34 **Lee**, R. D., and others, eds., *Population Patterns in the Past*, 1977. Lee's introduction discusses models of low population growth under conditions of natural fertility. Also contains area case-studies, and essays on combining aggregate statistics with family reconstitution techniques.

5.35 **Le Roy Ladurie**, E., 'From Waterloo to Colyton', in Le Roy Ladurie (4.35), 223-34. Historiographical essay.

5.36 —— 'History that stands still', in his *The Mind and Method of the Historian*, 1981, 1-27. Well-known expression of "Malthusian" interpretation of early modern demographic regime, originally given as Collège de France lecture, 1973. See another brief exposition in 5.111; and his major thesis, 7.56.

5.37 **Loschky**, D. J., 'Economic change, mortality and Malthusian Theory', *Pop.Stud.*, 30, 1976, 439-52. Asks whether variation or decline in mortality rates was due primarily to economic factors.

5.38 **McKeown**, T., and others, 'Interpretation of the modern rise of population in Europe', *Pop.Stud.*, 26, 1972, 345-82. Attributes rise mainly to improvement in diet. Arguments challenged by P. E. Razzell, *ib.* 28, 1974, 5-17, who prefers hypothesis of smallpox inoculation and improvements in hygiene.

5.39 —— *The Modern Rise of Population*, 1976. Book-length development of argument in previous entry. For critical review see A.

B. Appleby, 'Disease, diet and history', *J.Interdisc.Hist.*, 8, 1978, 725-35.

5.40 **Marcy**, P. T., 'Factors affecting the fecundity and fertility of historical populations: a review', *J.Family Hist.*, 6, 1981, 309-26. Useful introduction to recent work.

5.41 **Matossian**, Mary K., 'Mold poisoning and population growth in England and France, 1750-1850', *J.Ec.Hist.*, 44, 1984, 669-86. Suggests that ergot on rye may have been major factor in mortality before 1750, then mitigated by climatic and dietary changes.

5.42 **Mendels**, F. F., 'Recent research in European historical demography', *Am.Hist.Rev.*, 75, 1970, 1065-73. Review article useful for its comments on methodology.

5.43 **Moller**, H., 'Population and society during the Old Regime, c.1640-1770', in his *Population Movements in Modern European History*, New York, 1964, 19-42. Argues that migration, war and disease created labour shortage important in promoting more liberal society.

5.44 **Mols**, R., *Introduction à la Démographie Historique des Villes d'Europe du 14e au 18e Siècle*, 3 vols., Louvain, 1954-6. Still very valuable synthesis of data. Review article: K. F. Helleiner, *J.Ec.Hist.*, 18, 1958, 56-61.

5.45 —— 'Population in Europe, 1500-1700', in *Fontana Economic History of Europe*, 2 (2.24), 15-82.

5.46 **Mosk**, C., 'The evolution of pre-modern demographic regimes: a research note', *Explor.Ec.Hist.*, 18, 1981, 199-208. On differences between population behaviour in Sweden and Japan (c.1650-1850) despite similarities of family system in two countries.

5.47 **Noonan**, J. T., 'Intellectual and demographic history', *Daedalus*, 97, 1968, 463-85. Repr. in Glass and Revelle (5.18), 115-36. Considers influence of such factors as preaching and use of confession on social mores affecting demography.

5.48 **Ohlin**, G., 'Historical evidence of Malthusianism', in P. Deprez, ed., *Population and Economics. Proceedings of the Historical Demography Section, 4th Congress of the International Economic History Association*, Winnipeg, c.1970, 3-9. Looks at what demographic research has shown about Malthusian and other models of relation between population trends and economic factors.

.49 —— 'Mortality, marriage and growth in pre-industrial populations', *Pop.Stud.*, 14, 1961, 190-7. Model designed to show that population should remain stable despite considerable variation in mortality rates if marriage is linked to inheritance.

.50 **Peller**, S., 'Births and deaths among Europe's ruling families since 1500', in Glass and Eversley (5.22), 87-100. Summarises findings of his series of articles, 'Studies on mortality since the Renaissance', *Bull.Hist.Medicine*, 13, 1943, 427-61; 16, 1944, 362-81; 21, 1947, 51-101. These examined mortality in Europe's ruling families, c.1500-1900, with data taken from Isenburg's genealogical tables and Almanach de Gotha.

.51 **Phillips**, J. A., 'Achieving a critical mass while avoiding an explosion. Letter-cluster sampling and nominal record linkage', *J.Interdisc.Hist.*, 9, 1979, 493-508. Method which avoids some disadvantages of random sampling in demographic sources.

.52 **Reinhard**, M., and others, *Histoire Générale de la Population Mondiale*, 3rd ed., Paris, 1968. Useful text-book. Early modern period covered in pp. 102-285, with special attention to France.

.53 **Schofield**, R. S., 'Historical demography. Some possibilities and some limitations', *Trans.Roy.Hist.Soc.*, 5th ser., 21, 1971, 119-32. Raises general issues, though examples mostly drawn from England.

.54 —— 'The relationship between demographic structure and environment in pre-industrial Western Europe', in W. Conze, ed., *Sozialgeschichte der Familie*, Stuttgart, 1976, 147-60.

.55 **Sharlin**, A. N., 'Historical demography as history and demography', *Am. Behavioral Sci.*, 21, 1977, 245-62.

.56 —— 'Methods for estimating population total, age distribution and vital rates in family reconstitution studies', *Pop.Stud.*, 32, 1978, 511-21.

.57 **Smith**, D. S., 'A homeostatic demographic regime. Patterns in West European family reconstitution studies', in Lee (5.34), 19-51. Correlates data in published studies, and finds that large variations in mortality, fertility and age at marriage tend to zero sum.

.58 **Spencer**, Barbara, and others, 'Spectral analysis and the study of seasonal fluctuations in historical demography', *J.Eur.Ec.Hist.*, 5, 1976, 171-90. Method for establishing cycles of conception, tested on data from Belgium and Italy in seventeenth and eighteenth centuries.

5.59 **Spengler**, J., 'Demographic factors and early modern economic development', *Daedalus*, 97, 1968, 433-46. Repr. in Glass and Revelle (5.18), 87-98. Argues that West European pattern of late marriage was favourable to productivity, capital formation, and relatively high income.

5.60 'Techniques et méthodes en démographie historique, 17e-18e siècles. Actes du Colloque de Florence', *Ann.Démographie Hist.*, 1972, whole issue. Conference papers, mainly methodological.

5.61 **Tilly**, C., 'The historical study of vital processes', in Tilly (5.13), 3-55. State-of-the-art review and agenda, dealing in particular with determinants of fertility variation.

5.62 **Van de Walle**, E., and Kantrow, Louise, 'Historical demography. A bibliographical essay', *Pop.Index*, 40, 1974, 611-22.

5.63 **Wachter**, K. W., and others, *Statistical Studies of Historical Social Structure*, New York, 1978. Papers describing computer simulations and other statistical models of (mainly) pre-industrial demography. For critical review article, see Nancy Fitch, *Hist.Methods*, 13, 1980, 127-37.

5.64 **Weir**, D. R., 'Life under pressure. France and England, 1670-1870', *J.Ec.Hist.*, 44, 1984, 27-47. Questions usefulness of Malthusian model for early modern history (as expounded, for example, in 5.36).

5.65 **Willigan**, J. D., and Lynch, Katherine A., *Sources and Methods of Historical Demography*, 1982. Fairly demanding in its chapters on statistical analysis and demographic modelling. Review article: R. Schofield, *Hist.Methods*, 18, 1985, 71-5.

5.66 **Winchester**, I., 'Linkage of historical records by man and computer', *J.Interdisc.Hist.*, 1, 1970, 107-24. Computer techniques for linking names of variant spelling. (Examples use Canadian data. For a French example of problem, see 5.76).

5.67 **Wrigley**, E. A., 'Fertility strategy for the individual and the group', in Tilly (5.13), 135-54. Model, based on life tables, which sees pre-industrial marriage and household patterns as functional for population stability.

5.68 —— ed., *Identifying People in the Past*, 1973. Six essays on methodology of nominal record linkage for family reconstitution. Review article: M. P. Gutmann, *J.Family Hist.*, 2, 1977, 151-8.

5.69 —— *Population and History*, 1969. Valuable popularisation, especially strong on early modern period.

FRANCE
See also 3.5,8,37,49,57; 5.10,41,52,64; 6.58,87,109; 7.30; 9.460-3; 11.283.

5.70 **Ackerman**, Evelyn B., 'The commune of Bonnières-sur-Seine in the eighteenth and nineteenth centuries', *Ann.Démographie Hist.*, 1977, 85-100. Demography of small town near Mantes. Her book on Bonnières, *Village on the Seine*, Ithaca, N.Y., 1978, is restricted to nineteenth century.

5.71 **Baehrel**, R., 'Sur des communes-échantillons', *Annales*, 15, 1960, 702-31. Attacks sampling method proposed by Fleury and Henry (5.90) for leaving many geographical environments unrepresented.

5.72 **Baratier**, E., *La Démographie Provençale du 13e au 16e Siècle*, Paris, 1961. Includes comparison with eighteenth-century figures.

5.73 **Benedict**, P., 'Catholics and Huguenots in sixteenth-century Rouen. The demographic effects of the Religious Wars', *Fr.Hist.Stud.*, 9, 1975, 209-34. Study based on rates of baptisms and deaths recorded in church registers.

5.74 **Biraben**, J.-N., 'Inventaire par sondage des registres paroissiaux de France', *Population*, 15, 1960, 25-58. Results of enquiry into preservation of pre-1789 parish registers, to serve as basis for project outlined by Fleury and Henry (5.90)

5.75 —— and Blanchet, D., 'Le mouvement naturel de la population en France avant 1670. Présentation d'une enquête par sondage', *Population*, 37, 1982, 1099-1130. Reports further project to cover period before 1670, allowing for poorer sources. Progress report by Biraben, *ib.*, 40, 1985, 47-70.

5.76 **Blayo**, Y., 'Name variations in a village in Brie, 1750-1860', in Wrigley (5.68), 57-63. Example of difficulties encountered in computerised family reconstitution.

5.77 —— and Henry, L., 'Données démographiques sur la Bretagne et l'Anjou de 1740 à 1829', *Ann. Démographie Hist.*, 1967, 91-171.

5.78 **Burguière**, A., 'From Malthus to Max Weber. Belated marriage and the spirit of enterprise', in R. Forster and O. Ranum, eds., *Family and Society. Selections from the Annales*, Baltimore, Md., 1976, 237-50. Transl. from *Annales*, 27, 1972, 1128-38. Hypotheses about prevalence of late marriage and spread of contraception in pre-industrial France.

5.79 **Chamoux**, Antoinette, and Dauphin, Cécile, 'La contraception avant la Révolution. L'exemple de Châtillon-sur-Seine', *Annales*, 24, 1969, 662-84. Analysis of fertility in 87 marriages contracted between 1772-84 finds evidence for use of contraception.

5.80 **Charbonneau**, H., *Tourouvre-au-Perche au 17e et 18e siècles. Étude de démographie historique*, Paris, 1970. One of a number of model parish reconstitution studies; others incl.5.92-3.

5.81 **Croix**, A., *Nantes et le Pays Nantais au 16e Siècle. Étude Démographique*, Paris, 1974. Review article, and reply: J. Dupâquier, *Annales*, 30, 1975, 394-401, 1585-93.

5.82 **Deniel**, R., and Henry, L., 'La population d'un village du Nord de la France, Sainghin-en-Mélantois, de 1665 à 1851', *Population*, 28, 1965, 563-602.

5.83 **Derouet**, B., 'Une démographie différentielle. Clés pour un système auto-régulateur des populations rurales d'ancien régime', *Annales*, 35, 1980, 3-41. Discusses differences in demographic behaviour between peasant proprietors and wage labourers of Chartres region in eighteenth century.

5.84 **Dreyer-Roos**, Suzanne, *La Population Strasbourgeoise sous l'Ancien Régime*, Strasbourg, 1969. Detailed demographic study, though reconstitution methods not attempted; covers period 1681-1789.

5.85 **Dupâquier**, J., 'French population in the seventeenth and eighteenth centuries', in Cameron and others (3.251), 150-69. Transl. from *Rev.Hist.*, 239, 1968, 43-79. Useful survey of work published or then in progress.

5.86 —— *La Population Française aux 17e et 18e Siècles*, Paris, 1980. Handy textbook in *Que Sais-Je* series.

5.87 —— *La Population Rurale du Bassin Parisien à l'Époque de Louis XIV*, Paris, 1979. Interpretative distillation of his massive statistical compilation, *Statistiques Démographiques du Bassin Parisien, 1636-1720*, Paris, 1977.

5.88 —— and others, 'Villes et villages de l'ancienne France', *Ann.Démographie Hist.*, 1969, 10-292. Group of parish studies (mainly eighteenth-century data) involving Paris region, Normandy, Brittany, Touraine, and Alsace.

5.89 **Fleury**, M., and Henry, L., *Nouveau Manuel de Dépouillement et d'Exploitation de l'État Civil Ancien*, Paris, 1965. Classic exposition of family reconstitution from parish registers, updating an earlier version, *Des Registres Paroissiaux à l'Histoire de la Population* (1956). Further corrections and amplifications in Henry's *Techniques d'Analyse en Démographie Historique*, Paris, 1980.

5.90 —— 'Pour connaître la population de la France depuis Louis XIV', *Population*, 13, 1958, 663-86. Outlines project for large-scale sampling of parish registers on representative regional and sociological lines.

5.91 **Galliano**, P., 'La mortalité infantile dans la banlieue sud de Paris à la fin du 18e siècle (1774-94)', *Ann.Démographie Hist.*, 1966, 139-77. Sets out to compare ordinary child mortality with that of wet-nursed infants.

5.92 **Ganiage**, J., *Trois Villages d'Ile de France au 18e Siècle. Étude Démographique*, Paris, 1963. Belongs to same series as more celebrated following entry.

5.93 **Gautier**, E., and Henry, L., *La Population de Crulai, Paroisse Normande*, Paris, 1958. Pioneer study in family reconstitution technique.

5.94 **Goubert**, P., 'Historical demography and the reinterpretation of early modern French history', *J.Interdisc.Hist.*, 1, 1970, 37-48. Repr. in Rotberg and Rabb, *Family in History* (5.33), 16-27. Brief review of French contribution to demographic research.

5.95 —— 'Legitimate fecundity and infant mortality in France during the eighteenth century: a comparison', *Daedalus*, 97, 1968, 593-603. Repr. in Glass and Revelle (5.18), 321-30. Points to higher rates of fertility and mortality in Brittany as opposed to South-West France.

5.96 —— 'Recent themes and research in French population between 1500 and 1700', in Glass and Eversley (5.22), 457-73.

5.97 **Gouhier**, P., *Port en Bessin, 1597-1792. Étude d'Histoire Démographique*, Caen, 1962. Of special interest as study of a maritime community.

5.98 **Gutierrez**, H., and Houdaille, J., 'La mortalité maternelle en France au 18e siècle', *Population*, 38, 1983, 975-93. Data derived from project outlined in 5.90.

5.99 **Henry**, L., 'Fécondité des mariages dans le quart sud-ouest de la France de 1720 à 1829', *Annales*, 27, 1972, 612-40, 977-1023. Further geographical analyses by Henry and J. Houdaille cover the North-West (*Population*, 28, 1973, 873-922); the South-East (*ib.*, 33, 1978, 855-82); and the North-East (*Ann.Démographie Hist.*, 1976, 341-92).

5.100 —— 'The population of France in the eighteenth century', in Glass and Eversley (5.22), 434-56. General summary of research on all aspects of demography.

5.101 —— and Blayo, Y., 'La population de la France de 1740 à 1860', *Population*, 30, 1975, special issue, 71-122. Estimates of population by sex and age groups at 5-year intervals. In supplementary articles, Blayo deals with annual births, deaths and marriages (*ib.* 15-70); and sex specific mortality rates (*ib.* 123-41). For earlier period see Rebaudo (5.115)

5.102 —— and Houdaille, J., 'Célibat et age au mariage aux 18e et 19e siècles en France', *Population*, 33, 1978, 43-83; 34, 1979, 403-41. More material from project begun in 5.99.

5.103 —— and Levy, C., 'Quelques données sur la région autour de Paris au 18e siècle', *Population*, 17, 1962, 297-326. Some first results of sampling survey outlined in 5.90.

5.104 **Lachiver**, M., *La Population de Meulan du 17e au 19e Siècle*, Paris, 1969. Study of small town near Paris, using family reconstitution and illustrating precocious decline in birth-rate in late eighteenth century.

5.105 **Lebras**, H., and Dinet, Dominique, 'Mortalité des laïcs et mortalité des religieux. Les Bénédictins de Saint-Maur aux 17e et 18e siècles', *Population*, 35, 1980, 347-82. Shows that monks had better than average life expectancy to middle age, but poorer in late life.

5.106 **Lebrun**, F., 'Les crises démographiques

en France aux 17e et 18e siècles', *Annales*, 35, 1980, 205-34. General study of effects of plague, war and food shortages; see also case-study on Bordeaux by J.-P. Poussu, which argues that mortality surges cannot be directly attributed to subsistence crises (*ib*. 235-52).

5.107 —— *Les Hommes et la Mort en Anjou aux 17e et 18e Siècles. Essai de Démographie et de Psychologie Historiques*, Paris, 1971. As sub-title indicates, both causes and attitudes to death are investigated in rich detail. Review article: J. Delumeau, *Annales*, 27, 1972, 1389-99. For further material on psychological aspects of death, see 14.106-25.

5.108 **Lecuir**, J., 'La *Gazette de l'Agriculture, du Commerce, et de Finance* et le débat sur la population à la fin du 18e siècle', *Ann. Démographie Hist.*, 1979, 363-441. Reproduces statistics collected and cited by this journal in running debate on population trends and policy, 1777-81.

5.109 **Lefebvre-Teillard**, Anne, *La Population de Dôle au 18e Siècle*, Paris, 1969. Short study aiming to establish some aggregate indices.

5.110 **Lepetit**, B., 'Démographie d'une ville en gestation. Versailles sous Louis XIV', *Ann.Démographie Hist.*, 1977, 49-83. Finds urban characteristics heavily underlined – mobility, high birth and mortality rates, frequent pre-marital conceptions.

5.111 **Le Roy Ladurie**, E., 'Zero population growth. Population and subsistence in sixteenth-century rural France', *Peasant Stud.Newsl.*, 1, 1972, 60-5. Views population rise of sixteenth century as recuperation within fundamentally homeostatic system.

5.112 **Meuvret**, J., 'Demographic crisis in France from the sixteenth to the eighteenth century', in Glass and Eversley (5.22), 507-22. On causes of mortality.

5.113 **Pinède**, C., 'La population de Quercy à la fin du 18e siècle', *Actes Congrès Nat.Soc.Savantes*, 82, 1957, 51-103. Documentation of 1770s and '80s for *généralité* of Montauban.

5.114 **Radeff**, Anne, 'Naissance d'une communauté agro-industrielle du Jura. Vallorbe, 1397-1614', *Ét.Rurales*, 68, 1977, 107-40. Finds little correlation between land clearance and population cycles.

5.115 **Rebaudo**, Danièle, 'Le mouvement annuel de la population française rurale de 1670 à 1740', *Population*, 34, 1979, 589-603.

5.116 **Valmary**, P., *Familles Paysannes au 18e Siècle en Bas-Quercy*, Paris, 1965. Based on registers of two parishes, using family reconstitution.

5.117 **Van de Walle**, E., 'The French fertility decline until 1850', in Tilly (5.13), 257-88. Discusses regional variations in fertility and mortality, but presents no firm conclusions on causality of decline which began in eighteenth century.

5.118 —— 'Motivations and technology in the decline of French fertility', in R. Wheaton and Tamara K. Hareven, eds., *Family and Sexuality in French History*, Philadelphia, Pa., 1980, 135-78. Speculates on contraceptive practices which may have contributed to decline.

LOW COUNTRIES
See also 5.58.

5.119 **Alter**, G., 'Plague and the Amsterdam annuitant', *Pop.Stud.*, 37, 1983, 23-41. Compares mortality experiences of two groups of annuity purchasers in 1580s and 1670s respectively.

5.120 **Bruneel**, C., *La Mortalité dans les Campagnes. Le Duché de Brabant aux 17e et 18 Siècles*, Louvain, 1977. Concludes that fertility rise must underlie population increase of this area, as mortality rate improved only marginally.

5.121 **Deprez**, P., 'The demographic development of Flanders in the eighteenth century', in Glass and Eversley (5.22), 608-30.

5.122 **De Vries**, J., 'The population and economy of the preindustrial Netherlands', *J.Interdisc.Hist.*, 15, 1985, 661-82. State of the art survey based on comparison with Wrigley and Schofield's *Population History of England*.

5.123 **Faber**, J. A., and others, 'Population changes and economic developments in the Netherlands', *A.A.G.Bijd.*, 12, 1965, 47-113. Aggregate trends from 1500 onwards. Briefer account in *Proc. Third International Conference of Economic History*, Paris, 1968-74, 4, 67-78.

5.124 **Gutmann**, M. P., 'Reconstituting Wandre. An approach to semi-automatic family reconstitution', *Ann.Démographie*

Hist., 1977, 315-41. Explains use of computer in small-scale reconstitution of village near Liège (1666-1729).

5.125 —— 'Why they stayed. The problem of wartime population loss', *Tijd.Geschied.*, 91, 1978, 407-28. Examines comparative stability of population of Lower Meuse region despite continual disruptions of war between 1618 and 1748. See Gutmann's full-length study of region in 10.504.

5.126 —— and Wyrick, R., 'Adapting methods to needs. Studying fertility and nuptiality in seventeenth- and eighteenth-century Belgium', *Hist.Methods*, 14, 1981, 163-71.

5.127 **Hélin**, E., *La Démographie de Liège aux 17e et 18e Siècles*, Brussels, 1963. Valuable. See also his preliminary work on aggregate population, *La Population des Paroisses Liégeoises* (Liège, 1959).

5.128 **Slicher van Bath**, B. H., 'Contrasting demographic development in some parts of the Netherlands during the depression period of the seventeenth and eighteenth centuries', in Bechhofer (5.11), 209-19. Seeks explanation of population decline in Holland and considerable increase in Overijssel.

5.129 —— 'Historical demography and the social and economic development of the Netherlands', *Daedalus*, 97, 1968, 604-21. Repr. in Glass and Revelle (5.18), 331-46. General account of trends between 1500 and 1800, based on research in 5 provinces.

5.130 —— 'Report on the study of historical demography in the Netherlands', *A.A.G.Bijd.*, 11, 1964, 182-90. Data on sources and some rather miscellaneous statistics.

5.131 **Van der Woude**, A. M., 'Population developments in the Northern Netherlands (1500-1800) and the validity of the "urban graveyard" effect', *Ann.Démographie Hist.*, 1982, 55-75. Questions automatic association of pre-industrial city with very high mortality (only combatted by in-migration).

5.132 —— and Mentink, G. J., 'La population de Rotterdam au 17e et au 18e siècle', *Population*, 21, 1966, 1165-90.

SPAIN AND PORTUGAL
On Spain see also 3.112,117; 5.8; 7.99,105,289; 8.75,82; 10.124; 12.80. On Portugal, 11.144.

5.133 **Ansón Calvo**, María, *Demografía y*

Sociedad Urbana en la Zaragoza del Siglo 17, Zaragoza, 1977. Much detail on computer methods used.

5.134 **Bustelo García**, F., 'La población española en la segunda mitad del siglo 18', *Moneda y Crédito*, 123, 1972, 53-104.

5.135 **Cachinero-Sánchez**, B., 'Estimating levels of adult mortality in eighteenth-century Spain', *Hist.Methods*, 18, 1985, 63-70. Explains new procedure by application to census data of 1768-97.

5.136 **Fernández Vargas**, Valentina, *La Población de León en el Siglo 16*, Madrid, 1968. Covers city and province.

5.137 **García-Baquero López**, G., *Estudio Demográfico de la Parroquia de San Martín de Sevilla, 1551-1749*, Seville, 1982. Deals in turn with data from baptismal, marriage, and mortality registers.

5.138 **Gutiérrez Nieto**, J. I., 'Evolución demográfica de la cuenca del Segura en el siglo 16', *Hispania*, 111, 1969, 25-115. River valley in South-Eastern Spain.

5.139 **Larquié**, C., 'Une approche quantitative de la pauvreté. Les Madrilènes et la mort au 17e siècle', *Ann.Démographie Hist.*, 1978, 175-96. Explores relations of poverty and poor life expectancy.

5.140 —— 'Étude de démographie madrilène. La paroisse de San Ginés de 1650 à 1700', *Mél.Casa de Velazquez*, 2, 1966, 225-58.

5.141 —— 'Quartiers et paroisses urbaines. L'exemple de Madrid au 17e siècle', *Ann.Démographie Hist.*, 1974, 165-95. Looks at densities of population, and class profiles.

5.142 **López-Salazar Pérez**, J., 'Evolución demográfica de La Mancha en el siglo 18', *Hispania*, 133, 1976, 233-99. Uses parish records to plot vital rates for whole of century.

5.143 **Marcos Martín**, A., *Auge y Declive de un Núcleo Mercantil y Financiero de Castilla la Vieja. Evolución Demográfica de Medina del Campo durante los Siglos 16 y 17*, Valladolid, 1978.

5.144 **Martín Galán**, M., 'Fuentes y metodes para el estudio de la demografía histórica castellana durante la edad moderna', *Hispania*, 148, 1981, 231-325. Important survey of availability and uses of censuses, hearth lists, parish registers, and other sources.

5.145 **Mauleon Isla**, Mercedes, *La Población de Bilbao en el Siglo 18*, Valladolid, 1961.

5.146 **Molinié-Bertrand**, Annie, *Au Siècle*

d'Or. L'Espagne et ses Hommes. La Population du Royaume de Castille au 16e Siècle, Paris, 1985. Based esp. on 1591 census; contains province by province analysis as well as general conclusions.

5.147 **Nadal**, J., *La Población Española, Siglos 16 a 20*, Barcelona, 1966; 2nd ed. 1984. Basic survey.

5.148 —— and Giralt, E., *La Population Catalane de 1553 à 1717. L'Immigration Française et les autres Facteurs de son Développement*, Paris, 1960. Using hospital records and small sample of parishes, develops material on demographic rates, epidemics, etc., as well as major question of French settlement.

5.149 **Pérez Moreda**, V., *Las Crisis de Mortalidad en la España Interior, Siglos 16-19*, Madrid, 1980. Based on burial registers of wide selection of Castilian parishes. Rural emigration rather than epidemics or famine seen as major cause of depopulation.

5.150 **Pérez-Moreda**, V., 'Matrimonio y familia. El modelo matrimonial español en la edad moderna', *Bol.Assoc.Demografia Hist.*, 4, 1986, 3-51. Seeks to differentiate local variations in age of marriage.

5.151 **Rodríguez Sánchez**, A., *Cáceres: Población y Comportamientos Demográficos en el Siglo 16*, Cáceres, 1977.

5.152 **Romero de Solís**, P., *La Población Española en los Siglos 18 y 19*, Madrid, 1973. Substantial chapter on period 1715-87.

5.153 **Sentlaurens**, J., 'Séville dans la seconde moitié du 16e siècle. Population et structures sociales. Le recensement de 1561', *Bull.Hispanique*, 77, 1975, 321-90. Interesting data, despite author's claim to be no historian.

5.154 **Vincent**, B., 'Récents travaux de démographie historique en Espagne (14e-18e siècles)', *Ann.Démographie Hist.*, 1977, 463-91. Valuable bibliographical article.

ITALY

See also 5.8,58; 6.153,162; 8.95,99-101; 11.238,240,329.

5.155 **Aleati**, G., *La Popolazione di Pavia durante il Dominio Spagnolo*, Milan, 1957. Review article: G. Felloni, *Annales*, 15, 1960, 774-8.

5.156 **Aymard**, M., 'Une croissance selective. La population sicilienne au 17e siècle', *Mél.Casa de Velazquez*, 4, 1968, 203-27. Compares data from fiscal enquiries of 1623 and 1681.

5.157 **Bellettini**, A., *La Popolazione di Bologna dal Secolo 15 all'Unificazione Italiana*, Bologna, 1961.

5.158 **Beltrami**, D., *Storia della Popolazione di Venezia dalla Fine del Secolo 16 alla Caduta della Repubblica*, Padua, 1954.

5.159 **Cipolla**, C. M., 'The "bills of mortality" of Florence', *Pop.Stud.*, 32, 1978, 543-8. Concerns two series of mortality registers extending from c.1400 to 1800, and discrepancies between them.

5.160 —— 'Four centuries of Italian demographic development', in Glass and Eversley (5.22), 570-87.

5.161 **Comitato Italiano per lo Studio della Popolazione**, *Le Fonti della Demografia Storica in Italia*, 2 vols., Rome, 1974; followed by *Problemi di Utilizzazione delli Fonti...*, Rome, 1977. Massive compilation of sources and methodology produced as seminar proceedings.

5.162 **Delille**, G., *Agricoltura e Demografia nel Regno di Napoli nei Secoli 18 e 19*, Naples, 1977. Primarily a demographic study.

5.163 **Del Panta**, L., *Una Traccia di Storia Demografica della Toscana nei Secoli 16-18*, Florence, 1974. Brief outline of global trends, based on Florentine and Sienese censuses.

5.164 —— and Livi Bacci, M., 'Chronologie, intensité, et diffusion des crises de mortalité en Italie, 1600-1850', *Population*, 32, 1977, special issue, 401-40.

5.165 **Ginatempo**, Maria, 'Per la storia demografica del territorio Senese nel Quattrocento, Problemi di fonti e di metodo', *Arch.Stor.Ital.*, 142, 1984, 511-87.

5.166 **Herlihy**, D., 'Deaths, marriages, births, and the Tuscan economy (c.1300-1550)', in Lee (5.34), 135-64. Emphasis on economic factors affecting marriage rates.

5.167 —— 'The population of Verona in the first century of Venetian rule', in J. R. Hale, ed., *Renaissance Venice*, 1973, 91-120. Period coincides roughly with fifteenth century.

5.168 **Litchfield**, R. B., 'Demographic characteristics of Florentine patrician families, sixteenth to nineteenth centuries', *J.Ec.Hist.*, 29, 1969, 191-205. Attributes decline of patrician numbers to limitations on cadet marriages for sake of concentrating family wealth.

5.169 **Società Italiana di Demografia Storica,** *La Popolazione Italiana nel Settecento,* Bologna 1980.

5.170 —— *La Demografia Storica delle Città Italiane*, Bologna, 1982. This and preceding entry are essay collections rather than comprehensive works. Note also on urban demography 8.95.

GERMANY, SWITZERLAND, AND AUSTRIA
See also 3.227; 5.10; 9.588; 11.259.

5.171 **Blaschke**, K., *Bevölkerungsgeschichte von Sachsen bis zur Industriellen Revolution*, Weimar, 1967. Review article: H. Harnisch, *Jb.Wirtschaftsgesch.*, 1973 (iv), 205-20.

5.172 **Braun**, R., 'Early industrialisation and demographic changes in the canton of Zurich', in Tilly (5.13), 289-334. Proponent of proto-industrialisation thesis, finding high population growth in regions with cottage industry opportunities, thanks to earlier marriage and lack of out-migration. See comment on 5.14; and related studies at 5.363-4,423.

5.173 **Burri**, H.-R., *Die Bevölkerung Luzerns im 18. und Frühen 19. Jahrhundert*, Luzern, 1975.

5.174 **François**, E., 'La mortalité urbaine en Allemagne au 18e siècle', *Ann. Démographie Hist.*, 1978, 135-65. General synthesis.

5.175 —— 'La population de Coblence au 18e siècle. Déficit démographique et immigration dans une ville de résidence', *ib.*, 1975, 291-341. For François' general study of Koblenz see 8.126.

5.176 **Gschwind**, F., *Bevölkerungsentwicklung und Wirtschaftsstruktur der Landschaft Basel im 18. Jahrhundert*, Liestal, 1977. Aggregate study, based on rich census records.

5.177 **Helczmanovski**, H., ed., *Beiträge zur Bevölkerungs- und Sozialgeschichte Österreichs*, Vienna, 1973. Contains sketch of population history in early modern period by K. Klein, and demographic study of parish of Stockerau by J.-P. Lehners.

5.178 **Henry**, L., *Anciennes Familles Genevoises. Étude Démographique, 16e-18e Siècle*, Paris, 1956. Works through genealogies of 19 prominent families admitted to citizenship before 1550.

5.179 **Imhof**, A. E., ed., *Historische Demographie als Sozialgeschichte. Giessen und Umgebung vom 17. zum 19. Jahrhundert*, 2 vols., Darmstadt, 1975. Large-scale collective research on town in Hesse, ending with comparative essays on other regions in Germany, Switzerland and Scandinavia. See following articles by Imhof based on this work.

5.180 —— 'The analysis of eighteenth-century causes of death. Some methodological considerations', *Hist.Methods*, 11, 1978, 3-35.

5.181 —— 'An approach to historical demography in Germany', *Soc.Hist.*, 4, 1979, 345-66.

5.182 —— 'Historical demography as social history. Possibilities in Germany', *J.Family Hist.*, 2, 1977, 305-32.

5.183 —— 'Reconstructing biological frameworks of populations in the past', in Clubb and Scheuch (1.5), 71-83.

5.184 **Keyser**, E., *Die Bevölkerungsgeschichte Deutschlands*, Leipzig, 1938. 3rd ed., 1943. Massive work, which laid good foundations for subsequent research.

5.185 **Knodel**, J., 'Child mortality and reproductive behaviour in German village populations in the past', *Pop.Stud.*, 36, 1982, 177-200. This and following articles by Knodel rely considerably on sample of villages providing data on eighteenth- and nineteenth-century demography via methods outlined in 5.190.

5.186 —— 'Natural fertility in pre-industrial Germany', *ib.*, 32, 1978, 481-510. Suggests that family limitation was largely absent before 1850.

5.187 —— 'Seasonal variation in infant mortality. An approach with applications', *Ann.Démographie Hist.*, 1983, 208-30. Article in issue largely devoted to infancy questions.

5.188 —— 'Two and a half centuries of demographic history in a Bavarian village', *Pop. Stud.*, 24, 1970, 353-76. Shows constant pattern of late marriage, high fertility and high infant mortality from 1700 to 1900.

5.189 —— and De Vos, Susan, 'Preferences for the sex of offspring and demographic behaviour in eighteenth and nineteenth-century Germany', *J.Family Hist.*, 5, 1980, 145-66. Finds that preference for male children is only very weakly discernible.

5.190 ——and Shorter, E., 'The reliability of family reconstitution data in German village genealogies (*Ortssippenbücher*)', *Ann.Démographie Hist.*, 1976, 115-53. Favourable assessment of accuracy of these local genealogical compilations.

5.191 —— and Wilson, C., 'The secular increase in fecundity in German village populations. Couples married 1750-1899', *Pop.Stud.*, 35, 1981, 53-84.

5.192 **Kronshage**, W., *Die Bevölkerung Göttingens. Ein Demographischer Beitrag zur Sozial- und Wirtschaftsgeschichte vom 14. bis 17. Jahrhundert*, Göttingen, 1960.

5.193 **Lee**, W. R., 'The mechanism of mortality change in Germany, 1750-1850', *Medizinhist.J.*, 15, 1980, 244-68. Rejects any monocausal explanation such as McKeown's (5.39).

5.194 —— *Population Growth, Economic Development, and Social Change in Bavaria, 1750-1850*, New York, 1977. Important study of connections between demographic change and society in region that remained primarily agrarian (Freising region provides case-study).

5.195 **Mathis**, F., *Zur Bevölkerungsstruktur Österreichischer Städte im 17. Jahrhundert*, Vienna, 1977. Copious statistics for Salzburg, Innsbruck, and Hall, but lacks comparative and analytical dimension.

5.196 **Monter**, E. W., 'Historical demography and religious history in sixteenth-century Geneva', *J.Interdisc.Hist.*, 9, 1979, 399-427. Demographic patterns correlated with city's role as Protestant refugee centre.

5.197 **Perrenoud**, A., *La Population de Genève du 16e au Début du 19e Siècle*, Geneva, 1979. Based on reconstitution of 500 families. Second vol.scheduled to follow. Following articles derive from this material.

5.198 —— 'Malthusianisme et protestantisme. Un modèle démographique weberien', *Annales*, 29, 1974, 975-88. Looks at family limitation and possible link with Protestant ethic.

5.199 —— 'L'inégalité sociale devant la mort à Genève au 17e siècle', *Population*, 30, 1975, special issue, 221-43. Explores differences in mortality rates between social classes.

5.200 **Rödel**, W. G., *Mainz und seine Bevölkerung im 17. und 18. Jahrhundert*, Stuttgart, 1985.

EAST CENTRAL EUROPE (BOHEMIA, HUNGARY, AND POLAND)
See also 3.274 (Hungary); 10.149 (Poland).

5.201 **Andorka**, R., 'Birth control in the eighteenth and nineteenth centuries in some Hungarian villages', *Local Pop.Stud.*, 22, 1979, 38-43. Examines low fertility rates in 4 villages over period 1760-1850. More fully developed in *Ann.Démographie Hist.*, 1972, 25-53 (in French).

5.202 **Gieysztorowa**, Irena, 'Introduction à la démographie de l'ancienne Pologne (16e-18e siècles)', *Ann.Démographie Hist.*, 1977, 357-77. Résumé of recently published work in Polish by author.

5.203 —— 'Research into the demographic history of Poland. Provisional summing up', *Acta Poloniae Hist.*, 18, 1968, 5-17. Considers aggregate population figures over whole span of Polish history.

5.204 **Horvath**, R., 'Interdependence of economic and demographic development in Hungary (from the middle of the eighteenth to the middle of the nineteenth century)', in Deprez (5.48), 127-40.

5.205 **Hunyadi**, I., 'Étude comparée des sources fiscales Turques et Hongroises du 16e siècle comme base de calcul de la population', *Turcica*, 12, 1980, 125-55. On possibilities of control afforded by overlapping documents for certain regions.

5.206 **Kovacsics**, J., 'Population of Hungary in the eighteenth century (1720-86)', in *Proc. Third International Conference of Economic History* (5.123), 4, 137-45.

TURKEY AND THE BALKANS
See also 11.88.

5.207 **Barkan**, O. L., 'Essai sur les données statistiques des registres de recensement dans l'empire Ottoman au 15e et 16e siècles', *J.Ec.& Soc. Hist.Orient*, 1, 1958, 9-36. Includes estimate of population around 1520-30. See comment and further data by J. C. Russell, *ib.*, 3, 1960, 265-74; and shorter English version of Barkan's paper in M. A. Cook, ed., *Studies in the Economic History of the Middle East*, 1970, 163-71.

5.208 **Cook**, M. A., *Population Pressure in Rural Anatolia, 1450-1600*, 1972. Sets out to test Braudel's thesis of decline in Turkish grain exports due to expanding population.

5.209 **Erder**, Leila, 'The measurement of pre-industrial population changes. The Ottoman Empire from the fifteenth to the seventeenth century', *Mid.E.Stud.*, 11, 1975, 284-301. Largely a discussion of sources and methods of extrapolating from them.

5.210 —— and Faroqhi, Suraiya, 'Population rise and fall in Anatolia, 1550-1620', *ib.*, 15, 1979, 322-45. Repr. in Faroqhi (4.82). Based on tax registers of two contrasting provinces.

5.211 **Papadopoulos,** T., *Social and Historical Data on Population (1570-1881)*, Nicosia, 1965. Documentary collection on Cyprus population history.

5.212 **Željazkova**, Antonina L., 'Ottoman-Turkic colonization in Albania and some aspects of the ensuing demographic changes', *Ét.Balkaniques*, 20 (ii), 1984, 67-84.

SCANDINAVIA
See also 5.46; 6.213-14; 10.151,154.

5.213 **Åkerman**, S., and others, eds., *Chance and Change. Social and Economic Studies in Historical Demography in the Baltic Area*, Odense, 1978. Essay collection, mostly case studies dealing with Scandinavia in the eighteenth and nineteenth centuries.

5.214 **Backer**, Julie E., and Ofstad, K., 'Population statistics and population registration in Norway', *Pop.Stud.*, 1, 1947, 212-28; 2, 1948, 318-38; 3, 1949, 66-75. On sources available for study of Norwegian demographic history.

5.215 **Drake**, M., *Population and Society in Norway, 1735-1865*, 1969. See also following articles, drawing on this material. Critical review article by S. Tveite (with author's reply), *Scan.Ec.Hist.Rev.*, 20, 1972, 78-88.

5.216 —— 'Fertility controls in pre-industrial Norway', in Glass and Revelle (5.18), 185-98.

5.217 —— 'The growth of population in Norway, 1735-1855', *Scan.Ec.Hist.Rev.*, 13, 1965, 97-142.

5.218 **Dyrvik**, S., and others, *Demographic Crises in Norway in the Seventeenth and Eighteenth Centuries*, Bergen, 1976. Brief publication which examines annual mortality figures in a number of parishes.

5.219 —— 'Historical demography in Norway, 1660-1801', *Scan.Ec.Hist.Rev.*, 20, 1972, 27-44. Historiographical article.

5.220 **Friberg**, N., 'Population growth in a mining district in Sweden, 1650-1750, and its economic background', in *Proc. Third International Conference of Economic History* (5.123), 4, 79-90. Investigates central Swedish district of Grangärde in period before official collection of statistics.

5.221 **Fridlizius**, G., 'Some new aspects on Swedish population growth', *Ec.& Hist.*, 18, 1975, 3-33, 126-54. Examines trends between 1750 and 1860 in various counties.

5.222 **Gaunt**, D., 'Family planning and preindustrial society. Some Swedish evidence', in K. Agren and others, eds., *Aristocrats, Farmers, Proletarians. Essays in Swedish Demographic History*, Uppsala, 1973, 28-59. Family reconstitution methods applied to parishes in eighteenth-century Gotland.

5.223 —— 'Pre-industrial economy and population structure. The elements of variance in early modern Sweden', *Scan.J.Hist.*, 2, 1977, 183-210. Study of 5 villages showing higher fertility and household size among freeholders with extra income opportunities in mining, haulage, etc.

5.224 **Gille**, H., 'The demographic history of the Northern European countries in the eighteenth century', *Pop.Stud.*, 3, 1949, 3-65. Includes comprehensive description of sources.

5.225 **Heckscher**, E. F., 'Swedish population trends before the Industrial Revolution', *Ec.Hist.Rev.*, 2nd ser., 2, 1950, 266-77. Analysis begins from start of official record-keeping in 1749.

5.226 **Imhof**, A. E., *Aspekte der Bevölkerungsentwicklung in den Nordischen Ländern, 1720-50*, 2 vols., Bern, 1976. Vast range of demographic and medical data, esp. for Sweden and Finland; despite title, includes some material on second half of century.

5.227 —— and Larsen, O., 'Social and medical history. Methodological problems in interdisciplinary quantitative research', *J.Interdisc.Hist.*, 7, 1977, 493-8. Note on Scandinavian mortality registers of eighteenth century which permit unusually detailed analysis of morbidity factors.

5.228 **Johansen**, H. C., and others, 'Current research in economic history in Scandinavia: historical demography', *Scan.Ec.Hist.Rev.*, 20, 1972, 71-7. Brief, country-by-country survey of research. See 5.236 for succeeding period.

5.229 —— 'Some aspects of Danish rural population structure in 1787', *ib.*, 20, 1972, 61-70. Data from one per cent random sample of 1787 census.

5.230 **Jutikkala**, E., 'Can the population of Finland in the seventeenth century be calculated?', *ib.*, 5, 1957, 155-72. Discusses reliability of poll-tax lists as population source, using example of Tavastland province.

5.231 —— 'Finland's population movement in the eighteenth century', in Glass and Eversley (5.22), 549-69.

5.232 **Kälvemark**, Ann-S., 'The country that kept track of its population. Methodological aspects of Swedish population records', *Scan.J.Hist.*, 2, 1977, 211-30.

5.233 **Lassen**, A., 'Population of Denmark in 1660', *Scan.Ec.Hist.Rev.*, 13, 1965, 1-30. Argues that heavy plague mortality in late 1650s reduced population below half a million.

5.234 —— 'Population of Denmark, 1660-1960', *ib.*, 14, 1966, 134-57. Despite title, deals principally with trends up to census of 1801.

5.235 **Pitkänen**, K., 'Reliability of registration of births and deaths in Finland in the eighteenth and nineteenth centuries', *ib.*, 25, 1977, 138-59. Contends that tests on three parishes reveal considerable omissions from parish registers, esp. in cases of infant mortality. See comment by E. Jutikkala, *ib.*, 26, 1978, 168-9; and reply, *ib.*, 27, 1979, 67.

5.236 **Sogner**, S., 'Bilan de la recherche en démographie historique dans les pays scandinaves, 1976-85', *Ann.Démographie Hist.*, 1986, 275-310.

5.237 —— 'A demographic crisis averted?', *ib.*, 24, 1976, 114-28. Argues from experience of Akershus diocese in 1782-83 that mere threat of economic crisis may affect birth-rate.

5.238 **Thestrup**, P., 'Methodological problems of a family reconstruction study in a Danish rural parish before 1800', *ib.*, 20, 1972, 1-26.

5.239 **Tomasson**, R. F., 'A millenium of misery. The demography of the Icelanders', *Pop.Stud.*, 31, 1977, 405-27.

5.240 **Turpeinen**, O., 'Infant mortality in Finland, 1749-1865', *Scan.Ec.Hist.Rev.*, 27, 1979, 1-21. Describes temporal, regional and class variations.

5.241 —— 'Infectious diseases and regional differences in Finnish death rates, 1749-73', *Pop.Stud.*, 32, 1978, 523-33. Contends that disease counts for more than economic factors in differing mortality rates.

5.242 **Utterström**, G., 'Population and agriculture in Sweden, c.1700-1830', *Scan.Ec.Hist.Rev.*, 9, 1961, 176-94. Presents evidence that population increase created larger class of labourers and tenants-at-will.

5.243 —— 'Population in eighteenth-century Scandinavia', in Glass and Eversley (5.22), 523-48. Main emphasis on Sweden.

5.244 —— 'Some population problems in pre-industrial Sweden', *Scan.Ec.Hist.Rev.*, 2, 1954, 103-65. Thorough survey of aggregate trends in period 1750-1850, drawing attention to higher death rates in east of country.

RUSSIA AND BALTIC PROVINCES
See also 8.166.

5.245 **Czap**, P., 'Russian history from a demographic perspective', in L. A. Kosinski, ed., *Demographic Developments in Eastern Europe*, New York, 1977, 120-37. Indication of where research would be most fruitful rather than contribution or overview.

5.246 **Palli**, H., 'Parish registers and revisions. Research strategies in Estonian historical demography and agrarian history', *Soc.Sci.Hist.*, 7, 1983, 289-310. Assessment of sources by Estonian historian.

5.247 **Ransel**, D. L., 'Recent Soviet studies in demographic history', *Russian Rev.*, 40, 1981, 143-57.

SEXUAL BEHAVIOUR
See also 2.55 and 5.430.
On prostitution note some further material in sub-section on crime, 10.370-461, esp. 372-3,400,408-10).

5.248 Bullough, V. L., *History of Prostitution*, New Hyde Park, N.Y., 1964. Rather pedestrian survey history from classical Greece to Wolfenden Report. Another attempt at overview, somewhat anecdotal, is F. Henriques, *Prostitution and Society. A Survey*, 3 vols., 1962-68 (material on early modern period in vol.2).

5.249 —— *Homosexuality: a History*, New York, 1979. Brave attempt at synoptic view from ancient times onward.

5.250 —— *Sexual Variance in Society and History*, New York, 1976. Covers attitudes to homosexuality, transvestism, masturbation, etc. without restriction of period or place. See also shorter related study (with Bonnie Bullough), *Sin, Sickness and Sanity. A History of Sexual Attitudes*, New York, 1977.

5.251 Coward, D. A., 'Eighteenth-century attitudes to prostitution', *Stud.on Voltaire*, 189, 1980, 363-99. Based somewhat uncritically on miscellaneous literary sources.

5.252 Crompton, L., 'The myth of lesbian impunity', *J.Homosexuality*, 6, 1980-81, 11-25. Shows that legal codes of ancien regime demanded severe penalties for lesbian practices. See also account of German trial of 1721, *ib.*, 27-40. Both articles repr. in S. J. Licata and R. P. Petersen, eds., *The Gay Past*, New York, 1985.

5.253 Darmon, P., *Trial by Impotence*, 1985. Transl. from French ed. of 1979. Role of church courts in establishing impotence as ground for divorce. Spares no details. Notes omitted in English version.

5.254 Elmroth, I., 'Family planning as a diffusion phenomenon during l'ancien régime', in G. Rystad, ed., *Europe and Scandinavia. Aspects of the Process of Integration in the Seventeenth Century*, Lund, 1983, 245-56.

5.255 Faderman, Lillian, *Surpassing the Love of Men. Romantic Friendship and Love between Women from the Renaissance to the Present*, New York, 1981. Early modern section mainly cites literary examples or concerns England.

5.256 Flandrin, J.-L., 'Contraception, marriage and sexual relations in the Christian West', in R. Forster and O. Ranum, eds., *The Biology of Man in History. Selections from the* Annales, Baltimore, Md., 1975, 23-47. Transl. from *Annales*, 24, 1969, 1370-90. Looks at evidence in medieval and early modern penitentials, works of casuistry, etc.

5.257 —— *L'Église et le Contrôle des Naissances*, Paris, 1970. Brief account ranging from early Christian to modern times.

5.258 —— 'Mariage tardif et vie sexuelle. Discussions et hypothèses de recherche', *Annales*, 27, 1972, 1351-78. Answers objections to his arguments in 5.256, and contends for unlikelihood of general chastity among unmarried in seventeenth and eighteenth centuries.

5.259 —— 'Repression and change in the sexual life of young people in medieval and early modern times', *J.Family Hist.*, 2, 1977, 196-210. Repr. in Wheaton and Hareven (5.118), 27-48. Argues that early modern period saw campaign against traditional sexual outlets at same time as age at marriage considerably increased.

5.260 —— 'Sentiments et civilisation. Sondage au niveau des titres d'ouvrages', *Annales*, 20, 1965, 939-66. Comparison of sixteenth- and late twentieth-century views on sexuality as reflected in vocabulary of book titles.

5.261 Laslett, P., ed., *Bastardy and its Comparative History*, 1980. Mainly of interest for Laslett's long introductory essay comparing illegitimacy over time and between cultures; and those of J. Meyer on early modern France (249-63), and D. Gaunt on East Sweden in seventeenth and eighteenth centuries (313-26).

5.262 Shorter, E., 'Illegitimacy, sexual revolution, and social change in modern Europe', *J.Interdisc.Hist.*, 2, 1971, 237-72. Repr. in Rotberg and Rabb, *Family in History*, 48-84; and *Marriage and Fertility*, 85-120 (see 5.33). Influential and controversial thesis that increase in illegitimacy over period 1750-1880 was token of greater freedom and opportunity for women.

5.263 —— 'Female emancipation, birth control,

and fertility in European history', *Am.Hist.Rev.*, 78, 1973, 605-40. Similar in theme to previous.

5.264 —— 'Sexual change and illegitimacy: the European experience', in R. J. Bezucha, ed., *Modern European Social History*, Lexington, Mass., 1972, 231-69.

5.265 —— 'On writing the history of rape', *Signs*, 3, 1977, 471-82. Reviewing Susan Brownmiller's polemical *Against our Will* (New York, 1975), argues that rape was endemic in pre-industrial village society. See criticism of this view, *ib.*, 931-5.

5.266 **Solé**, J., *L'Amour en Occident à l'Époque Moderne*, Paris, 1976. Popular but reasonably scholarly survey, with heavy emphasis on France.

5.267 **Tilly**, Louise A., and others, 'Women's work and European fertility patterns', *J.Interdisc.Hist.*, 6, 1976, 447-76. Contends, against Shorter (5.262-4), that increased illegitimacy rates represent desertion of would-be wives rather than change in women's sexual outlook.

5.268 **Walters**, R. G., 'Sexual matters as historical problems. A framework of analysis', *Societas*, 6, 1976, 157-75. Using example of prostitution, suggests dichotomy between values, norms and behaviour as appropriate framework for research.

FRANCE
See also 5.79,118,261,266.

5.269 **Badalo-Dulong**, Claude, *L'Amour au 17e Siècle*, Paris, 1969. Semi-popular work on sentiment of love, principally in fashionable society.

5.270 **Benabou**, Erica-M., *La Prostitution et la Police des Moeurs au 18e Siècle*, Paris, 1987. Posthumous work, ed. by P. Goubert. Thorough archival study, though almost entirely confined to Parisian evidence.

5.271 **Coward**, D. A., 'Attitudes to homosexuality in eighteenth-century France', *J.Eur.Stud.*, 10, 1980, 231-55. Treatment extends to lesbianism.

5.272 **Cummings**, M., 'Elopement, family, and the courts. The crime of rape in early modern France', *Proc.West.Soc.Fr.Hist.*, 4, 1976, 118-25. Deals with efforts to strengthen paternal authority in cases involving elopement of minors.

5.273 **Depauw**, J., 'Illicit sexual activity and society in eighteenth-century Nantes', in Forster and Ranum (5.78), 145-91. Transl. from *Annales*, 27, 1972, 1155-82. Computer analysis of declarations of pregnancy made by unmarried mothers.

5.274 **Fairchild**, Cissie, 'Female sexual attitudes and the rise of illegitimacy: a case study', *J.Interdisc.Hist.*, 8, 1978, 627-67. Repr. in Rotberg and Rabb, *Marriage and Fertility* (5.33), 163-217. Examines eighteenth-century pregnancy declarations at Aix-en-Provence and questions Shorter's thesis about rise in illegitimacy rate (5.262-4). See also debate with J.-L. Flandrin arising from this article, *J.Interdisc.Hist.*, 9, 1978, 309-21.

5.275 **Flandrin**, J.-L., *Les Amours Paysannes. Amour et Sexualité dans les Campagnes de l'Ancienne France, 16e-19e Siècle*, Paris, 1975. Popular account with brief extracts from sources and some pleasant illustrations.

5.276 **Friedman**, Adele C., 'Love, sex, and marriage in traditional French society. The documentary evidence of folksongs', *Proc.West.Soc.Fr.Hist.*, 5, 1977, 146-54. Argues that importance of love articulated in folksong reflects aspirations if not practice.

5.277 **Gouesse**, J.-M., 'En Basse-Normandie aux 17e et 18e siècles. Le refus de l'enfant au tribunal de la pénitence', *Ann. Démographie Hist.*, 1973, 231-61. On casuistry of hearing confessions about contraceptive practices.

5.278 **Jones**, C., 'Prostitution and the ruling class in eighteenth-century Montpellier', *Hist.Workshop*, 6, 1978, 7-28.

5.279 **Lottin**, A., 'Naissances illégitimes et filles-mères à Lille au 18e siècle', *Rev.Hist.Mod.et Contemp.*, 17, 1970, 278-322.

5.280 **Ranum**, O., and Ranum, Patricia, eds., *Popular Attitudes towards Birth Control in Pre-industrial France and England*, New York, 1972. Collection of essays and extracts, including 2 translated papers by P. Ariès.

5.281 **Rossiaud**, J., 'Prostitution, sex, and society in French towns in the fifteenth century', in P. Ariès and A. Béjin, eds., *Western Sexuality. Practice and Precept in Past and Present Times*, 1985, 76-94. Transl. from French ed. of 1982. Evidence comes mainly from Dijon.

5.282 —— 'Prostitution, youth, and society in

the towns of Southeastern France in the fifteenth century', in R. Forster and O. Ranum, eds., *Deviants and the Abandoned in French Society. Selections from the Annales*, Baltimore, Md., 1978, 1-46. Transl. from *Annales*, 31, 1976, 289-325. Concentrates on towns of Rhone Valley between 1440-90.

OTHER REGIONS
See also 5.261 (Sweden); 10.447 (Italy); 14.73 (Netherlands); 14.87,89 (Germany).

.283 **Perry**, Mary E., 'Deviant insiders. Legalized prostitutes and a consciousness of women in early modern Seville', *Comp.Stud.Soc.& Hist.*, 27, 1985, 138-58. Stresses contradictions involved in legalising prostitution (also reveals ambivalence of feminist historians about this subject). See also her earlier treatment, ' "Lost women" in early modern Seville. The politics of prostitution', *Feminist Stud.*, 4 (i), 1978, 195-214.

.284 **Redondo**, A., ed., *Amours Légitimes, Amours Illégitimes en Espagne (16e-17e Siècles)*, Paris, 1985. Conference papers on theme of marriage and sexual behaviour in practice and in literary representation.

.285 **Brucker**, G., *Giovanni and Lusanna. Love and Marriage in Renaissance Florence*, 1986. Touching study of sexual liaison across classes, ending in disputed secret marriage (mid-fifteenth century).

.286 **Pavan**, Elisabeth, 'Police des moeurs, société, et politique à Venise à la fin du Moyen Age', *Rev.Hist.*, 264, 1980, 241-88.

On attitudes to prostitution and sodomy.

5.287 **Trexler**, R. C., 'La prostitution florentine au 15e siècle. Patronages et clientèles', *Annales*, 36, 1981, 983-1015. Account of officially licensed and superintended system.

5.288 **Beck**, R., 'Illegitimät und voreheliche Sexualität auf dem Land. Unterfinning, 1671-1770', in R. van Dülmen, ed., *Kultur der Einfachen Leute. Bayerisches Volksleben vom 16. bis zum 19. Jahrhundert*, Munich, 1983, 112-50. Study of parish in Augsburg region.

5.289 **Lee**, W. R., 'Bastardy and the socioeconomic structure of South Germany', *J.Interdisc.Hist.*, 7, 1977, 403-25. Repr. in Rotberg and Rabb, *Marriage and fertility* (5.33), 121-62. Sees rise in real wages of lower peasantry as key to illegitimacy increase in century 1750-1850. See also debate with E. Shorter, *J.Interdisc.Hist.*, 8, 1978, 459-76.

5.290 **Monter**, E. W., 'Sodomy and heresy in early modern Switzerland', *J. Homosexuality*, 6, 1980-81, 41-55. Repr. in Licata and Petersen (5.252). Compares trials in urban Geneva and rural Fribourg.

5.291 **Roper**, L., 'Discipline and respectability. Prostitution and the Reformation in Augsburg', *Hist.Workshop*, 19, 1985, 3-28. Good account of conflicting attitudes about sexual roles and drives. Cf.5.283.

5.292 **Stevnsborg**, H., 'Aims and methods of the official campaign against prostitution in Copenhagen, 1769-1780', *Scan.J.Hist.*, 6, 1981, 207-27.

FAMILY, KINSHIP, AND HOUSEHOLD. MARRIAGE AND INHERITANCE

BIBLIOGRAPHIES
See also bibliographical material in 5.297,312,325,369,386,411.

5.293 **Milden**, J. W., *The Family in Past Time. A Guide to the Literature*, New York, 1977. Restricted to English-language citations.

5.294 **Soliday**, G. L., and others, *History of the Family and Kinship. A Select International Bibliography*, New York, 1980. Indispensable work, with over 3000 entries on Europe (incl. Britain); includes much

on general demography as well as family in narrow sense. Multilingual, but not annotated.

GENERAL
See also 5.599; 6.45; 9.451; 13.4-5.

5.295 **Anderson**, M., *Approaches to the History of the Western Family, 1500-1914*, 1980. Excellent but brief "state of the art", with emphasis on pre-industrial family.

5.296 **Barbier**, J.-M., *Le Quotidien et son Économie. Essai sur les Origines Historiques et Sociales de l'Économie Familiale*, Paris, 1981. Surveys emergence of "home" as separate sphere of activity and woman's role as its manager. Mainly French context.

5.297 **Berkner**, L. K., 'Recent research on the history of the family in Western Europe', *J.Marriage & Family*, 35, 1973, 395-405.

5.298 —— 'Rural family organization in Europe. A problem in comparative history', *Peasant Stud.Newsl.*, 1, 1972, 145-56. Argues need to control for legal, economic, and class variables, when comparing proportion of extended families in different regions via census data.

5.299 —— 'The use and misuse of census data for the historical analysis of family structure', *J.Interdisc.Hist.*, 5, 1975, 721-38. Develops previous article, criticising Laslett's views on primacy of nuclear families (see 5.313-15).

5.300 —— and Mendels, F., 'Inheritance systems, family structure, and demographic patterns in Western Europe (1700-1900)', in Tilly (5.13), 209-23. Argues that market conditions tended to have more influence on marriage and family than formal inheritance systems, which were often circumvented.

5.301 **Bossy**, J., 'Godparenthood. The fortunes of a social institution in early modern Christianity', in K. von Greyerz, ed., *Religion and Society in Early Modern Europe, 1500-1800*, 1984, 194-201. Suggests reasons why practice fell into some discredit in sixteenth century.

5.302 **Burguière**, A., 'The formation of the couple', *J.Family Hist.*, 12, 1987, 39-53. Contribution to debate on emergence of married couple as unit with its own "private space" (cf. work of Ariès, Shorter, and others).

5.303 **Clawson**, Mary A., 'Early modern fraternalism and the patriarchal family', *Feminist Stud.*, 6, 1980, 368-91. Shows how guilds and fraternities expressed duties of membership by evoking those of kinship.

5.304 'The craft of family history', *J.Family Hist.*, 12, 1987, 263-301. Reflective essays by P. Laslett, R. Wheaton, and Louise Tilly.

5.305 **Dupâquier**, J., and others, eds., *Marriage and Remarriage in Populations of the Past*, 1981. Over 40 papers (English and French) from international colloquium at Kristiansand on aspects of remarriage. Strong emphasis on preindustrial Europe.

5.306 **Goody**, J., *The Development of the Family and Marriage in Europe*, 1983. Ranges widely, but gives rather more space to medieval societies than those of early modern era.

5.307 —— 'Strategies of heirship', *Comp. Stud. Soc. & Hist.*, 15, 1973, 3-20. Useful starting-point in theorising how varieties of property succession may be related to social priorities.

5.308 **Hammel**, E. A., and Laslett, P., 'Comparing household structure over time and between cultures', *ib.*, 16, 1974, 73-109. Suggests usefulness of anthropological methods of recording kinship relations and also computerized analysis.

5.309 **Hareven**, Tamara K., 'The family as process. The historical study of the family cycle', *J.Soc.Hist.*, 7, 1974, 322-9. Advocates life-cycle approach to historical study of the family.

5.310 —— 'Cycles, courses, and cohorts. Reflections on theoretical and methodological approaches to the historical study of family development', *ib.* 12, 1978, 97-109. Modifies previous article by arguing that since individuals usually impinge on more than one family, studying individual life cycle may be more profitable than family cycle.

5.311 —— 'The history of the family as an interdisciplinary field', *J.Interdisc.Hist.*, 2, 1971, 399-414.

5.312 **Harris**, Barbara J., 'Recent work on the history of the family. A review article', *Feminist Stud.*, 3 (iii-iv), 1976, 159-72. Some overlap with 5.297.

5.313 **Laslett**, P., 'Characteristics of the Western family considered over time', *J.Family Hist.*, 2, 1977, 89-116. Repr. (revised) in Laslett (5.33), 12-49. Main suggested characteristics include nuclear household (but sometimes with servants); late child-bearing; and small age gap between spouses.

5.314 —— 'The stem-family hypothesis and its privileged position', in Wachter and others (5.63), 89-111. Further argument against prevalence of extended household.

5.315 —— and Wall, R., eds., *Household and Family in Past Time*, 1972. Introductory methodological essays by Laslett, T. K. Burch, and J. Goody, followed by case-studies. Review articles: P. M. G. Harris, *J.Eur.Ec.Hist.*, 3, 1974, 765-77; A. Collomp, *Annales*, 29, 1974, 777-86.

316 **Medick**, H., and Sabean, D., 'Call for papers. Family and kinship, material interest and emotion', *Peasant Stud.*, 8 (ii), 1979, 139-60. Argues that family historians have been too prone to view love and money as mutually exclusive.

.317 **Mendels**, F. F., 'Notes on the age of maternity, population growth, and family structure in the past', *J.Family Hist.*, 3, 1978, 236-50. Argues that while importance of age of first maternity as demographic variable is well recognized, less attention has been paid to age of paternity and its importance in shaping household structure.

.318 **Mitterauer**, M., and Sieder, R., *The European Family. Patriarchy to Partnership from the Middle Ages to the Present*, 1982. Transl. from German ed. of 1977. Topical rather than chronological treatment, mostly drawing on Central European evidence.

.319 **Noonan**, J. T., *Power to Dissolve. Lawyers and Marriages in the Courts of the Roman Curia*, Cambridge, Mass., 1972. Looks at Catholic divorce system through lengthy examination of a few individual cases, three drawn from early modern period.

.320 **Rapp**, Rayna, and others, 'Examining family history', *Feminist Stud.*, 5, 1979, 174-200.

.321 **Sabean**, D., 'Aspects of kinship behaviour and property in rural Western Europe before 1800', in J. Goody and others, eds., *Family and Inheritance. Rural Society in Western Europe, 1200-1800*, 1976, 96-111. Explores effects of inheritance and dowry systems on family ties and reverse effects of family life-cycle on legal formalities.

.322 **Shorter**, E., *The Making of the Modern Family*, New York, 1975. Controversial thesis, positing growth of sentimental ties in marriage and child-rearing, and greater stress on privacy, from eighteenth century onwards. Review article: R. T. Vann, *J.Family Hist.*, 1, 1976, 106-17.

.323 **Skolnick**, Arlene, 'The family revisited. Themes in recent social science research', *J.Interdisc.Hist.*, 5, 1975, 703-19. Concentrates on research and concepts that might be useful to historians.

5.324 **Thirsk**, Joan, 'The European debate on customs of inheritance, 1500-1700', in Goody and others (5.321), 177-91. Brief account of polemics about expediency of primogeniture.

5.325 **Tilly**, Louise A., and Cohen, Miriam, 'Does the family have a history? A review of theory and practice in family history', *Soc.Sci.Hist.*, 6, 1982, 131-79. Bibliographical survey. Major emphasis is on industrialisation and after.

5.326 **Verdon**, M., 'The stem family. Toward a general theory', *J.Interdisc.Hist.*, 10, 1979, 87-105. Argues that only a few societies (including, in Europe, Basque country and Alpine region) have adopted this structure.

5.327 **Wall**, R., and others, eds., *Family Forms in Historic Europe*, 1983. As well as general essays on household size and family economy, includes studies on eighteenth-century Poland, Estonia, and Hungary, and one on Austria since the seventeenth century. Papers on more limited topics separately noted. Review articles: D. I. Kertzer, *J.Family Hist.*, 10, 1985, 98-107; F. Mendels, *J.Soc.Hist.*, 11, 1986, 81-7.

5.328 **Wheaton**, R., 'Family and kinship in Western Europe. The problem of the joint family household', *J.Interdisc.Hist.*, 5, 1975, 601-28. Another exponent of view that census data may obscure wider kinship system and developmental cycle. Cf. 5.298-9.

5.329 **Wrigley**, E. A., 'Reflections on the history of the family', in Alice S. Rossi and others, eds., *The Family*, New York, 1978, 71-85. (This work originally appeared as issue 2 of *Daedalus*, 106, 1977.)

FRANCE
See also 3.53; 5.116,272,296,493; 6.61,111; 9.460-3; 13.31,117.

5.330 **Armengaud**, A., *La Famille et l'Enfant en France et en Angleterre du 16e au 18e Siècle. Aspects Démographiques*, Paris, 1975. *Agrégation* lecture course. The two countries are separately treated rather than explicitly compared.

5.331 **Baulant**, Micheline, 'The scattered family. Another aspect of seventeenth-century demography', in Forster and Ranum (5.78), 104-16. Transl. from *Annales*, 27, 1972, 959-68. Examines guardianship arrangements for children affected by death or remarriage of parents.

5.332 **Berkner**, L. K., and Shaffer, J. W., 'The joint family in the Nivernais', *J.Family Hist.*, 3, 1978, 150-62. Argues that joint family arrangements had largely died out among land-owning peasants by end of eighteenth century, but persisted with share-croppers.

5.333 **Bideau**, A., 'A demographic and social analysis of widowhood and remarriage. The example of the castellany of Thoissey-en-Dombes, 1670-1840', *J.Family Hist.*, 5, 1980, 28-43.

5.334 **Biraben**, J.-N., 'A Southern French village. The inhabitants of Montplaisant in 1644', in Laslett and Wall (5.315), 237-54. Examines household structure.

5.335 **Bourdieu**, P., 'Marriage strategies as strategies of social reproduction', in Forster and Ranum (5.78), 117-44. Transl. from *Annales*, 27, 1972, 1105-25. Views variety of marriage options practised in a Béarn village until recent times as strategy for preserving family property and influence.

5.336 **Chrisman**, Miriam, 'Family and religion in two noble families, French Catholic and English Puritan', *J.Family Hist.*, 8, 1983, 190-210. Comparison of personal relationships and moral outlook in families of Mme. de Sévigné and the Verneys.

5.337 **Collomp**, A., *La Maison du Père. Famille et Village en Haute-Provence aux 17e et 18e Siècles*, Paris, 1983. Deals with system of family property transmission in context of economic and political power within village. Review article: K. P. Luria, *Peasant Stud.*, 13, 1986, 207-21. Following articles derive from this research.

5.338 —— 'Alliance et filiation en Haute Provence au 18e siècle', *Annales*, 32, 1977, 445-77. Analysis of several hundred marriage contracts from St. André-les-Alpes for evidence on marriage strategy and kinship relations.

5.339 —— 'Tensions, dissensions, and rupture inside the family in seventeenth- and eighteenth-century Haute Provence', in H. Medick and D. Sabean, eds., *Interest and Emotion. Essays on the Study of Family and Kinship*, 1984, 145-70. Instances disagreements within stem family context, esp. over disposal of property.

5.340 **Darrow**, Margaret H., 'Popular concepts of marital choice in eighteenth-century France', *J.Soc.Hist.*, 19, 1986, 261-72. Study of attitudes derived from dispensation cases handled by ecclesiatical court at Montauban.

5.341 **Davis**, Natalie Z., 'Ghosts, kin, and progeny. Some features of family life in early modern France', *Daedalus*, 106 (ii), 1977, 87-114. Repr. in Rossi (5.329), 87-114. More data on strategies for safeguarding patrimony and status over long term.

5.342 **Diefendorf**, Barbara B., 'Widowhood and remarriage in sixteenth-century Paris', *J.Family Hist.*, 7, 1982, 379-95. Deals principally with arrangements in Robe and mercantile elite.

5.343 **Dupâquier**, J., 'Naming-practices, godparenthood, and kinship in the Vexin, 1540-1900', *J.Family Hist.*, 6, 1981, 135-55. Mainly on changing fashions in choice of christian names. See also on this topic, for other regions and various chronological periods, conference papers ed. by Dupâquier and others, *Le Prénom. Mode et Histoire*, Paris, 1984.

5.344 —— and Jadin, L., 'Structure of household and family in Corsica, 1769-71', in Laslett and Wall (5.315), 283-97. Charts variations in household type according to age of principals.

5.345 **Flandrin**, J.-L., *Families in Former Times. Kinship, Household, and Sexuality*, 1979. Transl. from French ed. of 1976. Sometimes rather speculative and idiosyncratic. Considerable emphasis on Southern France. New French ed., 1984.

5.346 —— and others, 'Le 17e siècle et la famille', *Dix-Septième Siècle*, 102-3, 1974, whole issue. Symposium with general papers by Flandrin and J. Gaudemet; Y. Castan on father-son relations in Languedoc; J.-M. Gouesse on choice of partner in Normandy; A. Lottin on marital discord in Cambrai diocese (on latter subject, see also 5.353).

5.347 **Gay**, J. L., *Les Effets Pécuniaires du Mariage en Nivernais du 14e au 18e Siècles*, Paris, 1953.

5.348 **Girard**, R., 'Marriage in Avignon in the second half of the fifteenth century', *Speculum*, 28, 1953, 485-98. Evidence from notarial records.

5.349 **Goubert**, P., 'Family and province. A contribution to the knowledge of family structure in early modern France', *J.Family Hist.*, 2, 1977, 179-95. Indicates three major types of household structure, rooted in economic differences between

North, South, and East.

5.350 **Lafon**, J., *Les Époux Bordelais, 1450-1550. Régimes Matrimoniaux et Mutations Sociales*, Paris, 1972. Analyses large number of Guyenne marriage contracts.

5.351 **Lebrun**, F., *La Vie Conjugale sous l'Ancien Régime*, Paris, 1975. Brief and popular, but with scholarly grounding.

5.352 **Le Roy Ladurie**, E., 'A system of customary law. Family structures and inheritance customs in sixteenth-century France', in Forster and Ranum (5.78), 75-103; and in Goody and others (5.321), 37-70. Transl. from *Annales*, 27, 1972, 825-46. Explains Yver's geographical classification of inheritance customs (see 5.361).

5.353 **Lottin**, A., and others, *Désunion du Couple sous l'Ancien Régime. L'Exemple du Nord*, Lille, 1975. Team research into broken marriages and engagements in Cambrai diocese during eighteenth century.

5.354 **Mousnier**, R., *La Famille, L'Enfant, et l'Éducation en France et en Grande-Bretagne du l6e au 18e Siècle*, 2 vols., Paris, 1975. Another course of *agrégation* lectures on this theme (see also 5.330,355).

5.355 **Pillorget**, R., *La Tige et le Rameau. Familles Anglaises et Françaises, 16e-18e Siècle*, Paris, 1979. Further lectures on this theme; marked emphasis on Christian teaching regarding rights of the wife.

5.356 **Poster**, M., 'Patriarchy and sexuality. Restif and the peasant family', *Eighteenth Century: Theory & Interpretation*, 25, 1984, 217-40. Peasant family life as recorded in Restif de la Bretonne's autobiographical writings. Compare E. Le Roy Ladurie (7.57).

5.357 **Shaffer**, J. W., *Family and Farm. Agrarian Change and Household Organization in the Loire Valley, 1500-1900*, Albany, N.Y., 1982. Charts gradual decay of joint family landownership and *métayage* in Nivernais.

5.358 **Traer**, J. F., *Marriage and the Family in Eighteenth-Century France*, Ithaca, N.Y., 1980. Argues that changes in family relations discerned by Shorter, Stone and others (cf.5.322), were product of Enlightenment ideas.

5.359 **Wheaton**, R., 'Affinity and descent in seventeenth-century Bordeaux', in Wheaton and Hareven (5.118), 111-34. Looks at potential conflict between marital harmony and lineage claims in disposal of property.

5.360 —— 'Recent trends in the historical study of the French family', *ib.*, 3-26.

5.361 **Yver**, J., *Égalité entre Héritiers et Exclusion des Enfants Dotés. Essai de Géographie Coutumière*, Paris, 1966. Technical essay on provincial customary law which has provided much evidence for historians dealing with family and inheritance.

5.362 **Zonabend**, Françoise, 'Baptismal kinship at Minot (Côte d'Or)', in R. Forster and O. Ranum, eds., *Ritual, Religion, and the Sacred. Selections from the* Annales, 7, Baltimore, Md., 1982, 57-80. Transl. from *Annales*, 33, 1978, 656-76. Longitudinal study of godparentage in Burgundian village up to present day.

LOW COUNTRIES

5.363 **Gutmann**, M. P., and Leboutte, R., 'Rethinking protoindustrialization and the family', *J.Interdisc.Hist.*, 14, 1984, 587-607. Finds that industrial activity did not lower age of marriage in East Belgian villages investigated over period 1650-1850.

5.364 **Mendels**, F., 'Industry and marriages in Flanders before the Industrial Revolution', in Deprez (5.48), 81-93. Finds correlation between marriage rate and buoyancy in demand for agricultural and textile exports.

5.365 **Mook**, Bertha, *The Dutch Family in the Seventeenth and Eighteenth Centuries*, Ottawa, 1977. Slight work relying heavily on literary evidence.

5.366 **Spierenburg**, P., 'Imprisonment and the family. An analysis of petitions for confinement in Holland, 1680-1805', *Soc.Sci.Hist.*, 10, 1986, 115-46. Concerns not criminal imprisonment, but confinement for unacceptable private conduct, e.g. insanity, alcoholism, immorality.

5.367 **Van der Woude**, A. M., 'Variations in the size and structure of the household in the United Provinces of the Netherlands in the seventeenth and eighteenth centuries', in Laslett and Wall (5.315), 299-318. Examines possible links between regional farming systems and differences in household structure.

5.368 **Wyntjes**, Sherrin M., 'Survivors and

status. Widowhood and family in the early modern Netherlands', *J.Family Hist.*, 7, 1982, 396-405. Draws on material from study of Netherlands gentry during War of Independence. See 6.113 for full context.

SPAIN AND ITALY
On Spain see also 5.150,284; 7.103; 10.431; on Italy, 5.285,418; 6.148,157.

5.369 **Kertzer**, D. I., and Brettell, Caroline, 'Advances in Italian and Iberian family history', *J.Family Hist.*, 12, 1987, 87-120. Surveys work of last decade or so.

5.370 **Chacon Jiménez**, F., 'Introducción a la historia de la familia española. El ejemplo de Murcia y Orihuela (siglos 17-19)', *Cuadernos de Hist.*, 10, 1983, 235-66. Relatively rare example of detailed research on Spanish household.

5.371 **García Carcel**, R., and others, 'La familia en España (siglos 16-18)', *Historia*, 57, 1981, 47-73. General outline for non-specialist audience.

5.372 **Barbagli**, M., *Sotto lo Stesso Tetto. Mutamenti della Famiglia in Italia dal 15 al 20 Secolo*, Bologna, 1984. Concentrates mainly on Northern and Central Italy, dealing in turn with household structure and with transition from patriarchal to conjugal primacy in personal relations (largely concerned with aristocracy in latter respect).

5.373 **Caiati**, V., 'The peasant household under Tuscan *mezzadria*. A socioeconomic analysis of some Sienese *mezzadri* households, 1591-1640', *J.Family Hist.*, 9, 1984, 111-26. Discusses effects of tenurial system on household size and family relationships.

5.374 **Delille**, G., *Famille et Propriété dans le Royaume de Naples (15e-19e Siècle)*, Rome, 1985. Kinship, marriage strategy, inheritance and control of property, studied at both noble and peasant levels.

5.375 **Douglass**, W. A., 'The South Italian family: a critique', *J.Family Hist.*, 5, 1980, 338-59. Examines family structures in Agnone (Molise region) now and in the eighteenth century and seeks to modify anthropologists' views about social atomism of South Italy.

5.376 **Herlihy**, D., 'Mapping households in medieval Italy', *Cath.Hist.Rev.*, 58, 1972, 1-21. Mainly on Florentine *catasto* of 1427, but also makes comparisons with later

fifteenth-century data. For more on *catasto* see Herlihy and Christiane Klapisch-Zuber, *Les Toscans et leurs Familles. Une Étude du Catasto Florentin de 1427*, Paris, 1978. Abridged transl., New Haven, Conn., 1985.

5.377 **King**, Margaret L., 'Caldiera and the Barbaros on marriage and the family. Humanist reflections of Venetian realities', *J.Med.& Renaiss.Stud.*, 6, 1976, 19-50. Examines three fifteenth-century treatises for light they throw on aristocratic family norms.

5.378 **Klapisch-Zuber**, Christiane, *Women, Family and Ritual in Renaissance Italy*, Chicago, 1985. Collection of essays, originally publ. in French journals, dealing mainly with Tuscany between 1300 and 1500.

5.379 **Merzario**, R., *Il Paese Stretto. Strategie Matrimoniali nella Diocesi di Como, Secoli 16-18*, Turin, 1981. Examines reasons why consanguinity dispensations were so frequently sought in mountainous regions.

5.380 **Swain**, Elizabeth, 'Faith in the family. The practice of religion by the Gonzaga', *J.Family Hist.*, 8, 1983, 177-89. Correspondence within Mantuan ruling family, 1418-84, showing how much family supportiveness and piety went hand in hand.

GERMANY, SWITZERLAND, AUSTRIA
See also 5.318,327,415; 7.183,185;13.91.

5.381 **Berkner**, L. K., 'Inheritance, land tenure, and peasant family structure. A German regional comparison', in Goody and others (5.321), 71-95. Compares areas of Lower Saxony with partible and impartible inheritance laws, finding more tendency to stem family households in the latter.

5.382 —— 'The stem family and the developmental cycle of the peasant household. An eighteenth-century Austrian example', *Am.Hist.Rev.*, 77, 1972, 398-418. Illustrates his view that census data underestimate extended family structure (see 5.299) with examples from region east of Linz.

5.383 —— 'Peasant household organization and demographic change in Lower Saxony (1689-1766)', in Lee and others (5.34), 53-70. Again compares villages with partible and impartible inheritance laws.

5.384 **Jütte**, R., 'Household and family life in late sixteenth-century Cologne. The Weinsberg family', *Sixteenth-Cent.J.*, 17, 1986, 165-82. Evidence provided by bulky diaries and household book of town councillor Hermann Weinsberg.

5.385 **Knodel**, J., and Lynch, Katherine A., 'The decline of remarriage. Evidence from German village populations in the eighteenth and nineteenth centuries', *J.Family Hist.*, 10, 1985, 34-59. Charts secular decline, partly age-specific, partly related to increase in life-spans.

5.386 **Lee**, W. R., 'Past legacies and future prospects. Recent research on the history of the family in Germany', *J.Family Hist.*, 6, 1981, 156-76. Bibliographical essay.

5.387 **Mitterauer**, M., 'Auswirkungen von Urbanisierung und Frühindustrial-isierung auf die Familienverfassung an Beispielen des österreichischen Raums', in Conze (5.54), 53-146. Major study of changes in household structure in selected villages around Vienna and Salzburg between seventeenth and early nineteenth centuries.

5.388 —— 'Familienformen und Illegitimität in ländlichen Gebieten Österreichs', *Arch.Sozialgesch.*, 19, 1979, 123-88. Study of rise in illegitimacy extending from c. 1750 to end of nineteenth century.

5.389 —— 'Marriage without co-residence. A special type of historic family forms in rural Carinthia', *J.Family Hist.*, 6, 1981, 177-81. Some eighteenth-century examples of servant married couples normally living apart.

5.390 —— 'Vorindustrielle Familienformen. Zur Funktionsentlastung des "ganzen Hauses" im 17. und 18. Jahrhundert', in F. Engel-Janosi and others, *Fürst, Bürger, Mensch. Untersuchungen zu Politischen und Soziokulturellen Wandlungsprozessen in Vorrevolutionären Europa*, Munich, 1975, 123-85. Based on censuses of Salzburg region.

5.391 —— 'Zur Familienstruktur in ländlichen Gebieten Österreichs im 17. Jahrhundert', in Helczmanovski (5.177), 167-224.

5.392 **Möller**, H., *Die Kleinbürgerliche Familie im 18.Jahrhundert*, Berlin, 1969. On family life of urban artisanate; substantial, but largely from published sources.

5.393 **Ozment**, S., *When Fathers Ruled. Family Life in Reformation Europe*, Cambridge,

Mass., 1983. Concentrates on Protestant Germany and Switzerland, and (mainly on evidence of vernacular literature) emphasises warmth and co-operation in family relations. Review article: K. P. Luria, *Peasant Stud.*, 13, 1986, 149-70. See also Ozment's *Magdalena and Balthasar*, New York, 1986, study of husband and wife in Nuremberg merchant class, based on their correspondence over two decades; and 5.454.

5.394 **Pedlow**, G. W., 'Marriage, family size, and inheritance among Hessian nobles, 1650-1900', *J.Family Hist.*, 7, 1982, 333-52. Shows partible inheritance system nevertheless effectively preserved estates.

5.395 **Rebel**, H., 'Peasant stem families in early modern Austria. Life plans, status tactics, and the grid of inheritance', *Soc.Sci.Hist.*, 2, 1978, 255-91. See also Rebel's major work on Austrian peasantry (7.183).

5.396 **Safley**, T. M., *Let No Man Put Asunder. The Control of Marriage in the German Southwest, 1550-1600*, Kirksville, Mo., 1984. Compares handling of marriage disputes by courts of Catholic Konstanz and Protestant Basel. Following articles derive from this research.

5.397 —— 'Marital litigation in the diocese of Constance, 1551-1620', *Sixteenth Cent.J.*, 12 (ii), 1981, 61-77.

5.398 —— 'Protestantism, divorce, and the breaking of the modern family', in Sessions and Bebb (13.225), 35-56.

5.399 —— 'To preserve the marital state. The *Basler Ehegericht*, 1550-1592', *J.Family Hist.*, 7, 1982, 162-79.

5.400 **Schneider**, L., *Der Arbeiterhaushalt im 18. und 19. Jahrhundert*, Berlin, 1967. Contrasts household and family conditions of pre-industrial and factory workers.

5.401 **Weber-Kellermann**, Ingeborg, *Die Deutsche Familie. Versuch einer Sozialgeschichte*, Frankfurt, 1974. Long-range introductory study. See also her similar work, with illustrations, *Die Familie: Geschichte, Geschichten, und Bilder*, Frankfurt, 1977.

EASTERN AND NORTHERN EUROPE
See also 3.309; 5.327.

5.402 **Granasztói**, G., 'The Hungarian bourgeois family in the late Middle Ages', *Acta Hist.Acad.Sci.Hungaricae*, 30, 1984, 257-320. Study of household structures revealed by two sixteenth-century listings of town of Kassa (present-day Košica).

5.403 **Kula**, W., 'Seigneury and peasant family in eighteenth-century Poland', in Forster and Ranum (5.78), 192-203. Transl. from *Annales*, 27, 1972, 949-58. Shows how manorial regulations aimed at maintaining stable, adequately-sized holdings against demographic vagaries.

5.404 **Byrnes**, R. F., ed., *Communal Families in the Balkans. The Zadruga*, Notre Dame, Ind., 1976. *Festschrift* for Philip Mosely (incl. 4 essays by Mosely). All deal with general or local aspects of *zadruga*, except Mosely's 'Russian family, old style and new' and D. Chirot's 'The Romanian communal village, an alternative to the zadruga'.

5.405 **Gavazzi**, M., 'The extended family in Southeastern Europe', *J.Family Hist.*, 7, 1982, 89-102. Brief general introduction to Balkan zadruga.

5.406 **Hammel**, E. A., 'The zadruga as process', in Laslett and Wall (5.315), 335-73.

5.407 **Laslett**, P., and Clark, Marilyn, 'Houseful and household in an eighteenth-century Balkan city. A tabular analysis of the listing of the Serbian sector of Belgrade in 1733-34', *ib.*, 375-400.

5.408 **Stoianovich**, T., 'The Balkan domestic family. Geography, commerce, demography', *Rev.Et.Sud-Est Eur.*, 14, 1976, 465-75. Ranges over period of Turkish occupation, and speculates that domestic (i.e. extended) family may be inverse function of population density.

5.409 **Grønseth**, E., 'Notes on the historic development of the relation between nuclear family, kinship system, and the wider social structure in Norway', in R. Hill and R. Konig, eds., *Families in East and West*, Paris, 1970, 225-47. Rapid sketch spanning prehistoric times to nineteenth century.

5.410 **Sogner**, S., '...a prudent wife is from the Lord. The married peasant woman of the eighteenth century in a demographic perspective', *Scan.J.Hist.*, 9, 1984, 113-33. More a general picture of marriage than looked at from woman's point of view.

5.411 **Aleksandrov**, V. A., 'Typology of the Russian peasant family in the feudal period', *Soviet Stud.in Hist.*, 21 (ii), 1982, 26-62. General review of Soviet historiography on pre-industrial family.

5.412 **Czap**, P., 'Marriage and the peasant joint family in the era of serfdom', in D. L. Ransel, ed., *The Family in Imperial Russia*, Urbana, Ill., 1978, 103-23. Quantitative study of serf marriage patterns on two estates in Riazan Province, showing norm of marriage at very early ages.

5.413 —— 'The perennial multiple family household. Mishino, Russia, 1782-1858', *J.Family Hist.*, 7, 1982, 5-26. Based on twelve successive censuses of a peasant estate in Riazan Province.

5.414 **Kahk**, J., and others, 'Peasant family and household in Estonia in the eighteenth and the first half of the nineteenth centuries', *J.Family Hist.*, 7, 1982, 76-88.

5.415 **Mitterauer**, M., and Kagan, A., 'Russian and Central European family structure: a comparative view', *J.Family Hist.*, 7, 1982, 103-31. Concentrates on province of Yaroslavl' in eighteenth century, as contrasted in particular with Austrian structures.

5.416 **Plakans**, A., 'Identifying kinfolk beyond the household', *J.Family Hist.*, 2, 1977, 3-27. Case-study of estate in Courland (mainly based on 1797 census).

5.417 —— 'Parentless children in the soul revisions', in Ransel (5.412), 77-102. Data from Courland on orphans and children living apart from parents.

5.418 —— 'Peasant families East and West. A comment on L. K. Berkner's "Rural family organization in Europe" ', *Peasant Stud.Newsl.*, 2 (iii), 1973, 11-16. Uses Courland evidence to point out that Berkner's model is biased to West European pattern. For Berkner's article see 5.298. See also note by F. Mcardle, *ib.*, 3 (iii), 1974, 11-14, on some similarities between Tuscany and Courland.

5.419 —— 'Peasant farmsteads and households in the Baltic littoral, 1797', *Comp. Stud. Soc. & Hist.*, 17, 1975, 2-35. More data from Courland revealing marked tendency to extended family groupings on farmsteads.

5.420 —— 'Seigneurial authority and peasant family life. The Baltic area in the eighteenth century', *J.Interdisc.Hist.*, 5, 1975, 629-54. Further evidence of co-residential kinship groups from large Courland parish.

5.421 —— 'Ties of kinship and kinship roles in an historical Eastern European peasant community', *J.Family Hist.*, 7, 1982, 52-75. Examines estate of Spahren in

Courland.

5.422 **Rabinovich**, M. G., 'The Russian urban family at the beginning of the eighteenth century', *Soviet Stud.in Hist.*, 21 (ii), 1982, 63-87. Uses census of 1713 for iron manufactures town of Ustiuzhna.

5.423 **Rudolph**, R. L., 'Family structure and proto-industrialization in Russia', *J.Ec.Hist.*, 40, 1980, 111-8. Argues that phenomenon of proto-industrialization can be identified, but did not involve same changes in marriage patterns and mobility as claimed for West Europe.

LIFE CYCLE: CHILDHOOD, YOUTH, OLD AGE

5.424 **Spitzer**, A. B., 'The historical problem of generations', *Am.Hist.Rev.*, 78, 1973, 1353-85. Outlines six, sometimes overlapping, ways in which life-cycle or cohort effects may show up in historical situations.

5.425 **Wells**, R. V., 'The dangers of constructing artificial cohorts in times of rapid social change', *J.Interdisc.Hist.*, 9, 1978, 103-10. On pitfalls of using single census-type sources to deduce age-specific characteristics.

INFANCY, CHILDHOOD, AND ADOLESCENCE

See also 14.126-237 (subsection on education): and 11.266,278; 13.306. For bibliography see 5.293-4,429,433.

5.426 **Ariès**, P., *Centuries of Childhood*, 1962. Transl. from French ed. of 1960. Influential and engaging survey of increasing emphasis during early modern period on children as separate age group. For round-up of several review articles provoked by it, see R. T. Vann, *Hist.& Theory*, 21, 1982, 279-97. C. Tilly, 'Population and pedagogy in France', *Hist.Educ.Q.*, 13, 1973, 113-28, chides Ariès, Hunt (5.441), and others for not perceiving demographic and economic rationale of changes in attitudes.

5.427 **De Mause**, L., ed., *History of Childhood*, New York, 1974. De Mause's introduction, also publ. in *Hist.Childhood Q.*, 1, 1974, 503-75 (with comments and reply, 576-606), is characterised by Lawrence Stone as "bold, challenging, dogmatic, enthusiastic, perverse". Treatment of children from antiquity to present day is seen as generally brutal acting out of phobias and fantasies of parents' own childhood. Review articles:

D. Calhoun, *Hist.Educ.Q.*, 14, 1974, 371-7; M. F. Shore, *J.Interdisc.Hist.*, 6, 1976, 495-505. See also 5.439.

5.428 **De Molen**, R. L., 'Childhood and the sacraments in the sixteenth century', *Arch.Reformationsgesch.*, 66, 1975, 49-71. Discusses changes made by Reformers and some Catholic areas in administration of sacraments to make more definite cleavage between childhood and adult status.

5.429 **Ende**, Aurel, 'Children in history. A personal review of the past decade's published research', *J.Psychohist.*, 11, 1983, 65-88.

5.430 **Flandrin**, J.-L., 'L'attitude à l'égard du petit enfant et les conduites sexuelles dans la civilisation occidentale', *Ann. Démographie Hist.*, 1973, 143-210. Looks at theological views on parent-child relations, and on legitimacy of restricting families.

5.431 **Gélis**, J., *L'Arbre et le Fruit. La Naissance dans l'Occident Moderne, 16e-19e Siècle*, Paris, 1984. Copious material on rituals of pregnancy and delivery, problems of infant and maternal mortality or birth injury, etc.

5.432 **Halla**, F. L., 'Childhood, culture, and society in psychoanalysis and history', *Historian*, 39, 1977, 423-38. Examines particularly Lawrence Stone's criticisms of psychohistory (reviewing Ariès, De Mause, and others), in *New York Rev.of Books*, Nov.14, 1974, 25-31.

5.433 **Lopez**, M. D., 'A guide to the interdisciplinary literature of the history of childhood', *Hist.Childhood Q.*, 1, 1974, 463-94. Rather heavily slanted towards Anglo-Saxon world.

5.434 **Neuman**, R. P., 'Masturbation, madness, and the modern concepts of childhood and adolescence', *J.Soc.Hist.*, 8 (iii), 1975, 1-27. Associates anxiety about masturbation with socio-economic developments after c.1700 which tended to delay adult status of young people.

5.435 **Schofield**, R., 'Did the mothers really die? Three centuries of maternal mortality in "the world we have lost" ', in L. Bonfield and others, eds., *The World We Have Gained. Histories of Population and Social Structure. Essays Presented to Peter Laslett*, 1986, 231-60. Argues that risks of childbirth were somewhat less than commonly thought.

5.436 **Shorter**, E., 'Maternal sentiment and death in childbirth. A new agenda for psycho-medical history', in Patricia Branca, ed., *The Medicine Show. Patients, Physicians, and the Perplexities of the Health Revolution in Modern Society*, New York, 1977, 67-88. Suggests that degree of risk in childbearing may be crucial variable in changing maternal attitudes.

5.437 **Sommerville**, C. J., *The Rise and Fall of Childhood*, Beverley Hills, Calif., 1982. Summarises recent historiography of Western child-rearing (and serves as illustration of its rather dubious quality).

5.438 **Stewart**, Abigail, and others, 'Coding categories for the study of child-rearing from historical sources', *J.Interdisc.Hist.*, 5, 1975, 687-701. Offers coding system for analysis of child-rearing manuals.

5.439 **Wilson**, S., 'The myth of motherhood a myth. The historical view of European child-rearing', *Soc.Hist.*, 9, 1984, 181-98. Criticises Elisabeth Badinter's *The Myth of Motherhood*, 1981, a popularisation of view that children enjoyed little family affection before eighteenth century, and blames more reputable historians for propagating misconceptions along these lines. In same vein see Linda A. Pollock's *Forgotten Children. Parent-Child Relations from 1500 to 1900*, 1983, which uses British and American diarists for evidence of parental tenderness.

5.440 **Wrightson**, K., 'Infanticide in European history', *Criminal Justice Hist.*, 3, 1982, 1-20. Brief overview, not confined to this period.

5.441 **Hunt**, D., *Parents and Children in History. The Psychology of Family Life in Early Modern France*, New York, 1970. Heavily Freudian. Sweeping title disguises fact that main sources concern childhood of Louis XIII and Richelieu. Review articles: E. van de Walle, *J.Interdisc.Hist.*, 2, 1972, 359-65; J. Demos, *Comp.Stud.in Soc.&*

Hist., 15, 1973, 493-503.

5.442 **Lorence**, B. W., 'Parents and children in eighteenth-century Europe', *Hist. Childhood Q.*, 2, 1974, 1-30. Evidence drawn only from England and France.

5.443 **Marvick**, Elizabeth W., 'Childhood history and decisions of state. The case of Louis XIII', *ib.*, 135-80. Overlaps with 5.441. Comments by O. Ranum and others, 181-99.

5.444 —— 'Nature versus nurture. Patterns and trends in seventeenth-century French child-rearing', in de Mause (5.427), 259-302. Argues that Counter-Reformation morality was hostile to excessive parental authority over children.

5.445 **Otis**, Leah L., 'Municipal wet nurses in fifteenth-century Montpellier', in Barbara A. Hanawalt, ed., *Women and Work in Preindustrial Europe*, Bloomington, Ind., 1986, 83-93. Financial documents, 1460-98, show employment for care of foundlings.

5.446 **Senior**, Nancy, 'Aspects of infant feeding in eighteenth-century France', *Eighteenth-Cent.Stud.*, 16, 1983, 367-88. Deals with opinion about breast-feeding and use of wet-nurses. Note that Valerie Fildes' *Breasts, Bottles, and Babies. A History of Infant Feeding*, 1986, though focussed on period 1500-1800, is based mainly on English diaries and medical treatises.

5.447 **Sussman**, G. D., *Selling Mothers' Milk. The Wet-Nursing Business in France, 1715-1914*, Urbana, Ill., 1982. Review article: J. R. Lehning, *Peasant Stud.*, 9, 1982, 250-57.

5.448 **Vassberg**, D. E., 'Juveniles in the rural work force of sixteenth-century Castile', *J.Peasant Stud.*, 11, 1983, 62-75. Briefly sketches evidence of employment on family plots, as community herdsmen, etc.

5.449 **Ross**, J. B., 'The middle-class child in urban Italy, fourteenth to early sixteenth century', in de Mause (5.427), 183-228.

5.450 **Trexler**, R. C., 'Infanticide in Florence', *Hist.Childhood Q.*, 1, 1973, 98-116. Argues from number of absolutions granted where children have been suffocated.

5.451 —— 'Ritual in Florence. Adolescence and salvation in the Renaissance', in C. Trinkaus and H. A. Oberman, eds., *The Pursuit of Holiness in Late Medieval and Renaissance Religion*, Leiden, 1974, 200-64. On confraternities for boys as means of social control.

5.452 **Lindemann**, Mary, 'Love for hire. Regulation of the wet-nursing business in eighteenth-century Hamburg', *J.Family Hist.*, 6, 1981, 379-95.

5.453 —— 'Maternal politics. The principles and practice of maternity care in eighteenth-century Hamburg', *ib.*, 9, 1984, 44-63. Essentially deals with provision for destitute mothers.

5.454 **Ozment**, S., 'The family in Reformation Germany. The bearing and rearing of children', *ib.*, 8, 1983, 159-76. Material from medical texts, educational treatises, and catechisms.

5.455 **Schlumbohm**, J., ed., ' "Traditional" collectivity and "modern" individuality. Some questions and suggestions for the historical study of socialization. The German lower and upper bourgeoisies around 1800', *Soc.Hist.*, 5, 1980, 71-103. Contrasts relatively isolated upbringing of upper class children with "street" socialisation of artisans. See also his documentary exploration of this theme in *Kinderstuben. Wie Kinder zu Bauern, Bürgern, Aristokraten Würden, 1700-1850*, Munich, 1983.

5.456 **Robisheaux**, T., 'Peasants and pastors. Rural youth control and the Reformation in Hohenlohe, 1540-1680', *Soc.Hist.*, 6, 1981, 281-300. Deals esp. with stricter parental control over marriage encouraged by Lutheran Church.

5.457 **Gorer**, G., 'Some aspects of the psychology of the people of Great Russia', *Am.Slavic & E.Eur.Rev.*, 8, 1949, 155-67. Hypothesises traumatic effects on Russian psychology and politics of practice of swaddling infants. See criticism by I. Goldman, *ib.*, 9, 1950, 151-61.

5.458 **Okenfuss**, M., *The Discovery of Childhood in Russia. The Evidence of the Slavic Primer*, Newtonville, Mass., 1980. Argues that change in nature of primers between sixteenth and eighteenth centuries parallels reception of western model of childhood as separate sphere requiring its own educational material.

5.459 **Tovrov**, Jessica, 'Mother-child relationships among the Russian nobility', in Ransel (5.412), 15-43. Based on manuals, memoirs, and fiction of late eighteenth and early nineteenth centuries.

OLD AGE
See also 5.385 (Germany); 10.49 (Italy).

5.460 **Bever**, E., 'Old age and witchcraft in early modern Europe', in P. N. Stearns, ed., *Old Age in Preindustrial Society*, New York, 1982, 150-90. Stresses particular vulnerability of old women to both accusation and self-incrimination.

5.461 **Gaunt**, D., 'Property and kin relationships of retired farmers in Northern and Central Europe', in Wall and others (5.327), 249-79. Surveys intra-family retirement provisions over several centuries.

5.462 **Gilbert**, C., 'When did a man in the Renaissance grow old?', *Stud.in Renaiss.*, 14, 1967, 7-32. Evidence taken largely from Vasari's *Lives of the Painters*.

5.463 **Laslett**, P., 'History of aging and the aged', in Laslett (5.33), 174-213. Mostly considered in English context, but with a good deal of comparison.

5.464 **Bois**, J.-P., 'Le veillard dans la France moderne, 17e-18e siècle', *Hist.,Éc., et Soc.*, 1984, 67-94. Outlines objectives and methods for tackling subject.

5.465 **Poitrineau**, A., 'Minimum vital catégoriel et conscience populaire. Les retraites conventionelles des gens âgés dans le pays de Murat au 18e siècle', *Fr.Hist.Stud.*, 12, 1981, 165-76. Interesting study, from Auvergne notarial records, of pensions thought appropriate to different levels of rural society.

5.466 **Troyansky**, D. G., 'Old age in the rural family of enlightened Provence', in Stearns (5.460), 209-31. Based on archives of large village near Aix during eighteenth century.

5.467 'Vieillir autrefois', *Ann.Démographie Hist.*, 1985, 7-169. Symposium containing several papers on treatment of elderly in eighteenth-century France; see also *ib.*, 283-321, for additional documentation.

5.468 **Trexler**, R. C., 'A widows' asylum of the Renaissance. The Orbatello of Florence', *ib.*, 119-49.

5.469 **Held**, T., 'Rural retirement arrangements in seventeenth- to nineteenth-century Austria. A cross-community analysis', *J.Family Hist.*, 7, 1982, 227-54. Finds that formal retirement arrangements between parents and heirs were rare before nineteenth century.

5.470 **Johansen**, H. C., 'The position of the old in the rural household in a traditional society', *Scan.Ec.Hist.Rev.*, 24, 1976,

129-42. Danish data showing that in late eighteenth century only about half parents over seventy lived with married children.

WOMEN IN FAMILY AND SOCIETY
See also 5.296; 13.165,308,344,359; 14.143,356 (general material). On France see 9.460-3,552;
10.398,400,410; 13.59,266; 14.48,149,158,247. On Italy 5.378; 6.260-1; 13.333. On the Netherlands 6.113;
13.279. On Germany 6.254; 9.113; 14.200,208. On Denmark 10.454. On Russia 6.273; 13.164; 14.229.
Note that prostitution is covered in subsection 5.248-92 passim.

5.471 **Frey,** Linda, and others, *Women in Western European History. A Select Chronological, Geographical, and Topical Bibliography*, 2 vols., 1982-84. Magnificently all-embracing. Vol.1 covers antiquity to late eighteenth century. See also 5.476 and 480 for bibliographical survey articles.

5.472 **Ankarloo,** B., 'Agriculture and women's work. Directions of change in the West, 1700-1900', *J.Family Hist.*, 4, 1979, 111-20. Suggests that impact of capitalism and technology in agriculture was to exclude women from farming labour force, other than as wives and mothers.

5.473 **Bridenthal,** Renate, and Koonz, Claudia, eds., *Becoming Visible. Women in European History*, Boston, Mass., 1976. Collective work offering more or less continuous survey from earliest times. Contributions on early modern period (by E. W. Monter, Joan Kelly-Gadol, and others) run from pp.119-235.

5.474 **Bullough,** V. L., *The Subordinate Sex. A History of Attitudes toward Women*, Urbana, Ill., 1973. Sweeping survey, full of righteous indignation. For another synoptic work written before heyday of women's movement see Mary R. Beard, *Women as Force in History. A Study in Traditions and Realities*, New York, 1946.

5.475 **Carroll,** Berenice A., ed., *Liberating Women's History. Theoretical and Critical Essays*, Urbana, Ill., 1976. Methodological interest only.

5.476 **Davis,** Natalie Z., ' "Women's history" in transition. The European case', *Feminist Stud.*, 3 (iii-iv), 1976, 83-103. Historiographical essay, with considerable emphasis on early modern period.

5.477 **Goody,** J., 'Inheritance, property, and women. Comparative considerations', in Goody and others (5.321), 10-36. On property transfer between generations, or involving women, in peasant society

5.478 **Howell,** Martha C., *Women, Production, and Patriarchy in Late Medieval Cities*, Chicago, 1986. Changing patterns of work opportunities for women in Köln and Leiden (fourteenth-sixteenth centuries) form basis for comparison with other North European cities.

5.479 —— 'Women, the family economy, and the structure of market production in cities of Northern Europe during the late Middle Ages', in Hanawalt (5.445), 198-222. Suggests that women only had access to skilled work where production was organised on family basis.

5.480 **Hufton,** Olwen, 'Women in history. Early modern Europe', *P.& P.*, 101, 1983, 125-41. Bibliographical survey.

5.481 **Kelly-Gadol,** Joan, 'Did women have a Renaissance?', in her *Women, History, and Theory*, Chicago, 1984, 19-50. Pessimistic view, based on literary evidence. See Merry E. Wiesner's gloss on this: 'Women's defence of their public role', in Mary B. Rose, ed., *Women in the Middle Ages and the Renaissance. Literary and Historical Perspectives*, Syracuse, N. Y., 1986, 1-27.

5.482 **Kelso,** Ruth. *Doctrine for the Lady of the Renaissance*, Urbana, Ill., 1956. Analyses copious literature produced between 1400 and 1600 setting out ideals of education and conduct for gentlewomen.

5.483 **Labalme,** Patricia H., ed., *Beyond their Sex. Learned Women of the European Past*, New York, 1980. Contributors include P. O. Kristeller and Natalie Z. Davis. Most papers deal fairly narrowly with women scholars; Labalme's on women in early modern Venice somewhat broader in scope. Review article: Penelope D. Johnson, *Hist.Educ.Q.*, 24, 1984, 137-41.

5.484 **Maclean,** I., *The Renaissance Notion of Woman. A Study in the Fortunes of Scholasticism and Medical Science in*

European Intellectual Life, 1980. Describes continuing intellectual tradition of woman's innate inferiority in Renaissance discourse, but little reference to social context of discussion.

5.485 **O'Faolain**, Julia, and Martines, L., eds., *Not in God's Image. Women in History from the Greeks to the Victorians*, New York, 1973. Source reader (diaries, medical views, legal codes, etc.)

5.486 **Shorter**, E., *A History of Women's Bodies*, New York, 1982. Some interesting medical history, but takes questionable view of preindustrial sexual relations as unremitting brutality. Review article: S. R. Johansson, *Hist.Methods*, 17, 1984, 33-6.

5.487 **Beech**, Beatrice, 'Charlotte Guillard. A sixteenth-century business woman', *Renaiss.Q.*, 36, 1983, 345-67. Ran printing business in Paris after being widowed.

5.488 **Darrow**, Margaret H., 'French noblewomen and the new domesticity, 1750-1850', *Feminist Stud.*, 5, 1979, 41-65. On reshaping of feminine aristocratic mores by experiences of Revolution.

5.489 **Davis**, Natalie Z., 'Women in the crafts in sixteenth-century Lyon', *Feminist Stud.*, 8, 1982, 46-80. Repr. in Hanawalt (5.445), 167-97. Looks at women both as wage-earners and unpaid family helpers.

5.490 **Dulong**, Claude, *La Vie Quotidienne des Femmes au Grand Siècle*, Paris, 1984. Tends like many such works to concentrate unduly on Paris and Court circles.

5.491 **Hufton**, Olwen H., 'Women and the family economy in eighteenth-century France', *Fr.Hist.Stud.*, 9, 1975, 1-22. Discusses work prospects and expectations of working-class and peasant women, before and after marriage, stressing their vital economic role.

5.492 —— 'Women without men. Widows and spinsters in Britain and France in the eighteenth century', *J.Family Hist.*, 9, 1984, 355-76. Examines options for single women at various social levels.

5.493 —— 'Women, work, and marriage in eighteenth-century France', in R. B. Outhwaite, ed., *Marriage and Society. Studies in the Social History of Marriage*, 1981, 186-203. Concentrates on economics of getting married, esp. how girls might hope to earn dowry.

5.494 **Lougee**, Carolyn C., *Le Paradis des Femmes. Women, Salons, and Social Stratification in Seventeenth-Century France*, Princeton, N.J., 1976. Salon participants (principally daughters of Robe families marrying into older nobility) shown as champions of intellectual education for women as against finishing school approach of Saint Cyr, leading school for daughters of *noblesse d'épée*.

5.495 —— 'Noblesse, domesticity, and social reform. The education of girls by Fénélon and Saint-Cyr', *Hist.Educ.Q.*, 14, 1974, 87-113.

5.496 **Norberg**, Kathryn, 'Women, the family, and the Counter-Reformation. Women's confraternities in the seventeenth century', *Proc.Western Soc.Fr.Hist.*, 6, 1978, 55-63. Explores values promoted by elite women's religious confraternity at Grenoble.

5.497 **Phillips**, R., 'Gender solidarities in late eighteenth-century urban France. The example of Rouen', *Hist.Sociale/Social Hist.*, 13, 1980, 325-38. On women's mutual support over domestic conflicts at neighbourhood level.

5.498 **Spencer**, Samia I., ed., *French Women and the Age of Enlightenment*, Bloomington, Ind., 1984. Includes essays on various social themes (women and family, women and work, etc.), though majority deal with aspects of intellectual life.

5.499 **Brown**, Judith C., 'A woman's place was in the home. Women's work in Renaissance Tuscany', in Margaret W. Ferguson and others, eds., *Rewriting the Renaissance. The Discourses of Sexual Difference in Early Modern Europe*, Chicago, 1986, 206-24. Finds evidence of increasing participation in labour force.

5.500 —— and Goodman, J., 'Women and industry in Florence', *J.Ec.Hist.*, 40, 1980, 73-80. Women's role in Florentine labour force between fifteenth and seventeenth centuries.

5.501 **Cavallo**, Sandra, and Cerutti, Simona, 'Onore femminile e controllo sociale della riproduzione in Piemonte tra sei e settecento', *Quad.Stor.*, 44, 1980, 346-83. Investigates concept of female honour as revealed in matrimonial law cases, esp. for breach of promise.

5.502 **Martin**, J., 'Out of the shadow. Heretical and Catholic women in Renaissance Venice', *J.Family Hist.*, 10, 1985, 21-33.

5.503 **Martines**, L., 'A way of looking at women in Renaissance Florence', *J.Medieval & Renaiss.Stud.*, 4, 1974, 15-28. Examines life of patrician women via correspondence of Alessandra Strozzi (1447-70).

5.504 **Karant-Nunn**, Susan C., 'Continuity and change. Some effects of the Reformation on the women of Zwickau', *Sixteenth-Cent.J.*, 13 (ii), 1982, 16-42. Areas explored: education, marital disputes, prostitution, etc.

5.505 **Petschauer**, P., 'Eighteenth-century German opinions about education for women', *Central Eur.Hist.*, 19, 1986, 262-92.

5.506 —— 'Growing up female in eighteenth-century Germany', *J.Psychohist.*, 11, 1983, 167-207. Based mainly on autobiographies and correspondence.

5.507 **Quataert**, Jean H., 'The shaping of women's work in manufacturing. Guilds, households, and the state in Central Europe, 1648-1870', *Am.Hist.Rev.*, 90, 1985, 1122-48. Broad view of disintegration of guild system in Prussia under pressure from domestic system and official espousal of freer trade.

5.508 **Roper**, L., ' "The common man", the "common good", "common women". Gender and meaning in the German commune', *Soc.Hist.*, 12, 1987, 1-21. Points out some ambiguities of term *gemein* and *gemeinde*, esp. in relation to women's status in community.

5.509 **Wensky**, Margret, 'Women's guilds in Cologne in the later middle ages', *J.Eur.Ec.Hist.*, 11, 1982, 631-50. Fifteenth- and early sixteenth-century evidence. Note also her monograph on this theme, *Die Stellung der Frau in der Stadtkölnischen Wirtschaft im Spät-mittelalter*, Köln, 1981.

5.510 **Wiesner**, Merry E., *Working women in Renaissance Germany*, New Brunswick, N.J., 1986. Chronicles occupations allowed to women in six South German cities, c.1480-1620, arguing there was increase in exclusiveness of guilds and restrictive moral attitudes of councils. See also 9.113 and 593.

5.511 **Monter**, E. W., 'Women in Calvinist Geneva, 1500-1800', *Signs*, 6, 1980, 189-209.

5.512 **Gerber**, H., 'The social and economic position of women in an Ottoman city, Bursa, 1600-1700', *Int.J.Mid.E.Stud.*, 12, 1980, 231-44.

5.513 **Jennings**, R. C., 'Women in early seventeenth-century Ottoman judicial records', *J.Ec.& Soc.Hist.Orient*, 18, 1975, 53-114. Surprising testimony on status of women from records of *sharia* court of Kayseri in Anatolia.

5.514 **Jacobsen**, Grethe, 'Women, marriage, and magisterial Reformation. The case of Malmø, Denmark', in Sessions and Bebb (13.225), 57-77. Concludes that Reformation had only temporary and marginal effect on position of women.

5.515 —— 'Women's work and women's role. Ideology and reality in Danish urban society, 1300-1550', *Scan.Ec.Hist.Rev.*, 31, 1983, 3-20. On fairly widespread employment of women in trades and crafts.

5.516 **Manninen**, Merja, 'The opportunities of independent life for women in an eighteenth-century Finnish provincial town', *Scan.J.Hist.*, 9, 1984, 149-68. Data from town of Oulu, port on Gulf of Bothnia.

5.517 **Stadin**, K., 'Women in the Swedish taxation records', *ib.*, 135-47. Chiefly on evidence that can be deduced from eighteenth-century records.

5.518 **Atkinson**, Dorothy, 'Society and the sexes in the Russian past', in Atkinson and others, eds., *Women in Russia*, Stanford, Calif., 1977, 3-38. General survey from medieval times.

5.519 **Kollmann**, Nancy S., 'The seclusion of elite Muscovite women', *Russ.Hist.*, 10, 1983, 170-87. On virtual purdah for female kin of princes and boiars down to Peter the Great's reforms.

5.520 **Levy**, Sandry, 'Women and the control of property in sixteenth-century Muscovy', *ib.*, 201-12. Evidence from land donations to prestigious Volokolamsk Monastery.

5.521 **Lewitter**, L. R., 'Women, sainthood, and marriage in Muscovy', *J.Russ.Stud.*, 37, 1979, 3-12. Evidence from three literary sources about women's lot in sixteenth and seventeenth centuries.

5.522 **Nash**, Carol S., 'Educating new mothers. Women and the Enlightenment in Russia', *Hist.Educ.Q.*, 21, 1981, 301-16. Rather limited in scope and approach.

MIGRATION, SETTLEMENT, AND COLONISATION
See also 8.23; 9.506,517-18 (general material). On France see 3.62; 8.39. On Spain 11.231. On Italy 5.658. On Germany and Switzerland 9.538; 10.518. On Scandinavia 9.374.

5.523 **Åkerman**, S., 'Towards an understanding of emigrational processes', *Scan.J.Hist.*, 3, 1978, 131-54. General methods and models. See also F. D. Scott, 'Study of the effects of emigration', *Scan.Ec.Hist.Rev.*, 8, 1960, 161-74, which raises question of emigration as factor for social change in mother country.

5.524 **Kirchner**, W., 'Emigration. Some eighteenth-century considerations', *Comp.Stud.Soc.& Hist.*, 5, 1963, 346-56. Repr. in Kirchner (9.183), 210-17. On generally negative attitude of European governments at this period.

5.525 **Lucassen**, J., *Migrant Labour in Europe, 1600-1900. The Drift to the North Sea*, 1987. Adapted from Dutch ed. of 1984. Notes that coastal area from Calais to Bremen strongly attracted seasonal labour, and seeks to trace rise and fall of this phenomenon and compare it with other "push-pull" migration.

5.526 **Debien**, G., *Les Engagés pour les Antilles, 1634-1715*, Paris, 1952. By leading specialist on French West Indies; data mainly from Dieppe and La Rochelle.

5.527 **Henry**, L., and Courgeau, D., 'Deux analyses de l'immigration à Paris au 18e siècle', *Population*, 26, 1971, 1073-92. Henry studies volume of immigration (1740-92); Courgeau provenance of immigrants (1789-1815).

5.528 **Poitrineau**, A., *Remues d'Hommes. Essai sur les Migrations Montagnardes en France aux 17e et 18e Siècles*, Paris, 1983. Study of seasonal migration of workers from Auvergne and Pyrenees.

5.529 **Poussu**, J.-P., 'Les mouvements migratoires en France et à partir de France de la fin du 15e au début du 19e siècle', *Ann.Démographie Hist.*, 1970, 11-78. Substantial synthesis of research and methodology.

5.530 **Schilling**, H., 'Innovation through migration. The settlement of Calvinistic Netherlanders in sixteenth- and seventeenth-century Central and Western Europe', *Hist.Sociale/Social Hist.*, 16, 1983, 7-33. Sketches economic impact on many German localities, drawing on full scale-study *Niederländische Exulanten im 16. Jahrhundert*, Gütersloh, 1972.

5.531 **Boyd-Bowman**, P., *Patterns of Spanish Emigration to the New World*, Buffalo, N.Y., 1973.

5.532 —— 'Patterns of Spanish emigration to the Indies until 1600', *Hisp.Am.Hist.Rev.*, 56, 1976, 580-604.

5.533 —— 'Spanish emigrants to the Indies, 1595-98: a profile', in Chiapelli and others (4.100), 723-35. Draws on detailed interviews with emigrants recorded in *informaciones de pasajeros*.

5.534 **Corbett**, T. G., 'Migration to a Spanish imperial frontier in the seventeenth and eighteenth centuries. St. Augustine', *Hisp.Am.Hist.Rev.*, 54, 1974, 414-30. Uses marriage records to establish provenance of immigrants to Florida colonial capital.

5.535 **Friede**, J., 'The *Catálogo de Pasajeros* and Spanish emigration to 1550', *ib.*, 31, 1951, 333-48. Criticises lacunae in this series of published emigrant lists begun in 1940.

5.536 **Hauben**, P. J., 'First decade of an agrarian experiment in Bourbon Spain. The "new towns" of Sierra Morena and Andalusia, 1766-76', *Agric.Hist.*, 39, 1965, 34-40. Recounts recruitment of German settlers to open up land in depopulated region.

5.537 **Meijide Pardo**, A., *La Emigración Gallega Intrapeninsular en el Siglo 18*, Madrid, 1960. Short study dealing with scarcity factors driving Galicians to migrate to Castile, Portugal and Andalusia.

5.538 **Mörner**, M., 'Spanish migration to the New World prior to 1810. A report on the state of research', in Chiapelli and others (4.100), 737-82. Valuable survey.

5.539 **Augel**, J., *Italienische Einwanderung und Wirtschaftätigkeit in Rheinischen Städten des 17. und 18. Jahrhunderts*, Bonn, 1971. Includes biographical appendix of some 1800 settlers, mainly from Lombardy.

5.540 **Levi**, G., 'Mobilità della popolazione e immigrazione a Torino nella prima metà del Settecento', *Quad.Stor.*, 17, 1971, 510-54.

5.541 **Hippel**, W., *Auswanderung aus Südwestdeutschland. Studien zur Württembergischen Auswanderung und Auswanderungspolitik im 18. und 19.*

Jahrhundert, Stuttgart, 1984. About equally divided between the two centuries.

5.542 **Hochstadt**, S., 'Migration in preindustrial Germany', *Central Eur.Hist.*, 16, 1983, 195-224. Suggests, mainly from urban sources, a high rate of mobility.

5.543 **Schelbert**, L., *Einführung in die Schweizerische Auswanderungsgeschichte der Neuzeit*, Zurich, 1976. Most comprehensive treatment of Swiss emigration, both military and civilian, incl. selection of documents. Note also 5.547.

5.544 **Armstrong**, T. E., *Russian Settlement in the North*, 1965. Charts Russian expansion into Arctic regions of both Europe and Asia.

5.545 **Bartlett**, R. P., *Human Capital. The Settlement of Foreigners in Russia, 1762-1804*, 1979. Deals primarily with agricultural immigrants and role of state in attracting and settling them in Russia's underpeopled regions.

5.546 **Duran**, J. A., 'Catherine II, Potemkin, and colonization policy in Southern Russia', *Russ.Rev.*, 28, 1969, 23-36. Settlement of what became Ekaterinoslav Province.

5.547 **Kirchner**, W., 'Emigration to Russia', *Am.Hist.Rev.*, 55, 1950, 552-66. Repr. in

Kirchner (9.183), 192-209. Deals primarily with Swiss response to Russian efforts to attract immigrants in eighteenth and nineteenth centuries.

5.548 **Lantzeff**, G. V., and Pierce, R. A., *Eastward to Empire. Exploration and Conquest on the Russian Open Frontier to 1750*, Montreal, 1973. Mainly on opening up of Siberia.

5.549 **Nol'de**, B. E., *La Formation de l'Empire Russe. Études, Notes, et Documents*, 2 vols., Paris, 1952-53. Deals with Russian expansion, both via migration and conquest. Useful material on Urals region.

5.550 **Portal**, R., 'Les Russes en Sibérie au 17e siècle', *Rev.Hist.Mod.et Contemp.*, 5, 1958, 5-38.

5.551 **Treadgold**, D. D., 'Russian expansion in the light of Turner's study of the American frontier', *Agric.Hist.*, 26, 1952, 147-52.

5.552 **Wieczynski**, J. L., *The Russian Frontier. The Impact of Borderlands upon the Course of Early Russian History*, Charlottesville, Va., 1976. Suggests, not very convincingly, that, as in America, open frontiers nourished social mobility and egalitarian values.

ETHNIC GROUPS. MINORITIES

RACIAL-RELIGIOUS INTOLERANCE IN SPAIN. 1. GENERAL WORKS. ANTISEMITISM

See also 13.326-35 (general works on Inquisition); and 5.601; 13.386.

5.553 **Singerman**, R., *The Jews in Spain and Portugal. A Bibliography*, New York, 1975. Mainly chronological arrangement, plus some sections on special subjects.

5.554 **Beinart**, H., *Trujillo. A Jewish Community in Extremadura on the Eve of the Expulsion from Spain*, Jerusalem, 1980. Microstudy, about two-thirds consisting of documents.

5.555 **Caro Baroja**, J., *Los Judios en la España Moderna y Contemporánea*, 3 vols., Madrid, 1961-2. Deals with Sephardi community from sixteenth to nineteenth centuries, i.e. during period of crypto-Jewry or forced conversion. Review article: A. M. Salazar, *Jewish J.Sociol.*, 7, 1965, 118-28. See also 13.386.

5.556 **Domínguez Ortiz**, A., *Los Conversos de Origen Judío después de la Expulsión*, Madrid, 1955. Reissued as *Los Judeoconversos en España y América*, 1971.

5.557 —— 'Historical research on Spanish conversos in the last fifteen years', in M. P. Hornik, ed., *Collected Studies in Honour of Américo Castro's Eightieth Year*, 1965, 63-82. In festschrift devoted mainly to interactions of Jewish and Hispanic culture; see 3.93 for Castro's influence in this area.

5.558 **Edwards**, J. H., 'Religious belief and social conformity. The "converso" problem in late-medieval Córdoba', *Trans.Roy.Hist.Soc.*, 5th ser., 31, 1981, 115-28. Considers implications of introduction of Inquisition following anti-converso riot of 1473.

5.559 **Friedman**, J., 'Jewish conversion, the Spanish blood laws, and Reformation. A revisionist view of racial and religious antisemitism', *Sixteenth-Cent.J.*, 18, 1987, 3-29. Argues that converso problem had European-wide dimension and fostered antisemitism more than did Jewish aloofness from Christianity. See 5.617-19 and 623 for Italian hostility to lapsed converts.

560 **Gutiérrez Nieto**, J. I., 'La estructura castizo-estamental de la sociedad castellana del siglo 16', *Hispania*, 125, 1973, 519-63. Examines how converso question complicated Spanish social structure by adding racial descent to profession in accordance of esteem.

561 **Haliczer**, S. H., 'The Castilian urban patriciate and the Jewish expulsions of 1480-92', *Am.Hist.Rev.*, 78, 1973, 35-62. Contends that converso elements in town elites demanded expulsions to protect themselves against Inquisition arbitrariness.

562 **Kriegel**, M., 'La prise d'une décision. L'expulsion des juifs d'Espagne en 1492', *Rev.Hist.*, 260, 1978, 49-90. Views decision as government initiative rather than response to popular pressure.

563 **Mackay**, A., 'The Hispanic-converso predicament', *Trans.Roy.Hist.Soc.*, 5th ser., 35, 1985, 159-79. Surveys period from fourteenth to sixteenth centuries, and notes reflections of hostility in literary works by converts.

564 —— 'Popular movements and pogroms in fifteenth-century Castile', *P.& CP.*, 55, 1972, 33-67. Aims to show that problem of antisemitism was linked to other causes of unrest.

565 **Moore**, K., *Those of the Street. The Catholic-Jews of Mallorca*, Notre Dame, Ind., 1976. Anthropological and historical study of group known as *Xuetas*.

566 **Netanyahu**, B., *The Marranos of Spain from the Late Fourteenth to the Early Sixteenth Century*, New York, 1966. 2nd ed., 1971. Based on Hebrew sources. Contends that Inquisition caused reversion to Judaism which great majority of Marranos had genuinely abandoned. See also his 'The Marranos according to the Hebrew sources of the fifteenth and early sixteenth centuries', *Proc.Am.Acad.Jewish Res.*, 31, 1963, 81-164.

567 **Roth**, C., *A History of the Marranos*, 4th ed., New York, 1974. First publ. in 1932. Minor revisions only.

568 **Redondo**, A., ed., *Les Problèmes de l'Exclusion en Espagne (16e-17e Siècles). Idéologie et Discours*, Paris, 1983. Papers of conference dealing with repressive attitudes towards minorities and deviants, particularly as shown in literary or juridical discourse.

5.569 **Sicroff**, A., *Les Controverses des Statuts de "Pureté de Sang" en Espagne du 15e au 17e Siècle*, Paris, 1960. On formal discrimination measures.

2. THE MORISCOS
See also previous sub-section; and 3.146; 11.326.

5.570 **Aranda Doncel**, J., *Los Moriscos en Tierras de Córdoba*, Cordoba, 1984. Unit of study is diocese of Córdoba.

5.571 **Carande**, R., 'Los Moriscos de Henri Lapeyre, los de Julio Caro, y algun Morisco mas', *Moneda y Crédito*, 78, 1961, 9-26. Review article covering material in 5.573,580,583,589.

5.572 **Cardaillac**, L., *Morisques et Chrétiens. Un Affrontement Polemique, 1492-1640*, Paris, 1977. Principally a study of propaganda war, but social setting well described.

5.573 **Caro Baroja**, J., *Los Moriscos del Reino de Granada*, Madrid, 1957. 2nd ed., 1976 (only introduction is new material).

5.574 **Casey**, J., 'Moriscos and the depopulation of Valencia', *P.& P.*, 50, 1971, 19-40. Concludes that Valencian depression of seventeenth century was too broad to be attributed wholly to expulsions of 1609. See also 5.584,586.

5.575 **Chejne**, A. G., *Islam and the West. The Moriscos, a Cultural and Social History*, Albany, N.Y., 1983. Attempts to reconstruct Morisco culture and self-image from writings produced in *Aljamiado* (Spanish dialect in Arabic script).

5.576 **Domínguez Ortiz**, A., and Vincent, B., *Historia de los Moriscos. Vida y Tragedia de una Minoría*, Madrid, 1978.

5.577 **Dressendörfer**, P., *Islam unter der Inquisition. Die Morisco-Prozesse in Toledo, 1575-1610*, Wiesbaden, 1971. Classification of accusations raised in trials.

5.578 **García Arenal**, Mercedes, *Inquisición y Moriscos. Los Procesos del Tribunal de Cuenca*, Madrid, 1978. Similar study of Inquisition trials at local level. See also related article, *Hispania*, 138, 1978, 151-99.

5.579 —— *Los Moriscos*, Madrid, 1975.

Collection of documents and readings.

5.580 **Halperin Donghi**, T., *Un Conflicto Nacional. Moriscos y Cristianos Viejos en Valencia*, Valencia, 1980. See also earlier article, 'Les Morisques du royaume de Valence au 16e siècle', *Annales*, 11, 1956, 154-82.

5.581 **Hess**, A. C., 'The Moriscos. An Ottoman fifth column in sixteenth-century Spain', *Am.Hist.Rev.*, 74, 1968, 1-25. Argues that threat of links between Turks and Moriscos was main motive of expulsion, and that Turkish archives show definite attempts to foment rebellion.

5.582 **Ladero Quesada**, M. A., *Los Mudejares de Castilla en Tiempos de Isabel I*, Valladolid, 1969.

5.583 **Lapeyre**, H., *Géographie de l'Espagne Morisque*, Paris, 1959. On distribution of Morisco population preceding expulsion of 1609. Review article: P. Chaunu, *Rev.Hist.*, 225, 1961, 81-98.

5.584 **Magraner Rodrigo**, A., *La expulsión de los Moriscos, sus Razones Juridicas y Consecuencias Economicas para la Región Valenciana*, Valencia, 1975. See also 5.574,586.

5.585 *Les Morisques et leur Temps*, Paris, 1983. Substantial volume of essays delivered at Table Ronde Internationale, Montpellier, 1981.

5.586 **Palau García**, F., 'La situación histórica del Morisco en el Reino de Valencia en el transito del siglo 16-17', *Hispania*, 149, 1981, 515-62. Discusses expulsion of Moriscos in context of Marxist debate over transition from feudalism to capitalism.

5.587 **Phillips**, Carla R., 'The Moriscos of La Mancha, 1570-1614', *J.Mod.Hist.*, 50, 1978, 1067-95 (on demand article). On community which settled around Ciudad Real between deportation from Granada and final expulsion from Spain.

5.588 **Pike**, Ruth, 'An urban minority. The Moriscos of Seville', *Int.J.Mid.E.Stud.*, 2, 1971, 368-77. Material from census of 1580 covering five city parishes.

5.589 **Regla**, J., *Estudios sobre los Moriscos*, Valencia, 1964. 3rd ed., Barcelona, 1974, adds fourth paper.

5.590 **Vincent**, B., 'L'Albaicin de Grenade au 16e siècle', *Mél.Casa de Velazquez*, 7, 1971, 187-223. On Morisco quarter of Granada.

5.591 —— 'L'expulsion des Morisques du Royaume de Grenade et leur répartition en

Castille (1570-71)', *ib.*, 6, 1970, 211-46. Useful maps.

JEWS IN OTHER EUROPEAN COUNTRIES
See also 2.129,131; 9.521; 10.254; 11.82,160; 13.322. Note bibliographical items at 5.593 (general), 5.603 (France); 5.553 (Spain); 5.625 (Germany); 5.635 (Poland).

5.592 **Baron**, S. W., *A Social and Religious History of the Jews*, 18 vols. to date, New York, 1937- . Vols. 9 onwards deal with period 1200-1650, sometimes thematically, sometimes by region.

5.593 —— 'Some recent literature on the history of the Jews in the pre-emancipation era (1300-1800)', *J.World Hist.*, 7, 1962, 137-71.

5.594 **Coser**, L. A., 'The alien as a servant of power. Court Jews and Christian renegades', *Am.Sociol.Rev.*, 37, 1972, 574-81. Argues that German court Jews and Christian employees of Ottoman Empire typify partiality of autocratic governments for operating through "ghetto" officials.

5.595 **Farine**, A., 'Charity and study societies in Europe of the sixteenth-eighteenth centuries'. *Jewish Q. Rev.*, 64, 1973, 16-47, 164-75. On Jewish welfare organisations – data drawn from Italy, Germany, and Eastern Europe.

5.596 **Gross**, N., ed., *Economic History of the Jews*, New York, 1975. Collective work, First third of book is a chronological survey from Biblical period onwards; remainder deals in turn with agriculture, industry, and service trades.

5.597 **Israel**, J. I., *European Jewry in the Age of Mercantilism, 1550-1750*, 1985. Wide-ranging synthesis.

5.598 **Katz**, J., *Exclusiveness and Tolerance. Studies in Jewish-Gentile Relations in Medieval and Modern Times*, 1961. See also his *Jews and Freemasons in Europe, 1723-1939*, Cambridge, Mass., 1970, on importance and limitations of Freemasonry as vehicle for Jewish assimilation.

5.599 —— 'Family, kinship, and marriage among Ashkenazim in the sixteenth to eighteenth centuries', *Jewish J.Sociol.*, 1, 1959, 4-22. Only literary sources seem to be used.

5.600 **Oelsner**, T., 'The place of the Jews in

economic history as viewed by German scholars', *Yrbk.Leo Baeck Inst.*, 7, 1962, 183-212. Critical examination of views of Roscher, Sombart, and Weber on Jewish drive to commercial success.

601 **Poliakov**, L., *The History of Anti-Semitism*, 4 vols., 1966-85. Transl. from French. Vol. 1 deals with Europe in general up to 1700; vol. 2 largely with Spain; vol. 3 contains section on eighteenth century.

602 **Stow**, K. R., 'The burning of the Talmud in 1553', *Bibl.d'Humanisme et Renaiss.*, 34, 1972, 435-59. General background to heightened Catholic intolerance of Jewish religious publications. For an Italian example see Grendler, 5.615.

603 **Blumenkranz**, B., *Bibliographie des Juifs en France*, Toulouse, 1974.

604 —— ed., *Histoire des Juifs en France*, Toulouse, 1972. Collective history, from earliest settlements to modern times.

605 **Calmann**, Marianne, *The Carrière of Carpentras*, 1984. Study of ghetto in Comtat Venaissin. Richer and more comprehensive is R. Moulinas, *Les Juifs du Pape. Les Communautés d'Avignon et du Comtat Venaissin aux 17e et 18e Siècles*, Toulouse, 1982.

606 **Hertzberg**, A., *The French Enlightenment and the Jews*, New York, 1968.

607 **Posener**, S., 'Social life of the Jewish communities in France in the eighteenth century', *Jewish Soc.Stud.*, 7, 1945, 195-232. Looks at communities of Bordeaux, Avignon, and Alsace-Lorraine regions on eve of Revolution, stressing weakening of rabbinical authority.

608 **Szajkowski**, Z., 'The Jewish problem in Alsace, Metz, and Lorraine on the eve of the Revolution of 1789', *Jewish Q.Rev.*, 44, 1954, 205-43. Some moves and counter-moves in struggle for liberalisation of status.

609 —— 'Jewish status in eighteenth-century France and the *droit d'aubaine*', *Hist.Judaica*, 19, 1957, 147-61. Legal controversy over whether Jews were aliens, and thus liable to estate confiscation.

610 **Swetschinski**, D. M., 'The Portuguese Jews of seventeenth-century Amsterdam. Cultural continuity and adaptation', in Frances Malino and Phyllis C. Albert, eds., *Essays in Modern Jewish History*, Rutherford, N.J., 1982, 56-80. Principally on intellectual life of community (books, theatre, etc.).

5.611 **Bachi**, R., 'The demographic development of Italian Jewry from the seventeenth century', *Jewish J.Sociol.*, 4, 1962, 172-91. Discusses aggregate statistics, including changes in geographical distribution. See also his contribution in following entry.

5.612 **Boesch Gajano**, Sofia, and Luzzati, M., eds., 'Ebrei in Italia', *Quad.Stor.*, 54, 1983, 779-939. Group of articles, several dealing with early modern period. See also R. Bachi and S. Della Pergola, 'Gli Ebrei italiani nel quadro della demografia della diaspora', *ib.*, 55, 1984, 155-97, a longitudinal study spanning longer period than 5.611.

5.613 **Bonazzoli**, Viviana, 'Gli Ebrei del Regno di Napoli all'epoca della loro espulsione', *Arch.Stor.Ital.*, 137, 1979, 495-559; 139, 1981, 179-287. Covers period 1456 to 1541. Much broader study of Jewish community than older paper on expulsion by F. Ruiz Martín in *Hispania*, 9, 1949, 28-76, 179-240.

5.614 **Finlay**, R., 'The foundation of the ghetto. Venice, the Jews, and the War of the League of Cambrai', *Proc.Am.Phil.Soc.*, 126, 1982, 140-54. Introduction of segregation for refugee Jews made scapegoats for disasters of war.

5.615 **Grendler**, P. F., 'The destruction of Hebrew books in Venice, 1568', *Proc.Am.Acad.Jewish Res.*, 45, 1978, 103-30.

5.616 **Pullan**, B., *The Jews of Europe and the Inquisition of Venice*, 1983. Deals not with Jewish ghetto but with converted Jews suspected of lapsing. See following two articles for case-studies involving Portuguese Jews at Venice drawn from this research.

5.617 —— ' "A ship with two rudders". "Righetto Marrano" and the Inquisition in Venice', *Hist.J.*, 20, 1977, 25-58.

5.618 —— 'The Inquisition and the Jews of Venice. The case of Gasparo Ribeiro, 1580-81', *Bull.John Rylands Lib.*, 62, 1979, 207-31.

5.619 **Ravid**, B., 'Socio-economic background of the expulsion and readmission of the Venetian Jews, 1571-73', in Malino and Albert (5.610), 27-55. Arose from divisions of Senate about utility of Jewish moneylenders.

5.620 **Roth**, C., *The History of the Jews of Italy*, Philadelphia, 1946. See also his 'Jewish society in the Renaissance environment',

J.World Hist., 11, 1968, 239-50, which deals only with Italy.

5.621 **Saperstein**, M., 'Martyrs, merchants, and rabbis. Jewish communal conflict as reflected in the *responsa* on the boycott of Ancona', *Jewish Soc.Stud.*, 43, 1981, 215-28. Attempt by Ottoman Jewish merchants to boycott port of Ancona after papal execution of lapsed Portuguese marranos (1556).

5.622 **Shulvass**, M. A., 'Jewish population in Renaissance Italy', *ib.*, 13, 1951, 3-24. Collects scattered data on local population figures over period 1300-1600. See also 5.611-12.

5.623 ——*Jews in the World of the Renaissance*, Leiden, 1973. Transl. from Hebrew ed. of 1955. General work on Italian communities.

5.624 **Simonsohn**, S., *History of the Jews in the Duchy of Mantua*, New York, 1977. Transl. from Hebrew ed. of c.1964. Covers fourteenth to eighteenth centuries in great detail. Note also author's projected documentary history of Italian Jewry, beginning with *Jews in the Duchy of Milan*, Jerusalem, 1982.

5.625 **Wolff**, I. R., *German Jewry, its History, Life, and Culture (Wiener Library Catalogue Series, 3)*, 1958. Bibliography; material on early modern period somewhat dispersed by topical approach.

5.626 **Arnheim**, A., 'German court Jews and Denmark during the Great Northern War', *Scan.Ec.Hist.Rev.*, 14, 1966, 115-33. Largely confined to financial dealings of Isaak Liebmann, head of Jewish community in Berlin.

5.627 **Carsten**, F. L., 'The court Jews. A prelude to emancipation', *Yrbk.Leo Baeck Inst.*, 3, 1958, 140-56. Repr. in his *Essays in German History*, 1985, 127-44. Extended review and discussion of books by Stern and Schnee (5.633 and 10.254).

5.628 **Frey**, W., 'Passionsspiel und geistliche Malerei als Instrumente der Judenhetze in Frankfurt am Main um 1500', *Jb.Inst.Dt.Gesch.*, 13, 1984, 15-57. Interesting illustrations of anti-Jewish art.

5.629 **Glanz**, R., *Geschichte des Niederen Judischen Volkes in Deutschland*, New York, 1968. Interesting, privately publ. study of marginal and criminal Jewish groups in pre-industrial Germany.

5.630 **Israel**, J. I., 'Central European Jewry during the Thirty Years' War', *Central Eur.Hist.*, 16, 1983, 3-30. Suggests that Jewish communities of Holy Roman Empire fared surprisingly well in this period.

5.631 **Pollack**, H., *Jewish Folkways in Germanic Lands (1648-1806). Studies in Aspects of Daily Life*, Cambridge, Mass., 1971. Area dealt with is essentially that of Holy Roman Empire. Thematic arrangement of material somewhat obscures regional variations.

5.632 **Richarz**, Monika, *Eintritt der Juden in die Akademischen Berufe*, Tübingen, 1974. Two chapters deal with limited Jewish access to higher education in seventeenth and eighteenth centuries.

5.633 **Stern**, Selma, *Der Preussische Staat und die Juden*, 4 vols. in 8, Tübingen, 1962-75. Enormous scholarly work (including documentary volumes), dealing with government policies towards, and financial relations with, Jews in seventeenth and eighteenth centuries. Earlier sketch publ. as *The Court Jew*, Philadelphia, 1950.

5.634 —— 'Principles of German policy toward the Jews at the beginning of the modern era', *Yrbk.Leo Baeck Inst.*, 1, 1956, 15-27. Brief survey of attitudes in fifteenth and early sixteenth centuries.

5.635 **Hundert**, G. D., and Bacon, G. C., *The Jews in Poland and Russia. Bibliographical Essays*, Bloomington, Ind., 1984. In section 1 Hundert deals with Jews of Poland-Lithuania from twelfth century to 1772; remainder is on modern Poland and Russia.

5.636 **Abramsky**, C., and others, eds., *The Jews in Poland*, 1986. Conference papers. Essays 2-4 (of 17) deal with aspects of early modern period.

5.637 **Goldberg**, J., 'Poles and Jews in the seventeenth and eighteenth centuries. Rejection or acceptance?', *Jb. Gesch. Osteuropas*, 22, 1974, 248-82.

5.638 **Hundert**, G. D., 'Jewish urban residence in the Polish Commonwealth in the early modern period', *Jewish J.Sociol.*, 26, 1984, 25-34. Suggests that ghetto residence was not enforced in many towns in eighteenth and nineteenth centuries.

5.639 —— 'Jews, money, and society in the seventeenth-century Polish Commonwealth. The case of Krakow', *Jewish Soc.Stud.*, 43, 1981, 261-74. Stresses importance of banking services to gentry.

5.640 **Shulman**, N. E., *Authority and Community*

Polish Jewry in the Sixteenth Century, New York, 1986. Based mainly on rabbinic responsa; part 2 summarises those of Rabbi Slonik to variety of queries on Jewish law in everyday practice.

5.641 **Weinryb**, B. D., *The Jews of Poland. A Social and Economic History of the Jewish Community in Poland from 1100 to 1800*, Philadelphia, 1973. Broad survey, but including more religious and intellectual history than title suggests.

5.642 —— 'Texts and studies in the communal history of Polish Jewry', *Proc. Am. Acad. Jewish Res.*, 19, 1950, 1-110. Lengthy introduction to texts in Hebrew; author's summaries give detailed picture of communities at Poznan, Cracow, and Wlodawa in seventeenth and eighteenth centuries.

5.643 **Wischnitzer**, M., 'Origins of the Jewish artisan class in Bohemia and Moravia, 1500-1648', *Jewish Soc.Stud.*, 16, 1954, 335-50. Charts increase in artisan practitioners and opposition of Christian guilds.

5.644 **Arbel**, B., 'Jews in Cyprus. New evidence from the Venetian period', *ib.*, 41, 1979, 23-40. Data on immigrant Jews recently settled at Famagusta and ordered to be expelled, 1568.

5.645 **Braude**, B., and Lewis, B., eds., *Christians and Jews in the Ottoman Empire. The Functioning of a Plural Society. Vol.1: The Central Lands*, New York, 1982. Several relevant essays on religious/national minorities and *millet* system. See also 5.655.

5.646 **Heyd**, U., 'The Jewish communities of Istanbul in the seventeenth century', *Oriens*, 6, 1953, 299-314. Data culled from poll-tax registers.

5.647 **Klier**, J. D., 'The ambiguous legal status of Russian Jewry in the reign of Catherine II', *Slavic Rev.*, 35, 1976, 504-17.

5.648 **Pipes**, R., 'Catherine II and the Jews. The origins of the Pale of Settlement, *Soviet Jewish Affairs*, 5, 1975, 3-20. Argues that basic rules bearing on Russian Jewry were laid down under Catherine and relatively benign in intent (twisted by local hostility and later governments).

OTHER GROUPS
See also 10.346.

5.649 **Asséo**, Henriette, 'Le traitement administratif des Bohémiens. Marginalité et exclusion', in *Problèmes Socio-Culturels en France au 17e Siècle*, Paris, 1974, 9-87. Valuable essay on treatment of gypsies. See also 5.654.

5.650 **Cassia**, P. S., 'Religion, politics, and ethnicity in Cyprus during the *Turkocratia* (1571-1878)', *Arch.Eur.Sociol.*, 27, 1986, 3-28. Argues that neither religion nor ethnicity were major sources of cleavage in pre-modern Cyprus.

5.651 **Fisher**, A., *The Crimean Tatars*, Stanford, Calif., 1978. History under Russian rule from origins to Second World War deportation.

5.652 **Hoffman**, G. W., 'Evolution of the ethnographic map of Yugoslavia. A historical geographic interpretation', in Carter (4.20), 437-99.

5.653 **Jennings**, R. C., 'Zimmis (non-muslims) in early seventeenth-century Ottoman judicial records', *J.Ec.& Soc.Hist.Orient*, 21, 1978, 225-93. Material on status and rights of Armenian and Orthodox Christians from records of *sharia* court of Kayseri in Anatolia.

5.654 **Kappen**, O. van, 'Histoire des Tsiganes aux Pays-Bas. L'évolution du statut des "païens" ou "Egyptiens" dans les Pays-Bas du Nord (c.1420-1750)', *Acta Hist.Neerlandica*, 3, 1968, 160-88. Summary of his monograph in Dutch (Assen, 1965). See also 5.649.

5.655 **Karpat**, K. H., *An Inquiry into the Social Foundations of Nationalism in the Ottoman State*, Princeton, N.J., 1973. On factors giving rise to nationalities problem from eighteenth century onwards. See also 5.645.

5.656 **Longworth**, P., *The Cossacks*, 1969. History up to 1917; useful introduction, but little depth on social aspects. Review article: I. L. Rudnytsky, *Slavic Rev.*, 31, 1972, 870-75. See also 5.660.

5.657 **McCloy**, S. T., *The Negro in France*, Lexington, Ky., 1961. Note author's rather anecdotal earlier essay 'Negroes and mulattoes in eighteenth-century France', *J.Negro Hist.*, 30, 1945, 276-92; 39, 1954, 284-97.

5.658 **Mitler**, L., 'The Genoese in Galata, 1453-1682', *Int.J.Mid.E.Stud.*, 10, 1979, 71-91. On Genoese community near Istanbul which stayed on after Turkish conquest.

5.659 **Pescatello**, Ann M., 'The *leyenda negra*

and the African in sixteenth- and seventeenth-century Iberian thought', *Cath.Hist.Rev.*, 66, 1980, 169-83. Documents various expressions of concern for treatment of negro slaves.

5.660 **Seaton**, A., *The Horsemen of the Steppes.*

The Story of the Cossacks, 1985. See also 5.656.

5.661 **Stone**, G., *The Smallest Slavonic Nation. The Sorbs of Lusatia*, 1972. Small enclave in German territory.

6

SOCIAL STRATIFICATION. ESTATES AND ORDERS

GENERAL WORKS. STATUS, WEALTH, AND MOBILITY

Much additional material will be found in Sections 7 and 8 on rural and urban society. See also sources listed in 2.8,10,11; and 10.480.

.1 **Arriaza**, A., 'Mousnier and Barber. Theoretical underpinning of the "society of orders" in early modern Europe', *P.& P.*, 89, 1980, 39-57. Suggests that Mousnier's *Social Hierarchies* (6.8), though influenced by sociologist Bernard Barber's work on social stratification, fails to assimilate his emphasis on dysfunctions and questionable norms that may be involved.

.2 **Barber**, B., and Barber, Elinor G., eds., *European Social Class. Stability and Change*, New York, 1965. Readings, about half concerned with early modern period.

.3 **Corvisier**, A., 'La représentation de la société dans les danses des morts du 15e au 18e siècle', *Rev.Hist.Mod.et Contemp.*, 16, 1969, 489-535. Looks at depiction of social hierarchy in processions that are typical of this art form.

.4 **Duplessis**, R., 'Class and class-consciousness in Western European cities, 1400-1650', *Radical Hist.Rev.*, 3, 1975, 74-91. Suggests that small-scale production, citizenship bonds, and difficulties of inter-city communication made conflicts relatively short-lived.

.5 **Hobsbawm**, E. J., 'Class consciousness in history', in I. Meszaros, ed., *Aspects of History and Class Consciousness*, 1971, 5-21. Opening lecture of series centering on G.

Lukacs' *History and Class Consciousness*.

6.6 **Katz**, M. B., 'Occupational classification in history', *J.Interdisc.Hist.*, 3, 1972, 63-88. Useful on methodology, though examples drawn from nineteenth century Canada. See also 6.12.

6.7 **Mousnier, R., ed.**, *Problèmes de Stratification Sociale. Actes du Colloque International (1966)*, Paris, 1968. Conference revolving around application of terms "caste", "estate", and "class" in European social history. Early modern contributions to note incl. H. Stuke (on what Germans meant by "Stand"); I. Schöffer (seventeenth-century Netherlands); F. L. Carsten (Prussian nobility); V. Giuntella (eighteenth-century Roman society).

6.8 —— *Social Hierarchies, 1450 to the Present*, 1973. Transl. from French ed. of 1969. Very brief comparative survey, with a certain amount of twentieth-century polemics.

6.9 **Mendels**, F. F., 'Social mobility and phases of industrialization', *J.Interdisc.Hist.*, 7, 1976, 193-216. Repr. in T. K. Rabb and R. I. Rotberg, eds., *Industrialization and Urbanization*, Princeton, N.J., 59-82. Observations on social factors promoting mobility (e.g. inheritance systems) and on feedback between mobility and advancing levels of industrialisation.

6.10 **Rotelli**, E., 'La structure sociale dans l'itinéraire historiographique de Roland Mousnier', *Rev.Hist.Mod.etContemp.*, 51, 1973, 145-82. Taken from introduction to Italian ed. of 6.8.

6.11 **Thernstrom**, S., 'Notes on the historical study of social mobility', *Comp. Stud. Soc. & Hist.*, 10, 1967, 162-72. Repr. in Drake (5.30), 221-32; and in D. K. Rowney and J. Q. Graham, eds., *Quantitative History. Selected Readings in Quantitative Analysis of Historical Data*, Homewood, Ill., 1969, 99-108. General, though somewhat biased towards modern U.S. history.

6.12 **Treiman**, D. J., 'A standard occupational prestige scale for use with historical data', *J.Interdisc.Hist.*, 7, 1976, 283-304. Claims that occupational status hierarchies prove to be relatively invariant across time and space. See also 6.6.

FRANCE
See also 8.43; 14.251.

6.13 **Bluche**, F., and Solnon, J.-F., *La Véritable Hiérarchie Sociale de l'Ancienne France. Le Tarif de la Première Capitation (1695)*, Geneva, 1983. Evidence on wealth and prestige from classifications of poll tax introduced in 1695.

6.14 **Daumard**, Adeline, and Furet, F., *Structures et Relations Sociales à Paris au Milieu du 18e Siècle*, Paris, 1961. Analysis of over 2000 marriage contracts of year 1749 for light they throw on social structure and relationships.

6.15 **Clouatre**, D. J., 'The concept of class in French culture prior to the Revolution', *J.Hist.Ideas*, 45, 1984, 219-44. Concerns linguistic evolution of term "classe" towards its modern sense of elements of social stratification.

6.16 **Furet**, F., 'Structures sociales parisiennes au 18e siècle', *Annales*, 16, 1961, 939-58. Further light on Parisian hierarchies from poor relief assessments of 1743.

6.17 **Giesey**, R. E., 'Rules of inheritance and strategies of mobility in prerevolutionary France', *Am.Hist.Rev.*, 82, 1977, 271-89. Stresses importance of *rentes* and office-holding in maintaining stability of family fortunes.

6.18 **Hickey**, D., 'The introduction of absolutism in Dauphiné. Fiscal and social

structures', *Proc.Western Soc.Fr.Hist.*, 10, 1982, 189-97. Examines changes in taxation system for evidence on distribution of wealth.

6.19 **Jensen**, C. R., and Bitton, D., 'Social mobility in Clairac, 1680-1780', *ib.*, 7, 1979, 24-33. Brief study of marriage patterns, property transactions, etc., in two extensive families in small Guyenne town.

6.20 **Jouanna**, Arlette, *Ordre Social. Mythes et Hiérarchies dans la France du 16e Siècle*, Paris, 1977. On values underpinning hierarchy, especially concept of inherited nobility.

6.21 **Mandrou**, R., *Classes et Luttes de Classe en France au Début du 17e Siècle*, Messina, 1965. Argues that class consciousness is essential to class conflict, and that only social elite was affected by either.

6.22 **Mousnier**, R., *Recherches sur la Stratification Sociale à Paris aux 17e et 18e Siècles. L'Échantillon de 1634, 1635, 1636*, Paris, 1976. From sample of marriage contracts and inventories seeks to identify status attached to various professions and trades.

6.23 —— 'Les concepts d'"ordres", d'"états", de "fidelité", et de "monarchie absolue" en France de la fin du 15e à la fin du 18e', *Rev.Hist.*, 247, 1972, 289-312. Clear exposition of social hierarchy as perceived by lawyers, corporations, political theorists, etc.

6.24 —— and others, 'La mobilité sociale au 17e siècle', *Dix-Septième Siècle*, 122, 1979, whole issue. Mousnier provides introduction and summing up to symposium which includes studies of financiers, the Army, Parisian artisans, and links between mobility and rebellion.

6.25 **Roche**, D., and Labrousse, C. E., eds., *Ordres et Classes. Colloque d'Histoire Sociale, Saint-Cloud...1967*, Paris, 1973. Articles of main interest for early modern France are J.-C. Perrot on hierarchy in eighteenth-century towns (141-66); and J. Dupâquier and J. Jacquart on seventeenth-century countryside (167-80).

6.26 **Sewell**, W. H., '*État, corps,* and *ordre.* Some notes on the social vocabulary of the French Old Regime', in H.-U. Wehler, ed., *Sozialgeschichte Heute. Festschrift für Hans Rosenberg zum 70. Geburtstag*, Göttingen, 1974, 49-68.

6.27 **Taylor**, G. V., 'Noncapitalist wealth and

the origins of the French Revolution', *Am.Hist.Rev.*, 72, 1967, 469-96. Argues that commonest form of wealth, both noble and non-noble, was "proprietary" (rent-yielding and low-risk); thus conflict between orders concerned political rather than economic issues.

OTHER STATES AND REGIONS

See also 6.7 (Netherlands); 3.112,129 and 5.153 (Spain); 6.7 (Italy); 7.150,155 (Germany); 5.199 (Switzerland).

6.28 **Dijk**, H. van, and Roorda, D. J., 'Social mobility under the regents of the Republic', *Acta Hist.Neerlandica*, 9, 1976, 76-102. United Provinces in seventeenth and eighteenth centuries.

6.29 **Donézar Díez de Ulzurrun**, J. M., *Riqueza y Propriedad en la Castilla del Antiguo Régimen. La Provincia de Toledo en el Siglo 18*, Madrid, 1984. Analysis of wealth and landed property drawn from tax reform survey of Enseñada in 1750s.

6.30 **De Rosa**, L., *Studi sugli Arrendamenti del Regno di Napoli. Aspetti della Distribuzione della Richezza Mobiliare nel Mezzogiorno Continentale*, Naples, 1958. Data on non-landed wealth derived from complex indirect tax system.

6.31 **Romani**, M. A., *La Gente, le Occupazioni, i Redditi del Piacentino (da un Estimo della Fine del Secolo 16)*, Parma, 1969. Analysis of urban and rural cadasters for Piacenza area drawn up for Ottavio Farnese.

6.32 **Greve**, K., and Krüger, Kersten, 'Steurstaat und Sozialstruktur. Finanzsoziologische Auswertung der Hessischen Katastervorbeschreibungen für Waldkappel (1744) und Herleshausen (1748)', *Gesch.und Gesellschaft*, 8, 1982, 295-332. Points to usefulness of Hesse cadasters as source for wealth distribution among more modest levels of society.

6.33 **Saalfeld**, D., 'Die ständische Gliederung der Gesellschaft Deutschlands im Zeitalter des Absolutismus. Ein Quantifizierungs-versuch', *VSWG*, 67, 1980, 457-83. Offers estimates of relative size of broad social strata in eighteenth century.

6.34 **Walker**, M., ' "Rights and functions". The social categories of eighteenth-century German jurists and cameralists', *J.Mod.Hist.*, 50, 1978, 234-51. Contrasts jurists' emphasis on rights and privileges of ranks (e.g. Moser), with that of cameralists on their function in general economy (e.g.Justi).

6.35 **Inalcik**, H., 'Capital formation in the Ottoman Empire', *J.Ec.Hist.*, 29, 1969, 97-140. Repr. in Inalcik (3.299). Argues that great wealth was only to be attained in mercantile sphere.

6.36 **Todorov**, N., 'Social structures in the Balkans during the eighteenth and nineteenth centuries', *Ét.Balkaniques*, 21 (iv), 1985, 48-71. Somewhat schematically forced into mould of transition from feudalism to capitalism.

6.37 **Carlsson**, S., 'The dissolution of the Swedish estates', *J.Eur.Ec.Hist.*, 1, 1972, 574-624. Discusses process of social assimilation that led to abolition of separate political representation.

6.38 **Dahlgren**, S., 'Estates and classes [in Sweden]', in Roberts (3.345), 102-31.

6.39 **Jutikkala**, E., 'The distribution of wealth in Finland in 1800', *Scan.Ec.Hist.Rev.*, 1, 1953, 81-103. Evidence from capital levy imposed throughout Sweden and Filand.

6.40 **Soltow**, L., 'Wealth distribution in Denmark in 1789', *ib.*, 27, 1979, 121-38. Sample data from inventories produced under revenue law of 1789.

6.41 **Hassell**, J., 'Implementation of the Russian table of ranks during the eighteenth century', *Slavic Rev.*, 29, 1970, 283-95. Stresses conflict between ostensibly meritocratic system and realities of hierarchy of birth.

ELITES. NOBILITY, PATRICIANS, AND UPPER BOURGEOISIE

For nobility as landlords and agriculturalists see also Section 7; and on political role and employment as bureaucra and soldiers, Section 10. On entrepreneurial activity and participation in commerce see Section 9.

6.42 **Billacois**, F., 'La crise de la noblesse européenne, 1550-1650', *Rev.Hist.Mod.et Contemp.*, 23, 1976, 258-77. Literature survey.

6.43 **Burke**, P., *Venice and Amsterdam. A Study of Seventeenth-Century Elites*, 1974. Excellent short comparison of these markedly differing ruling classes.

6.44 **Bush**, M. L., *Noble Privilege*, 1983. Invaluable comparative study, arranged by type of privilege, and ranging widely in geography and chronology.

6.45 **Cooper**, J. P., 'Patterns of inheritance and settlement by great landowners from the fifteenth to the eighteenth centuries', in Goody and others (5.321), 192-327. Extensive survey of entails, family settlements, and marriage portions of aristocracy in England, Castile, France, and Italy.

6.46 **Cowan**, A. F., *The Urban Patriciate. Lübeck and Venice, 1580-1700*, Köln, 1986. Another first-class comparative work, based on extensive archival research for both cities. Begins with useful discussion on identification of this class.

6.47 'Études sur la noblesse', *Acta Poloniae Hist.*, 36, 1977, 5-176. Essays on French and Polish nobilities, mainly in early modern period arising from Franco-Polish symposium at Lublin, 1975.

6.48 **Goodwin**, A., ed., *The European Nobility in the Eighteenth Century. Studies of the Nobilities of the Major European States in the Pre-Reform Era*, 1953. Essays on France, Spain, Lombardy, Prussia, Austria, Hungary, Sweden, Poland, and Russia.

6.49 **Jones**, M., ed., *Gentry and Lesser Nobility in Late Medieval Europe*, 1986. Relevant essays on Netherlands and France (two each), Castile, Germany.

6.50 **Köpeczi**, B., and Balázs, Eva H., eds., *Noblesse Française, Noblesse Hongroise, 16e-19e Siècles*, Budapest, 1981. Conference proceedings. All papers in French.

6.51 **Labatut**, J. P., *Les Noblesses Européennes de la Fin du 15e Siècle à la Fin du 18e Siècle*, Paris, 1978. Studies hierarchy, values, and relation to state – but with tendency to regard France as paradigmatic.

6.52 **Meyer**, J., *Noblesses et Pouvoirs dans l'Europe d'Ancien Régime*, Paris, 1973. Divided into thematic (part 1) and area sections(part 2).

6.53 **Vierhaus**, R., ed., *Der Adel vor der Revolution*, Göttingen, 1971. Comprises three essays, on French, Polish, and German aristocracies of eighteenth century.

6.54 **Woolf**, S., 'The aristocracy in transition. A continental comparison', *Ec.Hist.Rev.*, 2nd ser., 23, 1970, 520-31. Review of Lawrence Stone's work on Elizabethan and early Stuart peerage, *Crisis of the Aristocracy*, pointing to parallels and contrasts elsewhere in Europe.

FRANCE
See also 5.488,494-5; 6.47,49,50,53; 7.335.

6.55 **Barber**, Elinor G., *The Bourgeoisie in Eighteenth-Century France*, Princeton, N.J., 1955. Brief, conceptual study, with emphasis on conflicting appeals of hierarchy and mobility.

6.56 **Behrens**, Betty, 'Nobles, privileges, and taxes in France at the end of the ancien régime', *Ec.Hist.Rev.*, 2nd ser., 15, 1963, 451-75. Argues that nobility was, in practice, by no means immune from taxation. See criticism of this view by G. J. Cavanaugh, *Fr.Hist.Stud.*, 8, 1974, 681-92; and further debate, *ib.*, 9, 1976, 521-31.

6.57 **Bitton**, D., *The French Nobility in Crisis, 1560-1640*, Stanford, Calif., 1969. Study of public opinion and polemic about noble status, rather than of nobility's economic position.

6.58 **Blacker**, J. G. C., 'Social ambitions of the bourgeoisie in eighteenth-century France, and their relation to family limitation', *Pop.Stud.*, 11, 1957, 46-63. Postulates connection between need for capital (to finance office-holding or noble life style) and spread of family limitation. Not supported by any empirical investigation.

59 **Bluche**, F., *La Vie Quotidienne de la Noblesse Française au 18e Siècle*, Paris, 1973. Good popularisation.

.60 **Bohanan**, Donna, 'The education of nobles in seventeenth-century Aix-en-Provence', *J.Soc.Hist.*, 20, 1987, 757-64. Briefly indicates graduations at Aix University, and contents of some aristocratic libraries.

.61 —— 'Matrimonial strategies among nobles of seventeenth-century Aix-en-Provence', *ib.*, 19, 1986, 503-10. Chiefly illustrates frequency of alliance between old and new aristocracy.

.62 *La Bourgeoisie Alsacienne. Études d'Histoire Sociale*, Strasbourg, 1954. Substantial volume of essays on capitalist and professional elite since late medieval period.

.63 **Chaussinand-Nogaret**, G., *The French Nobility in the Eighteenth Century. From Feudalism to Enlightenment*, 1985. Transl. from French ed. of 1976.

.64 ——, ed., *Histoire des Élites, 1700-1848. Recueil de Textes*, Paris, 1975. Reader consisting of extracts from such historians as J. Tulard, F. Bluche, R. Forster.

.65 **Constant**, J.-M., *La Vie Quotidienne de la Noblesse Française aux 16e-17e Siècles*, Paris, 1985. Partly based on author's thesis on nobility of Beauce region.

.66 **Crouzet**, D., 'Recherches sur la crise de l'aristocratie en France au 16e siècle. Les dettes de la Maison de Nevers', *Hist.Ec.et Soc.*, 1, 1982, 7-50. On finances of one of most important French ducal families.

.67 **Devyver**, A., *Le Sang Épuré. Les Préjugés de Race chez les Gentilshommes Français de l'Ancien Régime, 1560-1720*, Brussels, 1973. Lengthy study of defences of blue blood.

.68 **Deyon**, P., 'Relations between the French nobility and the absolute monarchy during the first half of the seventeenth century', in R. F. Kierstead, ed., *State and Society in Seventeenth-Century France*, New York, 1975, 25-43. Transl. from *Rev.Hist.*, 231, 1964, 341-56. Repr. in P. J. Coveney, ed., *France in Crisis, 1620-75*, 1977, 231-46. Sees level of fiscal pressure as key to restiveness of nobility.

.69 **Di Corcia**, J., '*Bourg, bourgeois, bourgeois de Paris* from the eleventh to the eighteenth century', *J.Mod.Hist.*, 50, 1978, 207-33. Defines obligations and privileges of those Parisians having status of *bourgeois* – and shows that these overlapped in many respects with attributes of nobility. See also 6.105.

6.70 **Diefendorf**, Barbara B., *Paris City Councillors in the Sixteenth Century. The Politics of Patrimony*, Princeton, N.J., 1983. Prosopography of ninety councillors nominated between 1535 and 1575.

6.71 **Doyle**, W., 'Was there an aristocratic reaction in pre-Revolutionary France?', *P.&P.*, 57, 1972, 97-122. Repr. in D. Johnson, ed., *French Society and the Revolution*, 1976, 3-28. Finds no marked change in aims or practices of nobility which justify this term.

6.72 **Du Puy de Clinchamps**, P., *La Noblesse*, Paris, 1959. Brief primer, concentrating on legal aspects.

6.73 **Ellis**, H. A., 'Genealogy, history, and aristocratic reaction in early eighteenth-century France. The case of Henri de Boulainvilliers', *J.Mod.Hist.*, 58, 1986, 414-51. How Norman seigneur saw position of nobility and reasons for its perceived decline.

6.74 **Ford**, F. L., *Robe and Sword. The Regrouping of the French Aristocracy after Louis XIV*, Cambridge, Mass., 1953. Portrays high Robe as tactical and intellectual leaders of eighteenth-century aristocracy, with which they were now almost totally assimilated.

6.75 **Forster**, R., *The House of Saulx-Tavannes. Versailles and Burgundy, 1700-1830*, Baltimore, Md., 1971. How one important aristocratic family lived, spent, managed its estates, and fared in the Revolution.

6.76 —— *Merchants, Landlords, Magistrates. The Depont Family in Eighteenth-Century France*, Baltimore, Md., 1980. Case study of social mobility, showing rise of La Rochelle merchant family into bureaucracy and landed gentry.

6.77 —— *The Nobility of Toulouse in the Eighteenth Century. A Social and Economic Study*, Baltimore, Md., 1960. Looks at both Robe and Sword in city and surrounding countryside.

6.78 —— 'The provincial noble. A reappraisal', *Am.Hist.Rev.*, 68, 1963, 681-91. Shows us "active, shrewd, and prosperous landlords" rather than poverty-stricken *hobereaux* in Toulouse region.

6.79 **Goodwin**, A., 'Social origins and privileged status of the French eighteenth-century nobility', *Bull.J.Rylands Lib.*, 47,

1965, 382-403. Tends to play down extent of privilege and exclusiveness.

6.80 —— 'Social structure and economic and political attitudes of the French nobility in the eighteenth century', in *Reports Twelfth International Congress of Historical Sciences*, Vienna, 1965, 1, 356-68.

6.81 **Hunt**, L. A., 'Local elites at the end of the old regime. Troyes and Reims, 1750-89', *Fr.Hist.Stud.*, 9, 1976, 379-99. Describes restricted access to city councils and *baillage* offices, and residential patterns.

6.82 **Huppert**, G., *Les Bourgeois Gentilshommes. An Essay on the Definition of Elites in Renaissance France*, Chicago, 1977. Deals with Robe and higher clerics, i.e. professional elite who lacked noblesse de race.

6.83 **Jouanna**, Arlette, *L'Idée de Race en France au 16e Siècle et au Début du 17e Siècle (1498-1614)*, 3 vols., Lille, 1976. Large-scale doctoral thesis on propagation of notion that nobility's privileges spring from inherited virtues (courage, ability to judge, etc.).

6.84 **Kalas**, R. J., 'The Selve family of Limousin. Members of a new elite in early modern France', *Sixteenth-Cent.J.*, 18, 1987, 147-72. Case study of upward mobility.

6.85 **Labatut**, J. P., *Les Ducs et Pairs de France au 17e Siècle. Étude Sociale*, Paris, 1972. On highest echelon of French nobility.

6.86 **Le Roy Ladurie**, E., 'In Normandy's woods and fields', in Le Roy Ladurie (4.35), 133-71. Transl. of his introduction to journal of Sire du Gouberville, country gentleman of mid-sixteenth century (reissue of Tollemer's edition of 1873). See also 6.102.

6.87 **Levy**, C., and Henry, L., 'Ducs et pairs sous l'ancien régime. Caractéristiques démographiques d'une caste', *Population*, 15, 1960, 807-30. Demography of over 50 families between 1650 and 1800.

6.88 **Major**, J. R., 'Crown and aristocracy in Renaissance France', *Am.Hist.Rev.*, 69, 1964, 631-45. Looks principally at clientage system of fifteenth-seventeenth centuries.

6.89 —— 'Noble income, inflation, and the Wars of Religion in France', *ib.*, 86, 1981, 21-48. Largely based on experiences of Albret family. Contends there is little reason to believe nobility lost its relative position.

6.90 **Meyer**, J., *La Noblesse Bretonne au 18e Siècle*, 2 vols., Paris, 1966. Richly documented account of all levels of nobility, their revenues and mode of life.

6.91 **Mousnier**, R., and others, eds., *Problèmes de Stratification Sociale. Deux Cahiers de la Noblesse pour les États Généraux de 1649-51*, Paris, 1965. Mousnier's introduction is a preliminary draft of his work on social hierarchies (6.8).

6.92 **Neuschel**, K. B., 'The Picard nobility in the sixteenth century', *Proc.Western Soc.Fr.Hist.*, 9, 1981, 42-9. Short account of Condé family's clientage.

6.93 **Nicolas**, J., *La Savoie au 18e Siècle. Noblesse et Bourgeoisie*, 2 vols., Paris, 1978. Sorbonne doctoral thesis, with luxuriant description of property, family structure, and mental world of Savoyard elite.

6.94 **Reinhard**, M., 'Élite et noblesse dans la seconde moitié du 18e siècle', *Rev. Hist. Mod. et Contemp.*, 3, 1956, 5-37. Tries to assess elements of rupture and continuity between elites of old regime and Napoleonic France.

6.95 **Roche**, D., 'Aperçus sur la fortune et les revenus des princes de Condé à l'aube du 18e siècle', *Rev.Hist.Mod.et Contemp.*, 14, 1967, 217-43.

6.96 —— 'Recherches sur la noblesse parisienne au milieu du 18e siècle. La noblesse du Marais', *Actes Congrès Nat.Soc.Savantes*, 86, 1961, 541-78. Details on nobility with residences in Marais quarter, whether Robe or Sword, property outside Paris, etc.

6.97 **Salmon**, J. H. M., 'Storm over the noblesse', *J.Mod.Hist.*, 53, 1981, 242-57. Review essay, discussing treatment of relations between Robe and Sword in Mousnier's *Institutions of France* (3.15) and other recent works.

6.98 **Schalk**, E., *From Valor to Pedigree. Ideas of Nobility in France in the Sixteenth and Seventeenth Centuries*, Princeton, N.J., 1986. Argues that at beginning of period nobility was regarded as coterminous with military profession; only gradually did hereditary caste aspect come to be emphasised. Following entries stem from research.

6.99 —— 'The appearance and reality of nobility in France during the Wars of Religion. An example of how collective attitudes can change', *J.Mod.Hist.*, 48, 1976, 19-31.

6.100 —— 'Ennoblement in France from 1350 to 1660', *J.Soc.Hist.*, 16 (ii), 1982, 101-10. Brief statistical treatment based on ennoblements registered in the Paris Chambre des Comptes.

6.101 **Sturdy**, D. J., 'Tax evasion, the *faux nobles*, and state fiscalism. The example of the Généralité of Caen, 1634-35', *Fr.Hist.Stud.*, 9, 1976, 549-72. Interesting example of an enquiry into titles (and hence tax exemptions) of nobility; about eleven per cent of families examined found to be unjustifiably claiming status.

6.102 **Teall**, Elizabeth, 'The myth of royal centralization and the reality of neighbourhood. The journals of the Sire de Gouberville, 1549-62', in Miriam U. Chrisman and O. Gründler, eds., *Social Groups and Religious Ideas in the Sixteenth Century*, Kalamazoo, Mich., 1978, 1-11. On informal authority and leadership displayed by a local seigneur. See also 6.86.

6.103 —— 'The seigneur of Renaissance France. Advocate or oppressor?', *J.Mod.Hist.*, 37, 1965, 131-50. Comments on paternalism of nobility – ideal and reality.

6.104 **Temple**, Nora, 'Municipal elections and municipal oligarchies in eighteenth-century France', in J. F. Bosher, ed., *French Government and Society, 1500-1850*, 1973, 70-91.

6.105 **Vovelle**, M., and Roche, D., 'Bourgeois, rentiers, propriétaires. Éléments pour la définition d'une catégorie sociale à la fin du 18e siècle', *Actes Congrès Nat. Soc. Savantes*, 84, 1959, 419-52. Uses notarial documents from Chartres and Marais quarter of Paris to investigate legal meaning of ascription "bourgeois" (term which, in this sense, ended with Revolution).

6.106 **Weary**, W. A., 'The House of La Trémoille, fifteenth through eighteenth centuries', *J.Mod.Hist.*, 49, 1977, 1001-38 (on demand article). Emphasises importance of long-term perspective in assessing adequacy of a noble family's economic base.

6.107 **Wiley**, W. L., *The Gentleman of Renaissance France*, Cambridge, Mass., 1954. Portrait of way of life, mainly derived from literary sources.

6.108 **Wood**, J. B., *The Nobility of the Élection of Bayeux, 1463-1666*, Princeton, 1980. Argues that nobility, at least in this area, consolidated its wealth, absorbed newcomers without tension, and was not in state of crisis. Review article: A. Grant, *Eur.Stud.Rev.*, 12, 1982, 87-95. See following articles for material from this study.

6.109 —— 'Demographic pressure and social mobility among the nobility of early modern France', *Sixteenth-Cent.J.*, 8 (i), 1977, 3-16.

6.110 —— 'The decline of the nobility in sixteenth- and early seventeenth-century France: myth or reality?', *J.Mod.Hist.*, 48, 1976, on demand article.

6.111 —— 'Endogamy and *mésalliance*. The marriage patterns of the nobility of the Élection of Bayeux, 1430-1669', *Fr.Hist.Stud.*, 10, 1978, 375-92.

LOW COUNTRIES
See also 6.43,49; 13.61.

6.112 **Lamet**, S. A., 'The *vroedschap* of Leiden, 1550-1600. The impact of tradition and change on the governing elite of a Dutch city', *Sixteenth-Cent.J.*, 12 (ii), 1981, 15-42.

6.113 **Marshall**, Sherrin, *The Dutch Gentry, 1500-1650. Family, Faith, and Fortune*, New York, 1987. Data mostly from Utrecht province. Concentrates particularly on family relations and experience of women; material also on impact of Netherlands Revolt.

6.114 —— [as S. Marshall Wyntjes], 'Raising hell or raising the rent. The gentry's response to inflation in sixteenth-century Holland and Utrecht', in N. Schmukler and E. Marcus, eds., *Inflation through the Ages*, New York, 1983, 170-82. Examines flexibility of gentry incomes and possible role of financial difficulties in Netherlands Revolt.

6.115 **Muinck**, B. E. de, 'A regent's family budget about the year 1700', *Acta Hist.Neerlandica*, 2, 1967, 222-32. Summary of Dutch-language book publ. in 1965.

6.116 **Roorda**, D. J., 'Ruling classes in Holland in the seventeenth century', in J. S. Bromley and E. H. Kossman, eds., *Britain and the Netherlands*, 2, Groningen, 1964, 109-32. Discusses urban patriciate of province of Holland (i.e. not United Provinces in general).

SPAIN
See also 3.117; 6.45,49.

6.117 **Amelang**, J. S., *Honored Citizens of Barcelona. Patrician Culture and Class Relations, 1490-1714*, Princeton, N.J., 1986. Important study with enlightening comparative perspective; concentrates esp. on patrician views of hierarchy and class identity.

6.118 **Atienza Hernandez**, I., 'La "quiebra" de la nobleza castellana en el siglo 17. Autoridad real y poder señorial. El secuestro de los bienes de la Casa de Osuna', *Hispania*, 156, 1984, 49-81. Case study of debt problems of grandees and their dependence on Crown for rescue. Cf. 6.125.

6.119 **Domínguez Ortiz**, A., *Las Clases Privilegiadas en la España del Antiguo Régimen*, Madrid, 1973. About equally divided between noble and clerical estates.

6.120 **Gerbet**, Marie-C., *La Noblesse dans le Royaume de Castille. Étude sur les Structures Sociales en Estrémadure de 1454 à 1516*, Paris, 1979.

6.121 **Haliczer**, S., 'The Castilian aristocracy and the mercedes reform of 1478-82', *Hisp.Am.Hist.Rev.*, 55, 1975, 449-67. Argues that resumption of these grants of Crown revenues was not aimed at weakening noble incomes.

6.122 **Highfield**, J. R. L., 'The De La Cerda, the Pimentel, and the so-called "price revolution" ', *Eng.Hist.Rev.*, 87, 1972, 495-512. Finances of two grandee families in period 1490-1550.

6.123 **Hiltpold**, P., 'Noble status and urban privilege. Burgos, 1572', *Sixteenth-Cent.J.*, 12 (iv), 1981, 21-44. Examines differences within municipal council over tax privileges of nobles.

6.124 **Jago**, C., ' "Crisis of the aristocracy" in seventeenth-century Castile', *P.& P.*, 84, 1979, 60-90. Study of finances of Dukes of Bejar.

6.125 —— 'The influence of debt on the relations between Crown and aristocracy in seventeenth-century Castile', *Ec. Hist. Rev.*, 2nd ser., 26, 1973, 218-36. Argues that Crown enhanced its power through ability to aid noble debtors by various legal strategems. For example see 6.118.

6.126 **Lambert-Gorges**, Martine, *Basques et Navarrais dans l'Ordre de Santiago (1580-1620)*, Paris, 1985. Material on Basque nobility derived from enquiries held on applicants for membership of Order. See also her article on nature of these enquiries, *Mél.Casa de Velazquez*, 18, 1982, 165-98.

6.127 **Liehr**, R., *Sozialgeschichte Spanischer Adelskorporationen. Die Maestranzas de Caballería (1670-1808)*, Wiesbaden, 1981. On noble fraternities, active principally in organisation of festivals and horsemanship training (including bullfights), and to some extent in general education.

6.128 **Maravall**, J. A., *Poder, Honor, y Elites en el Siglo 17*, Madrid, 1979. Collection of essays dealing with theme of honour in Spanish society, and with nobility's justification of its own status and privileges.

6.129 **Molinié-Bertrand**, Annie, 'Les "hidalgos" dans le Royaume de Castile à la fin du 16e siècle. Approche carto-graphique', *Rev.Hist.Ec.et Soc.*, 52, 1974, 51-82. Based on tax document of 1591 showing distribution of noble households.

6.130 **Nader**, Helen, *The Mendoza family in the Spanish Renaissance, 1350-1550*, New Brunswick, N.J., 1979. Devoted mostly to family's part in literary and political culture, but draws also on estate papers. Her 'Noble income in sixteenth-century Castile. The case of the Marquises of Mondejar, 1480-1580', *Ec.Hist.Rev.*, 2nd ser., 30, 1977, 411-28, shows how one branch of family was able to maintain real income.

6.131 **Owens**, J. B., 'Diana at the bar. Hunting, aristocrats, and the law in Renaissance Castile', *Sixteenth-Cent.J.*, 8 (i), 1977, 17-36. Account of a lawyer's cautionary book about hunting abuses. For hunting privileges of German nobility, see 6.179.

6.132 **Thompson**, I. A. A., 'Neo-noble nobility. Concepts of *hidalguía* in early modern Castile', *Eur.Hist.Q.*, 15, 1985, 379-406. Examines justifications put forward by recipients of ennoblement charters obtained from Crown.

6.133 —— 'Purchase of nobility in Castile, 1552-1700', *J.Eur.Ec.Hist.*, 8, 1979, 313-60. Suggests that less than 300 patents of nobility were sold in this period, since price was so high that it did not pay in terms of tax privileges. See comment by J. S. Amelang, *ib.*, 11, 1982, 219-26.

6.134 **Wright**, L. P., 'Military orders in sixteenth- and seventeenth-century Spanish society', *P.& P.*, 43, 1969, 34-70.

Stresses importance of knighthood in these orders as proof of social prestige and racial purity. Cf. 6.126.

ITALY
See also 3.158; 5.168,372,377,380,503; 6.43,46; 7.141; 13.138; 14.190.

6.135 **Capra**, C., 'Nobili, notabili, élites. Dal "modello" francese al caso italiano', *Quad.Stor.*, 37, 1978, 12-47. Seeks to identify differences in ruling castes of France and Italy.

6.136 **Cipolla**, C. M., 'The professions. The long view', *J.Eur.Ec.Hist.*, 2, 1973, 37-52. Makes some attempt to quantify numbers of lawyers and doctors practising in various Italian towns between thirteenth and seventeenth centuries.

6.137 **Martines**, L., 'The gentleman in Renaissance Italy. Strains of isolation in the body politic', in R. S. Kinsman, ed., *The Darker Vision of the Renaissance. Beyond the Fields of Reason*, Berkeley, Calif., 1974, 77-93. Background to Castiglione's *Book of the Courtier*.

6.138 **Mozzarelli**, C., and Schiera, P., eds., *Patriziati e Aristocrazie Nobiliari. Ceti Dominanti e Organizzazione del Potere nell'Italia Centro-Settentrionale dal 16 al 18 Secolo*, Trento, 1978. Symposium mainly dealing with urban aristocracies.

6.139 **Tagliaferri**, A., ed., *I Ceti Dirigenti in Italia nell'Età Moderna e Contemporanea*, Udine, 1984. Symposium. Majority of papers deal with nobility of Veneto. Note also useful comparison of Florentine and Piedmontese elites in seventeenth century by E. Stumpo.

6.140 **Baker**, G. F., 'The "antiquarian" Francesco Piccolomini and the crisis of the Sienese nobility at the turn of the eighteenth century', *Rassegna Arch.di Stato*, 31, 1971, 690-701. Piccolomini compiled memoranda on decline in numbers and quality of his fellow patricians.

6.141 —— 'Nobiltà in declino. Il caso di Siena sotto i Medici e gli Asburgo-Lorena', *Riv.Stor.Ital.*, 84, 1972, 584-616. Longitudinal study covering period 1560-1779. Preceding article provides subjective perspective.

6.142 **Berner**, S., 'The Florentine patriciate in the transition from republic to *principato*, 1530-1609', *Stud.in Med.& Renaiss.Hist.*, 9, 1972, 3-15.

6.143 **Bizzocchi**, R., 'La dissoluzione di un clan familiare. I Buondelmonti di Firenze nei secoli 15 e 16', *Arch.Stor.Ital.*, 140, 1982, 3-46. On difficulties of sustaining noble family fortune because of inheritance partitions.

6.144 **Cooper**, Roslyn P., 'The Florentine ruling group under the "governo populare", 1494-1512', *Stud.Med.& Renaiss.Hist.*, n.s., 7, 1985, 69-181. Detailed prosopographical study.

6.145 **Goldthwaite**, R. A., 'The Florentine palace as domestic architecture', *Am.Hist.Rev.*, 77, 1972, 977-1012. Examines palazzi as evidence for patricians' way of life and domestic arrangements.

6.146 —— *Private Wealth in Renaissance Florence. A Study of Four Families*, Princeton, N.J., 1968. On four patrician families in fifteenth and sixteenth centuries.

6.147 **Hurtubise**, P., *Une Famille-Témoin. Les Salviati*, Rome, 1985. Exceptionally thorough longitudinal study of Florentine-Roman noble family, deriving much of its prestige from high Church office.

6.148 **Kent**, F. W., *Household and Lineage in Renaissance Florence. The Family Life of the Capponi, Ginori, and Rucellai*, Princeton, N.J., 1977. On patrician family clans. Mainly fifteenth century evidence. Review article: A. Molho, *J.Mod.Hist.*, 50, 1978, 304-11; see also 3.182.

6.149 **Malanima**, P., *I Riccardi di Firenze. Una Famiglia e un Patrimonio nella Toscana dei Medici*, Florence, 1977. Charts social ascent of originally modest family.

6.150 **Grendi**, E., 'Capitazioni e nobiltà genovese in età moderna', *Quad.Stor.*, 26, 1974, 403-44. On increasingly closed nature of Genoan aristocracy, and its wealth as compared to other classes of city.

6.151 **Bueno de Mesquita**, D. M., 'Ludovico Sforza and his vassals', in E. F. Jacob, ed., *Italian Renaissance Studies*, 1960, 184-216. Deals with principal Lombard families in later fifteenth century.

6.152 **Pino**, F., 'Patriziato e decurionato a Milano nel secolo 18', *Società e Storia*, 5, 1979, 339-78.

6.153 **Zanetti**, D. E., 'The *patriziato* of Milan from the domination of Spain to the unification of Italy. An outline of the social and demographic history', *Soc.Hist.*, [1],

6.154 **Woolf**, S. J., 'Economic problems of the nobility in the early modern period. The example of Piedmont', *Ec.Hist.Rev.*, 2nd ser., 17, 1964, 267-83. Finds little evidence that problems were very severe. For more detailed treatment see following entry.

6.155 —— *Studi sulla Nobiltà Piemontese nell'Epoca dell'Assolutismo*, Turin, 1963. Studies of three noble families and their fortunes in seventeenth and eighteenth centuries. Review article: R. Forster and R. B. Litchfield, *Comp.Stud.Soc.& Hist.*, 7, 1965, 324-32.

6.156 **Coffin**, D. R., *The Villa in the Life of Renaissance Rome*, Princeton, N.J., 1979. Principally architectural history; administrative aspects and social impact touched on in a minor way.

6.157 **Kolsky**, S., 'Culture and politics in Renaissance Rome. Marco Antonio Altieri's Roman weddings', *Renaiss.Q.*, 40, 1987, 49-90. Examines early sixteenth-century marriage treatise for light it sheds on social preoccupations of Roman patrician.

6.158 **Beltrami**, D., *Forze di Lavoro e Proprietà Fondiaria nelle Campagne Venete dei Secoli 17 e 18. La Penetrazione economica dei Veneziani in Terraferma*, Venice, 1961. Deals with switch from commercial to landed investment by Venetian patriciate. See useful summary by S. J. Woolf, 'Venice and the Terraferma. Problems of the change from commercial to landed activities', in Pullan (3.156), 174-203.

6.159 **Borelli**, G., *Un Patriziato della Terraferma Veneta tra 17 e 18 Secolo. Ricerche sulla Nobiltà Veronese*, Milan, 1974. Major section of book is a survey, alphabetically ordered, of 29 leading families of Verona.

6.160 **Chojnacki**, S., 'Kinship ties and young patricians in fifteenth-century Venice', *Renaiss.Q.*, 38, 1985, 240-70. Looks at registrations for *Balla d'Oro* (lottery for choosing early entrants to Grand Council) between 1408 and 1497.

6.161 **Cowan**, A., 'Rich and poor among the patriciate in early modern Venice', *Studi Veneziani*, n.s., 6, 1982, 147-60. Perceives considerable increase in relatively poor patricians from late sixteenth century onwards.

6.162 **Davis**, J. C., *The Decline of the Venetian Nobility as a Ruling Class*, Baltimore, Md., 1962. Deals with shrinking demographic and economic base of "Venetian oligarchy".

6.163 —— *A Venetian Family and its Fortune, 1500-1900. The Donà and the Conservation of their Wealth*, Philadelphia, 1975. Preservation of this family's papers permits unusual study in continuity of wealth.

6.164 **Dooley**, B., 'Crisis and survival in eighteenth-century Italy. The Venetian patriciate strikes back', *J.Soc.Hist.*, 20, 1986, 323-34. Presents some evidence of economic and intellectual adaptability.

6.165 **Pullan**, B., 'Occupation and investments of the Venetian nobility in the middle and late sixteenth century', in Hale (5.167), 379-408. Based on petitions to Senate of some 140 patrician families.

6.166 —— 'Service to the Venetian state. Aspects of myth and reality in the early seventeenth century', *Studi Secenteschi*, 5, 1964, 95-147. Substantial essay on opportunities of Venetian aristocracy in commerce, state service, and the Church.

6.167 **Queller**, D. E., *The Venetian Patriciate. Reality versus Myth*, Urbana, Ill., 1986. Devoted to demonstrating that governing class was as corrupt in fourteenth and fifteenth centuries as in late Republic. Principally a study of political conduct.

6.168 **Rapp**, R. T., 'Real estate and rational investment in early modern Venice', *J.Eur.Ec.Hist.*, 8, 1979, 269-90. Case study of Alberto Gozzi, magnate who divided his investments about equally between land and commerce.

6.169 **Ventura**, A., *Nobiltà e Popolo nella Società Veneta del '400 e '500*, Bari, 1964. Sees society and politics throughout Venetian territories as increasingly dominated by aristocratic interests and values.

6.170 **Aymard**, M., 'Une famille de l'aristocratie sicilienne aux 16e et 17e siècles. Les ducs de Terranova', *Rev.Hist.*, 247, 1972, 29-66. Charts building up of large-scale landed domain, largely by marriage and inheritance, and its generally successful exploitation.

6.171 **Davies**, T., *Famiglie Feudali Siciliane. Patrimoni, Redditi, Investimenti, tra '500 e '600*, Rome, 1985. Investigates financial management of four major aristocratic families.

6.172 **Labrot**, G., 'Le comportement collectif de

l'aristocratie napolitaine du 16e au 18e siècle', *Rev.Hist.*, 258, 1977, 45-71. Deals with style of life of aristocracy which adopted urban residence as norm. For fuller development, see his *Baroni in Città. Residenza e Comportamenti dell'Aristocrazia Napoletana, 1503-1734*, Naples, 1980.

GERMANY, SWITZERLAND, AND AUSTRIA
See also 5.178,394; 6.7,46,49,53; 14.204,207.

6.173 **Asch**, J., *Rat und Bürgerschaft in Lübeck, 1598-1669. Die Verfassungsrechtlichen Auseinandersetzungen im 17. Jahrhundert und ihre Sozialen Hintergründe*, Lübeck, 1961. On political and social challenge to Hanseatic city's governing oligarchy.

6.174 **Bátori**, Ingrid, and Weyrauch, E., *Die Bürgerliche Elite der Stadt Kitzingen. Studien zur Sozial- und Wirtschaftsgeschichte einer Landesherrlichen Stadt im 16. Jahrhundert*, Stuttgart, 1982. Detailed prosopographical exercise.

6.175 **Benecke**, G., 'Ennoblement and privilege in early modern Germany', *History*, 56, 1971, 360-70. On devolved system of selling honours and patents via Imperial *Hofpfalzgrafen*.

6.176 **Berdahl**, R. M., 'The *Stände* and the origins of conservatism in Prussia', *Eighteenth-Cent.Stud.*, 6, 1973, 298-321. Argues that late eighteenth-century Prussian aristocracy was constructing a static social philosophy just as its economic circumstances were changing radically.

6.177 **Brady**, T. A., 'Patricians, nobles, merchants. Internal tensions and solidarities in South German urban ruling classes at the close of the Middle Ages', in Chrisman and Gründler (6.102), 38-45. Argues that dominance of guilds did not imply any gulf between merchants and nobles, who were closely interlocked by marriage, investment, land purchase, etc.

6.178 **Brunner**, O., *Adeliges Landleben und Europäischer Geist. Leben und Werk Wolf Helmhards von Hohberg, 1612-88*, Salzburg, 1949. Austrian country gentleman used as focus for essay on noble values and traditions.

6.179 **Eckardt**, H. W., *Herrschaftliche Jagd, Bäuerliche Not, und Bürgerliche Kritik. Zur Geschichte der Fürstlichen und Adligen Jagdprivilegien vornehmlich im Südwestdeutschen Raum*, Göttingen, 1976. Emphasis on criticism and abolition of game laws (Württemberg and Baden). See 6.131 for hunting in Spanish context.

6.180 **Glas-Hochstettler**, T. J., 'The Imperial Knights in post-Westphalian Mainz. A case study of corporatism in the Old Reich', *Central Eur.Hist.*, 11, 1978, 131-49. Study of families who monopolised positions in Chapter and electoral court of Mainz.

6.181 **Guyer**, P., *Die Soziale Schichtung der Bürgerschaft Zürichs vom Ausgang des Mittelalters bis 1798*, Zürich, 1952. Short study examining social composition of citizenry and corporation at intervals between 1600 and 1800.

6.182 **Hahn**, P.-M., *Struktur und Funktion des Brandenburgischen Adels im 16. Jahrhundert*, Berlin, 1979. Useful synthesis, arguing among other things that narrow elite shared power with Margrave via loans to ruler.

6.183 **Hintze**, O., 'The Hohenzollern and the nobility', in F. Gilbert, ed., *The Historical Essays of Otto Hintze*, New York, 1975, 33-63. Originally publ. in *Hist.Zeitschr.*, 112, 1914, 494-524. Sketches relations over several centuries, giving somewhat idealised view of evolution into state servants in eighteenth century. Compare with Rosenberg (10.341).

6.184 **Hitchcock**, W. R., *Background of the Knights' Revolt, 1522-23*, Berkeley, Calif., 1958. Outlines grievances of Imperial Freiherren. For an E. German view, see M. Meyer, 'Sickingen, Hutten, und die reichsritterschaftlichen Bewegungen', *Jb.Gesch.Feudalismus*, 7, 1983, 215-46.

6.185 **Kramm**, H., *Studien über die Oberschichten der Mitteldeutschen Städte im 16. Jahrhundert. Sachsen, Thuringen, Anhalt*, 2 vols., Köln, 1981. Mine of information on crafts and guilds, residential patterns, etc.

6.186 **Lampe**, J., *Aristokratie, Hofadel, und Staatspatriziat in Kurhannover. Die Lebenskreise der Höheren Beamten an den Kurhannoverschen Zentral- und Hofbehörden, 1714-60*, 2 vols., Göttingen, 1963. Excellent study of court society, with substantial genealogical appendix.

6.187 **Legates**, Marlene J., 'The Knights and the problems of political organizing in sixteenth-century Germany', *Central Eur.Hist.*, 7, 1974, 99-136. On cantonal organisation of Franconian gentry; useful sidelight on corporate bonds among elite.

6.188 —— 'Princes, parliaments, and privilege. German research in European context', *Eur.Stud.Rev.*, 10, 1980, 151-76. Contrasts Bavaria and Franconia to show that though political power of nobility might vary widely, similarities of privilege and status were more significant.

6.189 **Liebel**, Helen P., 'The bourgeoisie in Southwestern Germany, 1500-1789. A rising class?', *Int.Rev.Soc.Hist.*, 10, 1965, 283-307. Paints static picture of patrician class monopolising government and professions in Imperial cities and Württemberg towns.

6.190 **Messmer**, K., and Hoppe, P., *Luzerner Patriziat. Sozial- und Wirtschaftsgeschichtliche Studien zur Entstehung und Entwicklung im 16. und 17. Jahrhundert*, Luzern, 1976. Two separate studies, not originally meant for joint publication, but with joint bibliography.

6.191 **Nicolini**, Ingrid, *Die Politische Führungsschicht in der Stadt Köln gegen Ende der Reichsstädtischen Zeit*, Köln, 1979. Good on power stucture, but lacks economic and cultural dimensions.

6.192 **Richarz**, Irmintraut, *Herrschaftliche Haushalte in Vorindustrieller Zeit im Weserraum*, Berlin, 1971. Stresses importance of agricultural market for income and consumption of manorial lords in seventeenth and eighteenth centuries.

6.193 **Rössler**, H., ed., *Deutscher Adel, 1430-1740. Büdinger Vortrage, 1963-64*, 2 vols., Darmstadt, 1965. Essays from two colloquia; dividing line between vols. is 1555.

6.194 —— *Deutsches Patriziat, 1430-1740. Büdinger Vorträge, 1965*, Limburg, 1968. Another valuable symposium.

6.195 **Turner**, R. S., 'The *Bildungsbürgertum* and the learned professions in Prussia, 1770-1830', *Histoire Sociale/Social Hist.*, 13, 1980, 105-35.

EASTERN EUROPE (GENERAL)

6.196 **Banac**, I., and Bushkovitch, P., eds., *The Nobility in Russia and Eastern Europe*, New Haven, Conn., 1983. Eight essays, mainly on eighteenth and nineteenth centuries, covering Poland and Hungary as well as Russia.

6.197 **Kann**, R. A., 'Aristocracy in the eighteenth-century Habsburg Empire', *E.Eur.Q.*, 7, 1973, 1-13. Very general (delivered as conference paper).

6.198 **Subtelny**, O., *Domination of Eastern Europe. Native Nobilities and Foreign Absolutism, 1500-1715*, 1986. Studies impact of foreign rule on noble-dominated societies of Hungary, Poland, Moldavia, Ukraine, and Livonia.

BOHEMIA, HUNGARY, AND POLAND
See also 6.47,53 (Poland); 6.50 (Hungary).

6.199 **Odlozilik**, O., 'The nobility of Bohemia, 1620-1740', *E.Eur.Q.*, 7, 1973, 15-30. Principally on political attitudes.

6.200 **Polisensky**, J. V., *War and Society in Europe, 1618-48*, 1978. Mainly on campaigns and diplomacy of Thirty Years' War; but see chap. 9, "Changes in the composition of the Bohemian nobility".

6.201 **Lukowski**, G. T., *The Szlachta and the Confederacy of Radom, 1764-67/68*, Rome, 1977. Interesting analysis of large section of Polish nobility who joined pro-Russian Confederacy.

6.202 **Maczak**, A., 'Money and society in Poland and Lithuania in the sixteenth and seventeenth centuries', *J.Eur.Ec.Hist.*, 5, 1976, 69-104. Deals especially with income and expenses of nobility.

6.203 —— 'The social distribution of landed property in Poland from the sixteenth to the eighteenth century', in *Proc. Third International Conference of Economic History* (5.123), 1, 455-69. Mainly on increasing differentiation within nobility.

6.204 **Opalinski**, E., 'Great Poland's power elite under Sigismund III, 1587-1632. Defining the elite', *Acta Poloniae Hist.*, 42, 1980, 41-66. Indicates those elements of nobility most involved in politics and administration.

6.205 **Pospiech**, A., and Tygielski, W., 'The social role of magnates' courts in Poland', *ib.*, 43, 1981, 75-100. "Court" used here in sense of household serving as administrative headquarters for estates.

6.206 **Roos**, H., 'The Polish nobility in prerevolutionary Europe', in W. J. Stankiewicz, ed., *The Tradition of Polish Ideals*, 1981, 85-111. Concentrates mostly on its political role.

BALKANS

6.207 **Georgescu**, V., 'The Romanian boyars in the eighteenth century. Their political ideology', *E.Eur.Q.*, 7, 1973, 31-40. On political status and views of native nobility after imposition of Phanariot governors.

6.208 **Sadat**, D. R., 'Rumeli Ayanlari. The eighteenth century', *J.Mod.Hist.*, 44, 1972, 346-63. Deals with group known as *ayan*, and their transformation from municipal officials into landed aristocracy and warlords.

6.209 **Zlatar**, Z., 'The crisis of the patriciate in early seventeenth-century Dubrovnik', *Balcanica*, 6, 1975, 111-30. Criticises thesis that patriciate had withdrawn from trade and came into conflict with new mercantile class.

SCANDINAVIA

6.210 **Ågren**, K., 'Breadwinners and dependents. An economic crisis in the Swedish aristocracy during the 1600s?', in Ågren and others (5.222), 9-27.

6.211 —— 'Rise and decline of an aristocracy', *Scan.J.Hist.*, 1, 1976, 55-80. Discusses Swedish political elite during seventeenth century, and argues that its cohesiveness (as measured by inter-marriage) had begun to decline by 1680.

6.212 **Christianson**, J. R., 'The reconstruction of the Scandinavian aristocracy, 1350-1660', *Scan.Stud.*, 53, 1981, 289-301. Short bibliographical overview.

6.213 **Elmroth**, I., 'Demography as history. A study of the living conditions of the Swedish nobility from 1600 to 1800', in J. Zitomersky, ed., *On Making Use of History*, Lund, 1982, 179-206. Studies career choices, marriage rates, and size of family, of succesive generations of newly ennobled.

6.214 **Hansen**, S. A., 'Changes in the wealth and the demographic characteristics of the Danish aristocracy, 1470-1720', in *Proc. Third International Conference of Economic History* (5.123), 4, 91-122. Summarises findings of his *Adelsvaeldens Grundlag*, Copenhagen, 1964, especially on decline in marriage rates which followed extensive land sales of seventeenth century.

6.215 **Mörner**, M., 'The evolution of Swedish society, 1620-1920, as reflected in the history of a noble family', *Scan.Stud.*, 52, 1980, 381-413. Demography, properties, professions, etc., of author's own family examined over 40- or 50-year spans.

6.216 **Petersen**, E. L., 'The crisis of the Danish nobility, 1580-1660', in *Social Historians in Contemporary France* (3.4), 156-79. Transl. from *Annales*, 23, 1968, 1237-61.

RUSSIA AND BALTIC PROVINCES
See also 5.459.

6.217 **Alef**, G., *Rulers and Nobles in Fifteenth-Century Muscovy*, 1983. Journal reprints, mostly from *Forsch.zur Osteur.Gesch.*, dealing with political status of aristocracy.

6.218 **Augustine**, W. R., 'Notes toward a portrait of the eighteenth-century Russian nobility', *Can.Slavic Stud.*, 4, 1970, 373-425. Preoccupations of nobility as revealed in grievances drawn up by *uezd* assemblies for Great Commission of 1767-68. See also 6.228,230.

6.219 **Backus**, O. P., 'Mortgages, alienations, and redemptions. The rights in land of the nobility in sixteenth-century Lithuanian and Muscovite law and practice compared', *Forsch.Osteur.Gesch.*, 18, 1973, 139-68. Discusses important aspect of financial and inheritance strategy of nobles.

6.220 —— 'The problem of feudalism in Lithuania, 1506-48', *Slavic Rev.*, 21, 1962, 639-59. Examination of rights and duties of boyars – in particular whether they owed military service for lands.

6.221 **Bennett**, H. A., 'Evolution of the meanings of *chin*...from...Peter the Great's Table of Ranks to the Bolshevik Revolution', *California Slavic Stud.*, 10, 1977, 1-43. First part deals with impact on nobility down to Charter of Nobility in 1785.

6.222 **Confino**, M., 'Histoire et psychologie. A propos de la noblesse russe au 18e siècle', *Annales*, 22, 1967, 1163-1205. Compares Marc Raeff's interpretation (6.239) with classic analysis of Klyuchevskii in part 5 of his *History of Russia*.

6.223 **Crummey**, R. O., *Aristocrats and Servitors. The Boyar Elite in Russia, 1613-89*, Princeton, N.J., 1983. Prosopographical study of military and administrative elite. See also following articles associated with this research.

6.224 —— 'Crown and boiars under Fedor Ivanovich and Michael Romanov', *Can.-Am.Slavic Stud.*, 6, 1972, 549-74.

6.225 —— 'Peter and the boiar aristocracy, 1689-1700', *ib.*, 8, 1974, 274-87.

6.226 —— 'The reconstitution of the boiar aristocracy, 1613-45', *Forsch. Osteur. Gesch.*, 18, 1973, 187-220. Attempt to assess how much social mobility was engendered in recruitment to Duma.

6.227 —— 'Russian absolutism and the nobility', *J.Mod.Hist.*, 49, 1977, 456-67. Review article of recent work on nobility of early modern Russia and its role in state-building.

6.228 **Dukes**, P., *Catherine the Great and the Russian Nobility. A Study Based on the Materials of the Legislative Commission of 1767*, 1967. Review article: L. Bushkoff, *Can.Slavic Stud.*, 3, 1969, 121-7.

6.229 **Esper**, T., 'The *Odnodvortsy* and the Russian nobility', *Slavonic & E.Eur.Rev.*, 45, 1967, 124-34. Class intermediate between peasantry and gentry, which some nobles adopted to avoid service obligations.

6.230 **Givens**, R. D., 'Supplication and reform in the instructions of the nobility', *Can.-Am.Slavic Stud.*, 11, 1977, 483-502. Another analysis of *nakazy* for 1767 Legislative Commission. See also 6.218,228.

6.231 **Jones**, R. E., *The Emancipation of the Russian Nobility, 1762-85*, Princeton, N.J., 1973. Sees re-enlistment of nobility into state service, and concessions on serfdom, as reaction to Pugachev Rebellion.

6.232 **Kahan**, A., 'The costs of "westernization" in Russia. The gentry and the economy in the eighteenth century', *Slavic Rev.*, 25, 1966, 40-66. Repr. in M. Cherniavsky, ed., *The Structure of Russian History. Interpretive Essays*, New York, 1970, 224-66. Examines ways in which gentry sought to increase income to cope with higher living costs implicit in "western" mode of life.

6.233 **Kleimola**, Ann M., 'The changing face of the Muscovite aristocracy. The sixteenth century: sources of weakness', *Jb. Gesch. Osteuropas*, 25, 1977, 481-93. Offers various reasons why nobility was unable to impede power of Grand Princes.

6.234 —— 'Up through servitude. The changing condition of the Muscovite elite in the sixteenth and seventeenth centuries', *Russ.Hist.*, 6, 1979, 210-29. Argues that because of service obligations top levels of Russian society were first to suffer increasing control of state.

6.235 **Kohut**, Z. E., 'The Ukrainian elite in the eighteenth century and its integration into the Russian nobility', in Banac and Bushkovitch (6.196), 65-97.

6.236 **Leitsch**, W., 'The Russian nobility in the eighteenth century', *E.Eur.Q.*, 11, 1977, 317-40. General outline of political and social position, given as conference paper.

6.237 **McGrew**, R. E., 'The politics of absolutism. Paul I and the Bank of Assistance for the Nobility', *Can.-Am.Slavic Stud.*, 7, 1973, 15-38. Short-lived scheme to alleviate noble indebtedness.

6.238 **Raeff**, M., 'Home, school, and service in the life of the eighteenth-century Russian nobleman', *Slavonic & E.Eur.Rev.*, 40, 1962, 295-307. Repr. in Cherniavsky (6.232), 212-23. Generalised picture of aristocratic upbringing.

6.239 —— *Origins of the Russian Intelligentsia. The Eighteenth-Century Nobility*, New York, 1966. Review article: L. Bushkoff, *Can.Slavic Stud.*, 3, 1969, 121-7; and see 6.222.

6.240 —— 'The Russian nobility in the eighteenth and nineteenth centuries. Trends and comparisons', in Banac and Bushkovitch (6.196), 99-121.

6.241 **Shatz**, M. S., 'The noble landowner in Russian comic operas of the time of Catherine the Great. The patriarchal image', *Can.Slavic Stud.*, 3, 1969, 22-38.

MIDDLING AND LOWER CLASSES

On Peasantry see Section 7. On industrial working conditions and organisation see Section 9.
Note also 11.31 (France); 9.75 Spain); 5.392 and 12.98-9(Germany); 8.167-71; 9.140; and 10.157 (Russia).

6.242 **Kuczynski**, J., *The Rise of the Working Class*, 1967. Popular illustrated work with a good deal of material on eighteenth century.

6.243 **Darnton**, R., 'Workers revolt. The great cat massacre of the Rue Saint-Séverin', in his *The Great Cat Massacre and Other Episodes in French Cultural History*, New York, 1984, 75-104. Draws some inferences about workers' attitudes to masters from curious episode in Parisian printing shop in 1730s. Review articles (concentrating on this essay): R. Chartier, *J.Mod.Hist.*, 57, 1985, 682-95; (in Italian) P. Benedict and G. Levi, *Quad.Stor.*, 58, 1985, 257-77.

6.244 **Kaplow**, J., *The Names of Kings. The Parisian Laboring Poor in the Eighteenth Century*, New York, 1972. Well-documented study of resident and migrant labour in Paris, and importance of Revolution in raising political consciousness of lower classes. See also 11.212.

6.245 **Lottin**, A., ed., *Chavatte, Ouvrier Lillois. Un Contemporain de Louis XIV*, Paris, 1979. Takes us into mental world of a Lille weaver by interpreting and supplementing diary-chronicle he left.

6.246 **Roche**, D., ed., *Journal de Ma Vie. Jacques-Louis Ménétra, Compagnon Vitrier au 18e Siècle*, Paris, 1982. Autobiography of travelling workman, with lengthy commentary as postscript. Transl., with foreword by R. Darnton, New York, 1986 – brave attempt to capture semi-literate style of original.

6.247 **Sewell**, W. H., *Work and Revolution in France. The Language of Labor from the Old Régime to 1848*, 1980. By analysing vocabulary of artisan protest and ideals, shows debt of early socialism to corporatist tradition of pre-Revolutionary France. Review article: L. Hunt and G. Sheridan, *J.Mod.Hist.*, 58, 1986, 813-44.

6.248 **Cohn**, S. K., *The Laboring Classes in Renaissance Florence*, New York, 1980. Social history of *popolo minuto* in fourteenth and fifteenth centuries. Review article: see 3.182.

6.249 **Tagliaferri**, A., *Consumi e Tenore di Vita di una Famiglia Borghese del '600*, Milan, 1968. Based on account books of a Verona notary for 1650s.

6.250 **Engelsing**, R., *Zur Sozialgeschichte Deutscher Mittel- und Unterschichten*, Göttingen, 1973. Collection of essays dealing principally with living standards and reading habits of different classes during eighteenth and nineteenth centuries.

6.251 **Friedrichs**, C. R., 'Capitalism, mobility, and class formation in the early modern German city', *P.& P.*, 69, 1975, 24-49. Repr. in P. Abrams and E. A. Wrigley, eds., *Towns in Societies. Essays in Economic History and Historical Sociology*, 1978, 187-213. On emergence of a "lower middle class" of craftsmen, shopkeepers, etc., following breakdown of guild solidarity and growth of putting-out system.

6.252 **Lutz**, R. H., *Wer War der Gemeine Mann? Der Dritte Stand in der Krise des Spätmittelalters*, Munich, 1979. On fifteenth-century origins and context of this concept popularised by work of P. Blickle (see 10.53 and 12.98).

6.253 **Weiss**, Hildegard, *Lebenshaltung und Vermögensbildung des "Mittleren" Bürgertums. Studien zur Sozial- und Wirtschaftsgeschichte der Reichsstadt Nürnberg zwischen 1400-1600*, Munich, 1980. Note overlapping study of M. Toch, *Die Nürnberger Mittelschichten im 15. Jahrhundert*, Nuremberg, 1978, which compares non-patrician means and structures in 1440s and period 1497-1504.

6.254 **Wiesner**, Merry E., 'Making ends meet. The working poor in early modern Europe', in Sessions and Bebb (13.225), 79-88. Interesting short paper on workers (often female) not eligible for guild membership. Material drawn from German urban records.

6.255 **Kahan**, A., 'The "hereditary workers" hypothesis and the development of a factory labor force in eighteenth- and nineteenth-century Russia', in C. A. Anderson and Mary J. Bowman, eds., *Education and Economic Development*, Chicago, 1965, 291-7. Contrasts some data on parentage and literacy of industrial workers available for 1730s and for 1897.

6.256 **Jones**, R. E., 'Jacob Sievers, enlightened reform, and the development of a "third estate" in Russia', *Russ.Rev.*, 36, 1977, 424-37. Efforts of Novgorod governor to loosen legal constraints attached to urban citizenship.

SERVANTS
See also 5.389.

6.257 **Fairchilds**, Cissie, *Domestic Enemies. Servants and their Masters in Old Regime France*, Baltimore, Md., 1984. Finds more mobility and greater importance attached to wages after mid-century, drawing mainly on evidence from Toulouse, Bordeaux, and Paris. Some preliminary findings in her 'Masters and servants in eighteenth-century France', *J.Soc.Hist.*, 12, 1979, 368-93.

6.258 **Gutton**, J.-P., *Domestiques et Serviteurs dans la France de l'Ancien Régime*, Paris, 1981.

6.259 **Maza**, Sarah C., *Servants and Masters in Eighteenth-Century France*, Princeton, N.J., 1983. Good on mutual relationship aspects. See also her 'Anatomy of paternalism. Masters and servants in eighteenth-century France', *Eighteenth-Cent.Life*, 7 (i), 1981, 1-24.

6.260 **Klapisch-Zuber**, Christiane, 'Célibat et service féminins dans la Florence du 15e siècle', *Ann.Démographie Hist.*, 1981, 289-302. Investigates how far entry to domestic service was tied to single state.

6.261 —— 'Women servants in Florence during the fourteenth and fifteenth centuries', in Hanawalt (5.445), 56-80. Emphasises role of servants and slaves as household "property".

6.262 **Engelsing**, R., 'Einkommen der Dienstboten in Deutschland zwischen dem 16. und 20. Jahrhundert', *Jb. Inst. Dt. Gesch.*, 2, 1973, 11-65; 3, 1974, 227-56.

SLAVES
See also 5.657,659; 10.346,379,488.

6.263 **Miller**, J. C., *Slavery. A Worldwide Bibliography, 1900-82*, New York, 1985. Includes sections on medieval and early modern Europe, and on slave-trade.

6.264 **Larquié**, C., 'Les esclaves de Madrid à l'époque de la décadence (1650-1700)', *Rev.Hist.*, 244, 1970, 41-74.

6.265 **Pike**, Ruth, 'Sevillian society in the sixteenth century. Slaves and freedmen', *Hisp.Am.Rev.*, 47, 1967, 344-59. On use of negroes for domestic service, etc.

6.266 **Saunders**, A. C. de C. M., *A Social History of Black Slaves and Freedmen in Portugal, 1441-1551*, 1982. Rare study of black slavery in Old World setting.

6.267 **Gioffrè**, D., *Il Mercato degli Schiavi a Genova nel Secolo 15*, Genoa, 1971. All-round study of commerce and utilisation of slaves at Genoa.

6.268 **Inalcik**, H., 'Servile labor in the Ottoman Empire', in A. Ascher and others, eds., *Mutual Effects of the Islamic and Judeo-Christian Worlds. The East European Pattern*, New York, 1979, 25-52. Repr. in Inalcik (3.290). Covers supply of slaves and their employment in crafts and agriculture.

6.269 **Hellie**, R., *Slavery in Russia, 1450-1725*, Chicago, 1982. Russian slavery, mainly for discharge of debt, persisted into eighteenth century. Hellie offers wide range of comparison with other slave systems, ancient and modern.

6.270 —— 'Muscovite slavery in comparative perspective', *Russ.Hist.*, 6, 1979, 133-209. Preliminary outline of findings in previous entry.

6.271 —— 'Recent Soviet historiography on medieval to early modern Russian slavery', *Russ.Rev.*, 35, 1976, 1-32. See also discussion with H. Leventer, ib., 36, 1977, 64-75.

6.272 —— 'Slavery among the early modern peoples on the territory of the U.S.S.R.', *Can.-Am. Slavic Stud.*, 17, 1983, 454-65. Describes slavery (and slave-raiding into Muscovy) practised by Central Asian khanates.

6.273 —— 'Women and slavery in Muscovy', *Russ.Hist.*, 10, 1983, 213-29. Discusses women as slaves and (more rarely) slave-owners.

7

RURAL SOCIETY

See Section 6 for general material on landowning nobility; 9.340-63 for material on trade in agricultural produce; and Section 11.1-170 passim on agricultural prices and regulation of food supplies. Peasant revolts are covered in Section 12.

GENERAL WORKS. PEASANT ECONOMY AND TENURE. ESTATE MANAGEMENT.
See also 5.19,472; 9.446; 10.480.

1 **Abel**, W., *Agricultural Fluctuations in Europe, from the Thirteenth to the Twentieth Centuries*, 1980. Transl. of pioneering German study, charting long-term movements in rural economy (prices, wages, rents, productivity, etc.). First publ. 1935, and extensively revised in 1966. Transl. is of 3rd ed. (1978). Review articles: H. Freudenberger, *Central Eur.Hist.*, 2, 1969, 170-6; R. Berthold, *Jb.Wirtschaftsgesch.*, 1971 (iv), 231-65.

2 **Aston**, T. H., and Philpin, C. H. E., eds., *The Brenner Debate. Agrarian Class Structure and Economic Development in Pre-Industrial Europe*, 1985. Collects contributions to long-running debate in *P.& P.*, inauguarated by R. Brenner's 'Agrarian class structure and economic development in pre-industrial Europe' (*ib.*, 70, 1976, 30-75), which argued that landlord-tenant relations, rather than demographic factors or purely market forces, determined agrarian development. Among those joining in general debate, esp. as regards comparison of French and English experience: G. Bois, J. P. Cooper, Patricia Croot and D. Parker, E. Le Roy Ladurie. Other case studies noted below in regional context.

7.3 **Banaji**, J., 'The peasantry in the feudal mode of production. Towards an economic model', *J.Peasant Stud.*, 3, 1976, 299-320. Emphasises market orientation of both peasant-producer and demesne-producer forms of feudalism.

7.4 **Blum**, J., 'The condition of the European peasantry on the eve of emancipation', *J.Mod.Hist.*, 46, 1974, 395-424. General survey of tenurial obligations, housing, diet, etc., in late eighteenth and early nineteenth centuries.

7.5 —— *The End of the Old Order in Rural Europe*, Princeton, N.J., 1978. Brave attempt at comprehensive history of serf emancipation throughout Europe. Review article: J. Komlos, *J.Eur.Ec.Hist.*, 14, 1985, 515-20.

7.6 —— 'The European village as community. Origins and functions', *Agric.Hist.*, 45, 1971, 157-78. Very wide-ranging survey, looking at medieval origins of common-field farming; and different degrees of communal control of tenures and farming methods.

7.7 —— 'Internal structure and polity of the European village community, fifteenth to nineteenth century', *J.Mod.Hist.*, 43, 1971, 541-76. Comparative study of collective self-government, its limitations and possible inequities.

7.8 ——, ed., *Our Forgotten Past. Seven Centuries of Life on the Land*, 1982. Illustrated, collaborative work of popularisation. Contributors incl. Blum, Joan Thirsk, Y.-M. Bercé. Main focus of interest is early modern European peasantry, their economy and mentality.

7.9 **De Maddalena**, A., 'Rural Europe, 1500-1750', in *Fontana Economic History of Europe*, 2 (2.24), 273-353, 595-622 (statistical appendix). Also separately publ., 1970.

7.10 **Godechot**, J. ed., *Abolition de la Féodalité dans le Monde Occidental*, 2 vols., Paris, 1971. International conference, with papers (all French-language) on most European countries or regions. Review article: A. Massafra, *J.Eur.Ec.Hist.*, 3, 1974, 203-8.

7.11 **Grigg**, D., *The Dynamics of Agricultural Change. The Historical Experience*, 1982. General conceptual work, not confined to one place or period. Examples mainly drawn from English experience.

7.12 **Gunst**, P., and Hoffmann, T., eds., *Large Estates and Small Holdings in Europe in the Middle Ages and Modern Times*, Budapest, 1982. Papers on most European regions prepared for Eighth International Conference of Economic History (French, English, and German language). Most deal with late medieval and early modern periods.

7.13 **Huggett**, F. E., *The Land Question and European Society*, 1975. General history of agriculture and agrarian problems from seventeenth century onwards. Generously illustrated.

7.14 **Jones**, E. L., and Woolf, S. J., 'The historical role of agrarian change in economic development', in their *Agrarian Change and Economic Development. The Historical Problems*, 1969, 1-22. Posits conditions of population rate, social development, and agricultural innovation necessary to foster manufacturing growth.

7.15 **Kahan**, A., 'Notes on serfdom in Western and Eastern Europe', *J.Ec.Hist.*, 33, 1973, 86-99. Mainly definitional (part of symposium on property rights and slavery).

7.16 **Kay**, C., 'Comparative development of the European manorial system and the Latin American hacienda system', *J.Peasant Stud.*, 2, 1974, 69-98. Very schematic.

7.17 **Kjaergaard**, T., 'Origins of economic growth in European societies since the sixteenth century. The case of agriculture', *J.Eur.Ec.Hist.*, 15, 1986, 591-8. In correlating growth of agricultural productivity with that in number of agricultural treatises published offers unconditional support for Eisenstein's views on printing revolution (see 14.276-80).

7.18 **Köpeczi**, B., and Balázs, Eva H., eds., *Paysannerie Française, Paysannerie Hongroise, 16e-20e Siècles*, Budapest, 1973. Papers presented at Franco-Hungarian historical conference. French contributors include E. Le Roy Ladurie, J. Meyer, R. Mandrou.

7.19 **Le Roy Ladurie**, E., 'Rural civilization', in Le Roy Ladurie (4.35), 79-110. Very general characterisation of Western European peasant society down to early twentieth century, written for encyclopedia.

7.20 **Slicher Van Bath**, B. H., 'Accounts and diaries of farmers before 1800 as a source for agricultural history', *AAG Bijd.*, 8, 1962, 5-33. Examples from a number of W. European countries.

7.21 —— *The Agrarian History of Western Europe, 500-1850*, 1966. Extremely valuable synthesis.

7.22 —— 'Agriculture in the vital revolution', in *Cambridge Economic History of Europe*, 5 (2.15), 42-132. Excellent survey of early modern centuries (title somewhat anachronistic for most of period covered).

7.23 **Stankiewicz**, Z., 'Remarks on the typology of transition from feudalism to capitalism in agriculture', *Acta Poloniae Hist.*, 28, 1973, 169-89.

7.24 **Vincent**, Joan, 'Agrarian society as organised flow', *Peasant Stud.*, 6, 1977, 56-75. Suggests shifting focus of research from farms and administrative boundaries to individuals and their activity fields.

7.25 **Wyczanski**, A., and Topolski, J., 'The peasant economy before and during the first stage of industrialisation', in *Sixth International Congress on Economic History. Themes* (4.91), 11-31. With comments in *ib. Proceedings*, 13-45.

FRANCE
See also 3.16,37; 4.7,9; 5.357; 6.25;
7.18,279-84,306-7; 10.191,281; 13.116,118.

?6 **Marduel**, Marie-L., and Robert, M., *Les Sociétés Rurales Françaises. Éléments de Bibliographie*, Paris, 1979. Spreads net wide enough to include many historical works (monographs only). Usefully arranged by region and annotated.

?7 **Baehrel**, R., *Une Croissance. La Basse-Provence Rurale de la Fin du 16e Siècle à 1789*, 2 vols., Paris, 1961. According to Baehrel, Lower Provence enjoyed continuing prosperity for most of seventeenth century; methodological arguments involved put him rather at odds with fellow masters of French regional history. Review article: E. Le Roy Ladurie, *Annales*, 20, 1965, 1268-80.

?8 **Bastier**, J., *La Féodalité au Siècle des Lumières dans la Région de Toulouse, 1730-90*, Paris, 1975. Part 1 deals with landowners and agents; part 2 with legal framework.

?9 **Bloch**, M., *French Rural History. An Essay on its Basic Characteristics*, 1966. Transl. of Bloch's famous *Caractères Originaux de l'Histoire Rurale Française* as publ. in 1931. Volume of supplementary material (assembled from articles and reviews), which appeared with reissue of *Caractères* in 1956, is not covered by transl.

?0 **Bois**, G., *The Crisis of Feudalism. Economy and Society in Eastern Normandy, c.1300-1550*, 1984. Influential thesis, important for its demographic as well as agrarian material. Transl. from French ed. of 1976. Review article: J. Day, *Annales*, 34, 1979, 305-24.

?1 **Boutruche**, R., *Une Société Provinciale en Lutte contre le Régime Féodal. L'Alleu en Bordelais et en Bazadais du 11e au 18e Siècle*, Rodez, 1947. Rather technical study of persistence of freehold tenures in this region.

?2 **Cabourdin**, G., *Terre et Hommes en Lorraine (1550-1635). Toulois et Comté de Vaudémont*, 2 vols., Nancy, 1977. Another massive doctoral thesis – on region interesting for its half-French, half-German patterns.

?3 **Constant**, J.-M., 'Gestion et revenus d'un grand domaine au 16e et 17e siècles, d'après les comptes de la baronnie d'Auneau', *Rev.Hist.Éc.et Soc.*, 50, 1972,

165-202. Principal property of Charles d'Escoubleau, governor of Amboise and the Orléannais.

7.34 **Costamagna**, H., 'Aspects et problèmes de la vie agro-pastorale dans le comté de Nice (1699-1792), *ib.*, 49, 1971, 508-49.

7.35 **Davies**, A., 'The origins of the French peasant revolution of 1789', *History*, 49, 1964, 24-41. Useful view of agrarian scene and grievances on eve of Revolution, based on research in Calvados.

7.36 **Descadeillas**, R., *Rennes et ses Derniers Seigneurs, 1730-1820. Contribution à l'Étude Économique et Sociale de la Baronnie de Rennes (Aude) au 18e Siècle*, Toulouse, 1964. Traces development of medium-sized barony near Carcassonne through vicissitudes of Revolution.

7.37 **Devèze**, M., 'Les communautés rurales de Bourgogne en 1665', *Actes Congrès Nat.Soc.Savantes*, 84, 1959, 77-117. Derived from fiscal enquiry which throws general light on economic position of peasantry, notably in baillage of Arnay-Le Duc.

7.38 **Duby**, G., and Wallon, A., eds., *Histoire de la France Rurale. Vol.2: L'Age Classique des Paysans, 1340-1789*, Paris, 1975. Part of sumptuous four-volume set featuring contributions by leading social historians such as Le Roy Ladurie, J. Jacquart, and M. Agulhon. As well as matters strictly agrarian, climate, popular culture, diet, crime, sex, etc. are amply covered.

7.39 **Dupâquier**, J., *La Propriété et l'Exploitation Foncières à la Fin de l'Ancien Régime dans le Gâtinais Septentrional*, Paris, 1956. Study of evidence in terriers and tax rolls of various parishes of region.

7.40 **Fitch**, Nancy, 'The demographic and economic effects of seventeenth-century wars. The case of the Bourbonnais', *Review*, 2, 1978, 181-206. Deals with forced land sales of peasantry faced with steep tax rises and troop depredations of period 1630-60.

7.41 **Forster**, R., 'The noble as landlord in the region of Toulouse at the end of the Old Régime', *J.Ec.Hist.*, 17, 1957, 224-44. Supports view that rural nobility relied on demesne agriculture rather than seigneurial rights for prosperity.

7.42 —— 'Seigneurs and their agents', in E. Hinrichs and others, eds., *Vom Ancien Regime zur Französischen Revolution*,

Göttingen, 1978, 169-87. Work of estate stewards illustrated by records of four considerable aristocratic proprietors.

7.43 —— 'The "world" between seigneur and peasant', *Stud.in Eighteenth-Cent.Culture*, 5, 1976, 401-21. Choiseul properties in Lorraine used to illustrate use of middlemen in estate administration.

7.44 **Goldsmith**, J. L., 'The agrarian history of preindustrial France. Where do we go from here?', *J.Eur.Ec.Hist.*, 13, 1984, 175-99. Charts quarrel between *Annales* serial historians and advocates of national accounting methods, but views structural analysis as more promising approach than either.

7.45 **Goubert**, P., *The French Peasantry in the Seventeenth Century*, 1986. Transl. of French ed. of 1982. Excellent general summary of life-cycle, tenure, and work in various types of regional economy.

7.46 —— 'The French peasantry of the seventeenth century. A regional example', *P.& P.*, 10, 1956, 55-77. Repr. in Aston (2.72), 141-66. Some findings from his research on Beauvais region (see 8.36).

7.47 **Hoffman**, P. T., 'The economic theory of sharecropping in early modern France', *J.Ec.Hist.*, 44, 1984, 309-20. Suggests this tenure was rational approach to risk, incentives, and transaction costs, and not a cause of stagnation. See also short preliminary paper on this subject, *ib.*, 42, 1982, 155-9.

7.48 **Hufton**, Olwen, 'The seigneur and the rural community in eighteenth-century France. The seigneurial reaction: a reappraisal', *Trans.Roy.Hist.Soc.*, 5th ser., 29, 1979, 21-39. Finds concept of seigneurial reaction on the whole implausible. For more traditional view see, e.g., 7.68-9.

7.49 **Jacquart**, J., *La Crise Rurale en Ile-de-France, 1550-1670*, Paris, 1974. Wider in thematic range than Venard (7.71), though also deals with latter's theme of rich Parisians buying up their hinterland.

7.50 **Jones**, P. M., 'Parish, seigneurie, and the community of inhabitants in Southern Central France during the eighteenth and nineteenth centuries', *P.& P.*, 91, 1981, 74-108. Argues that parish was main focus of rural life for scattered settlements of southern Massif Central.

7.51 —— 'Rural bourgeoisie of the southern Massif-Central. A contribution to the

study of the social structure of ancien régime France', *Soc.Hist.*, 4, 1979, 65-83. Describes non-noble, non-peasant rural elite of rentiers, minor officials, and land agents in isolated upland region. This and preceding article anticipate material in Jones' later book, *Politics and Rural Society. The Southern Massif-Central, c.1750-1880*, 1985, whose main focus, however, is post-Revolution.

7.52 **Labrousse**, E., 'A view of the allocation of agricultural expansion among social classes', *Review*, 2, 1978, 149-78. Transl. extract from vol.2 of Braudel and Labrousse (3.6), dealing with property distribution and wages in rural sector of eighteenth-century economy.

7.53 **Léon**, P., ed., *Structures Économiques et Problèmes Sociaux du Monde Rural dans la France du Sud-Est (Fin du 17e Siècle-1835)*, Paris, 1966. Studies four communities in region south of Lyon.

7.54 **Le Roy Ladurie**, E., *The French Peasantry, 1450-1660*, 1987. Transl. of his contribution to Braudel and Labrousse (3.6), with updating introduction and conclusion.

7.55 —— 'French peasants in the sixteenth century', in Le Roy Ladurie (5.36), 97-122. General view, contributed to festschrift for Ernest Labrousse (1974).

7.56 —— *Les Paysans de Languedoc*, 2 vols., Paris, 1966. Another landmark of post-war French scholarship, in which agrarian conditions of sixteenth and seventeenth centuries are seen as working out of Malthusian process (population expansion leading to pauperisation and exodus). Abridged version, publ. in 1969, transl. *The Peasants of Languedoc*, Urbana, Ill., 1974 (last chapter repr. as 'A long agrarian cycle' in Earle (3.71), 143-64). Review articles: L. Bergeron, *Hist.& Theory*, 7, 1968, 367-76; D. Ligou, *Rev.Hist.Éc.et Soc.*, 45, 1967, 406-14; P. Chaunu, *Rev.Hist.*, 237, 1967, 359-80.

7.57 —— 'Rétif de la Bretonne as a social anthropologist. Rural Burgundy in the eighteenth century', in Le Roy Ladurie (5.36), 211-69. Transl. of section from 7.38, dealing with Rétif's portrait of village life in *La Vie de Mon Père*.

7.58 **Mackrell**, J. Q. C., *The Attack on Feudalism in Eighteenth-Century France*, 1973. Defends polemicists against "feudalism" as having genuine target in seigneurial rights and ethos that still pervaded France.

7.59 **Meadwell**, H., 'Exchange relations between lords and peasants', *Arch.Eur.Sociol.*, 28, 1987, 3-49. Examines peasant unrest leading to Revolution in light of "exchange model" of tenurial relations.

7.60 **Merle**, L., *La Métairie et l'Evolution Agraire de la Gâtine Poitevine de la Fin du Moyen Age à la Révolution*, Paris, 1958. On métayage, i.e. share-cropping, tenure. Review article: P. Massé, *Annales*, 15, 1960, 350-8.

7.61 **Michaud**, C., 'Redistribution foncière et rentière en 1569. Les aliénations du temporel ecclésiastique dans quatre diocèses du centre de la France', *Rev.Hist.*, 267, 1982, 305-56. Detailed assessment of purchases of church land in dioceses of Orléans, Bourges, Tours, and Chartres.

7.62 **Morineau**, M., 'Y a-t-il eu une révolution agricole en France au 18e siècle?', *Rev.Hist.*, 239, 1968, 299-326. Abridged transl. in Cameron and others (3.251), 170-82. Finds French improvements modest in comparison with levels long attained in regions of Netherlands. See also 3.37.

7.63 **Plaisse**, A., *La Baronnie de Neubourg. Essai d'Histoire Agraire, Économique, et Sociale*, Paris, 1961. Substantial analysis of Norman *seigneurie* from late Middle Ages to eighteenth century. Review article: P. Chaunu, *Annales*, 17, 1962, 1152-68.

7.64 **Poitrineau**, A., *La Vie Rurale en Basse Auvergne au 18e Siècle, 1726-89*, 2 vols., Paris, 1965. Highly rated.

7.65 **Rascol**, P., *Les Paysans de l'Albigeois à la Fin de l'Ancien Régime*, Aurillac, 1961. Study of Albi region.

7.66 **Raveau**, P., *L'Agriculture et les Classes Paysannes. La Transformation de la Propriété dans le Haut Poitou au l6e Siècle*, Paris, 1926. Remains valued account of changing attitudes to landownership and its exploitation.

7.67 **Root**, H. L., 'Challenging the seigneurie. Community and contention on the eve of the French Revolution', *J.Mod.Hist.*, 57, 1985, 652-81. Documents increasing litigation of Burgundian communities against feudal dues, suggesting it sprang from perception that state had displaced seigneur as source of authority. See also

Root's book, 10.39.

7.68 **Saint-Jacob**, P. de, *Les Paysans de la Bourgogne du Nord au Dernier Siècle de l'Ancien Régime*, Paris, 1960. Finds ample evidence of "agrarian individualism" and 'seigneurial reaction' transforming relations. See also *Documents Relatifs à la Communauté Villageoise en Bourgogne, du Milieu du 17e Siècle à la Révolution*, Paris, 1962, a documentary addendum.

7.69 **Soboul**, A., 'De la pratique des terriers à la veille de la Révolution', *Annales*, 19, 1964, 1049-65. Valuable article on so-called "feudal reaction" in estate administration.

7.70 —— 'The French rural community in the eighteenth and nineteenth centuries', *P.&P.*, 10, 1956, 78-95. Outlines his view of transition from feudal to capitalist rural structure.

7.71 **Venard**, M., *Bourgeois et Paysans au 17e Siècle. Recherche sur le Rôle des Bourgeois Parisiens dans la Vie Agricole au Sud de Paris*, 1957. Assesses effects of land investment by prosperous Parisians. Review article: P. Massé, *Annales*, 15, 1960, 350-58. See also 7.49.

7.72 **Walter**, G., *Histoire des Paysans de France*, Paris, 1963. Rather one-dimensional in its concentration on grievances and revolts.

7.73 **Woloch**, I., *The Peasantry in the Old Régime. Conditions and Protests*, New York, 1970. Reader comprising excerpts from books and articles by Goubert, Bloch, Mandrou, etc.

FRENCH VILLAGE STUDIES
See also 7.37,67; 9.460-3; 10.39; 14.54.

7.74 **Bouchard**, G., *Le Village Immobile. Sennely-en-Sologne au 18e Siècle*, Paris, 1972. Depicts deprived and stagnating community, but only by impressionistic use of sources (e.g. *cahiers de doléances*). Review article: C. Johnson, *Peasant Stud.Newsl.*, 2 (iv), 1973, 9-16.

7.75 **Brunet**, C., *Une Communauté Rurale au 18e Siècle. Le Plessis-Gassot (Seine-et-Oise)*, Paris, 1964. Extended essay length.

7.76 **Cameron**, J. B., 'Village government in Provence in the eighteenth century', *Proc.Western Soc.Fr.Hist.*, 1, 1974, 98-107. Machinery of local government seen as mirror of social structure (village of Allauch).

7.77 **Collier**, R., 'Essai sur le "socialisme"

communal en Haute-Provence', *Actes Congrès Nat.Soc.Savantes*, 90 (i), 1965, 303-33. Notes strength of communal organisation in this region, and close regulation of economic and welfare activity it exercised.

7.78 **Gutton**, J.-P., *Villages du Lyonnais sous la Monarchie, 16e-18e Siècles*, Lyon, 1978. Short study of functioning of rural communities, allotment of fiscal burdens, etc., with appendix of documents.

7.79 **Higonnet**, P. L. R., *Pont-de-Monvert. Social Structure and Politics in a French Village, 1700-1914*, Cambridge, Mass., 1971. Long-term trends in largely Protestant village of Cévennes region. Review article: P. Dawson, *J.Soc.Hist.*, 6, 1973, 344-58.

7.80 **Leclercq**, Paulette, *Garéoult. Un Village de Provence dans la Deuxième Moitié du 16e Siècle*, Paris, 1979. Short, but intensively researched.

7.81 **Lefebvre**, H., *La Vallée de Campan. Étude de Sociologie Rurale*, Paris, 1963. Based on archives of Pyrenean village up to Revolution, tracing growing encroachment of state power and inequality of property.

7.82 **Levi-Pinard**, Germaine, *La Vie Quotidienne à Vallorcine au 18e Siècle*, Annecy, 1974. Based on papers of Savoyard artisan and hill farmer.

7.83 **Rambaud**, P., *Économie et Sociologie de la Montagne. Albiez-le-Vieux en Maurienne*, Paris, 1962. Longitudinal study of Savoyard commune since medieval period.

7.84 **Sheppard**, T. F., *Lourmarin in the Eighteenth Century. A Study of a French Village*, Baltimore, Md., 1971. Thorough, all-round survey of Provençal village. Review articles: as for 7.74 and 7.79.

7.85 **Zink**, Anne, *Azereix. La Vie d'une Communauté Rurale à la Fin du 18e Siècle*, Paris, 1969. General social history of a Pyrenean village near Tarbes.

LOW COUNTRIES
See also 7.285; 10.504,506; 11.143.

7.86 **Bieleman**, J., 'Rural change in the Dutch province of Drenthe in the seventeenth and eighteenth centuries', *Agric.Hist.Rev.*, 33, 1985, 105-18. Attributes intensification of production (with more emphasis on arable) to increased burden of taxation.

7.87 **De Vries**, J., *The Dutch Rural Economy in the Golden Age, 1500-1700*, New Haven, Conn., 1974. Portrays a growingly progressive and specialised agricultural economy.

7.88 —— 'Peasant demand patterns and economic development. Friesland, 1550-1750', in W. N. Parker and E. L. Jones, eds., *European Peasants and their Markets. Essays in Agrarian Economic History*, Princeton, N.J., 1975, 205-66. Detailed tables of peasant expenditure, showing that, despite increasing prosperity, demand was satisfied by small-scale, local production.

7.89 **Jansen**, J. C. G. M., 'Agrarian development and exploitation in South Limburg, 1650-1850', *Acta Hist.Neerlandica*, 5, 1971, 243-70.

7.90 **Sivery**, G., *Structures Agraires et Vie Rurale dans le Hainaut à la Fin du Moyen Age*, 2 vols., Lille, 1977-80. Spans period from fourteenth to early sixteenth centuries.

7.91 **Slicher van Bath**, B. H., 'Agriculture in the Low Countries, c.1600-1800', in *Relazioni del 10 Congresso Internazionale di Scienze Storiche*, Rome, 1955, 4, 169-203.

7.92 **Van der Woude**, A. M., 'The *A.A.G. Bijdragen* and the study of Dutch rural history', *J.Eur.Ec.Hist.*, 4, 1975, 215-42. Survey of Dutch agrarian history in light of contributions made by this influential journal.

7.93 **Verhulst**, A., 'L'histoire rurale de la Belgique jusqu'à la fin de l'Ancien Régime. Aperçu bibliographique, 1969-83', *Rev.Hist.*, 271, 1984, 419-37.

SPAIN AND PORTUGAL
See also 3.91,130; 4.13,16; 5.448; 6.29; 7.286-9; 9.241.

7.94 **Amalric**, J.-P., and Ponsot, P., eds., *L'Exploitation des Grands Domaines dans l'Espagne d'Ancien Régime*, Paris, 1985. Collection of case studies.

7.95 **Andrés-Gallego**, J., 'Datos de economía rural castellana (1676-1840)', *Hispania*, 125, 1973, 597-627.

7.96 **Anes Alvarez**, G., *Las Crisis Agrarias en la*

España Moderna, Madrid, 1970. General study of period 1680-1840, with emphasis on market problems.

7.97 **Artola**, M., and others, *El Latifundio. Propriedad y Explotación, ss. 18-20*, Madrid, 1978. Studies great estates of Andalusia. Two of the three contributors deal principally with eighteenth century.

7.98 **Behar**, Ruth, *Santa María del Monte. The Presence of the Past in a Spanish Village*, Princeton, N.J., 1986. Anthropological study of León community with frequent reference back to eighteenth-century village ordinances. Review article: W. A. Douglass, *Peasant Stud.*, 14, 1987, 119-30.

7.99 **Borrero Fernández**, Mercedes, *El Mundo Rural Sevillano en el Siglo 15. Aljarafe y Ribera*, Seville, 1983. On demography and landowners of Andalusian district strongly influenced by owners from Seville.

7.100 **Brumont**, F., *Campo y Campesinos de Castilla la Vieja en Tiempos de Felipe II*, Madrid, 1984. Study of Bureba, rural region in vicinity of Burgos. Based on French thesis, *La Bureba à l'Époque de Philippe II*. (*Dissertations on European Economic History*), New York, 1977.

7.101 —— 'La rente de la terre en Rioja occidentale à l'époque moderne', *Mél.Casa de Velazquez*, 16, 1980, 237-72. Looks at rentable value of land over whole period 1500-1800.

7.102 **Cabrera Muñoz**, E., *El Condado de Belalcázar (1444-1518). Aportación al Estudio del Régimen Señorial en la Baja Edad Media*, Cordoba, 1977. Study of workings of large Castilian fief created for Sotomayor family.

7.103 **Clavero**, B., *Mayorazgo. Propriedad Feudal en Castilla, 1369-1836*, Madrid, 1974. Effects of primogeniture on land system.

7.104 **Fernández Izquierdo**, F., 'Las ventas de bienes de las ordenes militares en el siglo 16 como fuente para el estudio del régimen señorial. La provincia de Calatrava de Zorita', *Hispania*, 151, 1982, 419-62. Investigates whether purchasers profited from seigneurial rights involved as part of "refeudalisation" process in Castile.

7.105 **Floristán Imízcoz**, A., *La Merindad de Estella en la Edad Moderna. Los Hombres y la Tierra*, Pamplona, 1982. Demographic and agrarian study of district in Navarre, c.1500-1800.

7.106 **García-Lombardero**, J., *La Agricultura y*

el Estancamiento de Galicia en la España del Antiguo Régimen, Madrid, 1973. Brief study emphasising role of agrarian sector in general provincial economy of eighteenth century.

7.107 **Guilarte**, A. M., *El Régimen Señorial en el Siglo 16*, Madrid, 1962. Written primarily from viewpoint of legal historian. See also 7.109-11.

7.108 **López-Salazar Pérez**, J., 'Una empresa agraria capitalista en la Castilla del 17. La hacienda de D. Gonzalo Muñoz Treviño de Loaisa', *Hispania*, 148, 1981, 355-407. Evidence of close attention to business detail of a Ciudad Real *caballero*.

7.109 **Morant Deusa**, Isabel, *El Declive del Señorio. Los Dominios del Ducado de Gandía, 1705-1837*, Valencia, 1984. Case-study of swelling opposition to feudal powers of nobility.

7.110 **Moxo**, S. de, *La Incorporacíon de los Señoríos en la España del Antiguo Régimen*, Valladolid, 1959.

7.111 —— *La Disolucíon del Régimen Señorial en España*, Madrid, 1963. This and preceding work are standard works on legal-institutional aspects of land system before liberal reforms.

7.112 **Phillips**, Carla R., 'Urban landownership in Castile. Additional evidence from seventeenth-century Ciudad Real', *Societas*, 3, 1973, 313-35. Analyses social groups involved in purchases of agricultural land in vicinity of city (800 notarial transactions analysed).

7.113 **Rau**, Virginia, 'Large-scale agricultural enterprise in post-medieval Portugal', in *Contributions [to] First International Conference of Economic History*, Paris, 1960, 425-32. Very brief overview of development of land tenure in modern Portugal.

7.114 **Ruiz Torres**, P., *Señores y Proprietarios. Cambio Social en el Sur del Pais Valenciano, 1650-1850*, Valencia, 1981. Concentrates on Marquisate of Elche.

7.115 **Salomon**, N., *La Campagne de Nouvelle Castille à la Fin du 16e Siècle, d'après les "Relaciones Topograficas"*, Paris, 1964. Based on government surveys of 1570s; peasants may have exaggerated burdens on suspicion that they were compiled for tax purposes.

7.116 **Silbert**, A., *Le Portugal Méditerranéen à la Fin de l'Ancien Régime. Contribution à l'Histoire Agraire Comparée*, 2 vols., Paris,

1966. Massive study of agriculture and rural conditions in regions of Beira and Alentejo in late eighteenth and early nineteenth centuries. Review article: O. Ribeiro, *Ét.Rurales*, 41, 1971, 94-103.

7.117 **Torras**, J., 'Class struggle in Catalonia. A note on Brenner', *Review*, 4, 1980, 253-65. Contends that rise in Catalonian agricultural productivity did not conform to "capitalist" model postulated by Brenner (see 7.2).

7.118 **Vassberg**, D. E., *Land and Society in Golden Age Castile*, Cambridge, 1984. Concentrates on Crown resumptions and sales of communal land. Note also following articles based on this research.

7.119 —— 'Peasant communalism and anti-communal tendencies in early modern Castile', *J.Peasant Stud.*, 7, 1980, 477-91.

7.120 —— 'The sale of *Tierras Baldías* in sixteenth-century Castile', *J.Mod.Hist.*, 47, 1975, 629-54.

7.121 —— 'The *Tierras Baldías*. Community property and public lands in sixteenth-century Castile', *Agric.Hist.*, 48, 1974, 383-401.

7.122 **Weisser**, M. R., *The Peasants of the Montes. The Roots of Rural Rebellion in Spain*, Chicago, 1976. Brief study of locality in Toledo region, which argues that social tensions of sixteenth and early seventeenth centuries have persisted into twentieth.

ITALY
See also 3.185,203; 5.162,373; 6.158,170; 7.290-1; 10.237.

7.123 'Agricoltura, proprietà, mercati', *Quad.Stor.*, 21, 1972, 781-1052. Journal issue which includes four long micro-studies on early modern agrarian economy and society.

7.124 **Beltrami**, D., *Saggio di Storia dell' Agricoltura nello Repubblica di Venezia durante l'Età Moderna*, Florence, 1956. Short (78pp.) account of rural economy and society in seventeenth and eighteenth centuries.

7.125 **Casali**, Elide, *Il Villano Dirozzato. Cultura, Società, e Potere nelle Campagne Romagnole della Contrariforma*, Florence, 1982. Takes form of commentary on advice manual (both moral and agricultural) publ. by gentleman of Ravenna region (Bernardino Caroli, *Instrutione del Giovane*

ben Creato).

7.126 **Cattini**, M., *I Contadini di San Felice. Metamorfesi di un Mundo Rurale nell'Emilia dell'Età Moderna*, Turin, 1984. Microstudy of Modenese commune during "long seventeenth century", under broad headings of environment, demography, economy, and social structure.

7.127 *Contadini e Proprietari nella Toscana Moderna. Atti del Convegno di Studi in Onore di Giorgio Giorgetti*, 2 vols., Florence, 1979-81. Papers ranging from medieval to contemporary history of Tuscan rural society. All relevant to early modern period are in vol.1. Title echoes Giorgetti's own best-known book, *Contadini e Proprietari nell'Italia Moderna. Rapporti di Produzione e Contratti Agrari dal Secolo 16 a Oggi*, Turin, 1974, whose main emphasis, however, is on nineteenth and early twentieth centuries.

7.128 **Corazzol**, L., 'Prestatori e contadini nella campagna Feltrina intorno alla prima metà del '500', *Quad.Stor.*, 26, 1974, 445-500. On rural money-lenders.

7.129 **Delille**, G., *Croissance d'une Société Rurale. Montesarcho et la Vallée Caudine aux 17e et 18e Siècles*, Naples, 1973.

7.130 **De Maddalena**, A., 'Il mondo rurale italiano nel cinque- e nel seicento. Rassegna di studi recenti', *Riv.Stor.Ital.*, 76, 1964, 349-426. Valuable bibliographical article.

7.131 **Doria**, G., *Uomini e Terre di un Borgo Collinare dal 16 al 18 Secolo*, Milan, 1968. Detailed picture of rural community in Apennines, based on estate papers of its Genoese overlord.

7.132 **Georgelin**, J., 'A great estate in Venetia in the eighteenth century: Anguillara', in *Social Historians in Contemporary France* (3.4), 100-130. Transl. from *Annales*, 23, 1968, 483-519. On administration of Tron family estate near Rovigo.

7.133 **Laurent**, Jane K., 'The peasant in Italian agrarian treatises', *Agric.Hist.*, 58, 1984, 565-83. Examines outlook of landlords as expressed in treatises written between fourteenth and seventeenth centuries.

7.134 **Lepre**, A., *Feudi e Masserie. Problemi della Società Meridionale nel '600 e nel '700*, Naples, 1973. Comparative study of landlords operating fief tenures (mainly in Abruzzo) and those running estate farms (predominant in Puglia).

7.135 **Levi**, G., ed., 'Villagi. Studi di

antropologia storica', *Quad.Stor.*, 46, 1981, 7-152. Three village studies: E. Grendi on politics of a Ligurian commune in sixteenth and seventeenth centuries; Patrizia Bigi and others, and Renata Ago, on eighteenth-century villages in Piedmont and Campagna respectively.

.136 **Lo Giudice**, G., *Communità Rurali della Sicilia Moderna. Bronte, 1747-1853*, Catania, 1969. Tenurial and agricultural developments in Sicilian latifundia region.

.137 **McArdle**, F., *Altopascio. A Study in Tuscan Rural Society, 1587-1784*, 1978. Excellent microstudy of estate belonging to Grand Duke.

.138 **Massafra**, A., 'Giurisdizionalismo feudale e rendita fondiaria nel Settecento napoletano', *Quad.Stor.*, 19, 1972, 187-252. Deals with wealth and estate administration of Pignatelli and Revertera families.

.139 **Mazzi**, M. S., and Raveggi, S., *Gli Uomini e le Cose nelle Campagne Fiorentine del Quattrocento*, Florence, 1983. Attempts to document wealth and standard of living of peasantry from inventories.

.140 **Pansini**, G., 'Per una storia del feudalismo nel Granducato di Toscana durante il periodo Mediceo', *Quad.Stor.*, 19, 1972, 131-86. Part of journal issue concentrating on rural class relations.

.141 **Pescosolido**, G., *Terra e Nobiltà. I Borghese*, Rome, 1979. Deals with estates of princely family in Papal States from seventeenth to early twentieth centuries.

.142 **Poni**, C., ed., 'Azienda agraria e microstoria', *Quad.Stor.*, 39, 1978, 801-1035. Eleven case-studies of early modern estates in Central and Northern Italy.

.143 **Sereni**, E., *Storia del Paesaggio Agrario Italiano*, Bari, 1961. Attempts similar outline to Bloch's for France (7.29). Review article: G. Duby, *Annales*, 18, 1963, 352-62.

.144 —— and others, 'Agricoltura e sviluppo del capitalismo', *Studi Stor.*, 9, 1968, 477-812. Notable for pieces by A. Ventura on early modern Veneto and G. Giorgetti on eighteenth-century Tuscany. (Also contains short general papers by W. Kula on Poland and S. Pach on Hungary).

.145 **Spaggiari**, P. L., *L'Agricoltura negli Stati Parmensi dal 1750 al 1859*, Milan, 1966. Conditions in Duchy of Parma, an important wheat-growing area.

7.146 **Visceglia**, Maria A., 'Rendita feudale e agricoltura in Puglia nell'età moderna (16-18 sec.)', *Società e Storia*, 3, 1980, 527-60. See also associated article by Michèle Benaiteau on returns in Principato Ultra of Naples, *ib.*, 561-611.

7.147 **Zangheri**, R., 'The historical relationship between agricultural and economic development in Italy', in Jones and Woolf (7.14), 23-39. Some reasons why agriculture, though technically advanced at an early stage in some Italian regions, did not fuel industrial take-off.

GERMANY, SWITZERLAND, AUSTRIA

See also 3.221; 5.381-3; 6.192; 7.292-3; 9.104,128; 14.90.

7.148 **Abel**, W., *Geschichte der Deutschen Landwirtschaft vom Frühen Mittelalter bis zum 19. Jahrhundert*, Stuttgart, 1962. 2nd ed., 1967. Concentrates on technological and economic aspects. See also 7.158 and 7.177 in same series.

7.149 **Achilles**, W., *Die Lage der Hannoverschen Landbevölkerung im Späten 18. Jahrhundert*, Hildesheim, 1982. Comprehensive description of agrarian conditions in North-West Germany, based on official enquiry in 1766. Review articles: R. Berthold, *Jb.Wirtschaftsgesch.*, 1985 (iii), 109-23; G. Heitz, ib. (iv), 149-66.

7.150 —— *Vermögensverhältnisse Braunschweig-ischer Bauernhöfe im 17. und 18. Jahrhundert*, Stuttgart, 1965. Investigates values of land and farm stock from inventories, etc., in a number of Brunswick districts.

7.151 **Berdahl**, R. M., 'Christian Garve on the German peasantry', *Peasant Stud.*, 8 (ii), 1979, 86-102. Translates a portion of Garve's *Über den Charakter der Bauern* (1786).

7.152 —— 'Paternalism, serfdom, and emancipation in Prussia', in E. Angermann and Marie-L. Frings, eds., *Oceans Apart? Comparing Germany and the United States*, Stuttgart, 1981, 29-44. Includes some comparison with American slavery (cf. 7.195).

7.153 **Boelcke**, W. A., 'Bäuerlicher Wohlstand in Württemberg, Ende des 16. Jahrhunderts', *Jb.Nationalökonomie*, 176, 1964, 241-80. See also his article on peasant credit facilities in fifteenth- and sixteenth-century Württemberg, ib., 319-58.

7.154 **Bog**, I., *Die Bäuerliche Wirtschaft im Zeitalter des Dreissigjährigen Krieges*, Coburg, 1952. Based mainly on sources from district of Heilsbronn, between Nuremberg and Ansbach.

7.155 —— *Dorfgemeinde, Freiheit, und Unfreiheit in Franken*, Stuttgart, 1956. On social structure of rural communities in Würzburg and Bamberg areas.

7.156 **Carsten**, F. L., 'The origins of the Junkers', *Eng.Hist.Rev.*, 62, 1947, 145-78. Repr. in his *Essays in German History*, 1985, 17-50. Investigates conditions which led to decline and revival of demesne farming by East German nobility, c.1375-1625.

7.157 **Cole**, J. W., and Wolf, E. R., *The Hidden Frontier. Ecology and Ethnicity in an Alpine Valley*, New York, 1974. Anthropological study of one German and one Romance-speaking village in South Tyrol, with strong emphasis on historical factors.

7.158 **Franz**, G., *Geschichte des Deutschen Bauernstandes vom Frühen Mittelalter bis zum 19. Jahrhundert*, Stuttgart, 1970. Companion vol. to 7.148 and 7.177.

7.159 —— ed., *Bauernschaft und Bauernstand, 1500-1970. Büdinger Vorträge, 1971-72*, Limburg an der Lahn, 1975. Valuable essay collection.

7.160 **Fresacher**, W., *Der Bauer in Kärnten*, 3 vols., Klagenfurt, 1950-55. Concentrates on tenurial law.

7.161 **Gagliardo**, J. G., *From Pariah to Patriot. The Changing Image of the German Peasant, 1770-1840*, Lexington, Ky., 1969. Tries to account for shift in publicists' attitude to peasantry, which came to be extolled as upholder of national virtues. See also his 'Moralism, rural ideology, and the German peasant in the late eighteenth century', *Agric.Hist.*, 42, 1968, 79-102.

7.162 **Hagen**, W. W., 'How mighty the Junkers? Peasant rents and seigneurial profits in sixteenth-century Brandenburg', *P.& P.*, 108, 1985, 80-116. Revisionist thesis that expansion of demesne farming was not so oppressive of peasantry as traditionally painted.

7.163 —— 'The Junkers' faithless servants. Peasant insubordination and the breakdown of serfdom in Brandenburg-Prussia, 1763-1811', in R. J. Evans and W. R. Lee, eds., *The German Peasantry. Conflict and Community in Rural Society*

from the Eighteenth to the Twentieth Centuries, 1986, 71-101. Case study of Brandenburg estate of Stavenow, showing increased dissatisfaction of tenants with tenurial obligations.

7.164 —— 'Working for the Junker. The standard of living of manorial labourers in Brandenburg, 1584-1810', *J.Mod.Hist.*, 58, 1986, 143-58. Another paper on Stavenow estate, painting relatively favourable picture of conditions.

7.165 **Harnisch**, H., *Bauern, Feudaladel, Städtebürgertum*, Weimar, 1980. Reconstructs marketing of farm produce, rents, prices, and wages of Magdeburg region.

7.166 —— 'Die Gutsherrschaft. Forschungs-geschichte, Entwicklungszusammen-hänge, und Strukturelemente', *Jb. Gesch. Feudalismus*, 9, 1985, 189-240; 10, 1986, 251-74. Survey article on East German agrarian structure; later part deals with periodisation and regional typology. Interesting to compare with earlier treatment, 'Die Gutsherrschaft in Brandenburg. Ergebnisse und Probleme', *Jb.Wirtschaftsgesch.*, 1969 (iii), 117-48.

7.167 —— *Die Herrschaft Boitzenburg. Untersuchungen zur Entwicklung der Sozialökonomischen Struktur Ländlicher Gebiete in der Mark Brandenburg vom 14. bis zum 19. Jahrhundert*, Weimar, 1968. Traces evolution of estate belonging to von Arnim family.

7.168 —— 'Peasants and markets. The background to the agrarian reforms in feudal Prussia east of the Elbe, 1760-1807', in Evans and Lee (7.163), 37-70. Stresses important effect on tenurial questions of late eighteenth-century rise in grain prices.

7.169 —— 'Rechnungen und Taxationen. Quellenkundliche Betrachtungen zu einer Untersuchung der Feudalrente, vornehmlich vom 16. bis zum 18. Jahrhundert', *Jb.Gesch.Feudalismus*, 6, 1982, 337-70.

7.170 —— 'Rechtsqualität des Bauernlandes und Gutsherrschaft', *ib.*, 3, 1979, 311-63. Looks at historical reasons for differing oppressiveness of peasant tenures and repercussions for demesne farming.

7.171 **Henning**, F. W., *Bauernwirtschaft und Bauerneinkommen im Fürstentum Paderborn im 18. Jahrhundert*, Berlin, 1970. Valuable, especially on size of holdings.

7.172 —— *Dienste und Abgeben der Bauern im 18.Jahrhundert*, Stuttgart, 1969. Presents useful contrast between East and West European peasant conditions by case studies of East Prussia, on one hand, and Bishopric of Paderborn, on other.

7.173 —— and others, 'Bäuerliche Einkommen im 18. Jahrhundert', *Jb.Wirtschaftsgesch.*, 1970 (i), 165-97. Associated short articles by Henning, R. Berthold, and H. Harnisch.

7.174 **Hirschfelder**, H., *Herrschaftsordnung und Bauerntum im Hochstift Osnabrück im 16. und 17. Jahrhundert*, Osnabrück, 1971.

7.175 **Lehmann**, R., *Die Verhältnisse der Niederlausitzischen Herrschafts- und Gutsbauern in der Zeit vom Dreissigjährigen Kriege bis zu den Preussischen Reformen*, Köln, 1956.

7.176 **Lütge**, F., *Die Bayerische Grundherrschaft. Untersuchungen über die Agrarverfassung Altbayerns im 16.- 18. Jahrhundert*, Stuttgart, 1949. Gives somewhat static picture.

7.177 —— *Geschichte der Deutschen Agrarverfassung vom Frühen Mittelalter bis zum 19. Jahrhundert*, Stuttgart, 1963. 2nd ed., 1967. Companion vol. to 7.148 and 7.158, concentrating on tenurial aspects. Review article: D. Lösche, *Jb.Wirtschafts-gesch.*, 1967 (i), 381-406.

7.178 —— *Die Mitteldeutsche Grundherrschaft und ihre Auflösung*, Stuttgart, 1957. Reworking of book first publ. in 1934, and with somewhat legalistic and institutional approach then common to agrarian history.

7.179 **Mayhew**, A., *Rural Settlement and Farming in Germany*, 1973. Historical geographer's perspective. Covers earliest times to present day.

7.180 **Müller**, H.-H., 'Domänen und Domänenpächter in Brandenburg-Preussen im 18. Jahrhundert', *Jb.Wirtschaftsgesch.*, 1965, 152-92. Repr. in Büsch and Neugebauer (3.248), 1, 316-59.

7.181 **Nichtweiss**, J., *Das Bauernlegen in Mecklenburg. Eine Untersuchung zur Geschichte der Bauernschaft und der Zweiten Leibeigenschaft in Mecklenburg bis zum Beginn des 19. Jahrhunderts*, Berlin, 1954. Some useful information under layers of Marxist terminology.

7.182 —— 'The second serfdom and the so-called "Prussian way". The development

of capitalism in Eastern German agricultural institutions', *Review*, 3, 1979, 99-153. Includes discussion between author and J. Kuczynski. Transl.from *Zeitschr.Geschichtswissenschaft*, 1-2, 1953-54, complete with allusions to Stalin and Marxist early fathers, and publ. for alleged relevance to continuing debate on nature of market-oriented estate agriculture.

7.183 **Rebel**, H., *Peasant Classes. Bureaucratization of Property and Family Relations under Early Habsburg Absolutism, 1511-1636*, Princeton, N.J., 1983. Examines social and family structures in Upper Austria, and argues that their authoritarian nature had unofficial police function. Review article: T. Fox, *Peasant Stud.*, 12, 1985, 217-25.

7.184 **Saalfeld**, D., *Bauernwirtschaft und Gutsbetrieb in der Vorindustriellen Zeit*, Stuttgart, 1960. Deals essentially with Lower Saxon region in early modern period.

7.185 **Sabean**, D., 'Family and land tenure. A case study of conflict in the German Peasants' War (1525)', *Peasant Stud.Newsl.*, 3 (i), 1974, 1-15. Originally publ. (in French) in *Annales*, 27, 1972, 903-22. Region examined is Upper Swabia (around Ravensburg), with emphasis on disputes concerning inheritance law.

7.186 —— German agararian institutions at the beginning of the sixteenth century. Upper Swabia as an example', *J.Peasant Stud.*, 3, 1975, 76-88. Population pressure, new market relationships, and increasing demands from state seen as factors producing change and protest.

7.187 —— *Landbesitz und Gesellschaft am Vorabend des Bauernkriegs. Eine Studie der Sozialen Verhältnisse im Südlichen Oberschwaben in den Jahren vor 1525*, Stuttgart, 1972. Detailed account of conditions in countryside around Ravensburg, c.1450-1525, with attention to factors influencing peasant discontent.

7.188 **Schissler**, Hanna, *Preussische Agrargesellschaft im Wandel. Wirtschaftliche, Gesellschaftliche, und Politische Transformationsprozesse von 1763 bis 1847*, Göttingen, 1978. Good synthesis of research on agrarian society during "era of reform" and peasant emancipation.

7.189 **Winkler**, K., *Landwirtschaft und Agrarverfassung im Fürstentum Osnabrück*

nach dem Dreissigjährigen Kriege,
Stuttgart, 1959.

7.190 **Wunder**, Heide, *Bäuerliche Gemeinde in
Deutschland*, Göttingen, 1986.
Examination of how rural communes
functioned by leading specialist on early
modern German peasantry (covers early
medieval to modern times).

7.191 —— 'Peasant organization and class
conflict in East and West Germany',
P.&P., 78, 1978, 47-55. Repr. in Aston
and Philpin (7.2), 91-100. Argues that
East-West contrast in peasant obligations
so marked from sixteenth century on,
cannot be traced back to medieval patterns
of class domination.

7.192 —— 'Serfdom in later medieval and early
modern Germany', in T. H. Aston and
others, eds., *Social Relations and Ideas.
Essays in honour of R. H. Hilton*, 1983,
249-72. Compares situation in S. W.
Germany, Bavaria, and east of the Elbe.

EASTERN EUROPE (GENERAL)
*For material on "Gutsherrschaft" system in German
lands, see preceding sub-section, notably
7.152,156,162-70,172,175,181-2,184,188,191-2.
See also 9.169.*

7.193 **Blum**, J., 'Land tenure in the Austrian
monarchy before 1848', *Agric.Hist.*, 19,
1945, 87-98. Sketch of conditions
prevailing in Habsburg Empire,
c.1760-1848.

7.194 —— 'The rise of serfdom in Eastern
Europe', *Am.Hist.Rev.*, 62, 1957, 807-36.

7.195 **Chirot**, D., 'Growth of the market and
service labour systems in agriculture',
J.Soc.Hist., 8 (ii), 1975, 67-80. Compares
E. European serfdom, American slavery,
and colonial forced labour as "servile"
mode of production differing from classical
feudalism in arising from combination of
market forces and labour shortage. Cf.
7.152.

7.196 **Hunt**, V. F., 'The rise of feudalism in
Eastern Europe. A critical appraisal of the
Wallerstein "world-system" thesis', *Sci.&
Soc.*, 42, 1978, 43-61. Attributes second
serfdom to endogenous factors such as
labour shortage rather than dependence on
western markets.

7.197 **Kahan**, A., 'Infringement of the market
upon the serf-economy in Eastern Europe',
Peasant Stud.Newsl., 3 (ii), 1974, 7-13.
Sketches adjustments to market forces by

both landlords and serfs in later eighteenth
century.

7.198 **Link**, Edith M., *The Emancipation of the
Austrian Peasant, 1740-98*, New York,
1949. Useful study of chequered agrarian
reforms of Maria Theresa and Joseph II.
("Austrian" used in wider sense).

7.199 **Makkai**, L., and others, '[Symposium on
neo-serfdom in East Central Europe]',
Slavic Rev., 34, 1975, 225-78. General
survey by Makkai, and separate articles on
Bohemia, Poland, and Hungary.

7.200 **Millward**, R., 'An economic analysis of the
organization of serfdom in Eastern
Europe', *J.Ec.Hist.*, 42, 1982, 513-48.
Argues that a manorial structure with
forced labour is logical economic outcome
of institutional serfdom. See also further
discussion with S. Fenoaltea, *ib.*, 43, 1983,
705-12; and 9.453.

7.201 **Schöffer**, I., 'The second serfdom in
Eastern Europe as a problem of historical
explanation', *Hist.Stud.(Australia &
N.Z.)*, 9, 1959, 46-61. Argues that by-
passing of towns during expansion of corn
exports is most plausible explanation.

7.202 **Topolski**, J., 'Continuity and
discontinuity in the development of the
feudal system in Eastern Europe (tenth to
seventeenth centuries)', *J.Eur.Ec.Hist.*,
10, 1981, 373-400. Useful for discussion of
"refeudalisation" process.

7.203 —— 'The manorial-serf economy in
Central and Eastern Europe in the
sixteenth and seventeenth centuries',
Agric.Hist., 48, 1974, 341-52. Sees "new
serfdom" as part of European-wide search
by nobility for new sources of income.

BOHEMIA, HUNGARY, AND POLAND
See also 6.203; 7.18,144,232,294-7; 11.85.

7.204 **Blodgett**, Linda L., 'The "second
serfdom" in Bohemia. A case study of the
Rozmberk estates in the sixteenth
century', in I. Volgyes, ed., *The Peasantry
of Eastern Europe*, New York, 1979, 1,
1-18. Shows that on most important private
estates in Bohemia there was no switch
from a rentier to a domain economy in this
period.

7.205 **Klíma**, A., 'Agrarian class structure and
economic development in pre-industrial
Bohemia', *P.& P.*, 85, 1979, 49-67. Repr.
in Aston and Philpin (7.2), 192-212.

Sketches rise and decline of demesne labour service in seventeenth and eighteenth centuries.

7.206 **Stark**, W., 'Die Abhängigkeits-verhältnisse der gutsherrlichen Bauern Böhmens im 17. und 18. Jahrhundert', *Jb.Nationalökonomie*, 164, 1952, 270-92, 348-74, 440-53.

7.207 **Wright**, W. E., *Serf, Seigneur, and Sovereign. Agrarian Reform in Eighteenth-Century Bohemia*, Minneapolis, Minn., 1966. Concentrates on Joseph II's measures to restrict peasant burdens.

7.208 **Erdei**, F., 'Peasant society', *Peasant Stud.Newsl.*, 4 (ii), 1975, 5-12. Brief general survey of Hungarian peasantry's history.

7.209 **Eszlary**, C. d', 'La situation des serfs en Hongrie de 1514 à 1848', *Rev.Hist.Éc.et Soc.*, 38, 1960, 385-417.

7.210 **Gates-Coon**, Rebecca, 'The Esterhazy princes as landlords. Estate management in Hungary during the late eighteenth century', in K. Hitchins, ed., *Studies in East European Social History*, Leiden, 1977-81, 2, 157-89.

7.211 **Kállay**, I., 'Management of big estates in Hungary between 1711 and 1848', in *Études Historiques Hongroises…15e Congrès International des Sciences Historiques*, 2 vols., Budapest, 1980, 1, 341-60.

7.212 **Komjáthy**, A., 'Hungarian *jobbágyság* in the fifteenth century', *E.Eur.Q.*, 10, 1976, 77-111. Deals with peasant conditions leading up to major revolt of 1514.

7.213 **Liebel-Weckowicz**, Helen, and Szabo, F. J., 'Modernization forces in Maria Theresa's peasant policies, 1740-80', *Hist.Sociale/Social Hist.*, 15, 1982, 301-31. Argues that aim was property-owning peasantry through conversion of onerous tenures to freehold.

7.214 **Pach**, Z. P., 'The development of feudal rent in Hungary in the fifteenth century', *Ec.Hist.Rev.*, 2nd ser., 19, 1966, 1-14. Argues that in later fifteenth century Hungarian agrarian structure was still developing on same lines as in W. Europe.

7.215 —— *Die Ungarische Agrarentwicklung im 16-17. Jahrhundert*, Budapest, 1964. Attempts to explain why Hungary followed E. European pattern.

7.216 **Kieniewicz**, S., *The Emancipation of the Polish Peasantry*, Chicago, 1969. Contains some material on later eighteenth century.

7.217 **Kula**, W., *An Economic Theory of the Feudal System. Towards a Model of the Polish Economy, 1500-1800*, 1976. Transl. from French ed. of 1970. Presents much-discussed and influential model of manorial system of production in widest context. Review article: M. Postan, *New Left Rev.*, 103, 1977, 72-7.

7.218 —— 'Money and serfs in eighteenth-century Poland', in E. J. Hobsbawm and others, eds., *Peasants in History. Essays in Honour of Daniel Thorner*, Calcutta, 1980, 30-41. Charts certain areas in which cash dealings by peasants were important despite theoretical self-sufficiency.

7.219 **Zytkowicz**, L., 'The peasant's farm and the landlord's farm in Poland from the sixteenth to the middle of the eighteenth century', *J.Eur.Ec.Hist.*, 1, 1972, 135-54. General review of agrarian history.

TURKEY AND THE BALKANS
See also 3.304; 7.298; 10.526; 13.154.

7.220 **Asdrachas**, S. I., 'Aux Balkans du 15e siècle. Producteurs directs et marché', *Et.Balkaniques*, 6 (iii), 1970, 36-69. Investigates whether agricultural markets existed at village level, and how far Ottoman society had Asiatic mode of production (in Marxist terminology).

7.221 **Columbeanu**, S., *Grandes Exploitations Domaniales en Valachie au 18e Siècle*, Bucharest, 1974.

7.222 **Faroqhi**, Suraiya, 'Rural society in Anatolia and the Balkans during the sixteenth century', *Turcica*, 9, 1977, 161-95; 11, 1979, 103-53. Major survey.

7.223 —— 'The peasants of Saideli in the late sixteenth century', *Arch.Ottomanicum*, 8, 1983, 215-50. Repr. in Faroqhi (4.82). Pieces together social history of small group of Anatolian villages north of Konya.

7.224 **Inalcik**, H,, 'The emergence of big farms, *çiftliks*. State, landlords, and tenants', in Inalcik (3.290). Eighteenth-century development.

7.225 —— 'The Ottoman decline and its effects upon the *reaya*', in Inalcik (3.299). On increasing burdens of peasantry from late sixteenth century.

7.226 **Mioc**, D., and others, 'L'évolution de la rente féodale en Valachie et en Moldavie du 14e au 17e siècle', in *Nouvelles Études d'Histoire… 11e Congrès des Sciences*

Historiques, Bucharest, 1960, 221-52.

7.227 **Otetea**, A., 'Le second asservissement des paysans roumains (1746-1821)', in *Nouvelles Études d'Histoire...10e Congrès des Sciences Historiques*, Bucharest, 1955, 299-312.

7.228 **Prodan**, D., 'Serfdom in sixteenth-century Transylvania', *Review*, 9, 1986, 649-78. General conclusion transl. from 3-vol. work in Romanian (1967-68).

7.229 **Stahl**, H. H., *Les Anciennes Communautés Villageoises Roumaines. Asservissement et Pénétration Capitaliste*, Bucharest, 1969. History of internal functioning and feudal burdens of villages from late Middle Ages to early twentieth century (thematic rather than chronological).

7.230 **Stoianovich**, T., 'Land tenure and related sectors of the Balkan economy, 1600-1800', *J.Ec.Hist.*, 13, 1953, 398-411. Describes rise of *çiftlik* estates, and subsequent diffusion of cotton and maize cultivation.

7.231 **Sugar**, P. F., 'Major changes in the life of the Slav peasantry under Ottoman rule', *Int.J.Mid.E.Stud.*, 9, 1978, 297-305. Survey lecture.

7.232 **Zytkowicz**, L., 'Directions of agrarian development in South-Eastern Europe in the sixteenth-eighteenth centuries', *Acta Poloniae Hist.*, 43, 1981, 31-73. Useful summary, dealing in turn with Hungary, Romanian principalities, and Ottoman-occupied Balkans.

SCANDINAVIA
See also 4.23; 5.242; 10.455; 11.96.

7.233 **Aspvall**, G., 'The sale of Crown land in Sweden. The introductory epoch, 1701-23', *Ec.& Hist.*, 9, 1966, 3-28. Investigates social distribution of sales in county of Skaraborg.

7.234 **Aunola**, T., 'Indebtedness of North-Ostrobothnian farmers to merchants, 1765-1809', *Scan.Ec.Hist.Rev.*, 13, 1965, 163-85. Credit arrangements in region of Raahe and Oulu ports – argued that inflation gave farmers a favourable rate.

7.235 **Bjørn**, C., 'The peasantry and agrarian reform in Denmark', *ib.*, 25, 1977, 117-37. Discusses government's regulation of labour dues, and argues that enclosures were not altogether unpopular. (Later eighteenth century).

7.236 **Ericsson**, Birgitta, 'Central power and the local right to dispose over the forest commune in eighteenth-century Sweden', *Scan.J.Hist.*, 5, 1980, 75-92. Micro-study of one parish's struggle against local iron foundry, and methods of appeal used.

7.237 **Hansen**, V., 'A Danish land survey from the seventeenth century', in A. R. H. Baker and M. Billinge, eds., *Period and Place. Research Methods in Historical Geography*, 1982, 281-8. Brief study of research possibilities offered by Christian V's national survey of 1688.

7.238 **Holmsen**, A., 'Landowners and tenants in Norway', *Scan.Ec.Hist.Rev.*, 6, 1958, 121-31. Review of book by H. Bjørkvik on Ryfylke district of Stavanger, tracing pattern of landholding back from 1661 to pre-Reformation times.

7.239 —— 'The transition from tenancy to freehold peasant ownership in Norway', *ib.*, 9, 1961, 152-64. Discusses regional differences in growth of freehold farms between mid-seventeenth century and 1835.

7.240 **Jutikkala**, E., 'Finnish agricultural labour in the eighteenth and early nineteenth centuries', *ib.*, 10, 1962, 203-19. On use of hired hands and establishment of crofts as sources of estate labour.

7.241 —— 'Large scale farming in Scandinavia in the seventeenth century', *ib.*, 23, 1975, 159-66. Short survey of extent of demesne farming (found to be very limited, even in Denmark).

7.242 **Lárusson**, B., 'Valuation and distribution of landed property in Iceland', *Ec.& Hist.*, 4, 1961, 34-64. Based on land registers compiled at beginning of eighteenth century.

7.243 **Lunden**, K., 'Some causes of change in a peasant economy. Interactions between cultivated area, farming population, climate, taxation, and technology', *Scan.Ec.Hist.Rev.*, 22, 1974, 117-35. Examines Norwegian peasant economy from c.800 to 1600 in light of theoretical models.

7.244 **Luuko**, A., 'The "annual budget" of North Finnish farmers at the end of the seventeenth century', *ib.*, 6, 1958, 132-43. Attempts to use export figures to assess economic position of farmers.

7.245 **Mäkelä**, A., 'Deserted lands and tenements in Hattula and Porvoo to 1607', *ib.*, 25, 1977, 62-87. Widespread (if sometimes temporary) abandonment of holdings in two Finnish districts deduced from tax records.

.246 **Munck**, T., *The Peasantry and the Early Absolute Monarchy in Denmark, 1660-1708*, Copenhagen, 1979. Mainly on Crown administrative policy concerning tenurial relations and burdens of taxation and conscription.

.247 —— 'The economic and social position of peasant freeholders in late seventeenth-century Denmark', *Scan.Ec.Hist.Rev.*, 25, 1977, 37-61. Emphasises limited numbers and precarious status of freeholds.

.248 **Oakley**, S., 'Reconstructing Scandinavian farms, 1660-1860. Sources in Denmark, Iceland, Norway, and Sweden', *ib.*, 34, 1986, 181-203. Case-studies to illustrate methods for tracing history of individual peasant farms over long time span.

.249 **Østerud**, Ø., *Agrarian Structure and Peasant Politics in Scandinavia. A Comparative Study of Rural Response to Economic Change*, Oslo, 1978. Begins with seventeenth- and eighteenth-century developments; main emphasis on Norway.

.250 **Salvesen**, H., 'The strength of tradition. A historiographical analysis of research into Norwegian agrarian history during the late Middle Ages and the early modern period', *Scan.J.Hist.*, 7, 1982, 75-133. Traces development of research tradition since about 1920.

.251 **Skrubbeltrang**, F., 'Developments in tenancy in eighteenth-century Denmark as a move towards peasant proprietorship', *Scan.Ec.Hist.Rev.*, 9, 1961, 165-75. Discusses copyhold tenure as precursor of freehold, and regional lags in this process.

.252 —— 'History of the Finnish peasant', *ib.*, 12, 1964, 165-80. Review and summary of work in Finnish by Eino Jutikkala (Helsingfors, 1963).

.253 **Sogner**, S., 'Freeholder and cottar. Property relationships and the social structure in the peasant community in Norway during the eighteenth century', *Scan.J.Hist.*, 1, 1976, 181-99.

.254 **Tønnesson**, K., 'Tenancy, freehold, and enclosure in Scandinavia from the seventeenth to the nineteenth century', *ib.*, 6, 1981, 191-206. Explores differences in trend towards freehold tenure between Sweden, Denmark, and Norway. See also short supplementary on Finland by E. Jutikkala, *ib.*, 7, 1982, 339-44.

RUSSIA AND BALTIC PROVINCES
See also 7.329; 8.173; 10.537.

7.255 **Bartlett**, R. P., 'J. J. Sievers and the Russian peasantry under Catherine II', *Jb.Gesch.Osteuropas*, 32, 1984, 16-33. Mainly on Sievers' admiration for Livonian agriculture, and unsuccessful attempts to apply methods to model estate in his Novgorod government.

7.256 **Blum**, J., *Lord and Peasant in Russia from the Ninth to the Nineteenth Century*, Princeton, N.J., 1963. Pioneering study of rise and consolidation of serfdom.

7.257 **Confino**, M., *Domaines et Seigneurs en Russie vers la Fin du 18e Siècle. Étude de Structures Agraires et de Mentalités Économiques*, Paris, 1963. Makes especial use of publications of Economic Society of St. Petersburg, founded in 1765. Review article: F. Dovring, *Comp.Stud.Soc.& Hist.*, 7, 1965, 309-23.

7.258 **Indova**, E. I., 'Les activités commerciales de la paysannerie dans les villages du Tsar de la région de Moscou (première moitié du 18e siècle)', *Cah.Monde Russe et Sov.*, 5, 1964, 208-28. Describes peasant enterprise in marketing produce or as artisans, sometimes on considerable scale.

7.259 **Madariaga**, Isabel de, 'Catherine II and the serfs', *Slavonic & E.Eur.Rev.*, 52, 1974, 34-62. Points to some uncertainties in evidence that serf numbers and burdens increased markedly under Catherine.

7.260 **Dunsdorfs**, E., *Der Grosse Schwedische Kataster in Livland, 1681-1710*, Stockholm, 1950. On survey of land ownership and use in Latvia.

7.261 —— *The Livonian Estates of Axel Oxenstjerna*, Stockholm, 1981. Material on both peasant and demesne agriculture during Swedish occupation of Latvia.

7.262 **Grekov**, B. D., *Die Bauern in der Rus von den Ältesten Zeiten bis zum 17. Jahrhundert*, 2 vols., Berlin, 1958-59. Transl. from Russian ed. of 1954. Grekov shaped standard Marxist interpretation of Russian peasant history, and this work represents his most considered synthesis.

7.263 **Hellie**, R., *Enserfment and Military Change in Muscovy*, Chicago, 1971. Sees advancement of serfdom in sixteenth and seventeenth centuries as quid pro quo for role of service nobility in the army. Review article: S. L. Parsons, *Can.-Am.Slavic Stud.*, 6, 1972, 478-89.

7.264 **Sakharov**, A. N., 'The seventeenth-century Russian village; based on data from the Patriarchy's holdings', *Soviet Stud.in Hist.*, 6 (ii), 1967, 3-43. Transl. of introduction and chaps.3-4 of book of this title (Moscow, 1966), followed by review by I. A. Tikhonov and Z. K. Ianel'. Extracts deal with rents and peasant mobility.

7.265 **Smith**, R. E. F., *The Enserfment of the Russian Peasantry*, 1968. Collection of documents in transl.

7.266 —— *Peasant Farming in Muscovy*, 1977. Deals with peasant economy from Mongol invasions to seventeenth century, and gradual erosion of independence as tsars became more powerful.

7.267 **Vernadsky**, G., 'Serfdom in Russia', in *10 Congresso Internazionale di Scienze Storiche*

(7.91), 3, 247-72. Brief outline of main stages from origins to emancipation.

7.268 **Von Loewe**, K., 'Commerce and agriculture in Lithuania, 1400-1600', *Ec.Hist.Rev.*, 2nd ser., 26, 1973, 23-37. On relation between tenure and nature of markets.

7.269 —— 'Juridical manifestations of serfdom in West Russia', *Can.-Am.Slavic Stud.*, 6, 1972, 390-9. Difficulties of tracing evolution of serfdom in Lithuania before late sixteenth century.

7.270 **Zorn**, J., 'New Soviet work on the old-Russian peasantry', *Russ.Rev.*, 39, 1980, 339-47. Discusses three Russian works about peasants on monastery lands in seventeenth and early eighteenth centuries.

AGRICULTURAL PRODUCTIVITY, CROPS, AND TECHNIQUES

GENERAL PRODUCTIVITY. CEREALS CULTIVATION AND YIELDS
See also 4.33,36 (general); 3.65 and 7.62 (France); 11.50 (Low Countries); 11.146 (Spain); 4.39 (Switzerland).

7.271 **Goy**, J., and Le Roy Ladurie, E., eds., *Les Fluctuations du Produit de la Dîme. Conjoncture Décimale et Dominiale de la Fin du Moyen Age au 18e Siècle*, Paris, 1972. Reports of research team investigating tithe receipts in various European regions, mainly French, as measure of agricultural production. For brief description of project, see Le Roy Ladurie (4.35), 193-202, or *Annales*, 24, 1969, 826-32.

7.272 —— 'Peasant dues, tithes, and trends in agricultural production in pre-industrial societies', in *Proc. Seventh International Economic History Congress* (4.45), 1, 113-61, 541-50. Papers, mainly in French, covering Netherlands, Italy, Spain, Germany, and Eastern Europe (en bloc).

7.273 —— *Tithe and Agrarian History from the Fourteenth to the Nineteenth Century*, 1982. Two separate essays: one on methodology (Goy), one attempting synthesis of research results (Le Roy Ladurie).

7.274 **Kahk**, J., and Remmel, M., 'Studying cycles of agrarian development through

pattern recognition methods', in D. K. Rowney, ed., *Soviet Quantitative History*, Beverly Hills, Calif., 1984, 89-112. Comparative analysis of early modern harvest cycles by graphical methods.

7.275 **Morineau**, M., 'History and tithes', *J.Eur.Ec.Hist.*, 10. 1981, 437-80. Long critique of some conclusions drawn from tithe investigations, notably by Le Roy Ladurie (see 7.271-2).

7.276 **Slicher van Bath**, B. H., *Yield Ratios, 810-1820*, Wageningen, 1963. Pioneering tabulation.

7.277 —— and Dovring, F., 'Eighteenth-century agriculture on the continent of Europe. Evolution or revolution?', *Agric.Hist.*, 43, 1969, 169-86. Both writers agree that productivity gains of century were fairly modest; even England was only catching up with standards already achieved in Netherlands.

7.278 **Wrigley**, E. A., 'Some reflections on corn yields and prices in pre-industrial economies', in his *People, Cities, and Wealth. The Transformation of Traditional Society*, 1987, 92-130. Largely speculative; seeks to emphasise non-linear relationship of price to yield.

7.279 **Forster**, R., 'Obstacles to agricultural growth in eighteenth-century France',

Am.Hist.Rev., 75, 1970, 1600-15.

7.280 **Le Roy Ladurie**, E., 'The fantastical accounts of Gregory King', in *Social Historians in Contemporary France* (3.4), 141-56; and in Le Roy Ladurie (4.35), 173-91. Transl. from *Annales*, 23, 1968, 1086-1102. Questions King's and Vauban's estimates of agricultural production in France c.1700.

7.281 **Meuvret**, J., *Le Problème des Subsistances à l'Époque Louis XIV. La Production des Céréales*, 2 vols. in 3, Paris, 1977-87. Part of vast study on food supply system of old regime which Meuvret did not complete for publication, and which is being assembled from drafts. Review article (vol.1): S. L. Kaplan, *Annales*, 36, 1981, 294-300.

7.282 **Neveux**, H., *Vie et Déclin d'une Structure conomique. Les Grains du Cambrésis (Fin du 14e-Début du 17e Siècle)*, Paris, 1980. Finds evidence of decline in grain yields over this period (tithe sources) and seeks explanation in social structure.

7.283 **Sexauer**, B., 'English and French agriculture in the late eighteenth century', *Agric.Hist.*, 50, 1976, 491-505. Primarily using figures of Arthur Young, attempts comparative estimates of product per acre and product per unit of labour.

7.284 **Toutain**, J. C., *Le Produit de L'Agriculture Française de 1700 à 1958. (Cahiers de l'I.S.E.A., Histoire Quantitative de l'Économie Française, 1-2)*, Paris, 1961. Part of ambitious statistical history.

7.285 **Van der Wee**, H., and Cauwenberghe, E. van, eds., *Productivity of Land and Agricultural Innovation in the Low Countries, 1250-1800*, Louvain. 1978. Contains nine papers assessing regional variations.

7.286 **Anes Alvarez**, G., and Le Flem, J. P., 'Las crisis del siglo 17. Producción agrícola, precios y ingresos en tierras de Segovia', *Moneda y Crédito*, 93, 1965, 3-55.

7.287 **Juan Vidal**, J., 'La evolución de la producción agrícola en Mallorca durante la edad moderna', *ib.*, 145, 1978, 67-99.

7.288 **Ladero Quesada**, M. A., and González Jiménez, M., *Diezmo Ecclesistico y Producción de Cereales en el Reino de Sevilla (1408-1503)*, Seville, 1979. Uses tithes of Archbishopric as measure of production along lines of 7.271-3.

7.289 **Weisser**, M. R., 'The agrarian depression in seventeenth-century Spain', *J.Ec.Hist.*, 42, 1982, 149-54. Short conference paper, mainly on sustained loss of population and stagnant production of Segovia and Toledo provinces.

7.290 **Cattini**, M., 'Produzione, auto-consumo, e mercato dei grani a San Felice sul Panaro (1590-1637)', *Riv.Stor.Ital.*, 85, 1973, 698-753. Microstudy of production patterns in commune near Modena.

7.291 **Paci**, R., 'Rese, commercio ed esportazione dei cereali nella Legazione di Urbino nei secoli 17-18', *Quad.Stor.*, 28, 1975, 87-149. On yields of wheat and vegetables in Northern Marche, and increasing export trade of eighteenth century

7.292 **Berthold**, R., 'Entwicklungstendenzen der spätfeudalen Getreidewirtschaft in Deutschland', *Jb.Wirtschaftsgesch.*, 1981, suppl., 7-134. On technical aspects of grain cultivation, sixteenth-eighteenth centuries.

7.293 **Dickler**, R. A., 'Organization and change in productivity in Eastern Prussia', in Parker and Jones (7.88), 269-92. Looks at effects of profit inflation and agrarian reforms in period 1750-1850.

7.294 **Kirilly**, Z., and Kiss, I. N., 'Production de céréales et exploitations paysannes en Hongrie aux 16e et 18e siècles', *Annales*, 23, 1968, 1211-36.

7.295 **Topolski**, J., 'Economic decline in Poland from the sixteenth to the eighteenth centuries', in Earle (3.71), 127-42. Transl. from *Acta Poloniae Hist.*, 7, 1962, 28-49 (in French). Attributes decline in peasant agricultural productivity to intensification of serfdom and (to lesser extent) seventeenth-century wars.

7.296 **Zytkowicz**, L., 'Grain yields in Poland, Bohemia, Hungary, and Slovakia in the sixteenth to eighteenth centuries', *Acta Poloniae Hist.*, 24, 1971, 51-72. Few firm conclusions.

7.297 —— 'Agricultural production in Masovia in the first half of the seventeenth century', *ib.*, 18, 1968, 98-118. Inventories from Bishopric of Plock used to investigate and compare yields of peasant and demesne farms, and their marketable surplus.

7.298 **Neamtu**, V., *La Technique de la Production Céréalière en Valachie et en Moldavie jusqu'au 18e Siècle*, Bucharest, 1975. Remains fairly narrowly within confines of tools, crops, rotations, harvesting methods, etc.

FARMING METHODS AND INNOVATIONS. NEW CROPS

See also 11.116,123,158 (general); 7.62 and 11.124 (France); 4.55 (Spain); 9.355-6 (Italy); 4.25; 7.230; 9.183,604 (Eastern Europe).

7.299 **Fussell**, G. E., *The Classical Tradition in West European Farming*, 1972. Deals with long succession of writers (from Pliny through Tusser, de Serres, etc.), but without investigating how far their influence percolated. See also article of same title (restricted to sixteenth century) in *Ec.Hist.Rev.*, 2nd ser., 22, 1969, 538-51.

7.300 **Masefield**, G. B., 'Crops and livestock', in *Cambridge Economic History of Europe, 4* (2.15), 276-301. New crops and changes in diet brought about by Europe's colonial expansion.

7.301 **Bourde**, A. J., *Agronomie et Agronomes en France au 18e Siècle*, 3 vols., Paris, 1967. Enormous work on agricultural theorists and improvers, which is also a mine of information about actual rural conditions and obstacles to change. Review article: D. Roche, *Rev.Hist.Mod.et Contemp.*, 16, 1969, 672-7. See also Bourde's earlier work *The Influence of England on the French Agronomes, 1750-89*, 1953.

7.302 **Brandenburg**, D. J., 'Agriculture in the *Encyclopédie*', *Agric.Hist.*, 24, 1950, 96-108. Contends that agricultural techniques advocated were fairly conservative in nature.

7.303 **Davies**, A., 'The new agriculture in Lower Normandy, 1750-89', *Trans. Roy. Hist. Soc.*, 5th ser., 8, 1958, 129-46.

7.304 **Debien**, G., *Défricheurs au Travail en Haut-Poitou, 15e-18e Siècles*, Paris, 1952. Study of land reclamation.

7.305 —— 'Du Béarn en Poitou. L'expansion du maïs du 17e au 19e siècle', *Actes Congrès Nat.Soc.Savantes*, 91 (ii), 1966, 75-103.

7.306 **Fel**, A., '*Petite culture*, 1750-1850', in Clout (4.7), 215-46. Social and technical aspects of small-scale landownership and share-cropping, where peasants lacked such resources as heavy ploughs.

7.307 **Jacquart**, J., 'French agriculture in the seventeenth century', in Earle (3.71), 165-84. Transl. from *Dix-Septième Siècle*, 70/71, 1966, 21-46. On technology, crops, and returns.

7.308 **Rigaudière**, A., 'La Haute-Auvergne face à l'agriculture nouvelle au 18e siècle', in *Études d'Histoire Économique Rurale au 18e Siècle*, Paris, 1965, 2-104. Deals with efforts to diffuse new agricultural methods.

7.309 **Rozental**, A. A., 'The enclosure movement in France', *Am.J.Ec.& Sociol.*, 16, 1956, 55-71. Describes limited progress on this question in last years of old regime.

7.310 **Roessingh**, H. K., 'Tobacco growing in Holland in the seventeenth and eighteenth centuries. A case study of the innovative spirit of Dutch peasants', *Acta Hist.Neerlandica*, 11, 1978, 18-54.

7.311 **Slicher van Bath**, B. H., 'The rise of intensive husbandry in the Low Countries', in J. S. Bromley and E. H. Kossman, eds., *Britain and the Netherlands, 1*, 1960, 137-53. Repr. in C. K. Warner, ed., *Agrarian Conditions in Modern European History*, New York, 1966, 24-42. Deals with sixteenth- and seventeenth-century developments.

7.312 **Peset**, M., and Peset, J. L., 'Cultivos de arroz y paludismo en la Valencia del siglo 18', *Hispania*, 121, 1972, 277-375. On rice cultivation see also 7.315,321.

7.313 **Vilar**, P., 'Agricultural progress and the economic background in eighteenth-century Catalonia', *Ec.Hist.Rev.*, 2nd ser., 11, 1958, 113-20. Concerns demand for madder.

7.314 **Coppola**, G., *Il Mais nell'Economia Agricola Lombarda*, Bologna, 1979. On diffusion of maize cultivation over period 1600-1850.

7.315 **Faccini**, L., *L'Economia Risicola Lombarda dagli Inizi del 18 Secolo all'Unità*, Milan, 1977. Useful brief account.

7.316 **Poni**, C., *Gli Aratri e l'Economia Agraria nel Bolognese dal 17 al 19 Secolo*, Bologna, 1963. Deduces considerable economic and social consequences from alternative types of plough available to peasants. Review article: F. Dovring, *Comp.Stud.Soc.& Hist.*, 7, 1965, 309-23.

7.317 **Rebora**, G., *Un'Impresa Zuccheriera del Cinquecento*, Naples, 1968. Detailed picture of wages and conditions of workers at sugar plantation and refinery near Palermo in 1580s.

7.318 **Schröder**, K. H., 'Farmstead development in Central Europe since the Middle Ages', in R. H. Buchanan and others, eds., *Fields, Farms, and Settlement* in Europe, 1976, 143-51. Brief typology of farm buildings layout.

7.319 **Demidowicz**, G., 'Planned landscapes in North-East Poland. The Suraz estate, 1550-1760', *J.Hist.Geog.*, 11, 1985, 21-47. Describes imposition of *wlocka* system on a Crown estate. See next entry for general principles involved.

7.320 **French**, R. A., 'The three-field system of sixteenth-century Lithuania', *Agric.Hist.Rev.*, 18, 1970, 106-25. Allocation of uniform tenurial blocks in three-field rotation.

7.321 **Inalcik**, H., 'Rice cultivation and the *çeltükci-re'âyâ* system in the Ottoman Empire', *Turcica*, 14, 1982, 69-141. Repr. in Inalcik (3.290). Mainly on labour system established in rice-growing areas.

7.322 **Islamoğlu**, H., and Faroqhi, Suraiya, 'Crop patterns and agricultural production trends in sixteenth-century Anatolia', *Review*, 2, 1979, 401-36.

7.323 **Dahl**, S., 'Strip fields and enclosure in Sweden', *Scan.Ec.Hist.Rev.*, 9, 1961, 56-67. On consolidation of agricultural holdings in period 1750-1830.

7.324 **Frandsen**, K.-E., 'Danish field systems in the seventeenth century', *Scan.J.Hist.*, 8, 1983, 293-317.

7.325 **Friedmann**, Karen J., 'Fencing, herding, and tethering in Denmark. From open-field agriculture to enclosure', *Agric.Hist.*, 58, 1984, 584-97.

7.326 **Pred**, A., *Place, Practice, and Structure. Social and Spatial Transformation in Southern Sweden, 1750-1850*, 1986. Studies environmental effects of enclosures, and consequences for village power relations.

7.327 **Soininen**, A. M., 'Burn-beating as the technical basis of colonisation in Finland in the sixteenth and seventeenth centuries', *Scan.Ec.Hist.Rev.*, 7, 1959, 150-66. Describes slash and burn cultivation techniques which persisted into nineteenth century in Finland.

7.328 **Blum**, J., 'Russian agriculture in the last 150 years of serfdom', *Agric.Hist.*, 34, 1960, 3-12. Material on crops, tools, field systems, etc.

7.329 **Confino**, M., *Systèmes Agraires et Progrès Agricole. L'Assolement Triennal en Russie aux 18e-19e Siècles*, Paris, 1969. Despite its title, not a narrowly technical work; deals widely with social importance of traditional farming practices. Review articles: J. Blum, *J.Mod.Hist.*, 43, 1971,

495-8; J. L. van Regemorter, *Annales*, 26, 1971, 40-45; E. D. Vinogradoff, *Peasant Stud.Newsl.*, 4 (iii), 1975, 6-19.

7.330 **Smith**, R. E. F., 'The pattern of forest cultivation in Toropets uezd in the mid-sixteenth century', *Forsch.Osteur.Gesch.*, 18, 1973, 125-37. From register which explains something of field systems and settlements in forest area.

VITICULTURE
See also 9.353-4 on wine trade.

7.331 **Huetz de Lemps**, A., and others, eds., *Géographie Historique des Vignobles. Colloque de Bordeaux...1977*, 2 vols., Paris, 1978. Conference papers. First vol. deals with France; second with countries other than France.

7.332 **Beauroy**, J., *Vin et Société à Bergerac du Moyen Age aux Temps Modernes*, Saratoga, Calif., 1976. History of south-western wine producing region up to decline of Dutch market in eighteenth century.

7.333 **Dion**, R., *Histoire de la Vigne et du Vin en France des Origines au 19e Siècle*, Paris, 1959. Pioneering, large-scale work, dealing with commerce and consumption as well as production.

7.334 **Durand**, G., *Vin, Vigne, et Vignerons en Lyonnais et Beaujolais, 16e-18e Siècles*, Paris, 1979. Detailed account of production for Lyon market, concentrating on seventeenth and eighteenth centuries.

7.335 **Forster**, R., 'The noble wine producers of the Bordelais in the eighteenth century', *Ec.Hist.Rev.*, 2nd ser., 14, 1961, 18-33.

7.336 **Lachiver**, M., *Vin, Vigne, et Vignerons en Région Parisienne du 17e au 19e Siècle*, Pontoise, 1982. Lengthy study of economic and demographic behaviour of sector that gradually gave way to more profitable crops.

7.337 *Vignobles et Vins d'Aquitaine. Histoire-Économie-Art*, Bordeaux, 1970. Proceedings of a regional studies conference: variety of themes and periods.

7.338 **Huetz de Lemps**, A., *Vignobles et Vins du Nord-Ouest de l'Espagne*, 2 vols., Bordeaux, 1967. Important longitudinal survey.

7.339 'Produzione e commercio del vino nella storia d'Europa', *Ann.Cisalpines d'Hist.Soc.*, 3, 1972, whole issue. Mainly devoted to studies of Italian production in eighteenth and nineteenth centuries.

ANIMAL HUSBANDRY
See also 7.300; 9.561.

7.340 **Blanchard**, I., 'The continental European cattle trades, 1400-1600', *Ec.Hist.Rev.*, 2nd ser., 39, 1986, 427-60. Useful synthesis, charting growing recourse of western markets to supply from Denmark and Central Europe. Draws extensively on case-studies in E. Westermann, ed., *Internationaler Ochsenhandel, 1350-1750. Akten des Seventh International Economic History Congress*, Stuttgart, 1979.

7.341 **Wiese**, H., and Bölts, J., *Rinderhandel und Rinderhaltung im Nordwest-europäischen Küstengebiet vom 15. bis zum 19. Jahrhundert*, Stuttgart, 1966. Two complementary studies dealing with cattle raising and trade in Denmark, North Germany, and the Netherlands. Review article: E. L. Petersen, *Scan.Ec.Hist.Rev.*, 18, 1970, 69-85.

7.342 **Goldsmith**, J. L., 'Agricultural specialization and stagnation in early modern Auvergne', *Agric.Hist.*, 47, 1973, 216-34. Examines trend towards dairy farming in Cantal.

7.343 **Bishko**, C. J., 'The peninsular background of Latin American cattle ranching', *Hisp.Am.Hist.Rev.*, 32, 1952, 491-515. Repr. in his *Studies in Medieval Spanish Frontier History*, 1980. On medieval and early modern cattle farming practices in Spain.

7.344 —— 'The Andalusian municipal mestas in the fourteenth-sixteenth centuries. Administrative and social aspects', in *Actas del 1 Congreso de Historia de Andalucía*, Cordoba, 1978, 1, 347-74. Repr. as in 7.343.

7.345 **Le Flem**, J. P., 'Las cuentas de la Mesta, 1510-1709', *Moneda y Crédito*, 121, 1972, 23-104. See also 7.347.

7.346 **Lemeunier**, G., 'Les estremeños, ceux qui viennent de loin. Contribution à l'étude de la transhumance ovine dans l'Est castillan (16e-19e s.)', *Mél.Casa de Velazquez*, 13, 1977, 321-59. Information on Cuenca branch of Mesta.

7.347 **Mickun**, Nina, *La Mesta au 18e Siècle*, Budapest, 1983. Work by Russian historian, mainly based on government legislation and enquiries. Old work of J. Klein, *The Mesta*, Cambridge, Mass., 1920, remains only comprehensive longitudinal study of institution; but see also valuable new evidence of Le Flem (7.345).

7.348 **Dorwart**, R. A., 'Cattle disease (Rinderpest?) – prevention and cure in Brandenburg, 1665-1732', *Agric.Hist.*, 33, 1959, 79-85. Epidemic at its most serious in 1711.

7.349 **Westermann**, E., 'Zur Erforschung des nordmitteleuropäischen Ochsenhandels der frühen Neuzeit (1480-1620) aus hessischer Sicht', *Zeitschr.Agrargesch.*, 23, 1975, 1-31.

7.350 **Buza**, J., 'Die grossbäuerliche Viehzucht auf der ungarischen Tiefebene im 17. Jahrhundert', *ib.*, 32, 1984, 165-209.

7.351 **Bjørkvik**, H., 'Norwegian *seter*-farming', *Scan.Ec.Hist.Rev.*, 11, 1963, 156-66. Review article of monumental 3-vol. book by Lars Reinton on this traditional form of out-pasture farming.

8

CITIES AND TOWNS

GENERAL WORKS

HISTORIOGRAPHY AND METHODOLOGY
See also 1.12; and national bibliographies at 8.28,61,112-14,161.

8.1 **Abrams**, P., 'Towns and economic growth. Some theories and problems', in Abrams and Wrigley (6.251), 9-33. Argues that "urbanism" is not a determining social factor in itself, and that urban history should be approached bearing in mind "complex of domination" in larger social context.

8.2 **Bédarida**, F., 'The growth of urban history in France. Some methodological trends', in H. J. Dyos, ed., *The Study of Urban History*, 1968, 47-60. Suggests five areas where research should be concentrated.

8.3 **Burke**, P., 'Urban history and urban anthropology of early modern Europe', in D. Fraser and A. Sutcliffe, eds., *The Pursuit of Urban History*, 1983, 69-82.

8.4 **Perrot**, J.-C., 'Recherches sur l'analyse de l'économie urbaine au 18e siècle', *Rev.Hist.Éc.et Soc.*, 52, 1974, 350-83. Suggests some general goals and methods.

8.5 **Rozman**, G., 'Urban networks and historical stages', *J.Interdisc.Hist.*, 9, 1978, 65-91. Repr. in Rabb and Rotberg (6.9), 257-83. Suggests criteria for assessing levels and stages of urban development.

8.6 **Sjoberg**, G., *The Preindustrial City, Past and Present*, Glencoe, Ill., 1960. Argues that modern preindustrial cities (e.g. Bokhara, Lhasa) may offer parallels with European towns of Middle Ages and early modern period. Review article: N. P. Gist, *Ec.Dev.& Cultural Change*, 9, 1961, 660-2.

8.7 **Weyrauch**, E., 'Conditions and chances in the computer-aided analysis of historical record series. The case of early modern urban administrations', in Clubb and Scheuch (1.5), 112-19. Uses example of records available for town of Kitzingen in Margravate of Ansbach.

8.8 **Wolff**, P., ed., *Guide International d'Histoire Urbaine. 1; Europe*, Paris, 1977. Extremely useful. Provides for each country brief résumé of historiographical activity, principal sources, and often quite detailed bibliography. Publ. under auspices of International Commission Urban History. See cross-references at beginning of section for some national bibliographies sponsored by this body.

GENERAL HISTORY
See also 5.44; 6.4; 11.194,278; 12.21,47.

8.9 **Carter**, H., *An Introduction to Urban Historical Geography*, 1983. Deals in turn with function and physical and social structures, without chronological restriction.

8.10 **De Vries**, J., *European Urbanization,*

119

1500-1800, 1984. Remarkable work of statistical synthesis, charting growth of major population centres at 50 year intervals. Review article: P. Wheatley, *J.Interdisc.Hist.*, 17, 1986, 415-30.

8.11 —— 'Patterns of urbanization in pre-industrial Europe, 1500-1800', in H. Schmal, ed., *Patterns of European Urbanization since 1500*, 1981, 79-109. Outlines project leading to previous entry.

8.12 **Girouard**, M., *Cities and People. A Social and Architectural History*, New Haven, Conn., 1985. Highly readable and pleasantly-illustrated introduction to urban history, treated in broad chronological bands.

8.13 **Giuntella**, V. E., *La Città dell'Illuminismo*, Rome, 1982. Lively essay on eighteenth-century urban ideals and realities.

8.14 **Hohenberg**, P. M., and Lees, L. H., *The Making of Urban Europe, 1000-1950*, Cambridge, Mass., 1985. See section on "The protoindustrial age" (106-78).

8.15 **Katznelson**, I., 'Community, capitalist development, and the emergence of class', *Pol.& Soc.*, 9, 1980, 203-37. Political sociologist's sketch of changes in character and function of urban communities from feudal to industrial eras.

8.16 **Kindleberger**, C. P., 'European port cities', in his *Economic Response. Comparative Studies in Trade, Finance, and Growth*, Cambridge, Mass., 1978, 167-84.

8.17 **Langton**, J., and Hoppe, G., *Town and Country in the Development of Early Modern Western Europe*, 1983. Pamphlet-length essay arguing that economy of town and countryside was deeply interwoven, and neither can be typified as dynamic or inertial. Cf. 8.19,22,26.

8.18 **Livet**, G., and Vogler, B., eds., *Pouvoir, Ville, et Société en Europe, 1650-1750*, Paris, 1983. Large number of short conference papers on variety of urban themes. Mainly French emphasis, with special section on Strasbourg (venue of conference), but papers also on Central and Northern Europe and Mediterranean region.

8.19 **Merrington**, J., 'Town and country in the transition to capitalism', *New Left Rev.*,

93, 1975, 71-92. Sees towns as weakened force in period between outmoding of guild production and emergence of factory cities.

8.20 **Meyer**, J., and others, *Études sur les Villes en Europe Occidentale (Milieu du 17e Siècle à la Veille de la Révolution Française)*, 2 vols., Paris, 1983. Survey put together for *aggrégation* course. Covers France, England, Low Countries, and Rhenish Germany.

8.21 **Mumford**, L., *The City in History. Its Origins, its Transformations, and its Prospects*, New York, 1961. More, perhaps, a work of prophecy than of history (early advocacy of "small is beautiful"). Review article: A. Briggs, *Hist.Workshop*, 2, 1962, 296-301.

8.22 **Piuz**, Anne-M., 'Les relations économiques entre les villes et les campagnes dans les sociétés préindustrielles', in F. Bayard and others, eds., *Villes et Campagnes, 15e-20e Siècle*, Lyon, 1977, 1-53. Largely based on French research.

8.23 **Sharlin**, A., 'Natural decrease in early modern cities. A reconsideration', *P.&P.*, 79, 1978, 126-38. Suggests that excess of deaths over births may reflect preponderance of unmarried immigrants rather than unhealthy conditions. See debate with R. Finlay, *ib.*, 92, 1981, 169-80.

8.24 *La Ville au 18e Siècle*, Aix-en-Provence, 1975. Symposium dealing mainly with France and Poland.

8.25 **Wolff**, P., 'Pouvoirs et investissements urbains en Europe occidentale et centrale du 13e au 17e siècle', *Rev.Hist.*, 258, 1977, 277-311. Attempts broad picture of degree of public investment in utilities, education, etc. by city authorities.

8.26 **Wrigley**, E. A., 'Parasite or stimulus? The town in a pre-industrial economy', in Abrams and Wrigley (6.251), 295-309. Argues that this dichotomy is false one. Cf. 8.17,19,22.

8.27 —— 'Urban growth and agricultural change. England and the continent in the early modern period', *J.Interdisc.Hist.*, 15, 1985, 683-728. Relies heavily on 8.11 for European data.

REGIONAL SURVEYS AND HISTORY OF INDIVIDUAL CITIES

For works relating mainly to planning, spatial growth, and urban architecture, see 8.180-203.
For those relating mainly or exclusively to mercantile activity of cities see Section 9.

FRANCE

See also 3.44-5; 5.5; 6.25; 8.18,20,22,24,192-7; 10.204. 3.52 contains general material on Dijon; 3.8 on Grenoble; on Paris see 8.182-3 as well as entries in following sub-section; on Strasbourg see 8.18 and 8.135-6.

8.28 **Dollinger**, P., and Wolff, P., eds., *Bibliographie d'Histoire des Villes de France*, Paris, 1967. Compiled for International Commission for Urban History.

8.29 **Chevalier**, B., *Les Bonnes Villes de France du 14e au 16e Siècle*, Paris, 1982. Worthwhile popularisation which embraces social history, urban morphology and administration, and relations with state.

8.30 **Duby**, G., ed., *Histoire de la France Urbaine*, 4 vols., Paris, 1980-83. Parallel to earlier *France Rurale* (7.38). Sections of interest are J. Rossiaud, 'Crises et consolidations, 1330-1530' (2, 408-613); R. Chartier and H. Neveux, 'La ville dominante et soumise', covering sixteenth-seventeenth centuries (3, 16-285); E. Le Roy Ladurie and B. Quilliet, 'Baroque et Lumières' (3, 288-535).

8.31 **Perrot**, J.-C., 'Rapports sociaux et villes au 18e siècle', *Annales*, 23, 1968, 241-67.

8.32 **Deyon**, P., *Amiens, Capitale Provinciale. Étude sur la Société Urbaine au 17e Siècle*, Paris, 1967. Magisterial work in *Annales* tradition.

8.33 **Grimmer**, C., *Vivre à Aurillac au 18e Siècle*, Paris, 1983. Good picture of small urban society.

8.34 **El Kordi**, M., *Bayeux aux 17e et 18e Siècles. Contribution à l'Histoire Urbaine de la France*, Paris, 1970. Richly documented social and demographic history.

8.35 **Hufton**, Olwen H., *Bayeux in the Late Eighteenth Century*, 1967. Wears its learning a little more lightly than 8.34. Emphasises harsh effects of Revolution in dismantling ecclesiastical and legal institutions which town had serviced.

8.36 **Goubert**, P., *Beauvais et le Beauvaisis de 1600 à 1730. Contribution à l'Histoire Sociale de la France du 17e Siècle*, 2 vols.,

Paris, 1960. One of major monuments of *Annales* scholarship, depicting medium-sized city and its rural hinterland in economic depression. For summary of reviews and opinion see R. Harding, *Hist.& Theory*, 22, 1983, 178-98. Condensed version publ. as *Cent Mille Provinciaux au 17e Siècle*, Paris, 1968.

8.37 **Boutruche**, R., ed., *Bordeaux de 1453 à 1715*, Bordeaux, 1966. Part of excellent multi-volume history of city. Other relevant vol. is F. G. Pariset, ed., *Bordeaux au 18e Siècle*, Bordeaux, 1968. For more specialised material on Bordeaux as Atlantic port see 9.292-6.

8.38 **Butel**, P., and Poussu, J.-P., *La Vie Quotidienne à Bordeaux au 18e Siècle*, Paris, 1980. Good example of this popular series.

8.39 **Poussu**, J.-P., *Bordeaux et le Sud-Ouest au 18e Siècle. Croissance Économique et Attraction Urbaine*, Paris, 1983. Lengthy thesis, notable for its study of large-scale immigration into Bordeaux.

8.40 **Perrot**, J.-C., *Genèse d'une Ville Moderne. Caen au 18e Siècle*, 2 vols., Paris, 1975. Detailed socio-economic study of pre-Revolutionary city.

8.41 **Vovelle**, M., *Ville et Campagne au 18e Siècle. Chartres et la Beauce*, Paris, 1980. Collection of previously publ. articles. Distinctive theme is importance of ecclesistical property in town and region.

8.42 **Couturier**, M., *Recherches sur les Structures Sociales de Châteaudun, 1525-1789*, Paris, 1969. Demographic and social history of second-level administrative centre in Orléans region.

8.43 **Bois**, P., 'Structure socio-professionelle du Mans à la fin du 18e siècle', *Actes Congrès Nat.Soc.Savantes*, 87, 1962, 679-709.

8.44 **Garden**, M., *Lyon et les Lyonnais au 18e Siècle*, Paris, 1970. Major thesis. Also publ. in condensed form (same title), 1975. For Lyon in sixteenth century see Gascon's important work (9.27).

8.45 **Vieille**, P., 'Sociologie historique de Marseille, 12e-17e siècles', *Peuples Méditerr.*, 4, 1978, 77-111. Not original research, but uses various publ. city histories to point up peculiarities of southern urban society. Later history lightly treated in F. L. Tavernier, *La Vie Quotidienne à Marseille de Louis XIV à Louis Philippe*, Paris, 1973. Commercial history in 9.236-40.

8.46 **Darnton**, R., 'A bourgeois puts his world in order. The city as a text', in Darnton (6.243), 107-43. Considers a description of Montpellier and its society compiled anonymously in 1768.

8.47 **Bernard**, L., *The Emerging City. Paris in the Age of Louis XIV*, Durham, N.C., 1970. Chiefly account of urban infrastructure and municipal services.

8.48 **Denieul-Cormier**, Anne, *Paris à l'Aube du Grand Siècle*, Paris, 1971. Copiously illustrated portrait of Louis XIII's Paris; sections on physical appearance and services, on social classes, and on culture and entertainment.

8.49 **Farge**, Arlette, 'Les théatres de la violence à Paris au 18e siècle', *Annales*, 34, 1979, 984-1015. Anatomy of neighbourhood brawling.

8.50 ——— *La Vie Fragile. Violence, Pouvoirs, et Solidarités à Paris au 18e Siècle*, Paris, 1986. Based on judicial archives. Looks at three aspects of social history: tribulations of love and marriage; work, respectable and criminal; crowd behaviour.

8.51 ——— *Vivre dans la Rue à Paris au 18e Siècle*, Paris, 1979. Strings together snippets from police reports, travel accounts, etc., for picture of urban life as low life.

8.52 **Garrioch**, D., *Neighbourhood and Community in Paris, 1740-90*, 1986. Valuable study of what community ties and loyalties entailed, largely based on police records for six specimen *quartiers*.

8.53 **Mousnier**, R., *Paris, Capitale au Temps de Richelieu et de Mazarin*, Paris, 1978. Covers social, administrative, and cultural aspects.

8.54 **Pardailhé-Galabrun**, Annik, 'Les déplacements des Parisiens dans la ville aux 17e et 18e siècles', *Hist.,Éc.,et Soc.*, 2, 1983, 205-53. Somewhat on lines of Farge's research (8.49-51), but giving more space to better-off classes and their outdoor activities.

8.55 **Ranum**, O. A., *Paris in the Age of Absolutism*, New York, 1968. General history from about 1570 to 1700.

8.56 **Roche**, D., *The People of Paris. An Essay in Popular Culture in the Eighteenth Century*, 1987. Makes special study of clothing, housing, and popular reading.

8.57 **Bardet**, J.-P., *Rouen aux 17e et 18e Siècles. Les Mutations d'un Espace Social*, Paris, 1983. Brilliant thesis, concentrating especially on urban utilities. Review articles: E. Le Roy Ladurie, *Hist.,Éc.,et Soc.*, 2, 1983, 499-506; B. Lepetit, *Annales*, 39, 1984, 1086-92; A. Blum, *Population*, 40, 1985, 528-39. On Rouen as port see 9.290,305-6.

8.58 **Benedict**, P., *Rouen during the Wars of Religion*, 1981. Sets out to relate social structure of city to rival confessions and parties.

8.59 **Chevalier**, B., *Tours, Ville Royale, 1356-1520. Origine et Développement d'une Capitale à la Fin du Moyen Age*, Louvain, 1975. Adapted from doctoral thesis; considerable portion of treatment falls within relevant period.

8.60 **Le Goff**, T. J. A., *Vannes and its Region. A Study of Town and Country in Eighteenth-Century France*, 1981. Important for material on peasantry of Morbihan as well as urban history content.

LOW COUNTRIES
See also 5.131; 8.20,198.

8.61 **Herwijnen**, G. van, and others, *Bibliografie van de Stedengeschiedenis van Nederland*, Leiden, 1978. Bibliography sponsored by International Commission for Urban History.

8.62 **Houtte**, J. A. van, *Essays on Medieval and Early Modern Economy and Society*, Louvain, 1979. Reprints of journal articles, mostly in French or Dutch, principally on Flemish towns.

8.63 **Klep**, P. M. M., 'Regional disparities in Brabantine urbanisation before and after the Industrial Revolution, 1374-1970', in Bairoch and Levy-Leboyer (4.90), 259-69. Rather extreme example of *longue durée* perspective.

8.64 **Multhauf**, Lettie S., 'The light of lamp-lanterns. Street lighting in seventeenth-century Amsterdam', *Tech.& Culture*, 26, 1985, 236-52. Recounts system devised by Jan van der Heyden and used after 1670.

8.65 **Murray**, J. J., *Amsterdam in the Age of Rembrandt*, Norman, Okla., 1967. Brisk survey for general reader. See also 8.182.

Commercial and financial role dealt with in more depth in Section 9.

.66 **Regin**, D., *Traders, Artists, Burghers. A Cultural History of Amsterdam in the Seventeenth Century*, Assen, 1976. Rather derivative and breathless survey.

.67 **Murray**, J. J., *Antwerp in the Age of Plantin and Brueghel*, Norman, Okla., 1970. Same series as 8.65.

.68 **Sabbe**, E., *Anvers, Métropole de l'Occident (1492-1566)*, Brussels, 1952. Useful short survey. More specialised works on Antwerp as commercial centre in Section 9.

8.69 **Duplessis**, R. S., and Howell, Martha C., 'Reconsidering the early modern urban economy. The cases of Leiden and Lille', *P.&P.*, 94, 1982, 49-84. Describes organisation of small commodity production before eighteenth century.

SPAIN AND PORTUGAL
See also 10.326. On Alicante see 9.241; on Lisbon 8.199; and on Valencia notably 9.245.

8.70 **Saez**, E., and others, eds., *La Ciudad Hispanica durante los Siglos 13 al 16*, 2 vols., Madrid, 1985. Conference papers, mainly dealing with later end of titular period. Few general studies; most cover individual towns, in regionally arranged sections.

8.71 **Voltes Bou**, P., *Barcelona durante el Gobierno del Archiduque Carlos de Austria*, 2 vols., Barcelona, 1963. Vol.1 largely concerned with social structure and institutions.

8.72 **Phillips**, Carla R., *Ciudad Real, 1500-1750. Growth, Crisis, and Readjustment in the Spanish Economy*, Cambridge, Mass., 1979. Rather slight study of small provincial capital.

8.73 **Aranda Doncel**, J., *Historia de Córdoba. La Época Moderna (1517-1808)*, Córdoba, 1984. Social history predominant.

8.74 **Edwards**, J., *Christian Córdoba. The City and its Region in the Late Middle Ages*, 1982. Good study of post-Reconquest society, mainly based on fifteenth-century evidence.

8.75 **Fortea Pérez**, J. I., *Córdoba en el Siglo 16*, Córdoba, 1981. Examines population levels and economic activities.

8.76 **Sanz Sampelayo**, J., *Granada en el Siglo 18*, Granada, 1980. Thorough all-round study, with some attention to regional hinterland.

8.77 **Ringrose**, D. R., *Madrid and the Spanish Economy, 1560-1850*, Berkeley, Calif., 1983. Emphasises parasitic role of Madrid as consumer of weak natural resources of vast hinterland. See following entries for some preliminary findings, and longer outline (in Spanish) in *Moneda y Crédito*, 111, 1969, 65-122.

8.78 —— 'The impact of a new capital city. Madrid, Toledo, and New Castile, 1560-1660', *J.Ec.Hist.*, 33, 1973, 761-91.

8.79 —— 'Madrid and Spain, 1560-1860. Patterns of social and economic change', in P. Fritz and D. Williams, eds., *City and Society in the Eighteenth Century*, Toronto, 1973, 59-75. On urban design of eighteenth-century Madrid see 8.200.

8.80 **Chacon Jiménez**, F., *Murcia en la Centuria del Quinientos*, Murcia, 1979. Large-scale regional history of city and hinterland, emphasising dependence on raw silk production. For Murcia at time of Comunero Revolt see 12.86.

8.81 **Gelabert González**, J. E., *Santiago y la Tierra de Santiago de 1500 a 1640*, La Coruña, 1982.

8.82 **Collantes de Teran**, A., *Sevilla en la Baja Edad Media. La Ciudad y sus Hombres*, Seville, 1977. Analyses demography and wealth at intervals from 1384 to 1533 from tax assessment records. On period immediately following see 5.153.

8.83 **Morales Padrón**, F., ed., *Historia de Sevilla*, 5 vols., Seville, 1976-77. Enlarged ed., 5 vols. in 7, 1982. Morales Padrón covers sixteenth century, A. Domínguez Ortiz seventeenth, and F. Aguilar Piñal eighteenth. On Seville "underworld" see 10.436.

8.84 **Morell Peguero**, Blanca, *Mercadores y Artesanos en la Sevilla del Descubrimiento*, Seville, 1986. Notarial sources used for quantitative comparison of society in 1512 and in 1540, to assess effects of imperial trade expansion.

8.85 **Pike**, Ruth, *Aristocrats and Traders. Sevillian Society in the Sixteenth Century*, Ithaca, N.Y., 1972. General urban history, though with principal stress on mercantile activity. See also related article 'Seville in the sixteenth century', *Hisp. Am. Hist. Rev.*, 41, 1961, 1-30. For detailed work on Seville as a port see 9.311-16.

8.86 **Molenat**, J.-P., 'Tolède et ses finages au temps des Rois Catholiques. Contribution à l'histoire sociale et économique de la cité avant la Révolte des Comunidades', *Mél.Casa de Velazquez*, 8, 1972, 327-78.

8.87 **Montemayor**, J., 'Tolède en 1639', *ib.*, 18, 1982, 135-63. Social analysis provided by fiscal census of that year.

8.88 **Weisser**, M., 'The decline of Castile revisited. The case of Toledo', *J.Eur.Ec.Hist.*, 2, 1973, 614-40. Pictures Toledo's decline in population and economic activity as mirroring that of Castile as a whole.

8.89 **Bennassar**, B., *Valladolid au Siècle d'Or. Une Ville de Castille et sa Campagne au 16e Siècle*, Paris, 1967. Able study of Spain's most important sixteenth-century city, its population, economy, culture, and relations with rural hinterland. Review article: J.-P. Amalric, *Annales*, 26, 1971, 982-1002.

8.90 **Blasco Martínez**, Rosa M., *Zaragoza en el Siglo 18, 1700-70*, Zaragoza, 1977. Brief, but useful. See also her work on 8.92.

8.91 **Lopez González**, J.-J., *La Ciudad de Zaragoza a Finales del Siglo 18, 1782-92*, Zaragoza, 1977. Primarily based on diaries of Audiencia official.

8.92 **Maiso González**, J., and Blasco Martínez, Rosa M., *Las Estructuras de Zaragoza en el Primer Tercio del Siglo 18*, Zaragoza, 1984. Thorough study of social structure, primarily from fiscal census of 1723. For mainly demographic work on seventeenth-century Zaragoza see Ansón Calvo (5.133).

ITALY
General history of the major Italian city-states is covered in 3.173-207. See also 5.170; 8.181; 14.242-3 (general works); 8.182 (seventeenth-century Rome); 8.189 (topography of Florence); 11.247 (Udine)

8.93 **Blok**, A., 'South Italian agro-towns', *Comp.Stud.Soc.& Hist.*, 11, 1969, 121-35. On concentrated settlement patterns found in S. Italy.

8.94 *La Città nella Storia d'Italia*, Bari, 1980- . Well illustrated series of monographs on principal cities, under general editorship of Cesare De Seta. Each study is by single author. Volumes published so far have covered, among others, Palermo, Florence, Bologna, Rome, Genoa, Naples, Milan.

8.95 'Villes du passé', *Ann.Démographie Hist.*, 1982, 7-276. Symposium concentrating on Italian towns in early modern age; mainly, but not exclusively, demographic approach.

8.96 **Goy**, R. J., *Chioggia and the Villages of the Venetian Lagoon. Studies in Urban History*, 1985. Environmental and social history, written with architect's eye, and spanning origins to late eighteenth century.

8.97 **Berengo**, M., *Nobili e Mercanti nella Lucca del Cinquecento*, Turin, 1965. Well documented social history of Lucca and its hinterland.

8.98 **Mazzei**, Rita, *La Società Lucchese del Seicento*, Lucca, 1977. Continues some themes of preceding entry. See also 9.100.

8.99 **Petraccone**, C., *Napoli dal '500 al '800. Problemi di Storia Demografica e Sociale*, Naples, 1974. Patient use of parish records helps overcome some of source problems caused by destruction of city archives.

8.100 **Romani**, M. A., *Nella Spirale di una Crisi. Popolazione, Mercato, e Prezzi a Parma fra Cinque e Seicento*, Milan, 1975. Another rather pessimistic view of seventeenth-century trends in Italy.

8.101 **Blanshei**, Sarah R., 'Population, wealth, and patronage in medieval and Renaissance Perugia', *J.Interdisc.Hist.*, 9, 1979, 597-619. Widely-spaced comparison of society as revealed by fiscal sources of 1285 and of period 1498-1511.

8.102 **Brown**, Judith C., *In the Shadow of Florence. Provincial Society in Renaissance Pescia*, 1982. Study of Tuscan town from fourteenth to early seventeenth centuries.

8.103 **Andrieux**, M., *Daily Life in Papal Rome in the Eighteenth Century*, 1968. Transl. from French ed. of 1962. Fairly lightweight.

8.104 **Delumeau**, J., *Vie Économique et Sociale de Rome dans la Seconde Moitié du 16e Siècle*, 2 vols., Paris, 1957-59. Important, intensively researched work. Much condensed version publ. as *Rome du 16e Siècle*, 1975.

8.105 **Mitchell**, B., *Rome in the High Renaissance. The Age of Leo X*, Norman, Okla., 1973. Slight, and largely dominated by art history.

8.106 **Partner**, P., *Renaissance Rome, 1500-59. A Portrait of a Society*, Berkeley, Calif., 1976. Excellent, though not a work of original research.

8.107 **Stinger**, C. L., *The Renaissance in Rome*, Bloomington, Ind., 1985. Primarily cultural history, but provides long opening chapter on topographical and economic developments from mid-fifteenth century to Sack of 1527.

.108 **Fiumi**, E., *Storia Economica e Sociale di San Gimignano*, Florence, 1961. Able account of demography and changing distribution of wealth in small Tuscan city from twelfth century onwards.

.109 **Chiancone Isaacs**, Ann K., 'Popolo e monti nella Siena del primo Cinquecento', *Riv.Stor.Ital.*, 82, 1970, 32-80. Tax valuations used for social analysis of citizenry and their place in rival political clans (*monti*).

.110 **Hook**, Judith, *Siena. A City and its History*, 1979. Continues history up to present day, but medieval and Renaissance periods are dwelt on at most length.

.111 **Tagliaferri**, A., *L'Economia Veronese secondo gli Estimi dal 1409 al 1639*, Milan, 1966. Based on data from tax lists.

GERMANY, SWITZERLAND, AND AUSTRIA

Many items in Section 13.181-231 deal with urban nature of German Reformation (see 13.194 for useful bibliography). See also 5.195; 6.185,251; 8.20,140,163; 12.101-3,114,130. For early sixteenth-century topography of Augsburg see 8.189.

.112 **Guyer**, P., *Bibliographie der Städtegeschichte der Schweiz*, Zurich, 1960. Sponsored by International Commission for Urban History. Rather brief.

.113 **Keyser**, E., ed., *Bibliographie zur Städtgeschichte Deutschlands*, Vienna, 1969. Also Commission vol. Revised version by Brigitte Schröder and H. Stoob to be publ. shortly.

.114 **Rausch**, W., and others, *Bibliographie zur Geschichte der Städte Österreichs*, Linz, 1984. Again sponsored by International Commission.

.115 **Eitel**, P., *Die Oberschwäbischen Reichsstädte im Zeitalter der Zunftherrschaft. Untersuchungen zu ihrer Politischen und Sozialen Struktur*, Stuttgart, 1970. Considers four minor Imperial cities (Lindau, Memmingen, Ravensburg, and Uberlingen) in fifteenth and sixteenth centuries.

.116 **François**, E., 'Des républiques marchandes aux capitales politiques. Remarques sur la hiérarchie urbaine du Saint-Empire à l'époque moderne', *Rev.Hist.Mod.et Contemp.*, 25, 1978,

587-603. Sees cultural leadership passing from free cities to *Residenzstädte* between Reformation and Enlightenment.

8.117 **Mauersberg**, H., *Wirtschafts- und Sozialgeschichte Zentraleuropäischer Städte in Neuerer Zeit*, Göttingen, 1960. Draws on material from Basel, Frankfurt, Hamburg, Hanover, and Munich, though lacks integration into genuinely comparative study.

8.118 **Rublack**, H.-C., 'Political and social norms in urban communities in the Holy Roman Empire', in K. von Greyerz, ed., *Religion, Politics, and Social Protest. Three Studies on Early Modern Germany*, 1984, 24-60. Discusses continuity of ideals across Reformation divide. Review article: T. Scott, *Eur.Hist.Q.*, 16, 1986, 209-17.

8.119 **Walker**, M., *German Home Towns. Community, State, and General Estate, 1648-1871*, Ithaca, N.Y., 1971. Stresses inbred nature of society and politics in small towns, using example of Weissenburg in Franconia. Review articles: J. A. Vann, *Comp.Stud.Soc.& Hist.*, 15, 1973, 240-8; G. Strauss, *J.Urban Hist.*, 1, 1975, 238-42.

8.120 **Meyn**, M., *Die Reichsstadt Frankfurt vor dem Bürgeraufstand von 1612 bis 1614*, Frankfurt, 1980. Provides social and political background to revolt against city council.

8.121 **Soliday**, G. L., *A Community in Conflict. Frankfurt Society in the Seventeenth and Early Eighteenth Centuries*, Hanover, N.H., 1974. Also mainly concerned with city's constitutional conflicts.

8.122 **Scott**, T., *Freiburg and the Breisgau. Town-Country Relations in the Age of Reformation and Peasants' War*, 1986. Examines growing economic rivalry between city and hinterland (1450-1530), and holds that peasant-burgher cooperation in Peasants' Revolt was minimal (*pace* Blickle, 12.113).

8.123 **Monter**, E. W., *Calvin's Geneva*, New York, 1967. Emphasis on Reformation politics, but provides fair amount of background.

8.124 **Jacob**, F.-D., 'Städtisches Leben im Zeitalter der frühbürgerlichen Revolution im Spiegel des Görlitzer Steuerregisters von 1528', *Jb.Regionalgesch.*, 5, 1975, 110-41. Principal town of Upper Lusatia, at that time under Bohemian Crown.

8.125 **Loose**, H.-D., ed., *Hamburg. Geschichte*

der Stadt und ihrer Bewohner. 1: Von den Anfängen bis zur Reichsgründung, Hamburg, 1982. Excellent collective history. Chaps. by P. Gabrielsson, R. Postel, Loose, and F. Kopitzsch, cover period 1300-1806. Material on Hamburg's commercial life at 9.211-14.

8.126 **François**, E., *Koblenz im 18. Jahrhundert*, Göttingen, 1982. Comprehensive, though quite short, social history of Residenzstadt of Elector of Trier. See also 5.175.

8.127 **Blanning**, T. C. W., *Reform and Revolution in Mainz, 1743-1803*, 1974. Argues that Mainz was thriving economically on its inequalities, and had to have reform thrust upon it.

8.128 **Dreyfus**, F. G., *Sociétés et Mentalités à Mayence dans la Seconde Moitié du 18e Siècle*, Paris, 1968. More detailed on population and social structure than Blanning.

8.129 **Oberlé**, R., *La République de Mulhouse pendant la Guerre de Trente Ans*, Paris, 1965. Deals with both political fortunes and socio-economic life of this Alsatian city.

8.130 **Friedrichs**, C. R., *Urban Society in an Age of War. Nördlingen, 1580-1720*, Princeton, N.J., 1979. Richly documented portrait of middle-sized imperial city.

8.131 **Bog**, I., 'Wirtschaft und Gesellschaft Nürnbergs im Zeitalter des Merkantilismus (1648-1806)', *VSWG*, 57, 1970, 289-322.

8.132 **Pfeiffer**, G., ed., *Nürnberg, Geschichte einer Europäischen Stadt*, Munich, 1971. Excellent collective history, with substantial section on early modern period.

8.133 **Strauss**, G., *Nuremberg in the Sixteenth Century. City Politics and Life between Middle Ages and Modern Times*, New York, 1966. 2nd ed., Bloomington, Ind., 1976. Valuable, within limits it sets.

8.134 **Schultz**, Helga, *Soziale und Politische Auseinandersetzungen in Rostock im 18. Jahrhundert*, Weimar, 1974.

8.135 **Ford**, F. L., *Strasbourg in Transition, 1648-1789*, Cambridge, Mass., 1958. Admirable account of implications of French conquest. See also 8.18.

8.136 **Kintz**, J.-P., *La Société Strasbourgeoise du Milieu du 16e Siècle à la Fin de la Guerre de Trente Ans, 1560-1650*, Paris, 1984. Gets away from Reformation perspective which draws so much on this city's sources to concentrate on demography, diet, and economy.

8.137 **Straube**, M., 'Soziale Struktur und Besitzverhältnisse in Wittenberg zur Lutherzeit', *Jb.Gesch.Feudalismus*, 9, 1985, 145-88. Thorough study of wealth and residence patterns.

EAST CENTRAL EUROPE
See also 5.402,638; 8.25; 13.166.

8.138 **Kuklinska**, Krystyna, 'Central European towns and the factors of economic growth in the transition from stagnation to expansion between the seventeenth and eighteenth centuries', *J.Eur.Ec.Hist.*, 11, 1982, 105-15. Brief survey of E. Germany, Habsburg Empire, and Poland.

8.139 **Molenda**, Danuta, 'Mining towns in Central-Eastern Europe in feudal times', *Acta Poloniae Hist.*, 34, 1976, 165-88. Sketches social and spatial characteristics from later Middle Ages to seventeenth century.

8.140 **Rausch**, W., ed., *Beiträge zur Geschichte der Städte Mitteleuropas, 3-6*, Linz, 1974-82. Relevant vols. of series of miscellanies on towns of Germany and Austro-Hungary.

8.141 **Demonet**, M., and Granasztói, G., 'Une ville de Hongrie au milieu du 16e siècle. Analyse factorielle et modèle sociale', *Annales*, 37, 1982, 523-51. Topography, demography, and social structure of Kassa (now Košice) in Slovakia, analysed via census documents.

8.142 **Gyimesi**, S., 'Incomes, public constructions, and investments in the Hungarian towns in the eighteenth century', in *Études Historiques Hongroises Publiées à l'Occasion du 15e Congrès Int. des Sciences Historiques*, Budapest, 1980, 1, 365-77. Concerns public revenues and expenditure of free towns.

8.143 **Bogucka**, Maria, 'Les recherches Polonaises des années 1969-78 sur l'histoire des villes et de la bourgeoisie jusqu'au declin du 18e siècle', *Acta Poloniae Hist.*, 41, 1980, 239-57. Review of Polish-language material.

8.144 ——— 'Polish towns between the sixteenth and eighteenth centuries', in Fedorowicz and others (3.283), 135-52.

8.145 **Wynot**, E. D., 'Urban history in Poland', *J.Urban Hist.*, 6, 1979, 31-79. Bibliographical article.

8.146 **Wyrobisz**, A., 'Attitude of the Polish

nobility towards towns in the first half of the seventeenth century', *Acta Poloniae Hist.*, 48, 1983, 77-94. Deals with views expressed by literateur magnate K. Opalinski in work publ. in 1650.

147 —— 'Functional types of Polish towns in the sixteenth-eighteenth centuries', *J.Eur.Ec.Hist.*, 12, 1983, 69-103. See also rather sketchy preview in *Acta Poloniae Hist.*, 34, 1976, 153-64.

TURKEY AND THE BALKANS

148 **Carter**, F. W., 'Urban development in the Western Balkans, 1200-1800', in Carter (4.20), 147-96. Excellent starting-point.

149 **Erder**, Leila T., and Faroqhi, Suraiya, 'The development of the Anatolian urban network during the sixteenth century', *J.Ec.& Soc.Hist.Orient*, 23, 1980, 265-303. Repr. in Faroqhi (4.82).

150 **Faroqhi**, Suraiya, *Men of Modest Substance. House Owners and House Property in Seventeenth-Century Ankara and Kayseri*, 1987. Examines nature of property-holding in Ottoman urban society; material also on physical layout of houses and neighbourhoods.

151 —— 'Sixteenth-century periodic markets in various Anatolian *sancaks*', *J. Ec.& Soc. Hist. Orient*, 22, 1979, 32-80. Also repr. in 4.82. Investigates network of marketing centres and their considerable expansion in this century.

152 —— *Towns and Townsmen of Ottoman Anatolia. Trade, Crafts, and Food Production in an Urban Setting, 1520-1650*, 1984. Emphasises urban economics rather than social and cultural aspects.

153 **Jennings**, R. C., 'Urban population in Anatolia in the sixteenth century. A study of Kayseri, Karaman, Amasya, Trabzon, and Erzurum', *Int.J.Mid.E.Stud.*, 7, 1976, 21-57. Discerns marked urban growth.

154 **Rogič**, V., 'The changing urban pattern in Yugoslavia', in Carter (4.20), 409-36. Traces urban settlement patterns from antiquity onwards.

155 *Structure Sociale et Développement Culturel des Villes Sud-Est Européennes et Adriatiques aux 17e-18e Siècles*, Bucharest, 1975. Papers of conference held at Venice in 1971.

156 **Tekeli**, I., 'On institutionalized external relations of cities in the Ottoman Empire –

a settlement models approach', *Ét.Balkaniques*, 8 (ii), 1972, 49-72. Uses spatial analysis techniques to comment on Ottoman urban hierarchy in light of available production and transport technology.

8.157 **Todorov**, N., *The Balkan City, 1400-1900*, Seattle, Wash., 1983. Transl. from Bulgarian ed. of 1972. Highly regarded (has also been transl. into Russian and French). Provides outline of findings in 'The city in the Bulgarian lands from the fifteenth to the nineteenth century', in T. Butler, ed., *Bulgaria, Past and Present. Proceedings of the First International Conference on Bulgarian Studies…Univ. of Wisconsin, Madison*, Columbus, Ohio, 1976, 15-30.

8.158 **Karidis**, D. N., 'Town development in the Balkans, fifteenth-nineteenth centuries. The case of Athens', *Ét.Balkaniques*, 18 (ii), 1982, 48-57. Offers scheme of periodisation in terms of developments in Ottoman society (1456-1640; 1640-1760; 1760-1821).

8.159 **Lewis**, B., *Istanbul and the Civilization of the Ottoman Empire*, Norman, Okla., 1963. Urban history content relatively slight.

8.160 **Mantran**, R., *Istanbul dans la Seconde Moitié du 17e Siècle*, Paris, 1962. Work of brilliant and sustained research. See also 3.306.

SCANDINAVIA
See also 8.201.

8.161 **Swedish Institute for Urban History (Stockholm University)**, *International Bibliography of Urban History. Denmark-Finland-Norway-Sweden*, Stockholm, 1960. Needs revision and amplification.

8.162 **Jørgensen**, J., 'The economic condition of Zealand provincial towns in the eighteenth century', *Scan.Ec.Hist.Rev.*, 19, 1971, 1-11. Concerns depressed conditions in Danish Zealand. Evidence on wealth distribution from probate settlements.

8.163 **Riis**, T., 'Towns and central government in Northern Europe from the fifteenth century to the Industrial Revolution', *ib.*, 29, 1981, 33-52. General survey of political and economic role of towns in Baltic area (incl. Russia and N. Germany).

RUSSIA
See also 6.256; 8.163,202-3.

8.164 **Blackwell**, W. L., 'Modernization and urbanization in Russia. A comparative view', in M. F. Hamm, ed., *The City in Russian History*, Lexington, Ky., 1976, 291-330. Useful survey, with international comparisons. Includes section on pre-modern city down to 1860.

8.165 **Bushkovitch**, P., 'Towns, trade, and artisans in seventeenth-century Russia. The view from Eastern Europe', *Forsch.Osteur.Gesch.*, 27, 1980, 215-32. Argues that Russian urban society is better seen in general E. European context than stereotyped as "backward" via comparisons with western cities.

8.166 **Eaton**, H. L., 'Decline and recovery of the Russian cities from 1500 to 1700', *Can.-Am.Slavic Stud.*, 11, 1977, 220-52. Principally looked at in terms of population.

8.167 **Hellie**, R., 'Stratification of Muscovite society. The townsmen', *Russ.Hist.*, 5, 1978, 119-75. Reasons why Russia's urban population pressed for rigid restrictions on entry to trade, industry, and ownership of property introduced in early seventeenth century.

8.168 **Hittle**, J. M., 'Catherinean reforms, social change, and the decline of the *posad* commune', in D. K. Rowney and G. E. Orchard, eds., *Russian and Slavic History*, Columbus, Ohio, 1977, 274-300. Traces erosion of trade and artisanal privileges of urban estate (*posadkie lyudi*) and increasing stratification within it.

8.169 —— *The Service City. State and Townsmen in Russia, 1600-1800*, Cambridge, Mass., 1979. Useful synthesis of much Soviet historiography on urban commune.

8.170 **Hudson**, H. D., 'Urban estate engineering in eighteenth-century Russia. Catherine the Great and the elusive *meshchanstsvo*', *Can.-Am.Slavic Stud.*, 18, 1984, 393-410. Notes contradiction in government aims between fostering economic growth of towns and limiting access to them in social terms.

8.171 **Knabe**, B., *Die Struktur der Russischen Posadgemeinden und der Katalog der Beschwerden und Forderungen der Kaufmannschaft (1762-67)*, Berlin, 1975.

Forms vol.22 of *Forsch.Osteur.Gesch.* Wide-ranging study of urban communities at beginning of Catherine II's reign.

8.172 **Langer**, L. N., 'Historiography of the preindustrial Russian city', *J.Urban Hist.*, 5, 1979, 209-40. Surveys views on role and development of cities from S. M. Solov'ev to Pipes and Rozman.

8.173 **Milov**, L. V., 'On the so-called agararian towns of eighteenth-century Russia', *Soviet Stud.in Hist.*, 21 (i), 1982, 10-31. Contends that market gardening was characteristic of many towns bordering manufacturing districts.

8.174 **Rozman**, G., *Urban Networks in Russia, 1750-1800, and Premodern Periodization*, Princeton, N.J., 1976. Suggests that urban growth has been underestimated because of concentration on legal boundaries and functional criteria. Review article: D. H. Miller, *J.Urban Hist.*, 4, 1977, 117-26. Note summary of arguments in his 'Comparative approaches to urbanization. Russia, 1750-1800', in Hamm (8.164), 69-85.

8.175 **Shaw**, D. J. B., 'Urbanism and economic development in a pre-industrial context. The case of Southern Russia', *J. Hist. Geog.*, 3, 1977, 107-22. Traces evolution of towns in "black earth" region of Russia from defence outposts to economic growth points in seventeenth and eighteenth centuries.

8.176 **Fisher**, A. W., 'Azov in the sixteenth and seventeenth centuries', *Jb.Gesch.Osteur.*, 21, 1973, 161-73. On its importance as trading centre and point of contact between Russia and Ottoman Empire.

8.177 **Voyce**, A., *Moscow and the Roots of Russian Culture*, Norman, Okla., 1964. Semi-popular history, dealing largely with sixteenth- and seventeenth-century city.

8.178 **Alexander**, J. T., 'Catherine II, bubonic plague, and the problem of industry in Moscow', *Am.Hist.Rev.*, 79, 1974, 637-71. How Catherine II's project of expelling factories from Moscow on health grounds was paradoxically foiled by effects of plague of 1770-72 on labour supply.

8.179 —— 'Petersburg and Moscow in early urban policy', *J.Urban Hist.*, 8, 1982, 145-69. I.e. in early part of Catherine II's reign.

URBAN MORPHOLOGY AND DESIGN
See also 11.180; 14.25.

.180 **Argan**, G. C., *The Renaissance City*, 1969. Brief essay accompanying large section of plans and illustrations, mainly concentrating on town-planning ideals in Italy.

.181 **Benevolo**, L., *History of the City*, 1980. Transl. from Italian ed. of 1975. Lavishly illustrated survey, mainly in terms of spatial aspects. Note chapters on Italian Renaissance cities, and European capitals in baroque era.

.182 **Burke**, P., 'Investment and culture in three seventeenth century cities: Rome, Amsterdam, Paris', *J.Eur.Ec.Hist.*, 7, 1978, 311-36. Considers differing functions of building development in these cities.

.183 **Francastel**, P., ed., *L'Urbanisme de Paris et l'Europe, 1600-80*, Paris, 1969. Symposium mainly of architectural interest, but a few essays wider in scope (P. Goubert on economic implications of urban development, F. Thiriet on Venice, G. Labrot on Rome, J. Gállego on Madrid).

.184 **Gutkind**, E. A., *International History of City Development*, 8 vols., Glencoe, Ill., 1964-72. Monumental work, copiously illustrated, on urban form up to mid-nineteenth century. Volumes cover: 1, Central Europe; 2, Alpine and Scandinavian regions; 3, Spain and Portugal; 4, Italy and Greece; 5, France and Belgium; 6, Netherlands and British Isles; 7, Poland, Czechoslovakia, and Hungary; 8, Bulgaria, Romania, U.S.S.R. Each contains general notes, then city by city survey. Excellent bibliographies.

.185 **Jacob**, F.-D., 'Prolegomena zu einer quellenkundlichen Betrachtung historischer Stadtansichten', *Jb.Regionalgesch.*, 6, 1978, 129-66. Illustrated essay on uses that can be made of pictorial depictions of urban layout.

.186 **Konvitz**, J. W., *The Urban Millennium. The City-Buiding Process from the Early Middle Ages to the Present*, Carbondale, Ill., 1985. Sees urban development shaped according to relative dominance of users, investors, or planning authorities.

.187 **Lavedan**, P., and Hugueney, Jeanne, *Histoire de l'Urbanisme*, 3 vols., Paris,

1926-52. Classic work. Vol.2 (revised ed., 1959) covers Renaissance and early modern periods.

8.188 **Morris**, A. E. J., *History of Urban Form, Before the Industrial Revolutions*, 1974. 2nd ed., 1979. Chapters 5-7 relevant.

8.189 **Piper**, E., *Der Stadtplan als Grundriss der Gesellschaft. Topographie und Sozialstruktur in Augsburg und Florenz um 1500*, Frankfurt, 1982. Analysis of residential/occupational patterns.

8.190 *Storia dell'Urbanistica*, Bari, 1976- . Well-illustrated series giving general European coverage, though Italy receives pride of place. Relevant vols.: V. F. Pardo, *Dal Trecento al Quattrocento* (1982); E. Guidoni and A. Marino, *Il Cinquecento* (1982), and *Il Seicento* (1979); P. Sica, *Il Settecento* (1976).

8.191 **Vance**, J. E., *The Scene of Man. The Role and Structure of the City in the Geography of Western Civilization*, New York, 1977. Chapter 6 (201-69) covers morphology of early modern city.

8.192 **Konvitz**, J. W., *Cities and the Sea. Port City Planning in Early Modern Europe*, Baltimore, Md., 1978. Deals esp. with Colbert's creations of Sète, Rochefort, Brest, and Lorient, and compares with other developing ports such as Copenhagen and Gothenburg. See also Kindleberger's more purely economic treatment (8.16).

8.193 —— 'Grandeur in French city planning under Louis XIV. Rochefort and Marseille', *J.Urban Hist.*, 2, 1975, 3-42. Examines rejected as well as chosen plans for ways in which it was sought to link efficiency and aesthetics.

8.194 **Lavedan**, P., *Histoire de l'Urbanisme à Paris*, Paris, 1975. Part of series *Nouvelle Histoire de Paris*, now in progress, outside chronological divide of other vols.

8.195 **Nières**, C., *La Reconstruction d'une Ville au 18e Siècle. Rennes, 1720-1760*, Paris, 1972. Studies rebuilding of city after disastrous fire.

8.196 **Pringle**, J. K., 'Land use and political culture in later eighteenth-century Marseille', *Proc.Western Soc.Fr.Hist.*, 10, 1982, 285-94. Procedures for urban planning.

8.197 **Thomson**, D., *Renaissance Paris*.

Architecture and Growth, 1475-1600, 1984. Has social history dimension, though stylistic preoccupations tend to predominate.

8.198 **Burke**, G. L., *The Making of Dutch Towns. A Study in Urban Development from the Tenth to the Seventeenth Centuries*, 1956. Mainly on urban geography and architecture.

8.199 **França**, J.-A., *Une Ville des Lumières. La Lisbonne de Pombal*, Paris, 1965. Mainly deals with redevelopment after earthquake of 1755.

8.200 *Madrid y los Borbones en el Siglo 18. La Construcción de una Ciudad y su Territorio*, Madrid, 1984. Collaborative work designed to accompany exhibition.

8.201 **Jutikkala**, E., 'Town planning in Sweden and Finland until the middle of the nineteenth century', *Scan.Ec.Hist.Rev.*, 16, 1968, 19-46. Examines limited opportunities for geometrical planning, given strength of property rights.

8.202 **Jones**, R. E., 'Urban planning and the development of provincial towns in Russia, 1762-96', in J. G. Garrard, ed., *The Eighteenth Century in Russia*, 1973, 321-44. Describes determination of government to pursue western design and architecture.

8.203 **Munro**, G., 'Russia's non-Russian capital. Petersburg and the planning commission', *Eighteenth-Cent.Life*, 2, 1976, 49-53. Short account of Catherine II's commission to control growth of Petersburg (and Moscow).

9

COMMERCE AND INDUSTRY

TRADE, ENTERPRISE, AND INVESTMENT. GENERAL WORKS

Works on some major international commercial centres (e.g. Antwerp, Venice) have been included in this sub-section; but the majority of individual ports and their merchant communities are dealt with in the following sub-section on Routes and Ports. See also 10.160-263 for investment in public finance; and 4.61-3.

9.1 **Ball**, J. N., *Merchants and Merchandise. The Expansion of Trade in Europe, 1500-1630*, 1977. Useful summary, based on secondary literature.

9.2 **Bratchel**, M. E., 'Alien merchant colonies in sixteenth-century England. Community organization and social mores', *J.Med.& Renaiss.Stud.*, 14, 1984, 39-62. On differing senses of whether primary loyalties lay with host nation or country of origin.

9.3 **Brulez**, W., 'Shipping profits in the early modern period', *Acta Hist.Neerlandicae*, 14, 1981, 65-84. General coverage. Concludes that shipping rarely offered good profits per se, but only when combined with stake in cargo.

9.4 *Change and the Entrepreneur. Postulates and Patterns for Entrepreneurial History*, Cambridge, Mass., 1949. Essays by some notable pioneers of this approach to economic history (J. Schumpeter, A. Cole, etc.). Largely concerned with historiographical and philosophical issues: little period orientation.

9.5 **Christelow**, A., 'The economic background of the Anglo-Spanish War of 1762', *J.Mod.Hist.*, 18, 1946, 22-36. Examines commercial implications of Franco-Spanish Family Compact.

9.6 **Curtin**, P. D., *Cross-Cultural Trade in World History*, 1984. Describes trade routes and practices which have cut across cultural boundaries since ancient times.

9.7 **Glamann**, K., 'The changing patterns of trade', in *Cambridge Economic History of Europe*, 5 (2.15), 185-289.

9.8 —— 'European trade, 1500-1750', in *Fontana Economic History of Europe*, 2 (2.24), 427-526. Also publ. separately, 1971.

9.9 **Hoselitz**, B. F., 'The early history of entrepreneurial theory', *Explor. Entrepren. Hist.*, 3, 1951, 193-220. Discusses etymology and concept up to work of Physiocrats.

9.10 **Jeannin**, P., *Merchants of the Sixteenth Century*, New York, 1971. Transl. from French ed. of 1957. Short but vivid account of diversity of scale in European mercantile activity.

9.11 **Kellenbenz**, H., 'Marchands capitalistes et classes sociales', in [*Proc.*] *Fourth International Conference of Economic History*, Paris, 1973, 19-51. Outlines emergence of powerful merchant class in various European regions from late Middle Ages to c.1750. See also supplement (in English) on merchant archives, *ib.*, 131-49.

9.12 **Minchinton**, W., 'Patterns and structure

131

of demand, 1500-1750', in *Fontana Economic History of Europe*, 2 (2.24), 83-176. Shows refreshing novelty in looking at trade as shaped by consumer demand. Also provides much data on standards of diet, housing, etc. Similar article covering 1750-1914 in *ib.*, 3, 77-186.

9.13 **Pach**, S., 'Favourable and unfavourable conditions for capitalist growth. The shift of international trade routes in the fifteenth to seventeenth centuries', in *Proc.Fourth International Conference of Economic History*, (9.11), 53-68. Viewed in context of growing disparities between West and East European economic development.

9.14 —— 'The shifting of international trade routes in the fifteenth-seventeenth centuries', *Acta Hist.Acad.Sci.Hungaricae*, 14, 1968, 287-319. Valuable summary. But cf. also following entry.

9.15 **Rapp**, R. T., 'The unmaking of the Mediterranean trade hegemony. International trade rivalry and the commercial revolution', *J.Ec.Hist.*, 35, 1975, 499-525. Argues (from success of English textiles against Venetian) that aggressive competition in old markets rather than easier access to colonies is key to rise of North Atlantic commercial power.

9.16 **Roseveare**, H., ed., *Markets and Merchants in the Late Seventeenth Century. The Marescoe-David Letters, 1668-80*, 1987. Papers of major London firm, headed by French businessmen, active throughout Europe, esp. in imports from Sweden.

9.17 **Silva**, J. G. da, 'Fructification du capital et dynamique sociale dans les sociétés commerciales (16e-18e siècles', in *Proc.Third International Conference of Economic History* (5.123), 4, 63-132. Valuable survey of developments in business organisation: forms of partnership, chartered companies, etc.

9.18 **Sperling**, J., 'The international payments mechanism in the seventeenth and eighteenth centuries', *Ec.Hist.Rev.*, 2nd ser., 14, 1962, 446-68. Argues that satisfactory mechanism evolved via London and Amsterdam after 1660. For earlier arguments on settlement of trade balances see exchanges between C. Wilson and E. Heckscher, *ib.*, 2, 1949, 152-61; 3, 1950, 219-28; 4, 1951, 231-42.

9.19 **Supple**, B., 'The nature of enterprise', in *Cambridge Economic History of Europe*, 5

(2.15), 394-461. Deals with early modern entrepreneurial activity from variety of angles.

9.20 **Van der Wee**, H., and Peeters, T., 'Un modèle dynamique de croissance interséculaire du commerce mondial, 12e-18e siècles', *Annales*, 25, 1970, 100-26. Suggests that commercial growth was product of surplus and technical improvements, not so much of falling costs.

FRANCE
See also 3.16; 4.70; 9.49, 56, 164, 173, 175, 226, 231, 236-40, 242, 259-62, 268-73, 290-307, 320, 410-13.

9.21 **Bamford**, P. W., 'Entrepreneurship in seventeenth- and eighteenth-century France', *Explor.Entrepren.Hist.*, 9, 1957, 204-13. Activities of P. Babaud, timber merchant and iron-founder.

9.22 **Bosher**, J. F., 'The Paris business world and the seaports under Louis XV. Speculators in marine insurance, naval finances, and trade', *Hist.Sociale/Social Hist.*, 12, 1979, 281-97. Argues that Paris financiers were too preoccupied by public debt and speculation to be good source of mercantile credit.

9.23 **Bourgeon**, J. L., *Les Colbert avant Colbert. Destin d'une Famille Marchande*, Paris, 1973. Social ascent in early modern France illustrated by family origins of Louis XIV's great minister.

9.24 **Caster**, G., *Le Commerce du Pastel et de l'Épicerie à Toulouse, 1450 env. à 1561*, Toulouse, 1962. Thorough, but non-quantitative study.

9.25 **Davis**, Natalie Z., 'Sixteenth-century French arithmetics on the business life', *J.Hist.Ideas*, 21, 1960, 18-48. Examines ethos suggested by examples in a number of commercial arithmetic manuals.

9.26 **Favier**, J., 'Une ville entre deux vocations. La place d'affaires de Paris au 15e siècle', *Annales*, 28, 1973, 1245-79. Concerns conflicting pull of commerce and bureaucratic office.

9.27 **Gascon**, R., *Grand Commerce et Vie Urbaine au 16e Siècle. Lyon et ses Marchands, Environs de 1520-environs de 1580*, 2 vols., Paris, 1971. Imposing study of Lyon's heyday as commercial centre, and of its Italian and native entrepreneurial elite. Also deals, in considerable detail, with general urban affairs and social structure. Review article: P. Léon, *Rev.Hist.*, 249, 1973, 41-6.

9.28 **Goubert**, P., *Familles Marchandes sous l'Ancien Régime. Les Danse et les Motte de Beauvais*, Paris, 1959. Describes milieu of prosperous textile merchants.

9.29 **Hickey**, D., 'Politics and commerce in Renaissance France. The evolution of trade along the routes of Dauphiné', *Can.J.Hist.*, 6, 1971, 133-51. Considers impact of Lyon fairs and tax increases on traditional routes through province.

9.30 **Larmour**, Ronda, 'Business investment and social attitudes in sixteenth-century France. The Paris grocers', *Bus.Hist.Rev.*, 40, 1966, 491-8. Looks at inventories post mortem of wholesale grocers to see how far profits were being drained off into rural property.

9.31 —— 'A merchant guild of sixteenth-century France. The grocers of Paris', *Ec.Hist.Rev.*, 2nd ser., 20, 1967, 467-81. Emphasises social and economic predominance of wholesalers within guild.

9.32 **Leguay**, J. P., 'La confrérie des merciers de Rennes au 15e siècle', *Francia*, 3, 1975, 147-220.

9.33 **Morineau**, M., 'Le cifre, la balancia e la seta. Il commercio settecentesco tra Francia e Italia', *Riv.Stor.Ital.*, 95, 1983, 350-88. Considers reliability of registers of *Balance du Commerce* set up in 1716 to record French import-export balances.

9.34 **Scoville**, W. C., 'The French economy in 1700-01. An appraisal by the deputies of trade', *J.Ec.Hist.*, 22, 1962, 231-52. Reports of deputies from major towns to Council of Trade appointed to review condition of trade and manufactures.

9.35 **Taylor**, G. V., 'Notes on commercial travellers in eighteenth-century France', *Bus.Hist.Rev.*, 38, 1964, 346-53. Brief résumé of evidence for this occupation in later part of century.

9.36 —— 'The Paris *Bourse* on the eve of the Revolution, 1781-89', *Am.Hist.Rev.*, 67, 1962, 951-77. On speculative boom of 1780s.

9.37 —— 'Some business partnerships at Lyon, 1785-93', *J.Ec.Hist.*, 23, 1963, 46-70.

9.38 —— 'Types of capitalism in eighteenth-century France', *Eng.Hist.Rev.*, 79, 1964, 478-97. Distinguishes between merchant capitalism, involvement in state finances, and mining or manufacturing interests.

LOW COUNTRIES
See also 2.134; 3.71; 9.83, 166, 171, 181, 185-7, 192-3, 203-4, 263, 274-7, 325-30; 11.38.

9.39 **Brulez**, W., 'The balance of trade of the Netherlands in the middle of the sixteenth century', *Acta Hist.Neerlandica*, 4, 1970, 20-48.

9.40 —— 'L'exportation des Pays-Bas vers l'Italie par voie de terre au milieu du 16e siècle', *Annales*, 14, 1959, 461-91. Evidence based on records of export tax levied in 1543-45.

9.41 **Carter**, Alice, 'Dutch foreign investment, 1738-1800', *Economica*, n.s., 20, 1953, 322-40. Repr. in her *Getting, Spending, and Investing in Early Modern Times*, Assen, 1975, 23-52 (with related essay from *Tijd.Geschied.*, 66, 1953). Contends that only a small number of rentiers invested heavily abroad. See also discussion with C. Wilson, *Ec.Hist.Rev.*, 2nd ser., 12, 1960, 434-44.

9.42 —— *The Dutch Republic in Europe in the Seven Years War*, 1971. Contains three chaps. on financial and trading services as neutral power.

9.43 —— 'Financial activities of the Huguenots in London and Amsterdam in the mid-eighteenth century', in her *Getting, Spending...* (9.41), 91-106.

9.44 —— 'The family and business of Belesaigne, Amsterdam, 1689-1809', *ib.*, 107-22. Case study related to previous entry's general theme. Details of Huguenot family's progress from retail trade to rentier status.

9.45 **Davies**, D. W., *A Primer of Dutch Seventeenth-Century Overseas Trade*, The Hague, 1961. Short account of far-flung nature of Dutch commerce; relatively little about capital structure or domestic aspects.

9.46 **Klein**, P. W., 'Entrepreneurial behaviour and the economic rise and decline of the Netherlands in the seventeenth and eighteenth centuries', *Ann.Cisalpines d'Hist.Soc.*, 1, 1970, 7-19. Asks whether capital became too attached to purely financial and rentier investment.

9.47 —— 'The Trip family in the seventeenth century. A study of the behaviour of the entrepreneur on the Dutch staple market', *Acta Hist.Neerlandica*, 1, 1966, 187-211. Synopsis of Dutch-language book on powerful merchant family best known as arms dealers.

9.48 **Ormrod**, D., 'English re-exports and the Dutch staplemarket in the eighteenth century', in D. C. Coleman and P. Mathias, eds., *Enterprise and History. Essays in Honour of Charles Wilson*, 1984, 89-115. Emphasises political aspects of Anglo-Dutch commercial relations.

9.49 **Riley**, J. C., 'Dutch investment in France, 1781-87', *J.Ec.Hist.*, 33, 1973, 732-60. Clarifies Dutch part in boom on Paris *Bourse*.

9.50 **Steensgaard**, N., 'The Dutch East India Company as an institutional innovation', in M. Aymard, ed., *Dutch Capitalism and World Capitalism*, 1982, 235-57. Emphasises especially near-autonomy of directors in relation to passive share-holders.

9.51 **Wilson**, C. H., *Anglo-Dutch Commerce and Finance in the Eighteenth Century*, 1941. Basic work; repr. with brief foreword on subsequent research, 1966.

NETHERLANDS PORTS AND TRADING CENTRES

Other material on commerce and financial activities of Amsterdam at 9.43-4,167,176,184,197,414; on those of Antwerp, 9.72,177,197.

9.52 **Barbour**, Violet, *Capitalism in Amsterdam in the Seventeenth Century*, Baltimore, Md., 1950. Short account of how Amsterdam functioned as capital market and commercial clearing house.

9.53 **Dillen**, J. G. van, 'Amsterdam's role in seventeenth-century Dutch politics, and its economic background', in *Britain and the Netherlands*, 2 (6.116), 133-47. Asks how far commercial interests of city regents affected wider Netherlands diplomatic interests.

9.54 **Neal**, L., 'The integration and efficiency of the London and Amsterdam stock markets in the eighteenth century', *J.Ec.Hist.*, 47, 1987, 97-115. Compares quotations for English stock prices at London and at Amsterdam over period 1723-94.

9.55 **Smith**, W. D., 'The function of commercial centers in the modernization of European capitalism. Amsterdam as an information exchange in the seventeenth century', *J.Ec.Hist.*, 44, 1984, 985-1005. Looks at ways business information was disseminated and its part in lowering transaction costs and facilitating planning.

9.56 **Coornaert**, E., *Les Français et le Commerce International à Anvers, Fin du 15e-16e Siècle*, 2 vols., Paris, 1961. General work on Franco-Netherlands trade and French merchant community at Antwerp. Review articles: J. Craeybeckx, *Annales*, 17, 1962, 542-54; P. Jeannin, *Rev.Hist.Mod.et Contemp.*, 11, 1964, 65-70; Y. Renouard, *Rev.Hist.*, 228, 1062, 321-6. Complements older work of J. A. Goris, *Étude sur les Colonies Marchandes Méridionales (Portugais, Espagnols, Italiens) à Anvers de 1488 à 1567*, Louvain, 1925.

9.57 **Doehard**, Renée, *Études Anversoises. Documents sur le Commerce International à Anvers, 1488-1514*, 3 vols., Paris, 1962-63.

9.58 **Houtte**, J. A. van, 'Anvers aux 15e et 16e siècles. Expansion et apogée', *Annales*, 16, 1961, 248-78.

9.59 **Pitz**, E., 'Kapitalausstattung und Unternehmensformen in Antwerpen, 1488-1514', *VSWG*, 53, 1966, 53-91. Study of merchant organisation based largely on material in 9.57.

9.60 **Smolnar**, F. J., 'Resiliency of enterprise. Economic crisis and recovery in the Spanish Netherlands in the early seventeenth century', in C. H. Carter, ed., *From the Renaissance to the Counter-Reformation. Essays in Honour of Garrett Mattingly*, 1966, 247-68. Mainly on fortunes of some Anwerp merchant houses.

9.61 **Soly**, H., 'The "betrayal" of the sixteenth-century bourgeoisie: a myth? Some considerations of the behaviour pattern of the merchants of Antwerp in the sixteenth century', *Acta Hist.Neerlandica*, 8, 1975, 31-49. On alleged flight of capital from trade to land.

9.62 **Van der Wee**, H., *The Growth of the Antwerp Market and the European Economy (Fourteenth to Sixteenth Centuries)*, 3 vols., The Hague, 1963. Basic work on rise of Antwerp, massively documented. Vol.2 contains interpretative material; vols.1 and 3 statistical tables and graphs respectively. Review article: P. Jeannin, *Annales*, 20, 1965, 1222-41.

9.63 **Brulez**, W., 'Bruges and Antwerp in the fifteenth and sixteenth centuries: an antithesis?', *Acta Hist.Neerlandicae*, 6, 1973, 1-26. Sees no sharp contrast between type of trade or merchant community to account for relative decline of Bruges.

9.64 **Houtte**, J. A. van, 'Bruges as a trading

centre in the early modern period', in Coleman and Mathias (9.48), 71-88. History of port after its alleged downfall in early sixteenth century.

9.65 —— 'The rise and decline of the market of Bruges', *Ec.Hist.Rev.*, 2nd ser., 19, 1966, 29-47. Falls partly into our period.

9.66 **Phillips**, W. D., 'Local integration and long-distance ties. The Castilian community in sixteenth-century Bruges', *Sixteenth-Cent.J.*, 17, 1986, 33-50. Milieu of expatriate wool merchants analysed from wills of period 1544-69.

SPAIN AND PORTUGAL

On Spain see also 3.105, 130; 9.56, 66, 181, 211, 241-2, 244-6, 265, 267, 270, 276, 278-9, 281-2, 308-16, 415-20; 11.61. On Portugal, 3.150; 9.211, 243, 264, 266, 280, 283-5, 324, 331-4, 417.

9.67 **Basas Fernández**, M., *El Consulado de Burgos en el Siglo 16*, Madrid, 1963. Institutional account of merchant guild. For general work on such guilds see R. S. Smith, *The Spanish Guild Merchant*, Durham, N.C., 1940.

9.68 **Driesch**, W. von den, *Die Ausländischen Kaufleute während des 18. Jahrhunderts in Spanien und ihre Beteiligung am Kolonialhandel*, Köln, 1972. Lengthy work based on research in many European archives. On preceding period (from Peace of Pyrenees onwards) see still valuable A. Girard, *Le Commerce Français à Séville et Cadix au Temps des Habsbourg*, Paris, 1932.

9.69 **Fisher**, H. E. S., *The Portugal Trade. A Study of Anglo-Portuguese Commerce, 1700-70*, 1971. Mainly looked at from perspective of British economic history. See also his 'Anglo-Portuguese trade, 1700-70', *Ec.Hist.Rev.*, 2nd ser., 16, 1963, 219-33.

9.70 **La Force**, J. C., 'Royal joint-stock companies in Spain, 1700-1800', *Explor.Entrepren.Hist.*, 2nd ser., 1, 1964, 232-49. Considers nine industrial and commercial companies initiated by Crown.

9.71 **Lapeyre**, H., *El Comercio Exterior de Castilla a traves de las Aduanas de Felipe II*, Valladolid, 1981. Is also a technical study of customs duties themselves.

9.72 —— *Une Famille de Marchands, les Ruiz. Contribution à l'Étude du Commerce entre la France et l'Espagne au Temps de Philippe II*, Paris, 1955. Thorough study of milieu and activities of this important firm

(centred on Medina del Campo), whose archives have survived and provided material for a number of documentary studies. See J. G. da Silva, *Stratégie des Affaires à Lisbonne entre 1595 et 1607* (Paris, 1956), and its continuation *Marchandises et Finances* (2 vols., Paris, 1959-61), detailing dealings with Portuguese firm of Rodrigues D'Evora; V. Vazquez de Prada, *Lettres Marchandes d'Anvers* (4 vols., Paris, 1960-61), covering Antwerp correspondence, 1563-1606; and F. Ruiz Martin, *Lettres Marchandes changées entre Florence et Medina del Campo* (Paris, 1965), covering 1577-85.

9.73 **Lohmann Villena**, G., *Les Espinosa. Une Famille d'Hommes d'Affaires en Espagne et aux Indes à l'Époque de la Colonisation*, Paris, 1968.

9.74 **Martínez Gijón**, J., *La Compañia Mercantil en Castilla hasta las Ordenanzas del Consulado de Bilbao*, Seville, 1979. On legal position of trading companies up to mid-eighteenth century.

9.75 **Molas Ribalta**, P., *La Burguesía Mercantil en la España del Antiguo Régimen*, Madrid, 1985. Reworking of various publ. papers to comprise sections on general aspects (esp. relating to small traders); social status and honour; and regional studies.

9.76 **Reitzer**, L., 'Some observations on Castilian commerce and finance in the sixteenth century', *J.Mod.Hist.*, 32, 1960, 213-23. Bibliographical emphasis.

ITALY

See also 3.163; 9.56, 206, 227, 247-8, 251-3, 286, 421-34. On Genoa see 3.183; 9.249-50, 316, 428. On Venice 3.195; 9.222, 229-30, 431, 434; 11.70. On Florence 9.72, 228, 421, 424, 429, 567-8.

9.77 **Bratchel**, M. E., 'Italian merchant organization and business relationships in early Tudor London', *J.Eur.Ec.Hist.*, 7, 1978, 5-32.

9.78 —— 'Regulation and group-consciousness in the later history of London's Italian merchant colonies', *ib.*, 9, 1980, 585-610. Asks how far Italians were assimilated, or independent of ties with Italian firms.

9.79 **Ramsay**, G. D., 'The undoing of the Italian mercantile colony in sixteenth-century London', in N. B. Harte and K. G. Ponting, eds., *Textile History and Economic History*, 1973, 22-49. Attributes decline of colony to equivalent lack of vigour in merchant class in Italy itself.

9.80 **Bulferetti**, L., and Costantini, C., *Industria e Commercio in Liguria nell'Età del Risorgimento (1700-1861)*, Milan, 1966. Essentially a study of Genoese economy.

9.81 **Felloni**, G., *Gli Investimenti Finanziari Genovesi in Europa tra il Seicento e la Restaurazione*, Milan, 1971. Large-scale study, concentrating, despite chronology of title, on later eighteenth century. Review article: L. Dermigny, *Rev.Hist.Éc.et Soc.*, 52, 1974, 547-67.

9.82 'Genova e i Genovesi nel Seicento', *Riv.Stor.Ital.*, 84, 1972, 893-1059. Consists of general literature review (by E. Grendi), and articles on silk industry, capital and labour, and involvement in Sicilian finances.

9.83 **Brulez**, W., *Marchands Flamands à Venise*, Brussels, 1965. Provides summaries of notarial acts in Archivio di Stato; only vol.1 (1568-1605) of intended series appears to have been publ.

9.84 **Caizzi**, B., *Industria e Commercio della Republica Veneta nel 18 Secolo*, Milan, 1965. Concentrates on failure to exploit potential of Venetian mainland.

9.85 **Lane**, F. C., 'Public debt and private wealth, particularly in sixteenth-century Venice', in *Mélanges en l'Honneur de Fernand Braudel*, Toulouse, 1973, 1, 317-25. Looks at fortunes of bondholders involved in war loans.

9.86 —— *Venice and History. The Collected Papers of F. C. Lane*, Baltimore, Md., 1966. Reprints Lane's major papers on Venetian trade and business affairs, many published before 1945.

9.87 **Rapp**, R. T., *Industry and Economic Decline in Seventeenth-Century Venice*, Cambridge, Mass., 1976. Argues that while its commercial importance declined, Venice managed to sustain population and living standards by diversification. On Rapp's methodology see J. A. Marino, 'La crisi di Venezia e la New Economic History', *Studi Stor.*, 19, 1978, 79-107.

9.88 **Sella**, D., *Commerci e Industrie a Venezia nel Secolo 17*, Venice, 1961. Attempts to quantify extent of alleged economic decline.

9.89 —— 'Crisis and transformation in Venetian trade', in Pullan (3.156), 88-105. Again deals with seventeenth century.

9.90 **Tucci**, U., *Mercanti, Navi, Monete, nel Cinquecento Veneziano*, Bologna, 1981. Eight essays on Venetian commerce and currency.

9.91 —— 'The psychology of the Venetian merchant in the sixteenth century', in Hale (5.167), 346-78. Emphasises diversity and scope for social mobility in mercantile class.

9.92 **Caizzi**, B., *Industria, Commercio, e Banca in Lombardia nel 18 Secolo*, Milan, 1968.

9.93 **Caracciolo**, A., *L'Albero dei Belloni. Una dinastia di Mercanti del Settecento*, Bologna, 1982. On commercial family from Bologna which extended operations to Rome and attained nobility in 1740s.

9.94 —— 'Francesco Trionfi, capitalista e magnate d'Ancona', *Riv.Stor.Ital.*, 73, 1961, 660-98. Merchant and industrial entrepreneur active in mid-eighteenth century.

9.95 **Coniglio**, G., *Il Viceregno di Napoli nel Secolo 17. Notizie sulla Vita Commerciale e Finanziaria...*, Rome, 1955. Well documented, but poorly assembled.

9.96 **Goodman**, J., 'Financing pre-modern European industry. An example from Florence, 1580-1660', *J.Eur.Ec.Hist.*, 10, 1981, 415-35. Examines growth of equity holdings in silk manufactures by mercantile and banking groups.

9.97 **Mallett**, M. E., 'Anglo-Florentine commercial relations, 1465-91', *Ec.Hist.Rev.*, 2nd ser., 15, 1962, 250-65.

9.98 **Melis**, F., 'Consideration of some aspects of the rise of capitalist enterprise', in Marcelle Kooy, ed., *Studies in Economics and Economic History. Essays in Honour of H. M. Robertson*, 1972, 153-86. Concentrates on developments in Tuscan commercial enterprises, 1350-1500.

9.99 **Molho**, A., 'The Florentine "tassa dei traffichi" of 1451', *Stud.in Renaiss.*, 17, 1970, 73-118. Tax assessment on firms which offers much information on leading merchants and bankers.

9.100 **Mazzei**, Rita, 'La vita economica a Lucca agli inizi del secolo 17', *Arch.Stor.Ital.*, 128, 1970, 407-68. Account of mercantile companies active in period 1590-1610.

SWITZERLAND AND GERMANY

See also 9.128,201-5,211-17,287,435-6,484.

9.101 **Bergier**, J.-F., *Genève et l'Économie Européenne de la Renaissance*, 2 vols.,

Paris, 1963. Study of rise and decline of Geneva fairs in fifteenth and sixteenth centuries. Review article: J. Combes, *Annales*, 19, 1964, 804-8. For succeeding period see Anne-M. Piuz, *Affaires et Politique. Recherches sur le Commerce de Genève au 17e Siècle*, Geneva, 1964.

9.102 **Dietz**, A., *Frankfurter Handelsgeschichte*, 4 vols. in 5, Frankfurt, 1910-25. Remains standard source for city whose commercial importance increased in seventeenth and eighteenth centuries.

9.103 **Edlin-Thieme**, Margareta, *Studien zur Geschichte des Münchener Handelsstandes im 18. Jahrhunderts*, Stuttgart, 1969. Pictures mercantile community stifled by government restrictions. Rather limited on social side.

9.104 **Hildebrandt**, R., *Die "Georg Fuggerischen Erben". Kaufmännische Tätigkeit und Sozialer Status, 1555-1600*, Berlin, 1966. Deals with grandsons of Jakob Fugger (see 9.110), and their virtual absorption into landed aristocracy. See also on this theme R. Mandrou, *Les Fugger, Propriétaires Fonciers en Souabe, 1560-1618*, Paris, 1969.

9.105 **Irsigler**, F., 'Industrial production, international trade, and public finances in Cologne (fourteenth and fifteenth century)', *J.Eur.Ec.Hist.*, 6, 1977, 269-306.

9.106 **Kellenbenz**, H., 'Die Rolle der Verbindungsplätze zwischen Spanien und Augsburg im Unternehmen Anton Fuggers', *VSWG*, 56, 1978, 1-37.

9.107 **Lütge**, F., 'Der Handel Nürnbergs nach dem Osten im 15/16 Jahrhundert', in his *Beiträge zur Sozial- und Wirtschaftsgeschichte*, Stuttgart, 1970, 134-92. On increasing importance of eastward-going trade, ranging from European borderlands to Orient.

9.108 **Lutz**, E., *Die Rechtliche Struktur Süddeutscher Handelsgesellschaften in der Zeit der Fugger*, 2 vols., Tübingen, 1976. Straightforward technical study of contract law covering companies. Vol.2 consists of documents.

9.109 **Pölnitz**, G. von, *Die Fugger*, Frankfurt am Main, 1960. Based on deep knowledge of Fugger archives, of which author was custodian. See following entries for spacious biographies of firm's most important heads; and also 9.104,106. R. Ehrenberg's 1896 work on Fuggers also remains of interest, and in its translated

form *Capital and Finance in the Age of the Renaissance*, 1928, most substantial work accessible in English.

9.110 —— *Jakob Fugger*, 2 vols., Tübingen, 1949-51. L. L. Schick's *Un Grand Homme d'Affaires au Début du 16e Siècle. Jacob Fugger*, Paris, 1957 is less biographically orientated, with substantial sections on mining enterprises. In English, J. Strieder's *Jacob Fugger the Rich, 1459-1523*, New York, 1931, remains useful brief account.

9.111 —— *Anton Fugger*, 4 vols., Tübingen, 1958-71. Uncompleted (lacks vol. dealing with last six years of Anton's life).

9.112 **Redlich**, F., 'An eighteenth-century German guide for investors', *Bus.Hist.Rev.*, 26, 1952, 95-104. Describes *Der Kluge Capitalist* by J. F. Kobe, publ. in 1761.

9.113 **Wood**, Merry W., 'Paltry peddlers or essential merchants? Women in the distributive trades in early modern Nuremberg', *Sixteenth-Cent.J.*, 12 (ii), 1981, 3-13.

9.114 **Zorn**, W., *Handels- und Industriegeschichte Bayrisch-Schwaben, 1648-1870*, Augsburg, 1961. Main emphasis on Augsburg; section on entrepreneurs as class. See also sketch of findings on period 1648-1806 in *VSWG*, 43, 1956, 97-145.

EAST CENTRAL EUROPE AND THE BALKANS
See also 3.269,304; 6.35; 8.151-2; 9.221-7,232-5,254-7,437,490.

9.115 **Bog**, I., ed., *Der Aussenhandel Ostmitteleuropas, 1450-1650*, Köln, 1971. Symposium, mainly in German, covering Poland, Hungary, and Czech lands. Contributors include Maria Bogucka, A. Maczak, H. Samsonowicz, and A. Wyrobisz.

9.116 **Freudenberger**, H., 'An exploration in entrepreneurial motivation and action', *Explor.Ec.Hist.*, 7, 1970, 433-49. Account of four textile entrepreneurs of differing background in eighteenth-century Bohemia and Moravia.

9.117 **Pach**, Z. P., 'The role of East Central Europe in international trade (sixteenth-seventeenth centuries)', in *Études Historiques Publiées à l'Occasion du 13e Congrès Int. des Sciences Historiques*, Budapest, 1970, 217-64.

9.118 **Braude**, B., 'Venture and faith in the commercial life of the Ottoman Balkans, 1500-1650', *Int.Hist.Rev.*, 7, 1985, 519-42. Suggests that transaction costs of commerce in this region were so considerable that it had to function via ethnic networks.

9.119 **Bur**, Marta, 'Handelsgesellschaften-Organisationen der Kaufleute der Balkanländer in Ungarn im 17-18 Jahrhundert', *Balkan Stud.*, 25, 1984, 267-307. Appendix lists merchants subject to Ottoman Empire operating in Hungary, as registered in 1754.

9.120 **Clogg**, R., 'The Greek mercantile bourgeoisie, "progressive" or "reactionary"?', in Clogg, ed., *Balkan Society in the Age of Greek Independence*, 85-110. Questions view of Greek merchant magnates as patrons of new learning or nationalism in late eighteenth century.

9.121 **Faroqhi**, Suraiya, 'The early history of the Balkan fairs', *Südost-Forsch.*, 37, 1978, 50-68. Repr. in Faroqhi (4.82).

9.122 —— 'The Venetian presence in the Ottoman Empire (1600-30)', *J.Eur.Ec.Hist.*, 15, 1986, 345-84. Aims to throw light on relations between Ottoman and Venetian merchants, and attitude of Ottoman state towards them.

9.123 **Gerber**, H., 'The Muslim law of partnerships in Ottoman court records', *Studia Islamica*, 53, 1981, 109-19. Evidence on business partnerships drawn mainly from seventeenth-century Bursa.

9.124 **Inalcik**, H., 'The hub of the city. The *bedestan* of Istanbul', *Int.J.Turkish Stud.*, 1, 1980, 1-17. Repr. in Inalcik (3.290). Exchange for resident merchants.

9.125 **Mantran**, R., 'The transformation of trade in the Ottoman Empire in the eighteenth century', in Naff and Owen (3.308), 217-35. Full text is in French.

9.126 **Stoianovich**, T., 'The conquering Balkan Orthodox merchant', *J.Ec.Hist.*, 20, 1960, 234-313. Traces increasing status and wealth of merchant class from fourteenth to eighteenth centuries.

NORTHERN EUROPE

See also sub-section on Baltic trade: 9.156-220.
On Scandinavia see further 2.135;
9.288-9,317,335-6,438.
On Russia 7.258; 8.165; 9.337.

9.127 **Jeannin**, P., 'En Europe du Nord. Sources et travaux d'histoire commerciale', *Annales*, 23, 1968, 844-68. Useful review article on variety of recent work.

9.128 **Kellenbenz**, H., 'Bäuerliche Unternehmertätigkeit im Bereich der Nord- und Ostsee vom Hochmittelalter bis zum Ausgang der neueren Zeit', *VSWG*, 49, 1962, 1-40. Collects evidence for peasant investment, especially in shipping, in N. Germany and Scandinavia.

9.129 **Feldbaek**, O., 'The Danish trading companies of the seventeenth and eighteenth centuries', *Scan.Ec.Hist.Rev.*, 34, 1986, 204-18. Deals with overseas companies and those without fixed area of operations. See also 9.288-9.

9.130 **Baron**, S. H., *Muscovite Russia. Collected Essays*, 1980. Convenient collection of journal articles on early modern merchants and on aspects of Anglo-Russian trade.

9.131 —— 'Entrepreneurs and entrepreneurship in sixteenth/seventeenth century Russia', in G. Guroff and F. Carstensen, eds., *Entrepreneurship in Imperial Russia and the Soviet Union*, Princeton, N.J., 1983, 27-58.

9.132 **Bill**, V. T., *The Forgotten Class. The Russian Bourgeoisie from the Earliest Beginnings to 1900*, New York, 1959. Rather lightweight account of mercantile society.

9.133 **Bushkovitch**, P., *The Merchants of Moscow, 1580-1650*, 1980. Studies economic role of small merchant elite known as *gosti*. For article on *gosti* under Peter the Great see Baron's collection (9.130).

9.134 **Clendenning**, P. H., 'William Gomm. A case study of the foreign entrepreneur in eighteenth-century Russia', *J. Eur. Ec. Hist.*, 6, 1977, 533-848. On Gomm's attempt to establish timber monopoly in concert with Count Shuvalov (1750s and '60s).

9.135 **Daniel**, W., 'Grigorii Teplov and the conception of order. The Commission on Commerce and the role of the merchants in Russia', *Can.-Am. Slavic Stud.*, 16, 1982, 410-31. Part of economic policy debate under Catherine the Great. See also following related articles.

9.136 —— 'The merchantry and the problem of social order in the Russian state. Catherine II's Commission on Commerce', *Slavonic & E. Eur.Rev.*, 55, 1977, 185-203.

9.137 —— 'The merchants' view of the social

order in Russia as revealed in the town *nakazy* from Moskovskaia Guberniia to Catherine's Legislative Commission', *Can.-Am.Slavic Stud.*, 11, 1977, 503-22.

9.138 Kaufmann-Rochard, Jacqueline, *Origines d'une Bourgeoisie Russe, 16e et 17e Siècles. Marchands de Moscovie*, Paris, 1969. Valuable. Less focussed on Moscow than Bushkovitch's similarly titled work, 9.133, (whose bibliography does not cite it).

9.139 Kellenbenz, H., 'Marchands en Russie aux 17e-18e siècles', *Cah.Monde Russe et Sov.*, 11, 1970, 576-620; 12, 1971, 76-109. Compiled mainly from accounts of German travellers and merchants.

9.140 Rosovsky, H., 'The serf entrepreneur in Russia', *Explor.Entrepren.Hist.*, 6, 1954, 207-33. Repr. in H. G. J. Aitken, ed., *Explorations in Enterprise*, Cambridge, Mass., 1965, 341-70. Eighteenth-century examples, chiefly of industrial nature. Cf. 7.258.

ARISTOCRACY AND BUSINESS ENTERPRISE
See also 6.168; 9.580,597,625.

9.141 Redlich, F., 'European aristocracy and economic development', *Explor. Entrepren. Hist.*, 6, 1953, 78-90. Repr. in his *Steeped in Two Cultures. A Selection of Essays*, New York, 1971, 65-87. Introductory article of group on this theme.

9.142 Caron, X., 'Images d'une élite au 18e siècle. Quarante négociants anoblis face à la question sociale', *Hist., Éc., et Soc.*, 3, 1984, 381-426. Sees signs of "enterprise culture" in deliberate ennoblement of entrepreneurs.

9.143 Grassby, R. B., 'Social status and commercial enterprise under Louis XIV', *Ec.Hist.Rev.*, 2nd ser., 13, 1960, 19-38. Repr. in Kierstead (6.68), 200-32. Background to declaration of 1701 which eased restrictions on noble participation in commerce.

9.144 Hecht, Jacqueline, 'Un problème de population active au 18e siècle. La querelle de la noblesse commerçante', *Population*, 19, 1964, 267-90. Mainly on reactions to Abbé Coyer's pamphlet of 1757 encouraging business activity by nobility.

9.145 Richard, G., *Noblesse d'Affaires au 18e Siècle*, Paris, 1974. Fairly brief treatment. See also his related article 'La noblesse de France et les sociétés par actions à la fin du 18e siècle', *Rev.Hist.Éc.et Soc.*, 40, 1962, 484-523.

9.146 Callahan, W. J., *Honor, Commerce, and Industry in Eighteenth-Century Spain*, Boston, Mass., 1972. Mainly on question of how status was affected by participation in commerce and manufactures. See also related articles in following entries.

9.147 —— 'Crown, nobility, and industry in eighteenth-century Spain', *Int. Rev. Soc. Hist.*, 11, 1966, 444-64.

9.148 —— 'Don Juan de Goyeneche, hidalgo industrialist of eighteenth-century Spain', *Bus.Hist.Rev.*, 43, 1969, 152-70. Suggests this nobleman's experiments in manufacture on his estates were probably paternalistic rather than profit-minded.

9.149 Pike, Ruth, 'The Sevillan nobility and trade with the New World in the sixteenth century', *ib.*, 39, 1965, 439-65.

9.150 Litchfield, R. B., 'Les investissements commerciaux des patriciens florentins au 18e siècle', *Annales*, 24, 1969, 685-721. Computer analysis of registers of Mercanzia tribunal covering participation in limited liability companies.

9.151 Kellenbenz, H., 'German aristocratic entrepreneurship. Activities of the Holstein nobility in the sixteenth and seventeenth centuries', *Explor. Entrepren. Hist.*, 6, 1953, 103-14.

9.152 Zak, J., 'The role of aristocratic entrepreneurship in the industrial development of the Czech lands, 1750-1850', in M. Rechcigl, ed., *Czechoslovakia Past and Present*, The Hague, 1968, 2, 1259-73.

9.153 Pach, Z., 'Sixteenth-century Hungary. Commercial activity and market production by the nobles', in Burke (1.1), 113-33. Transl. from *Annales*, 21, 1966, 1212-31. Explores nobility's role in wine, cattle, and corn trades.

9.154 Ohlin, P. G., 'Entrepreneurial activities of the Swedish aristocracy', *Explor. Entrepren. Hist.*, 6, 1954, 147-62.

9.155 Kamendrowsky, V., and Griffiths, D. M.,

'The fate of the trading nobility controversy in Russia. A chapter in the relationship between Catherine II and the Russian nobility', *Jb.Gesch.Osteuropas*, 26, 1978, 198-221. Reviews ambivalent attitude to this question throughout eighteenth century.

REGIONAL AND COLONIAL TRADE. ROUTES AND PORTS

BALTIC AND NORTH SEA TRADE: GENERAL
See also 9.249,302,349-53,375-9.

9.156 **Alanen**, A. J., *Der Aussenhandel und die Schiffahrt Finnlands im 18. Jahrhundert*, Helsinki, 1957. Deals with shipbuilding, principal exports and imports, and mechanisms of trade.

9.157 'Anglo-Russian technological and commercial relations', in A. G. Cross, ed., *Great Britain and Russia in the Eighteenth Century. Contacts and Comparisons*, Newtonville, Mass., 1979, 137-89. Section consisting of papers by A. S. Fedorov, A. Kahan (brief general surveys), P. H. Clendenning, (on commercial treaty of 1766), and D. S. Macmillan (Scottish merchants and Russia). See also 9.179.

9.158 **Åstrom**, S.-E., 'The English Navigation Laws and the Baltic trade, 1660-1700', *Scan.Ec.Hist.Rev.*, 8, 1960, 3-18. Argues that banning Dutch carriers tended mostly to benefit Scandinavians.

9.159 —— *From Cloth to Iron. The Anglo-Baltic Trade in the Late Seventeenth Century*, Helsinki, 1963. Pattern of trade; and operations of English factors and merchant houses. On later period see Kent (9.182).

9.160 —— *From Stockholm to St. Petersburg. Commercial Factors in the Political Relations between England and Sweden, 1675-1700*, Helsinki, 1962. Describes how Russia began to displace Sweden as Britain's main Baltic supplier.

9.161 **Attman**, A., *The Russian and Polish Markets in International Trade, 1500-1650*, Göteborg, 1973. Concludes that Baltic ports generated large trade surpluses for Poland and Russia.

9.162 —— 'The Russian market in world trade, 1500-1860', *Scan.Ec.Hist.Rev.*, 29, 1981, 177-202.

9.163 —— *The Struggle for Baltic Markets. Powers in Conflict, 1558-1618*, Göteborg, 1979. Perhaps over-estimates economic motives in diplomatic rivalries of this period.

9.164 **Bamford**, P. W., 'French shipping in Northern Europe trade, 1660-1789', *J.Mod.Hist.*, 26, 1954, 207-19. Examines reluctance of French entrepreneurs to venture capital or ships in Baltic trade.

9.165 **Bjurling**, O., 'Sweden's foreign trade and shipping around the year 1700', *Ec.& Hist.*, 4, 1961, 3-33. Statistics calculated from customs records.

9.166 —— 'Swedish shipping and British-Dutch competition during the 1670s and 1680s', *ib.*, 14, 1971, 3-26. Effects of international relations on Baltic shipping and trade.

9.167 **Bogucka**, Maria, 'Amsterdam and the Baltic in the first half of the seventeenth century', *Ec.Hist.Rev.*, 2nd ser., 26, 1973, 433-47. Analyses freight contracts to establish main trading partners (Danzig and Riga greatly preponderant).

9.168 —— 'North European commerce as a solution to resource shortage in the sixteenth-eighteenth centuries', in Maczak and Parker (4.44), 9-42. Views development of Baltic trade as response to population increase elsewhere in Europe.

9.169 —— 'The role of Baltic trade in European development from the sixteenth to the eighteenth centuries', *J.Eur.Ec.Hist.*, 9, 1980, 5-20. Cf. rather similar 'North European commerce and the problem of dualism in the development of modern Europe', in Zimányi (3.269), 9-24. Both allude to arguments of 9.168 and to consequent divergences in social structure of East and West Europe.

9.170 **Cherepnin**, L. V., 'Russian seventeenth-century Baltic trade in Soviet historiography', *Slavonic & E.Eur.Rev.*, 43, 1964, 1-22.

9.171 **Christensen**, A. E., *Dutch Trade to the Baltic about 1600*, Copenhagen, 1941.

Basic work on establishment of Dutch commercial domination of area.

9.172 Cieslak, E., 'Aspects of Baltic sea-borne trade in the eighteenth century. The trade relations between Sweden, Poland, Russia, and Prussia', *J.Eur.Ec.Hist.*, 12, 1983, 239-70. Deals mainly with second half of century.

9.173 —— 'Sea-borne trade between France and Poland in the eighteenth century', *ib.*, 6, 1977, 49-62.

9.174 Esper, T., 'Russia and the Baltic, 1494-1558', *Slavic Rev.*, 25, 1966, 458-74. Looks at commercial relations with Western Europe from expulsion of Hanseatic League to acquisition of Narva.

9.175 Fox, F., 'A view of French-Russian trade relations in the eighteenth century. The ms. Le Gendre', *Jb.Gesch.Osteur.*, 16, 1968, 481-98. Summarises memorandum of 1780s on lack of direct French access to northern commerce.

9.176 Hart, S., 'Amsterdam shipping and trade to Northern Russia in the seventeenth century', *Meded.Nederlandse Vereniging Zeegeschied.*, 26, 1973, 5-30. On trade to Archangel; details of vessel charters from notarial archives.

9.177 Jeannin, P., 'Les relations économiques des villes de la Baltique avec Anvers au 16e siècle', *VSWG*, 43, 1956, 193-217, 323-55.

9.178 —— 'The sea-borne and the overland trade routes of Northern Europe in the sixteenth and seventeenth centuries', *J. Eur. Ec. Hist.*, 11, 1982, 5-59. Valuable essay on commercial logic of transport costs.

9.179 Kaplan, H. H., 'Russia's impact on the Industrial Revolution in Great Britain during the second half of the eighteenth century. The significance of international commerce', *Forsch.Osteur.Gesch.*, 29, 1981, 7-59. Supplemented by his 'Observations on the value of Russia's overseas commerce with Great Britain...', *Slavic Rev.*, 45, 1986, 85-94. See also 9.157 on this theme.

9.180 Kellenbenz, H., 'The economic significance of the Archangel route (from the late sixteenth to the late eighteenth century)', *J.Eur.Ec.Hist.*, 1973, 541-81. Shows that importance of route tended to depend on political difficulties impeding Baltic traffic.

9.181 —— 'Spanien, die nördlichen Niederlande und der skandinavisch-baltische Raum in der Weltwirtschaft und Politik um 1600', *VSWG*, 41, 1954, 289-332.

9.182 Kent, H. S. K., *War and Trade in Northern Seas. Anglo-Scandinavian Economic Relations in the Mid-Eighteenth Century*, 1973. Mainly looked at from British side, showing importance of trade during Seven Years War despite official attempts to foster colonial substitutes.

9.183 Kirchner, W., *Commercial Relations between Russia and Europe, 1400 to 1800. Collected Essays*, Bloomington, Ind., 1966. As well as general pieces, contains essays (mostly transl. from German and French journals) on sixteenth-century Narva, Danish-Russian treaty of 1562, Franco-Russian economic relations, and Ukrainian tobacco.

9.184 Knoppers, J., 'A comparison of the Sound accounts and the Amsterdam *galjootsgeldregisters*', *Scan.Ec.Hist.Rev.*, 24, 1976, 93-113. Sample comparisons of Baltic-Amsterdam traffic for 1724/5 and 1784/5 from these different sources.

9.185 —— *Dutch Trade with Russia from the Time of Peter I to Alexander I. A Quantitative Study in Eighteenth-Century Shipping*, 3 vols., Amsterdam, 1976. Strictly reference work: provides tables of shipping from Russian ports to Amsterdam and Rotterdam (not vice-versa), but without breakdown of cargo.

9.186 Lindblad, J. T., 'Structural change in the Dutch trade with the Baltic in the eighteenth century', *Scan.Ec.Hist.Rev.*, 33, 1985, 193-207. Measures cyclical changes within long-term structural and competitive decline.

9.187 —— *Sweden's Trade with the Dutch Republic, 1738-95*, Assen, 1982. Quantitative study tracing decline in volume of trade between these partners. Note his related article, 'Swedish shipping with the Netherlands in the second half of the eighteenth century', *Scan. Ec. Hist. Rev.*, 27, 1979, 139-65.

9.188 Maczak, A., 'The balance of Polish sea trade with the west, 1565-1646', *ib.*, 18, 1970, 107-42. Finds maritime trade, at least, to have been in surplus. Useful statistical appendix.

9.189 Malowist, M., 'A certain trade technique in the Baltic countries in the fifteenth-seventeenth centuries', in Geremek and Maczak (3.284), 103-16. Deals with

forward payments by merchants of
Danzig, Thorn, etc.

9.190 —— *Croissance et Régression en Europe,
14e-17e Siècles. Recueil d'Articles*, Paris,
1972. Articles mainly on Baltic commerce
(several in first transl. from Polish).

9.191 —— 'Poland, Russia, and the western
trade in the fifteenth and sixteenth
centuries', *P.& P.*, 13, 1958, 26-41.
Argues that growth of trade had rather
differing social effects on Poland and
Russia.

9.192 **Nolte**, H.-H., 'The Netherlands and
Russia in the seventeenth century.
Economic and social relations', *Review*,
10, 1986, 230-44. Briefly considers
whether centre-periphery model applies to
this relationship.

9.193 **Odén**, Birgitta, 'A Netherlands merchant
in Stockholm in the reign of Erik XIV',
Scan.Ec.Hist.Rev., 10, 1962, 3-37. Based
on account book of Nicolaes Verjuys, agent
for Antwerp merchants in 1560s.

9.194 **Öhberg**, A., 'Russia and the world market
in the seventeenth century', *ib.*, 3, 1955,
123-62. Examines three principal routes
for Russian trade with Western Europe,
and how prices affected or were affected by
their use.

9.195 **Shaskolskii**, I. P., 'New phenomena in the
Baltic trade of Russia in the seventeenth
century', *Scan.Ec.Hist.Rev.*, 34, 1986,
41-53. Focusses on Russia's difficulties of
direct access to Baltic.

9.196 **Soom**, A., 'Die merkantilische
Wirtschaftspolitik Schwedens und die
baltische Städte im 17. Jahrhundert',
Jb.Gesch.Osteur., 11, 1963, 183-222.
Examines both commercial and
manufacturing implications of Swedish
policy on Reval, Narva, and Riga.

9.197 **Stuijvenberg**, J. H. van, ed., *The
Interactions of Amsterdam and Antwerp with
the Baltic Region, 1400-1800*, Leiden,
1983. 19 brief conference papers (mainly
English and German) on aspects of trade
and balance of payments. Contributors
incl. H. Van der Wee, R. W. Unger, A.
Attman, M. Morineau, Maria Bogucka.

9.198 **Unger**, W. S., 'Trade through the Sound
in the seventeenth and eighteenth
centuries', *Ec.Hist.Rev.*, 2nd ser., 12,
1959, 206-21. Surveys general picture
presented by published tables of Sound
dues.

9.199 **Willan**, T. S., *The Early History of the
Russia Company, 1553-1603*, 1956.
Though main focus is on English chartered
company, contains a good deal of
information on Russian commercial policy
and conditions.

9.200 **Zins**, H., *England and the Baltic in the
Elizabethan Era*, 1972. Transl. from Polish
ed. of 1967. Recounts origins of Eastland
Company, and provides much incidental
information on Baltic conditions. See also
(though less helpful) R. W. K. Hinton, *The
Eastland Trade and the Common Weal in the
Seventeenth Century*, 1959.

BALTIC AND NORTH SEA PORTS
AND TRADING CENTRES

9.201 **Dollinger**, P., *The German Hansa*, 1970.
Transl. from French ed of 1964. Only two
chapters on period after 1500. Review
article: P. Jeannin, *Annales*, 22, 1967,
385-95.

9.202 **Olechnowitz**, K.-F., *Handel und
Seeschiffahrt der Späten Hanse*, Weimar,
1965. Concentrates on Wismar, Rostock,
and Stralsund in sixteenth and seventeenth
centuries, showing that economic, though
not political, decline of Hanse has been
exaggerated.

9.203 **Spading**, K., *Holland und die Hanse im 15.
Jahrhundert*, Weimar, 1973. Dutch capture
of Hanseatic markets seen in Marxist
context of transition from feudalism to
capitalism; not clearly explained why
Hanse remained locked to older system,
however.

9.204 **Winter**, W. L., 'Netherland regionalism
and the decline of the Hansa',
Am.Hist.Rev., 53, 1948, 279-87. On
increasing flouting of Hanseatic privileges
in Netherlands (early sixteenth century).

9.205 **Prange**, Ruth, *Die Bremische
Kaufmannschaft des 16. und 17.
Jahrhunderts in Sozialgeschichtlicher
Betrachtung*, Bremen, 1963. Study of
Bremen's merchant elite, incl.
considerable alien community.

9.206 **Obuchowska-Pysiowa**, Honorata, 'Trade
between Cracow and Italy from the
customs-house registers of 1604',
J.Eur.Ec.Hist., 9, 1980, 633-53.

9.207 **Bogucka**, Maria, 'Merchants' profits in
Gdansk [Danzig] foreign trade in the first
half of the seventeenth century', *Acta
Poloniae Hist.*, 23, 1971, 73-90. Provides
estimates of returns on various

commodities, arguing that in general profits remained high.

208 **Hoszowski**, S., 'The Polish Baltic trade in the fifteenth-eighteenth centuries', in *Poland at the 11th International Congress of Historical Sciences*, Warsaw, 1960, 117-54. Deals principally with role of Danzig.

209 **North**, M., 'A small Baltic port in the early modern period. The port of Elbing in the sixteenth and seventeenth century', *J.Eur.Ec.Hist.*, 13, 1984, 117-27.

210 **Grage**, Elsa-B., 'Capital supply in Gothenburg's foreign trade, 1765-1810', *Scan.Ec.Hist.Rev.*, 29, 1981, 97-128.

211 **Kellenbenz**, H., *Unternehmerkräfte im Hamburger Portugal- und Spanienhandel, 1590-1625*, Hamburg, 1954. Charts opportunities of north-south trade available to Hamburg because of Dutch-Spanish hostilities. Much detail on native and foreign merchant families. Review articles: S. Dalgård, *Scan.Ec.Hist.Rev.*, 9, 1961, 195-204; P. Jeannin, *Annales*, 11, 1956, 223-7.

212 —— 'Diego und Manoel Teixeira und ihr Hamburger Unternehmen', *VSWG.*, 42, 1955, 289-352. Case study in research area of previous entry.

213 **Newman**, Karin, 'Hamburg in the European economy, 1660-1750', *J.Eur.Ec.Hist.*, 14, 1985, 57-93. On Hamburg's eighteenth-century Atlantic role see 9.318. On conflict with Prussia see 10.144.

214 **Reissmann**, M., *Die Hamburgische Kaufmannschaft des 17. Jahrhunderts in Sozialgeschichtlicher Sicht*, Hamburg, 1975. More social than economic dimension.

215 **Glinski**, G. von, *Die Königsberger Kaufmannschaft des 17. und 18. Jahrhunderts*, Marburg, 1964. Has chaps. on Jews and foreign merchants.

216 **Jeannin**, P., 'Le commerce de Lübeck aux environs de 1580', *Annales*, 16, 1961, 36-65.

217 **Jørgensen**, J., 'Denmark's relations with Lübeck and Hamburg in the seventeenth century', *Scan.Ec.Hist.Rev.*, 11, 1963, 73-116. Carries appendix of Lübeck and Hamburg merchants trading in Denmark.

218 **Kuklinska**, Krystyna, 'Commercial expansion in eighteenth-century Poland. The case of Poznán', *J.Eur.Ec.Hist.*, 6, 1977, 443-60. Statistics on rapid growth of commodity exchange in period 1740-93.

9.219 **Etzold**, G., *Seehandel und Kaufleute in Reval nach dem Frieden von Nystad bis zur Mitte des 18. Jahrhunderts*, Marburg, 1975.

9.220 **Soom**, A., *Der Handel Revals im Siebzehnten Jahrhundert*, Wiesbaden, 1969. See also 9.196.

MEDITERRANEAN AND LEVANT TRADE: GENERAL
See also 4.62; 9.122,551; 11.89.

9.221 **Ashtor**, E., *Levant Trade in the Later Middle Ages*, Princeton, N.J., 1983. Gives much attention to European sources and traders in fifteenth century.

9.222 —— 'The Venetian supremacy in Levantine trade. Monopoly or pre-colonialism?', *J.Eur.Ec.Hist.*, 3, 1974, 5-53. Concludes that trade supremacy did not constitute monopoly or political hegemony.

9.223 —— 'The volume of Levantine trade in the later Middle Ages (1370-1498)', *J.Eur.Ec.Hist.*, 4, 1975, 573-612. Tries to estimate quantity of trade done by Southern European regions with Levant.

9.224 **Dan**, M., and Goldenberg, S., 'Le commerce Balkano-Levantin de la Transylvanie au cours de la seconde moitié du 16e siècle et au début du 17e siècle', *Rev.Ét.Sud-Est Eur.*, 5, 1967, 87-117. Deals with trade in so-called "Turkish goods".

9.225 **De Groot**, A. H., 'The organization of Western European trade in the Levant, 1500-1800', in L. Blussé and F. Gaastra, eds., *Companies and Trade. Essays on Overseas Trading Companies during the Ancien Régime*, The Hague, 1981, 231-41.

9.226 **Filippini**, J.-P., and others, *Dossiers sur le Commerce Français en Méditerranée Orientale au 18e Siècle*, Paris, 1976. Five essays dealing with aspects of Levant trade. Basic work in this field remains P. Masson, *Histoire du Commerce Français dans le Levant*, 2 vols., Paris, 1896-1911. See also Masson's *Histoire des Établissements et du Commerce Français dans l'Afrique Barbaresque (1560-1793)*, Paris, 1903.

9.227 **Goldenberg**, S., 'Notizie del commercio italiano in Transilvania nel secolo 16', *Arch.Stor.Ital.*, 121, 1963, 255-88.

9.228 **Mallett**, M. E., *The Florentine Galleys in the Fifteenth Century*, 1967. State-owned galleys leased for commercial ventures.

9.229 **Mallia-Milanes**, V., 'Some aspects of

Veneto-Maltese trade relations in the eighteenth century', *Studi Veneziani*, 16, 1974, 503-53. Mainly derived from correspondence of Venetian consul in Malta.

9.230 —— 'Towards an economic history of eighteenth-century Malta. Buzzaccarini Gonzaga's correspondence to the Venetian Magistracy of Trade, 1754-76', *J.Eur.Ec.Hist.*, 7, 1978, 461-97.

9.231 **Morineau**, M., 'Flottes de commerce et trafics français en Méditerranée au 17e siècle (jusqu'en 1669)', *Dix-Septième Siècle*, 86-87, 1970, 135-71. Questions *idée reçue* of commercial decline in this period.

9.232 **Romano**, R., *Le Commerce du Royaume de Naples avec la France et les Pays de l'Adriatique au 18e Siècle*, Paris, 1951. Two separate short studies.

9.233 **Pach**, Z. P., 'The Transylvanian route of Levantine trade at the turn of the fifteenth and sixteenth centuries', in *Études Historiques Hongroises...1980 (8.142)*, 1, 135-65. Mainly concerned with spice imports.

9.234 **Steensgaard**, N., 'Consuls and nations in the Levant from 1570 to 1650', *Scan.Ec.Hist.Rev.*, 15, 1967, 13-55. Examines workings of consular system developed by Venice, France, England, and Netherlands.

9.235 **Stoianovich**, T., 'Pour un modèle du commerce du Levant. Économie concurentielle et économie de bazar, 1500-1800', *Bull.Assoc.Int.Ét.Sud-Est Eur.*, 12, 1974, 61-120. Major attempt to categorise trade sectors and periodic shifts in importance of French participation.

MEDITERRANEAN PORTS AND TRADING CENTRES

9.236 **Baulant**, Micheline, ed., *Lettres de Négociants Marseillais. Les Frères Hermite (1570-1612)*, Paris, 1953. Documents giving vivid account of risks and profits of Levant trade.

9.237 **Bromley**, J. S., 'Projets et contrats d'armement en course Marseillais, 1705-12', *Rev.Hist.Éc.et Soc.*, 50, 1972, 74-109. Looks at business side of corsair activity during War of Spanish Succession.

9.238 **Carrière**, C., *Négociants Marseillais au 18e Siècle. Contributions à l'Étude des Économies Maritimes*, 2 vols., Marseille,

1973. Thorough all-round study of growth from regional to world port, with much material on mechanisms of trade. On Marseille grain trade in this period see 9.344.

9.239 —— and Courdurié, M., 'Un sophisme économique. Marseille s'enrichit en achetant plus qu'elle ne vend. Réflexions sur les mécanismes commerciaux levantins au 18e siècle', *Hist., Éc., et Soc.*, 3, 1984, 7-51. Deals principally with profits derived from favourable exchange rates. See also 9.551 on textile trade with Levant.

9.240 **Rambert**, G., ed., *Histoire du Commerce de Marseille*, 7 vols., Marseille, 1949-66. Scholarly cooperative work, mainly by city archivists. Vols.3-7 cover period 1480-1789.

9.241 **Giménez López**, E., *Alicante en el Siglo 18. Economía de una Ciudad Portuaria en el Antiguo Régimen*, Valencia, 1981. Contains material on demography and on agriculture of hinterland as well as commercial fortunes of city.

9.242 **Giralt y Raventos**, E., 'La colonia mercantil francesa de Barcelona a mediados del siglo 17', *Estud.de Hist.Mod.* 6, 1956-59, 217-78.

9.243 **Fisher**, H. E. S., 'Lisbon, its English merchant community, and the Mediterranean in the eighteenth century', in P. L. Cottrell and D. H. Aldcroft, eds., *Shipping, Trade, and Commerce. Essays in Memory of Ralph Davis*, 1981, 23-44. Covers importance of English vessels in freighting of Portugal's Mediterranean trade. On Lisbon see also 9.72 and 283.

9.244 **Castillo Pintado**, A., *Trafico Maritimo y Comercio de Importación en Valencia a Comienzos del Siglo 17*, Madrid, 1967. Study of tax registers of port of Valencia.

9.245 **Guiral-Hadziiossif**, Jacqueline, *Valence, Port Méditerranéen au 15e Siècle (1410-1525)*, Paris, 1986. Tackles not only trade and exchange in port and milieu of shipbuilders, dockers, and seamen; but also (in part 3) general social history of city

9.246 **Salvador**, Emilia, *La Economía Valenciana en el Siglo 16. Comercio de Importación*, Valencia, 1972.

9.247 **Caracciolo**, A., *Le Port Franc d'Ancône. Croissance et Impasse d'un Milieu Marchand au 18e Siècle*, Paris, 1965. Primarily a study of trade fluctuations. See also 9.94.

9.248 **Earle**, P., 'The commercial development

of Ancona, 1479-1551', *Ec.Hist.Rev.*, 2nd ser., 22, 1969, 28-44. Considers why Ancona briefly became major international entrepôt.

.249 **Grendi**, E., 'I Nordici e il traffico del porto di Genova, 1590-1666', *Riv.Stor.Ital.*, 83, 1971, 23-71.

.250 —— 'Traffico portuale, naviglio mercantile, e consolati Genovesi nel Cinquecento', *ib.*, 78, 1968, 593-629.

.251 **Braudel**, F., and Romano, R., *Navires et Marchandises à l'Entrée du Port de Livourne (1547-1611)*, Paris, 1951. Analysis of customs records for as total a picture as possible of commodities and destinations.

.252 **Carrière**, C., and Courdurié, M., 'Les grandes heures de Livourne au 18e siècle. L'exemple de la Guerre de Sept Ans', *Rev.Hist.*, 254, 1975, 39-80. Analyses brief surge in prosperity of Livorno thanks to exigencies of war.

.253 **Kaltenstadler**, W., 'Der österreichische Seehandel über Triest im 18. Jahrhundert', *VSWG.*, 55, 1968, 481-500; 56, 1969, 1-104.

.254 **Inalcik**, H., 'Bursa and the commerce of the Levant', *J.Ec.& Soc.Hist. Orient*, 3, 1960, 131-47. Repr. in Inalcik (3.299). Principally on eastward trade in late fifteenth century.

.255 **Carter**, F. W., 'The commerce of the Dubrovnik Republic, 1500-1700', *Ec.Hist.Rev.*, 2nd ser., 24, 1971, 370-94. On Ragusa and grain trade see Aymard (9.347).

.256 **Zlatar**, Z., 'Dubrovnik's investments in its Balkan colonies, 1594-1623. A quantitative analysis', *Balcanica*, 7, 1976, 103-16. Ragusan interests in Belgrade, Sofia, and other centres.

.257 **Svoronos**, N. G., *Le Commerce de Salonique au 18e Siècle*, Paris, 1956. Evidence taken almost entirely from French sources.

COLONIAL TRADE: GENERAL
See also 9.68; 11.16.

.258 **Coornaert**, E. L. J., 'European economic institutions and the New World. The chartered companies', in *Cambridge Economic History of Europe*, 4 (2.15), 220-74. New World here interpreted as overseas expansion in general, east and west.

9.259 **Bertin**, G. Y., 'Les aspects comptables et financiers du commerce colonial de la Compagnie des Indes entre 1719 et 1730', *Rev.Hist.Éc.et Soc.*, 40, 1962, 449-83. Fortunes of French company which amalgamated East and West Indies interests.

9.260 **Boulle**, P. H., 'French mercantilism, commercial companies, and colonial profitability', in Blussé and Gaastra (9.225), 97-117. General survey of seventeenth- and eighteenth-century French colonial companies.

9.261 —— 'Patterns of French colonial trade and the Seven Years' War', *Hist.Sociale/Social Hist.*, 7, 1974, 48-86. Ports which had over-specialised in transatlantic trade (e.g Nantes and La Rochelle) found to be worst affected.

9.262 **Stein**, R., 'The state of French colonial commerce on the eve of the Revolution', *J.Eur.Ec.Hist.*, 12, 1983, 105-17. Useful summary of trends from 1750s to '80s.

9.263 **Stols**, E., 'The Southern Netherlands and the foundation of the Dutch East and West India Companies', *Acta Hist.Neerlandicae*, 9, 1976, 30-47. Investigates effects of Dutch colonial companies on economy and opportunities of Belgian provinces.

9.264 **Magalhaes-Godinho**, V., *L'Économie de l'Empire Portugais aux 15e et 16e Siècles*, Paris, 1969. Large-scale work concentrating on trade in precious metals and spices. Review article: G. Chaussinand-Nogaret, *Annales*, 25, 1970, 1591-6.

9.265 **Walker**, G. J., *Spanish Politics and Imperial Trade, 1700-89*, Bloomington, Ind., 1980. Explores Spanish reluctance to abandon its inefficient fleet system of colonial trade.

9.266 **Winius**, G. D., 'Two Lusitanian variations on a Dutch theme. Portuguese companies in times of crisis, 1628-62', in Blussé and Gaastra (9.225), 119-34. Deals with two very short-lived India and Brazil companies.

ATLANTIC AND TRANSATLANTIC TRADE: GENERAL
See also 4.62,97-137 passim; 9.73,360,362,369,371,386-400,627; 10.121.

9.267 **Chaunu**, Huguette, and Chaunu, P., 'The Atlantic economy and the world economy', in Earle (3.71), 113-26. Partly an outline of their work on Seville (see 9.311).

9.268 **Bosher**, J. F., *The Canada Merchants, 1713-63*, 1987. Mainly social study of merchants involved at both ends of trade – their family, religious, and mercantile links. See also his 'French Protestant families in Canadian trade', *Hist.Sociale/ Social Hist.*, 7, 1974, 179-201; and 9.271.

9.269 **Harsin**, P., 'La création de la Compagnie d'Occident (1717). Contribution à l'histoire du système de Law', *Rev.Hist.Éc.et Soc.*, 34, 1956, 7-42. Company to exploit Louisiana. Principally analysis of subscribers.

9.270 **McNeill**, J. R., *Atlantic Empires of France and Spain. Louisbourg and Havana, 1700-63*, Chapel Hill, N.C., 1985. Comparative study of colonies of Cape Breton and Cuba, with much detail on their commercial importance.

9.271 **Miquelon**, D., *Dugard of Rouen. French Trade to Canada and the West Indies, 1729-70*, Montreal, 1978. Account of mainly Huguenot *Compagnie du Canada*, involving partners from Rouen, Bordeaux, and La Rochelle.

9.272 **Pritchard**, J., 'The pattern of French colonial shipping to Canada before 1760', *Rev.Fr.Hist.Outre-Mer*, 63, 1976, 189-210.

9.273 **Tarrade**, J., *Le Commerce Colonial de la France à la Fin de l'Ancien Régime. L'Évolution du Régime de l' "Exclusif" de 1763 à 1789*, 2 vols., Paris, 1972. Very detailed account of trade and policy, centering on monopoly access to West Indies market.

9.274 **Emmer**, P. C., 'The West India Company, 1621-1791: Dutch or Atlantic?', in Blussé and Gaastra (9.225), 71-95. General account of Dutch company (or series of companies); significance of question in title not altogether clear.

9.275 **Hoboken**, W. J. van, 'The Dutch West India Company. The political background of its rise and decline', in *Britain and the Netherlands, 1* (7.311), 41-61.

9.276 **Sluiter**, E., 'Dutch-Spanish rivalry in the Caribbean area, 1594-1609', *Hisp.Am.Hist.Rev.*, 28, 1948, 165-96. Study of both commercial and strategic implications of Dutch penetration.

9.277 **Van de Voort**, J. P., 'Dutch capital in the West Indies during the eighteenth century', *Acta Hist.Neerlandicae*, 14, 1981, 85-103. On debacle of wave of plantation loans in period 1750-75.

9.278 **Andrews**, K. R., *The Spanish Caribbean. Trade and Plunder, 1530-1630*, New Haven, Conn., 1978. Account of Spanish colonies most vulnerable to illicit trade or privateering by Northern Europeans.

9.279 **García Fuentes**, L., *El Comercio Español con América, 1650-1700*, Seville, 1980. Confirms that export trade was largely controlled by non-Castilian concerns; much detail on particular commodities.

9.280 **Hanson**, C. A., 'The European "renovation" and the Luso-Atlantic economy, 1560-1715', *Review*, 6, 1983, 475-530. Examines decline and recovery of Portuguese economy via increasing dependence on supplying Northern Europe with colonial produce.

9.281 **Haring**, C. H., *Trade and Navigation between Spain and the Indies in the Time of the Hapsburgs*, Cambridge, Mass., 1918. Pioneering work on official organisation of trade monopoly.

9.282 **Lorenzo Sanz**, E., *Comercio de España con América en la Epoca de Felipe II*, 2 vols., Valladolid, 1980. Adds much detail on commodities to Chaunu's global view of traffic (9.311).

9.283 **Mauro**, F., *Le Portugal et l'Atlantique au 17e Siècle (1570-1670)*, Paris, 1960. As complement to 9.311 rounds off pioneer attempts to quantify Iberian traffic with New World. Review article: P. Chaunu, *Annales*, 16, 1961, 1176-1207.

9.284 **Papagno**, G., 'Monopolio e libertà di commercio nell'Africa Orientale Portoghese', *Riv.Stor.Ital.*, 86, 1974, 266-330. Eighteenth-century experiments in allowing free trade with Mozambique.

9.285 **Smith**, D. G., 'Old Christian merchants and the foundation of the Brazil Company, 1649', *Hisp.Am.Hist.Rev.*, 54, 1974, 233-59. Analysis of major investors and directors of Portuguese enterprise.

9.286 **Verlinden**, C., 'From the Mediterranean to the Atlantic. Aspects of an economic shift (twelfth to eighteenth century)', *J.Eur.Ec.Hist.*, 1, 1972, 625-46. Details Italian influences in Iberian commerce, which prepared this shift.

9.287 **Schmitt**, E., 'The Brandenburg overseas trading companies in the seventeenth century', in Blussé and Gaastra (9.225), 159-76. On the African and African-American Companies founded in 1682 and 1692 respectively.

9.288 **Feldbaek**, O., 'The organization and

structure of the Danish East India, West India, and Guinea companies in the seventeenth and eighteenth centuries', *ib.*, 135-58.

9.289 **Gøbel**, E., 'Danish trade to the West Indies and Guinea, 1671-1754', *Scan.Ec.Hist.Rev.*, 31, 1983, 21-49. Deals with period before Danish colonial possessions were taken over by Crown.

ATLANTIC PORTS

9.290 **Mollat**, M., *Le Commerce Maritime Normand à la Fin du Moyen Age*, Paris, 1952. Concentrates on revival of trade of Rouen and Dieppe after 1470.

9.291 **Touchard**, H., *Le Commerce Maritime Breton à la Fin du Moyen Age*, Paris, 1967. Last third covers later fifteenth century. Review article: J. Favier, *Rev.Hist.Éc.et Soc.*, 46, 1968, 266-72.

9.292 **Bernard**, J., *Navires et Gens de Mer à Bordeaux, vers 1400-vers 1550*, 3 vols., Paris, 1968. Deals in remarkable detail with seafaring merchants and fishermen in Bordeaux' pre-colonial era. Vol.3 tabulates port traffic. Review article: M. Bataillon, *Annales*, 24, 1969, 1162-70.

9.293 **Butel**, P., *Les Négociants Bordelais. L'Europe et les Iles au 18e Siècle*, Paris, 1974. Part 1 deals with trade links; part 2 with commercial structures; part 3 with merchants' social position.

9.294 **Cavignac**, J., *Jean Pellet, Commerçant de Gros, 1694-1772. Contribution à l'Étude du Négoce Bordelais au 18e Siècle*, Paris, 1967. Study of middle-ranking import-export merchant, but also practically a general account of Bordeaux commerce.

9.295 **Cullen**, L. M., 'The Irish merchant communities of Bordeaux, La Rochelle, and Cognac in the eighteenth century', in Cullen and P. Butel, eds., *Négoce et Industrie en France et en Irlande aux 18e et 19e Siècles*, Paris, 1980, 51-63.

9.296 **Huetz de Lemps**, C., *Géographie du Commerce de Bordeaux à la Fin du Règne de Louis XIV*, The Hague, 1976. Survey of Bordeaux' various networks, based on analysis of traffic registers. Review article: P. Butel, *Rev.Hist.Éc.et Soc.*, 54, 1976, 581-6.

9.297 **Plaisse**, A., 'Le commerce du port de Brest à la fin du 16e siècle', *Rev.Hist.Éc.et Soc.*, 42, 1964, 499-545. Material on imports and exports during civil war of

1590s.

9.298 **Clark**, J. G., *La Rochelle and the Atlantic Economy in the Eighteenth Century*, Baltimore, Md., 1981. Studies c.90 leading shipping dynasties in both social and commercial terms. See also 9.295

9.299 **Trocmé**, E., and Delafosse, M., *Le Commerce Rochelais de la Fin du 15e Siècle au Début du 17e*, Paris, 1952.

9.300 **Richard**, R., 'Comptes et profits de navires Terreneuviers du Havre au 17e siècle', *Rev.Hist.Éc.et Soc.*, 54, 1976, 476-524. On Le Havre see also 9.306.

9.301 **Boulle**, P. H., 'Slave trade, commercial organization, and industrial growth in eighteenth-century Nantes', *Rev. Fr. Hist. Outre-Mer*, 59, 1972, 70-112. Asks how far slavery profits went into other economic investment. See also 9.393.

9.302 **Collins**, J. B., 'The role of Atlantic France in the Baltic trade. Dutch traders and Polish grain at Nantes, 1625-75', *J.Eur.Ec.Hist.*, 13, 1984, 239-89. Shows how Nantes overtook La Rochelle as principal French partner in Dutch traffic between Baltic and Spain.

9.303 **Meyer**, J., *L'Armement Nantais dans la Deuxième Moitié du 18e Siècle*, Paris, 1969. Attempts principally to trace origins and profitability of investment.

9.304 **Tanguy**, J., *Le Commerce du Port de Nantes au Milieu du 16e Siècle*, Paris, 1956. Brief survey, piecing together rather fragmentary evidence. Review article: M. Perrichet, *Rev.Hist.Éc.et Soc.*, 37, 1959, 144-51.

9.305 **Benedict**, P., 'Rouen's foreign trade during the era of the Religious Wars (1560-1600)', *J.Eur.Ec.Hist.*, 13, 1984, 29-74. For data on preceding period see 9.290.

9.306 **Dardel**, P., *Commerce, Industrie, et Navigation à Rouen et au Havre au 18e Siècle*, Rouen, 1966. On growing rivalry of these ports. Statistical evidence presented in *Navires et Marchandises dans les Ports de Rouen et du Havre au 18e Siècle*, Paris, 1963.

9.307 **Delumeau**, J., *Le Mouvement du Port de Saint-Malo à la Fin du 17e Siècle (1681-1700)*, Paris, 1962. Tabulation rather than exposition, classifying port traffic according to where or whence bound.

9.308 **Carrière**, C., 'Renouveau espagnol et prêt à la grosse aventure. Notes sur la place de Cadix dans la seconde moitié du 18e siècle', *Rev.Hist.Mod.et Contemp.*, 17, 1970, 321-52. Argues that commerce continued to be dominated by old-fashioned venture capital methods chiefly raised by foreigners.

9.309 **García Baquero**, A., *Cadiz y el Atlántico (1717-78)*, 2 vols., Seville, 1976. Takes up history of Atlantic fleets after Cadiz replaced Seville as official port for America. Important older work on this transition is A. Girard, *La Rivalité Commerciale et Maritime entre Séville et Cadix jusqu'à la Fin du 18e Siècle*, Paris, 1932.

9.310 **Palacio Atard**, V., *El Comercio de Castilla y el Puerto de Santander en el Siglo 18*, Madrid, 1960. Deals with Santander's rise as wool port, and rivalry with Bilbao.

9.311 **Chaunu**, Huguette, and Chaunu, P., *Séville et l'Atlantique, 1504-1650*, 8 vols. in 11, Paris, 1955-60. Monumental work based on exhaustive analysis and tabulation of city shipping registers. The 3 parts of vol.8 form interpretative nucleus. Review articles: R. S. Smith, *J.Ec.Hist.*, 22, 1962, 253-9; C. H. Haring, *Hisp.Am.Hist.Rev.*, 40, 1960, 53-62; F. Braudel (1.2), 91-104; J. Vidalenc, *Rev.Hist.Éc.et Soc.*, 40, 1962, 110-30; H. Lapeyre, *Rev.Hist.*, 228, 1962, 327-38.

9.312 **Domínguez Ortiz**, A., *Orto y Ocaso de Sevilla*, Seville, 1946. 2nd ed., 1974. From New World opportunities to relative decline of seventeenth century.

9.313 **García Baquero**, A., *Andalucía y la Carrera de Indias (1492-1824)*, Seville, 1986. Account of rise and fall of Seville's Atlantic monopoly, based on chaps. written for Domínguez Ortiz' *Historia de Andalucía* (3.138).

9.314 **Morales Padrón**, F., 'The commercial world of Seville in early modern times', *J.Eur.Ec.Hist.*, 2, 1973, 294-319.

9.315 **Moret**, Michèle, 'Aspects de la société marchande de Séville au début du 17e siècle', *Rev.Hist.Éc.et Soc.*, 42, 1964, 170-219, 546-90. Separately publ., Paris, 1967. Rather institutional and technical, based on correspondence of royal officials.

9.316 **Pike**, Ruth, *Enterprise and Adventure. The Genoese in Seville and the Opening of the New World*, Ithaca, N.Y., 1966. See also preliminary article of similar title in *J.Ec.Hist.*, 22, 1962, 348-78.

9.317 **Link**, T., *Flensburg's Überseehandel von 1755-1807*, Neumünster, 1960. On transatlantic trade of notable port then in Danish hands.

9.318 **Pohl**, H., *Die Beziehungen Hamburgs zu Spanien und dem Spanischen Amerika in der Zeit von 1740 bis 1806*, Wiesbaden, 1963.

TRADE WITH THE ORIENT
See also 4.62,97-137 passim; 9.50,357-9,653,659,661; 11.1,48,75.

9.319 **Chaudhuri**, K. N., 'The economic and monetary problem of European trade with Asia during the seventeenth and eighteenth century', *J.Eur.Ec.Hist.*, 4, 1975, 323-58. Seeks to explain why European trade balance was so unfavourable. See also debate between author and R. C. Blitz, *ib.*, 7, 1978, 214-31; and 11.1.

9.320 **Dermigny**, L., *La Chine et l'Occident. Le Commerce à Canton au 18e Siècle, 1719-1833*, 4 vols., Paris, 1964. Huge work, rather out of proportion to importance of trade, but exhaustive on impact of Chinese produce in Europe, esp. France.

9.321 —— and Glamann, K., 'Le fonctionnement des Compagnies des Indes', in M. Mollat, ed., *Sociétés et Compagnies de Commerce en Orient et dans l'Océan Indien (8e Colloque Int.d'Hist.Maritime)*, Paris, 1970, 443-79. Dermigny tackles English and French companies, Glamann (in English) the Danish.

9.322 **Furber**, H., *Rival Empires of Trade in the Orient, 1600-1800*, Minneapolis, Ma., 1976. Good account of Anglo-Dutch-French commercial rivalry.

9.323 **Keswani**, D. G., 'Western commercial enterprises in the East. Some oriental archival sources' in Mollat (9.321), 543-73.

9.324 **Steensgaard**, N., *Carracks, Caravans, and Companies. The Structural Crisis in the European-Asian Trade in the Early Seventeenth Century*, Copenhagen, 1973. Also publ. as *The Asian Trade Revolution of the Seventeenth Century*, Chicago, 1974. Deals esp. with decline of Portuguese supremacy as symbolised by fall of Hormuz, their Persian Gulf fort.

9.325 **Gaastra**, F., 'The shifting balance of trade of the Dutch East India Company', in Blussé and Gaastra (9.225), 47-69. Concerns overall trends in profit rather than types of trade.

326 **Glamann**, K., *Dutch-Asiatic Trade, 1620-1740*, Copenhagen, 1958. Comprehensive treatment of activities of Dutch East India Company. Review article: C. R. Boxer, *P.& P.*, 15, 1959, 82-6.

327 —— 'The Dutch East India Company's trade in Japanese copper, 1645-1736', *Scan.Ec.Hist.Rev.*, 1, 1953, 41-79. Covers both European and Asiatic markets.

328 **Jörg**, C. J. A., *Porcelain and the Dutch China Trade*, The Hague, 1982. Transl. from Dutch ed. of 1978. Handsomely illustrated, but primarily economic rather than fine art history.

329 **Kato**, E., 'Unification and adaptation. The early Shogunate and Dutch trade policies', in Blussé and Gaastra (9.225), 207-29. On establishment of the V.O.C. in Japan.

330 **Wills**, J. E., *Pepper, Guns, and Parleys. The Dutch East India Company and China, 1622-81*, Cambridge, Mass., 1974.

331 **Boxer**, C. R., *From Lisbon to Goa, 1500-1750. Studies in Portuguese Maritime Enterprise*, 1984. Miscellany of previously publ. articles, some very specialised. Similar is his *Portuguese Conquest and commerce in Southern Asia, 1500-1750*, 1985.

332 **Disney**, A. R., 'The first Portuguese India Company, 1628-33', *Ec.Hist.Rev.*, 2nd ser., 30, 1977, 242-58.

333 —— *Twilight of the Pepper Empire. Portuguese Trade in Southwest India in the Early Seventeenth Century*, Cambridge, Mass., 1978. Deals with both intra-Asian trade and procurement of pepper for Europe, including performance of Portuguese India Company.

9.334 **Souza**, G. B., *The Survival of Empire. Portuguese Trade and Society in China and the South China Sea, 1630-1754*, 1986. Mainly concerns inter-Asiatic commerce.

9.335 **Glamann**, K., 'The Danish Asiatic Company, 1732-72', *Scan.Ec.Hist.Rev.*, 8, 1960, 109-49. Useful all-round survey of structure and traffic. See also Feldbaek (9.288).

9.336 **Koninckx**, C., *The First and Second Charters of the Swedish East India Company (1731-66)*, Kortrijk, 1980. Detailed company history which also looks widely at Europe's oriental trade and investigates how much Swedish capital was involved. See also his essay on maritime routes of company, *Scan.Ec.Hist.Rev.*, 26, 1978, 36-65.

9.337 **Foust**, C. M., *Muscovite and Mandarin. Russia's Trade with China and its Setting, 1727-1805*, Chapel Hill, N.C., 1969. Very detailed but rather narrow in focus. See also his 'Russia's Peking caravan, 1689-1762', *S.Atlantic Q.*, 67, 1968, 108-24.

9.338 **Khachikian**, L., 'Le registre d'un marchand arménien en Perse, en Inde, et au Tibet (1682-93)', *Annales*, 22, 1967, 231-78.

9.339 **Nadel-Golobič**, Eleonora, 'Armenians and Jews in medieval Lvov. Their role in oriental trade, 1400-1600', *Cah.Monde Russe et Sov.*, 20, 1979, 345-88.

COMMODITIES TRADED

AGRICULTURAL PRODUCE: GENERAL WORKS

See also sub-sections on cereals and other crops, 7.271-330; and those on prices and subsistence, 11.1-170. For livestock-trade see 7.340-51.

340 **Kiss**, I. N., 'Der Agrarcharakter des ungarischen Exports vom 15. bis 18. Jahrhundert', *Jb.Wirtschaftsgesch.*, 1978 (i), 147-69.

341 **Panova**, Sneška, 'Die Beziehungen zwischen Stadt und Land und die Entwicklung des Handels in Südosteuropa im 16./17. Jahrhundert', *Jb.Gesch.Feudalismus*, 3, 1979, 281-309. On Balkan trade in agricultural produce.

GRAIN TRADE

9.342 **Frêche**, G., 'Études statistiques sur le commerce céréalier de la France méridionale au 18e siècle', *Rev.Hist.Éc.et Soc.*, 49, 1971, 5-43, 180-224. Concludes that cereal production, aided by improvements to infra-structure, greatly stimulated southern economy (arguing against P. Wolff's *Histoire de*

Toulouse, Toulouse, 1958).

9.343 **Le Goff**, T. J. A., 'An eighteenth-century grain merchant, Ignace Advisse Desruisseaux', in Bosher (6.104), 92-122. Grain exporter in Vannes, flourished in 1760s.

9.344 **Romano**, R., *Commerce et Prix du Blé à Marseille au 18e Siècle*, Paris, 1956. About equally devoted to description of trade structure and to price analysis.

9.345 **Usher**, A. P., *The History of the Grain Trade in France, 1400-1710*, 1913. Remains only synoptic view.

9.346 **Klein**, P. W., *Quantitative Aspects of the Amsterdam Rye-Trade during the Seventeenth Century*, Rotterdam, 1977. Short monograph publ. by Centrum voor Maatschappijgeschiedenis.

9.347 **Aymard**, M., *Venise, Raguse, et le Commerce du Blé pendant la Seconde Moitié du 16e Siècle*, Paris, 1966. Deals with period of significant shift of supply from Turkish Empire to Northern Europe.

9.348 **Davies**, T., 'Changes in the structure of the wheat trade in seventeenth-century Sicily and the building of new villages', *J.Eur.Ec.Hist.*, 12, 1983, 371-405. Switch from export to internal markets.

9.349 **Doroshenko**, V., and others, *Trade and Agrarian Development in the Baltic Provinces, Fifteenth-Nineteenth Centuries*, Tallinn, 1974. Brief pamphlet on grain trade.

9.350 **Faber**, J. A., 'Decline of the Baltic grain-trade in the second half of the seventeenth century', *Acta Hist.Neerlandica*, 1, 1966, 108-31. Argues that relatively slight fluctuations of demand in Southern Europe could have serious repercussions on Baltic suppliers.

9.351 **Maczak**, A., 'Export of grain and the problem of distribution of national income in Poland, 1550-1650', *Acta Poloniae Hist.*, 18, 1968, 75-98. Examines regional differences in grain trade, and trend towards larger estates.

9.352 **Soom**, A., *Der Baltische Getreidehandel im 17. Jahrhundert*, Stockholm, 1961. Principally from Swedish souces and viewpoint.

OTHER CROPS AND COMESTIBLES
On wine production see 7.331-9; on spice trade see also 9.233,333.

9.353 **Bizière**, J. M., 'The Baltic wine trade, 1563-1657', *Ec.Hist.Rev.*, 2nd ser., 20, 1972, 121-32. Concludes it was small beer...

9.354 **Craeybeckx**, J, *Un Grand Commerce d'Importation. Les Vins de France aux Anciens Pays Bas, 13-16 Siècles*, Paris, 1958.

9.355 **Ciriacono**, S., *Olio ed Ebrei nella Repubblica Veneta del Settecento*, Venice, 1975. Study of olive oil production and trade, and controversial part played in it by Jewish merchants.

9.356 **Mattozzi**, I., 'Crisi, stagnazione, e mutamento nello stato veneziano sei-settecentesco. Il caso del commercio e della produzione olearia', *Studi Veneziani*, n.s., 4, 1981, 199-276.

9.357 **Musgrave**, P., 'The economics of uncertainty. The structural revolution in the spice trade, 1480-1640', in Cottrell and Aldcroft (9.243), 9-21. Suggests that it was not so much because of maritime supremacy that English and Dutch companies took over trade as because of their success in reducing risks of investment.

9.358 **Wake**, C. H. H., 'The changing pattern of Europe's pepper and spice imports, c.1400-1700', *J.Eur.Ec.Hist.*, 8, 1979, 361-403.

9.359 —— 'The volume of European spice imports at the beginning and end of the fifteenth century', *ib.*, 15, 1986, 621-35. Responds to some criticisms by E. Ashtor of previous article, *ib.*, 9, 1980, 753-63.

9.360 **Stein**, R., 'The French sugar business in the eighteenth century. A quantitative study', *Bus.Hist.*, 22, 1980, 3-17. Attempts to quantify volume of production, imports, consumption, and price movements.

9.361 **Kirchner**, W., 'Ukrainian tobacco for France', *Jb.Gesch.Osteur.*, 10, 1962, 497-512. Abortive trade which briefly seemed promising in mid-eighteenth century.

9.362 **Price**, J. M., *France and the Chesapeake. A History of the French Tobacco Monopoly, 1674-1791, and of its Relationship to the British and American Tobacco Trades*, 2 vols., Ann Arbor, Mich., 1973. Large-scale work concentrating on entrepreneurs involved (i.e. not primarily colonial history).

9.363 **Cvetkova**, Bistra, 'Les *celep* et leur rôle dans la vie économique des Balkans à l'époque Ottomane (15e-18e siècles)', in

Cook (5.207), 172-92. Class charged with provision of sheepmeat to authorities for military and other victualling needs.

SALT
See also 10.388; 11.165.

364 **Delafosse**, M., and Laveau, C., *Le Commerce du Sel de Brouage aux 17e et 18e Siècles*, Paris, 1960.

365 **Dubois**, A., *Die Salzversorgung des Wallis, 1500-1610*, Winterthur, 1965. Lengthy and detailed study of importance of salt in economy of Valais.

366 **Hocquet**, J.-C., *Le Sel et la Fortune de Venise*, 2 vols., Lille, 1978-79. Deals notably with switch from local production to imports in later Middle Ages and reversion in seventeenth century.

367 **Schremmer**, E., 'Saltmining and the salt-trade…a case study in public enterprise and development in Austria and the South German states', *J.Eur.Ec.Hist.*, 8, 1979, 291-312. Working of state monopolies in sixteenth and seventeenth centuries.

368 **Keckova**, Antonina, 'Polish salt-mines as a state enterprise, thirteenth to eighteenth centuries', *ib.*, 10, 1981, 619-31. On salt-mines of Cracow and Ruthenia, important source of Crown revenue.

FISHERIES
See also 3.145; 9.300,469,649.

369 **Bosher**, J. F., 'A fishing company of Louisbourg, Les Sables d'Olonne, and Paris. La société du Baron d'Huart, 1750-75', *Fr.Hist.Stud.*, 9, 1975, 263-77.

370 **Gunnarsson**, G., *Monopoly Trade and Economic Stagnation. Studies in the Foreign Trade of Iceland, 1602-1787*, Lund, 1983. Principally a study of fisheries.

371 **La Morandière**, C. de, *Histoire de la Pêche Française de la Morue dans l'Amérique Septentrionale (des Origines à 1789)*, 2 vols., Paris, 1962-63. Mine of information.

372 **Michell**, A. R., 'The European fisheries in early modern history', in *Cambridge Economic History of Europe*, 5 (2.15), 134-84.

373 **Unger**, R. W., 'Dutch herring, technology, and international trade in the seventeenth century', *J.Ec.Hist.*, 40, 1980, 253-79. Suggests that Dutch limited exports to keep prices high, strategy that

failed when technological superiority was lost.

9.374 **Utterström**, G., 'Migratory labour and the herring fisheries of Western Sweden in the eighteenth century', *Scan. Ec. Hist. Rev.*, 7, 1959, 3-40. Describes important seasonal source of employment (particularly gutting and salting) till failure of shoals around 1800.

TIMBER
See also 9.134; 11.44.

9.375 **Åström**, S. E., 'North European timber exports to Great Britain, 1760-1810', in Cottrell and Aldcroft (9.243), 81-97. See also 9.378; and Åstrom's earlier article on English timber imports in *Scan. Ec. Hist. Rev.*, 18, 1970, 12-32.

9.376 —— 'Technology and timber exports from the Gulf of Finland, 1661-1740', *Scan.Ec.Hist.Rev.*, 23, 1975, 1-14. On development of sawmill technology in area of relatively free forest exploitation.

9.377 **Bamford**, P. W., *Forests and French Sea Power, 1660-1789*, 1956. Much material on timber trade and shortages of eighteenth century.

9.378 **Kent**, H. S. K., 'The Anglo-Norwegian timber trade in the eighteenth century', *Ec.Hist.Rev.*, 2nd ser., 8, 1955, 62-74. Primarily, but not exclusively, seen from British side.

9.379 **Kjaerheim**, S., 'Norwegian timber exports in the eighteenth century. A comparison of port books and private accounts', *Scan.Ec.Hist.Rev.*, 5, 1957, 188-201. Uses invoice books of a London importer (1772-85) as control of reliability of Norwegian customs declarations.

WOOL AND TEXTILE RAW MATERIALS
See also 9.66

9.380 **Israel**, J. I., 'Spanish wool exports and the European economy, 1610-40', *Ec.Hist.Rev.*, 2nd ser., 33, 1980, 193-211.

9.381 **Phillips**, Carla R., 'Spanish merchants and the wool trade in the sixteenth century', *Sixteenth-Cent.J.*, 14, 1983, 259-82.

9.382 —— 'The Spanish wool trade, 1500-1780', *J.Ec.Hist.*, 42, 1982, 775-95.

9.383 —— and Phillips, W. D., 'Spanish wool and Dutch rebels. The Middelburg incident of 1574', *Am.Hist.Rev.*, 82, 1977,

812-30. Provides evidence on Spanish wool exports and marine insurance system.

9.384 **Fisher**, R. H., *The Russian Fur Trade, 1550-1700* Berkeley, Calif., 1943. Workmanlike collation of scattered evidence.

9.385 **Rich**, E. E., 'Russia and the colonial fur trade', *Ec.Hist.Rev.*, 2nd ser., 7, 1955, 307-28. On usefulness of Russia to French and English colonial companies as market for surplus furs (later seventeenth century).

9.386 **Lee**, R. L., 'American cochineal in European commerce, 1526-1625', *J.Mod.Hist.*, 23, 1951, 205-24.

SLAVE TRADE
See also 6.263-73; 9.301.

9.387 **Hogg**, P. C., *The African Slave Trade and its Suppression. A Classified and Annotated Bibliography…*, 1973. Includes both source material and secondary works. French, Spanish, and other European participation well covered.

9.388 **Anstey**, R., 'The slave trade of the continental powers, 1760-1810', *Ec.Hist.Rev.*, 2nd ser., 30, 1977, 259-68. Brief look at volume of trade of significant carriers (France, Portugal, Netherlands, and Denmark).

9.389 **Curtin**, P. D., *The Atlantic Slave Trade. A Census*, Madison, Wis., 1969. Brave attempt to compute number of slaves shipped to different destinations in New World.

9.390 **Rawley**, J. A., *The Transatlantic Slave Trade. A History*, New York, 1981. Useful résumé, treating in turn each of major European participants.

9.391 **Reynolds**, E., *Stand the Storm. A History of the Atlantic Slave Trade*, 1985. Brief introductory study, with useful notes and bibliography.

9.392 **Stein**, R. L., *The French Slave Trade in the*

Eighteenth Century, Madison, Wis., 1979. Likely to become standard work. Based on considerable research in provincial archives.

9.393 —— 'The profitability of the Nantes slave trade, 1783-92', *J.Ec.Hist.*, 35, 1975, 779-93. Finds that net profits weren't spectacular but competitive with other investment possibilities.

9.394 **Viles**, P., 'The slaving interest in the Atlantic ports, 1763-92', *Fr.Hist.Stud.*, 7, 1972, 529-43. Rather scrappy essay on slavers of Nantes, Bordeaux, and La Rochelle, emphasising Protestant dominance of trade.

9.395 **Emmer**, P. C., 'The history of the Dutch slave trade: a bibliographical survey', *J.Ec.Hist.*, 32, 1972, 728-47.

9.396 —— and Van Den Boogart, E., 'The Dutch participation in the Atlantic slave trade, 1596-1650', in H. A. Gemery and J. S. Hogendorn, eds., *The Uncommon Market. Essays in the Economic History of the Atlantic Slave Trade*, New York, 1979, 353-75.

9.397 **Klein**, H. S., 'The Portuguese slave trade from Angola in the eighteenth century', *J.Ec.Hist.*, 32, 1972, 894-918.

9.398 **Miller**, J. C., 'Capitalism and slavery. The financial and commercial organization of the Angolan slave trade, according to the accounts of A. Coelho Guerreiro (1684-92)', *Int.J.African Hist.Stud.*, 17, 1984, 1-56. Enterprises of a colonial secretary exploiting Angola-Brazil-Lisbon trade network.

9.399 **Vogt**, J. L., 'The Lisbon Slave House and African trade, 1486-1521', *Proc. Am. Phil. Soc.*, 117, 1973, 1-16. On machinery of early slave trade, still mainly for internal employment.

9.400 **Green-Pedersen**, S. E., 'The scope and structure of the Danish negro slave trade', *Scan.Ec.Hist.Rev.*, 19, 1971, 149-97.

BANKING AND INSURANCE
See also sub-section on public finance, 10.160-263; and 2.23. On Italian banking and credit see also 3.195; 7.128, 9.81-2,92,99; 11.70. Other nationalities: 5.639 (Poland); 7.234 (Finland); 9.22 (France).

9.401 **Bergier**, J.-F., 'From the fifteenth century in Italy to the sixteenth century in Germany. A new banking concept?', in *The Dawn of Modern Banking*, New Haven,

Conn., 1979, 105-30. Part of symposium publ. by Center for Medieval and Renaissance Studies (UCLA). Other papers in this collection deal primarily with conditions before 1450.

9.402 **Boiteux**, L. A., *La Fortune de Mer. Le Besoin de Sécurité et les Débuts de l'Assurance Maritime*, Paris, 1968. Evolution of maritime insurance from Middle Ages to seventeenth century.

9.403 **De Roover**, R., *L'Évolution de la Lettre de Change*, Paris, 1953. Standard work outlining development of bills of exchange from c.1200 to beginning of eighteenth century.

9.404 —— 'New interpretations of the history of banking', *J.World Hist.*, 2, 1954, 38-76. Repr. in his *Business, Banking, and Economic Thought in Late Medieval and Early Modern Europe*, Chicago, 1974, 200-38. Survey of research on period 1300-1800.

9.405 **Dillen**, J. G. van, ed., *History of the Principal Public Banks*, The Hague, 1934. Remains very useful collection of essays, concentrating on pre-nineteenth century origins, by such outstanding historians as E. Heckscher, G. Luzzato, and P. Harsin. Substantial, though of course dated, bibliography.

9.406 **Kindleberger**, C. P., *A Financial History of Western Europe*, 1984. First half of book deals in turn with currency, banking, and finance up to 1914. Remainder devoted to twentieth century.

9.407 **Marx**, Anna V., ed., *Credito, Banche, e Investimenti, Secoli 13-20*, Florence, 1985. Late publication of 1972 conference papers, with contributions from several experts on early modern finance (R. Gascon, P. Jeannin, M. Morineau, U. Tucci, etc.).

9.408 **Parker**, G., 'The emergence of modern finance in Europe, 1500-1730', in *Fontana Economic History of Europe*, 2 (2.24), 527-94. Deals briefly with both mercantile credit and public finance.

9.409 **Van der Wee**, H., 'Monetary, credit, and banking systems', in *Cambridge Economic History of Europe*, 5 (2.15), 290-392. Covers sixteenth to eighteenth centuries, though later part of period is less thoroughly covered.

9.410 **Bayard**, Françoise, 'Les Bonvisi, marchands banquiers à Lyon, 1575-1629', *Annales*, 26, 1971, 1234-69. Business linked to family commercial empire extending over Italy, Spain, and Netherlands, which seems to have come to grief in 1629. For more general studies on

Lyon banking at this period see 9.27, and older works of M. Vigne, *La Banque à Lyon du 15e au 18e Siècle*, Paris, 1903; and M. Brésard, *Les Foires de Lyon au 15e et 16e Siècle*, Paris, 1914.

9.411 **Clark**, J. G., 'Marine insurance in eighteenth-century La Rochelle', *Fr. Hist. Stud.*, 10, 1978, 572-98.

9.412 **Kindleberger**, C. P., 'Financial institutions and economic development. A comparison of Great Britain and France in the eighteenth and nineteenth centuries', *Explor.Ec.Hist.*, 21, 1984, 103-24. Justifies traditional view of British superiority by reference to greater sophistication of their financial services.

9.413 **Luthy**, H., *La Banque Protestante en France de la Révocation de l'Édit de Nantes à la Révolution*, 2 vols., Paris, 1959-61. Explores reasons for Protestant predominance in development of French banking, esp. links with Geneva. Review article: J. Bouvier, *Annales*, 18, 1963, 779-93, transl. in Hatton (3.16), 263-80.

9.414 **Spooner**, F. C., *Risks at Sea. Amsterdam Insurance and Maritime Europe, 1776-80*, 1983. Painstaking and often technical study of insurance in period of maritime hostilities leading up to Armed Neutrality.

9.415 **Basas Fernández**, M., 'Burgos, plaza de cambios en el siglo 16', *Hispania*, 110, 1968, 564-93.

9.416 —— *El Seguro Maritimo en Burgos (Siglo 16)*, Bilbao, 1963. Uses archives of Consulate and of Ruiz firm.

9.417 **Boyajian**, J. C., *Portuguese Bankers at the Court of Spain, 1626-50*, New Brunswick, N.J., 1983. Important study in financing of Spain's part in Thirty Years' War, and decline of Genoese predominance in her finances.

9.418 **Hamilton**, E. J., 'Spanish banking schemes before 1700', *J.Pol.Ec.*, 57, 1949, 134-56. See also sequel, 'Plans for a national bank in Spain', *ib.*, 315-36; and his earlier studies on foundation of Bank of Spain (1782) and its first twenty years of operation, *ib.*, 53, 1945, 97-114; 54, 1946, 17-37, 116-40.

9.419 **Phillips**, Carla R., and Phillips, W. D., 'The Castilian fairs in Burgos, 1601-04', *J.Eur.Ec.Hist.*, 6, 1977, 413-29. Unsuccessful attempt to revive importance of Castilian fairs by move from Medina del Campo to Burgos.

9.420 **Zylberberg**, M., 'Un centre financier

"périphérique". Madrid dans la seconde moitié du 18e siècle', *Rev.Hist.*, 269, 1983, 265-309. Examines paradox that despite lack of flourishing commerce and industry "solo Madrid es banca" in Spain of this period.

9.421 **Bullard**, Melissa M., ' "Mercatores Florentini Romanam Curiam sequentes" in the early sixteenth century', *J.Med.& Renaiss.Stud.*, 6, 1976, 51-71. Contends that many Florentine bankers were already doing good business in Rome before accession of Medici Popes.

9.422 **Cova**, A., *Il Banco di S. Ambrogio nell'Economia Milanese dei Secoli 17 e 18*, Milan, 1972. Study of municipal bank set up to finance Milan's administration.

9.423 **De Maddalena**, A., 'Affaires et gens d'affaires lombards sur les foires de Bisenzone. L'exemple des Lucini (1579-1619)', *Annales*, 22, 1967, 939-90. Exchange operations of Milanese financiers at Piacenza fairs.

9.424 **De Roover**, R., *The Rise and Decline of the Medici Bank, 1397-1494*, Cambridge, Mass., 1963. Review article: Y. Renouard, *Annales*, 20, 1965, 160-8. Shorter preliminary work appeared in *J.Ec.Hist.*, 6, 1946, 24-52, 153-72; 7, 1947, 69-82; and separately, New York, 1948.

9.425 **De Rosa**, L., 'The price revolution, wars, and public banks in Naples', in *Mélanges...Braudel (9.85)*, 1, 159-75. Traces origins of government supported banks in seventeenth century. Cf. similar theme of D. Demarco (in French), *Proc.Third International Conference of Economic History (5.123)*, 4, 187-222, 241-54.

9.426 **Di Vittorio**, A., 'Financial history in Italy in the writings of the last 25 years', *J.Eur.Ec.Hist.*, 1, 1972, 181-92. Includes, but not limited to, work on early modern period.

9.427 **Gilbert**, F., *The Pope, his Banker, and Venice*, Cambridge, Mass., 1980. Complex story of Roman banker's dealings with Venice during War of League of Cambrai (1509-20).

9.428 **Gioffrè**, D., *Gênes et les Foires de Changes. De Lyon à Besançon*, Paris, 1960. How Italian wars of early sixteenth century affected Geneoese merchant financiers and their commercial relations.

9.429 **Goldthwaite**, R. A., 'Local banking in Renaissance Florence', *J.Eur.Ec.Hist.*, 14, 1985, 5-55. Chronicles local as opposed to international operations of Florentine banking by example of Cerchi firm (1472-85).

9.430 **Mandich**, G., *Le Pacte de Ricorsa et le Marché Italien des Changes au 17e Siècle*, Paris, 1953. Rather technical study of device (*ricorsa*) used for evading prohibitions on usury.

9.431 **Mueller**, R., 'The role of bank money in Venice, 1300-1500', *Studi Veneziani*, n.s., 3, 1979, 47-96. General study of clearing procedures via bank deposits.

9.432 **Poliakov**, L., *Jewish Bankers and the Holy See from the Thirteenth to the Seventeenth Centuries*, 1977. Abridged transl. of French ed. of 1965. Rather over-emphasises official Church pronouncements in bulls, sermons, etc.

9.433 **Silva**, J. G. da, *Banque et Crédit en Italie au 17e Siècle*, 2 vols., Paris, 1969. Though intended primarily as study of North Italian fairs known as Bisenzone (from their origins at Besançon), devotes almost half work to general history of European fairs and exchanges from their origins.

9.434 **Tenenti**, Branislava, 'I tassi assicurativi sulla piazza di Venezia, secc. 16-17', *Studi Veneziani*, n.s., 10, 1985, 15-55. See also 3.195.

9.435 **Baum**, H.-P., 'Annuities in late medieval Hanse towns', *Bus.Hist.Rev.*, 59, 1985, 24-48. Details Hamburg research project into this form of mortgage market (covers thirteenth to sixteenth centuries).

9.436 **Dorwart**, R. A., 'The earliest fire insurance company in Berlin and Brandenburg, 1705-11', *ib.*, 32, 1958, 192-203. Attempt at state-run compulsory insurance.

9.437 **Jennings**, R. C., 'Loans and credit in early seventeenth-century Ottoman judicial records. The *sharia* court of Anatolian Kayseri', *J.Ec.& Soc.Hist.Orient*, 16, 1973, 168-216. Judicial records showing well-developed credit system affecting both Muslims and Christians.

9.438 **Samuelsson**, K., 'International payments and credit movements by the Swedish merchant-houses, 1730-1815', *Scan.Ec.Hist.Rev.*, 3, 1955, 163-202.

INDUSTRY. GENERAL WORKS.
THE PROTO-INDUSTRIALISATION DEBATE
See also 4.92; 5.14.

9.439 **Berg**, Maxine, and others, eds., *Manufacture in Town and Country Before the Factory*, Cambridge, 1984. Contains introductory general essays by Berg, PAT Hudson, and M. Sonenscher; and area studies noted below.

9.440 **Clarkson**, L. A., *Proto-Industrialization. The First Phase of Industrialization?*, 1985. Pamphlet length. Takes fairly sceptical view of concept.

9.441 **Coleman**, D. C., 'Proto-industrialization. A concept too many?', *Ec.Hist.Rev.*, 2nd ser., 36, 1983, 435-48. Argues, mainly from English examples, that chronology and explanatory power of this model is very weak.

9.442 **Deyon**, P., and others, 'Les formes protoindustrielles', *Annales*, 39, 1984, 868-1008. Reproduces some papers given at Eighth International Congress of Economic History (Budapest, 1982). Most useful are contributions by C. Vandenbroeke and F. Mendels on Flanders, and Mendels' general summing-up.

9.443 **Freudenberger**, H., and Redlich, F., 'Industrial development of Europe. Reality, symbols, images', *Kyklos*, 17, 1964, 372-403. Principally concerned with what authors call "protofactory" in eighteenth century, when organisation of capital-intensive and -extensive enterprises moved closer together.

9.444 **Henderson**, W. O., 'The genesis of the industrial revolution in France and Germany in the eighteenth century', *ib.*, 9, 1956, 190-206. Emphasises role of state.

9.445 **Houston**, R., and Snell, K. D. M., 'Historiographical review. Proto-industrialization? Cottage industry, social change, and industrial revolution', *Hist.J.*, 27, 1984, 473-92. Argues that "less schematic and limiting approach" to transition from agrarian to industrial society is needed.

9.446 **Jones**, E. L., 'Environment, agriculture, and industrialization in Europe', *Agric.Hist.*, 51, 1977, 491-502. Supports thesis that cottage industry flourished in regions where environment was unfavourable to market farming; situation later complicated by availability of energy sources. See also earlier exposition 'The agricultural origins of industry', *P.& P.*, 40, 1968, 58-71.

9.447 **Kellenbenz**, H., 'The organization of industrial production', in *Cambridge Economic History of Europe*, 5 (2.15), 462-548. Comprehensive survey of such topics as technology, investment, state involvement, labour force, etc.

9.448 —— 'Rural industries in the West from the end of the Middle Ages to the eighteenth century', in Earle (3.71), 45-88. Transl. from *Annales*, 18, 1963, 833-82. Also appears in German version in *Proc. Second International Conference of Economic History*, Paris, 1965, 2, 377-428. Describes evolution in various European states and regions, and posits some general geographical and social factors involved in location.

9.449 **Kriedte**, P., and others, *Industrialization before Industrialization. Rural Industry in the Genesis of Capitalism*, 1981. Transl. from German ed. of 1977. Most fully worked out model of proto-industrial thesis, and notable for espousal of "demographic greenhouse" effect – i.e. that cottage industry encouraged large families for maximisation of earnings. Review articles: P. Jeannin, *Annales*, 35, 1980, 52-65; C. Poni, *Review*, 9, 1985, 305-14.

9.450 —— 'Der Proto-Industrialisierung auf dem Prüfstand der historischen Zunft. Antwort auf einige Kritiker', *Gesch.und Gesellschaft*, 9, 1983, 87-105. Summary of, and reply to, controversy stimulated by previous entry.

9.451 **Medick**, H., 'The proto-industrial family economy. Structural function of household and family during the transition from peasant society to industrial capitalism', *Soc.Hist.*, [1], no.3, 1976, 291-315. Repr. in Pat Thane and A. Sutcliffe, eds., *Essays in Social History*, 2, 1986, 23-52. Adapted from his contribution to 9.449.

9.452 **Mendels**, F. F., 'Proto-industrialization', *J.Ec.Hist.*, 32, 1972, 241-61. Early formulation of concept.

9.453 **Millward**, R., 'The early stages of European industrialization. Economic organization under serfdom', *Explor.Ec.Hist.*, 21, 1984, 406-28. Seeks to establish circumstances where contract labour might be more profitable than forced labour in East European serf economies.

9.454 **Mokyr**, J., 'Growing-up and the Industrial Revolution in Europe', *ib.*, 13, 1976, 371-96. Develops mathematical model of early industrialisation which emphasises importance of areas of surplus labour and low wages for capital formation.

9.455 **Nef**, J. U., *The Conquest of the Material World*, Chicago, 1964. Reprints articles on industry and technology of period 1500-1650, mostly written in 1930s and '40s.

9.456 **Sella**, D., 'European industries, 1500-1700', in *Fontana Economic History of Europe*, 2 (2.24), 354-426. Separately publ., 1970.

FRANCE AND THE LOW COUNTRIES
On France see also 3.16; 9.444; 10.111,492. On Netherlands, 5.363-4; 9.442,474.

9.457 **Crafts**, N. F. R., 'Industrial revolution in England and France. Some thoughts on the question, "Why was England first?" ', *Ec.Hist.Rev.*, 2nd ser., 30, 1977, 429-41. Uses probability theory to posit that England's primacy followed from "lucky" technological breakthrough rather than endogenous strengths.

9.458 **Deyon**, P., and Guignet, P., 'The royal manufactures and economic and technological progress in France before the Industrial Revolution', *J.Eur.Ec.Hist.*, 9, 1980, 611-32. Discusses whether regulatory approach of Sully and Colbert can be said to have yielded to laissez-faire philosophy after 1750.

9.459 **Guignet**, P., *Mines, Manufactures, et Ouvriers du Valenciennois au 18e Siècle*, 2 vols., New York, 1977. Large-scale dissertation, publ. unrevised. Distinguishes four differing kinds of artisans – guild workers and female lace-makers in Valenciennes itself (see also 9.552), miners and weavers in surrounding countryside.

9.460 **Gullickson**, Gay L., *The Spinners and Weavers of Auffay. Rural Industry and the Sexual Division of Labour in a French Village, 1750-1850*, 1986. Important as integrated study of community economy, proto-industrialisation, and demographic behaviour. Interesting to compare with Kriedte's work on Krefeld (9.588). See also following associated articles.

9.461 —— 'Agriculture and cottage industry. Redefining the causes of proto-industrialization', *J.Ec.Hist.*, 43, 1983, 831-50. On cotton manufacture in Pays de Caux (Normandy) – example of industry arising in commercial agriculture district because of seasonal unemployment and landlessness.

9.462 —— 'Proto-industrialization, demographic behaviour, and the sexual division of labour in Auffay, France, 1750-1850', *Peasant Stud.*, 9, 1982, 106-18. Contradicts hypothesis of lower marriage age in areas of rural industry.

9.463 —— 'Sexual division of labour in cottage industry and agriculture in the Pays de Caux. Auffay, 1750-1850', *Fr.Hist.Stud.*, 12, 1981, 177-99.

9.464 **Léon**, P., *La Naissance de la Grande Industrie en Dauphiné (Fin du 17e Siècle-1869)*, 2 vols., Paris, 1954. Conceived on heroic scale. Though main emphasis is on early nineteenth century, contains abundant detail on earlier conditions.

9.465 **Thomson**, J. K. J., 'Variations in industrial structure in pre-industrial Languedoc', in Berg and others (9.439), 61-91. Covers period 1600-1800.

9.466 **Zeller**, G., 'Industry in France before Colbert', in Cameron and others (3.251), 128-39. Transl. from *Rev.Hist.Éc.et Soc.*, 28, 1950, 1-20.

9.467 **Hasquin**, H., *Une Mutation. Le Pays de Charleroi aux 17e et 18e Siècles. Aux Origines de la Révolution Industrielle en Belgique*, Brussels, 1971. Shows growth of coal, iron, and other industry, in rural area free from guild restrictions.

9.468 **Mendels**, F. F., 'Agriculture and peasant industry in eighteenth-century Flanders', in Parker and Jones (7.88), 179-204. See also 9.442 and 474.

SPAIN AND ITALY
On Spain see also 3.130.

9.469 **Alonso Alvarez**, L., *Industrialización y Conflictos Sociales en la Galicia del Antiguo*

Régimen, 1750-1830, Madrid, 1976. Mainly concerns establishment of fish salting and preserving concerns.

9.470 **González Enciso**, A., 'La protoindustrialización en España', *Rev.Hist.Ec.*, 2, 1984, 11-44. Argues that only Galicia and Catalonia experienced something close to model of Mendels and Deyon.

9.471 **Malanima**, P., *La Decadenza di un'Economia Cittadina. L'Industria di Firenze nei Secoli 16-18*, Bologna, 1982. Does not, despite title, point to unrelieved decline. Review article: O. Raggio, *Quad.Stor.*, 52, 1983, 287-99.

9.472 **Poni**, C., ed., 'Protoindustria', *Quad.Stor.*, 52, 1983, 5-179; followed by 'Forme protoindustriali', *ib.*, 59, 1985, 341-528. Symposia with variety of relevant case-studies.

9.473 **Sella**, D., 'Industrial production in seventeenth-century Italy. A reappraisal', *Explor.Entrepren.Hist.*, 2nd ser., 6, 1969, 235-53. Presents material to temper impression of wholesale decline.

GERMANY, SWITZERLAND, AUSTRIA
See also 5.172; 9.444.

9.474 **Barkhausen**, M., 'Government control and free enterprise in Western Germany and the Low Countries in the eighteenth century', in Earle (3.71), 212-73. Transl. from *VSWG*, 45, 1958, 168-241. Describes political, social, and geographical factors which encouraged growth of entrepreneurial rural industry in Rhineland and Southern Belgium, untramelled by government regulations.

9.475 **Forberger**, R., *Die Manufaktur in Sachsen vom Ende des 16. bis zum Anfang des 19. Jahrhunderts*, Berlin, 1958. Thorough Marxist account, looking in turn at means of production (capital, material, and labour); at legal position within state; and at reasons for decline.

9.476 **Henderson**, W. O., 'The rise of the Berlin silk and porcelain industries', *Bus.Hist.*, 1, 1960, 84-98. Entrepreneurial cooperation between J. E. Gotzkowsky and Frederick the Great.

9.477 —— 'The rise of the metal and armament industries in Berlin and Brandenburg, 1712-95', *ib.*, 3, 1961, 62-74. Deals with multifarious activities of firm Splitgerber

and Daum, who moved from commission wholesaling into banking, shipping, and manufactures.

9.478 **Krüger**, H., *Zur Geschichte der Manufakturen und der Manufakturarbeiter in Preussen. Die Mittleren Provinzen in der Zweiten Hälfte des 18. Jahrhunderts*, Berlin, 1958. Deals with Brandenburg and Berlin. Informative, despite Marxist jargon; lengthy appendix of documents.

9.479 **Lange**, Gisela, *Das Ländliche Gewerbe in der Grafschaft Mark am Vorabend der Industrialisierung*, Cologne, 1976. In effect study of proto-industrialisation, though author seems unaware of historiographical dimensions of this concept.

9.480 **Mager**, W., 'Protoindustrialisierung und agrarisch-heimgewerbliche Verflechtung in Ravensberg während der frühen Neuzeit', *Gesch.und Gesellschaft*, 8, 1982, 435-74.

9.481 **Proesler**, H., *Das Gesamtdeutsche Handwerk im Spiegel der Reichsgesetzgebung von 1530 bis 1806*, Berlin, 1954. Survey of imperial regulation of industry; essay followed by texts.

9.482 **Reuter**, O., *Die Manufaktur in Fränkischen Raum. Eine Untersuchung Grossbetrieblicher Anfänge in den Fürstentümen Ansbach und Bayreuth*, Stuttgart, 1961. Eighteenth- and early nineteenth-century industrial enterprises in two small principalities.

9.483 **Schremmer**, E., 'Proto-industrialisation. A step towards industialisation?', *J.Eur.Ec.Hist.*, 10, 1981, 653-70. Bavarian examples of peasants combining farming and manufacture.

9.484 —— *Die Wirtschaft Bayerns vom Hohen Mittelalter bis zum Beginn der Industrialisierung. Bergbau, Gewerbe, Handel*, Munich, 1970.

9.485 **Schulte**, F., *Die Entwicklung der Gewerblichen Wirtschaft in Rheinland-Westfalen im 18. Jahrhundert*, Köln, 1959.

9.486 **Slawinger**, G., *Die Manufaktur in Kurbayern. Die Anfänge der Grossgewerbelichen Entwicklung...1740-1833*, Stuttgart, 1966.

9.487 **Wiest**, E., *Die Entwicklung der Nürnberger Gewerbes zwischen 1648 und 1806*, Stuttgart, 1968. Rather dependent on institutional sources and administrative regulations as evidence.

9.488 **Braun**, R., *Industrialisierung und Volksleben. Veränderungen der*

Lebensformen unter Einwirkung der Verlagsindustriellen Heimarbeit in einem ländlichen Industriegebiet (Zürcher Oberland) vor 1800, 2nd ed., Göttingen, 1979. Important study of impact of putting-out textile system on Swiss rural region. Some key passages (from first ed. of 1960) transl. in Landes (2.126), 53-64. See 5.172 for demographic data drawn from this research.

BOHEMIA, HUNGARY, POLAND

9.489 **Freudenberger**, H., 'Industrialization in Bohemia and Moravia in the eighteenth century', *J.Central Eur.Affairs*, 19, 1960, 347-56. Short account of government efforts to foster industry.

9.490 **Klima**, A., 'Industrial growth and entrepreneurship in the early stages of industrialization in the Czech lands', *J.Eur.Ec.Hist.*, 6, 1977, 549-74. Biographical material on late eighteenth- and early nineteenth-century industrialists.

9.491 —— 'The role of rural domestic industry in Bohemia in the eighteenth century', *Ec.Hist.Rev.*, 2nd ser., 27, 1974, 48-56.

SCANDINAVIA

9.492 **Barton**, H. A., 'Canton at Drottninghölm. A model manufacturing community from the mid-eighteenth century', *Scan.Stud.*, 49, 1977, 81-98. Set up by Swedish Crown in 1750s to encourage specialist manufactures.

9.493 **Ericsson**, Birgitta, and others, 'Central power and local community. Joint Nordic research on the granting of "privilegia" to industrial enterprises in Scandinavia during the eighteenth century', *J.Scan.Hist.*, 7, 1982, 173-254. Case studies from Denmark, Iceland, Norway, and Finland.

9.494 **Hornby**, O., and Oxenbøll, E., 'Proto-industrialisation before industrialisation? The Danish case', *Scan.Ec.Hist.Rev.*, 30, 1982, 3-33.

9.495 **Hovland**, E., and others, 'Proto-industrialisation in Norway, 1750-1850. Fact or fiction?', *Scan.Ec.Hist.Rev.*, 30, 1982, 45-56. Concludes that there was little manufacture which fits concept, and supplementary crafts remained closely tied to agriculture, fishing, and forestry.

9.496 **Isacson**, M., and Magnusson, L., *Proto-Industrialisation in Scandinavia. Craft Skills in the Industrial Revolution*, 1987. Some eighteenth-century material. Main emphasis on rural metal-working areas in Sweden, and their progress towards either more intensive industrialisation or de-industrialisation.

9.497 **Krantz**, O., 'Production and labour in the Swedish manufactories during the eighteenth century', *Ec.& Hist.*, 19, 1976, 27-48, 83-97. Seeks to establish statistics of productivity and volume.

RUSSIA
See also 5.423; 8.178; 10.532.

9.498 **Kahan**, A., 'Continuity in economic activity and policy during the post-Petrine period in Russia', *J.Ec.Hist.*, 25, 1965, 61-85. Repr. in Blackwell (3.362), 53-70; and Cherniavsky (6.232), 191-211. Maintains that economic impetus to manufactures given by Peter via state continued under private auspices under his successors.

9.499 **Portal**, R., 'Manufactures et classes sociales en Russie au 18e siècle', *Rev.Hist.*, 201, 1949, 161-85; 202, 1949, 1-23. Looks at various classes which participated in creation of industrial enterprises.

TECHNOLOGY AND ENGINEERING
See also 14.341-81 passim on relations between technology and scientific thought and practice. Also 4.132; 8.64; 9.157,566,572,610-11,644-8,658; 10.471.

9.500 **Ferguson**, E. S., *Bibliography of the History of Technology*, Cambridge, Mass., 1968. Of limited use, given bias towards modern, and particularly U.S., technology and sources.

9.501 **Adams**, N., 'Architecture for fish. The Sienese dam on the Bruna River – structures and designs, 1468-c.1530', *Tech.& Culture*, 25, 1984, 768-97.

9.502 'A bit of total history. The transfer of

technology between France and Great Britain during the eighteenth century', *Proc.Consortium on Revolutionary Eur.*, 1984, 45-86. Related papers by H. T. Parker (import of technology), J. R. Harris (nature of this technology), and W. M. Reddy (conservative influence of guilds on textile technology).

9.503 **Boyer**, Marjorie N., 'Resistance to technological innovation. The history of the pile driver through the eighteenth century', *Tech.& Culture*, 26, 1985, 56-68. Examines pile drivers in use between fourteenth and eighteenth centuries, and shows that practicable refinements don't necessarily find favour with artisans.

9.504 **Braun**, H.-J., *Technologische Beziehungen zwischen Deutschland und England von der Mitte des 17. bis zum Ausgang des 18. Jahrhunderts*, Düsseldorf, 1974. Chiefly on forging of links between various technically-minded societies ("agricultural", "patriotic", etc.), but also touches on individual visits of craftsmen.

9.505 **Cipolla**, C. M., *Clocks and Culture, 1300-1700*, 1967. On social and technological importance of clocks in Europe and China. See also 9.511.

9.506 —— 'The diffusion of innovations in early modern Europe', *Comp.Stud.Soc.& Hist.*, 14, 1972, 46-52. Sees migration of skilled craftsmen as main influence, and adduces reasons for their mobility.

9.507 **Gille**, B., ed., *The History of Techniques*, 2 vols., New York, 1986. Transl. from French encyclopedia of this title (1978). Ambitious attempt to relate technological developments to particular cultures and to progress in other disciplines. Vol.1 is general history; vol.2 essays on applications to science and social studies.

9.508 —— *The Renaissance Engineers*, 1966. Transl. from French ed. of 1964. Attractive illustrated work. Three chapters on Leonardo.

9.509 **Kellenbenz**, H., 'Technology in the age of the scientific revolution, 1500-1700', in *Fontana Economic History of Europe, 2* (2.24), 177-272. S. Lilley continues survey to 1914 in vol.3, 187-254.

9.510 **Kranzberg**, M., and Pursell, C. W., eds., *Technology in Western Civilization*, 2 vols.,

1967. Collaborative history designed to stress economic and social implications. For early modern period, to c.1830, see 79-321. Contributors incl. A. R. Hall, S. B. Clough, A. P. Usher, E. E. Lampard.

9.511 **Landes**, D. S., *Revolution in Time. Clocks and the Making of the Modern World*, Cambridge, Mass., 1983. Somewhat fuller and more technical than 9.505.

9.512 **O'Dea**, W. T., *A Social History of Lighting*, 1958. Organised by topics, e.g. home lighting, travel, workplace, entertainment. Not confined to early modern period.

9.513 **Pacey**, A., *The Maze of Ingenuity. Ideas and Idealism in the Development of Technology*, General outline from c.1100 to 1870. Attempts to show that humanitarian motives as spur to invention have been underestimated.

9.514 **Paulinyi**, A., 'Revolution and technology', in R. Porter and M. Teich, eds., *Revolution in History*, 1986, 261-89. Argues that decisive break in technological history lies in displacement of hand-tools by machines, irrespective of energy sources.

9.515 **Reynolds**, T. S., 'Scientific influences on technology. The case of the overshot waterwheel, 1752-54', *Tech.& Culture*, 20, 1979, 270-95. Case-study tending to show that theoretical solutions mattered much less than engineers' trial and error.

9.516 **Rosenberg**, N., 'Factors affecting the diffusion of technology', *Explor.in Ec.Hist.*, 10, 1972, 3-33. Argues that however spectacular a technological novelty may be, its economic impact tends to be gradual. Modern emphasis, but not exclusively so.

9.517 **Scoville**, W. C., 'The Huguenots and the diffusion of technology', *J.Pol.Ec.*, 60, 1952, 294-311, 392-411. Effects of forced emigration of Flemish and French Protestants.

9.518 —— 'Minority migrations and the diffusion of technology', *J.Ec.Hist.*, 11, 1951, 347-60.

9.519 **Singer**, C. J., and others, eds., *A History of Technology*, 7 vols., 1954-78. Standard detailed history. For early modern period vol.3 (1957) is central, covering c.1500-1750.

LABOUR ORGANISATION AND CONDITIONS

See also 5.523-52 for some material on migratory labour; and 6.242-73 for general studies of middling and lower classes. Women's participation in labour force is mostly dealt with in 5.471-522. For data on wages and standard of living see also 11.1-101 passim. Note also 10.378 (general); and on France 9.554,615; 10.401; 12.46; on the Netherlands 9.459,552,558,617,656-7; on Italy 9.573; on Central Europe 5.643; 6.185; 9.630; on the Balkans 10.150; on Scandinavia 9.634; 10.154; on Russia 9.608.

9.520 **Pallach**, U.-C., 'Fonctions de la mobilité artisanale et ouvrière – compagnons, ouvriers, et manufacturiers en France et aux Allemagnes. De la fin du 17e siècle au début de l'époque révolutionnaire en 1789', *Francia*, 11, 1983, 365-405. First part of enquiry, to be continued up to 1848.

9.521 **Wischnitzer**, M., *A History of Jewish Crafts and Guilds*, New York, 1965. General history from Biblical times onwards, but gives considerable space to European diaspora.

9.522 **Bouvier-Ajam**, M., *Histoire du Travail en France des Origines à la Révolution*, Paris, 1957. Little more than survey of government edicts.

9.523 **Coornaert**, E., *Les Compagnonnages en France du Moyen Age à nos Jours*, Paris, 1966. Unsatisfactory. J. P. Bayard, *Le Compagnonnage en France*, Paris, 1977, is also rather derivative and antiquarian.

9.524 —— *Les Corporations en France avant 1789*, Paris, 1941. 2nd ed., 1968. Standard work on French guilds. See very brief summary, 'French guilds under the Old Regime', in Cameron and others (3.251), 123-7.

9.525 **Davis**, Natalie Z., 'A trade-union in sixteenth-century France', *Ec.Hist.Rev.*, 2nd ser., 19, 1966, 48-69. Clandestine union among journeymen of Lyon printing industry.

9.526 **Garrioch**, D., and Sonenscher, M., '*Compagnonnages*, confraternities, and associations of journeymen in eighteenth-century Paris', *Eur.Hist.Q.*, 16, 1986, 25-45. Draws distinction between these various forms of association, since *compagnonnages* seem not to have existed in Paris before 1780s.

9.527 **Kaplan**, S. L., 'The character and implications of strife among the masters inside the guilds of eighteenth-century Paris', *J.Soc.Hist.*, 19, 1986, 631-47. Investigates hierarchy within guilds as opposed to better-known conflict between masters and journeymen.

9.528 —— and Koepp, Cynthia J., eds., *Work in France. Representation, Meaning, Organization, and Practice*, Ithaca, N.Y., 1986. Essays 2-8 deal with work and workers in eighteenth century, among them E. J. Shephard on guild receptions at Dijon (97-130); Cynthia M. Truant on journeymen of Nantes and Lyon (131-75); and Kaplan on Turgot's edict against corporations (176-228).

9.529 **Sonenscher**, M., 'Work and wages in Paris in the eighteenth century', in Berg and others (9.439), 147-72.

9.530 **Truant**, Cynthia M., 'Solidarity and symbolism among journeymen artisans. The case of *compagnonnage*', *Comp.Stud.Soc.& Hist.*, 21, 1979, 214-26. Details some myths and ceremonies of these illegal craft associations by which artisans dignified their calling.

9.531 **Santbergen**, R. van, *Les Bons Métiers des Meuniers, des Boulangers, et des Brasseurs de la Cité de Liège*, Liège, 1949. Organisation of guilds and their place in city life from fourteenth to eighteenth centuries.

9.532 **Capella Martínez**, M., and Matilla Tascón, A., *Los Cinco Gremios Mayores de Madrid*, Madrid, 1957. Exhaustive study of most important Madrid guilds.

9.533 **Molas Ribalta**, P., *Los Gremios Barceloneses del Siglo 18. La Estructura Corporativa ante el Comienzo de la Revolución Industrial*, Madrid, 1970. Substantial examination of guilds, both globally and in terms of individual industries.

9.534 **Redondo Veintemillas**, G., *Las Corporaciones de Artesanos de Zaragoza en el Siglo 17*, Zaragoza, 1982. Short work, with appendix of documents.

9.535 **Villas Tinoco**, S., *Los Gremios Malagueños, 1700-46*, 2 vols., Malaga, 1982. Trade by trade survey.

9.536 **Dal Pane**, L., *Storia del Lavoro in Italia dagli Inizi del Secolo 18 al 1815*, Milan, 1944. 2nd ed., 1958. Substantially revised in new ed.

9.537 **Mackenney**, R., *Tradesmen and Traders. The World of the Guilds in Venice and*

Europe, c.1250-1650, 1987. As title implies, some valuable comparative study is involved.

9.538 **Bade**, K. J., 'Altes Handwerk, Wanderzwang, und "Gute Policey". Gesellenwanderung zwischen Zunftökonomie und Gewerbereform', *VSWG*, 69, 1982, 1-37. On police problems posed by itinerant workers.

9.539 **Otruba**, G., *Berufsstruktur und Berufslaufbahn vor der Industriellen Revolution*, Vienna, 1952. History of craft guilds in Lower Austria from fifteenth century till abolition in 1859.

9.540 **Schwarz**, K., *Die Lage der Handwerksgesellen in Bremen während des 18. Jahrhunderts*, Bremen, 1975. Interesting case study of rearguard action by guild artisans, though lacks comparative dimension.

9.541 **Thamer**, H.-U., 'On the use and abuse of handicraft. Journeyman culture and enlightened public opinion in eighteenth- and nineteenth-century Germany', in S. L.

Kaplan, ed., *Understanding Popular Culture. Europe from the Middle Ages to the Nineteenth Century*, Berlin, 1984, 275-300. Details attacks on perceived inefficiencies and barbarities of guild customs.

9.542 **Wesoly**, K., *Lehrlinge und Handwerkgesellen am Mittelrhein. Ihre Soziale Lage und ihre Organisation vom 14. bis ins 17. Jahrhundert*, Frankfurt, 1985. Study of apprentices and itinerant journeymen, based on municipal records of Mainz, Frankfurt, Worms, and Speyer. Somewhat institutional in approach (much on journeymen fraternities).

9.543 **Jutikkala**, E., 'Labour policy and the urban proletariat in Sweden and Finland during the pre-industrial era', in Riis (11.194), 2, 133-44.

9.544 **Baer**, G., 'The Turkish guilds', in his *Fellah and Townsman in the Middle East*, 1982, 147-222. Links together three articles originally publ. in specialist journals.

PARTICULAR INDUSTRIES

TEXTILES

On trade in wool and other raw materials, see 9.380-6. See also 14.288; and on France 6.245; 9.460-3,502; 11.202; 12.46; on Italy 9.15,82,96; on Central and Eastern Europe 9.116,476,488.

9.545 **Ciriacono**, S., 'Silk manufacturing in France and Italy in the seventeenth century. Two models compared', *J.Eur.Ec.Hist.*, 10, 1981, 167-99. Examines how Lyon overtook Italian manufactures in production of best quality cloths.

9.546 **Coleman**, D. C., 'An innovation and its diffusion. The "new draperies" ', *Ec.Hist.Rev.*, 2nd ser., 22, 1969, 417-29. Looks at European market for these textiles, and manner of introduction of new techniques in England. See also comments of G. R. Hawke, *ib.*, 24, 1971, 258-61.

9.547 **Wilson**, C., 'Cloth production and international competition in the seventeenth century', *ib.*, 13, 1960, 209-21. Repr. in Wilson (3.83), 94-113. Shows that European cloth market had become single theatre of operations.

9.548 **Boyce**, Mary S., 'The Barbier manuscripts', *Textile Hist.*, 12, 1981, 37-58. Extracts from correspondence of Paris silk merchant, 1755-97.

9.549 **Chapman**, S. D., and Chassagne, S., *European Textile Printers in the Eighteenth Century. A Study of Peel and Oberkampf*, 1981. Compares two leading calico-printing enterprises in England and France.

9.550 **Descimon**, R., 'Structures d'un marché de draperie dans le Languedoc au milieu du 16e siècle', *Annales*, 30, 1975, 1414-46. Examines market at Lavaur, Albi, and Montagnac.

9.551 **Fukasawa**, K., *Toilerie et Commerce du Levant. D'Alep à Marseille*, Paris, 1987. Concerns eighteenth-century trade in cotton textiles from Middle East.

9.552 **Guignet**, P., 'The lacemakers of Valenciennes in the eighteenth century', *Textile Hist.*, 10, 1979, 96-113. Conditions of female labour force employed by Tribout manufactury. For wider context see 9.459.

9.553 **Markovitch**, T. J., *L'Industrie Française au 18e Siècle. L'Industrie Lainière à la Fin du Règne de Louis XIV et sous la Régence* (*Cahiers de l'I.S.E.A., Histoire Quantitative de l'Économie Française, 10*), Paris, 1968.

9.554 **Sonenscher**, M., 'Weavers, wage-rates, and the measurement of work in eighteenth-century Rouen', *Textile Hist.*, 17, 1986, 7-18.

9.555 **Tanguy**, J., 'La production et le commerce des toiles "bretagnes" du 16e au 18e siècle. Premiers résultats', *Actes Congrès Nat.Soc.Savantes*, 91 (i), 1966, 105-41. Deals principally with eighteenth-century fluctuations in industry.

9.556 **Thomson**, J. K. J., *Clermont-de-Lodève, 1633-1789. Fluctuations in the Prosperity of a Languedocian Cloth-Making Town*, 1982. Seeks reasons for increasing rigidity and lack of response to market changes.

9.557 **Endrei**, W., 'The productivity of weaving in late medieval Flanders', in N. B. Harte and K. G. Ponting, eds., *Cloth and Clothing in Medieval Europe. Essays in Memory of E. M. Carus-Wilson*, 1983, 108-19. Calculations based on data from Armentières in 1590s.

9.558 **Lebrun**, P., *L'Industrie de la Laine à Verviers pendant le 18e et le Début du 19e Siècle. Contribution à l'Étude des Origines de la Révolution Industrielle*, Liège, 1948. Contains sections on both workers and *patronat*.

9.559 **Ponting**, K. G., 'Sculptures and paintings of textile processes at Leiden', *Textile Hist.*, 5, 1974, 128-51. Describes works at city Lakenhal depicting processes of sixteenth and seventeenth century.

9.560 **Van der Wee**, H., 'Structural changes and specialization in the industry of the Southern Netherlands, 1100-1600', *Ec.Hist.Rev.*, 2nd ser., 28, 1975, 203-21. Concentrates on textile manufacture.

9.561 **Verhulst**, A., 'La laine indigène dans les anciens Pays-Bas entre le 12e et le 17e siècle', *Rev.Hist.*, 248, 1972, 281-322. On native sheep-rearing and textile industry based on it.

9.562 **Bejarano Robles**, F., *La Industria de la Seda en Málaga durante el Siglo 16*, Madrid, 1951.

9.563 **Iradiel Murugarren**, P., *Evolución de la Industria Textil Castellana en los Siglos 13-16. Factores de Desarrollo, Organización y Costes de la Producción Manufacturera en Cuenca*, Salamanca, 1974. Stress is on fifteenth and early sixteenth centuries. Establishes that Spain was not purely wool-exporting economy.

9.564 **La Force**, J. C., *The Development of the Spanish Textile Industry, 1750-1800*, Berkeley, Calif., 1965. Chequered history of Crown efforts to expand textile production. See also following articles.

9.565 —— 'Royal textile factories in Spain, 1700-1800', *J.Ec.Hist.*, 24, 1964, 337-63.

9.566 —— 'Technological diffusion in the eighteenth century. The Spanish textile industry', *Tech.& Culture*, 5, 1964, 322-43. On efforts to recruit foreign specialists.

9.567 **De Roover**, Florence E., 'Andrea Banchi, Florentine silk manufacturer and merchant in the fifteenth century', *Stud.Med.& Renaiss.Hist.*, 3, 1966, 223-85. Evidence spans years 1425-67.

9.568 **De Roover**, R., 'A Florentine firm of cloth manufacturers. Management and organization of a sixteenth-century business', in De Roover (9.404), 85-118. Firm involving Medici family.

9.569 **Lee**, E., 'Woad from Città di Castello, 1476-84', *J.Eur.Ec.Hist.*, 11, 1982, 141-56. Shows importance of small centre of production in upper Tiber valley for Tuscan textile industry.

9.570 **Mazzaoui**, Maureen F., *The Italian Cotton Industry in the Later Middle Ages, 1100-1600*, 1981.

9.571 **Morelli**, Roberta, *La Seta Fiorentina nel Cinquecento*, Milan, 1976. Briefly covers both manufacture and trade in silk cloth.

9.572 **Poni**, C., 'All'origine del sistema di fabbrica. Tecnologia e organizzazione produttiva dei mulini da seta nell'Italia settentrionale (sec. 17-18)', *Riv.Stor.Ital.*, 88, 1976, 444-97. Discusses technical changes in apparatus in relation to urban-rural distribution of manufacture.

9.573 —— 'Misura contro misura. Come il filo di seta divenne sottile e rotondo', *Quad.Stor.*, 47, 1981, 385-422. On changing labour conditions in Italian silk industry; offers some comparison with Lyon.

9.574 **Sella**, D., 'Venice. The rise and fall of the Venetian wool industry', in Pullan (3.156), 106-26. Repr. in E. W. Cochrane, ed., *The Late Italian Renaissance, 1525-1630*, 1970, 331-50. Transl. from *Annales*, 12, 1957, 29-45. Sees expansion and contraction as coinciding roughly with sixteenth and seventeenth centuries respectively, an orthodoxy now somewhat under challenge.

575 **Bodmer**, W., *Schweizerische Industriegeschichte. Die Entwicklung der Schweizerischen Textilwirtschaft im Rahmen der Übrigen Industrien und Wirtschaftszeige*, Zurich, 1960. Covers development of textile industry from sixteenth to mid-nineteenth century.

576 **Caspard**, P., 'Manufacture and trade in calico printing at Neuchâtel. The example of Cortaillod (1752-1854)', *Textile Hist.*, 8, 1977, 150-62. Caspard has publ. book length study of this enterprise in French: *La Fabrique-Neuve de Cortaillod*, Paris, 1979.

577 **Veyrassat**, Béatrice, *Négociants et Fabricants dans l'Industrie Cotonnière Suisse, 1760-1840*, Lausanne, 1982. Explains successful persistance of traditional handweaving methods in Eastern Switzerland.

578 **Clasen**, C.-P., *Die Augsburger Weber. Leistungen und Krisen des Textilgewerbes um 1600*, Augsburg, 1981. Excellent study of weavers in period between dissolution of guilds (1548) and Thirty Years' War.

579 **Friedrichs**, C. R., 'Early capitalism and its enemies. The Wörner family and the weavers of Nördlingen', *Bus.Hist.Rev.*, 50, 1976, 265-87. Stresses contrast between city council's support for artisans against powerful merchant family in late seventeenth century and their attitude in similar disputes a century later. For fuller context see Friedrichs' book (8.130).

580 **Grüll**, G., 'The Poneggen hosiery enterprise, 1763-1818. A study of Austrian mercantilism', *Textile Hist.*, 5, 1974, 38-79. Enterprise established by Count von Salburg in Upper Austria. Shortened version of monograph publ. in *Mitteil.Oberösterr.Landesarchivs*, 6, 1959, 5-135.

581 **Heitz**, G., *Ländliche Leinenproduktion in Sachsen, 1470-1555*, Berlin, 1961. Short but informative.

582 **Kellenbenz**, H., 'The fustian industry of the Ulm region in the fifteenth and early sixteenth centuries', in Harte and Ponting (9.557), 259-78.

583 **Kisch**, H., 'From monopoly to laissez-faire. The early growth of the Wupper Valley textile trades', *J.Eur.Ec.Hist.*, 1, 1972, 298-407. Deals with whole period from late Middle Ages to early nineteenth century.

9.584 —— 'Growth deterrents of a medieval heritage. The Aachen-area woolen trades before 1790', *J.Ec.Hist.*, 24, 1964, 517-37. Contrasts guild dominance in Aachen and less restrictive practices of surrounding countryside.

9.585 —— *Die Hausindustriellen Textilgewerbe am Niederrhein vor der Industriellen Revolution*, Göttingen, 1981. Posthumous work incorporating his work on Krefeld silk industry (see next entry), and dealing also with Wuppertal and Aachen in eighteenth century.

9.586 —— *Prussian Mercantilism and the Rise of the Krefeld Silk Industry. Variations upon an Eighteenth-Century Theme*, Philadelphia, 1968. Extended essay. Compare 9.588.

9.587 —— 'Textile industries in Silesia and the Rhineland. A comparative study in industrialization', *J.Ec.Hist.*, 19, 1959, 541-64. Differing success of these regions in nineteenth century traced back to early modern social structure.

9.588 **Kriedte**, P., 'Demographic and economic rhythms. The rise of the silk industry in Krefeld in the eighteenth century', *J.Eur.Ec.Hist.*, 15, 1986, 259-89. Study from forthcoming book on proto-industrialisation in Krefeld, aiming somewhat wider than Kisch's work (9.586); demographic background occupies about half article.

9.589 —— 'Proto-industrialisierung und grosses Kapital. Das Seidengewerbe in Krefeld und seinem Umland bis zum Ende des Ancien Régime', *Arch.Sozialgesch.*, 23, 1983, 219-66.

9.590 **Medick**, H., 'Privilegiertes Handels-kapital und "kleine Industrie". Produktion und Produktionsverhältnisse im Leinengewerbe des alt-württemberg-ischen Oberamts Urach im 18. Jahrhundert', *ib.*, 267-310. Case study, like preceding entry, by leading exponent of proto-industrialism model.

9.591 **Narweleit**, G., 'Die Standortverteilung des Textilgewerbes der Niederlausitz in der Mitte des 18. Jahrhunderts, und Tendenzen der Entwicklung bis 1800', *Jb.Wirtschaftsgesch.*, 1984 (i), 157-94. Discerns geographical structures of later industrialism already in formation in later eighteenth century.

9.592 **Schmitz**, Edith, *Leinengewerbe und Leinenhandel in Nordwestdeutschland, 1650-1850*, Köln, 1967. Deals with

Rhineland-Westphalia region.

9.593 **Wiesner**, Merry E., 'Spinsters and seamstresses. Women in cloth and clothing production', in Ferguson and others (5.499), 191-205. Argues that increasing specialisation in textile work was to detriment of women's opportunities. See 5.510 for Wiesner's wider exploration of theme.

9.594 **Wolf**, K., 'Stages in industrial organization', *Explor.Entrepren.Hist.*, 2nd ser., 1, 1963, 125-41. Discusses models of evolution of textile industry in Germany from *Kaufsystem* to *Manufaktur*.

9.595 **Freudenberger**, H., *The Industrialization of a Central European City. Brno and the Fine Woollen Industry in the Eighteenth Century*, 1977. Deals with state-fostered mill which at its peak employed c.2000 handloom weavers.

9.596 ——— 'Three mercantilistic proto-factories', *Bus.Hist.Rev.*, 40, 1966, 167-89. Using example of three woollen enterprises started with state aid in Habsburg territories, develops model of factories as method of introducing new techniques to areas without manufacturing experience.

9.597 ——— *The Waldstein Woolen Mill. Noble Entrepreneurship in Eighteenth-Century Bohemia*, Boston, Mass., 1963. Brief study of large-scale manorial industry.

9.598 ——— 'The woolen-goods industry of the Hapsburg monarchy in the eighteenth century', *J.Ec.Hist.*, 20, 1960. 383-406. Traces expansion of industry beyond bounds of guild restrictions after 1750.

9.599 **Klima**, A., 'English merchant capital in Bohemia in the eighteenth century', *Ec.Hist.Rev.*, 2nd ser., 12, 1959, 34-48. Activity of English entrepreneurs in Bohemian textile industry.

9.600 ——— 'Industrial development in Bohemia, 1648-1781', *P.&P.*, 11, 1957, 87-99. Concentrates on expansion of textile production.

9.601 **Braude**, B., 'International competition and domestic cloth in the Ottoman Empire, 1500-1650. A study in underdevelopment', *Review*, 2, 1979, 437-51. Looks at reasons for failure to nurture Balkan textile centres.

9.602 **Carter**, F. W., 'The woollen industry of Ragusa (Dubrovnik), 1450-1550. Problems of a Balkan textile centre', *Textile Hist.*, 2, 1971, 3-27. Shows that Ragusa was much more successful as entrepot than

as manufacturing centre.

9.603 **Çizakça**, M., 'Price history and the Bursa silk industry. A study in Ottoman industrial decline, 1550-1650', *J.Ec.Hist.*, 40, 1980, 533-50. Argues that price inflation forced abandonment of cloth manufacture and concentration on primary production.

9.604 **Faroqhi**, Suraiya, 'Notes on the production of cotton and cotton cloth in sixteenth- and seventeenth-century Anatolia', *J.Eur.Ec.Hist.*, 8, 1979, 405-17. Fragmentary indications on geography of cotton growing and weaving, from archival sources.

9.605 ——— 'Textile production in Rumeli and the Arab provinces. Geographical distribution and internal trade (1560-1650)', in Faroqhi (4.82), 61-83. General survey of Ottoman production.

9.606 **Tveite**, S., 'The Norwegian textile market in the eighteenth century', *Scan. Ec. Hist. Rev.*, 17, 1969, 161-78. Indicates that Norway was far from self-sufficient in textiles.

9.607 **Turnau**, Irene, 'Aspects of the Russian artisan. The knitter of the seventeenth to the eighteenth century', *Textile Hist.*, 4, 1973, 1-25. More on technique and types of garment than economic aspects.

9.608 **Zaozerskaja**, E. I., 'Le salariat dans les manufactures textiles russes au 18e siècle', *Cah.Monde Russe et Sov.*, 6, 1965, 189-222. Data on structure and numbers of labour force, but little on earnings and conditions.

MINING AND METALLURGY
See also 4.44; 8.139; 9.327; 10.441; 11.8.

9.609 **Blanchard**, I., 'Resource depletion in the European mining and metallurgical industries, 1400-1800', in Maczak and Parker (4.44), 85-113.

9.610 **Braunstein**, P., 'Innovations in mining and metal production in Europe in the late Middle Ages', *J.Eur.Ec.Hist.*, 12, 1983, 573-91. Mainly concerns technological developments in fifteenth and early sixteenth centuries.

9.611 **Hollister-Short**, G. J., 'Gunpowder and mining in sixteenth- and seventeenth-century Europe', *Hist.Tech.*, 10, 1985, 31-66. Explores early use of gunpowder for blasting operations.

9.612 **Kellenbenz**, H., ed., *Schwerpunkte der*

Eisengewinnung und Eisenverarbeitung in Europa, 1500-1650, Köln, 1974. Multilingual symposium, though deals principally with Germany. Note D. Sella 'The iron industry in Italy' (91-105).

9.13 —— *Schwerpunkte der Kupferproduktion und des Kupferhandels in Europa, 1500-1650*, Köln, 1977. Similar miscellany.

9.14 'Carrières, mines, et metallurgie de 1610 à nos jours', *Actes Congrès Nat. Soc. Savantes*, 98 (i), 1973, whole issue. Several relevant papers on French industries.

9.15 Gille, B., *Les Origines de la Grande Industrie Métallurgique en France*, Paris, 1947. Mainly concerned with eighteenth century. Includes material on social origins of entrepreneurs, and on sources and conditions of labour force.

9.16 Vidalenc, J., *La Petite Métallurgie Rurale en Haute Normandie sous l'Ancien Régime*, Paris, 1946.

9.17 Hansotte, G., *La Clouterie Liégeoise et la Question Ouvrière au 18e Siècle*, Brussels, 1972. Unusually detailed picture of labour unrest in early industrial enterprise (nail-making).

9.18 Alcalá Zamora, J., 'Producción de hierro y altos hornos en la España anterior a 1850', *Moneda y Crédito*, 128, 1974, 117-218.

9.19 Delumeau, J., *L'Alun de Rome, 15e-19e Siècle*, Paris, 1962. History of papal workings at Tolfa.

9.20 Klapisch-Zuber, Christiane, *Les Maîtres du Marbre. Carrare, 1300-1600*, Paris, 1969. Studies production and commercial outlets of principal marble quarries of Renaissance period.

9.21 Morelli, Roberta, 'The Medici silver mines', *J.Eur.Ec.Hist.*, 5, 1976, 121-39. Short account of ducal mining enterprise of Pietrasanta, probably abandoned in face of American competition.

9.22 Mori, G., 'L'estrazione di minerali nel Granducato di Toscana durante il periodo delle riforme (1737-90)', *Arch.Stor.Ital.*, 116, 1958, 207-46, 322-45.

9.23 Vergani, R., 'Technology and organization of labour in the Venetian copper industry (sixteenth-eighteenth centuries)', *J.Eur.Ec.Hist.*, 14, 1985, 173-86. Longitudinal study of mining and metallurgical centre in Imperina valley (Belluno).

9.24 Henschke, E., *Landesherrschaft und Bergbauwirtschaft. Zur Wirtschafts- und Verwaltungsgeschichte des Oberharzer Bergbaugebietes im 16. und 17. Jahrhundert*, Berlin, 1975. Sticks closely to organisation and technology, and hence somewhat weak on social aspects.

9.625 Redlich, F., 'A German eighteenth-century iron works during its first hundred years', *Bus.Hist.Rev.*, 27, 1953, 69-90, 141-57, 231-59. History of Lauchhammer works in Saxony, of interest as example of aristocratic enterprise, and for material on labour conditions.

9.626 Rimlinger, G. V., 'The legitimation of protest. A comparative study in labor history', *Comp.Stud.Soc.& Hist.*, 2, 1960, 329-43. Compares British and German coal-miners, seeing greater passivity of latter in industrial era as consequence of protection and patronage by state in early modern period.

9.627 Werner, T. G., 'Europäisches Kapital in ibero-amerikanischen Montanunter-nehmungen des 16. Jahrhunderts', *VSWG*, 48, 1961, 18-55, 289-328, 444-502. Deals mainly with Cuba copper interests of Tezel of Nuremberg (1545-71).

9.628 Westermann, E., *Das Eislebener Garkupfer und seine Bedeuting für den Europäischen Kupfermarkt, 1460-1560*, Köln, 1971. Sets copper mining industry of Thuringia in European context.

9.629 Molenda, Danuta, 'Investments in ore-mining in Poland from the thirteenth to the seventeenth century', *J.Eur.Ec.Hist.*, 5, 1976, 151-69. On sources of heavy investment needed for deeper seams in lead mines. See also *ib.*, 757-62, for A. Wyrobisz' review article of Molenda's books of 1963 and 1972 (in Polish) on lead and silver mining.

9.630 Myška, M., 'Pre-industrial iron-making in the Czech lands. The labour force and production relations, c.1350-c.1840', *P.& P.*, 82, 1979, 44-72. Argues that both capitalist and feudal labour relations were involved, latter esp. in auxiliary processes.

9.631 Faroqhi, Suraiya, 'Alum production and alum trade in the Ottoman Empire (about 1560-1830)', in Faroqhi (4.82), 153-75.

9.632 Hildebrand, K.-G., 'Foreign markets for Swedish iron in the eighteenth century', *Scan.Ec.Hist.*, 6, 1958, 3-52. Divides attention between British market and that of France and Mediterranean countries.

9.633 *Iron and Steel on the European Market in the*

Seventeenth Century. A Contemporary Swedish Account of Production Forms and Marketing, Stockholm, 1982. Original text (which was written in German), with transl. and copious background material.

9.634 **Montelius**, S., 'Recruitment and conditions of life of Swedish ironworkers during the eighteenth and nineteenth centuries', Scan.Ec.Hist.Rev., 14, 1966, 1-17.

9.635 **Fuhrman**, J. T., The Origins of Capitalism in Russia. Industry and Progress in the Sixteenth and Seventeenth Centuries, Chicago, 1972. Almost wholly devoted to iron industry.

9.636 **Hudson**, H. D., 'Free enterprise and the state in eighteenth-century Russia. The Demidov metallurgical empire', Can.Slavonic Pap., 26, 1984, 182-200. Urals enterprise which provided forty per cent of Russia's iron production by mid-century.

9.637 **Kahan**, A., 'Entrepreneurship in the early development of iron manufacturing in Russia', Ec.Dev.& Cultural Change, 10, 1962, 395-422.

9.638 —— 'A proposed mercantilist code in the Russian iron industry, 1734-36', Explor.Entrepren.Hist., 2nd ser., 2, 1965, 75-89. Proposal for state inspectorate of quality and working conditions.

9.639 **Portal**, R., L'Oural au 18e Siècle. Étude d'Histoire Économique et Sociale, Paris, 1950. On factory system in Urals. Review article: E. Koutaissoff, Ec.Hist.Rev., 2nd ser., 4, 1951, 252-5.

BUILDING
See also 4.44. Further material (mainly on wages of building workers): for France 11.21,179; for Spain 11.63; for Italy 11.76.

9.640 **Goldthwaite**, R., The Building of Renaissance Florence, Baltmore, Md., 1981. Detailed study of construction industry in all its aspects from architect to labourer. Fifteenth-century emphasis. Review article: see 3.182.

9.641 —— 'The building of the Strozzi Palace. The construction industry in Renaissance Florence', Stud.Med.& Renaiss.Hist., 10, 1973, 99-194. Case study from research for previous entry.

9.642 **Sella**, D., Salari e Lavoro nell'Edilizia Lombarda durante il Secolo 17, Pavia, 1968. Draws mainly on sources from Milan and Pavia.

9.643 **Barkan**, O. L., 'L'organisation du travail d'une grande mosquée à Istanbul au 16e siècle', Annales, 17, 1962, 1093-1106.

GLASSMAKING
See also 6.246.

9.644 **Harris**, J. R., 'Saint-Gobain et Ravenhead', Rev.Hist.Éc.et Soc., 55, 1977, 359-407. Comparative study of leading French and British plate-glass manufactures, and their mutual technical influence. See also short study on St-Gobain by C. Pris, ib., 52, 1974, 161-72.

9.645 —— and Pris, C., 'The memoirs of Delauney Deslandres', Tech.& Culture, 17 1976, 201-16. Describes unpubl. memoir by manager of major French glassworks i eighteenth century.

9.646 **Scoville**, W. C., Capitalism and French Glassmaking, 1640-1789, Berkeley, Calif. 1950. Good technical and business history but not very informative about capitalism

9.647 **Ludloff**, R., 'Industrial development in sixteenth-seventeenth century Germany', P.& P., 12, 1957, 58-75. History of glassmaking in Hesse and Thuringia used to illustrate transition from craft to capitalist production.

9.648 **Klíma**, A., 'Glassmaking industry and trade in Bohemia in the seventeenth and eighteenth centuries', J.Eur.Ec.Hist., 13 1984, 499-520. Technical side of industri process is main concern.

SHIPBUILDING AND SEAFARING
See also 4.61-2,121 and 10.471 (general); and on France 9.292; the Netherlands 10.501; Spain 10.507,509; Italy 9.228.

9.649 **Cabantous**, A., La Mer et les Hommes. Pêcheurs et Matelots Dunkerquois de Louis XIV à la Révolution, Dunkirk, 1980. Engaging study of main seagoing métiers fishermen, pilots, merchant seamen, privateers (excluding captains and officer

9.650 —— La Vergue et les Fers. Mutins et Déserteurs dans la Marine de l'Ancienne France, Paris, 1984. Examines disconten aboard men-of-war and merchant vessels during the eighteenth century.

9.651 **Merrien**, J., La Vie Quotidienne des Mari au Temps du Roi Soleil, Paris, 1964. Ligh but knowledgable.

9.652 **Pritchard**, J., 'From shipwright to naval

constructor. The professionalization of eighteenth-century French naval shipbuilders', *Tech.& Culture*, 28, 1987, 1-25. On training of shipwrights for warship construction and reasons for French excellence in this field.

653 **Boxer**, C. R., 'The Dutch East-Indiamen. Their sailors, their navigators, and life on board, 1602-1795', *Mariner's Mirror*, 49, 1963, 81-104.

654 ——'Sedentary workers and seafaring folk in the Dutch Republic', in *Britain and the Netherlands*, 2 (6.116), 148-68. On contemporary perception of shortage of seamen in second half of eighteenth century.

655 **Bruijn**, J. R., and Eyck van Heslinga, E. S. van, 'Seamen's employment in the Netherlands (c.1600-c.1800)', *Mariner's Mirror*, 70, 1984, 7-20. Describes five areas of employment: merchant shipping (European and E. Indian zones), fishing, whaling, and state navy.

656 **Unger**, R. W., *Dutch Shipbuilding before 1800. Ships and Guilds*, Assen, 1978. Interesting material on labour practices of guilds from fifteenth century onwards.

657 ——'Regulations of Dutch shipcarpenters in the fifteenth and sixteenth centuries', *Tijd.Geschied.*, 87, 1974, 503-20.

658 ——'Technology and industrial organization. Dutch shipbuilding to 1800', *Bus.Hist.*, 17, 1975, 56-72.

659 **Boxer**, C. R., 'The *Carreira da India*, 1650-1750', *Mariner's Mirror*, 46, 1960, 35-54. Conditions on round voyage between Lisbon and Goa.

660 **Clayton**, L. A., 'Ships and empire. The case of Spain', *ib.*, 62, 1976, 235-48. Notes on ship-building industry of sixteenth and seventeenth centuries.

661 **Russell-Wood**, A. J. R., 'Seamen ashore and afloat. The social environment of the *Carreira da India*, 1550-1750', *ib.*, 69, 1983, 35-52.

662 **Lane**, F. C., 'Wages and recruitment of Venetian *galeotti*, 1470-1580', *Studi Veneziani*, n.s., 6, 1982, 15-43. Repr. in Lane (3.191). Deals with period in which wages and conditions of war fleets became very different from those of merchant fleet.

663 **Romano**, R., 'Economic aspects of the construction of warships in Venice in the sixteenth century', in Pullan (3.156), 59-87. General survey of operations of

Arsenal. With main focus on rather earlier period F. C. Lane's *Venetian Ships and Shipbuilders of the Renaissance*, Baltimore, Md., 1934, remains standard account of Arsenal and private shipyards.

9.664 **Olechnowitz**, K. F., *Der Schiffbau der Hansischen Spätzeit*, Weimar, 1960. Ship-building industry of Hanseatic ports in sixteenth and seventeenth centuries.

OTHER INDUSTRIES AND CRAFTS

9.665 **Kaplan**, S. L., 'The luxury guilds in Paris in the eighteenth century', *Francia*, 9, 1981, 257-98.

9.666 **Stürmer**, M., 'Economy of delight. Court artisans of the eighteenth century', *Bus.Hist.Rev.*, 53, 1979, 496-528. On status and freedom from guild restrictions enjoyed by producers of luxury goods for French and German aristocracy. See also somewhat fuller version, 'Luxusgüter in der Knappheitsgesellschaft. Handwerks-kultur und höfisches Leben im 18. Jahrhundert', *Francia*, 6, 1978, 319-65.

9.667 **Scholz**, Traute, 'Produktivkraft-entwicklung, Arbeitskräftestruktur, und betriebliche Lohnarbeitsverhältnisse in der Porzellanmanufaktur Meissen im 18. und 19. Jahrhundert', *Jb.Wirtschaftsgesch.*, 1981 (ii), 51-103.

9.668 **Sonenscher**, M., *The Hatters of Eighteenth-Century France*, Berkeley, Calif., 1987. Describes undermining of urban beaver-hat industry by rural makers using indigenous furs.

9.669 **Turnau**, Irena, 'Techniques and organization of leather production in Poland from the sixteenth to the eighteenth century', *J.Eur.Ec.Hist.*, 1, 1972, 661-9.

9.670 **Scoville**, W. C., 'Government regulation and growth in the French paper industry during the eighteenth century', *Am.Ec.Rev.*, 57, 1967, 283-93. Argues that state intervention was mainly impediment to growth.

9.671 **Chauvet**, P., *Les Ouvriers du Livre en France des Origines à la Révolution de 1789*, Paris, 1959. Large-scale work on conditions, techniques, and labour organisations, though with rather narrow perspective. See also 5.487; 9.525; 13.240; and 14.319; as well as extensive material on printing and book trade in Section 14.

10

STATE AND SOCIETY

POLITICAL SOCIOLOGY. STATE FORMATION. COURTS AND CLIENTAGE SYSTEMS

See also Section 6 for some material on aristocracies and the state; also 2.22; 14.240.

10.1 **Anderson**, P., *Lineages of the Absolutist State*, 1974. Argues that despite differing agrarian structures of East and West Europe, absolutism co-existed in both regions symbiotically with aristocratic privilege. Influential Marxist work, open like most such bold syntheses to charge of squeezing complex developments into Procrustean bed. Review articles: Betty Behrens, *Hist.J.*, 19, 1976, 245-50; R. Porter and C. R. Whittaker, *Soc.Hist.*, [1], no.3, 1976, 367-76; W. G. Runciman, *Arch.Eur.de Sociol.*, 21, 1980, 162-78; P. Q. Hirst, *Marxism and Historical Writing*, 1985, 91-125.

10.2 **Armstrong**, J. A., *Nations before Nationalism*, Chapel Hill, N.C., 1982. Seeks to identify forces which shaped distinct ethnic identities in Europe and Islamic world before consolidation of modern nation states.

10.3 **Batchelder**, R. W., and Freudenberger, H., 'On the rational origins of the modern centralized state', *Explor.Ec.Hist.*, 20, 1983, 1-13. Uses economic arguments to buttress view that gunpowder was basis of early modern trend towards bureaucratic state.

10.4 **Behrens**, C. Betty A., 'Government and society', in *Cambridge Economic History of Europe*, 5 (2.15), 549-620. Deals with social basis of governments, and their attitudes to welfare and economic development.

10.5 —— *Society, Government, and the Enlightenment. The Experiences of Eighteenth-Century France and Prussia*, 1985. Excellent study of bureaucracy, government finance, and economic policy in these contrasted states.

10.6 **Bendix**, R., *Kings or People. Power and the Mandate to Rule*, Berkeley, Calif., 1978. Sociologist's view of structures of authority from medieval times. Examines mainly Europe, but also Japan. Review articles: A. Pizzorno, *Ec.Dev.& Cultural Change*, 31, 1982, 198-204; J. M. Wiener, *Hist.& Theory*, 20, 1981, 68-83.

10.7 **Checkland**, S. G., 'Stages and the state. How do they relate?', in Kindleberger and Di Tella (2.43), 1, 44-67. Examines various theories of how political and economic systems are interrelated, from Adam Smith to Rostow and Wallerstein.

10.8 *Culture et Idéologie dans la Genèse de l'État Moderne*, Rome, 1985. Franco-Italian symposium, dealing mainly with ritual, symbolism, and propaganda of state power in late medieval and early modern Europe.

10.9 **Durand**, Y., ed., *Hommage à Roland Mousnier. Clientèles et Fidélités en Europe à l'Époque Moderne*, Paris, 1981. Collection of French essays on importance of patronage in early modern politics.

Though most deal with France, also contains papers on sixteenth-century Rome, Olivares' Spain, and late seventeenth-century Sweden.

10.10 **Eisenstadt**, S. N., *The Political Systems of Empires*, New York, 1963. Ambitious comparative work where absolutist Europe is considered alongside Rome, Byzantium, China, etc. Review article: R. M. Adams, *Ec.Dev.& Cultural Change*, 13, 1965, 245-8.

10.11 **Elias**, N., *The Civilizing Process, 2. State Formation and Civilization*, 1982. First publ. in German (Basel, 1939). Work by influential historical sociologist which charts emergence of "civilised" norms of political behaviour. For vol.1 which deals with behaviour in private intercourse, see 14.12.

10.12 —— *Court Society*, 1983. Transl. from German ed. of 1969. Has been starting point for much recent research on role of courts in setting tone of political and social life. Mainly takes example of French court of later Bourbons.

10.13 **Grew**, R., ed., *Crises of Political Development in Europe and the United States*, Princeton, N.J., 1978. Series of comparative national histories where contributors are invited to discuss how states have dealt with five central issues: national identity, crises of legitimacy, participation, centralisation, distribution of wealth.

10.14 **Gundersheimer**, W. L., 'Patronage in the Renaissance. An exploratory approach', in G. F. Lytle and S. Orgel, eds., *Patronage in the Renaissance*, Princeton, N.J., 1982, 3-23. Patron-client relationships seen as pervasive social feature of early modern history.

10.15 **Hartung**, F., and Mousnier, R., 'Quelques problèmes concernant la monarchie absolue', in *10 Congresso Internazionale di Scienze Storiche*, (7.91), 4, 3-55. Classic exploration. Partial transl. in S. B. Clough and others, eds., *The European Past. Reappraisals in History from the Renaissance through Waterloo*, New York, 1964, 276-82.

10.16 **Huntington**, S. P., *Political Order in Changing Societies*, New Haven, Conn., 1966. Another influential work of historical political sociology, ranging widely in period and geography.

10.17 **Kiernan**, V. G., 'State and nation in Western Europe', *P.& P.*, 31, 1965, 20-38. Attempts to identify social features which made North-Western Europe cradle of modern nationalistic states.

10.18 **Lane**, F. C., 'The economic consequences of organized violence', *J.Ec.Hist.*, 18, 1958, 401-17. Repr. in Lane (9.86), 412-28: this collection also contains earlier papers on theme of military and police functions of government viewed as "protection service" and hence element in economy. An overlapping collection of Lane reprints on subject is *Profits from Power. Readings in Protection Rent and Violence-Controlling Enterprises*, Albany, N.Y., 1979. See also N. Steensgaard, 'Violence and the rise of capitalism. F. C. Lane's theory of protection and tribute', *Review*, 5, 1981, 247-73.

10.19 **Larner**, J., 'Europe of the courts', *J.Mod.Hist.*, 55, 1983, 669-81. Reflections on how to approach historiography of "the court", prompted by dissatisfaction with first publications of an Italian research centre set up for its study.

10.20 **Raeff**, M., *The Well-Ordered Police State. Social and Institutional Change through Law in the Germanies and Russia, 1600-1800*, New Haven, Conn., 1983. Contrasts varying success of rulers in trying to create disciplined, production-orientated social fabric. See 10.57 for discussion of its Prussian dimension.

10.21 **Ranum**, O., ed., *National Consciousness, History, and Political Culture in Early Modern Europe*, Baltimore, Md., 1975. Essay collection in which most contributors agree that nationalism is not appropriate concept for this period and offer alternative views of prevailing political ethos. Contributors include F. Gilbert (Italy), W. F. Church (France), L. Krieger (Germany), M. Cherniavsky (Russia), H. Koenigsberger (Spain).

10.22 **Roosen**, W., 'Early modern diplomatic ceremonial. A systems approach', *J.Mod.Hist.*, 52, 1980, 452-76. On importance of ceremonial as indicator of national status, current state of relations, etc.

10.23 **Shennan**, J. H., *The Origins of the Modern European State, 1450-1725*, 1974. More concerned with mechanics than with social background.

10.24 **Šindelař**, B., ' "The bronze rock of state power" and its problems, *Historica*, 20, 1980, 59-94. Marxist typology of absolutism, placing "Tudor" and "Spanish" varieties at opposite poles according to whether they fostered or retarded bourgeois forces.

10.25 **Tilly**, C., ed., *The Formation of National States in Western Europe*, Princeton, N.J., 1975. Important collection, with long general essays on state formation by Tilly and S. Rokkan, and a number tackling more specific aspects (see 10.243,266,470; and 11.122).

FRANCE
See also 6.68,88; 10.5,9,12,279; 14.312.

10.26 **Beik**, W., *Absolutism and Society in Seventeenth-Century France. State Power and Provincial Aristocracy in Languedoc*, 1985. Contends that absolutism functioned most efficiently when privileges of local elite were safeguarded, and plays down "modernising" role.

10.27 'Fidelity and clientage in seventeenth-century France', *Fr.Hist.Stud.*, 14, 1986, 391-446. Linked articles by J. R. Major and Sharon Kettering (former discussing client relationships in "Revolt of 1620", latter those involved in Fronde).

10.28 **Greengrass**, M., 'Noble affinities in early modern France. The case of Henri I de Montmorency, Constable of France', *Eur.Hist.Q.*, 16, 1986, 275-311. Clientage system of powerful governor of Languedoc during Wars of Religion.

10.29 **Harding**, R., 'Corruption and the moral boundaries of patronage in the Renaissance', in Lytle and Orgel (10.14), 47-64. Deals with shadier side of social and political patronage in sixteenth- and early seventeenth-century France.

10.30 **Holt**, M. P., 'Patterns of *clientèle* and economic opportunity at court during the Wars of Religion. The household of François, Duke of Anjou', *Fr.Hist.Stud.*, 13, 1984, 305-22.

10.31 **Kettering**, Sharon, *Patrons, Brokers, and Clients in Seventeenth-Century France*, New York, 1986. Most thorough-going study to date on how political patronage worked under Richelieu, Mazarin, and Colbert, drawing on author's detailed knowledge of Provence in this period.

10.32 **Lefebvre**, P., 'Aspects de la "fidelité" en France au 17e siècle. Le cas des agents des princes de Condé', *Rev.Hist.*, 250, 1973, 59-106. Another case study of clientage as

practised by important political family.

10.33 **Levron**, J., *La Vie Quotidienne à la Cour de Versailles aux 17e et 18e Siècles*, Paris, 1980. Informative on mechanics of sustaining a court. On sixteenth-century court see R. J. Knecht, 'The court of Francis I', *Eur.Stud.Rev.*, 8, 1978, 1-22; and his *Francis I*, 1982.

10.34 **Lublinskaya**, Aleksandra D., *French Absolutism. The Crucial Phase, 1620-29*, 1968. Transl. from Russian ed. of 1965. Narrative work by Soviet historian, but with wide perspective in introductory chapters (some trenchant criticism of "general crisis" thesis). But see 10.37.

10.35 **Major**, J. R., 'The electoral procedure for the Estates-General of France, and its social implications, 1483-1651', *Medievalia et Humanistica*, 10, 1956, 131-50. Elections examined for light they throw on leadership of local communities and relations between orders.

10.36 **Mousnier**, R., 'The development of monarchical institutions and society in France', in Hatton (3.16), 37-54. Transl. from *Dix-Septième Siècle*, 58-59, 1963, 57-72. Seeks social causes of three major developments: disappearance of Estates-General, use of intendants, and formalisation of seigneurial system. This and other papers by Mousnier on state apparatus and on popular risings collected in *La Plume, La Faucille, et le Marteau. Institutions et Société en France du Moyen Age à la Révolution*, Paris, 1970.

10.37 **Parker**, D., 'The social foundation of French absolutism, 1610-30', *P.& P.*, 53, 1971, 67-89. Offers convincing attack on Lublinskaya's view (10.34) that Louis XIII's ministers worked in alliance with "capitalist bourgeoisie" to defeat feudal grandees and foster commerce.

10.38 **Ranum**, O., 'Courtesy, absolutism, and the rise of the French state, 1630-60', *J.Mod.Hist.*, 52, 1980, 426-51. Views etiquette and granting or withholding of certain courtesies as coercive political instruments, particularly as used by intendants.

10.39 **Root**, H. L., *Peasants and King in Burgundy. Agrarian Foundations of French Absolutism*, Berkeley, Calif., 1987. Argues that it was to political and fiscal convenience of old regime monarchy to promote village communalism against both seigneurial assertiveness and agrarian individualism.

0.40 **Wallace-Hadrill**, J. M., and McManners, J., eds., *France: Government and Society*, 1957. Lecture course intended to stress interactions throughout French history. Chapters on early modern period by C. A. J. Armstrong, Menna Prestwich, and J. S. Bromley.

LOW COUNTRIES

0.41 **Riemersma**, J. C., 'Economic enterprise and political powers after the Reformation', *Ec.Dev.& Cultural Change*, 3, 1955, 297-308. Explores relation between Dutch commercial success and political pluralism, in comparison with more centralist powers.

0.42 **Spierenburg**, P., 'Model prisons, domesticated elites, and the state. The Dutch Republic and Europe', in Rystad (5.254), 219-35. Development of prisons and spread of French etiquette both seen as aspects of stabilisation and order contributing to state formation (seventeenth and eighteenth centuries).

SPAIN AND ITALY
See also 10.9,446; and (on Venice) 6.160,167; 14.445; (on Milan) 6.151; (on Siena) 8.109.

10.43 **Maravall**, J. A., *Estado Moderno y Mentalidad Social, Siglos 15 a 17*, 2 vols., Madrid, 1972. Tries to relate early modern government of Spain to changes in social composition and attitudes.

10.44 **Kent**, F. W., and others, eds., *Patronage, Art, and Society in Renaissance Italy*, 1987. Includes four papers on political and ecclesiastical patronage in Medicean Florence.

10.45 **Trexler**, R. C., *Public Life in Renaissance Florence*, New York, 1980. Part 4 deals with innovations in civic ritual to incorporate new social groups in period 1470-1530. For review article see 3.182.

10.46 **Waquet**, J.-C., *De la Corruption. Morale et Pouvoir à Florence aux 17e et 18e Siècles*, Paris, 1984. Interesting study which maintains that corruption was not taken for granted and posed real moral problems for perpetrators.

10.47 **Chojnacki**, S., 'Political adulthood in fifteenth-century Venice', *Am.Hist.Rev.*, 91, 1986, 791-810. Explains some rites of passage inducting young men of patrician

class into political participation.

10.48 **Finlay**, R., *Politics in Renaissance Venice*, 1980. Strong on social dimension, with useful data on patriciate of late fifteenth-early sixteenth centuries.

10.49 —— 'The Venetian Republic as a gerontocracy. Age and politics in the Renaissance', *J.Med.& Renaiss.Stud.*, 8, 1978, 157-78. Suggests that election of old men was of a piece with Venice's ideals of prudent and unflamboyant government.

10.50 **Muir**, E., *Civic Ritual in Renaissance Venice*, Princeton, N.J., 1981. Argues that state art and pageantry grew more elitist and celebratory of patrician power.

10.51 —— 'Images of power. Art and pageantry in Renaissance Venice', *Am.Hist.Rev.*, 84, 1979, 16-52.

HOLY ROMAN EMPIRE AND SWITZERLAND
See also 6.173,183,191; 10.5; 13.152.

10.52 **Benecke**, G., 'Maximilian I and his subjects. Aspects of town, court, and countryside in Renaissance Austria, c.1500', *Hist.Sociale/Social Hist.*, 12, no.23, 1979, 5-36. Most substantial section is on economy of Emperor's court at Innsbruck. See also Benecke's book on Maximilian (3.256).

10.53 **Blickle**, P., *Landschaften im Alten Reich. Die Staatliche Funktion des Gemeinen Mannes in Oberdeutschland*, Munich, 1973. Deals with representative institutions in South Germany and Austria and inter-relationship of social and political trends. Interesting to compare with Carsten's older treatment of assemblies (see 10.54-5).

10.54 **Carsten**, F. L., *The Origins of Prussia*, 1954. Covers relations between rulers of Brandenburg and their Estates from fifteenth to seventeenth centuries.

10.55 —— *Princes and Parliaments in Germany*, 1959. Wider study of decline of representative assemblies from sixteenth century onwards, stressing especially weakness of towns and their hostility to nobility. Review article: J. Elliott, *P.& P.*, 17, 1960, 82-7.

10.56 **Ehalt**, H. C., *Ausdrucksformen Absolutistischer Herrschaft. Der Wiener Hof im 17. und 18. Jahrhundert*, Vienna, 1980. Investigation of social and political functions of etiquette and ceremonial at Habsburg court.

10.57 **Melton**, J. van H., 'Absolutism and "modernity" in early modern Central Europe', *Ger.Stud.Rev.*, 8, 1985, 383-98. Argues that Raeff's *Well-Ordered Police State* (10.20) exaggerates modernising features in Hohenzollern administration.

10.58 **Schlumbohm**, J., *Freiheit. Anfänge der Bürgerlichen Emanzipationsbewegung in Deutschland (c.1760-c.1800)*, Düsseldorf, 1975. Seeks to relate changes in concept of "freedom" to changing social structure.

10.59 **Wegert**, K. H., 'Patrimonial rule, popular self-interest, and Jacobinism in Germany, 1763-1800', *J.Mod.Hist.*, 53, 1981, 440-67. Argues that pluralism, deference to vested interests, and fear of popular resistance all tempered old regime governments, and that Jacobinism paradoxically removed obstacles to autocracy.

10.60 **Barber**, B. R., *The Death of Communal Liberty. A History of Freedom in a Swiss Mountain Canton*, Princeton, N.J., 1974. History of Graubünden canton, displaying boundless admiration for Swiss tradition of participatory democracy.

10.61 **Monter**, E. W., 'The structure of Genevan politics', in his *Studies in Genevan Government (1536-1605)*, Geneva, 1964, 85-115. Deals with changing social characteristics of Genevan magistrature.

EASTERN AND NORTHERN EUROPE
On Poland see 6.204,206. Other material on Ottoman Empire at 3.307; 6.207. On Sweden 10.9. On Russia 3.371; 6.217,227,233-4; 10.367.

10.62 **Werner**, E., 'Despotie, Absolutismus, oder feudale Zersplitterung. Strukturwandlungen im Osmanenreich zwischen 1566 und 1699', *Jb.Wirtschaftsgesch.*, 1972 (iii), 107-28. Argues that feudal decentralisation increased in seventeenth-century Turkey, contrary to European norm.

10.63 'The emergence of the modern state in the Scandinavian countries during the sixteenth and seventeenth centuries', *Scan.J.Hist.*, 10, 1985, 271-363. Articles by L. Jespersen, J. Lindegren, and Ø. Rian on power structure and resources of Denmark, Sweden, and Norway respectively. Adapted from papers in E. L. Petersen. ed., *Magstaten i Norden i 1600-Talet*, Odense, 1984.

10.64 **Lehtinen**, E., 'Notions of a Finnish national identity during the period of Swedish rule', *Scan.J.Hist.*, 6, 1981, 277-95.

10.65 **Løgstrup**, Birgit, 'The landowner as public administrator. The Danish model', *ib.*, 9, 1984, 283-312. Description of power of local squirearchy in period 1660-1848.

10.66 **Petersen**, E. L., and Jespersen, K. J. V., 'Two revolutions in early modern Denmark', in Kouri and Scott (4.93), 473-501. On social realities behind aristocratic constitution of 1536 and its overthrow in 1660.

10.67 **Roberts**, M., 'On aristocratic constitutionalism in Swedish history, 1520-1720', in Roberts (3.349), 14-55.

10.68 **Maczak**, A., 'The structure of power in the Commonwealth of the sixteenth and seventeenth centuries', in Fedorowicz and others (3.283), 109-34. Concentrates on the forces for decentralisation in Polish social structure.

10.69 **Cherniavsky**, M., *Tsar and People. Studies in Russian Myths*, New Haven, Conn., 1961. On the notion of "Holy Russia", mystical idealisation of rulers and nation .

10.70 **Crummey**, R. O., 'Court spectacles in seventeenth-century Russia. Illusion and reality', in D. C. Waugh, ed., *Essays in Honor of A. A. Zimin*, Columbus, Ohio, 1985, 130-58. With pictorial appendix depicting processions, receptions, etc.

10.71 **Dukes**, P., *The Making of Russian Absolutism, 1613-1801*, 1982. Useful new synthesis of political history.

10.72 **Esper**, T., 'Recent Soviet views of Russian absolutism', *Can.-Am.Slavic Stud.*, 6, 1972, 620-30. Summarises debate over social basis of absolutism in work of A. I. Avrekh, A. N. Chistozvonov, A. L. Shapiro, and others.

10.73 **Fedosov**, I. A., 'The social essence and evolution of Russian absolutism (eighteenth and first half of the nineteenth centuries)', *Soviet Stud.in Hist.*, 11 (i), 1972, 56-92.

10.74 **Keenan**, E. L., 'Muscovite political folkways', Russ.Rev., 45, 1986, 115-81. In line of those who stress continuity of repressive government in Russia (cf. Hellie (3.368) and Pipes (3.371)); political culture of pre-Petrine Muscovy seen as formative.

10.75 **Keep**, J. L. H., 'The Muscovite elite and the approach to pluralism', *Slavonic & E.Eur.Rev.*, 48, 1970, 201-31. Examines abortive tendencies among military and aristocratic elite to support more flexible political order in seventeenth century.

10.76 Kollmann, Nancy S., 'Ritual and social drama at the Muscovite court', *Slavic Rev.*, 45, 1986, 486-502. Principally on precedence disputes.

10.77 Nazarov, V. D., and others, 'Problems in the sociopolitical history of feudal Russia in current historiography', *Soviet Stud.in Hist.*, 17 (iii), 1979, 3-51.

10.78 Pelenski, J., 'State and society in Moscovite Russia, and the Mongol-Turkic system in the sixteenth century', *Forsch.Osteur.Gesch.*, 27, 1980, 156-67. Compares early Tsardom and khanate successors of Golden Horde.

10.79 Yaney, G. L., *The Systematization of Russian Government. Social Evolution in the Domestic Administration of Imperial Russia, 1711-1905*, Urbana, Ill., 1973. Early chapters deal with social base of eighteenth-century "senatorial" government. Review article: J. Keep, *Can.-Am.Slavic Stud.*, 8, 1974, 569-80.

ECONOMIC THOUGHT AND POLICY

See also 11.108-70 passim on policy with regard to food supplies; and 11.188-261 on changing attitudes to work and poverty. Other general references: 2.121; 9.9; 11.172; 13.180.

10.80 Fundaburk, Emma L., *The History of Economic Thought and Analysis. A Selective International Bibliography. Vol.1*, Metuchen, N.J., 1973. Very large-scale work. Useful sections are (E) "Countries and areas" and (H) "Pre-classical period". For less comprehensive but annotated bibliography see Chap.1 of W. K. Hutchinson, *History of Economic Analysis. A Guide to Information Sources*, Detroit, Mich., 1976.

10.81 Blitz, R. C., 'Mercantilist policies and the pattern of world trade, 1500-1750', *J.Ec.Hist.*, 27, 1977, 39-55. Argues that realities of trade and currency justified preoccupation with favourable balances.

10.82 Coleman, D. C., 'Eli Heckscher and the idea of mercantilism', *Scan.Ec.Hist.Rev.*, 5, 1957, 3-25. Repr. in D. C. Coleman, ed., *Revisions in Mercantilism*, 1969, 92-117. Reviewing revised ed. (1957) of Heckscher's pre-war classic, *Mercantilism*, argues that while this term may describe a trend in economic thought it is fairly useless as a guide to actual policies pursued. See also reply by A. W. Coats, *ib.*, 173-87; and 1.57-8, 10.153.

10.83 De Roover, R., 'Monopoly theory prior to Adam Smith', *Q.J.Ec.*, 65, 1951, 492-524. Repr. in De Roover (9.404), 273-305.

10.84 —— 'Scholastic economics. Survival and lasting influence from the sixteenth century to Adam Smith', *Q.J.Ec.*, 69, 1955, 161-90. Also repr. in 9.404, 306-35, with useful introductory article by J. Kirshner, 'Raymond de Roover on scholastic economic thought', 15-36. See also 10.86,90,94,97.

10.85 Ekelund, R. B., and Tollison, R. D., *Mercantilism as a Rent-Seeking Society. Economic Regulations in Historical Perspective*, College Station, Tex., 1981. Conceptual essay, in which state monopolies and regulations of early modern period are viewed as opportunities for extracting "rent".

10.86 Gordon, B., *Economic Analysis before Adam Smith*, 1975. Useful chapters on scholastic economics, 1300-1600, esp. work of Lessius (1554-1623).

10.87 Jones, E. L., 'Disaster management and resource saving in Europe, 1400-1800', in Maczak and Parker (4.44), 114-36. Examines evolution of measures to contain or combat epidemics and famines.

10.88 Klaveren, J. van, 'Fiscalism, mercantilism, and corruption', in Coleman (10.82), 140-61. Transl. from *VSWG*, 47, 1960, 333-53. Indicates how often restrictive regulations on trade served corrupt purposes of officials.

10.89 Morazé, C., 'The domestic policies of Frederick the Great, Catherine the Great, Maria Theresa, and Joseph II', in Clough (10.15), 375-94. Transl. from *Annales*, 3, 1948, 279-96. Argues that practical example (e.g. English sophistication in public finance), rather than precepts of *philosophes*, fuelled policies of despots.

10.90 Noonan, J. T., *The Scholastic Analysis of Usury*, Cambridge, Mass., 1957. Contains section on Catholic adaptation to legitimacy of interest during period 1450-1750. See also J. Brodrick, *The Economic Morals of the Jesuits. An Answer to H. M. Robertson*, 1934 (Robertson's *Aspects of the Rise of Economic Individualism*, 1933, had sought examples of Catholic association with capitalist enterprise to refute implications of Weber thesis).

10.91 **Pribram**, K., *A History of Economic Reasoning*, Baltimore, Md., 1983. Last work of distinguished Austrian economist. Useful sketch of what he terms "Baconian and Cartesian economics", 31-135.

10.92 **Rimlinger**, G. V., 'Welfare policy and economic development', *J.Ec.Hist.*, 26, 1966, 556-76. Sees welfare provision as investment in human capital dictated by increasing demand for maximally productive labour.

10.93 **Schaeffer**, R. K., 'The entelechies of mercantilism', *Scan.Ec.Hist.Rev.*, 29, 1981, 81-96. In plain English, its objectives. Looks at historiography of term mercantilism, and at differing national versions of it.

10.94 **Schumpeter**, J. A., *History of Economic Analysis*, 1954. By celebrated theorist of trade cycles and entrepreneurship. Section on pre-classical economics notable for favourable view of scholastic approach. See R. De Roover, 'Joseph A. Schumpeter and scholastic economics', *Kyklos*, 10, 1957, 115-43.

10.95 **Venturi**, F., *Utopia and Reform in the Enlightenment*, 1971. Important in turning study of Enlightenment from genealogy of ideas to its place in practical politics. See further his detailed work on Italian enlightenment (10.130).

10.96 **Viner**, J., 'Power versus plenty as objectives of foreign policy in the seventeenth and eighteenth centuries', *World Pol.*, 1, 1948, 1-29. Repr. in Coleman (10.82), 61-91. Argues falsity of view that mercantilism subordinated wealth creation to pursuit of power and glory.

10.97 —— 'Religious thought and economic society', *Hist.Pol.Ec.*, 10, 1978, 1-192. Four chapters from projected book left uncompleted —— of interest are chap.3 on secularising tendencies in Catholic social thought from Renaissance to Jansenists; and chap.4 on Protestantism and rise of capitalism (the Weber thesis).

10.98 **Wilson**, C. H., ' "Mercantilism" '. Some vicissitudes of an idea', *Ec.Hist.Rev.*, 2nd ser., 10, 1957, 181-8. Repr. in Wilson (3.83), 62-72. Reviews meanings attached to this term from Adam Smith to Heckscher.

10.99 —— 'Trade, society, and the state', in *Cambridge Economic History of Europe, 4* (2.15), 487-575. General sketch of economic thought from late scholasticism to Adam Smith.

10.100 —— 'Treasure and trade balances. The mercantilist problem', *Ec.Hist.Rev.*, 2nd ser., 2, 1949, 152-61. Repr. in F. C. Lane and J. C. Riemersma, eds., *Enterprise and Secular Change. Readings in Economic History*, 1953, 337-49. Qualified defence of mercantilist concern about bullion exports, illustrated from English trade position vis-à-vis Baltic region. See also debate with Eli Heckscher, *ib.*, 3, 1950, 219-28; 4, 1951, 231-42.

FRANCE AND THE LOW COUNTRIES
See also 3.16; 7.301-2; 9.444,458; 10.5,207; 11.318.

10.101 **Buisseret**, D., *Sully and the Growth of Centralized Government in France, 1598-1610*, 1968.

10.102 **Cole**, C. W., *Colbert and a Century of French Mercantilism*, 2 vols., New York, 1939. Still major work on commercial and industrial policy in seventeenth century (less concerned with finance). Largely subsumes his *French Mercantilist Doctrines before Colbert*, 1931.

10.103 **Fox-Genovese**, Elizabeth, *The Origins of Physiocracy. Economic Revolution and Social Order in Eighteenth-Century France*, Ithaca, N.Y., 1976. Adopts broad socio-political approach rather than analysis in terms of intellectual pedigrees. See also 10.109,113,116-17.

10.104 —— 'The physiocratic model and the transition from feudalism to capitalism', *J.Eur.Ec.Hist.*, 4, 1975, 725-37. Written as review of Marguerite Kuczynski's edition of Quesnay's economic works (Berlin, 1971).

10.105 **Harsin**, P., *Les Doctrines Monétaires et Financiers en France du 16e au 18e Siècle*, Paris, 1928. Remains valuable.

10.106 **Hauser**, H., *La Pensée et l'Action Économique du Cardinal de Richelieu*,

Paris, 1944.

10.107 **King**, J. E., *Science and Rationalism in the government of Louis XIV, 1661-83*, Baltimore, Md., 1949. Argues that Colbert's style of administrative and economic regulation displayed not only quest for national power and glory but also application of scientific outlook.

10.108 **McCloy**, S. T., *The Humanitarian Movement in Eighteenth-Century France*, Lexington, Ky., 1957. Deals with advocacy of reform in treatment of criminals, slaves, religious dissenters, etc., and actual progress made during Revolution.

10.109 **Meek**, R. L., *The Economics of Physiocracy. Essays and Translations*, 1962. Principal English-language account of physiocratic movement. Most exhaustive narrative account remains 10.117.

10.110 **Meyer**, J., *Colbert*, Paris, 1981. Relatively brief but up-to-date account. See also R. Mousnier, ed., *Un Nouveau Colbert*, Paris, 1985 (Papers of conference held for tricentenary of his death).

10.111 **Parker**, H. T., *The Bureau of Commerce in 1781 and its Policies with respect to French Industry*, Durham, N.C., 1979. Intended as preliminary to a study of Bureau of Manufactures (as it became) in Revolutionary and Napoleonic periods. Reviews eighteenth-century industrial policy fairly widely.

10.112 **Payne**, H. C., *The Philosophes and the People*, New Haven, Conn., 1976. Aspects of social thought and welfare policy under discussion during French Enlightenment.

10.113 **Remond**, A., 'Trois bilans de l'économie française au temps des théories physiocratiques', *Rev.Hist.Éc.et Soc.*, 35, 1957, 416-56. Examines three phases of economy between 1756 and 1781 in terms of physiocratic theories.

10.114 **Rothkrug**, L., *Opposition to Louis XIV. The Political and Social Origins of the French Enlightenment*, Princeton, N.J., 1965. History of seventeenth-century French thought about state, esp. its role in economic regulation. Emphasises both Christian and secularist opposition to aggressive mercantilism. Review article: Rosalie L. Colie, *Hist.& Theory*, 6, 1967, 270-4.

10.115 **Schaeper**, T. J., *The French Council of Commerce, 1700-15. A Study of Mercantilism after Colbert*, Columbus,

Ohio, 1983. Experiment in regulation of trade and industry by mixed body of government officials and merchant representatives.

10.116 **Spurlock**, Janis, 'What price economic prosperity? Public attitudes to physiocracy in the reign of Louis XVI', *Brit. J. Eighteenth-Cent.Stud.*, 9, 1986, 183-96. Continues account of reaction to free-trade measures exhaustively chronicled for earlier period by Kaplan (11.133).

10.117 **Weulersse**, G., *Le Mouvement Physiocratique en France de 1756 à 1770*, Paris, 1910. 2nd ed., 1968. Work completed by three further posthumously publ. vols.: *La Physiocratie à la Fin du Règne de Louis XV, 1770-74* (1959); *La Physiocratie sous les Ministères de Turgot et de Necker, 1774-81* (1950); *La Physiocratie à l'Aube de la Révolution, 1781-92* (1985).

10.118 **Wilson**, A. M., 'The *philosophes* in the light of present-day theories of modernization', *Stud.on Voltaire & Eighteenth-Cent.*, 58, 1967, 1893-1913. Repr. in C. E. Black, ed., *Comparative Modernization. A Reader*, New York, New York, 1976, 116-30. *Philosophes* seen as advocating conditions now considered essential ingredients of successful modernisation. For more formal model which argues that crucial element of mass participation is ignored, see Harriet B. Applewhite and Darlene G. Levy, 'The concept of modernization and the French Enlightenment', *ib.*, 84, 1971, 53-98.

10.119 **Davis**, W. W., *Joseph II, an Imperial Reformer for the Austrian Netherlands*, The Hague, 1974. Opening background chaps. useful, as well as those on economic and welfare proposals which so alienated vested interests in 1780s.

SPAIN AND PORTUGAL
See also 3.119, 132; 9.70,564-5; 10.130.

10.120 **Anes Alvarez**, G., *Economía e Ilustración en la España del Siglo 18*, Barcelona, 1969. Collected articles.

10.121 **Bitar Letayf**, M., *Economistas Españoles del Siglo 18. Sus Ideas sobre la Libertad de Comercio con Indias*, Madrid, 1968. Rather narrow view, with much quotation and paraphrase.

10.122 **Callahan**, W. J., 'A note on the *Real y General Junta de Comercio, 1679-1814*', *Ec.Hist.Rev.*, 2nd ser., 21, 1968, 519-28.

Considers institutional difficulties faced by this principal instrument of Bourbon economic policy.

10.123 **Grice-Hutchinson**, Marjorie, *Early Economic Thought in Spain, 1177-1740*, 1978. See also her earlier *The School of Salamanca. Readings in Spanish Monetary Theory, 1544-1605*, 1952.

10.124 **Martín Rodríguez**, M., *Pensamiento Económico Español sobre la Población*, Madrid, 1984. Charts persistent debate over assumed population decline, and remedies needed to increase employment and subsistence.

10.125 **Rodrıguez Díaz**, Laura, *Reforma e Ilustración en la España del 18 Siglo. Pedro Rodríguez de Campomanes*, Madrid, 1975. Architect of reform drive under Carlos III. For English-language account, not very satisfactory, see A. Hull, *Charles II and the Revival of Spain*, Washington, D.C., 1981.

10.126 **Shafer**, R. J., *The Economic Societies in the Spanish World, 1763-1821*, Syracuse, 1958. First section deals with societies formed in Spain; major part of book with societies of Havana and Guatemala. See also on societies as protagonists of reform C. J. Crowley, '*Luces* and *hispanidad*. Nationalism and modernization in eighteenth-century Spain', in M. Palumbo and W. O. Shanahan, eds., *Nationalism. Essays in Honor of Louis L. Snyder*, Westport, Conn., 1981, 87-102.

10.127 **Vilar Berrogain**, J., *Literatura y Economía. La Figura Satírica del Arbitrista en el Siglo de Oro*, Madrid, 1973. Standard account of political pamphleteers whose jeremiads lent force to picture of economic crisis in early seventeenth century.

ITALY
See also 3.155.

10.128 **Klang**, D. M., 'Reform and enlightenment in eighteenth-century Lombardy', *Can.J.Hist.*, 19, 1984, 39-70. Argues that advocates of economic growth and rationalisation envisaged leadership from public spirited nobles and bureaucrats rather than business class.

10.129 **Symcox**, G., *Victor Amadeus II. Absolutism in the Savoyard State, 1675-1730*, 1983. Some useful material on economic and social policy, though somewhat swamped by diplomatic issues.

10.130 **Venturi**, F., *Italy and the Enlightenment. Studies in a Cosmopolitan Century*, 1972. (Ed. by S. Woolf). Valuable, in this context, for three concluding essays (first publ. in *Riv.Stor.Ital.*, 74-5, 1962-63) on reform in Southern Italy and Papal States, and on Spanish and Italian economists. Venturi's major work, which has had great influence on historiography of eighteenth-century Italy, and sets Italian developments in wide European context, is *Settecento Riformatore*, 3 vols. to date, Turin, 1969-79.

HOLY ROMAN EMPIRE
See also 3.215,262-3; 7.198,207,213;
9.444,489,541; 10.5,336; 11.352; 13.152.

10.131 **Blaich**, F., *Die Wirtschaftspolitik des Reichstags im Heiligen Römischen Reich*, Stuttgart, 1970. Study of Imperial Diet as forum for reconciling (or failing to reconcile) economic interests.

10.132 **Bog**, I., *Der Reichsmerkantilismus. Studien zur Wirtschaftspolitik des Heiligen Römischen Reiches im 17. und 18. Jahrhundert*, Stuttgart, 1959. Principally deals with Leopold I's attempts to wage economic war on France of Louis XIV.

10.133 —— 'Mercantilism in Germany', in Coleman (10.82), 162-89. Transl. from *Jb.Nationalökonomie*, 173, 1961, 125-45. Emphasises growing preoccupation with internal economy of Empire, and tension between fiscal requirements and desire to stimulate trade.

10.134 **Braun**, H.-J., 'Economic theory and policy in Germany, 1750-1800', *J.Eur.Ec.Hist.*, 4, 1975, 301-22. Survey of "cameralism", on which most substantial works remain A. W. Small, *The Cameralists. The Pioneers of German Social Polity*, Chicago, 1909; and Louise Sommer, *Die Österreichischen Kameralisten*, 2 vols., Vienna, 1920-25.

10.135 **Dorwart**, R. A., *The Prussian Welfare State before 1740*, Cambridge, Mass., 1971. Poor relief, public health, education, etc., studied mainly from government ordinances —— evidence apt to be misleading, as anachronistic title perhaps suggests.

10.136 **Eulen**, F., *Vom Gewerbefleiss zur Industrie*, Berlin, 1967. Deals with eighteenth-century German publicists' works on virtues of industriousness and gradual linkage with modern connotations of industry.

10.137 **Freudenberger**, H., 'State intervention as an obstacle to economic growth in the Habsburg monarchy', *J.Ec.Hist.*, 27, 1967, 493-509. Period dealt with is eighteenth century. Sins of omission rather than commission are implied.

10.138 **Henderson**, W. O., *Studies in the Economic Policy of Frederick the Great*, 1963. Isolated essays on aspects of Prussian economy, rather than overall interpretation of policy.

10.139 **Ingrao**, C. W., *The Hessian Mercenary State. Ideas, Institutions, and Reform under Frederick II, 1760-85*, 1987. Wide-ranging study of social policy in principality of Hesse-Cassel. Hessian mercenaries (notoriously employed in American War of Independence) feature less prominently than title suggests.

10.140 —— 'The problem of "enlightened absolutism" and the German State', *J.Mod.Hist.*, 58, 1986, suppl., 161-80. See also article on same subject by E. Weis, *ib.*, 181-97.

10.141 **Kann**, R. A., *A Study in Austrian Intellectual History. From Late Baroque to Romanticism*, 1960. Contains lengthy essays on two principal reform thinkers, Abraham a Sancta Clara and Joseph von Sonenfels. On latter see also K.-H. Osterloh, *Joseph von Sonenfels und die Österreichische Reformbewegung...*, Lübeck, 1970.

10.142 **Komlos**, J., 'Institutional change under pressure. Enlightened government policy in the eighteenth-century Habsburg monarchy', *J.Eur.Ec.Hist.*, 15, 1986, 427-82. Main thesis is that Austrian state acted (with good deal of success) to relieve pressure on living standards brought about by population growth.

10.143 **Kraschewski**, H.-J., *Wirtschaftspolitik im Deutschen Territorialstaat des 16. Jahrhunderts*, Köln, 1978. Looks at management of small principality of Brunswick-Wolfenbüttel by Duke Julius (1528-89).

10.144 **Liebel**, Helen P., 'Laissez-faire vs. mercantilism. The rise of Hamburg, and the Hamburg bourgeoisie vs. Frederick the Great, 1763', *VSWG*, 52, 1965, 207-38. On growing importance of port of Hamburg, and its Patriotic Society's arguments against Prussian tariff policies. See next entry for more comprehensive work on this theme.

10.145 **Mittenzwei**, Ingrid, *Preussen nach dem Siebenjährigen Krieg. Auseinandersetzungen zwischen Bürgertum und Staat um die Wirtschaftspolitik*, Berlin, 1979. E. German account with surprisingly favourable view of Frederick II; principally concerns disagreements with mercantile community over freer trade policy. See also long article in *Jb.Gesch.Feudalismus*, 1, 1977, 349-99.

10.146 **Otruba**, G., *Die Wirtschaftspolitik Maria Theresias*, Vienna, 1963. Limited to period of 1760s and to German provinces; does not offer much discussion of effectiveness of decisions.

10.147 **Tennstedt**, F., *Sozialgeschichte der Sozialpolitik in Deutschland, vom 18. Jahrhundert bis zum Ersten Weltkrieg*, Göttingen, 1981. Excellent short account of transformation of concepts and organisation.

10.148 **Vann**, J. A., *The Making of a State. Württemberg, 1593-1793*, Ithaca, New York, 1984. Good material on ducal bureaucracy.

EASTERN AND NORTHERN EUROPE
On Scandinavia see also 7.235,246; 9.196,492-3. On Russia 3.366,383,386; 7.255,257; 9.135-6; 14.272.

10.149 **Lipinski**, E., *De Copernic à Stanislas Leszczynski. La Pensée Économique et Démographique en Pologne*, Paris, 1961. Valuable for information, though little interpretation.

10.150 **Inalcik**, H., 'The Ottoman economic mind and aspects of the Ottoman economy', in Cook (5.207), 207-18. Repr. in Inalcik (3.299). Deals briefly with fostering of trade and attitude towards guilds.

10.151 **Hutchinson**, E. P., 'Swedish population thought in the eighteenth century', *Pop.Stud.*, 13, 1959, 81-102. Set in wider context of political economy. See also 10.154.

10.152 **Magnuson**, L., 'Economic thought and group interests. Adam Smith, Christopher Polhem, Lars Salvius, and classical political economy', *Scan.J.Hist.*, 2, 1977, 243-64. Asks how far laissez-faire economic theory may have represented special interests, and finds that its representative figures in Sweden did so.

10.153 —— 'Eli Heckscher, mercantilism, and the favourable balance of trade', *Scan.Ec.Hist.Rev.*, 26, 1978, 103-27.

Argues for mercantilism, and its Swedish practice in particular, as rational response to conditions.

10.154 **Utterström**, G., 'Labour policy and population thought in eighteenth-century Sweden', *ib.*, 10, 1962, 262-79. Gives more positive account of policy and debate on labour questions by government and Estates than E. P. Hutchinson (10.151).

10.155 **Blanc**, Simone, 'The economic policy of Peter the Great', in Blackwell (3.362), 21-49. Transl. from *Cah.Monde Russe et Sov.*, 3, 1962, 122-39.

10.156 **Dmytryshyn**, B., 'The economic content of the 1767 *nakaz* of Catherine II', *Am.Slavic & E.Eur.Rev.*, 19, 1960, 1-9. Tsarina's long memorandum to Legislative Commission, replete with "enlightened" views.

10.157 **Griffiths**, D. M., 'Eighteenth-century perceptions of backwardness. Projects for the creation of a Third Estate in Catherinean Russia', *Can.-Am.Slavic Stud.*, 13, 1979, 452-72.

10.158 **Letiche**, J. M., ed., *A History of Russian Economic Thought, Ninth through Eighteenth Centuries*, Berkeley, Calif., 1964. Transl. of collaborative work by A. I. Poshkov and others (1955), forming vol.1 of history of economic thought sponsored by U.S.S.R. Academy of Sciences.

10.159 **Lewitter**, L. R., 'Ivan Tikhonovich Pososhkov (1652-1726) and the "spirit of capitalism" ', *Slavonic & E.Eur.Rev.*, 51, 1973, 524-53. Gives wide background on traditional Russian ethics of wealth, as well as analysis of Pososhkov's *Poverty and Wealth* (1724). See also his lengthy introduction to edition of this work (with A. P. Vlasto), 1987.

TAXATION AND PUBLIC FINANCE
See also 9.401-38 for some material on public banks; and 11.1-101 for works on coinage and monetary policy.

10.160 **Ardant**, G., *Théorie Sociologique de l'Impôt*, 2 vols., Paris, 1965. Lengthy treatise on importance of taxation policies in shaping social and political institutions; contains much historical material. Review article: M. J. MacLeod, *Peasant Stud.Newsl.*, 4 (iii), 1975, 2-6. See also useful distillation of book, 'Financial policy and economic infrastructure of modern states and nations', in Tilly (10.25), 164-242.

10.161 **Bouvier**, J., and Perrot, J. C., eds., *États, Fiscalités, Économies. Actes du 5e Congrès de l'Association Française des Historiens Économistes*, Paris, 1985. Contains three papers on early modern French finances; and others on Austria and Venice.

10.162 **Buist**, M. G., 'The sinews of war. The role of Dutch finance in European politics (c.1750-1815)', in A. C. Duke and C. A. Tamse, eds., *Britain and the Netherlands, 6*, The Hague, 1977, 124-40. Loans to governments raised on Amsterdam capital market. See also 10.165.

10.163 **De Maddalena**, A., and Kellenbenz, H., eds., *Finanze e Ragion di Stato in Italia e in Germania nella Prima Età Moderna*, Bologna, 1984. Papers delivered at Italo-German conference, dealing mainly with political and constitutional aspects of public finance.

10.164 *La Fiscalité et ses Implications Sociales en Italie et en France aux 17e et 18e Siècles*, Rome, 1980. Miscellany (in Italian and French), mostly on workings of tax system or on financial officials.

10.165 **Riley**, J. C., *International Government Finance and the Amsterdam Capital Market, 1740-1815*, 1980. Investigates why Dutch investors were so ready to lend to untrustworthy foreign governments. See also 10.162.

10.166 **Waquet**, J.-C., 'Who profited from the alienation of public revenues in ancient regime societies. The examples of France, Piedmont, and Naples in the seventeenth and eighteenth centuries', *J.Eur.Ec.Hist.*, 11, 1982, 665-73. Introductory conference paper on social background of state creditors and tax-farmers.

FRANCE
See also 3.38; 6.13,18,56,101;
10.105,161,164,166,372,388,411-12; 12.33,45.

10.167 **Antoine**, M., 'L'administration centrale des finances de France du 16e au 18e siècle', in his *Le Dur Métier de Roi*, Paris, 1986, 31-60. Succinct summary of evolution of state financial apparatus.

10.168 —— 'Les Conseils des Finances sous le règne de Louis XV', *Rev.Hist.Mod.et Contemp.*, 5, 1958, 161-200.

10.169 —— 'Le régalement des tailles de 1623-25', *Rev.Hist.*, 265, 1981, 27-63. On mechanism of re-assessing tax dues.

10.170 **Bonney**, R. J., 'The failure of the French revenue farms, 1600-60', *Ec.Hist.Rev.*, 2nd ser., 32, 1979, 11-32. Seeks to explain why amalgamated farms tended to be more unprofitable than small-scale leases.

10.171 —— *The King's Debts. Finance and Politics in France, 1589-1661*, 1981. Attempts to make statistical sense of complicated revenue system, and to relate state of finances to domestic and foreign policy.

10.172 **Bosher**, J. F., 'Financing the French Navy in the Seven Years' War. Beaujon, Goossens, et Compagnie in 1759', *Bus.Hist.*, 28 (iii), 1986, 115-33. Episode showing growing tendency to involve merchant bankers in public finance (to their ruin in this case).

10.173 —— 'The French crisis of 1770', *History*, 57, 1972, 17-30.

10.174 —— *The Single Duty Project. A Study of the Movement for a French Customs Union in the Eighteenth Century*, 1964.

10.175 **Bouloiseau**, M., 'Une enquête de Calonne. Taillables et privilégiés en Haute-Normandie (1787)', *Fr.Hist.Stud.*, 7, 1972, 503-28.

10.176 **Charmeil**, J. P., *Les Trésoriers de France à l'Époque de la Fronde. Contribution à l'Histoire de l'Administration Financière sous l'Ancien Régime*, Paris, 1964. Useful for its material on social position and professional solidarity of financial Robe as well as administrative detail.

10.177 **Chaussinand-Nogaret**, G., *Les Financiers de Languedoc au 18e Siècle*, Paris, 1970. Many of this provincial group had national or even international links.

10.178 —— *Gens de Finance au 18e Siècle*, Paris, 1972. Brief. General description of public finance system, with one chap. on social background of financiers.

10.179 **Dent**, J., *Crisis in Finance. Crown, Financiers, and Society in Seventeenth-Century France*, 1973. Includes computer survey of social background and links of hundreds of men involved in financial administration and tax-farming system. Compare Dessert (10.182). See also following articles arising from research.

10.180 —— 'An aspect of the crisis of the seventeenth century. The collapse of the financial administration of the French monarchy, 1653-61', *Ec.Hist.Rev.*, 2nd ser., 20, 1967, 241-56.

10.181 —— 'The role of clientèles in the financial élite of France under Cardinal Mazarin', in Bosher (6.104), 41-69.

10.182 **Dessert**, D., *Argent, Pouvoir, et Société au Grand Siècle*, Paris, 1985. Shows how highly placed were financiers and receivers who dealt in state revenues (short biographies of several hundred *traitants* given in appendix). Compare Dent (10.179).

10.183 —— 'Finances et société au 17e siècle. À propos de la Chambre de Justice de 1661', *Annales*, 29, 1974, 847-81. Enquiry that led to fall of Fouquet provides one example of thesis in previous entry. Dessert attempts partial rehabilitation of minister in recent biography, *Fouquet*, Paris, 1987.

10.184 **Durand**, Y., *Les Fermiers Généraux au 18e Siècle*, Paris, 1971. All-round study of major tax-farmers. Condensed version publ. as *Finance et Mécénat. Les Fermiers Généraux au 18e Siècle*, Paris, 1976. Compare 10.195.

10.185 **Faure**, E., *La Banqueroute de Law, 17 Juillet, 1720*, Paris, 1977. Assessment of Law's "system" by politician with practical experience of public finance. On Law see also 10.201.

10.186 **Hamilton**, E. J., 'The political economy of France at the time of John Law', *Hist.Pol.Ec.*, 1, 1969, 123-49.

10.187 **Harris**, R. D., 'French finances and the American War, 1777-83', *J.Mod.Hist.*, 48, 1976, 233-58.

10.188 —— 'Necker's *Compte rendu* of 1781. A reconsideration', *ib.*, 42, 1970, 161-83. Tries to assess accuracy of this celebrated presentation of public accounts of Necker's ministry. See also Harris' general account, *Necker, Reform Statesman of the Ancien Régime*, Berkeley, Calif., 1979.

10.189 **Hickey**, D., *The Coming of French Absolutism. The Struggle for Tax Reform in the Province of Dauphiné, 1540-1640*, Toronto, 1986. Argues that central government's intervention in provincial affairs resulted from Third Estate pressure for tax reform rather than ministerial initiative.

10.190 **Hincker**, F., *Les Français devant l'Impôt sous l'Ancien Régime*, Paris, 1971. Useful short synthesis, with documents.

10.191 **Hoffman**, P. T., 'Taxes and agrarian life in early modern France. Land sales, 1550-1730', *J.Ec.Hist.*, 46, 1986, 37-55. Argues that tax exemptions of privileged fuelled large-scale transfer of land from peasantry to aristocracy of wealth. Cf. Italian case-study of this phenomenon, 10.237.

10.192 **Jennings**, R. M., and Trout, A. P., 'Internal control. Public finance in seventeenth-century France', *J.Eur.Ec.Hist.*, 1, 1972, 647-60. Deals with Paris *rentes* during Colbert's ministry.

10.193 **Ligou**, D., 'Un impôt en Bourgogne sous l'ancien régime. Les vingtièmes', *Actes Congrès Nat.Soc.Savantes*, 91 (ii), 1966, 184-215. Questions whether this eighteenth-century tax was assessed more equitably than personal *taille*.

10.194 **Mathias**, P., and O'Brien, P., 'Taxation in Britain and France, 1715-1810. A comparison of the social and economic incidence of taxes collected for the central governments', *J.Eur.Ec.Hist.*, 5, 1976, 601-50. Revisionist article which concludes that taxation was lighter and less socially regressive in France than in Britain. View challenged by D. N. McCloskey, *ib.*, 7, 1978, 209-13.

10.195 **Matthews**, G. T., *The Royal General Farms in Eighteenth-Century France*, New York, 1958. Basic work on tax-farming system. Lacks social dimension of Durand's work (10.184).

10.196 **Meuvret**, J., 'Fiscalism and public opinion under Louis XIV', in Hatton (3.16), 199-225.

10.197 **Michaud**, C., 'Notariat et sociologie de la rente à Paris au 17e siècle. L'emprunt du clergé de 1690', *Annales*, 32, 1977, 1154-79. Analyses investors in loan floated by clergy as part of its tax obligations.

10.198 **Morineau**, M., 'Budgets de l'État et gestion des finances royales en France au 18e siècle', *Rev.Hist.*, 264, 1980, 289-336. Finds that disorder of financial system has been exaggerated.

10.199 **Ravitch**, N., 'The taxing of the clergy in eighteenth-century France', *Church Hist.*, 33, 1964, 157-74. Explains incidence of taxation on and within clergy.

10.200 **Riley**, J. C., 'French finances, 1727-68', *J.Mod.Hist.*, 59, 1987, 209-43. Joins Morineau (10.198) in trying to put figures back into French budgets, this time from foreign sources.

10.201 **Sallon**, M. A., 'L'échec de Law', *Rev.Hist.Éc.et Soc.*, 48, 1970, 145-95. Finds much to admire in Law's ideas. See also 10.185.

10.202 **Schnapper**, B., *Les Rentes au 16e Siècle*, Paris, 1957. Examination of various kinds of rent, especially those used to finance municipal public debt.

10.203 **Sturgill**, C. C., 'Observations on the French Ministry of War budget, 1720-29', *Proc.Western Soc.Fr.Hist.*, 11, 1983, 100-10.

10.204 **Temple**, Nora, 'The control and exploitation of French towns during the ancien régime', *History*, 51, 1966, 16-34. Mainly on importance of municipal taxation in general scheme of public finance.

10.205 **Van Doren**, L. S., 'War taxation, institutional change, and social conflict in provincial France. The royal *taille* in Dauphiné, 1494-1559', *Proc. Am. Phil. Soc.*, 121, 1977, 70-96.

10.206 **Villain**, J., *Le Recouvrement des Impôts Directs sous l'Ancien Régime*, Paris, 1952. Rather restricted and institutional approach.

10.207 **Wolfe**, M., *The Fiscal System of Renaissance France*, New Haven, Conn., 1972. Clear exposition, extending from mid-fifteenth century to Richelieu's ministry. See also his 'French views on wealth and taxes from the Middle Ages to the Old Regime', *J.Ec.Hist.*, 26, 1966, 466-83, repr. in Coleman (10.82), 190-209.

LOW COUNTRIES
See also 10.162,165.

10.208 **Aalbers**, J., 'Holland's financial problems (1713-33) and the wars against Louis XIV', in *Britain and the Netherlands*, 6 (10.162), 79-93. Examines constraints imposed by burden of debt from wars of 1672-1713.

10.209 **Tracy**, J. D., *A Financial Revolution in the Netherlands. Renten and Renteniers in the County of Holland, 1515-65*, Berkeley, Calif., 1985. Municipal and States bonds and their purchasers; Tracy sees this as one of earliest examples of public debt funded on future revenues of entire province.

10.210 **Wilson**, C. H., 'Taxation and the decline of empires. An unfashionable theme', in Wilson (3.83), 114-27. Considers whether decline of Dutch power in the eighteenth century may have owed something to over-taxation. Theme now rather more in fashion.

SPAIN AND PORTUGAL
See also 3.121,150; 6.123; 9.71,417-18.

10.211 **Artola**, M., *La Hacienda del Antiguo Régimen*, Madrid, 1982. Major attempt at synthesising history of public finance from 1590 onwards.

10.212 **Carande**, R., *Carlos V y sus Banqueros*, 3 vols., Madrid, 1943-67. Revised ed. of vol.1, 1965. Vol.1 (introductory) forms virtually general history of population and economy; vol.2 covers institutions of public finance; vol.3 exploitation of American treasure as backing for state loans.

10.213 **Cepeda Adán**, J., 'Desamortización de tierras de las ordenes militares en el reinado de Carlos I', *Hispania*, 146, 1980, 487-528. Appropriation and sale of ecclesiastical property for state finances, 1537-51 – early example of long process of disentailment.

10.214 **Domínguez Ortiz**, A., *Política Fiscal y Cambio Social en la España del Siglo 17*, Madrid, 1984. Brief survey of public finance.

10.215 —— *Política y Hacienda de Felipe IV*, Madrid, 1960. Basic work on financing of Spain's part in Thirty Years War.

10.216 **Flynn**, D., 'Fiscal crisis and the decline of Spain (Castile)', *J.Ec.Hist.*, 42, 1982, 139-47. Short conference paper arguing that it was scale of profits from mining bullion, rather than quantities shipped, that first sustained and then failed Spanish Crown.

10.217 **Ladero Quesada**, M. A., *La Hacienda Real de Castilla en el Siglo 15*, La Laguna, 1973. Deals in turn with various sources of revenue.

10.218 **Lovett**, A. W., 'The account of Francisco de Lixalde', *Tijd.Geschied.*, 95, 1982, 163-78. Throws light on chaotic financing of early stages of action against Dutch rebels.

10.219 —— 'The Castilian bankruptcy of 1575', *Hist.J.*, 23, 1980, 899-911. Story continued in 'The general settlement of 1577', *ib.*, 25, 1982, 1-22.

10.220 **Moxo**, S. de, *La Alcabala. Sobre sus Orígines, Concepto, y Naturaleza*, Madrid, 1963. Principal Spanish excise tax.

10.221 **Ruiz Martín**, F., 'Las finanzas españolas

durante el reinado de Felipe II', *Cuadernos de Hist.*, 2, 1968, 109-73. Casts new light on Philip's unsuccessful attempts to "Castilianise" sources of loan finance on French model.

10.222 **Stewart**, P., 'The soldier, the bureaucrat, and fiscal records in the army of Ferdinand and Isabella', *Hisp.Am.Hist.Rev.*, 49, 1969, 281-92. Describes efforts to develop centralised bureaucratic control over military expenditure.

10.223 **Ulloa**, M., *La Hacienda Real de Castilla en el Reinado de Felipe II*, Rome, 1963. 2nd ed., Madrid, 1977. Standard work on Philip II's revenues from Castile. But see also 10.221.

ITALY
See also 10.164,166; 9.422 (Milan); 9.427 and 10.161 (Venice); 6.30 (Naples).

10.224 **Bueno de Mesquita**, D. M., 'The *deputati del denaro* in the government of Ludovico Sforza', in C. H. Clough, ed., *Cultural Aspects of the Italian Renaissance. Essays in honour of P. O. Kristeller*, 1976, 276-98. Fairly short-lived organisation for controlling state finances in late fifteenth-century Milan.

10.225 **Capra**, C., 'Riforme finanziarie e mutamento istituzionale nello Stato di Milano. Gli anni sessanta del secolo 18', *Riv.Stor.Ital.*, 91, 1979, 313-68.

10.226 **Klang**, D. M., *Tax Reform in Eighteenth-Century Lombardy*, Boulder, Colo., 1977.

10.227 **Vigo**, G., *Fisco e Società nella Lombardia del Cinquecento*, Bologna, 1979. Principally on principles and mechanisms of asessment.

10.228 **Stumpo**, E., *Finanza e Stato Moderno nel Piemonte del Seicento*, Rome, 1979.

10.229 **Dal Pane**, L., *La Finanza Toscana dagli Inizi del Secolo 18 alla Caduta del Granducato*, Milan, 1965.

10.230 **Marks**, L. F., 'The financial oligarchy in Florence under Lorenzo', in Jacob (6.151), 123-47. Deals with manipulation of *Monte Commune*, principal instrument of public finance.

10.231 **Bullard**, Melissa, *Filippo Strozzi and the Medici. Favour and Finance in Sixteenth-Century Florence and Rome*, 1980. Study of papal finances under Medici popes, and Strozzi's asset-stripping manipulation of Florentine funds on their behalf.

10.232 **Caravale**, M., *La Finanza Pontificia nel*

Cinquecento. Le Province del Lazio, Naples, 1974. Covers whole century. For case-study see 10.235.

10.233 **Partner**, P., 'The "budget" of the Roman Church in the Renaissance period', in Jacob (6.151), 256-78. Study of papal finances, c. 1420-1520.

10.234 —— 'Papal financial policy in the Renaissance and Counter-Reformation', *P.&P.*, 88, 1980, 17-62. Surveys income and expenditure of Curia, and workings of financial administration.

10.235 **Rotelli**, C., 'La finanza locale pontificia nel Cinquecento. Il caso di Imola', *Studi Stor.*, 9, 1968, 107-44.

10.236 **De Maddalena**, A., *Le Finanze del Ducato di Mantova all'Epoca di Guglielmo Gonzaga*, Milan, 1961. Good case study of economic management of small principality in later sixteenth century.

10.237 **Ferraro**, Joanne M., 'Feudal-patrician investments in the Bresciano, and the politics of the *Estimo*, 1426-1641', *Studi Veneziani*, n.s., 7, 1983, 31-57. Sees tax evasion by magnates as one means by which large estates were built up at cost of smaller proprietors.

10.238 **Ajello**, R., 'Il Banco di San Carlo. Organi di governo e opinione pubblica nel Regno di Napoli di fronte al problema della ricompra dei diritti fiscali', *Riv.Stor.Ital.*, 81, 1969, 812-81. On failure of state bank intended to resume alienated revenues (1725-33). See also preceding article by A. Di Vittorio on Neapolitan monetary and banking problems, *ib.*, 778-811.

10.239 **Mantelli**, R., *Burocrazia e Finanze Pubbliche nel Regno di Napoli a Metà del Cinquecento*, Naples, 1981. Based on records of extensive enquiry held over years 1559-64.

10.240 **Muto**, G., *Le Finanze Pubbliche Napolitane tra Riforme e Restaurazione (1520-1634)*, Naples, 1980. Brings out compromise between imperial standardisation and local institutions which Spanish administration had to forge.

HOLY ROMAN EMPIRE AND SWITZERLAND

See also 3.227; 5.626-7,633; 9.105; 10.161.

10.241 **Bérenger**, J., *Finances et Absolutisme Autrichien dans la Seconde Moitié du 17e Siècle*, Paris, 1975.

10.242 —— 'Public loans and Austrian policy in the second half of the seventeenth century', *J.Eur.Ec.Hist.*, 2, 1973, 657-69. Deals mainly with loan raised in 1665 for acquisition of Silesian dukedoms by Emperor.

10.243 **Braun**, R., 'Taxation, socio-political structure, and state-building. Great Britain and Brandenburg-Prussia', in Tilly (10.25), 243-327.

10.244 **Dickson**, P. G. M., *Finance and Government under Maria Theresia, 1740-80*, 2 vols., 1987. Magisterial account. Stresses importance of drive to finance standing army, and competition with nobility to tax peasant resources.

10.245 **Dollinger**, H., *Studien zur Finanzreform Maximilians I von Bayern in den Jahren 1598-1618*, Göttingen, 1969. Rather over-detailed account of Maximilian's succession and early years, with huge apparatus of notes.

10.246 **Ernstberger**, A., *Hans de Witte, Finanzmann Wallensteins*, Wiesbaden, 1954. Throws light on business opportunities provided by chaotic Imperial finances during Thirty Years' War. For review article see 10.483.

10.247 **Harnisch**, H., 'Gemeindeeigentum und Gemeindefinanzen im Spätfeudalismus', *Jb.Regionalgesch.*, 8, 1981, 126-74. Local community finance, examples mainly drawn from Saxony and Brandenburg.

10.248 **Holl**, B., *Hofkammerpräsident Graf Starhemberg und die österreichische Finanzpolitik der Barockzeit, 1703-15*, Vienna, 1976. Detailed study of pressures of prolonged war on Austrian public credit system.

10.249 **Eisenmann**, E., 'Reichsfinanzen und Reichssteuern im 15. Jahrhundert', *Zeitschr.Hist.Forschung*, 7, 1980, 129-218.

10.250 **Klein**, E., *Geschichte der öffentlichen Finanzen in Deutschland, 1500-1870*, Wiesbaden, 1974. Short text-book survey of public finance in major German states.

10.251 **Körner**, M. H., *Solidarités Financières Suisses au 16e Siècle*, Lausanne, 1980. Major work dealing with monetary history, municipal finance and banking, and (whence title) financial cooperation between cantons.

10.252 **Krüger**, Kersten, *Finanzstaat Hessen, 1500-67. Staatsbildung im Übergang vom Domänenstaat zum Steuerstaat*, Marburg, 1980. Solid study of moves towards more sophisticated (and onerous) state financial system.

10.253 **Monter**, E. W., 'Genevan public finance', in Monter (10.61), 9-56. Concentrates on sixteenth century.

10.254 **Schnee**, H., *Die Hoffinanz und der Moderne Staat. Geschichte und System der Hoffaktoren an Deutschen Fürstenhöfen im Zeitalter des Absolutismus*, 6 vols., Berlin, 1953-67. Enormously detailed study of Jewish court financiers of seventeenth and eighteenth centuries.

EASTERN AND NORTHERN EUROPE
On Hungary see 8.142. On Ottoman lands see also 3.304;10.527; and 11.162.

10.255 **Berindei**, M., and Veinstein, G., 'Règlements fiscaux et fiscalité de la province de Bender-Aqkerman, 1570', *Cah.Monde Russe et Sov.*, 22, 1981, 251-328. Structure of taxation in Turkish-occupied Moldavia.

10.256 **Di Vittorio**, A., *Finanze e Moneta a Ragusa nell'Età delle Crisi*, Naples, 1983. Concentrates on public finance during "long seventeenth century", but also gives broad picture of commercial cycles affecting republic.

10.257 **Hildebrand**, K.-G., 'Public finance and the national economy in early sixteenth-century Sweden', *Scan.Ec.Hist.Rev.*, 7, 1959, 95-106. Review of Swedish work by Ingrid Hammarström on early Vasa financial policy (*Finansförvaltning och Varuhandel, 1504-40*, Uppsala, 1956).

10.258 **Petersen**, E. L., 'From domain state to tax state', *Scan.Ec.Hist.Rev.*, 23, 1975, 116-48. Study of Danish Crown revenues in sixteenth and seventeenth centuries.

10.259 —— 'War, finance, and the growth of absolutism. Some aspects of the European integration of seventeenth-century Denmark', in Rystad (5.254), 33-49. Sees transformation from demesne finance to general taxation as process of conforming to European political norm.

10.260 **Ansimov**, E., 'Il contenuto sociale della riforma tributaria di Pietro I', *Riv.Stor.Ital.*, 97, 1985, 452-500. On implications of change to "souls" rather than "hearths" as basis of Russian tax assessment in 1720s.

10.261 **Bushkovitch**, P., 'Taxation, tax-farming, and merchants in sixteenth-century Russia', *Slavic Rev.*, 37, 1978, 373-98. Establishes considerable importance of sales taxes and their farmers but can provide little information on merchants involved.

10.262 **Kashtanov**, S. M., 'The centralised state and feudal immunities in Russia', *Slavonic & E.Eur.Rev.*, 49, 1971, 235-54. On ineffective attempts to lessen fiscal immunities in fifteenth and sixteenth centuries.

10.263 **Ledonne**, J. P., 'Indirect taxes in Catherine's Russia. 1: The salt code of 1781. 2: The liquor monopoly', *Jb.Gesch.Osteuropas*, 23, 1975, 161-90; 24, 1976, 173-207.

BUREAUCRATS AND LAWYERS. THE ADMINISTRATIVE ELITE
See also material on financial bureaucracy in previous sub-section. Also 5.594; 10.476; 11.173; 13.48; 14.2.

10.264 **Armstrong**, J.A., *The European Administrative Elite*, Princeton, N.J., 1973. Longitudinal study of recruitment, ethics, outlook, and career patterns, with early modern conditions treated on comparative basis.

10.265 'Old Regime governors. Bureaucratic and patrimonial attributes', *Comp.Stud.in Soc.& Hist.*, 14, 1972, 2-29. Comparison of French intendants (c. 1660-1789) and Russian *gubernatory* (c. 1760-1880) in terms of five characteristics held to distinguish

bureaucratic approach to office-holding from that based on family connections, local influence, etc.

10.266 **Fischer**, W., and Lundgreen, P., 'The recruitment and training of administrative and technical personnel', in Tilly (10.25), 456-561.

10.267 **Hintze**, O., 'The commissary and his significance in general European history', in Hintze (6.183), 267-301. Essay of lasting interest, first publ. (in German) in 1919.

10.268 —— 'The origins of the modern ministerial

system. A comparative study', *ib.*, 218-66.
Transl from *Hist.Zeitschr.*, 100, 1908,
53-111. Traces evolution of departments of
state from court officials and general
purpose councils.

10.269 **Malettke**, K., ed., *Ämterkäuflichkeit.
Aspekte Sozialer Mobilität im
Europäischen Vergleich (17.und 18.
Jahrhundert)*, Berlin, 1980. Essays (in
French and German) covering aspects of
venality of public office in France, Spain,
England, and Germany. Contributors
include R. Mousnier, F. Bluche, H.
Möller. For further material on this
subject note esp. 10.270,284,289,305,315.

10.270 **Swart**, K. W., *Sale of Offices in the
Seventeenth Century*, The Hague, 1949.
Valuable, though rather brief, comparative
treatment - with glance towards China and
Ottoman Empire as well as Western
Europe.

FRANCE

*See also 6.74,82; 10.265,396; 12.50;
13.314-15,375,382-3.*

10.271 **Baxter**, D. C., *The commissaires des guerres
in the 1660s'*, *Proc.Western Soc.Fr.Hist.*,
11, 1983, 91-9.

10.272 —— *Servants of the Sword. French
Intendants of the Army, 1630-70*, Urbana,
Ill., 1976. Mainly administrative, but
chapter devoted to social origins and
wealth of these officials.

10.273 **Berlanstein**, L. R., *The Barristers of
Toulouse in the Eighteenth Century, 1740-93*,
Baltimore, Md., 1975. Intensive statistical
treatment of this largely hereditary and
inter-marrying group practising in
Toulouse Parlement, emphasising strong
reaction against Revolution's legal
reforms.

10.274 —— 'Lawyers in pre-Revolutionary
France', in W. Prest, ed., *Lawyers in Early
Modern Europe and America*, 1981, 164-80.
On professional structures, social status,
and political importance in later eighteenth
century.

10.275 **Bien**, D. D., '*Secrétaires du Roi.*
Absolutism, corps, and privilege under the
ancien régime', in Hinrichs and others
(7.42),153-68. Chancellery officers in
sovereign courts, purchasable post offering
noble status after twenty years.

10.276 **Bluche**, F., *Les Magistrats de la Cour des
Monnaies de Paris au 18e Siècle, 1715-90*,

Paris, 1966. One of series of works giving
data on personnel of Paris sovereign courts.

10.277 —— *Les Magistrats du Grand Conseil au 18e
Siècle, 1690-1791*, Paris, 1966.

10.278 —— *Les Magistrats du Parlement de Paris
au 18e Siècle, 1715-71*, Paris, 1960.
Interpretative study on wealth and social
position; preliminary biographical
information, alphabetically arranged, in
*L'Origine des Magistrats du Parlement de
Paris au 18e Siècle*, Paris, 1956.

10.279 **Bonney**, R., *Political Change in France
under Richelieu and Mazarin, 1624-61*,
1978. Includes much material on social
background of officials of both Sword and
Robe, esp. intendants. Review article: A.
L. Moote, *Can.J.Hist.*, 14, 1979, 266-72.

10.280 **Bossenga**, Gail, 'From *corps* to citizenship.
The Bureaux des Finances before the
French Revolution', *J.Mod.Hist.*, 58,
1986, 610-42. Case-study of *bureau* at Lille,
showing how disillusion with monarchy's
violations of proprietorial rights of office
may account for acceptance of
revolutionary ideology among Robe.

10.281 **Cavanaugh**, G., 'Peasants, office holders,
and bureaucrats. The articulation of
liberalism in old regime France',
Proc.Western Soc.Fr.Hist., 8, 1980,
254-64. Argues that bureaucrats were
driving force in movement for legal and
fiscal equality and recognition of absolute
property rights, and sought to enlist
peasantry as main allies.

10.282 **Clarke**, J. A., 'Administration and culture
in the ancien régime. The Bignon
dynasty', *Societas*, 7, 1977, 193-207.
Traces continuity in high Robe offices of
Bignon family from 1620s to Revolution.

10.283 **Cubells**, Monique, *La Provence des
Lumières. Les Parlementaires d'Aix au 18e
Siècle*, Paris, 1984. Rich study of social
milieu, adopted from doctoral thesis.

10.284 **Cummings**, M., 'Social impact of the
Paulette. The case of the Parlement of
Paris', *Can.J.Hist.*, 15, 1980, 329-54.
Comparison of judges appointed fifty years
before and after introduction of Paulette
shows no significant trend towards closed
corporation, but some fall in entry age and
shorter tenures.

10.285 **Dawson**, P., 'The *bourgeoisie de robe* in
1789', *Fr.Hist.Stud.*, 4, 1965, 1-21. Details
various strands within legal profession, and
social attitudes displayed in their *cahiers de
doléances*.

10.286 **Dewald**, J., *The Formation of a Provincial Nobility. The Magistrates of the Parlement of Rouen, 1499-1610*, Princeton, N.J., 1980. Upholds view that distinction between Robe and Sword is superficial, and that two orders formed a cohesive, landed elite. Review article: A. Grant, *Eur.Stud.Rev.*, 12, 1982, 87-95.

10.287 —— 'Magistracy and political opposition at Rouen. A social context', *Sixteenth-Cent.J.*, 5 (ii), 1974, 66-78. Looks at professional reasons for discontent among Rouen *parlementaires* during Wars of Religion.

10.288 **Doyle**, W., *The Parlement of Bordeaux and the End of the Old Régime, 1771-70*, 1974. First part of study deals with social background of judges.

10.289 —— 'The price of offices in pre-Revolutionary France', *Hist.J.*, 27, 1984, 831-60. Argues that prices of most offices continued to rise, so that abolition of venality at 1771 values represented loss for majority.

10.290 **Giesey**, R. E., 'State-building in early modern France. The role of royal officialdom', *J.Mod.Hist.*, 55, 1983, 191-207. Offers model of Robe as dedicated to unified national administration and exemplars of social mobility.

10.291 **Gresset**, M., *Gens de Justice à Besançon, de la Conquête par Louis XIV à la Révolution Française, 1674-1789*, 2 vols. in 1, Paris, 1979.

10.292 **Gruder**, Vivian R., *The Royal Provincial Intendants. A Governing Elite in Eighteenth-Century France*, Ithaca, N.Y., 1968. Prosopography of about one hundred intendants serving during three selected periods of century.

10.293 **Hamscher**, A. N., *The Parlement of Paris after the Fronde, 1653-73*, Pittsburgh, Pa., 1976. Principally political and institutional history, but includes some material on recruitment and wealth.

10.294 **Harding**, R. R., *Anatomy of a Power Elite. The Provincial Governors of Early Modern France*, New Haven, Conn., 1978. Studies c.150 governors of the eleven major provinces between 1515 and 1650. Review article: A. Grant, *Eur.Stud.Rev.*, 12, 1982, 87-95.

10.295 —— 'Aristocrats and lawyers in French provincial government, 1559-1648. From governors to commissars', in Barbara C.

Malament, ed., *After the Reformation. Essays in Honor of J. H. Hexter*, 1980, 95-127. Warns against seeing intendants as necessarily in conflict with governors.

10.296 **Hardy**, J. D., *Judicial Politics in the Old Regime. The Parlement of Paris during the Regency*, Baton Rouge, La., 1967. Social dimension very limited.

10.297 **Kagan**, R. L., 'Law students and legal careers in eighteenth-century France', *P.&P.*, 68, 1975, 38-72. Traces social and geographical origins, and subsequent careers, of sample students from some law faculties (chiefly Dijon).

10.298 **Kaiser**, C., 'The deflation in the volume of litigation at Paris in the eighteenth century, and the waning of the old judicial order', *Eur.Stud.Rev.*, 10, 1980, 309-36. Suggests that diminution of litigation (and hence value of judicial office) was marked in Paris sovereign courts, and seems to have affected provinces also. But see 10.289.

10.299 **Kettering**, Sharon, *Judicial Politics and Urban Revolt in Seventeenth-Century France. The Parlement of Aix, 1629-59*, Princeton, N.J., 1978. Good case study of provincial Robe during Fronde. See also her general paper on judicial Fronde (12.64).

10.300 **Moote**, A. L., 'The French Crown versus its judicial and financial officials, 1615-83', *J.Mod.Hist.*, 34, 1962, 146-60.

10.301 —— 'The Parliamentary Fronde and seventeenth-century Robe solidarity', *Fr.Hist.Stud.*, 2, 1962, 330-55. Some preliminary findings amplified in full-length study of next entry.

10.302 —— *The Revolt of the Judges. The Parlement of Paris and the Fronde, 1643-52*, Princeton, N.J., 1971. In-depth study of grievances of established bureaucracy.

10.303 **Mousnier**, R., and others, *Le Conseil du Roi. De Louis XII à la Révolution*, Paris, 1970. Collaborative work on social status, family ties, and values of this apex of legal-administrative system.

10.304 —— 'The financial *officiers* during the Fronde', in Coveney (6.68), 201-30. Transl. from *Dix-Septième Siècle*, 42, 1959, 76-117.

10.305 —— *La Vénalité des Offices sous Henri IV et Louis XIII*, Rouen, 1946. Exhaustive study of origins of sale of office and its systemisation in *Paulette* system. Interpretation of political implications sometimes disputable.

10.306 **Powis**, J. K., 'Order, religion, and the magistrates of a provincial Parlement in sixteenth-century France', *Arch. Reformationsgesch.*, 71, 1980, 180-96. Case-study of Bordeaux. Suggests that religious crisis after 1559 raised acutely question how far magistrates were also local notables.

10.307 **Ranum**, O., 'Fathers and sons. Social values in seventeenth-century Robe society', *Proc.Western Soc.Fr.Hist.*, 10, 1982, 215-26.

10.308 **Roosen**, W. J., 'The true ambassador. Occupational and personal characteristics of French ambassadors under Louis XIV', *Eur.Stud.Rev.*, 3, 1973, 121-39.

10.309 **Rule**, J., 'The *commis* of the Department of Foreign Affairs under the administration of Colbert de Croissy and Colbert de Torcy, 1680-1715', *Proc.Western Soc.Fr.Hist.*, 8, 1980, 69-80. See also D. C. Baxter on *premier commis* of War Department in this period, ib., 81-9.

10.310 **Samoyault**, J. P., *Les Bureaux du Secrétariat d'État des Affaires Étrangères sous Louis XV*, Paris, 1971. Like preceding entry, on work and social standing of Foreign Ministry clerks.

10.311 'Serviteurs du roi. Quelques aspects de la fonction publique dans la société française du 17e siècle', *Dix-Septième Siècle*, 42-43, 1959, whole issue. P. Goubert deals with officials of provincial courts and *élections*; R. Mousnier with *Trésoriers-Généraux* during Fronde: V.-L. Tapié with seigneurial officials; A. Corvisier with military elite. F. Bluche's paper is transl. as 'The social origins of the secretaries of state under Louis XIV, 1661-1715', in Hatton (3.16), 85-97.

10.312 **Shennan**, J. H., *The Parlement of Paris*, 1968. Standard institutional and political study of Parlement from origins to demise. One chapter on social position of judges (110-48).

10.313 **Stocker**, C. W., 'The Calvinist officers of Orléans, 1560-72', *Proc.Western Soc.Fr.Hist.*, 6, 1978, 21-33. Emphasises clientage links in religious affiliations of judicial officials.

10.314 —— 'Office as maintenance in Renaissance France', *Can.J.Hist.*, 6,1971, 21-43. Discusses benefits accruing to nobility from provision of offices and influence over their distribution before system of Crown sales became established.

10.315 —— 'Public and private enterprise in the administration of a Renaissance monarchy. The first sales of office in the Parlement of Paris (1512-24)', *Sixteenth-Cent.J.*, 9 (ii), 1978, 4-29.

10.316 **Stone**, B., *The French Parlements and the Crisis of the Old Regime*, Chapel Hill, N.C., 1986. Portrait of high Robe on eve of Revolution, concentrating on political and social outlook, which is seen as not narrowly sectional. His *The Parlement of Paris, 1774-89*, Chapel Hill, N.C., 1981, is more on corporation's political attitudes than social milieu.

10.317 **Sturdy**, D. J., *The D'Aligres de la Rivière: Servants of the Bourbon State*, 1986. Studies three generations of one of most prominent Robe dynasties of seventeenth century. See also his 'Formation of a Robe dynasty. Étienne d'Aligre II (1560-1635), Chancellor of France', *Eng.Hist.Rev.*, 98, 1980, 48-73.

10.318 **Waquet**, J.-C., *Les Grands Maîtres des Eaux et Forêts de France de l689 à la Révolution*, Geneva, 1978. Study of officials administering Crown's woodland and riverine rights.

OTHER STATES AND PRINCIPALITIES

On Spain see also 14.180-2; on Italy 6.136,249; on Germany 6.186 and 10.148; on Ottoman state 6.208; on Russia 10.265.

10.319 **Prevenier**, W., 'Officials in town and countryside in the Low Countries. Social and professional developments from the fourteenth to the sixteenth century', *Acta Hist.Neerlandica*, 7, 1974, 1-17.

10.320 **Amelang**, J. S., 'Barristers and judges in early modern Barcelona', *Am.Hist.Rev.*, 89, 1984, 1264-84.

10.321 **Bernard**, G., *Le Secrétariat d'État et le Conseil Espagnol des Indes, 1700-1808*, Geneva, 1972. Rather narrowly institutional.

10.322 **Burkholder**, M. A., 'The Council of the Indies in the late eighteenth century', *Hisp.Am.Hist.Rev.*, 56, 1976, 404-23. Records shift in personnel recruitment from 1776 onwards to include men with colonial experience.

10.323 **Fayard**, Janine, *Les Membres du Conseil de Castille à l'Époque Moderne, 1621-1746*, Geneva, 1979. Social rather than administrative study, expertly charting patterns of wealth, family alliance, and moral values.

10.324 **García Marín**, J., *La Burocracia Castellana bajo los Austrias*, Seville, 1976. More study of bureaucratic ethos and constitutional position than social milieu or recruitment.

10.325 **Kagan**, R. L., 'Lawyers and litigation in Castile, 1500-1750', in Prest (10.274), 181-204. See also related book by Kagan (10.433).

10.326 **Lunenfeld**, M., *Keepers of the City. The corregidores of Isabella I of Castile (1474-1504)*, 1987. Recreates circumstances under which these originally ad hoc municipal chiefs became permanent administrators; and details their recruitment and training. See also preliminary general article in *J.Urban Stud.*, 9, 1982, 31-55.

10.327 **Molas Ribalta**, P., and others, *Historia Social de la Administración Española. Estudios sobre los Siglos 17 y 18*, Barcelona, 1980. Contains studies on various councils and audiencias, and on intendancy of Catalonia.

10.328 **Newitt**, M. 'Plunder and the rewards of office in the Portuguese Empire', in M. Duffy, ed., *The Military Revolution and the State, 1500-1800*, 1980, 10-24. On quasi-military nature of imperial administration, and factors which encouraged predatory behaviour.

10.329 **Pelorson**, J.-M., *Les Letrados. Juristes castillans sous Philippe III*, s.l., 1980. Important thesis detailing career opportunities, social status, and cultural role of jurists in early seventeenth century.

10.330 **Thompson**, I. A. A., 'The rule of the law in early modern Castile', *Eur.Hist.Q.*, 14, 1984, 221-34. Reviews work by Fayard (10.323), Pelorson (10.329), and Kagan (10.433).

10.331 **Brucker**, G., 'Bureaucracy and social welfare in the Renaissance. A Florentine case study', *J.Mod.Hist.*, 55, 1983, 1-21. On career structure provided for *familia*, i.e. minor civil servants at disposal of *Signoria* up to fall of Republic.

10.332 **Litchfield**, R. B., *Emergence of a Bureaucracy. The Florentine Patricians, 1530-1790*, Princeton, N.J., 1986. Discerns strong continuity between urban magistrature of republic and officialdom of Medici dukes, with patrician bureaucracy

beginning to crumble only in eighteenth century. See also his 'Office-holding in Florence after the Republic', in A. Molho and J. A. Tedeschi, eds., *Renaissance Studies in Honor of Hans Baron*, Dekalb, Ill., 1971, 531-55.

10.333 **Martines**, L., *Lawyers and Statecraft in Renaissance Florence*, Princeton, N.J., 1968. Comprehensive examination of guild of lawyers and notaries and its role in Florentine politics, 1380-1530, incl. chap. on background and education.

10.334 **Rovitto**, P. L., *Respublica dei Togati. Giuristi e Società nella Napoli del Seicento*, Naples, 1982. Charts growth of administrative elite and its formidable autonomy. Further vol. projected. See also overlapping study of V. I. Comparato, *Uffici e Società a Napoli (1600-47). Aspetti dell'Ideologia del Magistrato nell'Età Moderna*, Florence, 1974, which has substantial material on general structure and recruitment as well as political outlook.

10.335 **Hess**, U., *Geheimer Rat und Kabinett in den Ernestinischen Staaten Thüringens. Organisation, Geschäftsgang, und Personalgeschichte der Obersten Regierungssphäre im Zeitalter des Absolutismus*, Weimar, 1962. General conclusions hard to draw because territorial divisions of Ernestine state dominate book's structure.

10.336 **Johnson**, H. C., 'The concept of bureaucracy in Cameralism', *Pol.Sci.Q.*, 79, 1964, 378-402. Argues that enduring legacy of early modern German and Austrian jurists and political economists was "routine duty concept".

10.337 —— *Frederick the Great and his Officials*, New Haven, Conn., 1975. Primarily work of administrative history, but with constant reference to social matrix.

10.338 **Lanzinner**, M., *Fürst, Räte, und Landstände. Die Entstehung der Zentralbehörden in Bayern, 1511-98*, Göttingen, 1980. Prosopographical study of Bavarian ducal councillors. Succeeding period dealt with in rather more institutional work of R. Heydenreuter, *Der Landesherrliche Hofrat unter Herzog und Kurfürst Maximilian I von Bayern, 1598-1651*, Munich, 1981.

10.339 **Liebel**, Helen P., *Enlightened Bureaucracy Versus Enlightened Despotism in Baden, 1750-92*, Philadelphia, 1965. Short study dealing in part with social background of legal and administrative aristocracy.

10.340 **Mueller**, H.-E., *Bureaucracy, Education, and Monopoly. Civil Service Reforms in Prussia and England*, Berkeley, Calif., 1984. Chap.2 deals with eighteenth-century Prussian bureaucracy.

10.341 **Rosenberg**, H., *Bureaucracy, Aristocracy, and Autocracy. The Prussian Experience, 1660-1815*, Cambridge, Mass., 1958. Classic investigation of repercussions for nobility of growth of state apparatus.

10.342 **Wunder**, B., 'Die Sozialstruktur der Geheimratskollegien in den süddeutschen protestantischen Fürstentümern (1660-1720)', *VSWG*, 58, 1971, 145-220. Studies administrative elite of Baden-Durlach, Ansbach, Bayreuth, Hesse-Darmstadt, and Württemberg.

10.343 **Itzkowitz**, N., 'Eighteenth-century Ottoman realities', *Studia Islamica*, 16, 1962, 73-94. Criticises western historiography of Ottoman bureaucratic system.

10.344 **Jennings**, R. C., 'Kadi, court, and legal procedure in seventeenth-century Ottoman Kayseri', *Studia Islamica*, 48, 1978, 133-72; 50, 1979, 151-84. Wide-ranging study of Ottoman judicial and police system in action.

10.345 —— 'The office of *vekil* in seventeenth-century Ottoman sharia courts', *ib.*, 42, 1975, 147-68. Also draws on Kayseri sources for information about type of legal agent.

10.346 **Kunt**, M. I., 'Ethnic-regional (Cins) solidarity in the seventeenth-century Ottoman establishment', *Int. J. Mid. E. Stud.*, 5, 1974, 233-9. Discusses whether slave bureaucrats of Ottomans were as rootless in practice as system aimed at.

10.347 —— *The Sultan's servants. The transformation of Ottoman provincial government, 1550-1650*, New York, 1983. Prosopographic approach to career structure.

10.348 **Parry**, V. J., 'Elite elements in the Ottoman Empire', in R. Wilkinson, ed., *Governing Elites*, 1969, 59-73. Deals with administrative elite and its training.

10.349 **Shinder**, J., 'Career line formation in the Ottoman bureaucracy, 1648-1750', *J.Ec.& Soc.Hist.Orient*, 16, 1973, 217-37.

10.350 **Rystad**, G., 'The King, the nobility, and the growth of bureaucracy in seventeenth-century Sweden', in Rystad (5.254), 59-70.

On struggle between Crown and aristocracy for control of administrative appointments. Note additional information on Swedish system in 10.364.

10.351 **Alef**, G., 'Reflections on the boyar Duma in the reign of Ivan III', *Slavonic & E.Eur.Rev.*, 45, 1967, 76-123. Repr. in Alef (6.217). Prosopographical study of late fifteenth-century Muscovite council.

10.352 **Altbauer**, D., 'The diplomats of Peter the Great', *Jb.Gesch.Osteuropas*, 28, 1980, 1-16. On social and educational levels of diplomats.

10.353 **Clarkson**, J. D., 'Notes on bureaucracy, aristocracy, and autocracy in Russia, 1500-1800', in G. A. Ritter, ed., *Entstehung und Wandel der Modernen Gesellschaft. Festschrift für Hans Rosenberg*, Berlin, 1970, 187-220. Attempts some points of comparison with Rosenberg's well-known book on Prussia (10.341).

10.354 **Kleimola**, Ann M., 'Patterns of Duma recruitment, 1505-50', in Waugh (10.70), 232-58.

10.355 —— 'Status, place, and politics. The rise of *mestnichestvo* during the *boiarskoe pravlenie*', *Forsch.Osteur.Gesch.*, 27, 1980, 195-214. System of precedence governing elite bureaucratic and military appointments.

10.356 **Le Donne**, J. P., 'Appointments to the Russian Senate, 1762-96', *Cah.Monde Russe et Sov.*, 16, 1975, 27-56. Background and loyalties of 132 senators appointed by Catherine the Great.

10.357 —— 'Catherine's governors and governors-general, 1763-96', *ib.*, 20, 1979, 15-42.

10.358 —— *Ruling Russia. Politics and Administration in the Age of Absolutism*, Princeton, N.J., 1984. Concentrates more on describing system than personnel.

10.359 **Meehan-Waters**, Brenda, *Autocracy and Aristocracy. The Russian Service Elite of 1730*, New Brunswick, N.J., 1982. Study of *Generalitet* (top officials in state service, civil and military), as listed in 1730, emphasising that it provides little evidence of upward mobility in society. Following entries list some preliminary essays drawn from this research.

10.360 —— 'Elite politics and autocratic power', in Cross (9.157), 229-46.

10.361 —— 'Muscovite noble origins of the Russians in the Generalitet of 1730', *Cah.Monde Russe et Sov.*, 12, 1971, 28-75.

10.362 —— 'The Russian aristocracy and the reforms of Peter the Great', *Can.-Am.Slavic Stud.*, 8, 1974, 288-302.

10.363 **Orlovsky**, D. T., 'Recent studies on the Russian bureaucracy', *Russ.Rev.*, 35, 1976, 448-67. Review article dealing with both Soviet and western historiography. (Concerns only eighteenth century and later). Compare 10.366.

10.364 **Peterson**, C., *Peter the Great's Administrative and Judicial Reforms. Swedish Antecedents and the Process of Reception*, Stockholm, 1979. Rather narrowly institutional, but does contain incidental information on personnel.

10.365 **Pintner**, W. M., and Rowney, D. K., eds., *Russian Officialdom. The Bureaucratization of Russian Society from the Seventeenth to the Twentieth Century*, 1980. Collective work with broadly chronological chapters. Contributors include R. Crummey and Brenda Meehan-Waters.

10.366 **Raeff**, M., 'The bureaucratic phenomena of Imperial Russia, 1700-1905',

Am.Hist.Rev., 84, 1979, 399-411. Review article. Compare 10.363.

10.367 **Ransel**, D. L., 'Bureaucracy and patronage. The view from an eighteenth-century Russian letter-writer', in F. C. Jaher, ed., *The Rich, the Well Born, and the Powerful. Elites and Upper Classes in History*, Urbana, Ill., 1973, 154-78. Uses style manual of 1789 to show realities of patronage system behind façade of meritocracy introduced by Petrine reforms.

10.368 **Torke**, H. J., 'Continuity and change in the relations between bureaucracy and society in Russia, 1613-1861', *Can.Slavic Stud.*, 5, 1971, 457-76. Useful survey, emphasising continuity.

10.369 **Weickhardt**, G. G., 'Bureaucrats and boiars in the Muscovite Tsardom', *Russ.Hist.*, 10, 1983, 331-56. Analyses shift of power from professional bureaucrats to nobles in top administrative posts in course of seventeenth century.

POLICE. CRIME AND PUNISHMENT. LITIGATION

Prostitution dealt with mainly in Section 5.248-92. See also 13.336-402 for role of law in prosecution of witchcraft. Further references in 5.440; 10.18; 11.15; 13.277.

10.370 **Deyon**, P., *Le Temps des Prisons. Essai sur l'Histoire de la Délinquance et les Origines du Système Pénitentiaire*, Lille, 1975. Concentrates on eighteenth and early nineteenth centuries.

10.371 **Foucault**, M., *Discipline and Punish. The Birth of the Prison*, 1977. Transl. from French ed. of 1975. Covers roughly same period as Deyon, but in many ways more work of philosophy than historical research, arguing that prison design reflected industrial society's ideal of disciplined and supervised citizenry. For discussion of Foucault in this context see Patricia O'Brien, *J.Soc.Hist.*, 11, 1978, 508-20; more broadly, see 1.49-54.

10.372 **Geremek**, B., 'Criminalité, vagabondage, paupérisme. La marginalité à l'aube des temps modernes', *Rev.Hist.Mod.et Contemp.*, 21, 1974, 337-75. General intoductory essay for journal issue devoted to early modern criminality and poverty. Other papers by R. Chartier ('les élites et les gueux', 376-88); B. Vincent (Morisco

bandits in Andalusia, 389-400); J. Depauw (poor law legislation in France, 401-18); M. Lachiver (tax evasion in eighteenth-century French wine trade, 419-44); J. Lecuir (criminal statistics of 1780s as tabulated by Baron de Montyon, 445-93).

10.373 —— 'Men without masters. Marginal society during the pre-industrial era', *Diogenes*, 98, 1977, 28-54. Similar survey of authorities' attitudes to vagrants, prostitutes, outlaws, etc. See also his documentary reader *Truands et Misérables dans l'Europe Moderne (1350-1600)*, Paris, 1980. Geremek's related major work, *The Margins of Society in Late Medieval Paris*, 1987 (first publ. in Polish, 1971; French ed., 1976) draws mostly on pre-1450 evidence.

10.374 **Hobsbawm**, E. J., *Bandits*, 1969. Ranges widely in time and geographical coverage. Criticised as over-romantic by A. Blok, *Comp.Stud.Soc.& Hist.*, 14, 1972, 494-505. His article 'Social banditry', in H. A. Landsberger, ed., *Rural Protest*.

Peasant Movements and Social Change,
1974, 142-57 gives more emphasis than
book to limited, personal nature of protest
represented by bandit in agrarian society.

10.375 **Langbein**, J. H., *Prosecuting Crime in the
Renaissance. England, Germany, France*,
Cambridge, Mass., 1974. Somewhat
technical work, a prime concern being to
establish whether there were attempts to
introduce continental inquisitorial
methods into English procedure in
sixteenth century.

10.376 —— *Torture and the Law of Proof. Europe
and England in the Ancien Régime*,
Chicago, 1977. Again rather technical
work of legal history on conditions under
which evidence extracted by torture was
accepted as valid.

10.377 **Lenman**, B., and Parker, G., 'The state,
the community, and the criminal law in
early modern Europe', in V. A. C. Gatrell
and others, eds., *Crime and the Law. The
Social History of Crime in Western Europe
since 1500*, 1980, 11-48. Emphasises low
rates of detection and prosecution, and
hence that crime rates cannot be deduced
from court records.

10.378 **Lis**, Catharina, and Soly, H., 'Policing the
early modern proletariat, 1450-1850', in D.
Levine, ed., *Proletarianization and Family
History*, New York, 1984, 163-228.
Sketches drive by authorities against
idleness and disorder seen as
accompanying increases in waged labour
force, mobility, and urbanisation. Note
Kaplan's evidence from eighteenth-
century Paris on this theme (10.401).

10.379 **Sellin**, J. T., *Slavery and the Penal System*,
New York, 1976. Survey of penal systems
from earliest times, arguing that
punishment for common criminals (as
opposed to aristocratic malefactors) was
derived from slave societies.

10.380 **Soman**, A., 'Deviance and criminal justice
in Western Europe, 1300-1800', *Criminal
Justice Hist.*, 1, 1980, 3-28. Emphasises,
mainly from French sources, frequent
recourse to arbitration rather than
prosecution in criminal assaults. See
further evidence in 10.406,428.

10.381 **Spierenburg**, P., ed., *The Emergence of
Carceral Institutions. Prisons, Galleys, and
Lunatic Asylums, 1550-1900*, Rotterdam,
1984. Essay collection to which
Spierenburg contributes general survey of
spread of confinement as penal policy in

early modern period (9-77).

10.382 **Weisser**, M. R., *Crime and Punishment in
Early Modern Europe*, 1979. Perhaps rather
premature attempt at synthesising patchy
research done in this area; most confident
in dealing with Spanish material.

FRANCE
*See also 8.49-51; 10.372,380; 11.220;
14.44,308,322.*

10.383 **Abbiateci**, A., 'Arsonists in eighteenth-
century France', in Forster and Ranum
(5.282), 157-79. Transl. from *Annales*, 25,
1970, 229-48.

10.384 **Bamford**, P. W., *Fighting Ships and
Prisons. The Mediterranean Galleys of
France in the Age of Louis XIV*,
Minneapolis, Minn., 1973.

10.385 —— 'Procurement of oarsmen for French
galleys, 1660-1748', *Am.Hist.Rev.*, 65,
1959, 31-48. Interesting details on
treatment of convicts under escort to galley
service. See also Zysberg's work on French
galleys (10.423-6); and 10.442-3.

10.386 **Berlanstein**, L. R., 'The other side of
justice. Legal disputes among the Parisian
populace in the eighteenth century',
Proc.Western Soc.Fr.Hist., 4, 1976,
182-91. Typology of disputes brought
before *juge de paix* of poor Parisian quarter
(Arcis).

10.387 **Billacois**, F., *Le Duel dans la Société
Française des 16e-17e Siècles. Essai de
Psychosociologie Historique*, Paris, 1986.
Study in depth of conflicting values which
both sustained and condemned duelling.
See also 10.402,416.

10.388 **Bourquin**, Marie-Helène, and Hepp, E.,
Aspects de la Contrebande au 18e Siècle,
Paris, 1969. Two short studies: on
celebrated smuggler and bandit, Louis
Mandrin, and on tobacco smuggling. See
also Y. Durand, 'La contrebande du sel au
18e siècle aux frontières de Bretagne, du
Maine, et de l'Anjou', *Hist.Sociale/Social
Hist.*, 7, 1974, 227-69; and 10.412.

10.389 **Cameron**, I. A., *Crime and Repression in the
Auvergne and the Guyenne, 1720-90*, 1981.
Study of police and judicial functions of
prévôts des maréchaux in contrasted
provinces. See also associated article 'The
police of eighteenth-century France',
Eur.Stud.Rev., 7, 1977, 47-76.

10.390 **Castan**, Nicole, 'Arbitration of disputes
under the ancien régime', in J. Bossy, ed.,

Disputes and Settlements. Law and Human Relations in the West, 1983, 219-60. Transl. extract from 10.392.

).391 —— *Les Criminels de Languedoc, 1750-90*, Toulouse, 1980. Based on her work with criminal records of Parlement of Toulouse. Brings out distinction between "commonplace" crime and tensions of approaching revolutionary crisis. See transl. of oral defence of her thesis in *Criminal Justice Hist.*, 1, 1980, 175-84.

0.392 —— *Justice et Répression en Languedoc à l'Époque des Lumières*, Paris, 1980. Another major work using Parlement records, with more emphasis on court procedures and judges' penal views.

0.393 —— 'Summary justice', in Forster and Ranum (5.282), 111-56. Transl. from *Annales*, 31, 1976, 331-61. Deals with justice meted out by *prévôté* courts to offending vagrants (late eighteenth century).

0.394 —— and Castan, Y., eds., *Vivre Ensemble. Ordre et Désordre en Languedoc au 18e Siècle*, Paris, 1981. Documentary reader.

0.395 *Crimes et Criminalité en France sous l'Ancien Régime, 17e-18e Siècles*, Paris, 1971. Collective work on various types of crime and various criminal courts. Contributors include A. Abbiateci, F. Billacois, N. and Y. Castan.

0.396 **Dewald**, J., 'The "perfect magistrate". Parlementaires and crime in sixteenth-century Rouen', *Arch.Reformationsgesch.*, 67, 1976, 284-300. Seeks to illustrate judges' social outlook via analysis of over 500 decisions in criminal cases.

0.397 **Farge, Arlette**, *Délinquance et Criminalité. Le Vol d'Aliments à Paris au 18e Siècle*, Paris, 1974. Draws on Châtelet prosecutions of those caught stealing from shops, market stalls, etc.

0.398 **Greenshields**, M., 'Women, violence, and criminal justice records in early modern Haute Auvergne (1587-1664)', *Can.J.Hist.*, 22, 1987, 175-94. Investigates relatively few reported cases in which women were victims or accused.

0.399 **Hufton**, Olwen H., 'The urban criminal in eighteenth-century France', *Bull.J.Rylands Lib.*, 67, 1984, 474-99. Uses records of criminal courts in Paris, Bordeaux, and Toulouse.

0.400 'Justice et répression de 1610 à nos jours', *Actes Congrès Nat.Soc.Savantes*, 107 (i), 1982, whole issue. Numerous papers on crime and police under old regime, incl. section on aspects affecting women – matrimonial disputes, prostitution, etc. (77-134).

10.401 **Kaplan**, S., 'Réflexions sur la police du monde du travail, 1700-1815', *Rev.Hist.*, 261, 1979, 17-77. Detailed survey of policy and measures against worker combination and "indiscipline", mainly in Parisian context. See also 10.378.

10.402 **Kelly**, G. A., 'Duelling in eighteenth-century France. Archaeology, rationale, implications', *Eighteenth Cent. – Theory and Interpretations*, 21, 1980, 236-54. See also 10.387,416.

10.403 **Mogensen**, N. W., 'Crimes and punishments in eighteenth-century France. The example of the *pays d'Auge*', *Hist.Sociale/Social Hist.*, 10 (no.20), 1977, 337-53. Based on registers of *baillage* in Lower Normandy.

10.404 **Rader**, D. L., 'Beccarian reform in France. Too little and too late', *Proc.Western Soc.Fr.Hist.*, 6, 1978, 170-8. Statistics suggesting trend to more humane and lenient punishments for crime between 1769-89.

10.405 **Reinhardt**, S. G., 'Crime and royal justice in ancien régime France', *J. Interdisc. Hist.*, 13, 1983, 437-60. Analysis of late eighteenth-century cases before tribunal of Sarlat.

10.406 —— 'The selective prosecution of crime in ancien régime France. Theft in the *sénéchaussée* of Sarlat', *Eur.Hist.Q.*, 16, 1986, 3-24. More evidence that only small proportion of crimes were dealt with in formal proceedings.

10.407 **Riley**, P. F., 'Hard times, police, and the making of public policy in the Paris of Louis XIV', *Hist.Reflections*, 10, 1983, 313-34. Argues that last two decades of Louis' reign showed definite progress in combining welfare and security roles of Paris police. See 10.418 on subsequent period.

10.408 —— 'Louis XIV, watchdog of Parisian morality', *Historian*, 36, 1973, 19-33. General survey of police activity in such fields as prostitution, gambling, and drunkenness.

10.409 —— 'Police and the search for *bon ordre* in Louis XIV's Paris', *Proc.Western Soc.Fr.Soc.*, 7, 1979, 11-20.

10.410 —— 'Women and police in Louis XIV's Paris', *Eighteenth-Cent.Life*, 4, 1977,

37-42. Short account of police action against prostitution, abortion, etc.

10.411 **Robisheaux**, E., 'The "private army" of the tax farms. The men and their origins', *Hist.Sociale/Social Hist.*, 6 (no.12), 1973, 256-69. Studies sample of officers and men from brigades who policed collection of *gabelle* in Normandy.

10.412 **Roche**, D., and Michaut, C., ' "La veille aux advenues". (Gabellous et contrebandiers dans les hautes vallées piémontaises, 1662-63)', *Rev.Hist.Mod.et Contemp.*, 17, 1970, 161-220. Graphic account of anti-smuggling police activities.

10.413 **Ruff**, J. R., *Crime, Justice, and Public Order in Old Regime France. The Sénéchaussées of Libourne and Bazas, 1696-1789*, 1984.

10.414 —— 'Law and order in eighteenth-century France. The maréchaussée of Guyenne', *Proc,Western Soc.Fr.Hist.*, 4, 1976, 174-81; Maintains that provosts put more resources into pursuit of military and naval deserters than into their civilian police functions.

10.415 **Saint-Germain**, J., *La Reynie et la Police au Grand Siècle*, Paris, 1962. Biographical study of director of police in late seventeenth-century Paris.

10.416 **Schneider**, R. A., 'Swordplay and statemaking. Aspects of the campaign against the duel in early modern France', in C. Bright and Susan Harding, eds., *Statemaking and Social Movements. Essays in History and Theory*, Ann Arbor, Mich., 1984, 265-96. See also 10.387,402.

10.417 **Soman**, A., 'Criminal jurisprudence in ancien-régime France. The Parlement of Paris in the sixteenth and seventeenth centuries', in L. A. Knafla, ed., *Crime and Criminal Justice in Europe and Canada*, Waterloo, Ontario, 1981. Mainly on sentencing policy, suggesting that punishments were less gruesome and invariable than criminal codes suggest.

10.418 **Williams**, A., *The Police of Paris, 1718-89*, Baton Rouge, La., 1979. Useful guide to wide scope of "police" functions (fire service, public health, provisioning, etc., as well as crime prevention). Relies overmuch on evidence from official regulations. See also following entries drawing on research for this book; and 10.491. On policing of Paris at earlier periods see 10.407-10.415.

10.419 —— 'Domestic espionage and the myth of police omniscience in eighteenth-century Paris', *Proc.Consortium on Revolutionary Eur.*, 1979, 253-60. On alleged police informers.

10.420 —— 'Patterns of deviance in eighteenth-century Paris', *Proc.Western Soc.Fr.Hist.*, 6, 1978, 179-87. Argues that most historians of Paris crime have looked only at Châtelet records, which may overemphasise trials for theft.

10.421 —— 'The police and the administration of eighteenth-century Paris', *J.Urban Hist.*, 4, 1978, 157-82. Emphasises cooperation of various city authorities through *assemblée de police*.

10.422 —— 'The police and the poor in Paris', *Stud.on Voltaire*, 155, 1976, 2285-300.

10.423 **Zysberg**, A., *Les Galériens du Roi. Vie et Destins de 60,000 Forçats sur les Galères de France, 1680-1748*, Paris, 1987. Large-scale computer analysis of convicts sent to Mediterranean galleys. See also following related papers.

10.424 —— 'Galères et galériens en France à la fin du 17e siècle. Un image du pouvoir royal à l'âge classique', *Criminal Justice Hist.*, 1, 1980, 51-115.

10.425 —— 'Galleys and hard labour convicts in France, 1550-1850', in Spierenburg (10.381), 78-124.

10.426 —— 'Galley rowers in the mid-eighteenth century', in Forster and Ranum (5.282), 83-110. Transl. from *Annales*, 30, 1975, 43-65.

LOW COUNTRIES
See also 10.42.

10.427 **Backhouse**, M. F., 'Guerilla war and banditry in the sixteenth century. The Wood Beggars in the *westkwartier* of Flanders (1567-68)', *Arch. Reformationsgesch.*, 74, 1983, 232-51. Criminal band operating on pretext of anti-Catholic ideology.

10.428 **Diederiks**, H., 'Patterns of criminality and law enforcement during the ancien regime. The Dutch case', *Criminal Justice Hist.*, 1, 1980, 157-74. Once again emphasises small dimensions of formal criminal prosecutions.

10.429 —— 'Punishment during the Ancien Régime. The case of the eighteenth-century Dutch Republic', in Knafla (10.417), 273-96. Examines how far imprisonment was used as method of punishment.

10.430 Spierenburg, P., *The Spectacle of Suffering. Executions and the Evolution of Repression. From a Preindustrial Metropolis to the European Experience*, 1984. Draws particularly on records of sentences in Amsterdam, 1650-1750, to illustrate thesis of gradual erosion of cruel public punishments.

SPAIN
See also 10.382; 14.329.

10.431 **Casey**, J., 'Household disputes and the law in early modern Andalusia', in Bossy (10.390), 189-217.

10.432 **Colas Latorre**, G., and Salas Ausens, J. A., *Aragon en el Siglo 16. Alteraciones Sociales y Conflictos Politicos*, Zaragoza, 1982. Deals particularly with banditry and crime.

10.433 **Kagan**, R. L., *Lawsuits and Litigants in Castile, 1500-1700*, Chapel Hill, N.C., 1981. Charts seeming rise in litigiousness in seventeenth century, though admitting that surviving court records may distort long-term interpretation. Considerable material also on legal profession. Review article: R. F. E. Weissman, *Criminal Justice Hist.*, 3, 1982, 141-51.

10.434 —— 'A golden age of litigation. Castile, 1500-1700', in Bossy (10.390), 145-66. Focusses on those involved in lawsuits, and their motives.

10.435 **Kamen**, H., 'Public authority and popular crime. Banditry in Valencia, 1660-1714', *J.Eur.Ec.Hist.*, 3, 1974, 654-87.

10.436 **Perry**, Mary E., *Crime and Society in Early Modern Seville*, Hanover, N.H., 1980. Entertaining, though somewhat unstructured, portrait of Seville underworld. Review article: R. F. E. Weissman, *Criminal Justice Hist.*, 3, 1982, 141-51.

10.437 **Pike**, Ruth, *Penal Servitude in Early Modern Spain*, Madison, Wis., 1983. Brief work, looking first at retributive system of sixteenth and seventeenth centuries, then at development of utilitarian spirit and elements of rehabilitation in eighteenth. See also following articles based on this research.

10.438 —— 'Capital punishment in eighteenth-century Spain', *Hist.Sociale/Social Hist.*, 18, 1985, 375-86. Finds Spanish law more sparing of death penalty than English or French.

10.439 —— 'Crime and criminals in sixteenth-century Seville', *Sixteenth-Cent.J.*, 6 (i), 1975, 3-18. Based on royal enquiry of 1572.

10.440 —— 'Crime and punishment in sixteenth-century Spain', *J.Eur.Ec.Hist.*, 5, 1976, 689-704. Further data from 1572 enquiry.

10.441 —— 'Penal labor in sixteenth-century Spain. The mines of Almadén', *Societas*, 3, 1973, 193-206. Types of criminal sent to mercury mines (leased to Fuggers), and conditions of life there.

10.442 —— 'Penal servitude in early modern Spain. The galleys', *J.Eur.Ec.Hist.*, 11, 1982, 197-217.

10.443 **Thompson**, I. A. A., 'The map of crime in sixteenth-century Spain', *Ec.Hist.Rev.*, 2nd ser., 21, 1968, 244-67. Tentative conclusions on geographical distribution of crime based on lists of convicts sent to galleys. See discussion with H. Kamen, *ib.*, 22, 1969, 305-7.

10.444 **Weisser**, M., 'Crime and punishment in early modern Spain', in Gatrell and others (10.377), 76-96. General survey of judicial system and types of crime.

ITALY
See also 5.450; 11.241,245; 14.416.

10.445 **Cozzi**, G., ed., *Stato, Società e Giustizia nella Repubblica Veneta (Sec. 15-18)*, Rome, 1980. Essays on various aspects of criminal jurisdiction and punishment in Venetian territories.

10.446 **Hook**, Judith A., 'Justice, authority, and the creation of the ancien régime in Italy', *Trans.Roy.Hist.Soc.*, 5th ser., 34, 1984, 71-89. Discusses breakdown of both civil and criminal justice in late Renaissance communes as factor in rise of princely government.

10.447 **Trasselli**, C., 'Criminalité et moralité en Sicile au début de l'époque moderne', *Annales*, 28, 1973, 226-46. Deals particularly with sexual crimes and with criminality among clergy.

10.448 **Wright**, A. D., 'Venetian law and order. A myth?', *Bull.Inst.Hist.Res.*, 53, 1980, 192-202. Claims that Venice was as crime-ridden as any other Italian state at turn of sixteenth-seventeenth centuries.

GERMANY AND SWITZERLAND
See also 5.629; 12.97.

10.449 **Dülmen**, R. van, *Theater des Schreckens. Gerichtspraxis und Strafrituale in der Frühen Neuzeit*, Munich, 1985. Description of methods and rituals of punishment, esp. executions, under tribunals of Holy Roman Empire.

10.450 **Henry**, P., *Crime, Justice, et Société dans la Principauté de Neuchâtel au 18e Siècle (1707-1806)*, Neuchâtel, 1984. Very thorough examination of administrative and sociological aspects of crime in Swiss county under sovereignty of King of Prussia.

10.451 **Küther**, C., *Räuber und Gauner in Deutschland. Das Organisierte Bandenwesen im 18. und frühen 19. Jahrhundert*, Göttingen, 1976. Examines marginal groups from whom robber bands were drawn, their counter-culture and group solidarity.

10.452 **Monter**, E. W., 'Crime and punishment in Calvin's Geneva, 1562', *Arch. Reformationsgesch.*, 64, 1973, 281-6. Short analysis of unusually full list of criminal trials extant for 1562-63.

EASTERN AND NORTHERN EUROPE
See also 10.344 (Turkey); 14.99 (Russia).

10.453 **Swanson**, G. W., 'Ottoman police', *J.Contemp.Hist.*, 7 (i-ii), 1972, 243-60. Brief general account. See also similar essay in G. L. Mosse, ed., *Police Forces in History*, 1975, 39-56.

10.454 **Dübeck**, Inger, 'Poor women's criminality in eighteenth-century Denmark and Norway', in Riis (11.194), 2, 193-205.

10.455 **Österberg**, Eva, 'Violence among peasants. Comparative perspectives on sixteenth- and seventeenth- century Sweden', in Rystad (5.254), 257-75.

10.456 **Ylikangas**, H., 'Major fluctuations in crimes of violence in Finland', *Scan.J.Hist.*, 1, 1976, 81-103. Outlines fluctuations since sixteenth century, arguing that unofficial constraints of hierarchical society are major restraining factor.

10.457 **Backus**, O. P., 'Muscovite legal thought, the law of theft, and the problem of centralization, 1497-1589', in A. D. Ferguson and A. Levin, eds., *Essays in Russian History. A Collection Dedicated to George Vernadsky*, Hamden, Conn., 1964, 33-68. Finds continuing stress on local autonomy in administration of criminal justice.

10.458 **Dewey**, H. W., and Kleimola, Ann M., 'From the kinship group to every man his brother's keeper. Collective responsibility in pre-Petrine Russia', *Jb. Gesch. Osteuropas*, 30, 1982, 321-35. Explains police system based on communal pledges. See also their earlier outline, 'Suretyship and collective responsibility in pre-Petrine Russia', *ib.*, 18, 1970, 337-54.

10.459 **Eeckaute**, Denise, 'Les brigands en Russie du 17e au 19e siècle. Mythe et réalité', *Rev.Hist.Mod.et Contemp.*, 12, 1965, 161-202. Seeks explanations for persistence of problem well into nineteenth century.

10.460 **Keep**, J. L. H., 'Bandits and the law in Muscovy', *Slavonic & E.Eur.Rev.*, 35, 1956, 201-22. Principally concerns *guba* system of elective police officials in sixteenth and seventeenth centuries.

10.461 **Le Donne**, J. P., 'The provincial and local police under Catherine the Great, 1775-96', *Can.Slavic Stud.*, 4, 1970, 513-28.

ARMED FORCES AND THE IMPACT OF WAR
See also 10.18; 11.376; 12.72.

10.462 **Barker**, T. M., 'Military history, the social sciences, and early modern Europe', in Barker (10.516), 147-68. Reviews new directions in military historiography.

10.463 **Bean**, R., 'War and the birth of the nation state', *J.Ec.Hist.*, 33, 1973, 203-21. Argues that changes in military technology in fifteenth century led to increase in minimum efficient size of state. But see criticisms of D. R. Ringrose, *ib.*, 222 ff.

10.464 **Childs**, J., *Armies and Warfare in Europe, 1648-1789*, 1982. Much of book deals with social and political implications of standing armies.

10.465 **Cipolla**, C. M., *Guns and Sails in the Early Phase of European Expansion, 1400-1700*, 1965. Partly on impact of firearms in Asia, but contains much information on early armaments industry in Europe. For another, more specialised, aspect of naval technology see Guilmartin (10.471).

10.466 **Clark**, *Sir* G. N., *War and Society in the Seventeenth Century*, 1958. Brief, but a classic essay. Deals more with significance of war than with military sociology.

10.467 **Corvisier**, A., *Armies and Societies in Europe, 1494-1789*, Bloomington, Ind., 1979. Transl. from French ed. of 1976. Important work, dealing both with internal sociology of armies and with their increasing effect on government structures.

10.468 —— and others, 'Présence de la guerre au 17e siècle', *Dix-Septième Siècle*, 148, 1985, whole issue. Conference papers on various aspects of war and society, incl. its representation in literature and painting.

10.469 **Doorn**, J. van, *The Soldier and Social Change. Comparative Studies in the History and Sociology of the Military*, Beverly Hills, Calif., 1975. Part 1, "Emergence of the modern military", ranges widely over time and stresses parallels between military organisation and that (emerging later) of industry. Chapter on "The officer corps" appears more fully in *Arch.Eur.Sociol.*, 6, 1965, 262-82.

10.470 **Finer**, S. E., 'State- and nation-building in Europe. The role of the military', in Tilly (10.25), 84-163. Political scientist's view.

10.471 **Guilmartin**, J. F., *Gunpowder and Galleys. Changing Technology and Mediterranean Warfare at Sea in the Sixteenth Century*, 1974. Deals with implications for design and tactics of oared vessels of developments in naval artillery.

10.472 **Hale**, J. R., 'Military education of the officer class in early modern Europe', in Clough (10.224), 440-61. Repr. in his *Renaissance War Studies*, 1983, 225-46. On academies, teaching of horsemanship and fencing, etc.

10.473 —— 'Soldiers in the religious art of the Renaissance', *Bull.J.Rylands Lib.*, 69, 1986, 166-94; and 'The soldier in Germanic graphic art of the Renaissance', *J.Interdisc.Hist.*, 17, 1986, 85-114. Two studies of why soldiers became subject of representation, and what images of them were conveyed.

10.474 —— 'War and public opinion in the fifteenth and sixteenth centuries', *P.& P.*, 22, 1962, 18-35. Conference paper depicting contemporary views about morality of war and technological advances in weaponry; followed by discussion.

10.475 —— *War and Society in Renaissance Europe, 1450-1620*, 1985. Deals with impact of war through invasion, occupation, and taxation, as well as military sociology and values.

10.476 **Hintze**, O., 'Military organization and the organization of the state', in Hintze (6.183), 180-215. Lecture of 1906, broadly sketching importance of military factors in establishment of bureaucracies.

10.477 **Kiernan**, V. G., 'Foreign mercenaries and absolute monarchy', *P.& P.*, 11, 1957, 66-86. Repr. in Aston (2.72),117-40. On sources of recruitment.

10.478 **McNeill**, W. H., *The Pursuit of Power. Technology, Armed Force, and Society since A.D. 1000*, Chicago, 1982. Like all McNeill's work, stimulating and challenging in its generalisations.

10.479 **Parrott**, D. A., 'Strategy and tactics in the Thirty Years' War. The "military revolution" ', *Militärgesch.Mitteil.*, 38, 1985, 7-25. Argues that effects of innovations (popularised in M. Roberts' inaugural lecture *The Military Revolution*, 1956) pale alongside logistical inability to keep large armies adequately fed and paid.

10.480 **Pettengill**, J. S., 'The impact of military technology on European income distribution', *J.Interdisc.Hist.*, 10, 1979, 201-25. Argues that real income of peasantry fell everywhere in Europe between 1500 and 1650 as result of ruling class monopoly of firearms for coercive purposes – enabling increases in taxation, rents, or enserfment. Note echoes of Lane's formulation (10.18).

10.481 **Preston**, R. A., and others, *Men in Arms. A History of Warfare and its Interrelationships with Western Society*, 1956. Revised ed., 1962. Deals with warfare from earliest times, attempting to relate organisation and tactics to social and technological background.

10.482 **Redlich**, F., *De Praeda Militari. Looting and Booty, 1500-1815*, Wiesbaden, 1956. Brief essay arising out of his study of German military entrepreneurs (10.522), showing how state tried to take over from individuals in this aspect of warfare.

10.483 —— 'Military entrepreneurship and the credit system in the sixteenth and seventeenth centuries', *Kyklos*, 10, 1957, 186-93. Corrective review of A. Ernstberger's work on Hans de Witte (10.246).

10.484 **Teitler**, G., *The Genesis of the Professional Officers' Corps*, Beverly Hills, Calif., 1977. Transl. from Dutch ed. of 1974. Sociological history of professionalisation process. Devotes most space to European navies from late Middle Ages to Napoleonic Wars.

FRANCE
See also 7.40; 9.237; 10.384-5,423-6; 11.197.

10.485 **Aman**, J., *Les Officiers Bleus dans la Marine Française au 18e Siècle*, Paris, 1976. Study of auxiliary officers recruited to Navy in wartime. Suggests that aristocratic prejudice against them has been exaggerated. See also 10.490,497,499 on this question.

10.486 'L'Armée de 1610 à nos jours', *Actes Congrès Nat.Soc.Savantes*, 103 (i), 1978, whole issue. Several relevant articles, somewhat disparate in nature, on both land and sea forces.

10.487 **Asher**, E. L., *The Resistance to the Maritime Classes. The Survival of Feudalism in the France of Colbert*, Berkeley, Calif., 1960. Deals with resistance to naval conscription in maritime provinces. (Linkage with "feudalism" seems misplaced).

10.488 **Bamford**, P. W., 'Slaves for the galleys of France, 1665-1700', in J. Parker, ed., *Merchants and Scholars. Essays in the History of Exploration and Trade*, Minneapolis, Ma., 173-91. Approximately a third of oarsmen were slaves (mostly captured Moslems).

10.489 **Béchu**, P., 'Noblesse d'epée et tradition militaire au 18e siècle', *Hist.,Éc., et Soc.*, 2, 1983, 507-48. How important was military career to social prestige? Case study of Marquis de Beaupréau (of de Scépeaux family).

10.490 **Bien**, D. D., 'The Army in the French Enlightenment. Reform, reaction, and revolution', *P.& P.*, 85, 1979, 68-98. Argues that 1781 regulation restricting commissions to nobility was not altogether incompatible with drive for greater professionalism and uniformity of career structure. See also his 'La réaction aristocratique avant 1789. L'exemple de l'Armée', *Annales*, 29, 1974, 23-48, 505-34.

10.491 **Chagniot**, J., *Paris et l'Armée au 18e Siècle*, Paris, 1985. Deals both with role of military in police of Paris (rather restricted), and with Paris as headquarters of recruitment and supply.

10.492 **Contamine**, P., 'Les industries de guerre dans la France de la Renaissance. L'exemple de l'artillerie', *Rev.Hist.*, 550, 1984, 249-80. Looks at suppliers of bullets, gunpowder, weapons, etc.

10.493 **Corvisier**, A., *L'Armée Française de la Fin du 17e Siècle au Ministère de Choiseul. Le Soldat*, 2 vols., Paris, 1964. Immensely detailed and informative, both about army organisation and about social background of recruits. Review articles: J. C. Perrot, *Rev.Hist.Mod.et Contemp.*, 13, 1966, 313-19; J. Vidalenc, *Rev.Hist.Éc.et Soc.*, 46, 1968, 423-39.

10.494 **Jones**, C., 'The military revolution and the professionalisation of the French Army under the ancien régime', in Duffy (10.328), 29-47. On steps taken to lessen private enterprise recruitment and supply.

10.495 —— 'The welfare of the French foot-soldier', *History*, 65, 1980, 193-213. Sketches history of medical services, pension provision, etc., from Richelieu to Napoleon I.

10.496 **Léonard**, E. G., *L'Armée et ses Problèmes au 18e Siècle*. Paris, 1958. General work, not particularly strong on social aspects.

10.497 **Lynn**, J. A., 'A pattern of French military reform, 1750-90. Speculations concerning the officer corps', *Proc.Consortium on Revolutionary Eur.*, 1974 (publ. 1978), 113-28. Another look at question of how closed officer caste was.

10.498 **Wood**, J. B., 'The impact of the Wars of Religion. A view of France in 1581', *Sixteenth-Cent.J.*, 15, 1984, 131-68. Ingenious attempt to apply factor analysis (using data in Frumenteau's *Secret des Finances de France*, 1581), in assessing impact of war on particular localities.

10.499 **Wrong**, C. J., 'The *officiers de fortune* in the French infantry', *Fr.Hist.Stud.*, 9, 1976, 400-31. On social origins and restricted career opportunities of officers promoted from ranks in ten regiments of pre-Revolutionary Army.

LOW COUNTRIES

10.500 **Baetens**, R., 'The organization and effects of Flemish privateering in the seventeenth century', *Acta Hist.Neerlandica*, 9, 1976, 48-75. Mainly deals with economic repercussions. For privateering in the Republic see 10.502.

10.501 **Bruijn**, J. R., 'Dutch men-of-war. Those on board, c.1700-50', *ib.*, 7, 1974, 88-121. Social data on seamen and officers.

10.502 —— 'Dutch privateering during the Second and Third Anglo-Dutch Wars', *ib.*, 11, 1979, 79-93.

10.503 **Feld**, M. D., 'Middle-class society and the rise of military professionalism. The Dutch Army, 1589-1609', *Armed Forces & Soc.*, 1, 1975, 419-42. Perspective on military developments fostered by Maurice of Nassau and Oldenbarnevelt.

10.504 **Gutmann**, M. P., *War and Rural Life in the Early Modern Low Countries*, Princeton, N.J., 1980. Examines how much fought-over region of Lower Meuse, around Liège, coped with disruptions of war and disease between 1620 and 1750. Finds surprising powers of recovery. Some results anticipated in his 'Putting crises in perspective. The impact of war on civilian populations in the seventeenth century', *Ann.Démographie Hist.*, 1977, 101-28. And see also 5.125.

10.505 **Ruwet**, J., *Soldats des Régiments Nationaux au 18e Siècle*, Brussels, 1962. Provides information on origins and characteristics of recruits to Belgian regiments.

10.506 **Thoen**, E., 'Warfare and the countryside. Social and economic aspects of military destruction in Flanders during the late middle ages and early modern period', *Acta Hist.Neerlandica*, 13, 1980, 25-39. Deals particularly with effects on agricultural production and rent levels.

SPAIN
See also 10.222,442.

10.507 **Merino Navarro**, J. P., *La Armada Española en el Siglo 18*, Madrid, 1981. Deals esp. with finance, procurement of supplies, and naval construction.

10.508 **Parker**, G., 'Mutiny and discontent in the Spanish Army of Flanders, 1572-1607', *P.& P.*, 58, 1973, 38-52. Anatomy of the 46 mutinies over pay arrears and conditions of service staged in these years.

10.509 **Phillips**, Carla R., *Six Galleons for the King of Spain. Imperial Defense in the Early Seventeenth Century*, Baltimore, Md., 1986. Construction of six galleons at Bilbao for New World service (1625-28) provides framework for examination of shipbuilding industry; naval provisioning; shipboard life; and service record of vessels up to 1640. Interesting illustrations.

ITALY
See also 9.662-3.

10.510 **Barberis**, W., 'Continuità aristocratica e tradizione militare nel Piemonte sabaudo', *Società e Storia*, 4, 1981, 529-92. Looks back over nobility's military role in Piedmont from vantage point of defeat at Novara (1849).

10.511 **Hale**, J. R., 'Military academies on the Venetian terrafirma in the early seventeenth century', *Studi Veneziani*, 15, 1973, 273-95. Repr. in Hale (10.472), 285-308. Academies set up for training of cavalry officers.

10.512 —— 'Printing and military culture of Renaissance Venice', *Medievalia et Humanistica*, n.s., 8, 1977, 21-62. Repr. in Hale (10.472), 429-70. Seeks to explain why there was strong local market for books on military subjects.

10.513 **Mallett**, M. E., *Mercenaries and their Masters. Warfare in Renaissance Italy*, 1974. Important study; main emphasis on fourteenth and fifteenth centuries.

10.514 —— and Hale, J. R., *The Military Organization of a Renaissance State. Venice, c.1400 to 1617*, 1984. Comprehensive examination of recruitment, staffing, finances, fortification, and campaigns engaged in.

10.515 **Pieri**, P., *Il Renascimento e la Crisi Militare Italiana*, Turin, 1952. 2nd ed., 1970. Good background to Italian Wars of early sixteenth century.

HOLY ROMAN EMPIRE AND SWITZERLAND
See also 14.93.

10.516 **Barker**, T. M., *Army, Aristocracy, Monarchy. Essays on War, Society, and Government in Austria, 1618-1780*, New York, 1982. Revised versions of a number of journal articles on military entrepreneurship in Austrian nobility. Comprises three general chapters, followed by case studies of Piccolomini, Lobkovic, and Daun families, and of General Montecuccoli.

10.517 **Büsch**, O., *Militärsystem und Sozialleben im Alten Preussen, 1713-1807. Die Anfänge der Sozialen Militarisierung der Preussisch-Deutschen Gesellschaft*, Berlin, 1962. Valuable study of involvement of peasant and Junker in support of Prussian Army, and its integration into fabric of agrarian society.

10.518 **Casparis**, J., 'The Swiss mercenary system. Labor emigration from the semiperiphery', *Review*, 5, 1982, 593-642. Study conceived in terms of Wallerstein's centre-periphery model.

10.519 **Duffy**, C., *The Army of Frederick the Great*, 1974. Written for popular audience, but informative on everyday life in the service. His companion vol., *The Army of Maria Theresa, 1740-80*, 1977, is less good.

10.520 **Fann**, W. R., 'Peacetime attrition in the army of Frederick William I, 1713-40', *Central Eur.Hist.*, 11, 1978, 323-34. Contends that turn-over from desertion and discharge in the Prussian Army was much less than supposed, especially after 1726.

10.521 **Möller**, H.-M., *Das Regiment der Landsknechte. Untersuchungen zu Verfassung, Recht, und Selbstverständnis in Deutschen Söldnerheeren des 16. Jahrhunderts*, Wiesbaden, 1976. Good study of important mercenary forces continually involved in Valois-Habsburg and French civil wars.

10.522 **Redlich**, F., *The German Military Enterpriser and his Work Force*, 2 vols., 1964-65. Important study of transformation of military recruiting and service conditions from heyday of mercenaries to growth of standing armies and conscription.

EASTERN AND NORTHERN EUROPE
See also 3.281 (Poland); 7.263 (Russia); 11.168 (Sweden).

10.523 **Király**, B. K., and Rothenberg, G. E., eds., *War and Society in East Central Europe, 1. Special Topics and Generalizations on the Eighteenth and Nineteenth Centuries*, New York, 1979. Contains relevant papers on Habsburg

territories, Poland, Balkans, and Cossack regions.

10.524 **Rothenberg**, G. E., and others, eds., *East Central European Society and War in the Pre-Revolutionary Eighteenth Century*, New York, 1982. About thirty essays dealing with military institutions in Habsburg Empire, Poland, Balkans, and Cossack territories.

10.525 **Bak**, J. M., and Király, B. K., eds., *From Hunyadi to Rákóczi. War and Society in Late Medieval and Early Modern Hungary*, New York, 1982. Collection of essays, several of which provide social background to warfare against Turks, and also to anti-Habsburg insurrections, notably that of Rákóczi (1703-11).

10.526 **Fisher**, S. N., 'Ottoman feudalism and its influence upon the Balkans', *Historian*, 15, 1952, 3-22. Describes relation of land tenure and military service in Ottoman system, and its gradual demise from sixteenth century onwards with obsolescence of *sipahi* levies.

10.527 **Inalcik**, H., 'Military and fiscal transformation in the Ottoman Empire, 1600-1700', *Archivum Ottomanicum*, 6, 1980, 283-337. Repr. in Inalcik (3.290). On far-reaching social and fiscal implications of state's large-scale need for mercenaries equipped with handguns.

10.528 **Levy**, A., 'Military reform and the problem of centralization in the Ottoman Empire in the eighteenth century', *Mid.E.Stud.*, 18, 1982, 227-49. Charts attempts at both institutional and technical change.

10.529 **Jespersen**, K. J. V., 'Social change and military revolution in early modern Europe. Some Danish evidence', *Hist.J.*, 26, 1983, 1-13. Reasons for survival of knight service into late seventeenth century.

10.530 **Alef**, G., 'Muscovite military reforms in the second half of the fifteenth century', *Forsch.Osteur.Gesch.*, 18, 1973, 73-108. Repr. in Alef (6.217). Mainly on expansion of army and obligations to military service; little on financing.

10.531 **Duffy**, C., *Russia's Military Way to the West. Origins and Nature of Russian Military Power, 1700-1800*, 1981. Mainly deals with military machine and campaigns, but has chapters on soldiers and officers.

10.532 **Esper**, T., 'Military self-sufficiency and

weapons technology in Muscovite Russia', *Slavic Rev.*, 28, 1969, 185-208. On successful efforts to build up domestic manufacture of armaments.

10.533 **Keep**, J. L. H., 'Catherine's veterans', *Slavonic & E.Eur.Rev.*, 59, 1981, 385-96. Analyses data on veteran rankers (over 25 years service) of Yaroslavl' Regiment.

10.534 —— *Soldiers of the Tsar. Army and Society in Russia, 1462-1874*, 1985. Likely to be standard survey.

10.535 **Kimerling**, Elise, 'Soldiers' children, 1719-1856. A study of social engineering in imperial Russia', *Forsch.Osteur.Gesch.*, 30, 1982, 61-136. Detailed study of educational and other welfare provision made for children of non-commissioned soldiers (expected to continue in military service).

10.536 **Kleimola**, Ann M., 'Military service and elite status in Muscovy in the second quarter of the sixteenth century', *Russ.Hist.*, 7, 1980, 47-64. Considers significance of appointments to regimental commands.

10.537 **O'Brien**, C. B., 'Agriculture in Russian war economy in the later seventeenth century', *Am.Slavic & E.Eur.Rev.*, 8, 1949, 167-74. Use of land grants as means of financing army.

10.538 **Stevens**, Carol B., 'Belgorod. Notes on literacy and language in the seventeenth-century Russian Army', *Russ.Hist.*, 7, 1980, 113-24. Investigates literacy and nationality among regimental officers from account book evidence.

11

LIVING STANDARDS,
HEALTH, AND WELFARE

MONEY, PRICES, AND WAGES
Other general references: 7.278; 11.98.

11.1 **Attman**, A., *The Bullion Flow between Europe and the East, 1000-1750*, Gothenburg, 1981. Traces Europe's consistently unfavourable balance of trade with Asia. See also on this topic 9.319; 11.16,38,75.

11.2 **Braudel**, F., and Spooner, F., 'Prices in Europe from 1450 to 1750', in *Cambridge Economic History of Europe, 4* (2.15), 378-486. Explains difficulties of subject without itself being difficult. Accompanied by many graphs.

11.3 **Flynn**, D. O., 'Sixteenth-century inflation from a production point of view', in Schmukler and Marcus (6.114), 157-69. Reverts to view of inflation as primarily due to excess supply of silver.

11.4 **Grierson**, P., 'The monetary pattern of sixteenth-century coinage', *Trans. Roy. Hist. Soc.*, 5th ser. 21, 1971, 45-60. On factors governing issue of new coins.

11.5 **Gunnarsson**, G., 'A study in the historiography of prices', *Ec.& Hist.*, 19, 1976, 124-41. Short account of pioneers such as Thorold Rogers, Beveridge, and Hamilton.

11.6 **Hamilton**, E. J., 'The history of prices before 1750', in *Eleventh International Congress of Historical Sciences*, Stockholm, 1960, Rapports 1, 144-64.

11.7 —— 'Prices and progress', *J.Ec.Hist.*, 12, 1952, 323-49. Keynesian view of price trends since medieval times, stressing beneficial effects of modest inflation.

11.8 **Kellenbenz**, H., ed., *Precious Metals in the Age of Expansion. Papers of the 14th Int. Congress of Hist. Sciences*, Stuttgart, 1981. Papers (majority in English) on many aspects of production and trade of gold, silver, and copper in period 1450-1750. Well summarised in editor's concluding essay (307-61).

11.9 **McCusker**, J. J., *Money and Exchange in Europe and America, 1600-1775. A Handbook*, Chapel Hill, N.C., 1978. Tables of exchange rates prevailing at Amsterdam, Hamburg, Copenhagen, Paris, Cadiz, and Lisbon. See also his 'The rate of exchange on Amsterdam in London, 1590-1660', *J.Eur.Ec.Hist.*, 8, 1979, 689-705.

11.10 **Maczak**, A., 'Die Sundzollregister als eine preisgeschichtliche Quelle, 1557 bis 1647', *Jb.Wirtschaftsgesch.*, 1970 (iii), 179-220.

11.11 **Metz**, R., 'Long waves in coinage and grain price series from the fifteenth to the eighteenth century', *Review*, 7, 1984, 599-647. Applies filter method to price data to establish unbiased Kondratieff curves. For sceptical view of cycle-spotting in early modern economic history, see M. Morineau, 'Juglar, Kitchin, Kondratieff, et compagnie', *ib.*, 577-98.

11.12 **Miskimin**, H. A., 'Agenda for early modern economic history', *J.Ec.Hist.*, 31, 1971, 172-83. Deals almost exclusively with problem of sixteenth-century inflation.

11.13 **Morineau**, M., *Incroyables Gazettes et Fabuleux Métaux. Les Retours des Trésors Américains d'après les Gazettes Hollandaises (16e-18e Siècles)*, 1985. Reprint of five lengthy articles re-evaluating, from Dutch newsletters, quantities of bullion shipped from America to Europe. Strongly critical of "sixteenth-century boom, seventeenth-century stagnation" dichotomy.

11.14 **Phelps Brown**, E. H., and Hopkins, S. V., *A Perspective of Wages and Prices*, 1981. Brings together (1-105) articles on sixteenth-century inflation originally publ. in *Economica*.

11.15 **Redlich**, F., 'The eighteenth-century trade in "light ducats". A profitable illegal business', *Ec.& Hist.*, 16, 1973, 3-14. On clipping of Dutch and German coins.

11.16 **Richards**, J. F., ed., *Precious Metals in the Later Medieval and Early Modern Worlds*, Durham, N.C., 1983. 16 papers dealing principally with monetary flows rather than production. Strong emphasis on Asia and America.

11.17 **Zabinski**, Z., 'The biological index of the buying power of money', in Forster and Ranum (5.256), 179-90. Transl. from *Annales*, 23, 1968, 808-18. Suggests using value index based on daily minimum nutritional requirement.

11.18 **Vilar**, P., *A History of Gold and Money, 1450-1920*, 1976. Transl. from Spanish ed. of 1969. Useful starting point.

FRANCE
See also 3.16; 9.529.

11.19 **Baulant**, Micheline, 'Prix et salaires à Paris au 16e siècle. Sources et résultats', *Annales*, 31, 1976, 954-95. Evidence from accounts of hospitals, convents, and colleges.

11.20 —— and Meuvret, J., *Prix des Céréales extraits de la Mercuriale de Paris, 1520-1698*, 2 vols., Paris, 1960-62. Grain price series, based on records of Châtelet, court which fixed maximum bread prices. Review article: P. Chaunu, *Annales*, 16, 1961, 791-803; 19, 1964, 1171-81.

11.21 **Beutler**, Corinne, 'Bâtiment et salaires. Un chantier à Saint-Germain-des-Prés de 1644 à 1646', *ib.*, 26, 1971, 484-517. Detailed accounts kept during repairs to Abbey.

11.22 **Dermigny**, L., 'Circuits de l'argent et milieux d'affaires au 18e siècle', *Rev.Hist.*, 212, 1954, 239-78.

11.23 **Dupâquier**, J., and others, *Mercuriales du Pays de France et du Vexin Français, 1640-1792*, Paris, 1968. Price series for seven markets in Paris region.

11.24 **Frêche**, G., and Frêche, Geneviève, *Les Prix des Grains, des Vins, et des Légumes à Toulouse, 1486-1868*, Paris, 1967. Tables compiled from *mercuriales*.

11.25 **Glassman**, Debra, and Redish, Angela, 'New estimates of the money stock in France, 1493-1690', *J.Ec.Hist.*, 45, 1985, 31-46. Computations to allow for recoinage and losses through wear, export, etc.

11.26 **Hauser**, H., *Recherches et Documents sur l'Histoire des Prix en France de 1500 à 1800*, Paris, 1936. Takes form of tables of basic goods prices for various regions (largely excludes Midi).

11.27 **Labrousse**, E., *Esquisse du Mouvement des Prix et des Revenus en France au 18e Siècle*, 2 vols., Paris, 1933. Another fundamental statistical source. Note also early tables of Labrousse and others, *Prix du Froment en France au Temps de la Monnaie Stable, 1726-1913*, Paris, 1970 (average monthly prices arranged by *département*).

11.28 **Le Roy Ladurie**, E., 'Changes in Parisian rents from the end of the middle ages to the eighteenth century', in Le Roy Ladurie (4.35), 61-75. Transl. from *Annales*, 25, 1970, 1002-23. Based on computer analysis of many thousands of leases.

11.29 **Meuvret**, J., 'Monetary circulation and the use of coinage in sixteenth- and seventeenth-century France', in Cameron and others (3.251), 140-49. Repr. in Earle (3.71), 89-99.

11.30 **Miskimin**, H. A., *Money and Power in Fifteenth-Century France*, New Haven, Conn., 1984. Account of monetary system, with lengthy appendix detailing output of official mints, 1395-1495.

11.31 **Morineau**, M., 'Budgets populaires en France au 18e siècle', *Rev.Hist.Éc.et Soc.*, 50, 1972, 203-37, 449-81. Evidence for standard of living of wage-earners.

11.32 **Richet**, D., 'Causes of inflation in France in the sixteenth century', *J.Eur.Ec.Hist.*, 4, 1975, 707-15. Sketch of materials available and concepts to explore. Pioneer work still of interest on this theme is A. Liautey, *La Hausse des Prix et la Lutte contre la Cherté en France au 16e Siècle*, Paris, 1921.

11.33 —— 'Le cours officiel des monnaies étrangères circulant en France au 16e siècle', *Rev.Hist.*, 225, 1961, 359-96. Offers tables of exchange rates and coin quality.

11.34 **Riley**, J. C., 'Monetary growth and price stability. France, 1650-1700', *J. Interdisc. Hist.*, 15, 1984, 235-54. Attributes seeming paradox to widespread increase in hoarding, and looks for social explanations.

11.35 —— and McCusker, J. J., 'Money supply, economic growth, and the quantity theory of money. France, 1650-1788', *Explor. Ec. Hist.*, 20, 1983, 274-93. More evidence that fast growth of money supply accompanied stable prices, and vice versa.

11.36 **Spooner**, F. C., *The International Economy and Monetary Movements in France, 1493-1725*, Cambridge, Mass., 1972. Revised and extended English version of pioneering work publ. in French in 1956. Review article: J. Meuvret, *Annales*, 15, 1960, 569-77.

11.37 —— 'Monetary disturbance and inflation, 1590-93. The case of Aix-en-Provence', in *Mélanges...Braudel* (9.85), 1, 583-97. Example of economic disruption caused by rival mints of civil war parties.

LOW COUNTRIES
See also 11.141.

11.38 **Attman**, A., *Dutch Enterprise in the World Bullion Trade, 1550-1800*, Gothenburg, 1983. Relatively short study which tries to estimate outflow from Netherlands to "deficit zones" of Baltic, Levant, and Asia. See also 11.1.

11.39 **Cauwenberghe**, E. H. G. van, 'Inflation in the Southern Low Countries from the fourteenth to the seventeenth centuries', in Schmukler and Marcus (6.114), 147-56.

11.40 **De Vries**, J., 'An inquiry into the behaviour of wages in the Dutch Republic and the Southern Netherlands, 1580-1800', *Acta Hist.Neerlandica*, 10, 1978, 79-97. Repr. (with discussion) in Aymard (9.50), 37-72. Presents evidence that Dutch wage levels rose well above Flemish, and had deleterious effect in eighteenth century.

11.41 **Fanchamps**, M. L., *Recherches Statistiques sur le Problème Annonaire dans la Principauté de Liège de 1475 à la fin du 16e Siècle*, Liège, 1970. Study of prices and subsistence crises.

11.42 **Friis**, Astrid, 'Two crises in the Netherlands in 1557', *Scan.Ec.Hist.Rev.*, 1, 1953, 193-241. Deals with effects of grain crisis on financial confidence. Lengthy appendix provides tables of grain prices between 1556 and 1588 from Sound dues accounts.

11.43 **Koenigsberger**, H. G., 'Property and the price revolution. Hainault, 1474-1573', *Ec.Hist.Rev.*, 2nd ser. 9, 1956, 1-15. Repr. in his *Estates and Revolutions. Essays in Early Modern European History*, Ithaca, N.Y., 1971, 144-65. Argues that incomes of small property holders held up better than those of nobility.

11.44 **Middelhoven**, P. J., 'Auctions at Amsterdam of Northern European pinewood, 1717-1808. A contribution to the history of prices', *Acta Hist.Neerlandica*, 13, 1980, 65-89.

11.45 **Posthumus**, N. W., *Inquiry into the History of Prices in Holland*, 2 vols., Leiden, 1946-64. Vol. 1 tables wholesale prices on Amsterdam Exchange, 1585-1914; vol. 2 details prices recorded by institutions in Utrecht, Leiden, and Amsterdam. Review article: M. Morineau, *Annales*, 23, 1968, 178-205.

11.46 **Riemersma**, J. C., 'Monetary confusion as a factor in the economic expansion of Europe (1550-1650)', *Explor. Entrepren. Hist.*, 5, 1952, 61-74. Explores linkage between currency depreciations and commercial expansion in Netherlands.

11.47 **Ruwet**, J., and others, *Le Marché des Céréales à Ruremonde, Luxembourg, Namur et Diest aux 17e et 18e Siècles*, Louvain, 1966. Price tables taken from *mercuriales*.

11.48 **Schöffer**, I., and Gaastra, F., 'The import of bullion and coin into Asia by the Dutch East India Company in the seventeenth and eighteenth centuries', in Aymard (9.50), 215-33.

11.49 **Spufford**, P., *Monetary Problems and Policies in the Netherlands, 1433-96*, Leiden, 1970. Rather narrow, technical study.

11.50 **Tits-Dieuaide**, Marie-J., *La Formation des Prix Céréaliers en Brabant et en Flandre au 15e Siècle*, Brussels, 1975. Valuable data on local yields as well as price series.

11.51 **Van der Wee**, H., 'Prices and wages as development variables. Comparison between England and the Southern

Netherlands, 1400-1700', *Acta Hist.Neerlandica*, 10, 1978, 58-78. Tentative hypothesis that high-wage economy of Brabant may have hindered economic growth in later part of period.

11.52 **Verlinden**, C., 'Price and wage movements in Belgium in the sixteenth century', in Burke (1.1), 55-84. Transl. from *Annales*, 10, 1955, 173-98.

11.53 —— and others, eds., *Documents pour l'Histoire des Prix et des Salaires en Flandre et en Brabant, 15e-18e Siècle*, 2 vols. in 3, Bruges, 1959-65. Documents in Dutch and French, covering very wide range of places, commodities, and trades. Review article: M. Morineau, *Annales*, 24, 1969, 403-23.

SPAIN AND PORTUGAL
See also 7.286; 10.123; 11.147.

11.54 **Flynn**, D. O., 'A new perspective on the Spanish price revolution. The monetary approach to the balance of payments', *Explor.Ec.Hist.*, 15, 1978, 388-406. More a contribution to balance of payments theory than a historian's approach.

11.55 **Forsyth**, P. J., and Nicholas, S. J., 'The decline of Spanish industry and the price revolution. A neoclassical analysis', *J.Eur.Ec.Hist.*, 12, 1983, 601-10. Looks at effects of American bullion as typical of any natural resource boom rather than in terms of money supply.

11.56 **Gonzalez**, M. J., and Del Hoyo, J., 'Dinero y precios en la España del siglo 16. Una confirmación de la tesis de Hamilton', *Moneda y Crédito*, 166, 1983, 15-46.

11.57 **Hamilton**, E. J., *War and Prices in Spain, 1651-1800*, Cambridge, Mass., 1947. Sequel to his famous *American Treasure and the Price Revolution in Spain, 1501-1650*, 1934, which has continued to set terms of debate about price repercussions of silver imports. Data mostly from hospital archives.

11.58 **Le Flem**, J. P., 'Sociedad y precios en el siglo de oro. La mercurial de Segovia, 1540-1705', *Cuad.Investigación Hist.*, 1, 1977, 59-72. Interesting price series from major population centre.

11.59 **Mackay**, A., *Money, Prices, and Politics in Fifteenth-Century Castile*, 1981. Seeks tentatively to discern whether monetary factors shaped social situation or merely reflected more dynamic factors.

11.60 **Magalhaes Godinho**, V., *Prix et Monnaies au Portugal, 1750-1850*, Paris, 1955. Emphasis on price series.

11.61 **Taylor**, H., 'Price revolution or price revision? The English and Spanish trade after 1604', *Renaiss.& Mod.Stud.*, 12, 1968, 5-32. Uses experience of English merchants trading to Spain to evaluate Hamilton's evidence about Spanish currency and prices (11.57).

11.62 **Ulloa**, M., 'Castilian seigniorage and coinage in the reign of Philip II', *J.Eur.Ec.Hist.*, 4, 1975, 459-79. New information on history of Castilian mints.

11.63 **Vilar**, P., 'Élan urbain et mouvement des salaires. Le cas de Barcelone au 18e siècle', *Rev.Hist.Éc.et Soc.*, 28, 1950, 364-401. Draws largely on building contracts in notarial archives.

ITALY
See also 8.100; 9.90.

11.64 **Basini**, G. L., *Sul Mercato di Modena tra Cinque- e Seicento. Prezzi e Salari*, Milan, 1974. See also his *Zecca e Monete a Modena nei Secoli 16 e 17*, Parma, 1967.

11.65 **Cipolla**, C., *Mouvements Monétaires dans l'État de Milan, 1580-1700*, Paris, 1952. Based on statistics of output of Milan mint.

11.66 —— 'The so-called "price revolution". Reflections on the Italian situation', in Burke (1.1), 43-54. Transl. from *Annales*, 10, 1955, 513-6; 12, 1957, 269-74. Debate about quantity theory and inflation between Cipolla and A. R. E. Chabert.

11.67 **Damsholt**, T., 'Four series of Tuscan corn-prices, 1520-1630', *Scan. Ec. Hist. Rev.*, 12, 1964, 145-64. Analyses long-term rise, seasonal trends, relation to other commodities, etc.

11.68 **De Maddalena**, A., *Prezzi e Aspetti di Mercato in Milano durante il Secolo 17*, Milan, 1950. Continued by *Prezzi e Mercedi a Milano dal 1701 al 1860*, 2 vols., Milan, 1974. Price series based mainly on institutional expenditures.

11.69 **Felloni**, G., *Il Mercato Monetario in Piemonte nel Secolo 18*, Milan, 1968. Technical study of mint production and policy, on Spooner model (see 11.36).

11.70 **Lane**, F. C., and Mueller, R. C., *Money and Banking in Medieval and Renaissance Venice. Vol.1: Coins and Moneys of Account*, Baltimore, Md., 1985. Posthumous work in Lane's case. Often technical, but monetary history firmly placed in general context of commercial policy.

11.71 **Lombardini**, G., *Pane e Denaro a Bassano tra il 1501 e il 1799*, Vicenza, 1963. Grain price series (wholesale and retail) for a Venetian commune.

11.72 **Pullan**, B., 'Wage-earners and the Venetian economy, 1550-1630', *Ec.Hist.Rev.*, 2nd ser. 16, 1964, 407-26. Repr. in Pullan (3.156), 146-74. Finds little evidence of wage lag discerned in other European regions, perhaps because of large plague mortality of 1570s.

11.73 **Romano**, R., *Prezzi, Salari e Servizi a Napoli nel Secolo 18*, Milan, 1965. Repr. in his *Napoli dal Viceregno al Regno*, Turin, 1976. Largely consists of price and wage series.

11.74 **Silva**, J.-G. da, 'La dépréciation monétaire en Italie du Nord au 17e siècle. Le cas de Venise', *Studi Veneziani*, 15, 1973, 297-348.

11.75 **Tucci**, U., 'Les émissions monétaires de Venise et les mouvements internationaux de l'or', *Rev.Hist.*, 260, 1978, 91-122. On flow of European gold towards East, and supremacy of Venetian coinage in this process (sixteenth to eighteenth centuries).

11.76 **Vigo**, G., 'Real wages of the working class in Italy. Building workers' wages (fourteenth to eighteenth century)', *J.Eur.Ec.Hist.*, 3, 1974, 378-99.

CENTRAL, EASTERN, AND NORTHERN EUROPE
See also 6.202 (Poland); 9.603; 10.256 (Balkans).

11.77 **Hoszowski**, S., 'Central Europe and the sixteenth- and seventeenth-century price revolution', in Burke (1.1), 85-103. Transl. from *Annales*, 16, 1961, 441-56.

11.78 **Kiss**, I. N., 'Preis- und Kaufkraft-verschiebungen im deutschen, österreichischen, und ungarischen Donaugebiet vom 16. bis zum 18. Jahrhundert', *Jb.Gesch.Feudalismus*, 8, 1984, 311-40. See also 11.86.

11.79 **Elsas**, M. J., *Umriss einer Geschichte der Preise und Löhne in Deutschland vom ausgehenden Mittelalter bis zum Beginn des 19. Jahrhunderts*, 3 vols., Leiden, 1936-1949. Price tables for number of major German cities. See also recent valuable supplement by H.-J. Gerhard, *Löhne im Vor- und Frühindustriellen Deutschland. Materialen zur Entwicklung*

von Lohnsatzen von der Mitte des 18. bis zur Mitte des 19. Jahrhunderts, Göttingen, 1984.

11.80 **Heimpel**, C., *Die Entwicklung der Einnahmen und Ausgaben des Heiliggeistspitals zu Biberach an der Riss von 1500 bis 1630*, Stuttgart, 1966. Price study based on receipts and expenditure of a Swabian hospital.

11.81 **Irsigler**, F., 'La mercuriale de Cologne (1531-1797). Structure du marché et conjoncture des prix céréaliers', *Annales*, 33, 1978, 93-114. Reviews trends in agriculture and in provisioning policy that can be deduced from this very long price series.

11.82 **Redlich**, F., 'Jewish enterprise and Prussian coinage in the eighteenth century', *Explor.Entrepren.Hist.*, 3, 1951, 161-81. On leasing of Prussian mints.

11.83 **Bogucka**, Maria, 'The monetary crisis of the seventeenth century and its social and psychological consequences in Poland', *J.Eur.Ec.Hist.*, 4, 1975, 137-52. Argues that coinage crisis of 1620s was part of continental pattern, that of 1650s more local in cause.

11.84 **Hoszowski**, S., *Les Prix à Lwow (16e-17e siècles)*, Paris, 1954. Transl. of work first publ. in Polish in 1928.

11.85 —— 'The revolution of prices in Poland in the sixteenth and seventeenth centuries', *Acta Poloniae Hist.*, 2, 1959, 7-16. Claims rise in agricultural prices was wholly appropriated by nobility.

11.86 **Kiss**, I. N., 'Money, prices, values, and purchasing power from the sixteenth to the eighteenth centuries', *J.Eur.Ec.Hist.*, 9, 1980, 459-90. Observations using primarily Hungarian data.

11.87 **Klima**, A., 'Inflation in Bohemia in the early stage of the seventeenth century', in *Proc.Seventh International Economic History Congress* (4.45), 2, 375-86. Mainly on effects of coinage devaluation of 1622-23.

11.88 **Barkan**, O. L., 'The price revolution of the sixteenth century. A turning point in the economic history of the Near East', *Int.J.Mid.E.Stud.*, 6, 1973, 3-28. Deals with social upheaval in Ottoman Empire resulting from inflation and population pressure.

11.89 **Berov**, L., 'Changes in price conditions in trade between Turkey and Europe in the sixteenth-nineteenth century', *Ét.*

Balkaniques, 10 (ii-iii), 1974, 168-78. With graphs.

11.90 **Gerber**, H., 'The monetary system of the Ottoman Empire', *J. Ec. & Soc. Hist. Orient*, 25, 1982, 308-24. Brief outline of currency system and frequent debasements down to end of eighteenth century.

11.91 **Bengtsson**, T., and Jörberg, L., 'Market integration in Sweden during the eighteenth and nineteenth centuries. Spectral analysis of grain prices', *Ec.& Hist.*, 18, 1975, 93-106. Examines trend to greater uniformity in prices, seen as evidence of market integration.

11.92 **Bjurling**, O., 'Price developments in the Swedish realm during the latter part of the seventeenth century', *ib.*, 1, 1958, 3-20. Largely a critique of E. Heckscher's treatment of this question in his classic economic history of Sweden (3.340). For criticism of Heckscher on associated topic see 11.167.

11.93 **Eagly**, R. V., 'Monetary policy and politics in mid-eighteenth-century Sweden', *J.Ec.Hist.*, 29, 1969, 739-55. Controversy over inflation generated by credit expansion of state bank. See further debate with L. G. Sandberg, *ib.*, 30, 1970, 653-6.

11.94 **Friis**, Astrid, and Glamann, K., *A History of Prices and Wages in Denmark, 1660-1800*, 1958. Vol.1 (no further vols. publ.) deals with commodity prices at Copenhagen.

11.95 **Hammarström**, Ingrid, 'The "price revolution" of the sixteenth century. Some Swedish evidence', *Scan.Ec.Hist.Rev.*, 5, 1957, 118-54. As well as presenting table of Stockholm commodity prices, considers general European context of inflation.

11.96 **Jörberg**, L., 'The development of real wages for agricultural workers in Sweden during the eighteenth and nineteenth centuries', *Ec.& Hist.*, 15, 1972, 41-57.

11.97 —— *A History of Prices in Sweden, 1732-1914*, Lund, 1972. Consists mainly of year by year tabulation of regional variations.

11.98 **Söderberg**, J., 'Real wage trends in urban Europe, 1730-1850. Stockholm in a comparative perspective', *Soc.Hist.*, 12, 1987, 155-76. Finds marked deterioration in real wages in later eighteenth century

across broad band of European cities.

11.99 **Thestrup**, P., *The Standard of Living in Copenhagen, 1730-1800. Some Methods of Measurement*, Copenhagen, 1971.

11.100 **Mankov**, A. G., *Le Mouvement des Prix dans l'État Russe du 16e Siècle*, Paris, 1957. Transl. from Russian ed. of 1951. Shows from accounts of religious communities that inflation affected Russia to much same degree as Western Europe. See discussion of his work by J. Blum, *J.Ec.Hist.*, 16, 1956, 182-99.

11.101 **Mironov**, B. N., 'The "price revolution" in eighteenth-century Russia', *Soviet Stud.in Hist.*, 11 (iv), 1973, 325-52. Argues that increasing availability and cheapness of bullion led to price inflation.

METROLOGY
See also 14.105 (concerns Russia).

11.102 **Kula**, W., *Measures and Men*, Princeton, N. J., 1986. Part 1 considers importance of measures and their general historical development; part 2 concerns metrology of early modern Poland; and part 3 that of France (esp. late eighteenth-century pressure for standardisation).

11.103 **Lane**, F. C., 'Tonnages, medieval and modern', *Ec.Hist.Rev.*, 2nd ser., 17, 1964, 213-33. Repr. in Lane (9.86), 345-70. Useful summary of weights and measures still widely used in early modern period.

11.104 **Zupko**, R. E., *French Weights and Measures before the Revolution. A Dictionary of Provincial and Local Units*, Bloomington, Ind., 1978.

11.105 —— *Italian Weights and Measures from the Middle Ages to the Nineteenth Century*, Philadelphia, 1981. Two most useful handbooks.

11.106 **Witthöft**, H., *Umrisse einer Historischen Metrologie zum Nutzen der Wirtschafts- und Sozialgeschichtlichen Forschung*, 2 vols., Göttingen, 1979. Massive technical demonstration of common factors in diversity of measures, starting from those used in city of Lüneburg.

11.107 **Inalcik**, H., 'Introduction to Ottoman metrology', *Turcica*, 15, 1983, 311-48. Repr. in Inalcik (3.290).

FOOD SUPPLY AND DIET

*See preceding sub-section for serial data on food prices; and Section 12 passim
for popular violence over subsistence issues. Also 5.32,38-9; 7.300.*

11.108 **Abel**, W., *Massenarmut und Hungerkrisen in
Vorindustriellen Europa*, Hamburg, 1974.
Excellent history of agricultural and
subsistence crises from sixteenth to mid-
nineteenth centuries.

11.109 **Bizière**, J. M., 'Hot beverages and the
enterprising spirit in eighteenth-century
Europe', *Hist.Childhood Q.*, 7, 1979,
135-45. Psychohistorical explanation of
increasing consumption of tea, coffee, etc.
On coffee and cafés as social institution see
14.57.

11.110 **Bonnet**, J.-C., and Fink, Béatrice, eds.,
'Aliments et cuisine', *Dix-Huitième
Siècle*, 15, 1983, 5-210. Group of short
articles on eighteenth-century diet,
recipes, food themes in literature and
painting, etc.

11.111 **Braudel**, F., and others, 'Vie matérielle et
comportements biologiques', *Annales*,
16-24, 1961-69, *passim*. Valuable series of
articles on history and sociology of
European diet; many sections involve early
modern period.

11.112 **Flandrin**, J.-L., 'Le goût et la nécessité.
Sur l'usage des graisses dans les cuisines
d'Europe occidentale (14e-18e siècle)',
Annales, 38, 1983, 369-401. Discusses
implications of trend towards cooking with
fats, and Europe's division into olive oil
and dairy fat zones.

11.113 **Hémardinquer**, J. J., ed., *Pour une
Histoire de l'Alimentation. Recueil de
Travaux*, Paris, 1970. Anthology of essays,
mostly reprinted from *Annales* (see
11.111). Section on naval diet in early
modern period is of particular interest. For
comment see 11.117.

11.114 'Histoire de la consommation', *Annales*,
30, 1975, 402-631. Useful symposium,
containing several articles on early modern
Europe. See 11.129 and 11.154 for papers
in translation.

11.115 **Le Roy Ladurie**, E., 'Famine
amenorrhoea (seventeenth-twentieth
centuries)', in Le Roy Ladurie (4.35),
255-71; and in Forster and Ranum (5.256),
163-78. Transl. from *Annales*, 24, 1969,
1589-1601. On link between food shortage
and failure of menstruation.

11.116 **Morineau**, M., 'The potato in the

eighteenth century', in R. Forster and O.
Ranum, eds., *Food and Drink in History.
Selections from the Annales*, 5, Baltimore,
Md., 1979, 17-36. Transl. from *Annales*,
25, 1970, 1767-84. Critique of Dutch
article by C. Vandenbroeke on diffusion of
potato into France and Belgium (see 11.123
for English-language version).

11.117 **Neveux**, H., 'L'alimentation du 14e au 18e
siècle. Essai de mise au point',
Rev.Hist.Éc.et Soc., 51, 1973, 336-77.
Survey of recent literature, with particular
reference to Hémardinquer's collection
(11.113). See also comment by M.
Morineau, *ib.*, 54, 1976, 258-65.

11.118 **Post, J. D.**, *Food Shortage, Climatic
Variability, and Epidemic Disease in Pre-
Industrial Europe. The Mortality Peak in the
Early 1740s*, Ithaca, N.Y., 1985. Uses this
demographic crisis to test how far crop
diversification and poor relief systems
could temper effects of run of bad harvests.

11.119 **Revel**, J.-F., *Un Festin en Paroles. Histoire
Littéraire de la Sensibilité Gastronomique de
l'Antiquité à nos Jours*, Paris, 1979.
Pleasantly illustrated, and more
informative than title might suggest.

11.120 **Rotberg**, R. I., and Rabb, T. K., *Hunger
and History. The Impact of Changing Food
Production and Consumption Patterns on
Society*, 1985. Symposium. Most papers
non-specific in geography and period,
concentrating on methodological issues.
First publ. in *J.Interdisc.Hist.*, 14, 1983,
199-534.

11.121 **Tannahill**, Reay, *Food in History*, 1973.
Panoramic survey. Popular work, but well
researched. See part 5, 'The expanding
world, 1490-1800' (236-317).

11.122 **Tilly**, C., 'Food supply and public order in
modern Europe', in Tilly (10.25), 380-455.
Highly cogent survey, sharing some of
Rudé's insights on evolution of this issue
(see 12.13-17).

11.123 **Vandenbroeke**, C., 'Cultivation and
consumption of the potato in the
seventeenth and eighteenth century', *Acta
Hist.Neerlandica*, 5, 1971, 15-39.

FRANCE
See also 10.397.

1.124 **Appleby**, A. B., 'Grain prices and subsistence crises in England and France, 1590-1740', *J.Ec.Hist.*, 39, 1979, 865-87. Suggests that greater use of spring-sown crops may have made England less vulnerable than France to grain crises in later seventeenth century.

1.125 **Berger**, P., 'French administration in the famine of 1693', *Eur.Stud.Rev.*, 8, 1978, 101-28. Contends that response to crisis was traditionally local and does not show any sweeping moves towards centralisation. See also his 'Pontchartrain and the grain trade during the famine of 1693', *J.Mod.Hist.*, 48, 1976, on demand article. (Pontchartrain was Controller-General of Finance and secretary covering commerce and naval affairs).

1.126 **Bernard**, R.-J., 'Peasant diet in eighteenth-century Gévaudan', in Elborg Forster and R. Forster, eds., *European Diet from Pre-Industrial to Modern Times. Selections from the* Annales, New York, 1975, 19-46.

1.127 **Bricourt**, M., and others, 'La crise de subsistance des années 1740 dans le ressort du Parlement de Paris', *Ann.Démographie Hist.*, 1974, 281-333. Substantial study of authorities' management of shortages in 1740-41.

1.128 **Danière**, A., 'Feudal incomes and demand elasticity for bread in late eighteenth century France', *J.Ec.Hist.*, 18, 1958, 317-44. Argues, against E. Labrousse (see 3.33), that farmers could not count on inelasticity of demand for grain. Includes comments from D. S. Landes.

1.129 **Frijhoff**, W., and Julia, D., 'The diet in boarding schools at the end of the ancien régime', in Forster and Ranum (11.116), 73-85.

1.130 **Hémardinquer**, J.-J., 'The family pig of the ancien régime. Myth or fact?', *ib.*, 50-72. Transl. from *Annales*, 25, 1970, 1745-66. Questions idea that pig rearing was common or easy option to supplement diet of the poor in eighteenth-century France. Very similar paper appears in 11.131, 9-37.

1.131 'Histoire de l'alimentation', *Actes Congrès Nat.Soc.Savantes*, 93 (i), 1971, 9-241. Includes six papers on eighteenth-century aspects.

11.132 **Hufton**, Olwen, 'Social conflict and the grain supply in eighteenth-century France', *J.Interdisc.Hist.*, 14, 1983, 303-31. Repr. in Rotberg and Rabb (11.120), 105-33.

11.133 **Kaplan**, S. L., *Bread, Politics, and Political Economy in the Reign of Louis XV*, 2 vols., The Hague, 1976. Deals in great detail with government experiment of 1760s in free trade as opposed to traditional interventionism at times of dearth. Review article: K. M. Baker, *J.Mod.Hist.*, 50, 1978, 701-11.

11.134 —— *The Famine Plot Persuasion in Eighteenth-Century France*, Philadelphia, 1982. Short study dealing with rifeness of conspiracy theories at periods of grain shortage. Note Kaplan's paper on Paris bread riot of 1725 (12.38).

11.135 —— 'Lean years, fat years. The "community" granary system and the search for abundance in eighteenth-century Paris', *Fr.Hist.Stud.*, 10, 1977, 197-230. On attempts of Paris police to compel convents, hospitals, etc., to stock grain reserves.

11.136 —— *Provisioning Paris. Merchants and Millers in the Grain and Flour Trade during the Eighteenth Century*, Ithaca, N.Y., 1984.

11.137 **Lemarchand**, G., 'Economic crises and social atmosphere in urban society under Louis XIV', in Kierstead (6.68), 233-64. Transl. from *Rev.Hist.Mod.et Contemp.*, 14, 1967, 244-65. Deals with subsistence crises in Rouen and Dieppe.

11.138 **Mennell**, S., *All Manners of Food. Eating and Taste in England and France from the Middle Ages to the Present*, 1985. Looks at food in terms of status and fashion, influenced by approach of Norbert Elias (see 14.12).

11.139 **Rogers**, J. W., 'Subsistence crises and political economy in France at the end of the ancien régime', *Res.in Ec.Hist.*, 5, 1980, 249-301. On conflict between free trade theorists and administrators responsible for regulating food prices. See also 11.133.

11.140 **Wheaton**, Barbara K., *Savoring the Past. The French Kitchen and Table from 1300 to 1789*, Philadelphia, 1983. Concentrates on food of the wealthy, and evolution of *haute cuisine*.

OTHER REGIONS
See also 11.41 (Netherlands); 11.243,341 (Italy); 5.208 (Anatolia).

11.141 **Faber**, J. A., 'Dearth and famine in pre-industrial Netherlands', *Acta Hist.Neerlandica*, 13, 1980, 51-64. Contends that grain price fluctuations were less marked in Holland than in most of Europe.

11.142 **Tracy**, J. D., 'Habsburg grain policy and Amsterdam politics. The career of Willem Dirkszoon Baerdes, 1542-66', *Sixteenth-Cent.J.*, 14, 1983, 293-319. On tensions between grain merchants and government over price regulation.

11.143 **Vandenbroeke**, C., *Agriculture et Alimentation dans les Pays-Bas Autrichiens*, Ghent, 1975. On food production and markets during second half of eighteenth century.

11.144 **Cowgill**, U. M., and Johnson, H. B., 'Grain prices and vital statistics in a Portuguese rural parish, 1671-1720', *J.Biosoc.Sci.*, 3, 1971, 321-9. Postulates that women probably had less access to wheat diet than men, and that consequent poor nutrition in pregnancy helps account for rate of still-born male infants.

11.145 **Gibson**, C., 'An historical event and its interpretation. The Castilian grain crisis of 1506-07', *Soc.Sci.Hist.*, 2, 1978, 230-47. Criticises view that social structure accounts for inability to cope with natural disasters.

11.146 **Ibarra y Rodríguez**, E., *El Problema Cerealista en España durante el Reinado de los Reyes Católicos (1475-1516)*, Madrid, 1944. Pioneering work on production and distribution of grain; remains neglected subject in Iberian context.

11.147 **Palop Ramos**, J. M., *Hambre y Lucha Antifeudal. Las Crisis de Subsistencias en Valencia, Siglo 18*, Madrid, 1977. See also his *Fluctuaciones de Precios y Abastecimiento en la Valencia del Siglo 18*, Valencia, 1977.

11.148 **Basini**, G. L., *L'Uomo e il Pane. Risorse, Consumi, e Carenze Alimentari della Popolazione Modenese nel Cinque e Seicento*, Milan, 1970.

11.149 **Bullard**, Melissa M., 'Grain supply and urban unrest in Renaissance Rome. The crisis of 1533-34', in P. A. Ramsey, ed., *Rome in the Renaissance. The City and the Myth*, Binghampton, N.Y., 1982, 279-92. On unrest caused by papal government's grain monopoly policy.

11.150 **Grab**, A. I., 'The politics of subsistence. The liberalization of grain commerce in Austrian Lombardy under enlightened despotism', *J.Mod.Hist.*, 57, 1985, 185-210. Details considerable opposition aroused by programme of grain deregulation between 1765 and 1786.

11.151 **Grendi**, E., 'Genova alla metà del cinquecento. Una politica del grano?', *Quad.Stor.*, 13, 1970, 106-60. City's efforts to maintain ample grain supplies.

11.152 **Macry**, P., *Mercato e Società nel Regno di Napoli. Commercio del Grano e Politica Economica nel Settecento*, Naples, 1974.

11.153 **Pult Quaglia**, A. M., 'Controls over food supplies in Florence in the late sixteenth and early seventeenth centuries', *J.Eur.Ec.Hist.*, 9, 1980, 449-57.

11.154 **Revel**, J., 'A capital city's privileges. Food supplies in early-modern Rome', in Forster and Ranum (11.116), 37-49. Transl. from *Annales*, 30, 1975, 563-74.

11.155 **Venturi**, F., '1764. Napoli nell'anno della fame', *Riv.Stor.Ital.*, 85, 1973, 394-472. Subsistence crisis and its repercussions on economic debate and policy. See also parallel studies, '1764-67. Roma negli anni della fame', *ib.*, 514-43; and 'Quatro anni di carestia in Toscana (1764-67)', *ib.*, 88, 1976, 649-707.

11.156 **Zanetti**, D., *Problemi Alimentari di una Economia Preindustriale. Cereali a Pavia dal 1398 al 1700*, Turin, 1964.

11.157 **Abel**, W., *Massenarmut und Hungerkrisen im Vorindustriellen Deutschland*, Göttingen, 1972. Brief case-study of themes in his more general work (11.108).

11.158 **Denecke**, D., 'Innovation and diffusion of the potato in Central Europe in the seventeenth and eighteenth centuries', in Buchanan and others (7.318), 60-96. Distinguishes three phases: botanical curiosity, garden cultivar, outfield crop. Extensive tables and bibliography.

11.159 **Komlos**, J., 'Structure and nutrition in the Habsburg monarchy. The standard of living and economic development in the eighteenth century', *Am.Hist.Rev.*, 90, 1985, 1149-61. Attempts to assess changing nutritional standards from data on height of army recruits.

11.160 **Levine**, H., 'Gentry, Jews, and serfs. The rise of Polish vodka', *Review*, 4, 1980, 223-50. Jewish involvement in state monopoly of drink manufacture and retailing (sixteenth to eighteenth centuries).

11.161 **Wyczanski**, A., *La Consommation Alimentaire en Pologne aux 16e et 17e Siècles*, Paris, 1985.

11.162 **McGowan**, B., 'Food supply and taxation on the Middle Danube (1568-79)', *Archivum Ottomanicum*, 1, 1969, 139-96.

11.163 **Friedmann**, Karen J., 'Food marketing in Copenhagen, 1250-1850', *Agric.Hist.*, 50, 1976, 400-13. On system prevailing till city gates were taken down and tolls abolished in 1850s.

11.164 **Glamann**, K., 'Beer and brewing in pre-industrial Denmark', *Scan.Ec.Hist.Rev.*, 10, 1962, 128-40. Largely on brewing techniques and varieties of beer.

11.165 **Hildebrand**, K.-G., 'Salt and cloth in Swedish economic history', *ib.*, 2, 1954, 74-102. Mainly on relation between dietary conditions and salt imports in early modern period.

11.166 **Jutikkala**, E., 'The great Finnish famine in 1696-97', *ib.*, 3, 1955, 48-63. Estimates thirty per cent mortality in county of Tavastland-Nyland, and examines government attitude to relief.

11.167 **Morrell**, M., 'Eli F. Heckscher, the "food budgets", and Swedish food consumption from the sixteenth to the nineteenth century', *Scan.Ec.Hist.Rev.*, 35, 1987, 65-107. Reviews and augments criticism of Heckscher's evidence on dietary standards in his *Sveriges Ekonomiska Historia* (3.340). See also 11.92 on Heckscher's price data.

11.168 **Sandberg**, L. G., and Steckel, R. H., 'Soldier, soldier, what made you grow so tall? A study of height, health, and nutrition in Sweden, 1720-1881', *Ec.& Hist.*, 23, 1980, 91-105. Data drawn from records of provincial army regiment, showing secular trend towards greater height.

11.169 **Kahan**, A., 'Natural calamities and their effect upon the food supply in Russia', *Jb.Gesch.Osteur.*, 16, 1968, 353-77. Attempts chronology of bad harvest years from 867 to 1965.

11.170 **Smith**, R. E. F., and Christian, D., *Bread and Salt. A Social and Economic History of Food and Drink in Russia*, 1984. Period 1600-1850 forms principal focus of this excellent study. See also Smith's brief account of alcohol production and consumption, 'Drink in old Russia', in Hobsbawm and others (7.218), 42-54.

HOUSING AND CLOTHING
On housing see also 8.56 and 11.28 (France); 6.145,156 (Italy); 8.150 (Turkey); 14.429 (Rumania).

11.171 **Boucher**, F., *A History of Costume in the West*, 1966. 2nd ed., 1987. Originally publ. in French, 1965. Valuable for illustrations. Early modern period covered in pp.191-331.

11.172 **Freudenberger**, H., 'Fashion, sumptuary laws, and business', *Bus.Hist.Rev.*, 37, 1963, 37-48. On dress regulation as feature of mercantilist policy in seventeenth and eighteenth centuries, and its increasing ineffectiveness.

11.173 **Hargreaves-Mawdsley**, W. N., *A History of Legal Dress in Europe until the End of the Eighteenth Century*, 1963; and *A History of Academical Dress in Europe...*, 1963. Both somewhat antiquarian in approach.

11.174 **Mansel**, P., 'Monarchy, uniform, and the rise of the *frac*, 1760-1830', *P.& P.*, 96, 1982, 103-32. Discusses styles of elite male dress in this period.

11.175 **Ribeiro**, Aileen, *Dress in Eighteenth-Century Europe, 1715-89*, 1984.

Knowledgable and well-illustrated work by lecturer at Courtauld Institute; emphasis, however, on dress of wealthy, and on rise of couturier.

11.176 **Thornton**, P., *Seventeenth-Century Interior Decoration in England, France, and Holland*, New Haven, Conn., 1978. Well-illustrated history of furniture, carpeting, etc., and its actual disposition in more affluent households.

11.177 **Turnau**, Irena, 'Consumption of clothes in Europe between the sixteenth and eighteenth centuries', *J.Eur.Ec.Hist.*, 5, 1976, 451-68. Production capacity and consumer mentality ("fashion") seen as dual influences on consumption. D. E. Robinson, 'The importance of fashions in taste to business history', *Bus.Hist.Rev.*, 37, 1963, 5-36, also stresses importance of luxury textiles demand.

11.178 **Wright**, L., *Clean and Decent. The Fascinating History of the Bathroom and the*

Water Closet, 1960. Light-hearted. Well illustrated.

11.179 **Bardet**, J.-P., and others, *Le Bâtiment. Enquête d'Histoire Économique, 14e-19e Siècles. 1: Maisons Rurales et Urbaines dans la France Traditionelle*, Paris, 1971. Five extended essays on building methods, costs, and social context of housing in various regions of pre-industrial France.

11.180 **Gallet**, M., *Paris Domestic Architecture of the Eighteenth Century*, 1972. Adopts wider and less "architectural" approach than J.-P. Babelon's *Demeures Parisiennes sous Henri IV et Louis XIV*, Paris, 1965.

11.181 **Anderson**, Ruth M., *Hispanic Costume, 1480-1530*, New York, 1979. Well-illustrated and wide-ranging (extending to hair-styles and footwear). Portugal is included.

11.182 **Fayard**, Janine, and Larquié, C., 'Géographie pittoresque des hôtels Madrilènes en 1715', *Mél.Casa de Velazquez*, 3, 1967, 351-74. Stresses importance of accomodation provided by lodging-houses; further article (*ib.*, 4, 1968, 229-58) reproduces findings of report made on hotels in 1665. Useful maps in both cases.

11.183 **Hughes**, Diane O., 'Sumptuary law and social relations in Renaissance Italy', in Bossy (10.390), 69-99.

11.184 **Pavanini**, Paola, 'Abitazioni populari e borghesi nella Venezia cinquecentesca', *Studi Veneziani*, n.s., 5, 1981, 63-126. Evidence largely from inventories.

11.185 **Könenkamp**, W. D., *Wirtschaft, Gesellschaft, und Kleidungsstil in den Vierlanden während des 18. und 19. Jahrhunderts*, Göttingen, 1978. Detailed study of social aspects of dress, focussed on district in Hamburg region.

11.186 **Schmidt**, Maria, *Das Wohnungswesen der Stadt Münster im 17. Jahrhundert*, Münster, 1965. Recommended despite somewhat archaeological treatment, as material on German housing conditions of this period seems scanty.

11.187 **Turnau**, Irene, 'Varsovie au 18e siècle. Les Costumes bourgeois', *Annales*, 15, 1960, 1127-37. With numerous plates.

POVERTY AND CHARITY
See also 5.595; 10.372-3.

11.188 **Garraty**, J. A., *Unemployment in History*, New York, 1978. How problem has been perceived and dealt with since ancient times.

11.189 **Gutton**, J.-P., *La Société et les Pauvres en Europe, 16e-18e Siècles*, Paris, 1974. Covenient brief survey.

11.190 **Hunecke**, V., 'Überlegungen zur Geschichte der Armut in vorindustriellen Europa', *Gesch.u.Gesellschaft*, 9, 1983, 480-512. Useful bibliographically orientated discussion paper.

11.191 **Jütte**, R., 'Poor relief and social discipline in sixteenth-century Europe', *Eur.Stud.Rev.*, 11, 1981, 25-52. Tour d'horizon based mainly on quotations from contemporary commentators.

11.192 **Lis**, Catharina, and Soly, H., *Poverty and Capitalism in Pre-Industrial Europe*, 1975. Useful synthesis, extending from medieval period to c.1850, and concentrating more on causes and experience of poverty than on poor relief.

11.193 **Pullan**, B., 'Catholics and the poor in early modern Europe', *Trans.Roy.Hist.Soc.*, 5th ser., 26, 1976, 15-34. Attempts some rescue of concept that there were distinctive denominational approaches to charity.

11.194 **Riis**, T., ed., *Aspects of Poverty in Early Modern Europe*, 2 vols., Florence, 1981; Odense, 1986. Multilingual symposium. Some papers separately noted. Editor contributes general introduction on poverty and urban development.

11.195 **Woolf**, S. J., *The Poor in Western Europe in the Eighteenth and Nineteenth Centuries*, 1986. Contains introductory material on pre-Napoleonic period, but main emphasis is early nineteenth century.

FRANCE AND THE LOW COUNTRIES
See also 10.372-3,422.

11.196 **Adams**, T. M., 'Mendicity and moral alchemy. Work as rehabilitation', *Stud.on Voltaire.*, 151, 1976, 47-76. On new attitudes to poor relief and "reform" of vagrants in later eighteenth-century

France.

11.197 'Assistance et assistés de 1610 à nos jours', *Actes Congrès Nat.Soc.Savantes*, 97 (i), 1972, whole issue. Several relevant papers, esp. on welfare for military.

11.198 **Berger**, P., 'Rural charity in late seventeenth-century France. The Pontchartrain case', *Fr.Hist.Stud*, 10, 1978, 393-415. Documents extensive subsidies made by Comte de Pontchartrain to hospitals and schools on his estates because of low level of local community funds.

11.199 **Chill**, E., 'Religion and mendicity in seventeenth-century France', *Int.Rev.Soc.Hist.*, 7, 1962, 400-25. Influence of Company of Holy Sacrament in spread of workhouse type of hospital, with emphasis on discipline and confinement.

11.200 **Davis**, Natalie Z., 'Poor relief, humanism, and heresy. The case of Lyon', *Stud.in Med.& Renaiss.Hist.*, 5, 1968, 217-75. Repr. in her *Society and Culture in Early Modern France*, 1975, 17-64. Explains sixteenth-century relief provisions in Lyon, and effects of religious divisions on them.

11.201 **Delasselle**, C., 'Abandoned children in eighteenth-century Paris', in Forster and Ranum (5.282), 47-82. Transl. from *Annales*, 30, 1975, 187-218.

11.202 **Engrand**, C., 'Paupérisme et condition ouvrière dans la seconde moitié du 18e siècle. L'exemple Amiénois', *Rev. Hist. Mod. et Contemp.*, 29, 1982, 376-410. Sees prime cause of pauperism as poor wages in textile industry.

11.203 **Fairchilds**, Cissie S., *Poverty and Charity in Aix-en-Provence, 1640-1789*, Baltimore, Md., 1976. Argues that by mid-eighteenth century traditional sources of charity could not cope, necessitating state intervention.

11.204 **Gutton**, J.-P., *L'État et la Mendicité dans la Première moitié du 18e Siècle. Auvergne, Beaujolais, Forez, Lyonnais*, Paris, 1973. Mainly on royal edict of 1724 aimed at suppressing vagrancy.

11.205 —— *La Société et les Pauvres. L'Exemple de la Généralité de Lyon, 1534-1789*, Paris, 1971. Major thesis, of which previous entry is off-shoot.

11.206 **Hickey**, D., 'Changing expressions of charity in early modern France. Some hypotheses for a rural model', *Renaiss.& Reform*, 2, 1978, 12-22. Suggests, from evidence of South-East France, that decline in resources rather than change of ethos was affecting rural charities in late sixteenth century.

11.207 **Higgs**, D., 'Politics and charity at Toulouse, 1750-1850', in Bosher (6.104), 191-207.

11.208 **Hufton**, Olwen H., *The Poor of Eighteenth-Century France, 1750-89*, 1974. See following entries for articles prefiguring this excellent monograph.

11.209 —— 'Begging, vagrancy, vagabondage, and the law', *Eur.Stud.Rev.*, 2, 1972, 97-123.

11.210 —— 'Towards an understanding of the poor of eighteenth-century France', in Bosher (6.104), 145-65.

11.211 **Jones**, C., *Charity and "Bienfaisance". Treatment of the Poor in the Montpellier Region, 1740-1815*, 1982. Centres on contrasts between old regime and Revolution.

11.212 **Kaplow**, J., 'The culture of poverty in Paris on the eve of the Revolution', *Int.Rev.Soc.Hist.*, 12, 1967, 277-91. Attempts to characterise general outlook of urban labouring poor.

11.213 **McCloy**, S T., *Government Assistance in Eighteenth-Century France*, Durham, N.C., 1946. Describes routine poor relief and special measures taken in emergencies such as bad harvests and epidemics.

11.214 **Molinier**, A., 'Enfants trouvés, enfants abandonnés, et enfants illégitimes en Languedoc au 17e et 18e siècles', in Société de Démographie Historique, ed., *Sur la Population Française au 18e et au 19e Siècles. Hommage à Marcel Reinhard*, Paris, 1973, 445-73. On provision for parentless children.

11.215 **Norberg**, Kathryn, *Rich and Poor in Grenoble, 1600-1814*, Berkeley, Calif., 1985. Study of organisational developments and changing motivations behind charitable work, incl. medical and educational aspects.

11.216 —— 'Educating the poor. Charity schools and charitable attitudes, Grenoble, 1600-1789', *Proc.Western Soc.Fr.Hist.*, 8, 1980, 181-90.

11.217 'Les oeuvres de charité en France au 17e siècle', *Dix-Septième Siècle*, 90-91, 1971, whole issue. Of most interest are contributions by R. P. Chalumeau (medical charity), Y. Poutet (education of poor), M. Venard (charity at Avignon),

Mireille Forget (prison galley charities).

11.218 **Pugh**, Wilma J., 'Catholics, Protestants, and testamentary charity in seventeenth-century Lyon and Nîmes', *Fr.Hist.Stud.*, 11, 1980, 479-504. Examines differing pattern of charitable bequests among Catholics and Protestants in cities with contrasting majority faiths.

11.219 —— 'Social welfare and the Edict of Nantes. Lyon and Nîmes', *ib.*, 8, 1974, 347-76. Makes similar contrast for organisation of poor relief and private charity.

11.220 **Romon**, C., 'Mendiants et policiers à Paris au 18e siècle', *Hist., Éc., et Soc.*, 1, 1982, 259-95. Study of increasing "criminalisation" of able-bodied paupers.

11.221 —— 'Le monde des pauvres à Paris au 18e siècle', *Annales*, 37, 1982, 729-63. Analysis of records relating to beggars and vagabonds.

11.222 **Solomon**, H. M., *Public Welfare, Science, and Propaganda in Seventeenth-Century France. The innovations of Théophraste Renaudot*, Princeton, N.J., 1972. Interesting for Renaudot's prototype of a labour exchange.

11.223 **Blockmans**, W. P., and Prevenier, W., 'Poverty in Flanders and Brabant from the fourteenth to the mid-sixteenth century. Sources and problems', *Acta Hist.Neerlandica*, 10, 1978, 20-57.

11.224 **Haesenne-Peremans**, Nicole, *Les Pauvres et le Pouvoir. Assistance et Répression au Pays de Liège, 1685-1830*, Kortrijk, 1983. Rather narrowly institutional and administrative.

SPAIN
See also 5.139.

11.225 **Callahan**, W. J., *La Santa y Real Hermandad del Refugio y Piedad de Madrid, 1618-1832*, Madrid, 1980. History of leading charitable confraternity in early modern Madrid, offering much background material on poverty in city. Provides useful summary in 'Corporate charity in Spain. The *Hermandad del Refugio* of Madrid, 1618-1814', *Hist.Sociale/Social Hist.*, 9, 1976, 159-86.

11.226 —— 'The problem of confinement. An aspect of poor relief in eighteenth-century Spain', *Hisp.Am.Hist.Rev.*, 51, 1971, 1-24. Examines reasons for state policy of institutional confinement rather than

outdoor relief in later part of century.

11.227 —— 'A social contract. The poor, the privileged, and the Church in eighteenth-century Spain', in R. E. Morton and J. D. Browning, eds, *Religion in the Eighteenth Century (Pubs. McMaster Univ. Assoc. for Eighteenth-Cent.Stud., 6)*, New York, 1979, 103-16. On importance of ecclesiastical and private charity as mainstay of poor relief.

11.228 **Flynn**, Maureen M., 'Charitable ritual in late medieval and early modern Spain', *Sixteenth-Cent.J.*, 16, 1985, 335-48. Studies charitable work of confraternities.

11.229 **Marcos Martín**, A., *Economía, Sociedad, Pobreza en Castilla. Palencia, 1500-1814*, 2 vols., Palencia, 1985. Narrows down from general view of Palencia to detailed examination of Hospital of San Antolín in provincial capital; main focus is eighteenth century.

11.230 **Martz**, Linda, *Poverty and Welfare in Habsburg Spain. The Example of Toledo*, 1983. Concentrates on sixteenth century.

11.231 **Pérez Estevez**, Rosa M., *El Problema de los Vagos en la España del Siglo 18*, Madrid, 1976. General study of vagrancy and itinerants.

11.232 **Rumeu de Armas, A.**, *Historia de la Prevision Social en España*, Madrid, 1944. Emphasis on fraternities, guilds, and charitable pawnbroking facilities (early Middle Ages to eighteenth century).

11.233 **Soubeyroux**, J., *Paupérisme et Rapports Sociaux à Madrid au 18e Siècle*, Lille, 1978. Detailed thesis which looks principally at state and municipal policy, and also provides much statistical information on those needing relief.

ITALY

11.234 **Assereto**, G., 'Pauperismo e assistenza. Messa a punto di studi recenti', *Arch.Stor.Ital.*, 141, 1983, 253-71. Bibliographical review on Italian aspects of question.

11.235 **Branca**, L., 'Pauperismo, assistenza, e controllo sociale a Firenze (1621-32)', *ib.*, 141, 1983, 421-62. Concerns work of state vagrancy commission, notably in plague of 1631-33.

11.236 **Chaney**, E. P. de G., ' "Philanthropy in Italy". English observations on Italian hospitals, 1545-1789', in Riis (11.194), 1, 183-217. Chronicles generally admiring picture of Italian charitable institutions by English travellers.

1.237 **Cipolla**, C. M., 'Economic fluctuations, the poor, and public policy (Italy, sixteenth and seventeenth centuries)', *ib.*, 65-77. Brief sketch.

1.238 **Corsini**, C. A., 'Materiali per lo studio della famiglia in Toscana nei secoli 17-19. Gli esposti', *Quad.Stor.*, 33, 1976, 998-1052. Examines records of Florence's foundling hospital to establish rates of admittance, percentages legitimate, etc.

1.239 **Grendi**, E., 'Pauperismo e Albergo dei Poveri nella Genova del seicento', *Riv.Stor.Ital.*, 87, 1975, 621-65.

1.240 ——, ed., 'Sistemi di carità. Esposti e internati nella società di antico regime', *Quad.Stor.*, 53, 1983, 383-577. Seven case-studies, mainly dealing with eighteenth-century cities.

1.241 **Paglia**, V., *"La Pietà dei Carcerati". Confraternite e Società a Roma nei Secoli 16-18*, Rome, 1980. Concerns guild devoted to helping prisoners; study both of religious charities and of prison conditions.

1.242 **Pullan**, B., *Rich and Poor in Renaissance Venice. The Social Institutions of a Catholic State, to 1620*, 1971. Major study of urban poor relief. Review article: R. C. Mueller, *Studi Veneziani*, 14, 1972, 37-81. See also following articles which preceded this synthesis.

1.243 —— 'Famine in Venice and the new poor law, 1527-29', *Boll.Istituto di Storia della Società e dello Stato Veneziano*, 5-6, 1964, 141-202. Notes this measure as conforming to increasing European trend for secularised administration of charity.

1.244 —— 'Poverty, charity, and reason of state. Some Venetian examples', *ib.*, 2, 1960, 17-60.

1.245 —— 'The relief of prisoners in sixteenth-century Venice', *Studi Veneziani*, 10, 1968, 221-9. Mainly concerns Compagnia della Carità del Crocefisso, founded in 1591.

1.246 **Spicciani**, A., 'The "poveri vergognosi" in fifteenth-century Florence', in Riis (11.194), 1, 119-82. Detailed analysis of alms distributed in confidence by Congregation of Buonomini di S. Martino to socially respectable paupers (1466-70).

1.247 **Tagliaferri**, A., *Struttura e Politica Sociale in una Communità Veneta del '500 (Udine)*, Milan, 1969. Good local study, with emphasis on poor relief.

1.248 **Trexler**, R. C., 'Charity and the defence of

urban elites in the Italian communes', in Jaher (10.367), 64-109. Argues that *Monte di Pietà* and confraternity charities were aimed more at "distressed gentlefolk" than plebeian paupers.

GERMANY, SWITZERLAND, AND AUSTRIA
See also 5.453,629.

11.249 **Chrisman**, Miriam U., 'The urban poor in the sixteenth century. The case of Strasbourg', in Chrisman and Gründler (6.102), 59-67. Brief account of problems minuted by city welfare administrator.

11.250 **Fischer**, T., *Städtische Armut und Armenfürsorge im 15. und 16. Jahrhundert*, Göttingen, 1979. Uses records of Basel, Freiburg, and Strasbourg.

11.251 **Grimm**, H. J., 'Luther's contributions to sixteenth-century organization of poor relief', *Arch.Reformationsgesch.*, 61, 1970, 222-33. Shows that Luther encouraged provision of poor relief by secular authorities.

11.252 **Kingdon**, R. M., 'Social welfare in Calvin's Geneva', *Am.Hist.Rev.*, 76, 1971, 50-69. Mainly on foundation of General Hospital under Council control in 1535, seen as further trend towards laicisation of welfare, especially in Protestant cities.

11.253 **Küther**, C., *Menschen auf der Strasse. Vagierende Unterschichten in Bayern, Franken, und Schwaben in der Zweiten Hälfte des 18. Jahrhunderts*, Göttingen, 1983. Another considerable work on itinerants (see also 11.231).

11.254 **Lindberg**, C., ' "There should be no beggars among Christians." Karlstadt, Luther, and the origins of Protestant poor relief', *Church Hist.*, 46, 1977, 313-34. On measures adopted at Wittenberg in early 1520s.

11.255 **Midelfort**, H. C. E., 'Protestant monastery? A Reformation hospital in Hesse', in P. N. Brooks, ed., *Reformation Principle and Practice. Essays in Honour of A. G. Dickens*, 1980, 71-94. Details conversion of a monastic foundation at Haina for poor relief.

11.256 **Sachsse**, C., and Tennstedt, F., *Geschichte der Armenfürsorge in Deutschland vom Spätmittelalter bis zum 1. Weltkrieg*, Stuttgart, 1980. Carries documentary excerpts for various periods covered.

11.257 **Sothmann**, Marlene, *Das Armen-*,

Arbeits-, Zucht-, und Werkhaus in Nürnberg bis 1806, Nuremberg, 1970. Main focus is on eighteenth-century operation.

11.258 **Stekl**, H., *Österreichs Zucht- und Arbeitshauser, 1671-1920. Institutionen zwischen Fürsorge und Strafvollzug*, Munich, 1978. Pioneering study of institutional treatment of poverty in Austria.

11.259 **Ulbricht**, O., 'The debate about foundling hospitals in Enlightenment Germany. Infanticide, illegitimacy, and infant mortality rates', *Central Eur.Hist.*, 18, 1985, 211-56. Debate between proponents

of hospitals as means to foster population growth, and conservative opponents who stressed expense and encouragement of immorality.

11.260 **Wright**, W. J., 'A closer look at house poor relief through the common chest, and indigence in sixteenth-century Hesse', *Arch.Reformationsgesch.*, 70, 1979, 225-37. Compares post-Reformation system with almsgiving in pre-Reformation Marburg.

11.261 —— 'Reformation contributions to the development of public welfare policy in Hesse', *J.Mod.Hist.*, 49, 1977, 1145-80 (on demand article).

DISEASE AND MEDICAL SERVICES

See also preceding sub-section for some material on general welfare role of hospitals.
Also 4.37; 5.8-9,23; 11.118; 13.341,348.

11.262 **Appleby**, A. B., 'The disappearance of plague. A continuing puzzle', *Ec.Hist.Rev.*, 2nd ser. 33, 1980, 161-73. Sees partial explanation in development of immune rat population. P. Slack, commenting on this article, prefers effectiveness of quarantine: 'The disappearance of plague, an alternative view', *ib.*, 34, 1981, 469-76.

11.263 **Biraben**, J.-N., *Les Hommes et la Peste en France et dans les Pays Européens et Méditerranéens*, 2 vols., Paris, 1975-76. Fundamental. Vol.1 deals with course of epidemics from Black Death to nineteenth-century vestiges; vol.2 with beliefs and social reactions. Review article: M. W. Flinn, *J.Eur.Ec.Hist.*, 8, 1979, 131-48.

11.264 **Bullough**, Bonnie, and Bullough, V. L., *The Emergence of Modern Nursing*, New York, 1964. Broad survey, beginning with classical and medieval sick care.

11.265 **Burgess**, Renate, 'Notes on some plague paintings', *Medical Hist.*, 20, 1976, 422-8. On paintings by Raphael and Poussin, and their relation to actual experience.

11.266 **Forbes**, T. R., *The Midwife and the Witch*, New Haven, Conn., 1966. Rather miscellaneous account of superstitions concerning pregnancy and childbirth, with three chapters on history of midwifery. Evidence mainly from early modern Europe. For further material on midwives see 11.295,313,353.

11.267 **Foucault**, M., *The Birth of the Clinic. An Archaeology of Medical Perception*, 1973.

Transl. from French ed. of 1963. Another of Foucault's controversial essays on corrupting nature of "professional" expertise. Main chronological focus is late eighteenth century.

11.268 **Heller**, R., 'Educating the blind in the age of the Enlightenment', *Medical Hist.*, 23, 1979, 392-403. On schools, inventions prefiguring Braille, etc., c.1750-1800.

11.269 —— ' "Priest-doctors" as a rural health service in the age of the Enlightenment', *ib.*, 20, 1976, 361-83. Rudimentary medical help offered to parishioners by some rural priests, and abortive efforts to generalise this practice.

11.270 **Hopkins**, D. R., *Princes and Peasants. Smallpox in History*, Chicago, 1983. Diachronic survey by professional epidemiologist. Some relevant material.

11.271 **Imhof**, A., 'The hospital in the eighteenth century: for whom?', *Soc.Hist.*, 10, 1977, 448-70. Repr. in Branca (5.436), 141-64. Examines patient records of hospitals in Berlin, Copenhagen, and Kongsberg (Norway); as first two were military hospitals, their typicality is open to question.

11.272 —— ed., *Mensch und Gesundheit in der Geschichte*, Husum, 1980. Essay collection, mainly French and German context. A number have eighteenth-century interest.

11.273 **Le Roy Ladurie**, E., 'A concept: the unification of the globe by disease (fourteenth to seventeenth centuries)', in Le Roy Ladurie (5.36), 28-83. On continental intermingling of disease strains brought about by colonisation and increased trade.

11.274 **McKeown**, T., 'The sociological approach to the history of medicine', *Medical Hist.*, 14, 1970, 342-51. Argues that medical history with social dimension has operational value for current problems, and suggests various directions of relevance. Approach attacked by J. F. Hutchinson, 'Historical method and the social history of medicine', *ib.*, 17, 1973, 423-31. See also 11.279.

11.275 **McNeill**, W. H., *Plagues and People*, 1976. Deals with diffusion and social effects of epidemics from earliest times to present.

11.276 **Riley**, J. C., *The Eighteenth-Century Campaign to Avoid Disease*, 1987. Suggests that rubbish disposal and drainage measures in seventeenth and eighteenth centuries may have significantly diminished insect transmission of disease. See also his 'Insects and the European mortality decline', *Am.Hist.Eur.*, 91, 1986, 833-58.

11.277 **Rosen**, G., *History of Public Health*, New York, 1958. By pioneer of medical social history. Main emphasis on America and Britain, but some attention to European developments.

11.278 —— 'A slaughter of innocents. Aspects of child health in the eighteenth-century city', *Stud.in Eighteenth-Cent.Culture*, 5, 1976, 293-316.

11.279 —— 'People, disease, and emotion. Newer problems for research in medical history', *Bull.Hist.Medicine*, 41, 1967, 5-23. Plea for wider social context in medical historiography.

11.280 **Thompson**, J. D., and Goldin, Grace. *The Hospital. A Social and Architectural History*, New Haven, Conn., 1975. Part 1, by Goldin, discusses social aspects of hospital design with many historical examples and illustrations.

11.281 **Vigarello**, G., *Le Corps Redressé*, Paris, 1978. A history, rather à la Foucault, of prescriptions for posture and physical fitness, seen as imposition of social norms by dominant groups.

FRANCE
See also 11.263,272; 14.46.

11.282 **Adams**, T. M., 'Medicine and bureaucracy. Jean Colombier's regulation for the French *dépôts de mendicité*, 1785', *Bull.Hist.Medicine*, 52, 1979, 529-41. Hygiene regulations for type of workhouse set up in 1764.

11.283 **Biraben**, J.-N., 'Certain demographic characteristics of the plague epidemic in France, 1720-22', *Daedalus*, 97, 1968, 536-45. Repr. in Glass and Revelle (5.18), 233-42. Computes mortality figures in Provence for epidemic which began in Marseille (see following entry).

11.284 **Carrière**, C., and others, *Marseille, Ville Morte. La Peste de 1720*, Marseille, 1968. Presented without formal documentation, but substantial and well-researched. Review article: J.-N. Biraben, *Rev.Hist.*, 247, 1972, 407-26.

11.285 **Coleman**, W., 'Health and hygiene in the Encyclopédie. A medical doctrine for the bourgeoisie', *J.Hist.Medicine & Allied Sci.*, 29, 1974, 399-421. On articles of Arnulfe d'Aumont.

11.286 —— 'The people's health. Medical themes in eighteenth-century French popular literature', *Bull.Hist.Medicine*, 51, 1977, 55-74. On cures, charms, etc. scattered through almanacs and *bibliothèque bleue*, which, Coleman feels, had therapeutic value for population without accesss to doctors.

11.287 **Corbin**, A., *The Foul and the Fragrant. Odor and the French Social Imagination*, 1986. Transl. from French ed. of 1982. Inventory of smells afflicting or delighting eighteenth- or early nineteenth-century society – much detail on public and private hygiene.

11.288 **Desaive**, J. P., and others, *Médecins, Climat, et Épidémies à la Fin du 18e Siècle*, Paris, 1972. Series of studies built round enquiry of 1776-92 by Société Royale de Médecine on relations between climate and epidemics. Contributors include E. Le Roy Ladurie, J. Meyer, and J.-P. Goubert.

11.289 **Forster**, R., and Ranum, O., eds., *Medicine and Society in France. Selections from the Annales*, 6, Baltimore, Md., 1980. Transl. from *Annales*, 32, 1977, 849-1051, special issue dealing with health and medical problems in eighteenth and nineteenth centuries.

11.290 **Gelfand**, T., *Professionalizing Modern Medicine. Paris Surgeons and Medical Science and Institutions in the Eighteenth*

Century, Westport, Conn., 1980. Argues that surgeons constituted main medical profession of old regime, but were rapidly displaced by university-educated physicians after unification of professions during Revolution. See also following articles on aspects of this theme.

11.291 —— 'Demystification and surgical power in the French Enlightenment', *Bull.Hist.Medicine*, 57, 1983, 203-17. Role of Academy of Surgery in publicising secrets of craft.

11.292 —— 'Gestation of the clinic', *Medical Hist.*, 25, 1981, 169-80. Hospital experience of surgeons seen as part of process whereby clinical observation replaced abstract categories in mental approach of doctors.

11.293 —— 'A "monarchical profession" in the old regime. Surgeons, ordinary practitioners, and medical professionalisation in eighteenth-century France', in G. L. Geison, ed., *Professions and the French State, 1700-1900*, Philadelphia, Pa., 1984, 149-80.

11.294 —— 'Two cultures, one profession. The surgeons of France in the eighteenth century', *Proc.Consortium on Revolutionary Eur.*, 1978, 171-87. Highlights differences between professional surgeon and country barber-surgeon.

11.295 **Gelis**, J., 'L'enquête de 1786 sur les "sages-femmes du royaume"', *Ann.Démographie Hist.*, 1980, 299-343. Reproduces findings of enquiry into midwifery resources made at instigation of Société Royale de Médecine.

11.296 —— 'Miracle et médecine aux siècles classiques', *Hist.Reflections*, 9, 1982, 85-102. Discusses some cures regarded as miraculous.

11.297 **Goldstein**, J., ' "Moral contagion". A professional ideology of medicine and psychiatry in eighteenth- and nineteenth-century France', in Geison (11.293), 181-222. Concept of irrational crowd behaviour as analogous to disease epidemic.

11.298 **Goubert**, J.-P., 'The extent of medical practice in France around 1780', *J.Soc.Hist.*, 10, 1977, 410-27. Repr. in Branca (5.436), 211-28. Examines regional differences (northern *généralités* only), urban-rural ratios, and distribution as between doctors and surgeons.

11.299 —— *Malades et Médecins en Bretagne*,

1770-90, Rennes, 1974. Richly detailed and quantified.

11.300 **Greenbaum**, L. S., 'The cure of body and soul at the Paris Hospital at the end of the old regime', in J. D. Browning, ed., *Education in the Eighteenth Century (Pubs. McMaster Univ. Assoc. for Eighteenth-Cent. Stud., 7)*, 123-50. Deals with conflict of authority between nursing nuns and medical staff at Hôtel-Dieu in late 1780s. For further material on Hôtel-Dieu at this time, and proposals to replace it with newer and more "enlightened" institutions, see articles by Greenbaum in *Clio Medica*, 8, 1973, 261-84; *ib.*, 13, 1979, 347-68; *Proc.Consortium on Revolutionary Eur.*, 1973, 168-94; *ib.*, 1984, 26-40; *Stud.on Voltaire*, 152, 1976, 895-930; *Stud.in Eighteenth Cent.Cult.*, 10, 1981, 373-91; *Eighteenth-Cent. Life*, 9 (i), 1984, 1-15. See also 11.317

11.301 **Guillemot**, A., 'L'hôpital de Malestroit du milieu du 17e siècle à la Révolution', *Rev.Hist.Éc.et Soc.*, 48, 1970, 483-524. On revenues, administration, and work of hospital in small Breton town.

11.302 **Hammond**, E. A., and Sturgill, C. C., 'A French plague recipe of 1720', *Bull.Hist.Medicine*, 46, 1972, 591-7. "Remedy" called *aurifique minéral* circulated to intendants in Southern France during epidemic of 1720.

11.303 **Hannaway**, Caroline C., 'Veterinary medicine and rural health care in pre-Revolutionary France', *Bull. Hist. Medicine*, 51, 1977, 431-47. On schools for veterinary surgeons set up in 1760s; difficulties of this profession; and tendency to move over to human medicine.

11.304 **Jones**, C., and Sonenscher, M., 'The social functions of the hospital in eighteenth-century France. The case of the Hôtel-Dieu of Nîmes', *Fr.Hist.Stud.*, 13, 1983, 172-214. Analysis of admissions register.

11.305 **Klairmont**, Alison, 'The problem of the plague. New challenges to healing in sixteenth-century France', *Proc.Western Soc.Fr.Hist.*, 5, 1977, 119-27. Analysis of plague tracts.

11.306 **Lehoux**, Françoise, *Le Cadre de Vie des Médecins Parisiens aux 16e et 17e Siècles*, Paris, 1976. Substantial thesis. See also 11.309.

11.307 **Lebrun**, F., *Se Soigner Autrefois. Médecins, Saints, et Sorciers aux 17e et 18e Siècles*, Paris, 1983. Popular account of medical treatment, both orthodox and folk.

11.308 **Lingo**, Alison K., 'Empirics and charlatans in early modern France. The genesis of the classification of the "other" in medical practice', *J.Soc.Hist.*, 19, 1986, 583-603. Concentrates on arguments of two university-trained physicians against unlicensed healers (in works of 1580 and 1610 respectively).

11.309 **Millepierres**, F., *La Vie Quotidienne des Médecins au Temps de Molière*, Paris, 1964. Not research work like 11.306, but somewhat wider in range.

11.310 **Mitchell**, H., 'Politics in the service of knowledge. The debate over the administration of medicine and welfare in late eighteenth-century France', *Soc.Hist.*, 6, 1981, 185-207. Discusses views of intelligentsia and scientific establishment, notably on question of hospitals.

11.311 —— 'Rationality and control in French eighteenth-century medical views of the peasantry', *Comp.Stud.Soc.& Hist.*, 21, 1979, 82-112. Reports from doctors belonging to Société Royale de Médecine lamenting ignorance, passivity, and superstition of peasantry.

11.312 **Peter**, J.-P., 'Disease and the sick at the end of the eighteenth century', in Forster and Ranum (5.256), 81-124. Transl. from *Annales*, 22, 1967, 711-51. More evidence from archives of Société Royale de Médecine, chiefly on terminology and classification of disease.

11.313 **Petrelli**, R. L., 'Regulation of French midwifery during the ancien régime', *J.Hist.Medicine*, 26, 1971, 276-92. Rather derivative.

11.314 **Ramsey**, M. 'Repression of unauthorized medical practice in eighteenth-century France', *Eighteenth-Cent.Life*, 7 (ii), 1982, 118-35. In fact deals more with difficulties of repression, and with hopes placed in creation of Société Royale de Médecine (1776).

11.315 —— 'Traditional medicine and medical enlightenment. Regulation of secret remedies in the ancien régime', *Hist.Reflections*, 9, 1982, 215-32.

11.316 **Revel**, J., 'Autour d'une épidémie ancienne. La peste de 1666-70', *Rev.Hist.Mod.et Contemp.*, 17, 1970, 053-83. Last major outbreak in France (except for Marseilles outbreak of 1720), affecting North-East France and

Normandy.

11.317 **Richmond**, Phyllis A., 'The Hôtel-Dieu of Paris on the eve of the Revolution', *J.Hist.Medicine*, 16, 1961, 335-53. Conditions at Paris' most important general hospital, and proposals for reform in 1780s. See also 11.300.

11.318 **Rosen**, G., 'Mercantilism and health policy in eighteenth-century French thought', *Medical Hist.*, 3, 1959, 259-77. See similar article on Germany, 11.352.

11.319 **Sturgill**, C., 'The royal army and the plague of Marseilles, 1720-22', *Societas*, 1, 1971, 123-31. On use of troops to establish cordon sanitaire.

11.320 **Trout**, A. P., 'The municipality of Paris confronts the plague of 1668', *Medical Hist.*, 17, 1973, 418-23. Study of quarantine precautions successfully employed to prevent outbreaks at Amiens and Rouen reaching Paris.

LOW COUNTRIES
See also 5.119.

11.321 **Charlier**, J., *La Peste à Bruxelles de 1667 à 1669 et ses Conséquences Démographiques*, Brussels, 1969.

11.322 **Goldin**, Grace, 'A walk through a ward of the eighteenth century', *J.Hist.Medicine*, 22, 1967, 121-38. Documentation to be gleaned from view of sick ward of St. John's Hospital, Bruges (now Memling Museum). See also her 'Painting in Gheel', *ib.*, 26, 1971, 400-12, portraying hospice for sick and insane in 1639.

11.323 **Van Der Made**, R., *Le Grand Hôpital de Huy, 1263-1795*, Louvain, 1960. Longitudinal study of a municipal hospital.

SPAIN

11.324 **Ballesteros Rodríguez**, J., *La Peste en Córdoba*, Córdoba, 1982. General survey, but main emphasis on sixteenth and seventeenth centuries.

11.325 **Bennassar**, B., *Recherches sur les Grandes Épidémies dans le Nord de l'Espagne à la fin du 16e Siècle*, Paris, 1969. Examines and reproduces some sources for study of plague epidemic of 1596-1602, notably at Bilbao.

11.326 **García-Ballester**, L., 'Academicism versus empiricism in practical medicine in sixteenth-century Spain with regard to

Morisco practitioners', in A. Wear, and others, eds., *The Medical Renaissance of the Sixteenth Century*, 1985, 246-70. Deals in large part with way in which traditional healing practices could involve Moriscos in prosecution for heresy and superstition.

11.327 **Maiso González**, J., *La Peste Aragonesa de 1648 a 1654*, Zaragoza, 1982. Microstudy, but with excellent background and wide perspective.

11.328 **Peset**, M., and Peset, J. L., *Muerte en España. Politica y Sociedad entre la Peste y el Colera*, Madrid, 1972. Looks in broad context at issues of public health in eighteenth and early nineteenth centuries.

ITALY
See also 5.164; 11.235.

11.329 **Abrate**, M., *Popolazione e Peste del 1630 a Carmagnola*, Turin, 1972. Tries to estimate demographic effects on small Piedmont town.

11.330 **Bylebyl**, J. J., 'The school of Padua. Humanistic medicine in the sixteenth century', in C. Webster, ed., *Health, Medicine, and Mortality in the Sixteenth Century*, 1979, 335-70. Mainly on syllabus and science, but has some relevance to formation of physicians and their place in Italian society.

11.331 **Calvi**, Giulia, 'L'oro, il fuoco, le forche. La peste Napoletana del 1656', *Arch. Stor. Ital.*, 139, 1981, 405-58.

11.332 **Carmichael**, Ann G., *Plague and the Poor in Renaissance Florence*, 1986. Coverage extends patchily to 1500, but main emphasis on period from Black Death to c.1450.

11.333 —— 'Plague legislation in the Italian Renaissance', *Bull.Hist.Medicine*, 57, 1983, 508-25. Claims that only after 1450 did contagion theory of plague become widespread, with consequent sanitation measures, construction of isolation hospitals, etc.

11.334 **Cipolla**, C. M., *Christofano and the Plague. A Study in the History of Public Health in the Age of Galileo*, 1973. Case study of emergency measures taken at Prato in plague outbreak of 1629-31 (under direction of Christofano Ceffini).

11.335 —— *Faith, Reason, and the Plague. A Tuscan Story of the Seventeenth Century*, 1979. Transl. from Italian ed. of 1977. Detailed study of 1630-31 outbreak at

small village of Monte Lupo.

11.336 —— *I Pidocchi e il Granducato*, Bologna, 1979. On typhoid epidemic of early 1620s in Florence.

11.337 —— *Public Health and the Medical Profession in the Renaissance*, 1976. Second section of work provides social profile of doctors and surgeons practising in Tuscany around time of great plague of 1630.

11.338 **Del Lungo**, Mariella, 'Aspetti dell'organizzazione sanitaria nella Genova del settecento. La cura delle malattie veneree', *Società e Storia*, 6, 1983, 769-802.

11.339 **Del Panta**, L., *Le Epidemie nella Storia Demografica Italiana (Secoli 14-19)*, Turin, 1980. Fairly brief outline.

11.340 **De Rosa**, L., 'The "protomedicato" in Southern Italy, sixteenth-nineteenth centuries', *Ann.Cisalpines Hist.Soc.*, 4, 1973, 103-17. Official who superintended medical professions and services.

11.341 **Lombardi**, Daniela, '1629-31. Crisi e peste a Firenze', *Arch.Stor.Ital.*, 137, 1979, 3-50. Coincidence of grain crisis and epidemic.

11.342 **O'Neil**, Mary R., '*Sacerdote ovvero strione*. Ecclesiastical and superstitious remedies in sixteenth-century Italy', in Kaplan (9.541), 53-83. On difficulties of defining boundaries between orthodoxy and superstition in faith healing and exorcism.

11.343 **Palmer**, R., 'The Church, leprosy, and plague in medieval and early modern Europe', *Stud.Church Hist.*, 19, 1982, 79-99. In fact concentrates on Italian church.

11.344 —— 'Physicians and surgeons in sixteenth-century Venice', *Medical Hist.*, 23, 1979, 451-60. Documents showing that Venetian College of Surgeons was highly respected (i.e. not equated with barbers) and cooperated closely with physicians.

11.345 **Preto**, P., *Peste e Società a Venezia nel 1576*, Vicenza, 1978. More general treatment than earlier work by E. Rodenwaldt, *Pest in Venedig, 1575-77*, Heidelberg, 1952 (which was written by specialist in tropical hygiene, and rather technical in approach). See also 11.347.

11.346 **Trexler**, Bernice J., 'Hospital patients in Florence. San Paolo, 1567-68', *Bull.Hist.Medicine*, 48, 1974, 41-59. Analysis by complaint and occupation of patients at small Franciscan-run hospital over fifteen-month period.

11.347 *Venezia e la Peste, 1348-1798*, Venice, 1979. Large and sumptuous exhibition catalogue, with several valuable articles.

GERMANY AND SWITZERLAND
See also 11.271-2.

11.348 **Brügelmann**, J., 'Observations on the process of medicalization in Germany, 1770-1830, based on medical topographies', *Hist.Reflections*, 9, 1982, 131-49. Concerns growing practice of physicians reporting on medical and sanitary conditions of particular localities.

11.349 **Eckert**, E. A., 'Boundary formation and diffusion of plague. Swiss epidemics from 1562 to 1669', *Ann.Démographie Hist.*, 1978, 49-80. Attempt to chart plague routes both into and within a circumscribed area.

11.350 —— 'Spatial and temporal distribution of plague in a region of Switzerland in the years 1628 and 1629', *Bull.Hist.Medicine*, 56, 1982, 175-94. Charts spread and severity in area comprising cantons of Basel, Solothurn, Luzern, and Zürich.

11.351 **Kleiminger**, R., *Das Heiligengeisthospital von Wismar in Sieben Jahrhunderten*, Weimar, 1962. Comprehensive history of municipal hospital of a Hanse town.

11.352 **Rosen**, G., 'Cameralism and the concept of medical police', *Bull.Hist.Medicine*, 27, 1953, 21-42. On growing belief of German and Austrian mercantilists that state should involve itself with medical and welfare measures to foster population increase. Note similar article on France, 11.318.

11.353 **Wiesner**, Merry E., 'Early modern midwifery. A case study', in Hanawalt (5.445), 94-113. Examines practice of midwifery in Nuremberg in fifteenth and sixteenth centuries.

11.354 **Woehlkens**, E., *Pest und Ruhr im 16. und 17. Jahrhundert*, Hannover, 1954. Detailed study of effects of plague on one small town, Uelzen.

EASTERN AND NORTHERN EUROPE

11.355 **Bernard**, P. B., 'The limits of absolutism. Joseph II and the Allgemeines Krankenhaus', *Eighteenth-Cent.Stud.*, 9,

1976, 193-215. Background to creation of new Vienna hospital, opened in 1784.

11.356 **Sommer**, J. L., 'Hutterite medicine and physicians in Moravia in the sixteenth century and after', *Mennonite Q.Rev.*, 27, 1953, 111-27. With additional note by R. Friedmann, *ib.*, 128-36. Interesting information on health care, which seems to have been strongly developed in Moravian Church.

11.357 **Rothenberg**, G. E., 'The Austrian sanitary cordon and the control of bubonic plague, 1710-1871', *J.Hist.Medicine*, 28, 1973, 15-23. Details quarantine stations established along thousand-mile frontier zone with Ottoman Empire.

11.358 **Pulma**, P., 'The Riksdag, the state bureaucracy, and the administration of hospitals in eighteenth-century Sweden', *Scan.J.Hist.*, 10, 1985, 119-41. Includes material on Finland, and a survey of individual hospitals.

11.359 **Alexander**, J. T., *Bubonic Plague in Early Modern Russia. Public Health and Urban Disaster*, Baltimore, Md., 1980. Detailed monograph on plague outbreak of 1770-72, which especially affected Moscow.

11.360 —— 'Catherine the Great and public health', *J.Hist.Medicine*, 36, 1981, 185-204. Takes fairly favourable view of expansion of services during reign.

11.361 —— 'Medical developments in Petrine Russia', *Can.-Am.Slavic Stud.*, 8, 1974, 198-221. On beginnings of public health system and expansion of medical personnel and training.

11.362 —— 'Medical professionals and public health in "doldrums" Russia (1725-62)', *ib.*, 12, 1978, 116-35. With further note, 'Communicable disease, anti-epidemic policies, and the role of medical professionals', *ib.*, 154-69.

11.363 —— ed., 'Plague epidemics and anti-plague precautions in early modern Russia', *Soviet Stud.in Hist.*, 25 (iv), 1987, whole issue. Soviet articles (in transl.) on eighteenth-century epidemics in Ukraine and Moscow (incl. three concerning Moscow riot of 1771).

11.364 **Kahan**, A., 'Social aspects of the plague epidemics in eighteenth-century Russia', *Ec.Dev.& Cultural Change*, 27, 1979, 255-66.

MENTAL ILLNESS

11.365 **Boari**, M., *"Qui Venit contra Iura." Il "Furiosus" nella Criminalistica dei Secoli 15 e 16*, Milan, 1983. Legal opinion about insanity in Renaissance Roman law.

11.366 **Doerner**, K., *Madmen and the Bourgeoisie. A Social History of Insanity and Psychiatry*, 1981. Transl. from German ed. of 1969. Interesting material on British, French, and German medical attitudes to madness in eighteenth and early nineteenth centuries, with echoes of Foucault on links between industrialisation and coercive treatment (see 11.367,377).

11.367 **Foucault**, M., *Madness and Civilization. A History of Insanity in the Age of Reason*, New York, 1965. Transl. from French ed. of 1961. Review article: R. Mandrou, *Annales*, 17, 1962, 761-71. See also 11.370.

11.368 **Jones**, C., 'The treatment of the insane in eighteenth- and early nineteenth-century Montpellier', *Medical Hist.*, 24, 1980, 371-90. Emphasises extremely small numbers actually committed to asylum.

11.369 **Kinsman**, R. S., 'Folly, melancholy, and madness. A study in shifting styles of medical analysis and treatment, 1450-1675', in Kinsman (6.137), 273-320.

11.370 **Midelfort**, H. C. E., 'Madness and civilization in early modern Europe. A reappraisal of Michel Foucault', in Malament (10.295), 247-65.

11.371 —— 'Madness and the problems of psychological history in the sixteenth century', *Sixteenth-Cent.J.*, 12 (i), 1981, 5-12. Short "agenda" article, with illustrations mainly from Germany.

11.372 —— 'Sin, melancholy, obsession. Insanity and culture in sixteenth-century Germany', in Kaplan (9.541), 113-45. Examines differing attitudes and diagnoses of clergy, medical specialists, and local officials, regarding mental derangement.

11.373 **Mora**, G., 'Historical and sociopsychiatric appraisal of Tarantism', *Bull. Hist. Medicine*, 37, 1963, 417-39. Ailment relieved by frenetic dancing (hence tarentella), and supposed to be induced by tarantula bite, encountered in S. Italy in early modern period. See also Jean F. Russell, 'Tarantism', *Medical Hist.*, 23, 1979, 404-25, which includes musicology of tarentella; and 11.377.

11.374 **Rosen**, G., *Madness in Society. Chapters in the Historical Sociology of Mental Illness*, 1968. General survey, of which following entries give some flavour. Review article: E. J. Hundert, *J.Interdisc.Hist.*, 2, 1972, 669-88 (misnumbered as 453-72).

11.375 —— 'The mentally ill and the community in Western and Central Europe during the late Middle Ages and the Renaissance', *J.Hist.Medicine*, 19, 1964, 377-88. Charts beginnings of change in attitudes to treatment, incarceration becoming normal rather than reserved for dangerous lunatics. Succeeding period dealt with in 'Social attitudes to irrationality and madness in seventeenth- and eighteenth-century Europe', *J.Hist.Medicine*, 18, 1963, 220-40.

11.376 —— 'Nostalgia. A "forgotten" psychological disorder', *Clio Medica*, 10, 1975, 29-51. Rise and fall of view that homesickness constitutes an illness, frequently diagnosed in military recruits. See also J. Starobinski, 'The idea of nostalgia', *Diogenes*, 54, 1966, 81-103.

11.377 —— 'Psychopathology in the social process. Dance frenzies, demonic possession, revival movements...', *Bull.Hist.Medicine*, 36, 1962, 13-44. Describes wide variety of movements in Europe and America, which may have had therapeutic value despite hysterical aspects.

12

SOCIAL CONFLICT: PROTEST, REBELLION, CIVIL WAR

GENERAL SURVEYS

See also 11.108-70 for some material on food shortage and popular disturbances. Also 10.374; 13.18; 14.280.

12.1 **Bak**, J. M., and Benecke, G., eds., *Religion and Rural Revolt. Papers Presented to the Fourth Interdisciplinary Workshop on Peasant Studies*, 1984. Includes papers on Mediterranean Europe, 1500-1800; Normandy, Germany and Switzerland in sixteenth century; and Russia in seventeenth and eighteenth centuries.

12.2 **Bercé**, Y.-M., *Revolt and Revolution in Early Modern Europe*, 1987. Transl. from French ed. of 1980. Thematic approach: "leaders", "mechanisms of subversion", etc. See also his article 'Rural unrest' in Blum (7.8), 133-48; and his major works on French peasant risings (12.30-1).

12.3 'La crise européenne du 17e siècle, 1640-60', *Rev.Hist.Diplomatique*, 92, 1978, 5-232. Symposium on overlapping uprisings of mid-century which recalls R. B. Merriman's *Six Contemporaneous Revolutions*, 1938. Papers on anti-Spanish revolts of Portugal, Southern Italy, and Netherlands; on peasant movements in Switzerland (1653); and unrest in Baltic region.

12.4 **Elliot**, J. H., 'Revolution and continuity in early modern Europe', *P.& P.*, 42, 1969, 35-56. Repr. in Parker and Smith (2.78),110-31. Suggests that popular uprisings could only succeed when aided by alienated groups within ruling class, whose aims were always to conserve "ancient liberties".

12.5 **Forster**, R., and Greene, J. P., eds., *Preconditions of Revolution in Early Modern Europe*, Baltimore, Md., 1970. Contains substantial essays on Netherlands Revolt (J. W. Smit); revolts of 1640s in Spanish Empire (J. H. Elliot); the Fronde (R. Mousnier); and Pugachev's Rebellion (M. Raeff). Review article: H. G. Koenigsberger, *History*, 57, 1972, 394-8. See also 12.9

12.6 **François**, Martha E., 'Revolts in late medieval and early modern Europe. A spiral model', *J.Interdisc.Hist.*, 5, 1974, 19-43. Like Elliot (12.4) sees early modern revolts as essentially counter-revolutionary in nature.

12.7 **Holton**, R. J., 'The crowd in history. Some problems of theory and method', *Soc.Hist.*, 3, 1978, 219-33. Argues that G. Rudé's concern with crowd as vehicle of social protest (see 12.13) has obscured other interesting aspects (public ritual, community solidarity, etc.), and also elements of continuity between pre-industrial and modern crowd behaviour.

12.8 **Koenigsberger**, H. G., 'The organization of revolutionary parties in France and the Netherlands during the sixteenth century', *J.Mod.Hist.*, 27, 1955, 335-51. Repr. in Koenigsberger (11.43), 224-52. Now somewhat dated in its view of such "parties" as *Gueux* and League as prototypes of modern revolutionary organisations.

12.9 **Moote**, A. L., 'Preconditions of revolution in early modern Europe. Did they really exist?', *Can.J.Hist.*, 7, 1972, 207-34.

221

Repr. in Parker and Smith (2.78), 134-64. Starting point is Forster and Greene's book of this title (12.5), but rather wider in range than mere review article.

12.10 **Mousnier**, R., *Peasant Uprisings in Seventeenth-Century France, Russia, and China*, 1971. Transl. from French ed. of 1967. Attack on Marxist (or "vulgar Marxist") characterisation of peasant revolts as simple class-struggle. Review article: M. O. Gately and others, *P.& P.*, 51, 1971, 63-80.

12.11 **Mullett**, M., *Popular Culture and Popular Protest in Late Medieval and Early Modern Europe*, 1987. Aims to show how protest and rebellion were shaped by popular social values, esp. those derived from religious preaching.

12.12 **Nicolas**, J., ed., *Mouvements Populaires et Conscience Sociale, 16e-19e Siècles*, Paris, 1985. Papers from conference on social conflict. Mostly, but not exclusively, concerned with France before 1789.

12.13 **Rudé**, G., *The Crowd in History. A Study of Popular Disturbances in France and England, 1730-1848*, New York, 1964. Revised ed., 1981. Rather sketchy in many ways, but contains nub of Rudé's ideas about changing nature of popular protest. Review article: C. Tilly, *J.Soc.Hist.*, 1, 1968, 296-302.

12.14 —— *Ideology and Popular Protest*, 1980. Brief history of unrest in Europe and America from medieval times, built around concept that only when "derived" ideas are added to those "inherent" in popular notions of justice do truly revolutionary movements take shape, as opposed to strikes, food riots, peasant rebellions, etc.

12.15 —— 'Popular protest and ideology on the eve of the French Revolution', in Hinrichs and others (7.42), 420-35. Ranges over Europe as a whole. See also 12.47.

12.16 —— 'Popular protest in eighteenth-century Europe', in P. Fritz and D. Williams, eds., *The Triumph of Culture* (*Pubs. McMaster Univ. Assoc. for Eighteenth-Cent. Stud.,2*), Toronto, 1972, 277-97.

12.17 —— 'The study of popular disturbances in the pre-industrial age', *Hist. Stud.* (*Australia & N.Z.*), 10, 1963, 457-69. Conference paper.

12.18 **Sabean**, D., 'The communal basis of pre-1800 uprisings in Western Europe', *Comp.Pol.*, 8, 1976, 355-64. Offers several generalisations for testing (e.g. that lead was never taken by landless).

12.19 **Seibt**, F., *Revolution in Europa. Ursprung und Wege Innerer Gewalt. Strukturen, Elemente, Exempel*, Munich, 1984. Interesting pluralist view of nature of late medieval and early modern revolts; those analysed in detail incl. Hussite movement, German Reformation, Netherlands Revolt, and Bohemian insurrection of 1618.

12.20 **Tilly**, C., *From Mobilization to Revolution*, Reading, Mass., 1978. Methodological work on historical forms of collective action.

12.21 —— 'The web of contention in eighteenth-century cities', in Louise A. Tilly and C. Tilly, eds., *Class Conflict and Collective Action*, Beverly Hills, Calif., 1981, 27-51. Looks at types of popular collective action in London, Boston, Charleston, and Paris.

12.22 **Topolski**, J., 'Revolutionary consciousness in America and Europe from the mid-eighteenth to the early nineteenth century as a methodological and historical problem', in J. Pelenski, ed., *The American and European Revolutions, 1776-1848*, Iowa City, 1980, 75-93. Marxist analysis of some subtlety delivered at Conference of Polish and American Historians in 1976.

12.23 **Zagorin**, P., 'Prolegomena to the comparative history of revolution in early modern Europe', *Comp.Stud.Soc.& Hist.*, 18, 1976, 151-74. Criticises Marxist insistence on class conflict as essential ingredient of revolution, and proposes wide range of motives, in which rebellions and coups d'état can be comprehended.

12.24 —— *Rebels and Rulers, 1500-1660*, 2 vols., 1982. Large-scale survey of main rebellions, revolutions, and civil wars of early modern Europe; extremely useful, though fights shy of generalisation or Marxist interpretations. Review article: J. I. Israel, *Comp.Stud.Soc.& Hist.*, 27, 1985, 123-9.

12.25 —— 'Theories of revolution in contemporary historiography', *Pol.Sci.Q.*, 88, 1973, 23-52.

FRANCE: GENERAL
See also 6.21; 7.73; 10.27,36; 11.132; 12.10,12,13,21; 13.247.

12.26 **Beauroy**, J., 'The pre-Revolutionary crisis in Bergerac, 1770-89', *Proc.Western Soc.Fr.Hist.*, 1, 1974, 75-97. Principally an account, with documents, of grain riot by vineyard workers in 1773.

12.27 **Beik**, W. H., 'Magistrates and popular uprisings in France before the Fronde. The case of Toulouse', *J.Mod.Hist.*, 46, 1974, 585-608. Examines attitude of Parlement of Toulouse to popular unrest in 1630s, concluding that it is misleading to link magistrates' remonstrances to government with mob violence.

12.28 —— 'Two intendants face a popular revolt. Social unrest and the structure of absolutism in 1645', *Can.J.Hist.*, 9, 1974, 243-62. Anatomy of riots at Montpellier.

12.29 —— 'Urban factions and the social order during the minority of Louis XIV, *Fr.Hist.Stud.*, 15, 1987, 36-67. Analysis of endemic disorder in Languedoc towns between 1635 and 1660.

12.30 **Bercé**, Y.-M., *Croquants et Nu-Pieds. Les Soulèvements Paysans en France du 16e au 19e Siècle*, Paris, 1974. Analysis, punctuated by brief extracts from manifestos and other sources.

12.31 —— *Histoire des Croquants. Étude des Soulèvements Populaires au 17e Siècle dans le Sud-Ouest de la France*, Geneva, 1974. Thesis based on intensive research. Bread prices, troop billeting, and taxation seen as main causes of peasant risings, which reached peak in war years 1635-60. Review article: O. Ranum, *J.Interdisc.Hist.*, 8, 1977, 329-41.

12.32 **Bernard**, L., 'French society and popular uprisings under Louis XIV', *Fr.Hist.Stud.*, 3, 1964, 454-74. Repr. in Kierstead (6.68), 157-79. Analysis of several post-Fronde rebellions (incl. *Papier Timbré* in Brittany) gives support to view that class war was certainly involved, even when not among initial causes.

12.33 **Collins**, J. B., 'Taxation and peasant revolts in sixteenth- and seventeenth-century France', *Proc.Western Soc.Fr.Hist.*, 10, 1982, 164-80. With comment by A. G. Arthur.

12.34 **Foisil**, Madeleine, *La Révolte des Nu-Pieds et les Révoltes Normandes de 1639*, Paris, 1970. Analysis of one of most serious pre-Fronde tax revolts.

12.35 **Gallet**, J., 'Research on the popular movements at Amiens in 1635 and 1636', in Kierstead (6.68), 130-56. Transl. from *Rev.Hist.Mod.et Contemp.*, 14, 1967, 193-216.

12.36 **Garlan**, Y., and Nières, C., *Les Révoltes Bretonnes de 1675. Papier Timbré et Bonnets Rouges*, Paris, 1975. See also 12.32,41.

12.37 **Hufton**, Olwen H., 'Attitudes towards authority in eighteenth-century Languedoc', *Soc.Hist.*, 3, 1978, 281-302. From archives of governor's summary justice in diocese of Lodève, finds many examples of disrespect and violence towards seigneurs and priests, especially by youth groups.

12.38 **Kaplan**, S. L., 'The Paris bread riot of 1725', *Fr.Hist.Stud.*, 14, 1985, 23-56. Argues that appropriate lessons were learned, so that 50 years elapsed before Paris experienced another serious provision riot.

12.39 **Le Roy Ladurie**, E., 'Rural revolts and protest movements in France from 1675 to 1788', *Stud.Eighteenth-Cent.Culture*, 5, 1976, 423-51. Transl. from *Annales*, 29, 1974, 6-22. Perceives shift from anti-state to anti-seigneurial protest over this period.

12.40 **Mousnier**, R., 'Research into the popular uprisings in France before the Fronde', in Coveney (6.68), 136-68. Transl. from *Rev.Hist.Mod.et Contemp.*, 5, 1958, 81-113. Principally a critique of Porchnev (12.44)

12.41 —— 'La révolte dite du Papier Timbré en Basse-Bretagne en 1675', *Actes Congrès Nat.Soc.Savantes*, 92 (i), 1967, 325-57. Concerned to stress its mainly anti-state rather than anti-seigneurial nature. Cf. 12.32,36.

12.42 **Pillorget**, R., 'The Cascaveoux. The insurrection at Aix in the autumn of 1630', in Kierstead (6.68), 96-129. Transl. from *Dix-Septième Siècle*, 64, 1964, 3-30. See following entry for context.

12.43 —— *Les Mouvements Insurrectionnels de Provence entre 1596 et 1715*, Paris, 1975. Thesis of massive proportions. O. Ranum makes useful contrast between his typology and that of Bercé (12.31), *J. Interdisc.*

Hist., 8, 1977, 329-41.

12.44 **Porchnev**, B., *Die Volksaufstände in Frankreich vor der Fronde, 1623-48*, Leipzig, 1954. Transl. from Russian ed. of 1948. French version, *Les Soulèvements Populaires en France avant la Fronde*, Paris, 1963. Extracts in English publ. in Coveney (6.68), 78-135. Based on large collection of papers of Chancellor Séguier held in Leningrad. Beginning with Mousnier's article (12.40), generated much controversy as to whether revolts were primarily anti-seigneurial or anti-government. Another review article: D. Ligou, *Rev.Hist.Éc.et Soc.*, 42, 1964, 378-85.

12.45 **Powis**, J., 'Guyenne, 1548. The Crown, the province, and social order', *Eur.Stud.Rev.*, 12, 1982, 1-15. Revolt against *gabelles*.

12.46 **Reddy**, W., 'The textile trade and the language of the crowd at Rouen, 1752-1871', *P.& P.*, 74, 1977, 62-89. Notes symbolic nature of many worker protests (e.g. in what they attacked), and argues this reflects concern about erosion of status as much as economic grievances.

12.47 **Rudé**, G., 'The growth of cities and popular revolt, 1750-1850, with particular reference to Paris', in Bosher (6.104), 166-90.

12.48 **Salmon**, J. H. M., 'The Audijos revolt. Provincial liberties and institutional rivalries under Louis XIV', *Eur.Hist.Q.*, 14, 1984, 119-49. Anti-gabelle rising in Western Pyrenees, 1664-67. Repr. in his *Renaissance and Revolt*, 1987, 267-92.

12.49 —— 'Peasant revolt in Vivarais, 1575-80', *Fr.Hist.Stud.*, 11, 1979, 1-28. Repr. in Salmon (12.48), 211-34. Argues that revolt sprang not from taxation or feudal oppression, but from government's failure to prevent pillage by garrisons and war-bands.

12.50 —— 'Venal office and popular sedition in France', *P.& P.*, 37, 1967, 21-43. Repr. in Salmon (12.48), 191-210. Review of work of Porchnev and Mousnier (12.40,44), and subsequent research into connections between bureaucracy and popular risings.

12.51 **Tilly**, C., *The Contentious French*, Cambridge, Mass., 1986. How popular pressure, in form of riots, strikes, demonstrations, etc., has influenced French government and social order from seventeenth century onwards. Material on

early modern period is substantial.

12.52 —— 'Routine conflicts and peasant rebellions in seventeenth-century France', in R. P. Weller and S. E. Guggenheim, eds., *Power and Protest in the Countryside*, Durham, N.C., 1982, 13-41. Revised version of Tilly (1.20), 109-44. Attributes unrest far more to state exactions than to tenurial problems.

12.53 **Tilly**, Louise A., 'The food riot as a form of political conflict in France', *J. Interdisc. Hist.*, 2, 1971, 23-57. Overview of subsistence riots from seventeenth to nineteenth centuries.

WARS OF RELIGION IN FRANCE
See also 5.73; 8.58; 10.287; 11.37; 12.8; 13.22,106,238-70 passim; 14.58.

12.54 **Barnavi**, E., *Le Parti de Dieu. Étude Sociale et Politique des Chefs de la Ligue Parisienne*, Brussels, 1980. Corrects many misconceptions of Parisian League as democratic popular revolt; nevertheless criticised as anachronistic in some respects by Descimon (see following entry).

12.55 **Descimon**, R., *Qui Étaient les Seize? Mythes et Réalités de la Ligue Parisienne, 1585-94*, Paris, 1983. Full-scale prosopographical study. Review article: M. Greengrass, *History*, 69, 1984, 432-9. Note also substantial preliminary essay, 'La Ligue à Paris (1585-94): une révision', *Annales*, 37, 1982, 72-128.

12.56 **Diefendorf**, Barbara, 'Prologue to a massacre. Popular unrest in Paris, 1557-72', *Am.Hist.Rev.*, 90, 1985, 1067-91. Views St. Bartholomew Massacre as culmination of long break-down in public order in Paris. On St. Bartholomew in Protestant symbolism see 13.254.

12.57 **Greengrass**, M., 'The Sainte Union in the provinces. The case of Toulouse', *Sixteenth-Cent.J.*, 14, 1983, 469-96.

12.58 **Harding**, R., 'Revolution and reform in the Holy League. Angers, Rennes, Nantes', *J.Mod.Hist.*, 53, 1981, 379-416. Finds little evidence in these cities that elite split on any identifiable social basis or that League challenged basic institutions.

12.59 **Salmon**, J. H. M., 'The Paris Sixteen, 1584-94. Social analysis of a revolutionary movement', *J.Mod.Hist.*, 44, 1972, 540-76. Repr. in Salmon (12.48), 235-66. Shows that social status of League leaders varied with different phases of political structure, but was always considerably higher than portrayed by royalist propaganda. See further 12.54-5.

12.60 **Van Doren**, L. S., 'Revolt and reaction in the city of Romans, Dauphiné, 1579-80', *Sixteenth-Cent.J.*, 5 (i), 1974, 71-100. Social background to early League urban disturbances. For Le Roy Ladurie's very different treatment of this episode see 14.58.

THE FRONDE
See also 10.299-302,304; 12.5.

12.61 **Bercé**, Y.-M., and others, 'Retour à la Fronde', *Dix-Septième Siècle*, 145, 1984, whole issue. Five studies on major aspects, with bibliography of recent work in English by A. N. Hamscher.

12.62 **Bonney**, R., 'The English and French civil wars', *History*, 65, 1980, 365-82. Comparison of Fronde and English Civil War.

12.63 —— 'The French civil war, 1649-53', *Eur.Stud.Rev.*, 8, 1978, 71-100. Account of Fronde which stresses importance of

nobles' aims, as against Moote's emphasis on Robe (see 10.300-2).

12.64 **Kettering**, Sharon, 'The causes of the judicial Frondes', *Can.J.Hist.*, 17, 1982, 275-306. Seeks to discern why some provincial Parlements and not others followed Parisian lead.

12.65 **Knecht**, R. J., *The Fronde*, 1975. Useful short introduction (Historical Association pamphlet).

12.66 **Kossmann**, E. H., *La Fronde*, Leiden, 1954. French language account by Dutch historian. Finds it impossible to regard Fronde as coherent or classifiable movement.

12.67 **Mousnier**, R., 'Quelques raisons de la Fronde – les causes des journées révolutionnaires parisiennes de 1648', *Dix-Septième Siècle*, 2-3, 1949, 33-78. Still valuable examination of grievances.

12.68 **Westrich**, S. A., *The Ormée of Bordeaux. A Revolution during the Fronde*, Baltimore, Md., 1972. Tries to make sense of localist rising whose aims and leadership are particularly obscure.

LOW COUNTRIES
See also 3.80; 6.113-14; 12.3,5,8,19; 13.271,274,276,278.

12.69 **Griffiths**, G., 'The revolutionary character of the Revolt of the Netherlands', *Comp.Stud.Soc.& Hist.*, 2, 1960, 452-69. Followed by G. Nadel, 'The logic of *The Anatomy of Revolution* with reference to the Netherlands Revolt', *ib.*, 473-84. See also comment by I. Schöffer, *ib.*, 3, 1961, 470-7. Both essays attempt to fit Revolt to model of Crane Brinton's *Anatomy of Revolution*, New York, 1938.

12.70 **Israel**, J. I., 'A conflict of empires. Spain and the Netherlands, 1618-48', *P.& P.*, 76, 1977, 34-74. Mainly on economic aspects of second phase of Dutch Revolt.

12.71 **Parker**, G., *The Dutch Revolt*, 1977. Attractively written and scholarly.

12.72 —— 'War and economic change. The

economic costs of the Dutch Revolt', in J. M. Winter, ed., *War and Economic Development. Essays in Memory of David Joslin*, 1975, 49-71. Considers repercussions on economies of Spain, Portugal, and both parts of Netherlands.

12.73 **Wittman**, T., *Les Gueux dans les "Bonnes Villes" de Flandre, 1577-84*, Budapest, 1969. Interesting Marxist analysis of failure of Netherlands Revolt in Flemish cities.

12.74 **Weenink**, Hetty, 'Early eighteenth-century uprisings in the Low Countries', *Hist.Workshop*, 15, 1983, 95-116. Describes some little known struggles against oligarchic town rule in both Northern and Southern Netherlands.

SPAIN: GENERAL
See also 4.39; 5.558,564; 10.432.

12.75 **Elliott**, J. H., *The Revolt of the Catalans. A Study in the Decline of Spain, 1598-1640*, 1963. Masterly account of regional discontents. Review article: A. Domínguez Ortiz, *P.&P.*, 29, 1964, 105-11.

12.76 **García Carcel**, R., *Las Germanias de Valencia*, Barcelona, 1975. Revolt contemporaneous, though quite separate, from that of Castilian communes.

12.77 **Kamen**, H., 'A forgotten insurrection of the seventeenth century. The Catalan peasant rising of 1688', *J.Mod.Hist.*, 49, 1977, 210-30. Emphasises importance of split between aristocracy and peasantry in subsequent attitude of Catalonia to Spanish Succession War.

12.78 **Larquié**, C., 'Popular uprisings in Spain in the mid-seventeenth century', *Renaiss.& Mod.Stud.*, 26, 1982, 90-107. Rather sketchy survey transl. from *Rev.Hist.Diplomatique*, 92, 1978, 31-50 (symposium noted in 12.3).

12.79 **Rodriguez**, Laura, 'The Spanish riots of 1766', *P.&P.*, 59, 1973, 117-46. On widespread disturbances provoked by partial freeing of grain trade.

12.80 **Yun Casalilla**, B., *Crisis de Subsistencias y Conflictividad Social en Córdoba a Principios del Siglo 16*, Cordoba, 1980. Separate sections deal with demographic pressures and with more general sources of social tension.

THE COMUNERO REVOLT

12.81 **Gutiérrez Nieto**, J. I., *Las Comunidades como Movimiento Antiseñorial*, Barcelona, 1973. Contends that revolt had peasant as well as urban support.

12.82 **Haliczer**, S., *The Comuneros of Castile. The Forging of a Revolution, 1475-1521*, Madison, Wis., 1981. Only book-length modern treatment in English. Emphasises long-term antecedents.

12.83 —— 'Political opposition and collective violence in Segovia, 1475-1520', *J.Mod.Hist.*, 48, 1976 (on demand article). Local study of origins.

12.84 **Maravall**, J. A., *Las Comunidades de Castilla. Una Primera Revolución Moderna*, Madrid, 1963.

12.85 **Owens**, J. B., 'A city for the King. The impact of a rural revolt in Talavera during the Comunidades of Castile', *Societas*, 8, 1978, 53-64. Instance of municipality remaining loyal to Crown because of unrest in surrounding countryside.

12.86 —— *Rebelión, Monarquía, y Oligarquía. Murcia en la Epoca de Carlos V*, Murcia, 1980. Principally on city's participation in Comunero revolt; much background also on city and regional elite.

12.87 **Perez**, J., *La Révolution des Comunidades de Castille, 1520-21*, Bordeaux, 1970. Spanish ed., Madrid, 1977.

ITALY

12.88 **Burke**, P., 'The Virgin of the Carmine and the revolt of Masaniello', *P.&P.*, 99, 1983, 3-21. Repr. in Burke (14.81), 191-206. Essay on importance of ritual to both sides in insurrection. But see 12.91.

12.89 **Ferrante**, Lucia, ' "Tumulto di più persone per causa del calo del pane..." Saccheggi e repressione a Bologna (1671, 1677)', *Riv.Stor.Ital.*, 90, 1978, 770-809.

12.90 **Koenigsberger**, H. G., 'The revolt of Palermo in 1647', *Cambridge Hist.J.*, 8, 1946, 129-44. Repr. in Koenigsberger (11.43), 253-77.

12.91 **Villari**, R., 'Masaniello. Contemporary and recent interpretations', *P.&P.*, 108, 1985, 117-32. Takes issue with some of Burke's ideas in 12.88.

12.92 —— 'Naples: the insurrection of 1585', in Cochrane (9.574), 305-30. Transl. from *Studi Storici*, 8, 1967. Traces interconnection of popular bread riots and constitutional preoccupations of aristocracy. Forms early section of following work.

12.93 —— *La Rivolta Antispagnola a Napoli. Le Origini, 1585-1647*, Bari, 1967. Much-praised study of social and economic effects of Spanish rule. On Naples Revolt see also

3.201.

12.94 —— *Ribelli e Riformatori dal 16 al 18 Secolo*, Rome, 1979. Collected essays and reviews, some general, most interesting for our purposes concentrating on Southern Italy. Argues that some revolts had genuine revolutionary potential.

GERMANY, SWITZERLAND, AUSTRIA: GENERAL

See also 6.184; 12.3,139–40; 13.185.

12.95 **Barnett-Robisheaux**, T., 'Peasant revolts in Germany and Central Europe after the Peasants' War', *Central Eur.Hist.*, 17, 1984, 384-403. Review article, incl. comment on items 7.183; 12.96, 98, 107, 109.

12.96 **Blickle**, P., ed., *Aufruhr und Empörung? Studien zum Bäuerlichen Widerstand im Alten Reich*, Munich, 1980. Includes studies of three South German localities over several centuries, in attempt to generalise conditions making for peasant resistance; stresses political as well as economic motives of peasantry.

12.97 —— 'The criminalisation of peasant resistance in the Holy Roman Empire. Toward a history of the emergence of high treason in Germany', *J.Mod.Hist.*, 58, 1986, suppl., 88-97. Shows how treason legislation favoured increasing regulation of everyday life to prevent disorder ("polizei").

12.98 —— *Deutsche Untertanen. Ein Widerspruch*, Munich, 1981. Stresses community ideals and struggle for political voice, of lower social orders. See following entry for more detailed examination of one particular period.

12.99 —— 'Untertanen in der Frühneuzeit. Zur Rekonstruktion der politischen Kultur und der sozialen Wirklichkeit Deutschlands im 17. Jahrhundert', *VSWG*, 70, 1983, 483-522.

12.100 —— 'Peasant revolts in the German Empire in the late Middle Ages', *Soc.Hist.*, 4, 1979, 223-39.

12.101 **Friedrichs**, C. R., 'Citizens or subjects? Urban conflict in early modern Germany', in Chrisman and Gründler (6.102), 46-58. Argues that internal conflict is constant theme from fourteenth to eighteenth centuries, and Reformation did not usher in period of unchallenged oligarchical rule.

12.102 —— 'German town revolts and the seventeenth-century crisis', *Renaiss.&*

Mod.Stud, 26, 1982, 27-51. Finds marked differences between upheavals prior to Thirty Years War and those occuring after.

12.103 —— 'Urban conflicts and the imperial constitution in seventeenth-century Germany', *J.Mod.Hist.*, 58, 1986, suppl., 98-123. Footnote to previous entry, dealing with mediation by imperial commissions in these disputes.

12.104 **Grüll**, G., *Bauer, Herr, und Landesfürst. Sozialrevolutionäre Bestrebungen der Oberösterreichischen Bauern von 1650 bis 1848*, Graz, 1963.

12.105 —— *Der Bauer im Lande ob der Enns am Ausgang des 16.Jahrhunderts. Abgaben und Leistungen im Lichte der Beschwerden und Verträge von 1597-98*, Vienna, 1969. Grievances leading to peasant revolt in Upper Austria in 1597, area looked at in longer perspective in preceding entry.

12.106 **Harnisch**, H., 'Klassenkämpfe der Bauern in der Mark Brandenburg zwischen frühbürgerlicher Revolution und Dreissigjährigem Krieg', *Jb.Regionalgesch.*, 5, 1975, 142-72. "Early bourgeois revolution" is Marxist code for combined religious and social upheavals of 1520s.

12.107 **Schulze**, W., *Bäuerlicher Widerstand und Feudale Herrschaft in der Frühen Neuzeit*, Stuttgart, 1980. Charts forms of peasant resistance in German lands between 1525 and 1789 from open rebellions to action in law courts.

12.108 —— 'Peasant resistance in sixteenth- and seventeenth-century Germany in a European context', in Greyerz (8.118), 61-98. Very wide comparative perspective.

12.109 ——, ed., *Aufstände, Revolten, Prozesse. Beiträge zu Bäuerlichen Widerstands-bewegungen im Frühneuzeitlichen Europa*, Stuttgart, 1983. Essay collection, majority of which deal with unrest in German-speaking lands.

12.110 **Scott**, T., 'Peasant revolts in early modern

Germany', *Hist.J.*, 28, 1985, 455-68.
Review article, covering 7.183, 12.96,98,
107, 109. Compare 12.95.

THE GERMAN PEASANT WAR
OF 1525
See also 7.185; 8.122; 13.192,199,213.

12.111 **Winterhager**, F., *Bauernkriegsforschung*,
Darmstadt, 1981. Interesting survey of
historiography since Vormärz. For
further bibliography and historiographical
discussion see 2.55; 12.116,124-5,128,131;
13.192,230.

12.112 **Bak**, J., ed., *The German Peasant War of
1525*, 1975. Also forms *J.Peasant Stud.*, 3
(i), 1975. Contributors include R. W.
Scribner, Heide Wunder, P. Blickle, and
D. Sabean. Features discussion of Engels'
Peasant War in Germany.

12.113 **Blickle**, P., *The Revolution of 1525. The
German Peasants' War from a New
Perspective*, Baltimore, Md., 1981. Transl.
from German ed. of 1981. Vigorous
defence of rebels' aims as coherent and
largely uniform programme of both urban
and rural lower classes.

12.114 **Buck**, L. P., 'Civil insurrection in a
Reformation city. The *Versicherungsbrief* of
Windsheim, March 1525',
Arch.Reformationsgesch., 67, 1976, 100-17.
Light thrown on urban grievances which
played a part in disturbances of Peasants'
War.

12.115 —— 'Opposition to tithes in the Peasants'
Revolt. A case study of Nuremberg in
1524', *Sixteenth-Cent.J.*, 4 (ii), 1973,
11-22.

12.116 **Buszello**, H., and others, eds., *Der
Deutsche Bauernkrieg*, Paderborn, 1984.
Three-part symposium: part 1 deals with
historiography and background; part 2
with regional variations; part 3 with
general causes and aspects. Contributors
incl. P. Blickle, R. Endres, W. Schulze.

12.117 **Cohn**, H. J., 'Anticlericalism in the
German Peasants' War, 1525', *P.& P.*, 83,
1979, 3-31. Emphasises that Church was
primary focus of economic grievances.

12.118 **Heymann**, F. G., 'The Hussite Revolution
and the German Peasants' War',
Medievalia et Humanistica, n.s., 1, 1970,
141-59. Comparative study.

12.119 **Hillerbrand**, H. J., 'The German
Reformation and the Peasants' War', in L.
P. Buck and J. W. Zophy, eds., *The Social

History of the Reformation, Columbus,
Ohio, 1972, 106-36. Examines pamphlet
literature of early Reformation, and
expressed peasant grievances, finding little
connection.

12.120 **Kolb**, R., 'The theologians and the
peasants. Conservative evangelical
reactions to the German Peasants' Revolt',
Arch.Reformationsgesch., 69, 1978, 103-31.
Examines views of nine Reformation
leaders who took similar line to Luther's.

12.121 **Lau**, F., 'Did popular reformation really
stop with the peasants' defeat?', in K. C.
Sessions, ed., *Reformation and Authority.
The Meaning of the Peasants' Revolt*,
Lexington, Mass., 1968, 94-101.
Abbreviated transl. from *Luther-Jb.*, 26,
1959, 109-34. Argues that Lutheranism
continued to enjoy plenty of popular
support despite Martin's attitude in 1525.

12.122 **Macek**, J., *Der Tiroler Bauernkrieg und
Michael Gaismar*, Berlin, 1965. For attack
on Macek's view of Peasants' Revolt as
prototype "bourgeois revolution", see J.
Bücking, *Michael Gaismar, Reformer,
Sozialrebell, Revolutionär*, Stuttgart,
1978. For English treatment of Gaismar see
W. Klaasen, *Michael Gaismar*, Leiden,
1978, though this is less strong on social
background.

12.123 **Maurer**, J., *Prediger im Bauernkriege*,
Stuttgart, 1979. Seeks to chart relationship
between Reformation and revolt by noting
activities of over 200 evangelical pastors
during troubles.

12.124 **Midelfort**, H. C. E., 'The revolution of
1525? Recent studies of the Peasants' War',
Central Eur.Hist., 11, 1978, 189-206.
Reviews material produced in 1975 for
450th anniversary of Peasants' War,
concentrating particularly on challenges
they present to G. Franz' classic *Der
Deutsche Bauernkrieg* (1933).

12.125 **Scott**, T., 'The Peasants' War. A
historiographical review', *Hist.J.*, 22,
1979, 693-720, 953-74. Deals with 14
recent monographs and symposia.

12.126 —— 'Reformation and Peasants' War in
Waldshut and environs', *Arch.
Reformationsgesch.*, 69, 1978, 82-102;
70, 1979, 140-68. Impact of radical
ministry of Balthasar Hubmaier on local
peasantry.

12.127 **Scribner**, R. W., and Benecke, G., eds.,
*The German Peasant War of 1525. New
Viewpoints*, 1979. Collection of 14 articles

or extracts, mostly transl. from German journals or symposia. Contributors include P. Blickle, H. A. Oberman, Heide Wunder, D. Sabean. Good bibliography.

2.128 —— 'Revolutionary heritage. The German Peasant War of 1525', in Samuel (2.128), 242-55. On its place in socialist historiography.

2.129 **Sea**, T. F., 'The economic impact of the German Peasants' War. The question of reparations', *Sixteenth-Cent.J.*, 8 (iii), 1977, 74-97. Examines how Swabian League went about recouping costs of suppression.

2.130 —— 'Imperial cities and the Peasants' War in Germany', *Central Eur.Hist.*, 12, 1979, 3-37. On factors which led some cities to take a neutral stance or even submit to rebel armies.

2.131 **Sessions**, K. C., 'The war over Luther and the peasants. Old campaigns and new strategies', *Sixteenth-Cent.J.*, 3 (ii), 1972, 25-44. Historiographical article on relation between Reformation and revolt.

2.132 **Struck**, W.-H., *Der Bauernkrieg am Mittelrhein und in Hessen. Darstellung und Quellen*, Wiesbaden, 1975. Carries large

appendix of documents.

12.133 **Vogler**, G., *Die Gewalt Soll Gegeben Werden dem Gemeinen Volk. Der Deutsche Bauernkrieg*, 1525, Berlin, 1975. 3rd ed., 1983. Leading East German exposition.

12.134 **Waas**, A., *Die Bauern im Kampf um Gerechtigkeit, 1300-1525*, Frankfurt, 1964. Despite title, essentially a history of 1525 revolt, handsomely illustrated with prints and facsimile documents.

12.135 **Waring**, G. H., 'The silver miners of the Erzgebirge and the Peasants' War of 1525 in the light of recent research', *Sixteenth-Cent.J.*, 18, 1987, 231-47. Tries to account for relative passivity of miners.

12.136 **Wehler**, H.-U., ed., *Der Deutsche Bauernkrieg*, 1524-26, Göttingen, 1975. Important symposium. Some essays in it appear in transl. in Scribner and Benecke (12.127).

12.137 **Wohlfeil**, R., ed., *Der Bauernkrieg, 1524-26. Bauernkrieg und Reformation*, Munich, 1975. Another useful essay collection.

12.138 **Zins**, H., 'Aspects of the Peasant Rising in East Prussia in 1525', *Slavonic & E.Eur.Rev.*, 38, 1959, 178-87.

EASTERN AND NORTHERN EUROPE
See also 7.212 and 10.525 (Hungary); 11.363; 12.1,3,10 (Russia).

2.139 **Barton**, P. F., ed., *Sozialrevolution und Reformation. Aufsätze zur Vorreformation, Reformation, und zu den "Bauernkriegen" in Südmitteleuropa*, Vienna, 1975. Seven essays on links between Reformation and unrest in Austria, Bohemia, and Hungary.

2.140 **Heckenast**, G., ed., *Aus der Geschichte der Ostmitteleuropäischen Bauernbewegungen im 16.-17. Jahrhundert*, Budapest, 1977. Over 50 conference papers on unrest in Central and Eastern Europe, with special attention to Hungarian revolt of 1514.

2.141 **Heymann**, F. G., 'City rebellions in fifteenth-century Bohemia, and their ideological and sociological background', *Slavonic & E.Eur.Rev.*, 40, 1962, 324-40. Compares Prague struggle of 1420-21 with that of Breslau and Jihlava in 1458-59.

2.142 **Pelenski**, J., 'The *Haidamak* insurrections and the old regimes in Eastern Europe', in Pelenski (12.22), 228-47. Peasant-Cossack rebellions against Polish magnates and their Russian backers in the Ukraine (late

eighteenth century).

12.143 **Djordjevic**, D., and Fischer-Galati, S., *The Balkan Revolutionary Tradition*, New York, 1981. Survey of insurrections and revolutions from seventeenth century to end of Ottoman Empire.

12.144 **Griswold**, W. J., *The Great Anatolian Rebellion, 1000-20/1591-1611*, Berlin, 1983. Deals with widespread unrest and banditry known as Jelali outbreaks.

12.145 **Olson**, R. W., 'The *esnaf* and the Patrona Halil Rebellion of 1730', *J.Ec.& Soc.Hist.Orient*, 17, 1974, 329-44. Explains grievances of artisan class (*esnaf*) of Istanbul. Continued as 'Jews, janissaries, esnaf, and the revolt of 1740 in Istanbul', *ib.*, 20, 1977, 185-207.

12.146 **Prodan**, D., 'Emperor Joseph II and Horea's uprising in Transylvania', *S.E.Eur.*, 3, 1976, 135-44. Rising of Rumanian serfs in 1784. Narrative account, poor on analysis.

12.147 **Avrich**, P., *Russian Rebels, 1600-1800*,

New York, 1972. Account of popular risings, including those of Stenka Razin and Pugachev. Rather superficial.

12.148 **Gordon**, Linda, *Cossack rebellions. Social turmoil in the sixteenth-century Ukraine*, Albany, N.Y., 1983. Centres on rebellions in 1590s. Good on Cossack society, though assumes fairly detailed knowledge of political events.

12.149 **Longworth**, P., 'Popular protest in England and Russia. Some comparisons and suggestions', in Cross (9.157), 263-78. Finds certain similarities of belief and symbolism in pre-industrial riots and rebellions of the two countries (legendary heroes, pretenders, millenarianism).

12.150 —— 'The pretender phenomenon in eighteenth-century Russia', *P.& P.*, 66, 1975, 61-83. Considers involvement of pretenders to Crown in peasant social protest, springing from belief in Tsar as dispenser of divine justice. See also 12.154,156.

12.151 —— 'The subversive legend of Sten'ka Razin', in V. Strada, ed., *Rossiya/Russia. Studi e Ricerche*, 2, Turin, 1975, 17-40. Examines the many folk songs and legends about Razin as expression of peasant social aspirations.

12.152 **Mavrodin**, V. V., 'Soviet historical literature on the peasant wars in Russia during the seventeenth and eighteenth centuries', *Soviet Stud.in Hist.*, 1 (ii), 1962, 43-63.

12.153 **Miller**, D. H., 'Popular protests and urban violence in 1648 in Muscovy', *Soviet Stud.in Hist.*, 17 (i), 1978, 3-19, 20-114. Article followed by transl. extracts from book by E. V. Chistiakova on urban uprisings during 1630s and '40s in Moscow and Pomor'e (Voronezh, 1975).

12.154 **Perrie**, Maureen, ' "Popular socio-utopian legends" in the Time of Troubles', *Slavonic & E.Eur.Rev.*, 60, 1982, 221-43. Sceptical examination of K. V. Chistov's theory that pretender rumours conform to a pattern of folk myths about deliverers. See also 12.150,156.

12.155 **Pronshtein**, A. P., 'Resolved and unresolved problems in the history of peasant wars in Russia', *Soviet Stud.in Hist.*, 6 (iii), 1968, 27-39. Review of recent Soviet historiography, notably work by I.

I. Smirnov and others on seventeenth- and eighteenth-century peasant wars (Moscow, 1966).

12.156 **Siegelbaum**, L. H., 'Peasant disorders and the myth of the Tsar. Russian variations on a millenarian theme', *J.Relig.Hist.*, 10, 1979, 223-35. On myth of Tsar-deliverer in peasant disorders from seventeenth century to 1861. See also 12.150,154.

12.157 **Subtelny**, O., *The Mazepists. Ukrainian separatism in the early eighteenth century*, Boulder, Colo., 1981. Cossack rebellion of 1708; main emphasis, however, on political and dipomatic aspects.

12.158 **Yaresh**, L., 'The "peasant wars" in Soviet historiography', *Am.Slavic & E.Eur.Rev.*, 16, 1957, 241-59.

PUGACHEV'S REVOLT
See also 6.231; 12.5,147.

12.159 **Alexander**, J. T., *Autocratic Politics in a National Crisis. The Imperial Russian Government and Pugachev's Revolt, 1773-75*, Bloomington, Ind., 1969. As title indicates, deals more with repercussions than with revolt itself.

12.160 —— *Emperor of the Cossacks. Pugachev and the Frontier Jacquerie of 1773-75*, Lawrence, Kans., 1973. More general account, stronger on narrative than analysis.

12.161 —— 'Recent Soviet historiography on the Pugachev Revolt', *Can.Slavic Stud.*, 4, 1970, 602-17.

12.162 **Longworth**, P., 'Peasant leadership and the Pugachev Revolt', *J.Peasant Stud.*, 2, 1975, 183-205. Examines background and organisational abilities of Pugachev and his lieutenants, and motivation they sought to instil.

12.163 —— 'The Pugachev Revolt. The last great Cossack peasant rising', in Landsberger (10.374), 194-258. Valuable study, condensed and revised in *J.Eur.Stud.*, 3, 1973, 1-35.

12.164 **Peters**, Dorothea, *Politische und Gesellschaftliche Vorstellungen in der Aufstandsbewegung unter Pugačev (1773-75)*, Berlin, 1973. Forms vol.17 of *Forsch.Osteur.Gesch.*

13

RELIGION AND SOCIETY

GENERAL WORKS. CHURCH AND COMMUNITY. POPULAR PIETY

See sub-section 11.188-261 passim *for material on charitable activities.*
Also 5.301,428; 12.11; 13.277; 14.106-25.

3.1 **Carrier**, H., and Pin, E., *Sociology of Christianity. International Bibliography*, Rome, 1964. Comprises author, geographical, and topic indices. A good deal of historical material included. Note further bibliographical and historiographical material at 13.21,27,46,52,59,63,76.

3.2 **Bossy**, J., *Christianity in the West, 1400-1700*, 1985. Flavour of this work can be gained from following associated essays.

3.3 —— 'The Counter-Reformation and the people of Catholic Europe', *P.& P.*, 47, 1970, 51-70. Investigates some ways in which post-Tridentine Catholic discipline negated popular religious practice, esp. involvement of kinship groups.

3.4 —— 'Blood and baptism. Kinship, community, and Christianity in Western Europe from the fourteenth to the seventeenth centuries', *Stud.Church Hist.*, 10, 1973, 129-43. Views rites of marriage and baptism as imposing truce between potentially hostile groups.

3.5 —— 'Holiness and society', *P.& P.*, 75, 1977, 119-37. Again emphasises shift of social focus from kinship groups to nuclear families in post-Reformation religion. Review of Trinkaus and Oberman (5.451).

3.6 —— 'The mass as a social institution, 1200-1700', *P.& P.*, 100, 1983, 29-61.

13.7 —— 'The social history of confession in the age of the Reformation', *Trans. Roy. Hist. Soc.*, 5th ser., 25, 1975, 21-38. Revolves round hypothesis that purpose of confession shifted from community peace-making to individual, internal discipline.

13.8 **Callahan**, W. J., and Higgs, D., eds., *Church and Society in Catholic Europe of the Eighteenth Century*, 1979. Apart from editors' introduction, and chap. on popular religion by M. Venard, essays take country by country approach. Contributors include Callahan on Spain, Higgs on Portugal, Olwen Hufton on France, M. Rosa on Italy, G. Benecke on Germany, J. Bérenger on Austria, B. K. Kiraly on Hungary, J. Kloczowski on Poland.

13.9 **Certeau**, M. de, 'Du système religieux à l'éthique des Lumières (17e-18e siècles). La formalité des pratiques', in F. Malgeri, ed., *La Società Religiosa nell'Età Moderna. Atti del Convegno...Capaccio-Paestum, Naples*, 1973. Traces divorce between belief and systems of morality in this period.

13.10 **Davis**, Natalie Z., 'Some tasks and themes in the study of popular religion', in Trinkaus and Oberman (5.451), 307-36.

13.11 **Delumeau**, J., *Catholicism between Luther and Voltaire. A New View of the Counter-Reformation*, 1977. Transl. from French ed. of 1971. Substantial section on religious sociology.

13.12 —— *Le Péché et la Peur. La Culpabilisation en Occident (13e-18e Siècles)*, Paris, 1983. Lengthy study of imagery and literature which continually reminded Europeans of guilt and perils of after-life. See also 14.10 for some overlap of themes.

13.13 ——, ed., *Histoire Vécue du Peuple Chrétien*, 2 vols., Toulouse, 1979. Miscellany of articles, arranged chronologically but not forming continuous or comprehensive history. Contributions of interest are F. Rapp and B. Vogler on early modern Germany; Janine Estèbe on the Huguenots; and F. Lebrun on eighteenth-century preaching.

13.14 **Dolan**, J. P., 'Religious festivities during the Reformation and Counter-Reformation. Challenge and response', *Societas*, 2, 1972, 95-120. Points up similarities in Catholic and Protestant official denunciations of licentiousness and over-frequency of feast days.

13.15 **Duggan**, L. G., 'Fear and confession on the eve of the Reformation', *Arch. Reformationsgesch.*, 75, 1984, 153-75. Takes sceptical view of alleged angst generated by late medieval penitential system (see, e.g., 13.12,24).

13.16 **Frijhoff**, W. T. M., 'Official and popular religion in Christianity. The late Middle Ages and early modern times (thirteenth-eighteenth centuries)', in P. H. Vrijhof and J. Waardenburg, eds., *Official and Popular Religion*, The Hague, 1979, 71-116. Argues that "popular" religion tends to be equated with that which became marginal to values of elite.

13.17 **Ginzburg**, C., ed., 'Religioni delle classi popolari', *Quad.Stor.*, 41, 1979, 393-697. Italian language symposium, mostly case studies with Italian or French setting. Contributors incl. J. Bossy, P. Burke, M. Vovelle.

13.18 **Lewy**, G., *Religion and Revolution*, 1974. Major comparative survey, ranging over many periods and civilisations.

13.19 **Moller**, H., 'Social causation of affective mysticism', *J.Soc.Hist.*, 4, 1971, 305-38. Attempts to correlate geographical shifts in prevalence of quasi-erotic Christian spirituality (from St. Bernard onwards) with areas experiencing shortage of males.

13.20 **Monter**, W., *Ritual, Myth, and Magic in Early Modern Europe*, Athens, Ohio, 1983. Somewhat misleading title, as emphasis is on difficult birth of toleration. Reviewed in following article.

13.21 **Peters**, E. M., 'Religion and culture, popular and unpopular, 1500-1800', *J. Mod.Hist.*, 59, 1987, 317-30. Literature review; among items covered are Monter (13.20); Greyerz' collection (5.301); and Kaplan's (9.541).

13.22 **Sheils**, W. J., and Wood, Diana, eds., *Voluntary Religion (Stud. in Church Hist., 23)*, Oxford, 1986. Essays dealing mainly with confraternities and other special associations. Note J. Henderson on confraternities in Florence (69-83); R. Mackenney on those of Venice (85-95); and J. Bossy on leagues and associations during French Wars of Religion (171-89).

13.23 **Tazbir**, J., 'The cult of St. Isidore the Farmer in Europe', in Geremek and Maczak (3.284), 99-111. Cult of St. Isidore of Madrid, medieval peasant formally canonised in 1622.

13.24 **Tentler**, T. N., *Sin and Confession on the Eve of the Reformation*, Princeton, N.J., 1977. Examination of social and psychological impact of sacrament of confession, mainly from confessors' manuals.

13.25 **Trexler**, R. C., 'Reverence and profanity in the study of early modern religion', in Greyerz (5.301), 245-69. Comments (somewhat tortuously) on prejudices modern academics may import into their characterisation of beliefs and practices.

13.26 **Weinstein**, D., and Bell, R. M., *Saints and Society. The Two Worlds of Western Christendom, 1000-1700*, Chicago, 1982. Attempts to categorise sample of nearly 1000 saints (official or locally venerated) in terms of class, age, locality, style of sanctity, etc.

13.27 **Wilson**, S., ed., *Saints and their Cults*, 1983. Collection of reprinted articles, not bearing directly on early modern period; but contains excellent, annotated bibliography of cults, 309-417.

13.28 **Wirth**, J., 'Against the acculturation thesis', in Greyerz (5.301), 66-78. Attacks concept of inert and superstitious masses dragooned by elite to more acceptable practices (see esp. Muchembled, 13.48, 14.61), by producing examples of contrary tendency, e.g. popular iconoclasm.

13.29 **Wootton**, D., 'Unbelief in early modern

Europe', *Hist.Workshop*, 20, 1985, 82-100. Suggests that genuine atheism was reasonably common both at popular and literate levels: argument countering well-known contention of L. Febvre in *The Problem of Unbelief in the Sixteenth Century. The Religion of Rabelais*, Cambridge, Mass., 1982 (transl. of work first publ. in 1942).

FRANCE

See also 5.336,343,362,496; 11.218-19; 13.17; 14.108-9,111-12,115,118,123.

13.30 **Benedict**, P., 'The Catholic response to Protestantism. Church activity and popular piety in Rouen, 1560-1600', in J. Obelkevich, ed., *Religion and the People, 800-1700*, Chapel Hill, N.C., 1979, 168-90.

13.31 **Burguière**, A., 'Marriage ritual in France. Ecclesiastical practices and popular practices (sixteenth to eighteenth centuries)', in Forster and Ranum (5.362), 8-23. Transl. from *Annales*, 33, 1978, 637-49.

13.32 **Châtellier**, L., *Tradition Chrétienne et Renouveau Catholique dans le Cadre de l'Ancien Diocèse de Strasbourg (1650-1770)*, Paris, 1981. Multidimensional study of clergy and society in transition from ecclesiastical principality to French diocese.

13.33 **Crouzet**, D., 'Recherches sur les processions blanches, 1583-84', *Hist.,Éc., et Soc.*, 1, 1982, 511-63. Study of rash of penitential processions which accompanied crisis of League movement.

13.34 —— 'The sacred and the body social in sixteenth-century Lyon', *P.& P.*, 90, 1981, 40-70. Considers respective community life of Catholic and Calvinist confessions.

13.35 **Everdell**, W. R., 'The *Rosières* movement, 1766-89. A clerical precursor of the Revolutionary cults', *Fr.Hist.Stud.*, 9, 1975, 23-36. Spread of village festivals to honour virtuous young women, seen as new emphasis on utilitarian, social role of religion.

13.36 **Ferté**, Jeanne, *La Vie Religieuse dans les Campagnes Parisiennes, 1622-95*, Paris, 1962. Partly traditional institutional history of Paris diocese outside city; but contains substantial section on popular piety.

13.37 **Froeschlé-Chopard**, Marie H., 'Iconography of the sacred universe in the eighteenth century. Chapels and churches in the dioceses of Vence and Grasse', in Forster and Ranum (5.362), 146-81. Transl. from *Annales*, 31, 1976, 489-519. Sociological reading of church interiors.

13.38 —— *La Religion Populaire en Provence Orientale au 18e Siècle*, Paris, 1980.

13.39 **Galpern**, A. N., *The Religions of the People in Sixteenth-Century Champagne*, Cambridge, Mass., 1976. Mainly using evidence from wills, discerns shift in popular piety towards more individualistic expression. Review article: J. Butler, *J.Soc.Hist.*, 12, 1978, 159-67. See also his 'The legacy of late medieval religion in sixteenth-century Champagne', in Trinkaus and Oberman (5.451), 141-76.

13.40 **Gutton**, J.-P., 'Confraternities, curés, and communities in rural areas of the diocese of Lyons under the ancien régime', in Greyerz (5.301), 202-11. Sees parish become less traditional and integrated, more a secular, administrative unit.

13.41 **Hoffman**, P. T., *Church and Community in the Diocese of Lyon, 1500-1789*, New Haven, Conn., 1984. Central theme is struggle of clergy and devout urban elites to impose more puritan ethic of Counter-Reformation Catholicism on recalcitrant peasantry.

13.42 —— 'The Church and the rural community in the sixteenth and seventeenth centuries', *Proc.Western Soc.Fr.Hist.*, 6, 1978, 46-54. Outlines some themes of book noted in previous entry.

13.43 —— 'Wills and statistics. Tobit analysis and the Counter-Reformation in Lyon', *J.Interdisc.Hist.*, 14, 1984, 813-34. Explains a type of regression analysis used to measure variation in testamentary practice in rural Lyonnais over period 1550-1725.

13.44 **Kaplan**, S. L., 'Religion, subsistence, and social control. The uses of Saint Geneviève', *Eighteenth-Cent.Stud.*, 13, 1979-80, 142-68. On Parisian ceremonies invoking city's patron saint in times of bad weather or food shortage.

13.45 **Kreiser**, B. R., *Miracles, Convulsions, and Ecclesiastical Politics in Early Eighteenth-Century Paris*, Princeton, N.J., 1978. Study of internal conflicts in Gallican

Church sparked off by excesses of popular piety. Central episode described in 'Religious enthusiasm in early eighteenth-century Paris. The convulsionaries of Saint-Médard', *Cath.Hist.Rev.*, 61, 1975, 353-85.

13.46 **McManners**, J., *Popular Religion in Seventeenth- and Eighteenth-Century France. A New Theme in French Historiography*, 1982. Lecture delivered at London University.

13.47 **Mitchell**, H., 'The world between the literate and oral traditions in eighteenth-century France. Ecclesiastical instructions and popular mentalities', *Stud.Eighteenth-Cent.Culture*, 8, 1979, 33-67. On educational levels of priests and their congregations, and appropriate means of communication between them.

13.48 **Muchembled**, R., 'Lay judges and the acculturation of the masses (France and the Southern Low Countries, sixteenth to eighteenth centuries)', in Greyerz (5.301), 56-65. Illustrates tendency of lawyers to view themselves as custodians of morality, reverence, and repression of superstition.

13.49 **Perouas**, L., *Le Diocèse de La Rochelle de 1648 à 1724. Sociologie et Pastorale*, Paris, 1964. Review articles: P. Chaunu, *Rev.Hist.Mod.et Contemp.*, 12, 1965, 5-34; P. Deyon, *Annales*, 21, 1966, 367-71.

13.50 'La piété populaire de 1610 à nos jours', *Actes Congrès Nat.Soc.Savantes*, 99 (i), 1974, whole issue. Several relevant papers.

13.51 **Playoust-Chaussis**, Arlette, *La Vie Religieuse dans le Diocèse de Boulogne au 18e Siècle, 1725-90*, Arras, 1976.

13.52 **Plongeron**, B., ed., *La Religion Populaire. Approches Historiques*, Paris, 1976. Contains useful chap. by F. Lebrun on sources and published research for early modern period.

13.53 **Queniart**, J., *Les Hommes, l'Église, et Dieu dans la France du 18e Siècle*, Paris, 1978. Emphasises work of Church at grass roots.

13.54 **Ranum**, O. '*Lèse-majesté divine.* Transgressing boundaries by thought and action in mid-seventeenth century France', *Proc.Western Soc.Fr.Hist.*, 9, 1981, 68-80. Study of autodidact's heresy. Cf. Ginzburg's celebrated *The Cheese and the Worms* (14.85).

13.55 **Sanfaçon**, A., 'Society and ideology in early modern France. The sense of community in Chartres', *ib.*, 11, 1983, 12-20. Emphasises centrality of cathedral

cloister to social activity of town.

13.56 **Taveneaux**, R., *Le Catholicisme dans la France Classique, 1610-1715*, 2 vols., 1980. Institutions, currents of thought, and pastoral work all well covered.

13.57 **Viguerie**, J. de, 'Quelques aspects du catholicisme des Français au 18e siècle', *Rev.Hist.*, 265, 1981, 335-70. Distinguishes four types of Catholic, ranging from non-practising to devout.

13.58 **Vovelle**, M., *Piété Baroque et Déchristianisation en Provence au 18e Siècle. Les Attitudes devant la Mort d'après les Clauses des Testaments*, Paris, 1973. Attests marked falling-off in conventional piety from quantitative analysis of wills. Review article: J. Delumeau, *Rev.Hist.Mod.et Contemp.*, 22, 1975, 52-60.

13.59 **Weaver**, F. Ellen, 'Women and religion in early modern France. A bibliographical essay on the state of the question', *Cath.Hist.Rev.*, 67, 1981, 50-9.

LOW COUNTRIES

13.60 **Cloet**, M., 'Religious life in a rural deanery in Flanders during the seventeenth century. Tielt from 1609 to 1700', *Acta Hist.Neerlandica*, 5, 1971, 135-58. English summary of book publ. in 1968.

13.61 **Muchembled**, R., 'Un monde mental clos. Étude sémantique et historique du vocabulaire religieux d'un noble artésien à l'époque de Philippe II', *Tijd.Geschied.*, 88, 1975, 169-89. Examines religious terminology in correspondence of a family from petty nobility of Artois.

13.62 **Sprunger**, K. L., 'English and Dutch Sabbatarianism and the development of Puritan social theology (1600-60)', *Church Hist.*, 51, 1982, 24-38. Examines failure of English refugee churches in Netherlands to pass on strict sabbatarianism to host country.

13.63 **Tracy**, J. D., 'With and without the Counter-Reformation. The Catholic Church in the Spanish Netherlands and the Dutch Republic, 1580-1650. A review of the literature since 1945', *Cath.Hist.Rev.*, 71, 1985, 547-75. Includes much material on social aspects.

SPAIN AND PORTUGAL
See also 14.80,113.

13.64 **Caro Baroja**, J., *Las Formas Complejas de la Vida Religiosa. Religión, Sociedad, y Carácter en la España de los Siglos 16 y 17*, Madrid, 1978. Primarily study of mental attitudes and religious values.

13.65 **Christian**, W. A., *Apparitions in Late Medieval and Renaissance Spain*, Princeton, N.J., 1981. Explores types of visionary experience, and social attitudes towards such claims.

13.66 —— *Local Religion in Sixteenth-Century Spain, Princeton*, N.J., 1981. Uses material from sixteenth-century questionnaire to localities drawn up for a projected history of Spain.

13.67 **Dedieu**, J. P., ' "Christianisation" en Nouvelle Castille. Catéchisme, communion, messe, et confirmation dans l'Archevêché de Tolède, 1540-1650', *Mél.Casa de Velazquez*, 15, 1979, 261-93. Uses interrogation records of Inquisition to measure knowledge of basic beliefs and texts.

13.68 **Gerbet**, Marie-C., 'Les confréries religieuses à Cáceres de 1467 à 1523', *ib.*, 7, 1971, 75-113. Devotional guilds in principal town of Estremadura.

13.69 **Noel**, C. C., 'Missionary preachers in Spain. Teaching social virtue in the eighteenth century', *Am.Hist.Rev.*, 90, 1985, 866-92. Values expressed in sermons of four leading preachers spanning century.

ITALY
See also 5.380,451,502; 11.342-3; 13.17,22; 14.81,85,117.

13.70 **Bell**, R. M., *Holy Anorexia*, Chicago, 1985. Study, from Italian examples, of extreme ascetic practices by women, and their psycho-social significance. Includes chapter on seventeenth-century saint, Veronica Giuliani.

13.71 **Chittolini**, G., and Miccoli, G., eds., *La Chiesa e il Potere Politico*, Turin, 1986. Vol.9 of *Annali* section of Einaudi *Storia d'Italia* (3.168). Good material on social role of church, its property, recruitment of clergy, etc.

13.72 **De Maio**, R., *Società e Vita Religiosa a Napoli nell'Età Moderna (1656-1799)*, Naples, 1971. With dividing line at 1726, examines for earlier and later periods church structures, cultural levels of clergy and people, and devotional practices.

13.73 **Donati**, C., *Ecclesiastici e Laici nel Trentino del Settecento*, Rome, 1975. Portrait of clergy and popular religion in diocese of Trent round about mid-century.

13.74 **Galasso**, G., and Russo, Carla, eds., *Per la Storia Sociale e Religiosa del Mezzogiorno d'Italia*, 2 vols., Naples, 1980-82. Essays, some very substantial, covering many aspects of religious sociology, chiefly of Naples region, from sixteenth to early nineteenth centuries.

13.75 **Klapisch-Zuber**, Christiane, 'Zacharias; or the ousting of the father. The rites of marriage in Tuscany from Giotto to the Council of Trent', in Forster and Ranum (5.362), 24-56. Transl. from *Annales*, 34, 1979, 1216-43. Explores shift towards more Church-dominated ceremony of Counter-Reformation.

13.76 **Rosa**, M., 'Per la storia della vita religiosa e della Chiesa in Italia tra il '500 e il '600. Studi recenti e questioni di metodo', *Quad.Stor.*, 15, 1970, 673-758. Article heralding strong Italian involvement in historical sociology of religion.

13.77 —— *Religione e Società nel Mezzogiorno tra Cinque- e Seicento*, Bari, 1976. Volume of collected papers.

13.78 **Russo**, Carla, *Chiesa e Communità nella Diocesi di Napoli tra Cinque e Settecento*, Naples, 1984. Based on visitation records of rural parishes forming hinterland of city of Naples.

13.79 **Schutte**, Anne J., 'Printing, piety, and the people in Italy. The first thirty years', *Arch.Reformationsgesch.*, 71, 1980, 5-19. Examination of vernacular religious best-sellers during first years of printing in Italy (1465-94).

13.80 **Torre**, A., 'Village ceremonial life and politics in eighteenth-century Piedmont', in J. Obelkovich and others, eds., *Disciplines of Faith. Studies in Religion, Politics, and Patriarchy*, 1987, 194-207. On confraternities as focus of local power (and resistance to state bureaucracy on occasion).

13.81 **Trexler**, R. C., 'Florentine religious experience. The sacred image', *Stud.in Renaiss.*, 19, 1972, 7-41. On popular religion in fifteenth and early sixteenth centuries.

13.82 —— 'Ritual behaviour in Renaissance

Florence. The setting', *Medievalia et Humanistica*, n.s., 4, 1973, 125-44. On sacral nature of places and objects.

13.83 **Weinstein**, D., 'The Savonarola movement in Florence', in Sylvia L. Thrupp, ed., *Millennial Dreams in Action*, The Hague, 1962, 187-203. Essay in comparative perspective.

13.84 **Weissman**, R. F. E., *Ritual Brotherhood in Renaissance Florence*, New York, 1982. Study of pre-Tridentine religious confraternities.

GERMANY
See also 13.13; 14.124,201.

13.85 **Fulbrook**, Mary, *Piety and Politics. Religion and the Rise of Absolutism in England, Württemberg, and Prussia*, 1983. Seeks reasons why similar dissenting movements within established churches (English Puritanism and German Pietism) had markedly different political consequences in three states examined. Some valuable hypotheses. See useful summary in her 'Religion, revolution, and absolutist rule in Germany and England', *Eur.Stud.Rev.*, 12, 1982, 301-21.

13.86 **Greyerz**, K. von, 'Religion in the life of German and Swiss autobiographers (sixteenth and early seventeenth centuries)', in Greyerz (5.301), 223-41.

13.87 **Hinrichs**, C., *Preussentum und Pietismus*, Göttingen, 1971. Examines appeal of Pietism to various social groups (no quantification attempted).

13.88 **Hörger**, H., 'Organisational forms of popular piety in rural Old Bavaria (sixteenth to nineteenth centuries)', in Greyerz (5.301), 212-22. Mainly on rituals and where they took place.

13.89 **Hsia**, R. P., *Society and Religion in Münster, 1535-1618*, New Haven, Conn., 1984. Considers influence of Counter-Reformation in wide socio-political context. See also related article, 'Civic wills as sources for the study of piety in Münster, 1530-1618', *Sixteenth-Cent.J.*, 14, 1983, 321-48.

13.90 **Moeller**, B., 'Religious life in Germany on the eve of the Reformation', in Strauss (3.225), 13-42.

13.91 **Roper**, L., ' "Going to church and street". Weddings in Reformation Augsburg', *P.& P.*, 106, 1985, 62-101. Extensive essay on festivities and rituals of marriage

ceremony, and uneasy place of religion in it.

13.92 **Rothkrug**, L., *Religious Practices and Collective Perceptions. Hidden Homologies in the Renaissance and Reformation*, Waterloo, Ontario, 1980. (Forms no.1 of vol.7 of *Hist.Reflections*). Complex work, dealing esp. with distribution of pilgrimage shrines, whose density is correlated with resistance to Reformation. See also his paper on this theme in Obelkevich (13.30), 20-86.

13.93 **Sabean**, D., 'Communion and community. The refusal to attend the eucharist in sixteenth-century Protestant Württemberg', in *Mentalitäten und Lebensverhältnisse...Rudolf Vierhaus, zum 60. Geburtstag*, Göttingen, 1982, 95-107.

13.94 **Scharfe**, M., 'The distance between the lower classes and official religion. Examples from eighteenth-century Württemberg Protestantism', in Greyerz (5.301), 157-74. Illustrates various kinds of dissent.

13.95 **Scribner**, R. W., 'Cosmic order and daily life. Sacred and secular in pre-industrial German society', *ib.*, 17-32. Explores mingling of spiritual and material in popular piety which Reformers attacked as superstition.

13.96 —— 'Ritual and popular religion in Catholic Germany at the time of the Reformation', *J.Eccles.Hist.*, 35, 1984, 46-77.

13.97 **Veit**, L. A., and Lenhart, L., *Kirche und Volksfrömmigkeit im Zeitalter des Barock*, Freiburg, 1956. Deals with popular Catholic piety in South Germany.

13.98 **Warmbrunn**, P., *Zwei Konfessionen in Einer Stadt. Das Zusammenleben von Katholiken und Protestanten in den Paritätischen Reichstädten Augsburg, Biberach, Ravensburg, und Dinkelsbühl von 1548 bis 1648*, Wiesbaden, 1983. Detailed study of social repercussions of dual confessions coexisting in these South German cities. See also 13.100.

13.99 **Whaley**, D. P., *Religious Toleration and Social Change in Hamburg, 1529-1819*, 1985. Examines constraints on Catholic, Calvinist, and Jewish minorities in officially Lutheran city.

13.100 **Zschunke**, P., *Konfession und Alltag in Oppenheim*, Wiesbaden, 1984. Quantitative study of Catholic and Protestant communities in small biconfessional town (late seventeenth-eighteenth century).

EASTERN EUROPE
See also 14.94,221 (Bohemia); 14.227 (Russia).

13.101 **Skendi**, S. 'Crypto-Christianity in the Balkan area under the Ottomans', *Slavic Rev.*, 26, 1967, 227-46. Repr. in his *Balkan Cultural Studies*, Boulder, Colo., 1980,

233-57. On retention of Christian observances by nominal Moslems, and varied reasons for double allegiance.

13.102 **Željazkova**, Antonina L., 'Social aspects of the process of Islamization in the Balkan possessions of the Ottoman Empire', *Ét.Balkaniques*, 21 (iii), 1985, 107-22. Considers phenomenon to have been at its height in seventeenth and eighteenth centuries.

THE CLERGY. RECRUITMENT, FINANCES, AND INSTITUTIONS
See also sub-section on Inquisition, 13.326-35. Also 10.233-4; 11.269.

13.103 **Antonovics**, A. V., 'Counter-Reformation Cardinals, 1534-90', *Eur.Stud.Rev.*, 2, 1972, 301-28. Attempts some characterisation of the nearly 250 cardinals created in this period.

13.104 **Chambers**, D. S., 'The economic predicament of Renaissance cardinals', *Stud.Med.& Renaiss.Hist.*, 3, 1966, 289-313. Details of expenses and debts of various cardinals, c.1480-1530. See also 13.141,143.

13.105 **Hoppen**, Alison, 'The finances of the Order of St. John of Jerusalem in the sixteenth and seventeenth centuries', *Eur.Stud.Rev.*, 3, 1973, 103-19.

FRANCE
See also 5.105; 6.82; 8.41; 10.199; 13.55.

13.106 **Baumgartner**, F. J., *Change and Continuity in the French Episcopate. The Bishops and the Wars of Religion, 1547-1610*, Durham, N.C., 1986. Devotes considerable space to social origins and economic resources.

13.107 **Bergin**, J. A., *Cardinal Richelieu. Power and the Pursuit of Wealth*, New Haven, Conn., 1985. Study of Richelieu's personal fortune.

13.108 —— 'The Guises and their benefices, 1588-1641', *Eng.Hist.Rev.*, 99, 1984, 34-58. Study of revenues of ecclesiastical magnates Louis III and Henri II de Guise.

13.109 **Dolan**, Claire, *Entre Tours et Clochers. Les Gens d'Église à Aix-en-Provence au 16e Siècle*, Sherbrooke, Quebec, 1981. Well researched study of the many clerical communities in city.

13.110 **Edelstein**, Marilyn M., 'Social origins of

the episcopacy in the reign of Francis I', *Fr.Hist.Stud*, 8, 1974, 377-92. Finds that over two-thirds of identifiable French bishops came from nobility of the sword.

13.111 **Hayden**, J. M., 'The social origins of the French episcopacy at the beginning of the seventeenth century', *ib.*, 10, 1977, 27-40. Finds wider social range among bishops than in early sixteenth century or in eighteenth.

13.112 **Julia**, D., and McKee, D., 'Le clergé paroissial dans le diocèse de Reims sous l'épiscopat de Charles-Maurice Le Tellier', *Rev.Hist.Mod.et Contemp.*, 29, 1982, 529-83. Social profile of some 1500 parish priests ordained in period 1671-1710.

13.113 **Loupès**, P., *Chapitres et Chanoines de Guyenne*, Paris, 1985. Major study of recruitment and finance of cathedral and collegiate chapters. For article drawn from research see *Hist., Éc., et Soc.*, 4, 1985, 61-89.

13.114 **McManners**, J., 'Aristocratic vocations. The bishops of France in the eighteenth century', *Stud.Church Hist.*, 15, 1978, 305-25.

13.115 —— *French Ecclesiastical Society under the Ancien Régime. A Study of Angers in the Eighteenth Century*, 1960. Study of cathedral and regular clergy in a provincial capital.

13.116 ——'Tithe in eighteenth-century France. A focus for rural anticlericalism', in D. Beales and G. Best, eds., *History, Society, and the Churches. Essays in Honour of Owen Chadwick*, 1985, 147-68.

13.117 **Martin**, A. L., 'Jesuits and their families.

The experience in sixteenth-century France', *Sixteenth-Cent.J.*, 13 (i), 1982, 3-23. Shows that despite ideal of detachment Jesuits often retained affective family ties.

13.118 **Moran**, G. T., 'Bringing in the sheaves. Managing church property in Southern France, 1560-90', *J.Eur.Ec.Hist.*, 11, 1982, 165-95. Estate management of cathedral chapter of Montpellier.

13.119 **Peronnet**, M. C., *Les Evêques de l'Ancienne France*, 2 vols., Lille, 1977. Unrevised doctoral thesis. Valuable for its exhaustive research into family origins and patronage networks of bishops appointed between 1516 and 1789. For some previous studies of bishops within more limited chronological periods see 13.110-11, 114, 121-3.

13.120 **Plongeron**, B., *La Vie Quotidienne du Clergé Français au 18e Siècle*, Paris, 1974. Popular work by specialist historian.

13.121 **Ravitch**, N., *Sword and Mitre. Government and Episcopate in France and England in the Age of Aristocracy*, The Hague, 1966. On social background of the two episcopates. Claims that French nominations showed reversion to older aristocracy in comparison with late seventeenth century. See also following articles based on this research.

13.122 —— 'Robe and sword in the recruitment of French bishops', *Cath.Hist.Rev.*, 50, 1965, 494-508.

13.123 —— 'Social origins of French and English bishops in the eighteenth century', *Hist.J.*, 8, 1965, 309-25.

13.124 **Tackett**, T., *Priest and Parish in Eighteenth-Century France. A Social and Political Study of the Curés in a Diocese of Dauphiné*, 1750-91, Princeton, N.J., 1977. Diocese examined is Gap. Material on clerical grievances and reform projects also explored in following article.

13.125 —— 'The citizen priest. Politics and ideology among the parish clergy of eighteenth-century Dauphiné', *Stud.Eighteenth-Cent.Culture*, 7, 1978, 307-28.

13.126 —— 'The social history of the diocesan clergy in eighteenth-century France', in R. M. Golden, ed., *Church, State, and Society under the Bourbon Kings of France*, Lawrence, Kans, 1982, 327-79. Examines recruitment in fifteen sample dioceses throughout France. See also related article

in *Rev.Hist.Mod.et Contemp.*, 26, 1979, 198-234.

13.127 —— and Langlois, C., 'Ecclesiastical structures and clerical geography on the eve of the French Revolution', *Fr.Hist.Stud.*, 11, 1980, 352-70. Reconstruction of regional origins and distribution of French clergy in 1789, from pensions register of 1817.

13.128 **Thompson**, D. G., 'The fate of the French Jesuits' creditors under the ancien régime', *Eng.Hist.Rev.*, 91, 1976, 255-77. Study of debts left when Order was suppressed (1762-64).

13.129 —— 'French Jesuit wealth on the eve of the eighteenth-century suppression', *Stud.Church Hist.*, 24, 1987, 307-19. Reveals parlous finances of most Jesuit colleges.

13.130 **Ultee**, M., *The Abbey of St. Germain des Prés in the Seventeenth Century*, New Haven, Conn., 1981. Good on everyday life of monastic community and its place in local society; less informative on background of monks.

13.131 **Venard**, M., 'Pour une sociologie du clergé au 16e siècle. Le recrutement sacerdotal dans la province d'Avignon', *Annales*, 23, 1968, 987-1016. Examines ordinations in small province of five dioceses.

13.132 **Williams**, W. H., 'Perspectives on the parish clergy on the eve of the French Revolution', *Proc.Consortium on Revolutionary Eur.*, 1974 (publ. 1978), 52-64. Cf. Tackett's more ambitious surveys (13.126-7).

SPAIN AND ITALY
On Spain see also 3.117; 6.119. On Italy 6.147; 10.447; 13.73.

13.133 **Kamen**, H., 'Clerical violence in a Catholic society. The Hispanic world, 1450-1720', *Stud.Church Hist.*, 20, 1983, 201-16. Ranges from attitudes to war to everyday violent behaviour by clerics.

13.134 **Goodman**, D., 'Science and the clergy in the Spanish Enlightenment', *Hist.of Sci.*, 21, 1983, 111-40. Goes beyond narrow definition of science with general survey of attempts to "modernise" clerical education and attitudes.

13.135 **Hermann**, C., 'Les revenus des évêques espagnols au 18e siècle (1650-1830)', *Mél.Casa de Velazquez*, 10, 1974, 169-201.

13.136 **Molinié-Bertrand**, Annie, 'Le clergé dans le Royaume de Castille à la fin du 16e siècle. Approche cartographique', *Rev.Hist.Éc.et Soc.*, 51, 1973, 5-53. More findings from her investigation of tax census of 1591 (see 5.146), this time on geographical distribution of various orders of clergy.

13.137 **Rawlings**, H. E., 'The secularisation of Castilian episcopal office under the Habsburgs, c.1516-1700', *J.Eccles.Hist.*, 38, 1987, 53-79. Prosopographical study of episcopal appointments over this period.

13.138 **Bazzochi**, R., 'Chiesa e aristocrazia nella Firenze del Quattrocento', *Arch.Stor.Ital.*, 142, 1984, 191-282. Extensive study of part played by Church in patrician finances and patronage networks.

13.139 **Brambilla**, Elena, 'Società ecclesiastica e società civile. Aspetti della formazione del clero dal Cinquecento alla Restaurazione', *Società e Storia*, 4, 1981, 299-366. Longitudinal survey of clerical education in Italy.

13.140 **Deutscher**, T., 'Seminaries and the education of Novarese parish priests, 1593-1627', *J.Eccles.Hist.*, 32, 1981, 303-19. Material on seminary curriculum and quality of students.

13.141 **Lowe**, K. J. P., 'Questions of income and expenditure in Renaissance Rome. A case-study of Cardinal Francesco Armellini', *Stud.Church Hist.*, 24, 1987, 175-88. Includes analysis of household accounts, 1517-24.

13.142 **Toscani**, X., *Il Clero Lombardo dall'Ancien Regime alla Restaurazione*, Bologna, 1979. Using ordination records for 1750-1830 in the nine dioceses of Lombardy, examines social and geographical provenance of clergy.

13.143 **Volker**, R., *Kardinal Scipione Borghese, 1605-33. Vermögen, Finanzen, und Sozialer Aufstieg eines Papstnepoten*, Tübingen, 1984. Careful examination of wealth accumulated by family of Paul V's nephew during latter's pontificate.

GERMANY AND SWITZERLAND
See also 13.220.

13.144 **Boles**, Susan K., 'The economic position of Lutheran pastors in Ernestine Thuringia, 1521-55', *Arch.Reformations-gesch.*, 63, 1972, 94-125. Notes gradual improvement in resources after disruptions of 1520s.

13.145 **Gechter**, Marianne, *Kirche und Klerus in der Stadtkölnischen Wirtschaft im Spätmittelalter*, Wiesbaden, 1983. Details clerical participation in trade, investment, and property-holding. Extends well into sixteenth century.

13.146 **Hersche**, P., *Die Deutschen Domkapitel im 17. und 18. Jahrhundert*, 3 vols., Ursellen, 1984. Computerised study of 27 cathedral chapters and nearly 4,000 canons who held office over this period. Reformed chapters not dealt with. Vol. 2 comprises analysis; vols. 1 and 3 nominal list and tables respectively.

13.147 **Karant-Nunn**, S., *Luther's Pastors. The Reformation in the Ernestine Countryside (Trans. Am. Phil. Soc., 69, part 8)*, Philadelphia, Pa., 1979. Excellent short monograph on resources and training of clergy.

13.148 **Kingdon**, R. M., 'The economic behaviour of ministers in Geneva in the middle of the sixteenth century', *Arch.Reformationsgesch.*, 50, 1959, 33-9. Gives examples of property deals and money-lending by ministers.

13.149 **Kirk**, Linda, 'Godliness in a golden age. The church and wealth in eighteenth-century Geneva', *Stud.Church Hist.*, 24, 1987, 333-46. On finances of pastors and their attitudes to wealth and charity.

13.150 **Overfield**, J. H., 'University studies and the clergy in pre-Reformation Germany', in J. M. Kittelson and Pamela J. Transue, eds., *Rebirth, Reform, and Resilience. Universities in Transition, 1300-1700*, Columbus, Ohio, 1984, 254-92. Tabulates, down to 1520, number of matriculating students at German universities already regulars, canons, or parish clergy.

13.151 **Strauss**, G., 'The mental world of a Saxon pastor', in Brooks (11.255), 157-70. Evidence drawn from visitation questionnaire.

13.152 **Stroup**, J., *The Struggle for Identity in the Clerical Estate. Northwest German Protestant Opposition to Absolutist Policy in the Eighteenth Century*, Leiden, 1984. Charts opposition of Brunswick clergy to secular reformers' plans to turn them into a cultural bureaucracy.

13.153 **Vogler**, B., *Le Clergé Protestant Rhénan au Siècle de la Réforme, 1555-1619*, Paris, 1976. Condensation of doctoral thesis on social milieu and pastoral role of parish clergy in Palatinate and Zweibrücken.

TURKEY AND THE BALKANS

13.154 **Faroqhi**, Suraiya, 'Agricultural activities in a Bektashi center. The *tekke* of Kizil Deli, 1750-1830', *Südost-Forsch.*, 35, 1976, 69-96. Repr. in Faroqhi (4.82). On management of estates of dervish foundation in Western Thrace.

13.155 —— 'Seyyid Gazi revisited. The foundation as seen through sixteenth- and seventeenth-century documents', *Turcica*, 13, 1981, 90-122; repr. in Faroqhi (4.82). See also her 'The *tekke* of Haci Bektas. Social position and economic activities', *Int.J.Mid.E.Stud.*, 7, 1976, 183-208. Social history of two dervish convents in Anatolia.

13.156 —— 'Social mobility among the Ottoman *'ulemâ* in the late sixteenth century', *Int.J.Mid.E.Stud.*, 4, 1973, 204-18.

13.157 —— '*Vakif* administration in sixteenth-century Konya', *J.Ec.& Soc.Hist.Orient*, 17, 1974, 145-72. Deals with accounts and dues of a pious foundation.

13.158 **Hitchins**, K., 'An East European elite in the eighteenth century. The Rumanian Uniate hierarchy', in Jaher (10.367), 139-53. Uniate Church of Transylvania acknowledged Roman supremacy while retaining Orthodox rites, and was main focus of Rumanian peasantry in face of Magyar and German hegemony.

13.159 **Mandaville**, J. E., 'Usurious piety. The cash *waqf* controversy in the Ottoman Empire', *Int.J.Mid.E.Stud.*, 10, 1979, 289-308. Details arguments over legitimacy of pious foundations financed by interest.

13.160 **Zilfi**, Madeline C., 'Elite circulation in the Ottoman Empire. Great Mollas of the eighteenth century', *J.Ec.& Soc.Hist.Orient*, 26, 1983, 318-64. Prosopographical study of appointees to high office in religious hierarchy, showing their strong hereditary tendencies.

RUSSIA

13.161 **Freeze**, G. L., *The Russian Levites. Parish Clergy in the Eighteenth Century*, Cambridge, Mass., 1977. Excellent both on clergy's conditions of life, and on Church-State relations. See also his 'Social mobility and the Russian parish clergy in the eighteenth century', *Slavic Rev.*, 33, 1974, 641-62.

13.162 **Kollmann**, J. E., 'The *Stoglav* Council and parish priests', *Russian Hist.*, 7, 1980, 65-91. Evidence on life and role of parish priests from proceedings of reform council held in 1551.

13.163 **Thomas**, Marie A., 'Managerial roles in the Suzdal'skii Pokrovskii Convent during the seventeenth century', *Russ.Hist.*, 7, 1980, 92-112. Analyses work of convent *striapchii*, or professional steward.

13.164 —— 'Muscovite convents in the seventeenth century', *Russ.Hist.*, 10, 1983, 230-42. Social role of, and daily life in, nunneries.

THE IMPACT OF THE REFORMATION
See also 14.278.

13.165 **Blaisdell**, Charmarie J., 'The matrix of reform – women in the Lutheran and Calvinist movements', in R. L. Greaves, ed., *Triumph Over Silence. Women in Protestant History*, Westport, Conn., 1985, 13-44.

13.166 **Bogucka**, Maria, 'Towns in Poland and the Reformation. Analogies and differences with other countries', *Acta Poloniae Hist.*, 40, 1979, 55-74. Offers some reasons why Polish Reformation was not primarily urban movement.

13.167 **Chevalier**, B., and Sauzet, R., eds., *Les Réformes. Enracinement socio-culturel*, Paris, 1985. Conference papers, mainly but by no means exclusively dealing with France. Part 2 on urban aspects, and part 3 on cultural aspects, particularly relevant.

13.168 **Chrisman**, Miriam U., 'From polemic to propaganda. The development of mass persuasion in the late sixteenth century', *Arch.Reformationsgesch.*, 73, 1982, 175-95. Discusses shift from genuine theological argument to ritual abuse of religious opponents.

13.169 **Crofts**, R., 'Books, reform, and the Reformation', *ib.*, 71, 1980, 21-35. Attempts quantitative test of religious books published in period 1510-20 for presence of "reform" sentiments.

13.170 **Dickens**, A. G., *Reformation and Society in Sixteenth-Century Europe*, 1966. Popular illustrated work.

13.171 **Friesen**, A., *Reformation and Utopia. The Marxist Interpretation of the Reformation and its Antecedents*, Wiesbaden, 1974. See also his précis article, 'The Marxist interpretation of the Reformation', *Arch.Reformationsgesch.*, 64, 1973, 34-54.

13.172 **Hillerbrand**, H. J., 'The popular dimension of the Reformation. An essay in methodology and historiography', *Med.& Renaiss.Stud.*, 6, 1974, 55-86. Betrays certain uneasiness about topic.

13.173 —— 'The spread of the Protestant Reformation', in C. D. W. Goodwin and I. B. Holley, eds., *The Transfer of Ideas*, Durham, N.C., 1968, 65-86. Tries to account for immediacy with which Luther's message was taken up in Europe at large.

13.174 —— *The World of the Reformation*, New York, 1973. Emphasis on social impact.

13.175 **Monter**, E. W., 'Reformation history and social history', *Arch.Reformationsgesch.*, 72, 1981, 5-12. Brief presidential address to American Society for Reformation Research, urging that too much attention has been given to social causes of Reformation and not enough to effects.

13.176 **Petri**, F., ed., *Kirche und Gesellschaftlicher Wandel in Deutschen und Niederländischen Städten der Werdenden Neuzeit*, Köln, 1980. Symposium, of which most substantial contributions are C. von Looz-Corswarem on upheavals of 1525 in Köln; and H. Schilling on religion in early decades of United Provinces.

13.177 **Scribner**, R. W., 'Is there a social history of the Reformation?', *Soc.Hist.*, [1], iv, 1977, 483-505. Trenchant examination of areas of research required, prefaced by discussion of differing approaches of East and West German historians. Valuable bibliography.

13.178 —— 'Religion, society, and culture. Reorientating the Reformation', *Hist.Workshop*, 14, 1982, 2-22.

13.179 **Swanson**, G. E., *Religion and Regime. A Sociological Account of the Reformation*, Ann Arbor, Mich., 1967. Controversial work, which relates adoption or rejection of Reformation to political structure, classified into five types. Review articles:

W. J. Bouwsma, J. T. Flint (separately), *Comp.Stud.Soc.& Hist.*, 10, 1968, 486-509; Martha E. François, *ib.*, 14, 1972, 287-305; Natalie Z. Davis and others (incl. Swanson himself), *J.Interdisc.Hist.*, 1, 1971, 379-446.

13.180 **Yinger**, J. M., *Religion in the Struggle for Power. A Study in the Sociology of Religion*, Durham, N.C., 1946. Wide-ranging survey of Christian attitudes to social questions, with considerable section on Reformation and economic morality.

THE GERMAN REFORMATION

Question of Reformation and Peasants' War is discussed in 12.111-38. For bibliography and historiographical discussion see 2.55; 13.177,192,194,216,230. See also 5.291,504,514; 12.19; 13.144,147,176; 14.110,120,198-200,211-14,217,379,425-7.

13.181 **Abray**, Lorna J., *The People's Reformation. Magistrates, Clergy, and Commons in Strasbourg, 1550-98*, 1985. Investigates effects on lives and values of lay community.

13.182 **Bátori**, Ingrid, ed., *Städtische Gesellschaft und Reformation*, Stuttgart, 1980. Symposium. Contributors incl. T. Brady, R. Scribner, R. Postel (on Hamburg), and H. Rublack (on Esslingen).

13.183 **Birnbaum**, N., 'The Zwinglian Reformation in Zurich', *P.& P.*, 15, 1959, 27-47. Main concern is to look again at connections between Protestantism and capitalism.

13.184 **Blickle**, P., *Gemeindereformation*, Munich, 1985. Stresses part played by local communities (both urban and rural) in shaping German Reformation, and views princely role as one of blunting autonomy and personal responsibility initially displayed.

13.185 —— 'Social protest and Reformation theology', in Greyerz (8.118), 1-23.

13.186 **Brady**, T. A., *Ruling Class, Regime, and Reformation at Strasbourg, 1520-55*, Leiden, 1978. Adoption of Lutheranism seen as defensive strategy by patricians to head off social upheaval. See criticisms of this view by B. Moeller and R. W. Scribner in W. J. Mommsen and others, eds., *The Urban Classes, the Nobility, and the Reformation. Studies on the Social History of the Reformation in England and Germany*,

Stuttgart, 1979, 25-48.

13.187 **Broadhead**, P., 'Popular pressure for reform in Augsburg, 1524-34', in Mommsen and others (13.186), 80-7. Takes rather similar line to Brady's (see previous entry).

13.188 **Chrisman**, Miriam U., 'Lay response to the Protestant Reformation in Germany, 1520-28', in Brooks (11.255), 33-52. Takes evidence from pamphlets written by laymen.

13.189 —— *Strasbourg and the Reform. A Study in the Process of Change*, New Haven, Conn., 1967. Concludes that Reformation had little effect on distribution of power or wealth in city.

13.190 **Christensen**, C. C., 'Patterns of iconoclasm in the early Reformation. Strasbourg and Basel', in J. Gutmann, ed., *The Image and the Word. Confrontations in Judaism, Christianity, and Islam*, Missoula, Mont., 1977, 107-48. Shows that popular image-destruction and official image-destruction were sometimes quite distinct phenomena.

13.191 **Conrad**, F., *Reformation in der Bäuerlichen Gesellschaft. Zur Rezeption Reformatorischer Theologie im Elsass*, Stuttgart, 1984. Rare attempt to assess rural reactions in wider framework than Peasants' War.

13.192 **Foschepoth**, J., *Reformation und Bauernkrieg im Geschichtsbild der D.D.R.. Zur Methodologie einer Gewandelten Geschichtsverständnisses*, Berlin, 1971. Reviews East German historiography of Reformation. See also 13.230.

13.193 **Greyerz**, K. von, *The Late City Reformation in Germany. The Case of Colmar, 1522-1628*, Wiesbaden, 1980. Examines city where Reformation was not adopted till 1570s, comparing with similar cases such as Essen and Aachen.

13.194 —— 'Stadt und Reformation. Stand und Aufgaben der Forschungen', *Arch.Reformationsgesch.*, 76, 1985, 6-63. Excellent bibliographical survey.

13.195 **Grimm**, H. J., 'The Reformation and the urban social classes in Germany', in J. C. Olin and others, eds., *Luther, Erasmus, and the Reformation*, New York, 1969, 75-86. Brief conference paper.

13.196 —— 'Social forces in the German Reformation', *Church Hist.*, 31, 1962, 3-13. Presidential address to American Society of Church History.

13.197 **Hannemann**, M., *The Diffusion of the Reformation in South-Western Germany, 1518-34*, Chicago, 1975. Interesting essay on ideological diffusion and its geographical and social matrix.

13.198 **Kittelson**, J. M., 'Successes and failures in the German Reformation. The report from Strasbourg', *Arch.Reformationsgesch.*, 73, 1982, 153-74. A comment on 13.228, arguing from rural visitation reports in Strasbourg region that Strauss' pessimistic conclusions are not borne out there.

13.199 **Koenigsberger**, H. G., 'The Reformation and social revolution', in J. Hurstfield, ed., *The Reformation Crisis*, 1965, 83-94. Repr. in Koenigsberger (11.43), 211-23. Brief discussion of Peasants' War and Münster upheavals.

13.200 **Köhler**, H.-J., ed., *Flugschriften als Massenmedium der Reformationszeit*, Stuttgart, 1981. Essay collection, with general essays on importance of pamphlets (in English) by R. G. Cole and S. Ozment. Other contributors incl. R. Scribner, H. Oberman, and B. Moeller. Note 13.208 on this theme.

13.201 **Moeller**, B., *Imperial Cities and the Reformation. Three Essays*, Philadelphia, 1972. Most important of these studies is title essay, originally publ. separately (in German) in 1962, and starting point of much discussion on importance of cities to spread of Lutheranism. See, e.g., B. Hall, 'The Reformation city', *Bull.John Rylands Lib.*, 54, 1971, 103-48; and 13.204.

13.202 **Mörke**, O., *Rat und Burger in der Reformation. Soziale Gruppen und Kirklicher Wandel in den Welfischen Hansestädten Lüneburg, Braunschweig, und Göttingen*, Hildesheim, 1983. Interesting because northern cities have not been so intensively researched, and because of considerable differences between elites of these three.

13.203 **Oehmig**, S., 'Mönchtum – Reformation – Säkularisation. Zu den demographischen und sozialen Folgen des Verfalls der Klosterwesens in Mitteldeutschland', *Jb.Gesch.Feudalismus*, 10, 1986, 209-49. Consequences of dissolution of monasteries in Saxony and Thuringia.

13.204 **Ozment**, S. E., *The Reformation in the Cities. The Appeal of Protestantism to Sixteenth-Century Germany and Switzerland*, New Haven, Conn., 1975. Lays stress on shift of welfare responsibilities and institutions to charge of laymen as factor that particularly attracted city elites.

13.205 **Packull**, W. O., 'The image of the "common man" in the early pamphlets of the Reformation (1520-25)', *Hist.Reflections*, 12, 1985, 253-77. Sees positive image of peasants and artisans propounded by pamphleteers as "revolt from within" by lower clerical intelligentsia. See related theme of 13.208.

13.206 **Postel**, R., *Die Reformation in Hamburg, 1517-28*, Gütersloh, 1985. See also his contribution in 13.182.

13.207 **Rapp**, F., *Réformes et Réformation à Strasbourg. Église et Société dans le Diocèse de Strasbourg, 1450-1525*, Paris, 1974. Yet another study of Reformation Strasbourg (see also 13.181,186,189), though this one reaches further back in time and concentrates less exclusively on city.

13.208 **Russell**, P. A., *Lay Theology in the Reformation. Popular Pamphleteers in Southwest Germany, 1521-25*, Cambridge, 1986. Analyses works by propagandists having only limited education, including artisans and housewives. See also his ' "Your sons and your daughters shall prophesy..."'. Common people and the future of the Reformation in the pamphlet literature of Southwestern Germany to 1525', *Arch.Reformationsgesch.*, 74, 1983, 122-39.

13.209 **Schildhauer**, J., *Soziale, Politische, und Religiöse Auseinandersetzungen in der Hansestädten Stralsund, Rostock, und Wismar im Ersten Drittel des 16. Jahrhunderts*, Weimar, 1959. Marxist interpretation of Reformation in smaller Hanseatic cities.

13.210 **Schilling**, H., *Konfessionskonflikt und Staatsbildung. Eine Fallstudie über das Verhältnis von Religiösem und Sozialem Wandel in der Frühneuzeit am Beispiel der Grafschaft Lippe*, Gütersloh, 1981. Looks at social and constitutional impact of Reformation in this principality, down to early seventeenth century.

13.211 —— 'The Reformation in the Hanseatic cities', *Sixteenth-Cent.J.*, 14, 1983, 443-56.

13.212 **Schmidt**, H. R., *Reichsstädte, Reich, und Reformation. Korporative Religionspolitik, 1521-29*, Wiesbaden, 1985. Contributes to debate whether urban Reformation came from below, using evidence from South

German cities.

13.213 **Scott**, T., 'The "Volksreformation" of Thomas Müntzer in Allstedt and Mühlhausen', *J.Eccles.Hist.*, 34, 1983, 194-213. Explains how Müntzer came to be involved in Peasants' War.

13.214 **Scribner**, R. W., *For the Sake of Simple Folk. Popular Propaganda for the German Reformation*, 1981. Flavour of themes in this work by prolific historian of popular urban Protestantism will be evident from many of articles cited below. See also 13.177-8.

13.215 —— 'Civic unity and the Reformation in Erfurt', *P.& P.*, 66, 1975, 29-60. Analyses political and social motives which led city government to tolerate, without being dominated by, Lutheran influence.

13.216 —— *The German Reformation*, 1986. Good starting point, with useful annotated bibliography.

13.217 —— 'The image and the Reformation', in Obelkovich (13.80), 534-50. Characterises seven types of hostility to religious imagery, and seven ways in which it was considered legitimate or helpful to Protestant propaganda.

13.218 —— 'Incombustible Luther. The image of the Reformer in early modern Germany', *P.& P.*, 110, 1986, 38-68. How Lutheran Church spawned mythology of miraculous images and relics of its own founder.

13.219 —— 'Oral culture and the diffusion of Reformation ideas', *Hist.Eur.Ideas*, 5, 1984, 237-56. Argues that impact of Reformation message can hardly have come directly from print sources in most cases.

13.220 —— 'Practice and principle in the German towns. Preachers and people', in Brooks (11.255), 95-117. Material on background of early Protestant preachers and expectations of their congregations.

13.221 —— 'The Reformation as a social movement', in Mommsen (13.186), 49-79. Defines "social movement" as collective action to change existing order by non-institutional means, and examines events at Wittenberg, Zwickau and Leipzig in this light.

13.222 —— 'Reformation, carnival, and the world turned upside-down', *Soc.Hist.*, 3, 1978, 303-29. Repr. in Bátori (13.182), 234-64. Describes many German and Swiss anti-Catholic carnival demonstrations of 1520s and '30s, in pursuit of common features and relation to carnival tradition in general.

13.223 —— 'Why was there no Reformation in Cologne?', *Bull.Inst.Hist.Res.*, 49, 1976, 217-41. Explains in terms of institutional structure, esp. links between council and university.

13.224 **Seebass**, G., 'The Reformation in Nürnberg', in Buck and Zophy (12.119), 17-40. Rather weak as social history.

13.225 **Sessions**, K. C., and Bebb, P. N., eds., *Pietas et Societas. New Trends in Reformation Social History*, Kirksville, Mo., 1985. Miscellany on German Reformation, offered as festschrift for H. J. Grimm. Some items separately noted.

13.226 **Stalnaker**, J. C., '*Residenzstadt* and Reformation. Religion, politics, and social policy in Hesse, 1509-46', *Arch. Reformationsgesch.*, 64, 1973, 113-46. Centres on city of Marburg.

13.227 **Strauss**, G., 'Protestant dogma and city government. The case of Nuremberg', *P.& P.*, 36, 1967, 38-58. Conjectures that Lutheranism appealed to city governments because its stress on human depravity chimed with their minute regulation of morals.

13.228 —— 'Success and failure in the German Reformation', *ib.*, 67, 1975, 30-63. Argues that Lutheran vision of life made very little real impact on popular culture. Theme developed more fully in 14.211. See contradictory view of Kittelson (13.198).

13.229 **Wettges**, W., *Reformation und Propaganda. Studien zur Kommunikation des Aufruhrs in Süddeutschen Reichsstädten*, Stuttgart, 1978. For Nuremberg, Augsburg, and Regensburg, examines impact in turn on city elite, professions, and lower classes.

13.230 **Wohlfeil**, R., ed., *Reformation oder Frühburgerliche Revolution?*, Munich, 1972. Debate between East and West German historians on Marxist interpretation of Lutheran Reformation and Peasants' War. Contributors incl. T. Nipperdey, M. Steinmetz, G. Zschäbitz, G. Vogler. Cf. Foschepoth (13.192).

13.231 **Zins**, H., 'Political and social background of the early Reformation in Ermeland', *Eng.Hist.Rev.*, 75, 1960, 589-600. Area disputed between Poland and the Teutonic Knights of Prussia.

CALVINISM. HUGUENOTS. THE FRENCH AND DUTCH REFORMATIONS

See also 9.517-18. For material chiefly on France see also 8.58; 9.268,271,413; 10.306,313; 11.200; 13.13,30,34,167,376; 14.163. On Geneva 5.196,198; 8.123; 13.148-9. On Netherlands 5.530; 9.43-4; 10.427; 13.176.

13.232 **Howe**, D. W., 'The decline of Calvinism. An approach to its study', *Comp. Stud. Soc. & Hist.*, 14, 1972, 306-27. Postulates that the more economically comfortable societies became the more bland and diluted their versions of Calvinism tended to become.

13.233 **Kingdon**, R. M., 'Control of morals in Calvin's Geneva', in Buck and Zophy (12.119), 3-16. On role of Consistory. See 13.258,277,305 for further material on consistorial discipline.

13.234 —— 'Was the Reformation a revolution? The case of Geneva', *Stud.Church Hist.*, 12, 1975, 203-22. Argues that Genevan Reformation meets most criteria for definition of revolution. See article on similar lines, with extracts from sources, in R. M. Kingdon, ed., *Transition and Revolution. Problems and Issues of European Renaissance and Reformation History*, Minneapolis, Minn., 1974, 53-107.

13.235 **Scouloudi**, Irene, ed., *Huguenots in Britain and their French Background, 1550-1800*, 1987. Papers given at conference organised by Huguenot Society of London. Part 1 deals with economic activities in Britain, part 2 with situation in France between Edict of Nantes and its revocation. Note also A. Pettegree, *Foreign Protestant Communities in Sixteenth-Century London*, 1986, which looks at reception and impact of refugees from France, Netherlands, and Germany.

13.236 **Bien**, D. D., *The Calas Affair. Persecution, Toleration, and Heresy in Eighteenth-Century Toulouse*, Princeton, N.J., 1960. Case made famous by Voltaire. Contains useful background material on eighteenth-century French Protestantism. See also his 'The background of the Calas affair', *History*, 43, 1958, 192-206.

13.237 —— 'Catholic magistrates and Protestant marriage in the French Enlightenment', *Fr.Hist.Stud.*, 2, 1962, 409-29. Argues that by 1770 Parlements were largely turning a blind eye to proscription of Protestant marriages.

13.238 **Davies**, Joan, 'Persecution and Protestantism. Toulouse, 1562-78', *Hist.J.*, 22, 1979, 31-52. Social and economic profile of Huguenot community.

13.239 **Davis**, Natalie Z., 'The rites of violence. Religious riot in sixteenth-century France', *P.& P.*, 59, 1973, 51-91. Repr. in Davis (11.200), 152-88. Argues that crowds, in attacking symbols or persons of opposing party, tended to assume role of priest or pastor (purification) or magistrate (punishment). See dissenting note by Janine Estèbe, *ib.*, 67, 1975, 127-35, who finds this characterisation too divorced from economic motives and insufficiently distinctive between Catholic and Protestant types of violence.

13.240 —— 'Strikes and salvation at Lyon', *Arch.Reformationsgesch.*, 56, 1965, 48-64. Repr. in Davis (11.200), 1-16. Reasons why Lyon printing workers lost enthusiasm for Reformed Church in 1560s.

13.241 **Deursen**, A. T. van, *Professions et Métiers Interdits. Un Aspect de l'Histoire de la Révocation de l'Édit de Nantes*, Groningen, 1960. On attempts to exclude Protestants from law, medicine, military careers, etc.

13.242 **Deyon**, Solange, and Lottin, A., *Les "Casseurs" de l'Été 1566. L'Iconoclasme dans le Nord de la France*, Paris, 1981. Interesting complement to Crew (13.271).

13.243 **Farr**, J. R., 'Popular religious solidarity in sixteenth-century Dijon', *Fr.Hist.Stud.*, 14, 1985, 192-214. Emphasises importance of occupational and neighbourhood loyalties in determining confessional allegiance.

13.244 **Febvre**, L., *Au Coeur Religieux du 16e Siècle*, Paris, 1957. Collection of previously publ. essays broadly connected with theme of French Reformation, headed by celebrated essay noted (in transl.) in next entry. Review article: D. Cantimori, *Annales*, 15, 1960, 556-68.

13.245 —— 'The origins of the French Reformation. A badly-put question?', in P. Burke, ed., *A New Kind of History. From the Writings of [Lucien] Febvre*, 1973, 44-107. Originally publ. in *Rev.Hist.*, 161, 1929, 1-73. Emphasises complexity of popular faith in early sixteenth century, not easily categorisable as either Catholic or proto-Protestant.

13.246 **Fenlon**, D., 'Encore une question. Lucien Febvre, the Reformation, and the school of *Annales*', in *Historical Studies. Papers Read before the Irish Conference of Historians*, 9, 1974, 65-82. Gentle criticism of preceding entry.

13.247 **Frey**, Linda, and Frey, Marsha, 'The Camisards', *Proc.Western Soc.Fr.Hist.*, 13, 1986, 61-79. Two separate essays on resistance movement of Cévennes Protestants in first decade of eighteenth century.

13.248 **Garrisson-Estèbe**, Janine, *L'Homme Protestant*, Paris, 1980. Survey of culture and ethos of French Protestantism since its origins.

13.249 —— *Protestants du Midi, 1559-98*, Toulouse, 1980. Important study of heartland of French Protestantism, partly social and cultural, partly narrative.

13.250 **Greengrass**, M., 'Anatomy of a religious riot in Toulouse in May 1562', *J.Eccles.Hist.*, 34, 1983, 367-91. Uses attempted Huguenot seizure of city to assess nature and social context of religious split.

13.251 **Guggenheim**, Ann H., 'Calvinist notables of Nîmes during the era of the Religious Wars', *Sixteenth-Cent.J.*, 3, 1972, 80-96. Does not quantify or tabulate findings.

13.252 **Harding**, R. R., 'Mobilization of confraternities against the Reformation in France', *ib.*, 11 (ii), 1980, 85-107. On political and social importance of Catholic guilds during Wars of Religion, using case studies of Mâcon and Marseille.

13.253 **Heller**, H., 'Famine, revolt, and heresy at Meaux, 1521-25', *Arch.Reformationsgesch.*, 68, 1977, 133-57. Attempts to place reform movement at Meaux in social and economic setting.

13.254 **Kelley**, D. R., 'Martyrs, myths, and the Massacre. Background of St. Bartholomew', *Am.Hist.Rev.*, 77, 1972, 1323-42. Examines Massacre not "as it really happened", but for symbolic importance it took on as collective martyrdom.

13.255 **Lamet**, Maryélise S., 'French Protestants in a position of strength. The early years of the Reformation in Caen, 1558-68', *Sixteenth-Cent.J.*, 9 (iii), 1978, 35-55. Computer-aided attempt to reconstruct Protestant community from baptismal registers.

13.256 **Ligou**, D., *Le Protestantisme en France de 1598 à 1715*, Paris, 1968. Contains short sections on pastors and on sociology of Protestantism.

13.257 **McCloy**, S. T., 'Persecution of the Huguenots in the eighteenth century', *Church Hist.*, 20, 1951, 56-79.

13.258 **Mentzer**, R. A., '*Disciplina nervus ecclesiae*. The Calvinist reform of morals at Nîmes', *Sixteenth-Cent.J.*, 18, 1987, 89-115. Analyses some hundreds of consistory cases from 1560s and '70s for evidence on moral attitudes and offences.

13.259 —— *Heresy proceedings in Languedoc, 1500-60 (Trans. Am. Phil. Soc., 74, part 5)*, Philadelphia, 1984. Attempts some geographical and social analysis of hundreds prosecuted in earliest phase of French Reformation.

13.260 **Nicholls**, D. J., 'The nature of popular heresy in France, 1520-42', *Hist.J.*, 26, 1983, 261-75.

13.261 —— 'Social change and early Protestantism in France. Normandy, 1520-62', *Eur.Stud.Rev.*, 10, 1980, 279-308. Stresses that social diversity of early Protestantism was factor in its later disintegration.

13.262 —— 'The social history of the French Reformation. Ideology, confession, and culture', *Soc.Hist.*, 9, 1984, 25-43. Historiographical article.

13.263 **Parker**, D., 'The Huguenots in seventeenth-century France', in A. C. Hepburn, ed., *Minorities in History (Irish Conference of Historians, Historical Studies, 12)*, 1978, 11-30.

13.264 **Richard**, M., *La Vie Quotidienne des Protestants sous l'Ancien Régime*, Paris, 1966. Fairly light-weight.

13.265 **Richet**, D., 'Sociocultural aspects of religious conflicts in Paris during the second half of the sixteenth century', in Forster and Ranum (5.362), 182-212. Transl. from *Annales*, 32, 1977, 764-89.

13.266 **Roelker**, Nancy L., 'The appeal of Calvinism to French noblewomen in the sixteenth century', *J.Interdisc.Hist.*, 2, 1972, 607-34 (misnumbered 391-418).

13.267 **Salmon**, J. H. M., 'Religion and economic motivation. Some French insights on an old controversy', *J.Relig.Hist.*, 2, 1963, 181-203. Considers social background to religious adherance in sixteenth-century France.

13.268 **Scoville**, W. C., *The Persecution of Huguenots and French Economic Development, 1680-1720*, Berkeley, Calif.,

1960. Argues that persecution did not have alleged baneful effect on French economic performance.

13.269 —— 'The Huguenots in the French economy, 1650-1750', *Q.J.Ec.*, 67, 1953, 423-44.

13.270 **Wemyss**, Alice, *Les Protestants du Mas-d'Azil. Histoire d'une Résistance, 1680-1830*, Toulouse, 1961. Good study of effects of Revocation on small Pyreneen town.

13.271 **Crew**, Phyllis M., *Calvinist Preaching and Iconoclasm in the Netherlands, 1544-69*, 1978. Contends that what was labelled Calvinism masked very heterogenous movement, but does not see riots as primarily expression of economic discontent. See also (under name Phyllis Mack) her 'The wonderyear. Reformed preaching and iconoclasm in the Netherlands', in Obelkevich (13.30), 191-220. Further material on iconoclasm at 13.190,217,242,274,276.

13.272 **Duke**, A. C., 'Building heaven in hell's despite. The early history of the Reformation in the towns of the Low Countries', in A. C. Duke and C. A. Tamse, eds., *Britain and the Netherlands*, 7, The Hague, 1981, 45-75.

13.273 —— 'The face of popular religious dissent in the Low Countries, 1520-30', *J.Eccles.Hist.*, 26, 1975, 41-67. Evidence drawn mostly from heresy trials.

13.274 —— and Kolff, D. H. A., 'The time of troubles in the county of Holland, 1566-67', *Tijd.Geschied.*, 82, 1969, 316-37. Useful analysis of iconoclastic movement.

13.275 **Koch**, A. C. F., 'The Reformation at Deventer in 1579-80. Size and social structure of the Catholic section of the population during the religious peace', *Acta Hist.Neerlandica*, 6, 1973, 27-66.

13.276 **Maltby**, W. S., 'Iconoclasm and politics in the Netherlands, 1566', in Gutmann (13.190), 149-64. Tries to establish how far aristocratic dissidents fostered riots.

13.277 **Schilling**, H., ' "History of crime" or "history of sin"? Some reflections on the social history of early modern church discipline', in Kouri and Scott (4.93), 289-310. Emphasises that presbyterian discipline (as practised in Emden, Leiden, and Groningen) had quite different purpose from ecclesiastical jurisdiction that was part of government apparatus in many states.

13.278 **Wyntjes**, Sherrin M., 'Family allegiance and religious persuasion. The lesser nobility and the Revolt of the Netherlands', *Sixteenth-Cent.J.*, 12 (ii), 1981, 43-60. Study of c.200 dissidents identified in early stages of unrest

(1565-67).

13.279 —— 'Women and religious choices in the sixteenth-century Netherlands', *Arch. Reformationsgesch.*, 75, 1984, 276-89. Rather anecdotal.

MOVEMENTS AND SECTS

THE RADICAL REFORMATION. ANABAPTISM
See also 13.199.

13.280 **Barkun**, M., *Disaster and the Millennium*, New Haven, Conn., 1974. Attempts to isolate conditions which nurture millennarian movements. Not confined to Europe or any particular period.

13.281 **Brendler**, G., *Das Täuferreich zu Münster, 1534-35*, Berlin, 1966. East German view of anabaptist occupation as alliance between better-off opponents of episcopal government and poor. Other material on Münster episode at 13.287-8, 295, 299, 304.

13.282 **Clasen**, C.-P., *Anabaptism, a Social History, 1525-1618. Switzerland, Austria, Moravia, South and Central Germany*, Ithaca, N.Y., 1972. Major work.

13.283 —— 'The anabaptists in South and Central Germany, Switzerland, and Austria. A statistical study', *Mennonite Q.Rev.*, 52, 1978, 5-38. Concludes, after painstaking research into numbers area by area between 1525 and 1618, that anabaptism was never a mass movement.

13.284 —— 'The anabaptist leaders. Their numbers and background: Switzerland, Austria, South and Central Germany, 1525-1618', *ib.*, 49, 1975, 122-64. Includes long list of elected ministers and their professions.

13.285 —— 'Schwenckfeld's friends. A social study', *ib.*, 46, 1972, 58-69. Shows that anabaptism had some appeal to wealthier classes by looking at group around Caspar Schwenckfeld in Swabia (1530s and '40s).

13.286 —— 'The sociology of Swabian anabaptism', *Church Hist.*, 32, 1963, 150-80.

13.287 **Dülmen**, R. van, *Reformation als Revolution. Soziale Bewegung und Religiöser Radikalismus in der Deutschen*

Reformation, Munich, 1977. Attempt at comprehensive interpretation of early anabaptist movement, particularly Münster episode.

13.288 **Eichler**, Margrit, 'Charismatic prophets and charismatic saviors', *Mennonite Q.Rev.*, 55, 1981, 45-61. Contends that events at Münster during anabaptist occupation contradict theory that death of a charismatic leader leads to "routinisation" of leadership.

13.289 **Friedmann**, R., 'The Christian communism of the Hutterite Brethren', *Arch.Reformationsgesch.*, 46, 1955, 196-208. Generalised picture of anabaptist community as it might have functioned in sixteenth-century Moravia or Slovakia.

13.290 —— 'Economic aspects of early Hutterite life', *Mennonite Q.Rev.*, 30, 1956, 259-66. Short but useful sketch of economic organisation of communities.

13.291 **Friesen, A.**, 'The Marxist interpretation of anabaptism', *Sixteenth-Cent.Essays & Stud.*, 1, 1970, 17-34. Deals with a number of interpretations, from Engels to Zschäbitz (13.312). See also 13.302.

13.292 **Goertz**, H. J., *Die Täufer. Geschichte und Deutung*, Munich, 1980. Excellent general account.

13.293 **Horst**, I. B., ed., *The Dutch Dissenters. A Critical Companion to their History and Ideas*, Leiden, 1986. Collection on Dutch anabaptism. Essays most relevant to social history are L. G. Jansma on rise of movement (85-104); and A. F. Mellink on anabaptism at Amsterdam after Münster affair (127-42).

13.294 **Kirchner**, W., 'State and anabaptists in the sixteenth century. An economic approach', *J.Mod.Hist.*, 46, 1974, 1-25. Stresses diversity of economic status among anabaptists, and some economic considerations in authorities' handling of them.

13.295 **Kirchhoff**, K.-H., *Die Täufer in Münster, 1534-35. Untersuchungen zum Umfang und zur Sozialstruktur der Bewegung*, Münster, 1973. See also discussion of this work in 13.299.

13.296 **Klaasen**, W., 'The nature of anabaptist protest', *Mennonite Q.Rev.*, 45, 1971, 291-311. Attempts to sum up nature of protest in theological, economic, and political fields.

13.297 **Klassen**, P. J., *The Economics of Anabaptism, 1525-60*, 1964. Modifies notion of anabaptist "communism". See also his 'Mutual aid among the anabaptists. Doctrine and practice', *Mennonite Q.Rev.*, 37, 1963, 78-95.

13.298 **Krahn**, C., *Dutch Anabaptism. Origin, Spread, Life, and Thought, 1450-1600*, The Hague, 1968. Little explicit discussion of social context.

13.299 **Kuratsuka**, T., 'Gesamtgilde und Täufer. Der Radikalisierungsprozess in der Reformation Münsters', *Arch. Reformationsgesch.*, 76, 1985, 231-70. By further analysis of social composition, challenges Kirchhoff's thesis (13.295) that Münster movement embraced all classes.

13.300 **Mullett**, M. A., *Radical Religious Movements in Early Modern Europe*, 1980. Useful introductory work, though strongest on English sects.

13.301 **Ozment**, S. E., *Mysticism and Dissent. Religious Ideology and Social Protest in the Sixteenth Century*, New Haven, Conn., 1973. Deals with radical theologians like Münzer, Hut, and Denk, and social implications of their standpoints, rather than social history of their sects.

13.302 **Peachey**, P., 'Marxist historiography of the radical Reformation. Causality or covariation?', *Sixteenth-Cent.Essays & Stud.*, 1, 1970, 1-16. Call for dialogue between Marxist and more traditional "church history" approaches. See also 13.291.

13.303 —— 'The social background and social philosophy of the Swiss anabaptists, 1525-40', *Mennonite Q.Rev.*, 28, 1954, 102-27. Material drawn from court records. Appendix provides directory of urban sectaries, with occupations. For fuller treatment see his *Die Soziale Herkunft der Schweizer Täufer in der Reformationszeit*, Karlsruhe, 1954.

13.304 **Rammstedt**, O., *Sekte und Soziale Bewegung. Soziologische Analyse der Täufer in Münster, 1534-35*, Köln, 1966.

13.305 **Runzo**, Jean, 'Hutterite communal discipline, 1529-65', *Arch.Reformationsgesch.*, 71, 1980, 160-78. Analysis of cases recorded in sect's Great Chronicle.

13.306 **Schwartz**, H., 'Early anabaptist ideas about the nature of children', *Mennonite Q.Rev.*, 47, 1973, 102-14. Ideas dictating their rejection of infant baptism.

13.307 **Séguy**, J., 'Religion and agricultural success. Vocational life of the French anabaptists from the seventeenth to the nineteenth centuries', *ib.*, 47, 1973, 179-224. Material on agricultural practices. Movement strongest in Alsace and Vosges.

13.308 **Sprunger**, K. L., 'God's powerful army of the weak. Anabaptist women of the radical Reformation', in Greaves (13.165), 45-74.

13.309 **Waite**, G. K., 'The anabaptist movement in Amsterdam and the Netherlands, 1531-35. An initial investigation into its genesis and social dynamics', *Sixteenth-Cent.J.*, 18, 1987, 249-65.

13.310 **Williams**, G. H., *The Radical Reformation*, 1962. Book that did most to put anabaptism in forefront of Reformation research. Good narrative and doctrinal history, but left much work to do on social aspects. Review article: A. G. Dickens, *P.& P.*, 27, 1964, 123-5.

13.311 **Zeman**, J. K., 'Anabaptism. A replay of medieval themes, or a prelude to the modern age?', *Mennonite Q.Rev.*, 50, 1976, 259-71. Distinguishes personalism, pluralism, and egalitarianism as marking "modern" features of movement.

13.312 **Zschäbitz**, G., *Zur Mitteldeutschen Wiedertäuferbewegung nach dem Grossen Bauernkrieg*, Berlin, 1958. Marxist interpretation of anabaptists as craftsmen-victims of capitalist accumulation.

JANSENISM

13.313 **Kreiser**, B. R., 'Beyond Port-Royal. Popular Jansenism in eighteenth-century Paris', in J. Beauroy and others, eds., *The Wolf and the Lamb. Popular Culture in France*, Saratoga, Calif., 1976, 65-92.

13.314 **Goldmann**, L., *The Hidden God. A Study of Tragic Vision in the Pensées of Pascal and the Tragedies of Racine*, 1964. Transl. from French ed. of 1955. Influential study setting these writers in context of Robe milieu sympathetic to Jansenist outlook. See also his 'Remarques sur le Jansénisme', *Dix-Septième Siècle*, 19, 1953, 177-95.

13.315 **Hamscher**, A. N., 'The Parlement of Paris and the social interpretation of early French Jansenism', *Cath.Hist.Rev.*, 63, 1977, 392-410. Dissents from Goldmann's thesis that Jansenism had special appeal to Robe class (see previous entry).

13.316 **Taveneaux**, R., *La Vie Quotidienne des Jansénistes aux 17e et 18e Siècles*, Paris, 1973. Written for popular audience.

OTHER MOVEMENTS
See also 11.356 on Moravians;
3.366 on Russian Old Believers.

13.317 **Cameron**, E., *The Reformation of the Heretics. The Waldenses of the Alps, 1480-1580*, 1984. Deals with impact of wider Reformation on beliefs and culture of these older heretics.

13.318 **Brock**, P., *The Political and Social Doctrines of the Unity of Czech Brethren in the Fifteenth and Early Sixteenth Centuries*, The Hague, 1957.

13.319 **Gollin**, Gillian L., *Moravians in Two Worlds. A Study of Changing Communities*, New York, 1967. Contrasts Moravian settlement in Saxony (est. 1722) with daughter community in Pennsylvania (est. 1741), showing gradual divergence of social and economic systems despite identity of social ideals.

13.320 **Ward**, W. R., 'Zinzendorf and money', *Stud.Church Hist.*, 24, 1987, 283-305. On finances of early Moravian movement and its patron.

13.321 **Klein**, T., 'Minorities in Central Europe in the sixteenth and early seventeenth centuries', in Hepburn (13.263), 31-50. Deals essentially with religious minorities within Holy Roman Empire.

13.322 **Levine**, H., 'Frankism as a "cargo cult" and the Haskalah connection', in Malino and Albert (5.610), 81-94. Seeks to fit messianic movement of Jacob Frank among Polish and German Jews (1750s-1770s) into general sociology of religion.

13.323 **Cherniavsky**, M., 'The Old Believers and the new religion', *Slavic Rev.*, 25, 1966, 1-39. Repr. in Cherniavsky (6.232), 140-88. Social and cultural explanations of Russian schism of early eighteenth century.

13.324 **Clay**, J. E., 'God's people in the early eighteenth century. The Uglich affair of 1717', *Cah.Monde Russe et Sov.*, 26, 1985, 69-124. Account of millenarian sect (with long appendix of documents in Russian).

13.325 **Crummey**, R. O., *The Old Believers and the World of Antichrist. The Vyg Community and the Russian State, 1694-1855*, Madison, Wis., 1970. Includes material on social conditions and economic resources of this important settlement in Olonets region.

THE INQUISITION
See also subsection on racial minorities, 5.553-648; and 13.386-91; 14.329.

13.326 **Bennassar**, B., and others, *L'Inquisition Espagnole, 15e-19e Siècle*, Paris, 1979. Collaborative work, with chapters on personnel, repression of minorities, attitude to women, and enforcement of sexual morality.

13.327 **Contreras**, J., *El Santo Oficio de la Inquisición de Galicia. Poder, Sociedad, y Cultura*, Madrid, 1982. Detailed analysis of personnel employed and cases handled.

13.328 **García Carcel**, R., *Orígenes de la Inquisición Española. El Tribunal de Valencia, 1478-1530*, Barcelona, 1976. Followed by *Herejía y Sociedad en el Siglo 16. La Inquisición en Valencia, 1530-1609*, Barcelona, 1980. Major study of Inquisition's place in Valencian political institutions, with much material on officials and case-load.

13.329 **Haliczer**, S., ed., *Inquisition and Society in Early Modern Europe*, 1987. Comprises 9 essays, 6 on Hispanic and 3 on Italian tribunals – Judaising, Protestantism, and control of both popular and elite cultural expression all receive attention.

13.330 **Henningsen**, G., and Tedeschi, J., eds., *The Inquisition in Early Modern Europe. Studies on Sources and Methods*, Dekalb, Ill., 1986. 4 papers report on archival sources for Inquisition studies; further 4 provide statistical profiles of case loads of Spanish and Italian courts, and indicate usefulness for historical anthropology; and G. Gonnet contributes bibliographical essay.

13.331 **Kamen**, H., 'Confiscations in the economy of the Spanish Inquisition', *Ec.Hist.Rev.*, 2nd ser., 18, 1965, 511-25. Considers part which confiscations against *conversos* may have played in diminishing general prosperity of Spain.

13.332 **Monter**, E. W., 'The new social history and the Spanish Inquisition', *J.Soc.Hist.*, 17, 1984, 705-13. Review article on recent historiography.

13.333 —— 'Women and the Italian Inquisitions', in Rose (5.481), 73-87. Suggests that women offenders/accused tended to get off more lightly.

13.334 **Parker**, G., 'Some recent work on the Inquisition in Spain and Italy', *J.Mod.Hist.*, 54, 1982, 519-32. Bibliographical article.

13.335 **Pérez Villanueva**, J., ed., *La Inquisición Española. Nueva Visión, Nuevos Horizontes*, Madrid, 1980. Over fifty essays by leading specialists. Sections on Tribunal officials and on "grupos disidentes" (Moriscos, Lutherans, etc.) are of especial interest.

WITCHCRAFT AND THE OCCULT

For bibliography and historiography see 2.55; 13.340,346,354,358. Other general references: 5.460; 14.346.

13.336 **Anglo**, S., ed., *Damned Art. Essays in the Literature of Witchcraft*, 1977. Essays on some classic early modern witchcraft treatises (Bodin's *Démomanie*, the *Malleus Maleficarum*, etc.).

13.337 **Clark**, S., 'Inversion, misrule, and the meaning of witchcraft', *P. & P.*, 87, 1980, 98-127. Argues that both learned and popular culture thought in terms of polarities, so that every act attributed to witches reversed some divinely appointed ritual or order.

13.338 **Cohn**, N., *Europe's Inner Demons. An Enquiry Inspired by the Great Witch-Hunt*, 1975. Concentrates on medieval origins of sixteenth- and seventeenth-century persecution.

13.339 **Currie**, E. P., 'Crimes without criminals. Witchcraft and its control in Renaissance Europe', *Law & Society Rev.*, 3, 1968, 7-32. Repr. in D. Black and Maureen Mileski, eds., *The Social Organization of Law*, New York, 1973, 344-67. Contrasts bureaucratic persecution of continental countries with milder English conditions where denunciations were left to individual entrepreneurs.

13.340 **Estes**, L. L., 'Incarnation of evil. Changing perspectives on the European witch craze', *Clio*, 13, 1984, 133-47. Argues that historiography of witchcraft trials has frequently been affected by contemporary preoccupations.

13.341 —— 'Medical origins of the European witch craze. A hypothesis', *J.Soc.Hist.*, 17, 1983, 271-84. Suggests that breakdown of medieval patterns of diagnosis may have increased tendency of doctors to see symptoms as demonological.

13.342 **Febvre**, L., 'Witchcraft: nonsense or a mental revolution?', in Burke (13.245), 185-92. Transl. from *Annales*, 3, 1948.

13.343 **Garin**, E., *Astrology in the Renaissance*, 1983. Transl. from Italian ed. of 1976. Deals principally with learned tradition.

13.344 **Garrett**, C., 'Women and witches. Patterns of analysis', *Signs*, 3, 1977, 461-70. Examines witchcraft literature for clues as to why accused were almost always women. See also further comment by Claudia Honegger and Nelly Moia, *ib.*, 792-802.

13.345 **Ginzburg**, C., 'The witches' sabbat. Popular cult or inquisitorial stereotype?', in Kaplan (9.541), 41-51. Argues that mythology of sabbat incorporates elements of both learned and popular culture.

13.346 **Hess**, A. G., 'Hunting witches. A survey of some recent literature', *Criminal Justice Hist.*, 3, 1982, 47-79. Very useful bibliography.

13.347 **Hoak**, D., 'Art, culture, and mentality in Renaissance society. The meaning of Hans Baldung Grien's *Bewitched Groom*', *Renaiss.Q.*, 38, 1985, 488-510. Examines iconography of witchcraft. See also Linda C. Hults, 'Baldung's *Bewitched Groom* revisited', *Sixteenth-Cent.J.*, 15, 1984, 59-79.

13.348 **Horsley**, R. A., 'Who were the witches? The social roles of the accused in the European witchcraft trials',

J.Interdisc.Hist., 9, 1979, 689-715. Suggests that many accused were folk-healers more or less accepted by peasant society but caught by demonologists' doctrine that those who can cure by magic must have caused disease.

13.349 **Kieckhefer**, R., *European Witch-Trials. Their Foundations in Popular and Learned Culture, 1300-1500*, 1976. Good survey of late medieval developments.

13.350 **Klaits**, J., *Servants of Satan. The Age of the Witch Hunts*, Bloomington, Ind., 1985. General summmary, covering both medieval and early modern periods.

13.351 **Kors**, A. C., and Peters, E., eds., *Witchcraft in Europe, 1100-1700. A Documentary History*, 1972. Useful collection of extracts from documents. Peters' *The Magician, the Witch, and the Law*, 1978, gives primary emphasis to high Middle Ages.

13.352 **Larner**, Christina, 'Crimen exceptum? The crime of witchcraft in Europe', in Gatrell (10.377), 49-75. Repr. in her *Witchcraft and Religion. The Politics of Popular Belief*, 1985, 35-67. Considers whether witch trials reflect special social strains or more general changes in administering law and suppressing nonconformity.

13.353 **Levack**, B. P., *The Witch-Hunt in Early Modern Europe*, 1987. Includes chap. on influence of Reformation in intensifying prosecutions.

13.354 **Midelfort**, H. C. E., 'Recent witch-hunting research, or Where do we go from here?', *Pap.Bibliog.Soc.of America*, 62, 1968, 373-420. Survey of sources and research publ. in period 1940-67.

13.355 —— 'Were there really witches?', in Kingdon (13.234), 189-233. Lengthy documentary appendix.

13.356 —— 'Witch hunting and the domino theory', in Obelkevich (13.30), 277-88. Seeks general model for why witch panics tended to be self-limiting.

13.357 **Monter**, E. W., *European Witchcraft*, New York, 1969. Reader, combining sources and extracts from secondary works.

13.358 —— 'The historiography of European witchcraft. Progress and prospects', *J. Interdisc.Hist.*, 2, 1972, 651-68 (misnumbered 435-52).

13.359 —— 'The pedestal and the stake. Courtly love and witchcraft', in Bridenthal and Koonz (5.473), 119-36. Looks at the two faces of medieval and early modern image of women.

13.360 **Parrinder**, E. G., *Witchcraft, European and African*, 1958. By specialist in African religious anthropology. Interesting for comparative perspective, but needs caution.

13.361 **Quaife**, G. R., *Godly Zeal and Furious Rage. The Witch in Early Modern Europe*, 1987. Good synthesis, organised topically rather than geographically. Chaps. on popular and learned views of supernatural; sexual puritanism and misogyny; mechanics of persecution; village feuds and denunciations; subjective experience via dreams and delusions.

13.362 **Russell**, J. B., *A History of Witchcraft. Sorcerers, Heretics, and Pagans*, 1980. Popular illustrated work.

13.363 **Shumaker**, W., *The Occult Sciences in the Renaissance*, Berkeley, Calif., 1972. Best general introduction to systems of thought which embraced astrology, witchcraft and magic, and alchemy.

13.364 **Trevor-Roper**, H. R., 'The European witch-craze of the sixteenth and seventeenth centuries', in Trevor-Roper (2.82), 90-192. Repr. (slightly revised) as book, 1969. Concentrates on intellectual debate and persecutors, rather than victims and their environment.

13.365 **Walker**, D. P., *Unclean Spirits. Possession and Exorcism in France and England in the Late Sixteenth and Early Seventeenth Centuries*, 1981. Emphasises that exorcism was used against religious opponents as well as in connection with witchcraft.

13.366 —— 'Demonic possession used as propaganda in the later sixteenth century', in *Scienze, Credenze Occulte, Livelli di Cultura. Convegno Internazionale di Studi*, Florence, 1982, 237-48. Summarises one of main themes of previous entry.

13.367 **Zambelli**, Paola, 'Fine del mondo o inizio della propaganda? Astrologia, filosofia della storia, e propaganda politico-religiosa nel dibattito sulla congiunzione del 1524', *ib.*, 291-368. On mass of astrological material generated by planetary conjunctions of 1524. See also Ottavia Niccoli, 'Il diluvio del 1524', *ib.*, 369-92.

FRANCE, SWITZERLAND, AND THE LOW COUNTRIES
See also 13.365; 14.45,72.

13.368 **Briggs**, R., 'Witchcraft and popular mentality in Lorraine, 1580-1630', in B. Vickers, ed., *Occult and Scientific Mentalities in the Renaissance*, 1984, 337-49.

13.369 **Dupont-Bouchat**, Marie-S., and others, *Prophètes et Sorciers dans les Pays-Bas, 16e-18e Siècle*, Paris, 1978. Three separate essays covering Luxembourg (Dupont-Bouchat), Cambrésis (R. Muchembled), and United Provinces (W. Frijhoff).

13.370 **Garrett**, C., 'Witches and cunning folk in the Old Regime', in Beauroy and others (13.313), 53-64.

13.371 —— 'Witches, werewolves, and Henri Boguet', *Proc.Western Soc.Fr.Hist.*, 4, 1976, 126-34. Cases of possession in Jura region (1598, 1607) which influenced demonological treatise of investigating judge.

13.372 **Klaits**, J., 'Witchcraft trials and absolute monarchy in Alsace', in Golden (13.126), 148-72. Supplements Midelfort (13.396) for this region.

13.373 **Kreiser**, B. R., 'The Devils of Toulon. Demonic possession and religious politics in eighteenth-century Provence', *ib.*, 173-221. Episode (early 1730s) involving alleged abuse of confessional. Title echoes Aldous Huxley's famous account of seventeenth-century possession case, *The Devils of Loudun*, 1952.

13.374 **Le Roy Ladurie**, E., *Jasmin's Witch*, 1987. Transl. from French ed. of 1983. Traces real events behind narrative poem *Francouneto*, story of witchcraft set in sixteenth-century Gascony, by Occitan poet, Jean Jasmin.

13.375 **Mandrou**, R., *Magistrats et Sorciers en France au 17e Siècle. Une Analyse de Psychologie Historique*, Paris, 1968. Substantial doctoral thesis which concentrates on Robe as persecutors or sceptics. Review article: P. Chaunu, *Annales*, 24, 1969, 895-911. See also documentary appendage to this work, *Possession et Sorcellerie au 17e Siècle. Textes Inédits*, Paris, 1979.

13.376 **Monter**, E. W., *Witchcraft in France and Switzerland. The Borderlands during the Reformation*, Ithaca, N.Y., 1976. Explores trial records of Jura region over period

1560-1660, noting religious strife as complicating factor. Review article: J. Butler, *J.Soc.Hist.*, 12, 1978, 159-67. See also his 'Patterns of witchcraft in the Jura', *J.Soc.Hist.*, 5, 1971, 1-25.

13.377 —— 'Witchcraft in Geneva, 1537-1662', *J.Mod.Hist.*, 43, 1971, 179-204. Emphasises that most witch trials at Geneva originated in rural hinterland, and that judges were surprisingly lenient.

13.378 **Muchembled**, R., 'Witchcraft, popular culture, and Christianity in the sixteenth century, with emphasis upon Flanders and Artois', in Forster and Ranum (5.362), 213-36. Transl. from *Annales*, 28, 1973, 264-84.

13.379 —— 'The witches of the Cambrésis. The acculturation of the rural world in the sixteenth and seventeenth centuries', in Obelkevich (13.30), 221-76.

13.380 —— *La Sorcière au Village, 15e-18e Siècle*, Paris, 1979. Small collection of documentary extracts.

13.381 **Préaud**, M., *Les Sorcières*, Paris, 1973. Catalogue of exhibition held at Bibliothèque Nationale.

13.382 **Soman**, A., 'La décriminalisation de la sorcellerie en France', *Hist. Éc., et Soc.*, 4, 1985, 179-203. Stresses honourable role of Parlement of Paris in decline of prosecutions.

13.383 —— 'The Parlement of Paris and the great witch hunt, 1564-1640', *Sixteenth-Cent.J.*, 9, 1978, 31-44. Contradicts Mandrou's judgement (13.375) that Parlement routinely confirmed lower court sentences until well into seventeenth century. See also his longer (French) essay in *Annales*, 32, 1977, 790-814.

13.384 **Villette**, P., *La Sorcellerie et sa Répression dans le Nord de la France*, Paris, 1976. Posthumously publ. work of Cambrai priest and teacher, criticised by Muchembled (13.369) as weak in interpretation.

13.385 **Wilkins**, Kay S., 'Attitudes to witchcraft and demonic possession in France during the eighteenth century', *J.Eur.Stud.*, 3, 1973, 348-62. Examines literary expressions of scepticism.

SPAIN AND ITALY

13.386 **Caro Baroja**, J., *Inquisición, Brujería, y Criptojudaísmo*, Barcelona, 1970. Contains two separate studies; that on investigation of witchcraft occupies pp.183-315.

13.387 —— *Vidas Mágicas y Inquisición*, 2 vols., Madrid, 1967. In addition to general discussion, contains lengthy details of many individual cases, including some involving practice of astrology as well as magic and witchcraft.

13.388 —— *The World of the Witches*, Chicago, 1965. Transl. from Spanish ed. of 1961. General history of witchcraft from classical times. Part 3 (143-200) concentrates on Basque region in sixteenth and seventeenth centuries. Some materials on which this section is based publ. in his *Brujería Vasca*, San Sebastian, 1975.

13.389 **Darst**, D. H., 'Witchcraft in Spain. The testimony of Martín de Castañega's treatise (1529)', *Proc.Am.Phil.Soc.*, 123, 1979, 298-322. Mainly text of what is claimed to be oldest printed vernacular book on witchcraft.

13.390 **Henningsen**, G., *The Witches' Advocate. Basque Witchcraft and the Spanish Inquisition, 1609-14*, Reno, Nev., 1980. Based on dispassionate investigation by Inquisitor Alonso de Salazar, who tried to distinguish genuine popular beliefs from malicious accusations.

13.391 **Ginzburg**, C., *Night Battles. Witchcraft and Agrarian Cults in the Sixteenth and Seventeenth Centuries*, 1983. First publ. in Italian, 1966. Shows how practitioners of white magic in Friuli region were regarded by Inquisition as witches of standard pattern, and began to conform to it.

GERMANY AND AUSTRIA
See also 14.87.

13.392 **Kunstmann**, H. M., *Zauberwahn und Hexenprozess in der Reichstadt Nürnberg*, Nuremberg, 1970.

13.393 **Kunze**, M., *Strasse ins Feuer. Vom Leben und Sterben in der Zeit des Hexenwahns*, Munich, 1982. Episode involving persecution of Bavarian vagrant family arrested as suspected criminals and then implicated in diabolism.

13.394 **Lehmann**, H., 'Hexenverfolgung und Hexenprozesse im Alten Reich zwischen Reformation und Aufklärung', *Jb.Inst.Dt.Gesch.*, 7, 1978, 13-70. Good general survey of German witch hunts.

13.395 **Midelfort**, H. C. E., 'Witchcraft and religion in sixteenth-century Germany', *Arch.Reformationsgesch.*, 62, 1971, 266-78. Asks why Catholic authorities seem to have persecuted more vigorously than Protestant in early seventeenth century.

13.396 —— *Witch hunting in Southwestern Germany, 1562-1684. The Social and Intellectual Foundations*, Stanford, Calif., 1972.

13.397 **Schormann**, G., *Hexenprozesse in Nordwestdeutschland*, Hildesheim, 1977. Based on thorough study of archives of Lower Saxony and Westphalia.

13.398 —— *Hexenprozesse in Deutschland*, Göttingen, 1981. Uses a source collection assembled in 1930s to chart geography and chronology of persecutions, though, like previous entry, not strong on analysing reasons for fluctuations in intensity.

EASTERN EUROPE

13.399 **Tazbir**, J., 'Hexenprozesse in Polen', *Arch.Reformationsgesch.*, 71, 1980, 280-306.

13.400 **Zguta**, R., 'Ordeal by water (swimming of witches) in the East Slavic world', *Slavic Rev.*, 36, 1977, 220-30. Notes persistence of this practice in Ukraine into eighteenth and nineteenth centuries in times of drought or famine.

13.401 —— 'Witchcraft and medicine in pre-Petrine Russia', *Russ.Rev.*, 37, 1978, 438-48. Deals esp. with use of incantations by healers.

13.402 —— 'Witchcraft trials in seventeenth-century Russia', *Am.Hist.Rev.*, 82, 1977, 1187-1207. Finds persecution less intensive than in Western Europe but more prone to implicate men.

14

CULTURAL AND MENTAL HORIZONS

GENERAL WORKS. VALUES: BELIEFS: CUSTOMS AND RECREATIONS
See also 1.64; 2.62; 12.11.

14.1 **Bouwsma**, W. J., 'Anxiety and the formation of early modern culture', in Malament (10.295), 215-46. In Huizinga tradition of bold generalisation. See also 14.10,34.

14.2 —— 'Lawyers and early modern culture', *Am.Hist.Rev.*, 78, 1973, 303-27. Argues that lawyers' cast of mind was influential in growth of secularism, i.e. rejection of abstract systems in favour of specialisation, practicality, and historical perspective.

14.3 **Brinton**, C. C., *A History of Western Morals*, New York, 1959. Brave stab at history of social ethics from Babylonians to Bolsheviks: approx. 100 pages on early modern period.

14.4 **Burguière**, A., 'The fate of the history of *mentalités* in the *Annales*', *Comp. Stud. Soc. & Hist.*, 24, 1982, 424-37. Discusses what he contends are very different approaches of Lucien Febvre and Marc Bloch.

14.5 **Burke**, P., *Popular Culture in Early Modern Europe*, 1978. Concentrates on types and diffusion of popular entertainments and festivals, emphasising growing divergence from elite culture. Review article: W. Beik, *J.Interdisc.Hist.*, 11, 1980, 97-103.

14.6 —— 'Revolution in popular culture', in Porter and Teich (9.514), 206-25. General historiography. Finds "revolution" inappropriate concept for discussion of

popular culture. See also brief conference paper,'The "discovery" of popular culture', in Samuel (2.128), 216-26.

14.7 **Clark**, S., 'French historians and early modern popular culture', *P.& P.*, 100, 1983, 62-99. Castigates French historians for picture of early modern mentalities as stunted by ignorance and insecurity. Note similar arguments of Wirth (13.28).

14.8 **Cohen**, Esther, 'Law, folklore, and animal lore', *P.& P.*, 110, 1986, 6-37. On practice of animal trials, seen as conjunction of popular anthropomorphism and learned ideas of justice.

14.9 **Darnton**, R., 'Peasants tell tales. The meaning of Mother Goose', in Darnton (6.243), 9-72. Fairly general examination of eighteenth-century European folktales. See also 14.33,66-7,93.

14.10 **Delumeau**, J., *La Peur en Occident, 14e-18e Siècles. Une Cité Assiégée*, Paris, 1978. Portrays climate of pervasive fear (of riot, plague, evil spirits, etc.). See also case-studies of reaction to epidemics and earthquakes, mainly in Italian context, in 'Calamità, paure, risposte', *Quad.Stor.*, 55, 1984, 5-154; 60, 1985, 653-838. Note 13.28 and 14.7 on dangers of exaggerating popular credulity and fear.

14.11 **Eichberg**, H., *Leistung, Spannung, Geschwindigkeit. Sport und Tanz im Gesellschaftlichen Wandel des 18/19*

Jahrhunderts, Stuttgart, 1978. Tries to relate changes in sport and dance forms to greater social emphasis on equality and achievement throughout Western Europe.

14.12 **Elias**, N., *The Civilizing Process. The History of Manners*, 1978. German original first publ. in 1939, but remains principal history of domestic etiquette as it evolved in manuals of "correct" behaviour from late medieval period onwards.

14.13 **Foucault**, M., *The Order of Things. An Archaeology of the Human Sciences*, New York, 1970. Transl. from French ed. of 1966 (*Les Mots et les Choses*). Sets out linguistic, and hence perceptual, revolution in western thought between Renaissance and Enlightenment. Review article: Dorothy Leland, *Clio*, 4, 1975, 225-43.

14.14 **Gilbert**, F., 'Intellectual history: its aims and methods', *Daedalus*, 100, 1971, 80-97. Repr. in Gilbert and Graubard (1.5), 141-58. Discusses trend to analyse the history of ideas in relation to social groups rather than purely intrinsically.

14.15 **Ginzburg**, C., 'High and low. The theme of forbidden knowledge in the sixteenth and seventeenth centuries', *P.& P.*, 73, 1976, 28-41. Considers restrictive attitude to intellectual enquiry shown, for example, in emblem books.

14.16 **Gismondi**, M. A., ' "The gift of theory". A critique of the *histoire des mentalités*', *Soc.Hist.*, 10, 1985, 211-30. Discusses French historiographical tradition, with particular attention to Le Roy Ladurie.

14.17 **Hampson**, N., and Behrens, Betty, 'Cultural history as infra-structure', *Stud.on Voltaire*, 86, 1971, 7-24. Two separate short pieces seeking to extend range of cultural history.

14.18 **Heers**, J., *Fêtes des Fous et Carnavals*, Paris, 1983. Account of boisterous festivals (esp. those originating in society of collegiate churches) of medieval and early modern Europe, increasingly challenged by post-Reformation ethos.

14.19 **Hutton**, P. H., 'The history of mentalities. The new map of cultural history', *Hist.& Theory*, 20, 1981, 237-59. Examines work of Febvre, Bloch, Ariès, Elias, and Foucault.

14.20 **Larner**, Christina, 'Relativism and ethnocentrism. Popular and educated belief in pre-industrial culture', in Larner (13.352), 97-165. Gifford Lectures delivered in 1982. Entertaining debate about proper attitude of anthropologists (including those working on historical material) to belief systems they study.

14.21 **Le Goff**, J., and Schmitt, J.-C., eds., *Le Charivari*, Paris, 1981. Proceedings of conference held in 1977 on this widespread and long-lived custom. Relevant papers on France from A. Burguière, Nicole Castan, Natalie Davis, F. Lebrun, R. Muchembled; and on Italy from R. C. Trexler and Martine Boiteux. See also 14.41,47,50.

14.22 **Maravall**, J. A., *Culture of the Baroque. Analysis of a Historical Structure*, 1986. Transl. from Spanish ed. of 1975. Sees baroque culture (here treated mainly in Spanish examples) as directed to maintaining social hierarchy against potential disruption.

14.23 **Mitzman**, A., 'The civilizing offensive. Mentalities, high culture, and individual psyches', *J.Soc.Hist.*, 20, 1987, 663-87. Psychoanalytic view of popular-elite culture struggle, focussing on work of Elias, Muchembled, Le Roy Ladurie, and Darnton.

14.24 **Nef**, J. U., *Cultural Foundations of Industrial Civilization*, 1958. Argues that humanist and scientific ideals preceded and fostered industrialisation rather than being its product.

14.25 **Pahl**, J., 'The public square from the Middle Ages to the era of Baroque', *Cultures*, 5 (iv), 1978, 27-41. On square as focus of social intercourse.

14.26 **Park**, Katharine, and Daston, Lorraine J., 'Unnatural conceptions. The study of monsters in sixteenth-century France and England', *P.& P.*, 92, 1981, 20-54. Traces how monsters and marvels ceased to be taken seriously in learned culture.

14.27 **Payne**, H. C., 'Elite versus popular mentality in the eighteenth century', *Hist.Reflections*, 2, 1975, 183-208. Repr. in *Stud.in Eighteenth-Cent.Culture*, 8, 1979, 3-32. On growing perception of gulf between educated and masses.

14.28 **Redlich**, F., 'Ideas. Their migration in space and transmittal over time', *Kyklos*, 6, 1953, 301-20. Repr. in Redlich (9.141), 258-78. Attempts to systematise communication of ideas as historical phenomenon.

14.29 **Sennett**, R., *The Fall of Public Man*, New York, 1977. Traces growth of privacy and passiveness in social relations since flourishing public life of eighteenth-century London and Paris.

14.30 **Stearns**, P. N., and Stearns, Carol Z., 'Emotionology. Clarifying the history of emotions and emotional standards', *Am.Hist.Rev.*, 90, 1985, 813-36. Suggests methods of distinguishing between professed values and genuine emotional experience.

14.31 **Thomas**, K., 'Work and leisure in pre-industrial society', *P.& P.*, 29, 1964, 50-66. Conference paper offering wide-ranging survey of attitudes to work from medieval times onwards. Includes discussion.

14.32 **Vovelle**, M., *Idéologies et Mentalités*, Paris, 1982. Collection of occasional pieces, mainly general and historiographical.

14.33 **Weber**, E., 'Fairies and hard facts. The reality of folktales', *J.Hist.Ideas*, 42, 1981, 93-113. Contends that folktales reflect social realities rather than psychological fantasies (as postulated by, e.g., Bruno Bettelheim).

14.34 **White**, L., 'Death and the devil', in Kinsman (6.137), 25-46. Argues that period 1300-1650 was "the most psychically disturbed era in European history" due to natural disasters and cultural change. Cf. Delumeau (14.10).

FRANCE AND THE LOW COUNTRIES

See also 3.22,26,46; 10.387; 11.286,307; 12.37; 14.21,384.

14.35 **Agulhon**, M., *La Sociabilité Méridionale. Confréries et Associations dans la Vie Collective en Provence Orientale à la Fin du 18e Siècle*, 2 vols., Aix-en-Provence, 1966. Deals rather more widely than title suggests with confraternities, clubs, societies and other foci of social intercourse in late eighteenth century. Revised and shortened version publ. as *Pénitents et Francs-Maçons de l'Ancienne Provence*, Paris, 1968.

14.36 **Bakhtin**, M. M., *Rabelais and his World*, Cambridge, Mass., 1968. Transl. from Russian ed. of 1965 (probably written c.1940). Influential study of popular culture (in such forms as banquets, festivals, verbal and visual imagery, etc.) which fed into Rabelais' work.

14.37 **Beik**, W. H., 'Searching for popular culture in early modern France', *J.Mod.Hist.*, 49, 1977, 266-81. Examines many recent works on poverty, peasant revolt, and popular customs and beliefs.

14.38 **Belmont**, Nicole, *Mythes et Croyances dans l'Ancienne France*, Paris, 1973. Analysis of folklore. Review article: M. R. Marrus, *J.Soc.Hist.*, 8 (iii), 1975, 142-9 (also reviews her biography of Arnold Van Gennep, pioneer student of French folklore).

14.39 **Bercé**, Y.-M., *Fête et Révolte. Des Mentalités Populaires du 16e au 17e Siècle*, Paris, 1976. General work on subversive aspects of popular festivals. See Le Roy Ladurie (14.58) for detailed example.

14.40 **Brennan**, T., 'Beyond the barriers. Popular culture and Parisian *guingettes*', *Eighteenth-Cent.Stud.*, 18, 1984-85, 153-69. Suburban wine taverns outside Parisian excise limits and therefore offering cheaper refreshment.

14.41 **Burguière**, A., 'The charivari and religious repression in France during the ancien régime', in Wheaton and Hareven (5.118), 84-110.

14.42 —— 'Société et culture à Reims à la fin du 18e siècle…à travers les cahiers de doléances', *Annales*, 22, 1967, 303-33. Examines guild cahiers for clues to extent of diffusion of Enlightenemnt concepts.

14.43 **Caceres**, B., *Loisirs et Travail du Moyen Age à nos Jours*, Paris, 1973. Popular history of holidays in France.

14.44 **Castan**, Y., *Honnêteté et Relations Sociales en Languedoc, 1715-80*, Paris, 1974. Penetrating examination of criminal records of Toulouse Parlement for what they show of general attitudes to life, esp. questions of reputation and honour.

14.45 **Crouzet**, D., 'La représentation du temps à l'époque de la Ligue', *Rev.Hist.*, 270, 1983, 297-388. Long essay on prevalence of eschatology and astrological forecasts of doom. Cf.13.367.

14.46 **Davis**, Natalie Z., 'Proverbial wisdom and popular errors', in Davis (11.200), 227-67. Discusses printed collections of common proverbs and popular medical diagnoses and remedies.

14.47 —— 'The reasons of misrule. Youth groups and charivaris in sixteenth-century France', *P.& P.*, 50, 1971, 41-75. Repr. in Davis (11.200), 97-123. On social function of charivari, and some city-rural differences in emphasis and participation.

14.48 —— 'Women on top', in Davis (11.200), 124-51. Sex-role reversal in some popular rituals and festivities.

14.49 **Delumeau**, J., ed., *La Mort des Pays de Cocagne. Comportements Collectifs de la Renaissance à l'Age Classique*, Paris, 1976. Interesting collection of student research on popular culture and religion.

14.50 **Desplat**, C., *Charivaris en Gascogne. La "Morale des Peuples" du 16e au 20e Siècle*, Paris, 1982.

14.51 **Dunkley**, J., 'Gambling. A social and moral problem in France, 1685-1792', *Stud.on Voltaire*, 235, 1985, whole volume. Studies treatment of question in moralistic and imaginative literature of period. See also his 'Illegal gambling in eighteenth-century France. Incidence, detection, and penalties', *Brit.J.Eighteenth-Cent.Stud.*, 8, 1985, 129-37. Also 14.53,56.

14.52 **Febvre**, L., 'Amiens, from the Renaissance to the Counter-Reformation', in Burke (13.245), 193-207. Transl. from *Annales d'Hist.Soc.*, 3, 1941, 41-54. Traces changes in popular taste and piety revealed by household inventories.

14.53 **Grussi**, O., *La Vie Quotidienne des Joueurs sous l'Ancien Régime à Paris et à la Cour*, Paris, 1985. Lively introduction to history of gambling, though inevitably deals mainly with its place in high society. See also 14.51,56.

14.54 **Gutton**, J.-P., *La Sociabilité Villageoise dans l'Ancienne France. Solidarités et Voisinages du 16e au 18e Siècle*, Paris, 1979. Anthropology of village community life in early modern France. Excellent synthesis of current research.

14.55 *Images du Peuple au 18e Siècle*, Paris, 1973. Proceedings of conference at Centre Aixois d'Études et de Recherches sur le Dix-huitième Siècle. Essays both on popular culture and on concept of "the people" in literature and political thought.

14.56 *Le Jeu au 18e Siècle*, Aix-en-Provence, 1976. Another symposium of Centre Aixois (see previous entry). Many articles deal with gaming and sport in art and literature. See also 14.51,53.

14.57 **Leclant**, J., 'Coffee and cafés in Paris, 1644-93', in Forster and Ranum (11.116), 86-97. Transl. from *Annales*, 6, 1951, 1-12.

14.58 **Le Roy Ladurie**, E., *Carnival. A People's Uprising at Romans, 1579-80*, 1980. Transl. from French ed. of 1979. Much detail on small town's political and social strife, centrepiece being elaborate analysis of political importance of carnival demonstrations and rituals of disorder.

14.59 —— 'Mélusine down on the farm. Metamorphosis of a myth', in Le Roy Ladurie (4.35), 203-20. Transl. from *Annales*, 26, 1971, 604-22. Follows article by J. Le Goff on medieval fable, and traces its continuance in French folklore of sixteenth to eighteenth centuries.

14.60 **Moran**, G. T., 'Conceptions of time in early modern France', *Sixteenth-Cent.J.*, 12 (iv), 1981, 3-19. Examines leases of Montpellier chapter in terms of use of traditional church calendar or secular dates.

14.61 **Muchembled**, R., *Popular Culture and Elite Culture in France, 1400-1750*, Baton Rouge, La., 1985. Transl. from French ed. of 1978. Sees increasing attempt by authorities to suppress or divert many aspects of popular culture considered licentious or superstitious. Review article: W. Beik, *J.Interdisc.Hist.*, 11, 1980, 97-103. Note criticisms of some aspects of Muchembled's argument in, e.g., 13.28, 14.7, 14.62.

14.62 **Revel**, J., 'Forms of expertise. Intellectuals and "popular" culture in France, 1650-1800', in Kaplan (9.541), 255-73. Gives more nuanced picture than that which sees only widening rift between learned and popular.

14.63 **Rivière**, D., 'De l'avertissement à l'anathème. Le proverbe français et la culture savante (16e-17e siècle)', *Rev.Hist.*, 268, 1982, 93-130. Examines why *savants* became steadily more hostile to popular culture as exemplified in changing attitude to proverbs.

14.64 **Roubin**, Lucienne, 'Male space and female space within the Provençal community', in Forster and Ranum (4.86), 152-80. Transl. from *Annales*, 25, 1970, 537-60. Starts from present-day anthropology but looks back to roots in ancien régime.

14.65 **Shorter**, E., 'The *veillée* and the great transformation', in Beauroy and others (13.313), 127-40. Evening gatherings of villagers as socialisation process.

14.66 **Soriano**, M., *Les Contes de Perrault. Culture Savante et Traditions Populaires*, Paris, 1968. Study of origins and derivations of this famous seventeenth-century fairy tale collection. See author's interview with J. Le Goff, *Annales*, 25, 1970, 633-53.

14.67 **Thelander**, Dorothy R., 'Mother Goose and her goslings. The France of Louis XIV as seen through the fairy tale', *J. Mod. Hist.*, 54, 1982, 467-96. Examines fairy tales of late seventeenth-century France for glimpses of specific culture which produced them.

14.68 **Ultee**, J. M., 'The suppression of fêtes in France, 1666', *Cath.Hist.Rev.*, 62, 1976, 181-99. Unsuccessful attempt to reduce number of obligatory festivals in Paris diocese.

14.69 **Vartanian**, A., 'The *Annales* school and the Enlightenment', *Stud.in Eighteenth-Cent.Culture*, 13, 1984, 233-47. Comments on work by Vovelle, Roche, and Darnton.

14.70 **Vovelle**, M., and others, *Les Métamorphoses de la Fête en Provence de 1750 à 1820*, Paris, 1976. Argues that popular festivals were increasingly secularised well before Revolution turned them into political demonstrations.

14.71 —— 'Le tournant des mentalités en France, 1750-89. La "sensibilité" pré-révolutionnaire', *Soc.Hist.*, [1], no.5, 1977, 605-29. How far can changes in sexual attitudes, and increasing secularisation in ceremonies and village institutions be attributed to diffusion of elite opinions? (Written in English, in spite of title).

14.72 **Wilkins**, Kay S., 'Some aspects of the irrational in eighteenth-century France', *Stud.on Voltaire*, 138, 1975, 107-201. Largely a study of literary manifestations of interest in occult.

14.73 **Roodenburg**, H. W., 'The autobiography of Isabella de Moerloose. Sex, childrearing, and popular belief in seventeenth-century Holland', *J.Soc.Hist.*, 18, 1985, 517-40. Discusses curious autobiography publ. in 1695 by widow of elderly clergyman.

14.74 **Schama**, S., *The Embarrassment of Riches. An Interpretation of Dutch Culture in the Golden Age*, 1987. Main theme is Dutch self-perception, as revealed in art, literature, and material possessions – esp. conflicting drives of pleasure and puritanism. Generous in scale and engagingly written. His article 'The unruly realm. Appetite and restraint in seventeenth-century Holland', *Daedalus*, 108 (iii), 1979, 103-24, which starts from

Jan Steen's genre paintings, gives some flavour of work. See also 14.256.

SPAIN AND ITALY
On Spain see also 6.128; 14.22,327,394.
On Italy 11.342; 14.10,21.

14.75 **Bennassar**, B., *Spanish Character. Attitudes and Mentalities from the Sixteenth to the Nineteenth Century*, Berkeley, Calif., 1979. Transl. from French ed. of 1976. Fascinating, but largely based on impressionistic sources and generalisations.

14.76 **Callahan**, W. J., 'Utility, material progress, and morality in eighteenth-century Spain', in Fritz and Williams (12.16), 353-68. Details clerical hostility to over-energetic commercial profit-seeking.

14.77 **Caro Baroja**, J., 'Honour and shame. A historical account of several conflicts', in J.-G. Peristiany, ed., *Honour and Shame. The Values of Mediterranean Society*, 1965, 81-137. Some facts and ideas on changes which these concepts have undergone in Spanish society.

14.78 **Chauchadis**, C., *Honneur, Morale, et Société dans l'Espagne de Philippe II*, Paris, 1984. Study based on moralistic works of period.

14.79 **Redondo**, A., and Rochon, A., eds., *Visages de la Folie, 1500-1650 (Domaine Hispano-Italien)*, Paris, 1981. On importance of "folly" theme in Renaissance culture. Cf. 14.36,383.

14.80 **Saugnieux**, J., *Cultures Populaires et Cultures Savantes en Espagne, du Moyen Age aux Lumières*, Paris, 1982. Essays rather than connected narrative. Three deal with broad questions of eighteenth-century religion and culture.

14.81 **Burke**, P., *The Historical Anthropology of Early Modern Italy. Essays on Perception and Communication*, 1987. Sixteen self-contained but related essays, some previously publ., concentrating on codes of conduct, popular religion, rituals, etc.

14.82 **Camporesi**, P., *Il Paese della Fame*, Bologna, 1978. See also his *Il Pane Selvaggio*, Bologna, 1980; and *La Carne Impassibile*, Milan, 1983. Interesting but idiosyncratic works which pile up texts suggesting deranging effects of hunger, hallucigens, and charnel-house sights and smells on early modern mentalities. See also his essay in 14.265.

14.83 **Carroll**, Linda L., 'Carnival rites as vehicles of protest in Renaissance Venice', *Sixteenth-Cent.J.*, 16, 1985, 487-502. Relates social criticism in comedies of Angelo Beolco (Ruzante) to carnival tradition.

14.84 **Dundes**, A., *La Terra in Piazza. An interpretation of the Palio of Siena*, Berkeley, Calif., 1975. Some historical dimension. But see criticism of S. Silverman, 'On the uses of history in anthropology: the Palio of Siena', *Am.Ethnol.*, 6, 1979, 413-36, which views his symbolic interpretation and various other anthropological models as essentially ahistoric.

14.85 **Ginzburg**, C., *The Cheese and the Worms. The Cosmos of a Sixteenth-Century Miller*, 1980. Transl. from Italian ed. of 1976. Much admired exploration of ideas and beliefs revealed by heretic from Friuli region. See also abridged version in Obelkevich (13.30), 87-167.

14.86 **Hughes**, Diane O., 'Distinguishing signs. Ear-rings, Jews, and Franciscan rhetoric in the Italian Renaissance city', *P.& P.*, 112, 1986, 3-59. On fortunes of the ear-ring, mark of Jews and prostitutes which finally attained respectability.

CENTRAL, NORTHERN, AND EASTERN EUROPE

See also on Germany 13.222; on the Balkans 3.317; on Russia 14.396.

14.87 **Dülmen**, R. van, ed., *Kultur der Einfachen Leute. Bayerisches Volksleben vom 16. bis zum 19. Jahrhundert*, Munich, 1983. Essay collection. Those relevant to early modern period deal with houses as private space; witchcraft in Munich c.1600; village brawls; and premarital sex.

14.88 **Lottes**, G., 'Popular culture and the early modern state in sixteenth-century Germany', in Kaplan (9.541), 147-88. Examines various aspects of attempts by state and elite to tighten social discipline (tenurial obligations, dress, holidays, etc.).

14.89 **Medick**, H., 'Village spinning bees. Sexual culture and free time among rural youth in early modern Germany', in Medick and Sabean (5.339), 317-39. Mixed gatherings, ostensibly to allow women to work in sociable atmosphere, which caused concern to moralists when used for courtship and general boisterousness.

14.90 **Sabean**, D. W., *Power in the Blood. Popular Culture and Village Discourse in Early Modern Germany*, 1984. Studies interactions in small agricultural communities of Württemberg from sixteenth to eighteenth centuries. Review article: T. Robisheaux, *Peasant Stud.*, 14, 1987, 105-18.

14.91 **Schmidt**, J., 'Humanism and popular culture', in G. Hoffmeister, ed., *Renaissance and Reformation in Germany, an Introduction*, New York, 1977, 177-88.

14.92 **Smoller**, Laura A., 'Playing cards and popular culture in sixteenth-century Nuremberg', *Sixteenth-Cent.J.*, 17, 1986, 183-214. Suggests that card-playing (and earthy humour displayed on cards) continued to have cross-class appeal unaffected by Reformation.

14.93 **Taylor**, P., and Rebel, H., 'Hessian peasant women, their families, and the draft. A social-historical interpretation of four tales from the Grimm collection', *J.Family Hist.*, 6, 1981, 347-78. Claims these tales show response to inheritance patterns and destructive effects of military conscription system in eighteenth-century Hesse that is corroborated by other sources.

14.94 **Evans**, R. J. W., 'The significance of the White Mountain for the culture of the Czech lands', *Bull.Inst.Hist.Res.*, 44, 1971, 34-54. Examines broad cultural implications of resurgent Catholicism after 1621.

14.95 **Clogg**, R., 'Elite and popular culture in Greece under Turkish rule', in J. T. Koumoulides, ed., *Hellenic Perspectives. Essays in the History of Greece*, Lanham, Md., 1980, 107-43. Deals with period of "neo-Hellenic enlightenment" in late eighteenth century; literary evidence only.

14.96 'The Enlightenment in the Balkans', *E.Eur.Q.*, 9, 1975, 386-507. Conference proceedings dealing with broad cultural developments, role of Orthodox Church, etc.

14.97 **Mardin**, S., 'Some notes on an early phase in the modernization of communications in Turkey', *Comp.Stud.Soc.& Hist.*, 3, 1961, 250-76. On shaping of written Turkish in late eighteenth century and its importance in cultural modernisation.

14.98 **Schousboe**, Karen, 'The social dynamics of cultural signification in Denmark, 1400-1600', *Ethnol.Scan.*, 1984, 5-24.

Ritual of "shooting the parrot", practised by Danish guilds, explored as articulation of social relations.

14.99 **Dewey**, H. W., 'Old Muscovite concepts of injured honor (*Beschestie*)', *Slavic Rev.*, 27, 1968, 594-603. Charts increase in litigation of this type in sixteenth-century Russia.

14.100 —— and Stevens, K. B., 'Muscovites at play. Recreation in pre-Petrine Russia', *Can.-Am.Slavic Stud.*, 13, 1979, 189-203. Concentrates on ecclesiastical disapproval of many aspects of popular recreation.

14.101 **Martynova**, Antonina, 'The life of the pre-Revolutionary village as reflected in popular lullabies', in Ransel (5.412), 171-85. Based on collection of c.1,800 texts, mostly unpublished.

14.102 **Matossian**, Mary K., 'In the beginning God was a woman', *J.Soc.Hist.*, 6, 1973, 325-43. Suggests that some female personages and activities found in Russian peasant folklore and religion are survivals of prehistoric Mother Goddess cults.

14.103 **Perrie**, Maureen, *The Image of Ivan the Terrible in Russian Folklore*, 1987. Copious appendix of transl. texts. Favourable image of Tsar reveals problems of tracing chronology of folklore.

14.104 **Rogger**, H., *National Consciousness in Eighteenth-Century Russia*, Cambridge, Mass., 1960. Deals with growing self-awareness of specifically Russian culture.

14.105 **Smith**, R. E. F., 'Time, space, and use in early Russia', in Aston and others (7.192), 273-93. Examines vocabulary and measurement of time, distance, weight, etc.

ATTITUDES TO DEATH
See also 3.49; 5.107; 6.3; 13.58.

14.106 **Ariès**, P., *The Hour of our Death*, 1981. Transl. from French ed. of 1977. Challenging and lengthy survey of changing attitudes to death in Christian world since late antiquity. Lacks material on economics of dying. Review articles: J. P. Carse, *Hist.& Theory*, 21, 1982, 399-410; L. Stone (1.19), 242-59.

14.107 —— *Western Attitudes toward Death from the Middle Ages to the Present*, Baltimore, Md., 1974. Preliminary sketch of previous entry, given as lectures at Johns Hopkins University.

14.108 **Chartier**, R., 'Les arts de mourir,

1450-1600', *Annales*, 31, 1976, 51-75. Analysis of manuscripts and books on theme of preparation for death. Subsequent period dealt with in Roche (14.118).

14.109 **Chaunu**, P., *La Mort à Paris. 16e, 17e, et 18e Siècles*, Paris, 1978. Data drawn mostly from large-scale enquiry into wills. Three broad sections: theology of death; causes and patterns; preparations made by dying. Review article: J. Meyer, *Rev.Hist.*, 263, 1980, 403-16.

14.110 **Christensen**, C. C., 'The significance of the epitaph monument in early Lutheran ecclesiastical art. Some social and iconographical considerations', in Buck and Zophy (12.119), 297-314. Looks at social and religious values expressed in funeral monuments and tablets.

14.111 **Etlin**, R. A., *The Architecture of Death. The Transformation of the Cemetery in Eighteenth-Century Paris*, Cambridge, Mass., 1984. Copiously illustrated history of landscaping and monumental architecture of cemeteries. Many sidelights on treatment of death.

14.112 **Favre**, R., *La Mort dans la Littérature et la Pensée Françaises au Siècle des Lumières*, Lyon, 1978. As well as attitudes displayed by preachers, philosophers, and early romantics, studies efforts of doctors and administrators to prolong expectation of life.

14.113 **Highsmith**, Anne L., 'Religion and peasant attitudes toward death in eighteenth-century Portugal. The parish of São Cristóvão de Rio Mau, 1747-85', *Peasant Stud.*, 11, 1983, 5-18. Evidence from wills of parish in Minho region.

14.114 **Le Roy Ladurie**, E., 'Chaunu, Lebrun, Vovelle. The new history of death', in Le Roy Ladurie (4.35), 273-84. Three French historians who have explored this theme.

14.115 **McManners**, J., *Death and the Enlightenment. Changing Attitudes to Death among Christians and Unbelievers in Eighteenth-Century France*, 1981. Quarrels to some extent with Vovelle's hypothesis of "de-Christianisation" (see 13.58).

14.116 **Mitchell**, A., 'Philippe Ariès and the French way of death. *Fr.Hist.Stud.*, 10, 1978, 684-95. Notes some shifts of emphasis and unsatisfactory generalisations in Ariès' works (see 14.106-7). See also Mitchell's earlier criticism in *Proc.Western Soc.Fr.Hist.*, 4,

1976, 155-63.

14.117 **Prosperi**, A., ed., 'I vivi e i morti', *Quad.Stor.*, 50, 1982, 391-627; 51, 1982, 903-1025. Symposium on various aspects of death and belief in after-life, mainly in Italian context.

14.118 **Roche**, D., ' "La mémoire de la mort". Recherche sur la place des arts de mourir dans la librairie et la lecture en France aux 17e et 18e siècles', *Annales*, 31, 1976, 76-119. Continues 14.108.

4.119 **Tenenti**, A., *Il Senso della Morte e l'Amore della Vita nel Rinascimento (Francia e Italia)*, Turin, 1957. Expands an earlier, interestingly illustrated work, *La Vie et la Mort à travers l'Art du 15e Siècle*, Paris, 1952.

14.120 **Vogler**, B., 'La législation sur les sépultures dans l'Allemagne protestante au 16e siècle', *Rev.Hist.Mod.et Contemp.*, 22, 1975, 191-232. Charts considerable change in attitudes to death and after-life brought about by Reformation.

14.121 **Vovelle**, M., 'The history of mankind in the mirror of death', *Proc.Western Soc.Fr.Hist.*, 6, 1978, 91-109. Reflective piece on sources and interpretations involved in historiography of death.

14.122 —— *La Mort et l'Occident de 1300 à nos Jours*, Paris, 1983. Lengthy study, but often stronger on assertion than documented evidence.

14.123 —— *Mourir Autrefois. Attitudes Collectives devant la Mort au 17e et 18e Siècles*, Paris, 1974. Collection of source readings, virtually all from French material.

14.124 **Whaley**, J., ed., *Mirrors of Mortality. Studies in the Social History of Death*, 1981. Essays of interest for early modern period are Whaley on late seventeenth- and eighteenth- century funerals at Hamburg (80-105); J. McManners on 'Death and the French historians', historiographical study (106-30); and D. Irwin on design of monumental European tombs, 1750-1830 (131-53).

14.125 **Wilson**, S., 'Death and the social historians', *Soc.Hist.*, 5, 1980, 435-51.

EDUCATION AND LITERACY
See also 10.472; 11.173.

14.126 **Graff**, H. J., *Literacy in History. An Interdisciplinary Research Bibliography*, New York, 1981. Very thorough, though topical arrangement makes period approach somewhat cumbersome. Has short introductory section on primary sources. For other bibliographical and historiographical material see also 14.131,135,141,145.

14.127 **Bowen**, J., *A History of Western Education*, 3 vols., 1972-81. Useful broadly based account. Early modern period straddles vols.2-3.

14.128 **Bowman**, Mary J., and Arnold, C. A., 'Human capital and economic modernization in historical perspective', in *Proc.Fourth International Conference of Economic History* (9.11), 247-72. Wide-ranging discussion of economic effects of diffusion of education, beginning with early modern period.

14.129 **Chartier**, R., 'Student populations in the eighteenth century', *Brit.J.Eighteenth-Cent.Stud.*, 2, 1979, 150-62. Presents some data from research project, more fully described in *Rev.Hist.Mod.et Contemp.*, 25, 1978, 353-74.

14.130 **Cipolla**, C., *Literacy and Development in the West*, 1969. Opened up subject, but only a brief sketch.

14.131 **Fletcher**, J. M., and Deahl, J., 'European universities, 1300-1700. The development of research, 1969-81, and a summary bibliography', in Kittelson (13.150), 324-77.

14.132 **Garin**, E., *L'Éducation de l'Homme Moderne. La Pédagogie de la Renaissance*, Paris, 1968. First publ. in Italian, 1957. Study of educational thought and ideals, without much social context.

14.133 **Graff**, H. J., 'On literacy in the Renaissance. Review and reflections', *Hist.Educ.*, 12, 1983, 69-85.

14.134 **Hexter**, J. H., 'Education of the aristocracy in the Renaissance', *J.Mod.Hist.*, 22, 1950, 1-20. Repr. in his *Reappraisals in History*, 1961 (2nd ed., 1979), 45-70. Useful, though primary emphasis is on England.

14.135 **Houston**, R., 'Literacy and society in the

West, 1500-1850', *Soc.Hist.*, 8, 1983, 269-93. Valuable bibliographical essay.

14.136 **Leith**, J. A., ed., 'Facets of education in the eighteenth century', *Stud.on Voltaire*, 167, 1977, whole volume. Contains general surveys of most European countries or regions, concentrating on later eighteenth century and trend towards secular education. On universities note C. E. McClelland (on Germany), 169-89, and G. M. Addy (on Spain), 475-89.

14.137 **Maynes**, Mary J., *Schooling in Western Europe. A Social History*, New York, 1985. Useful approach from several angles, covering early modern and nineteenth-century Europe.

14.138 —— *Schooling for the People. Comparative Local Studies of Schooling History in France and Germany, 1750-1850*, New York, 1985. Compares schooling in villages of Vaucluse and Baden (respectively Catholic and Protestant areas): considers communal resources rather than religion is explanation for much higher attendance in Baden.

14.139 —— 'The virtues of archaism. The political economy of schooling in Europe, 1750-1850', *Comp.Stud.Soc.& Hist.*, 21, 1979, 611-25. Article based on research for previous entry.

14.140 **Ong**, W. J., 'Latin language study as a Renaissance puberty rite', *Stud.in Philology*, 56, 1959, 103-24.

14.141 **Parker**, G., 'An educational revolution? The growth of literacy and schooling in early modern Europe', *Tijd.Geschied.*, 93, 1980, 210-20. Good starting point. Discusses in particular Furet and Ozouf (14.160), Johansson (14.225), and Strauss (14.211).

14.142 **Pollard**, H. M., *Pioneers of Popular Education, 1760-1850*, Cambridge, Mass., 1957. First half of book deals with continental Europe.

14.143 **Stock**, Phyllis. *Better than Rubies. The History of Women's Education*, New York, 1978. Covers Europe and United States from Renaissance to twentieth century. Review article: Elizabeth S. Cohen, *Hist.Educ.Q.*, 19, 1979, 151-5.

14.144 **Talbott**, J. E., 'Education in intellectual and social history', *Daedalus*, 100, 1971, 133-50. Repr. in Gilbert and Graubard (1.9), 193-210. Many interesting questions raised, including functionalist approach. See also Gillian Sutherland, 'The study of

the history of education', *History*, 54, 1969, 49-59.

14.145 **Trenard**, L., 'Histoire des sciences de l'éducation (période moderne)', *Rev.Hist.*, 257, 1977, 429-72. Bibliographical review of work appearing since c.1950.

FRANCE AND THE LOW COUNTRIES

See also 5.494-5; 6.60; 10.297; 11.129,216-17; 13.47; 14.138.

14.146 **Artz**, F. B., *The Development of Technical Education in France, 1500-1850*, Cambridge, Mass., 1966. Rather perfunctory on period down to 1750.

14.147 **Bailey**, C. R., *French Secondary Education, 1763-90. The Secularization of ex-Jesuit collèges*, Philadelphia, 1978. Review article: D. Young, *Hist.Educ.Q.*, 20, 1980, 363-8.

14.148 —— 'Municipal *collèges*. Small-town secondary schools in France prior to the Revolution', *Fr.Hist.Stud.*, 12, 1982, 351-76. Examines work of 35 municipal schools in ressort of Parlement of Paris.

14.149 **Barnard**, H. C., *Girls at School under the Ancien Régime*, 1954. Short university lecture course. Mainly on convent schools, but gives some account of provision for poorer classes. See also 14.158.

14.150 **Brockliss**, L. W. B., *French Higher Education in the Seventeenth and Eighteenth Centuries. A Cultural History*, 1987. Principally on curriculum, but has long introductory section on environment of students and professoriate, and biographical appendix.

14.151 —— 'Patterns of attendance at the University of Paris, 1400-1800', *Hist.J.*, 21, 1978, 503-44. Shows that Paris, perhaps because of its exclusion of civil law, did not share boom in attendance noted elsewhere in Europe between 1550 and 1650.

14.152 **Chartier**, R., and others, *L'Éducation en France du 16e au 18e Siècle*, Paris, 1976. Attempt to quantify various aspects of education such as college attendance, literacy, distribution of schools, etc. Marked emphasis on conservative function of system.

14.153 **Chisick**, H., 'French charity schools in the seventeenth and eighteenth centuries, with special reference to the case of Amiens',

Hist.Sociale/Social Hist., 16, 1983, 241-77.
Notes that those granted free education
seem not to have been from poorest section
of community.

14.154 —— *Limits of Reform in the Enlightenment.
Attitudes towards the Education of the Lower
Classes in Eighteenth-Century France*,
Princeton, 1981. Examines background
and views of some sixty figures who
initiated or published projects for
appropriate education of artisans and
peasants.

14.155 —— 'Institutional innovation in popular
education in eighteenth-century France.
Two examples', *Fr.Hist.Stud.*, 10, 1977,
41-73. Work in progress for previous
entry, dealing with *École des Arts* at
Amiens and Comte de Thélis' *écoles
nationales*.

14.156 —— 'School attendance, literacy, and
acculturation. *Petites écoles* and popular
education in eighteenth-century France',
Europa, 3, 1980, 185-221. Argues that
primary aim of popular education was
socialisation through religion and not
literacy skills.

14.157 **Dainville**, F. de, 'Effectifs des collèges et
scolarité aux 17e et 18e siècles dans le
nord-est de la France', *Population*, 10,
1955, 455-88. Material drawn from records
of 21 Jesuit colleges. In further article, *ib.*,
12, 1957, 467-94, more scattered
information given on other regions.

14.158 **Dubois**, Elfrieda T., 'The education of
women in seventeenth-century France',
Fr.Stud., 32, 1978, 1-19. Offers little new
material. Same can be said of Samia I.
Spencer, 'Women and education in
eighteenth-century France', *Proc.Western
Soc.Fr.Hist.*, 10, 1982, 274-84.

14.159 **Frijhoff**, W. T. M., and Julia, D., *École et
Société dans la France d'Ancien Régime.
Quatre Exemples, Auch, Avallon, Condom,
et Gisors*, Paris, 1975. Well-researched
investigation into social origins and
destinies of students who got secondary
education in these small provincial towns
in eighteenth century.

14.160 **Furet**, F., and Ozouf, J., *Reading and
Writing. Literacy in France from Calvin to
Jules Ferry*, 1982. Transl. from French ed.
of 1977. For review article see 14.141.

14.161 **Grafton**, A., 'Teacher, text, and pupil in
the Renaissance classroom. A case study
from a Parisian college', *Hist.Univ.*, 1,
1981, 37-70. Teaching methods of classics

lecturer deduced from text annotations.

14.162 **Houdaille**, J., 'Les signatures au mariage
de 1740 à 1829', *Population*, 32, 1977,
65-89. Study of increasing literacy as
testified by marriage register signatures.

14.163 **Hudson**, Elizabeth K., 'The Protestant
struggle for survival in early Bourbon
France. The case of the Huguenot schools',
Arch.Reformationsgesch., 76, 1985, 271-95.
Finds close similarities of organisation and
curriculum between Protestant and Jesuit
colleges.

14.164 **Huppert**, G., *Public Schools in Renaissance
France*, Urbana, Ill., 1984. Deals with
municipal colleges for secondary education
created in some numbers well before
better-known spread of Jesuit institutions.
Review article: G. Strauss, *J.Soc.Hist.*, 19,
1985, 361-7.

14.165 **Julia**, D., 'L'enseignement primaire dans
le diocèse de Reims à la fin de l'ancien
régime', *Ann.Hist.Révol.Fr.*, 42, 1970,
233-86. Based on Archbishop's enquiry
sent out to all parishes in 1773.

14.166 —— and Pressly, P., 'La population
scolaire en 1789. Les extravagances du
Ministre Villemain', *Annales*, 30, 1975,
1516-61. Confronts a nineteenth-century
enquiry on educational resources before
the Revolution with contemporary
evidence.

14.167 **Leith**, J., 'The idea of the inculcation of
national patriotism in French educational
thought, 1750-89', in Browning (11.300),
59-77.

14.168 **Ligou**, D., 'The University of Dijon in the
eighteenth century', *Brit.J.Eighteenth-
Cent.Stud.*, 3, 1980, 47-57.

14.169 **Markoff**, J., 'Some effects of literacy in
eighteenth-century France',
J.Interdisc.Hist., 17, 1986, 311-33.
Examines parish *cahiers de doléances* to
establish whether there were significant
differences between areas of high and low
literacy levels.

14.170 **Palmer**, R. R., 'Free secondary education
in France before and after the Revolution',
Hist.Educ.Q., 14, 1974, 437-52. Argues
that free educational provision was
markedly more limited in 1850 than in
1780.

14.171 —— 'Old regime origins of the Napoleonic
educational structure', in Hinrichs and
others (7.42), 318-33.

14.172 **Parias**, L.-H., ed., *Histoire Générale de
l'Enseignement et de l'Éducation en France*,

2. *De Gutenberg aux Lumières*, Paris, 1981. Handsomely illustrated synthesis, part of 4-vol. history covering place of child in society and education at all levels. This vol. is by F. Lebrun, M. Venard, and J. Quéniart.

14.173 **Snyders**, G., *La Pédagogie en France aux 17e et 18e Siècles*, Paris, 1965. Concentrates on changing attitudes to child psychology, and hence shift from traditional curriculum to freer mode.

14.174 **Viguerie**, J. de, *L'Institution des Enfants. L'Éducation en France, 16e-18e Siècle*, Paris, 1978. Popular account, but takes fairly wide view.

14.175 **Vovelle**, M., 'Y a-t-il eu une révolution culturelle au 18e siècle? A propos de l'éducation populaire en Provence', *Rev.Hist.Mod.et Contemp.*, 22, 1975, 89-141. Presents pessimistic picture of educational stagnation.

14.176 **Frijhoff**, W. T. M, *La Société Néerlandais et ses Gradués, 1575-1814*, Amsterdam, 1981. Impressive computer study of graduates turned out by universities of United Provinces (omits those with incomplete register series).

SPAIN AND ITALY
On Spain see also 13.67; 14.136. On Italy 10.511; 13.139-40.

14.177 **Cobban**, A. B., 'Elective salaried lectureships in the universities of Southern Europe in the pre-Reformation era', *Bull.J.Rylands Lib.*, 67, 1985, 662-87. Shows that students still played important part in some appointments well into sixteenth century, esp. in Iberian faculties.

14.178 **Addy**, G. M., 'Alcalá before reform – the decadence of a Spanish university', *Hisp.Am.Hist.Rev.*, 48, 1968, 561-85. Describes conditions in early eighteenth century.

14.179 —— *The Enlightenment in the University of Salamanca*, Durham, N.C., 1966. On reforms in curriculum and appointments system between 1770 and 1807.

14.180 **Kagan**, R. L., *Students and Society in Early Modern Spain*, Baltimore, Md., 1974. Deals principally with increasing ties between universities and legal bureaucracy.

14.181 —— 'Universities in Castile, 1500-1810', in L. Stone, ed., *The University in Society*, Princeton, N.J., 1975, 2, 355-405. Stresses

dominance of legal studies, and offers suggestions as to why demand for lawyers should have lessened with consequent detriment to universities in seventeenth and eighteenth centuries.

14.182 —— 'Universities in Castile, 1500-1700', *P.& P.*, 49, 1970, 44-71. Covers similar ground to previous entry, with more emphasis on buoyant phase.

14.183 **Lanning**, J. T., 'The university in Spain and the Indies. Point and counterpoint', *Med.& Renaiss.Stud*, 4, 1968, 111-33. Impressionistic comparison of home and colonial universities.

14.184 **Larquié**, C., 'L'alphabétisation à Madrid en 1650', *Rev.Hist.Mod.et Contemp.*, 28, 1981, 132-57. Evidence on literacy culled from signatures in notarial archives.

14.185 **Peset**, M., and Peset, J. L., *La Universidad Española, Siglos 18 y 19. Despotismo Ilustrado y Revolución Liberal*, Madrid, 1974. Substantial work.

14.186 **Saugnieux**, J., 'Alphabétisation et enseignement élémentaire dans l'Espagne du 18e siècle', in his *Les Mots et les Livres. Études d'Histoire Culturelle*, Lyon, 1986, 113-237. Useful *mise au point* based on secondary sources or contemporary treatises.

14.187 **Varela**, Julia, *Modos de Educación en la España de la Contrarreforma*, Madrid, 1983. Mainly on doctrinal content of education.

14.188 **Baldo**, V., *Alunni, Maestri, e Scuole in Venezia alla Fine del 16 Secolo*, Como, 1977. Evidence based mainly on professions of faith collected from over 250 teachers in 1587.

14.189 **Black**, R., 'The *Studio Aretino* in the fifteenth and early sixteenth centuries', *Hist.Univ.*, 5, 1985, 55-82. On why decaying city of Arezzo sought to revive its university.

14.190 **Brizzi**, G. P., *La Formazione della Classe Dirigente nel Sei-Settecento. I Seminaria Nobilium nell' Italia Centro-Settentrionale*, Bologna, 1976. Valuable study of colleges for gentry at Bologna, Parma, Siena, and Modena.

14.191 **Chambers**, D. S., 'Studium Urbis and *gabella Studii*. The University of Rome in the fifteenth century', in Clough (10.224), 68-110. Good study of precarious finances and other aspects of Roman Studium.

14.192 **Goldthwaite**, R. A., 'Schools and teachers

of commercial arithmetic in Renaissance Florence', *J.Eur.Ec.Hist.*, 1, 1972, 418-33. Evidence provided by a teacher's contract of 1519.

14.193 **Grendler**, P. F., 'The organization of primary and secondary education in the Italian Renaissance', *Cath.Hist.Rev.*, 71, 1985, 185-205. Reaches well back into Middle Ages, but gives most emphasis to Venetian schools of late sixteenth century.

14.194 —— 'What Zuanne read in school. Vernacular texts in sixteenth-century Venetian schools', *Sixteenth-Cent.J.*, 13 (i), 1982, 41-54. Drawn from evidence mentioned in 14.188.

14.195 **Schutte**, Anne J., 'Teaching adults to read in sixteenth-century Venice. Giovanni Antonio Tagliente's *Libro Maistrevole*', *Sixteenth-Cent.J.*, 17, 1986, 3-16. Describes reading primer publ. in 1524.

GERMANY
See also 5.505,632; 13.150; 14.136,138.

14.196 **Evans**, R. J. W., 'German universities after the Thirty Years War', *Hist.Univ.*, 1, 1981, 169-90. General overview.

14.197 **Fletcher**, J. M., 'Change and resistance to change. A consideration of the development of English and German universities during the sixteenth century', *ib.*, 1-36. Mainly general administrative and curriculum history.

14.198 **Friedrichs**, C. R., 'Whose house of learning? Some thoughts on German schools in post-Reformation Germany', *Hist.Educ.Q.*, 22, 1982, 371-7. Title carries reference to book by G. Strauss (14.211), which is chided for saying too little on workings of schools themselves. Offers corrective examples from Brunswick and Frankfurt.

14.199 **Gawthrop**, R., and Strauss, G., 'Protestantism and literacy in early modern Germany', *P.& P.*, 104, 1984, 31-55. Contends that Bible-reading (insofar as it was stimulus to literacy) was promoted much more by eighteenth-century Pietism than by sixteenth-century Reformation.

14.200 **Green**, L., 'Education of women in the Reformation', *Hist.Educ.Q.*, 19, 1979, 93-116. Contends there was rapid expansion of educational provision for girls in sixteenth-century Protestant Germany.

14.201 **Helmreich**, E. C., *Religious Education in German Schools. An Historical Approach*, Cambridge, Mass., 1959. Standard work covering Reformation period onwards.

14.202 **La Vopa**, A. J., *Prussian Schoolteachers. Profession and Office, 1763-1848*, Chapel Hill, N.C., 1980. Mainly on conditions of rural primary teachers and their unsuccessful struggles for state salary and professional status.

14.203 —— 'Vocations, careers, and talent. Lutheran pietism and sponsored mobility in eighteenth-century Germany', *Comp.Stud.Soc.& Hist.*, 28, 1986, 255-86. Examines social context of ideas of August Hermann Francke of Halle Univ., who sought to strengthen recruitment of clergy by providing educational ladder for indigent.

14.204 **McClelland**, C. E., 'Aristocracy and university reform in eighteenth-century Germany', in L. Stone, ed., *Schooling and Society. Studies in the History of Education*, Baltimore, Md., 1976, 146-73. Chronicles founding of Göttingen University (1737) as deliberate attempt by Hanoverian state to provide curriculum attractive to nobility.

14.205 —— *State, Society, and University in Germany, 1700-1914*, 1980. Excellent discussion of social function of universities, and state's influence on them; recruitment of professoriate and student body; and relation to general process of modernisation.

14.206 **Neugebauer**, W., *Absolutischer Staat und Schulwirklichkeit in Brandenburg-Preussen*, New York, 1985. Lengthy study illustrating how far actuality was from government aims in eighteenth-century village schools; less concerned to ask what local society wanted of its schools.

14.207 **Overfield**, J. H., 'Nobles and paupers at German universities to 1600', *Societas*, 4, 1974, 175-210. Seeks explanation for increasing percentage of nobles and decline in "poor students" in matriculation lists.

14.208 **Petschauer**, P., 'Improving educational opportunities for girls in eighteenth-century Germany', *Eighteenth-Cent.Life*, 3, 1976, 56-62. Very short, but contains useful information, esp. in notes.

14.209 **Richter**, J., 'Zur Schriftkundigkeit mecklenburgischer Bauern im 17. Jahrhundert', *Jb.Wirtschaftsgesch.*, 1981 (iii), 79-102. Evidence from late seventeenth-century peasant letters on literacy levels and modes of expression.

14.210 **Schleunes**, K. A., 'Enlightenment, reform, reaction. The schooling revolution in Prussia', *Central Eur.Hist.*, 12, 1979, 315-42. On changing motivation of *Volksschule* policy as it developed from late eighteenth century to 1820s.

14.211 **Strauss**, G., *Luther's House of Learning. Indoctrination of the Young in the German Reformation*, Baltimore, Md., 1978. Important study of educational aims of Reformers, which argues that real impact on popular culture was extremely limited. Review article: M. U. Edwards, *Hist.Educ.Q.*, 21, 1981, 471-7. See also 13.228.

14.212 —— 'Lutheranism and literacy. A reassessment', in Greyerz (5.301), 109-23. Similar theme.

14.213 —— 'Reformation and pedagogy. Educational thought and practice in the Lutheran Reformation', in Trinkaus and Oberman (5.451), 272-93. With addendum by L. W. Spitz, 294-306.

14.214 —— 'The state of pedagogical theory, c.1530. What Protestant reformers knew about education', in Stone (14.204), 69-94.

14.215 **Turner**, R. S., 'University reformers and professorial scholarship in Germany, 1760-1806', in Stone (14.181), 2, 495-531.

14.216 **Vogler**, B., 'La politique scolaire entre Rhin et Moselle. L'exemple du Duché de Deux Ponts (1556-1619)', *Francia*, 3, 1975, 236-320; 4, 1976, 287-364. Extended study of elementary education provision and policy in small Protestant territory.

14.217 **Wright**, W. J., 'The impact of the Reformation on Hessian education', *Church Hist.*, 44, 1975, 182-98. Philip of Hesse's educational programme.

EASTERN AND NORTHERN EUROPE
On Russia see also 6.255; 10.538; 14.272.

14.218 **Adler**, P. J., 'Habsburg school reform among the Orthodox minorities, 1770-80', *Slavic Rev.*, 33, 1974, 23-45. On extension of education for Serbs and Rumanians.

14.219 **Domonkos**, L. S., 'The state of education in Hungary on the eve of the Battle of Mohács (1526)', *Can.-Am.Rev.Hungarian Stud.*, 2, 1975, 3-20. Brief survey ranging from university study to village schools.

14.220 **Melton**, J. V. H., 'From image to word. Cultural reform and the rise of literate culture in eighteenth-century Austria', *J.Mod.Hist.*, 58, 1986, 95-124. Why church and state came round to idea of universal literacy as desirable means of controlling opinion.

14.221 **Odlozilík**, O., 'Education, religion, and politics in Bohemia, 1526-1621', *J.World Hist.*, 13, 1971, 172-203. Survey, mainly of higher education, during period of religious pluralism.

14.222 **Litak**, S., 'The parochial school network in Poland prior to the establishment of the Commission of National Education (first half of the eighteenth century)', *Acta Poloniae Hist.*, 27, 1973, 45-66.

14.223 **Szreter**, R., 'Education for nation-saving. Poland between the partitions', in T. G. Cook, ed., *The History of Education in Europe*, 1974, 53-66. Efforts of Commission for National Education to foster patriotism by emphasis on Polish language, geography, and history in period 1773-94.

14.224 **Bagge**, S., 'Nordic students at foreign universities until 1660', *Scan.J.Hist.*, 9, 1984, 1-29. Survey extending from twelfth century onwards.

14.225 **Johansson**, E., *The History of Literacy in Sweden in Comparison with Some Other Countries*, Umeå, 1977. Lengthy extract, dealing with "reading campaign" fostered by parish examination system after 1686, in H. J. Graff, ed., *Literacy and Social Development in the West. A Reader*, 1981, 151-82.

14.226 **Nilehn**, L., 'Swedish society and Swedish students abroad in the seventeenth century', in Rystad (5.254), 101-17. Examines background and careers of over 2000 students who attended foreign universities, mostly German.

14.227 **Bissonnette**, G., 'Peter the Great and the Church as an educational institution', in Curtiss (1.70), 3-19. On Peter's increasing direction of church educational facilities towards secular admissions.

14.228 **Black**, J. L., *Citizens for the Fatherland. Education, Educators, and Pedagogical Ideals in Eighteenth-Century Russia*, Boulder, Colo., 1979. Study in plans, projects, and blue-prints, rather than actual conditions.

14.229 —— 'Educating women in eighteenth-century Russia. Myths and realities', *Can.Slavonic Pap.*, 20, 1978, 23-43. Mainly concerned with Catherine II's Smolny institutions.

14.230 **De Madariaga**, Isabel, 'Foundation of the

Russian educational system by Catherine II', *Slavonic & E.Eur.Rev.*, 57, 1979, 369-95.

14.231 **Hans**, N., 'Polish schools in Russia, 1772-1831', *ib.*, 38, 1960, 394-414. On educational provision for *szlachta* minority in Lithuanian and Ukrainian regions of former Polish kingdom.

14.232 **Jones**, W. G., 'The *Morning Light* charity schools, 1777-80', *ib.*, 56, 1978, 47-67. Charity schools partly financed by establishment of monthly magazine *Morning Light*.

14.233 **Krumbholz**, J., *Die Elementarbildung in Russland bis zum Jahre 1864*, Wiesbaden, 1982. Though main focus is on making of 1864 statute on primary education, system – or lack of it – is traced from seventeenth century onwards.

14.234 **Medlin**, W. K., 'Cultural crisis in Orthodox Rus' in the sixteenth and seventeenth centuries as a problem in education and social change',

Hist.Educ.Q., 9, 1969, 28-45. Principally on spread of education in Western Russia and Lithuania. See also similarly titled article in A. Blane, ed., *The Religious World of Russian Culture (Russia and Orthodoxy. Essays in Honor of G. Florovsky, 2)*, The Hague, 1975, 173-88.

14.235 **Okenfuss**, M. J., 'Education and empire. School reform in enlightened Russia', *Jb.Gesch.Osteuropas*, 27, 1979, 41-68. On values to be inculcated by new schools set up in 1780s.

14.236 —— 'The Jesuit origins of Petrine education', in Garrard (8.202), 106-30. Argues that Peter promoted education following humanistic model pioneered by Jesuits rather than on merely technological and utilitarian lines.

14.237 —— 'Technical training in Russia under Peter the Great', *Hist.Educ.Q.*, 13, 1973, 325-45. Deals principally with Moscow School of Mathematics and Navigation.

LEARNING AND THE ARTS

ELITE CULTURE. COURTS, ACADEMIES, AND THE LEARNED COMMUNITY

See also 2.19 (general); 3.25,35 (France); 3.137 (Spain); 3.161 (Italy); 3.240 (Germany).

14.238 **Burke**, P., 'Patrician culture. Venice and Amsterdam in the seventeenth century', *Trans.Roy.Hist.Soc.*, 5th ser., 23, 1973, 135-52.

14.239 **Corvisier**, A., *Arts et Sociétés dans l'Europe du 18e Siècle*, Paris, 1978. Brief and inevitably rather superficial, but touches on such questions as patronage, diffusion of taste, social position of artists and craftsmen, etc.

14.240 **Dickens**, A. G., ed., *The Courts of Europe. Politics, Patronage, and Royalty, 1400-1800*, 1977. Essays on most of principal courts of Europe from Burgundian dukes to Maria Theresa, with stress on patronage of art and learning.

14.241 **Gottschalk**, L., and others, *The Foundations of the Modern World (Unesco History of Mankind, 4)*, 2 parts, 1969. Largely history of elite culture.

14.242 **Koenigsberger**, H. G., 'Decadence or shift? Changes in the civilization of Italy and Europe in the sixteenth and seventeenth centuries', *Trans. Roy. Hist. Soc.*, 5th ser., 10, 1960, 1-18. Repr. in Koenigsberger (11.43), 278-97. Relates argued cultural decline of Italy to decline of civic vitality.

14.243 —— 'Republics and courts in Italian and European culture in the sixteenth and seventeenth centuries', *P.& P.*, 83, 1979, 32-56. Repr. in Koenigsberger (2.75), 237-61. Returns to theme of previous entry in somewhat wider context of decline of independent city states.

14.244 **Mandrou**, R., *From Humanism to Science, 1480-1700*, 1978. Transl. of French ed. of 1973. Overview of scientific and philosophical thought, emphasising secularisation of intellectual's role in society.

14.245 **Mousnier**, R., and Mesnard, J., eds., *L'Age d'Or du Mécénat, 1598-1661*, Paris, 1985. Conference proceedings. Over 40 short papers on cultural patronage, mainly, but not exclusively, in France.

14.246 **Porter**, R., and Teich, M., eds., *The Enlightenment in National Context*, 1981. Series of short essays on country by country basis. Good contributors (N. Hampson, S. Schama, T. C. W. Blanning, P. Dukes, E. Wangermann, etc.).

14.247 **Bodek**, Evelyn G., 'Salonières and bluestockings. Educated obsolescence and germinating feminism', *Feminist Stud.*, 3 (iii-iv), 1976, 185-99. Essay on French and English salons.

14.248 **Maland**, D., *Culture and Society in Seventeenth-Century France*, 1970. Survey of elite culture without any very clear theory of social determinants.

14.249 **Queniart**, J., *Culture et Société Urbaines dans la France de l'Ouest au 18e Siècle*, Paris, 1978. Rich study of literacy levels, book ownership, and general cultural life (at a more or less elite level) in nine cities.

14.250 **Rice**, E. F., 'The patrons of French humanism, 1490-1520', in Molho and Tedeschi (10.332), 687-702. Evidence taken from about 300 dedications.

14.251 **Roberts**, W., *Morality and Social Class in Eighteenth-Century French Literature and Painting*, Buffalo, N.Y., 1974. Argues that arts reflected aristocratic manners and values, even when intended for bourgeois audience.

14.252 **Roche**, D., *Le Siècle des Lumières en Province. Académies et Académiciens Provinciaux, 1680-1789*, 2 vols., Paris, 1978. Thorough study of membership and interests, with massive statistical appendix. Review article: K. M. Baker, *J.Mod.Hist.*, 53, 1981, 281-303.

14.253 —— 'La diffusion des lumières. Un exemple, l'Académie de Châlons-sur-Marne', *Annales*, 19, 1964, 887-922. Lengthy case-study from early phase of research for previous entry.

14.254 **Trenard**, L., *Lyon de l'Encyclopédie au Préromantisme*, 2 vols., Paris, 1958. Large-scale treatment of cultural institutions and political ideology of urban elite from c.1770 to 1815.

14.255 **Wiley**, W. L., *The Formal French*, Cambridge, Mass., 1967. Examines formalism in literature, ceremonial, art and architecture, etc., during old regime.

14.256 **Price**, J. L., *Culture and Society in the Dutch Republic during the Seventeenth Century*, 1974. Useful introduction, especially on reasons why painting remained popular as well as elite genre. See also 14.74,238.

14.257 **Linz**, J. J., 'Intellectual roles in sixteenth- and seventeenth-century Spain', *Daedalus*, 101 (iii), 1972, 59-108. Includes quantitative study of 300 writers published between 1500 and 1700.

14.258 **Benzoni**, G., *Gli Affanni della Cultura. Intellettuali e Potere nell'Italia della Contrariforma e Barocca*, Milan, 1978. Brings out often equivocal relationship of scholars and artists to world of power essential for their patronage. Similar themes in M. Cuaz, *Intellettuali, Potere, e Circolazione delle Idee nell'Italia Moderna, 1500-1700*, Turin, 1982.

14.259 **Burke**, P., *Culture and Society in Renaissance Italy, 1420-1540*, 1972. 2nd ed., 1974 (publ. as *Tradition and Innovation in Renaissance Italy*). 3rd ed., 1987 (with title *The Italian Renaissance. Culture and Society in Italy*). Fascinating attempt to tabulate social characteristics of Renaissance cultural elite and to test Burckhardt's intuitions about spirit of the age.

14.260 **Cochrane**, E., 'The profession of the historian in the Italian Renaissance', *J.Soc.Hist.*, 15, 1981, 51-72. Statistical survey of social provenance of historians and types of history to which they were drawn.

14.261 **Hay**, D., *The Italian Renaissance in its Historical Background*, 1962. 2nd ed., 1977.

14.262 'Intellettuali e centri di cultura', *Quad.Stor.*, 23, 1973, whole issue. Several articles on academies and learned societies in Italy.

14.263 **King**, Margaret L., *Venetian Humanism in an Age of Patrician Dominance*, Princeton, N.J., 1986. Analyses careers, social standing, and writings of almost one hundred core humanists.

14.264 **Logan**, O., *Culture and Society in Venice, 1470-1790. The Renaissance and its Heritage*, 1972. Main emphasis is on high culture, including useful chapters on patronage.

14.265 **Vivanti**, C., ed., *Intellettuali e Potere*, Turin, 1981. Vol.4 of *Annali* section of Einaudi *Storia d'Italia*. P. Camporesi, A. Prosperi, and A. Biondi in successive essays (81-304) deal with relations between intellectuals, Church, and common people. Other papers on education, publishing, etc.

14.266 **Brunschwig**, H., *Enlightenment and*

Romanticism in Eighteenth-Century Prussia, Chicago, 1974. Transl. from French ed. of 1947. Tends to see romanticism as product of professional blockages for educated young.

14.267 **Evans**, R. J. W., 'Learned societies in Germany in the seventeenth century', *Eur.Stud.Rev.*, 7, 1977, 129-51.

14.268 **Manheim**, E., 'The communicator and his audience. Liberals and traditionalists in eighteenth-century Germany', in W. J. Cahnman and A. Boskoff, eds., *Sociology and History. Theory and Research*, New York, 1964, 503-15. Discusses formation and methods of operation of literary and patriotic societies and masons.

14.269 **Wyrobisz**, A., 'The arts and social prestige in Poland between the sixteenth and eighteenth centuries', in Fedorowicz (3.283), 153-78. Mostly devoted to aristocratic patronage.

14.270 **Carmichael**, J., *The Cultural History of Russia*, 1968. Largely history of elite culture.

14.271 **Confino**, M., 'On intellectuals and intellectual tradition in eighteenth- and nineteenth-century Russia', *Daedalus*, 101 (ii), 1972, 117-49. Author defines as "halfway between an interpretative paper and a program of research".

14.272 **Tompkins**, S. R., *The Russian Mind from Peter the Great through the Enlightenment*, Norman, Okla., 1953. Contains chapters on education, press, and social thought, c.1700-1850.

PRINTING. BOOKS AND THEIR READERS

See also 13.169. On France 3.32; 9.671. On Holland 14.324. On Italy 10.512; 13.79. On Germany 6.250.

14.273 **Andries**, Lise, and others, eds., 'Littératures populaires', *Dix-Huitième Siècle*, 18, 1986, 5-187. Collection on popular reading; mainly, but not exclusively, French context.

14.274 **Barber**, G., 'The Cramers of Geneva and their trade in Europe between 1755 and 1766', *Stud.on Voltaire*, 30, 1964, 377-413. Business activities of Voltaire's printers.

14.275 **Darnton**, R., *The Business of Enlightenment. A Publishing History of the* Encyclopédie, *1775-1800*, Cambridge, 1979. Deals in great detail with production and finances of this international operation, and also analyses markets and

diffusion. Review articles: J. R. Censer, *J.Soc.Hist.*, 13, 1980, 629-38; K. M. Baker, *J.Mod.Hist.*, 53, 1981, 281-303; W. P. Vogt, *Hist.Educ.Q.*, 22, 1982, 89-98.

14.276 **Eisenstein**, Elizabeth L., *The Printing Press as an Agent of Change. Communications and Cultural Transformations in Early Modern Europe*, 2 vols., 1979. Brilliant polemic for view that the medium changed the message; others have argued that the message might have helped to produce the medium... Review articles: J. R. Censer, *J.Soc.Hist.*, 13, 1980, 629-38; A. T. Grafton, *J.Interdisc.Hist.*, 11, 1980, 265-86; C. G. Nauert, *Sixteenth-Cent.J.*, 11, 1980, 103-7. See following entries for various preliminary articles on themes tackled in book.

14.277 —— 'The advent of printing and the problem of the Renaissance', *P.& P.*, 45, 1969, 19-89. Argues that post-Gutenberg humanism had cumulative impact that would have been impossible in scribal culture. See further debate with T. K. Rabb, *ib.*, 52, 1971, 135-44.

14.278 —— 'The advent of printing and the Protestant revolt', in Kingdon (13.234), 235-70. Transl. from *Annales*, 26, 1971, 1355-82.

14.279 —— 'Some conjectures about the impact of printing on western society and thought', *J.Mod.Hist.*, 40, 1968, 1-56. Repr. (abridged) in Graff (14.225), 53-68.

14.280 —— 'On revolution and the printed word', in Porter and Teich (9.514), 186-205. On role of press in some early political revolutions or their making (mostly considers eighteenth-century France).

14.281 **Feather**, J., 'The commerce of letters. The study of the eighteenth-century book trade', *Eighteenth-Cent.Stud.*, 17, 1984, 405-24. General survey of European scene.

14.282 **Febvre**, L., and Martin, H.-J., *The Coming of the Book. The Impact of Printing, 1450-1800*, 1976. Transl. from French ed. of 1958. Mainly on production and marketing. Final chapter sketches some social repercussions along lines later elaborated by Eisenstein.

14.283 **Hirsch**, R., *Printing, Selling, Reading, 1450-1550*, Wiesbaden, 1967. Informative, though somewhat "bibliographical" in approach.

14.284 **Kingdon**, R. M., 'Patronage, piety, and printing in sixteenth-century Europe', in

D. H. Pinkney and T. Ropp, eds., *Festschrift for Frederick B. Artz*, Durham, N.C., 1964, 19-36. Looks at patronage and market for businesses of Plantin (Antwerp) and Estiennes (Geneva). On latter see also 14.311.

14.285 —— 'The Plantin breviaries. A case study in the sixteenth-century business operations of a publishing house', *Bibl.Humanisme et Renaiss.*, 22, 1960, 133-50. On how Plantin business more or less cornered market for breviaries in Spanish territories.

14.286 *Livre et Lecture en Espagne et en France sous l'Ancien Régime. Colloque de la Casa de Velazquez*, Paris, 1981. Fourteen papers on publishing and audience for books. Contributors incl. H.-J. Martin, M. Chevalier, R. Chartier, D. Roche.

14.287 **Mitchell**, J., 'The spread and fluctuation of eighteenth-century printing', *Stud.on Voltaire*, 230, 1985, 305-21. Makes some attempt at quantification of output and geographical distribution of European presses.

14.288 **Mukerji**, C., *From Graven Images. Patterns of Modern Materialism*, New York, 1983. Examines some repercussions of printing in generating mass market and culture of material acquisition, particularly via prints, maps, and patterned fabrics.

14.289 **Birn**, R., '*Livre et société* after ten years. Formation of a discipline', *Stud.on Voltaire*, 151, 1976, 287-312. Bibliographical article on new approaches to history of publishing, journalism, and literacy, concentrating on eighteenth-century France.

14.290 —— 'The profits of ideas. *Privilèges en librairie* in eighteenth-century France', *Eighteenth-Cent.Stud.*, 4, 1971, 131-68. Deals esp. with upheavals caused to traditional publishing practices by new regulations of 1777.

14.291 **Bollème**, Geneviève, *Les Almanachs Populaires aux 17e et 18e Siècles. Essai d'Histoire Sociale*, Paris, 1969.

14.292 —— *La Bibliothèque Bleue. Littérature Populaire en France du 16e au 19e Siècles*, Paris, 1971. Anthology of popular publications, with valuable introduction. See also her *La Bible Bleue* (Paris, 1975), another anthology; and thematic volumes of series *Bibliothèque Bleue*, published by Montalba under general editorship of D. Roche (Paris, 1982-). Note also 14.314-15.

14.293 **Censer**, J., 'Eighteenth-century journalism in France and its recruits', *Proc.Consortium on Revolutionary Eur.*, 1984 (publ. 1986), 165-79. Prosopographical study of 57 editorial journalists active in Paris, provinces, and neighbouring countries, between 1745-85.

14.294 **Chartier**, R., 'Culture as appropriation. Popular cultural uses in early modern France', in Kaplan (9.541), 229-53. Deals with book ownership, especially among urban small merchants and artisans.

14.295 —— *Lectures et Lecteurs dans la France d'Ancien Régime*, Paris, 1987. Collection of previously publ. articles (incl. three extracts from 14.318).

14.296 **Darnton**, R., 'The high Enlightenment and the low-life of literature in pre-Revolutionary France', *P.& P.*, 51, 1971, 81-115. Repr. in his *The Literary Underground of the Old Regime*, Cambridge, Mass., 1982, 1-40. Examines literary careerism in last years of old regime, and precarious existence of those who failed to secure government pensions.

14.297 —— 'Reading, writing, and publishing in eighteenth-century France. A case-study in the sociology of literature', *Daedalus*, 100, 1971, 214-56. Repr. in Darnton (14.296), 167-208; and Gilbert and Graubard (1.9), 238-80. Looks at pitfalls in some historians' attempts to quantify reading preferences; and goes on to deal with illegal publishing of political pornography.

14.298 —— 'Sounding the literary market in prerevolutionary France', *Eighteenth-Cent.Stud.*, 17, 1984, 477-92. Looks at market reports to Société Typographique de Neuchâtel in 1770s and '80s.

14.299 —— 'What is the history of books?', *Daedalus*, 111 (iii), 1982, 65-83. Seeks to illustrate new directions in social and economic history of literature with case study of a Montpellier bookseller's handling of Voltaire's *Questions sur l'Encyclopédie*.

14.300 —— 'The world of the underground booksellers in the Old Regime', in Hinrichs and others (7.42), 439-78.

14.301 **Davies**, Joan, 'Student libraries in sixteenth-century Toulouse', *Hist.of Univ.*, 3, 1983, 61-86. Inventory of unusually large collection of a law student.

14.302 **Davis**, Natalie Z., 'Beyond the market. Books as gifts in sixteenth-century

France', *Trans.Roy.Hist.Soc.*, 5th ser., 33, 1983, 69-88. On social significance of dedications and public and private donations.

14.303 —— 'Printing and the people', in Davis (11.200), 189-226. Repr. in Graff (14.225), 69-95. General discussion on how far, and what type of, books reached popular audience.

14.304 **Doucet**, R., *Les Bibliothèques Parisiennes au 16e Siècle*, Paris, 1956. Text of four personal library inventories, with introductory material based on examination of nearly two hundred such inventories (not systematically tabulated, however).

14.305 **Estivals**, R., *La Statistique Bibliographique de la France sous la Monarchie au 18e Siècle*, The Hague, 1965. Austere quantitative study of publishing and censorship based on records of official regulators. On years 1778-89 see also his 'La production des livres en France dans les dernières années de l'ancien régime', *Actes Congrès Nat.Soc.Savantes*, 90 (ii), 1965, 11-54.

14.306 **Furet**, F., ed., *Livre et Société dans la France du 18e Siècle*, 2 vols., The Hague, 1965-70. Important collection, with essays by Geneviève Bollème, D. Roche, J.-L. Flandrin, etc. For Furet's contribution, in transl., see following entry; that by A. Dupront, general survey of 'livre et culture', appeared as preview in *Annales*, 20, 1965, 867-98. Review article: B. Buczko, *Annales*, 26, 1971, 785-90.

14.307 —— 'Book licensing and book production in the kingdom of France in the eighteenth century', in Furet (1.25), 99-124. Looks at publishing trends in light of licence records. Transl. from previous entry.

14.308 **Hanley**, W., 'The policing of thought. Censorship in eighteenth-century France', *Stud.on Voltaire*, 183, 1980, 265-95.

14.309 **Harth**, Erica, *Ideology and Culture in Seventeenth-Century France*, Ithaca, N.Y., 1983. Examines developing genres of literature in terms of their social values and functions.

14.310 **Johnson**, N., 'Popular French almanacs of the eighteenth century', *Brit.J.Eighteenth-Cent.Stud.*, 8, 1985, 139-54. Looks at contents of four almanacs and doubts how far down social scale they penetrated.

14.311 **Kingdon**, R. M., 'The business activities of printers Henri and François Estienne',

in *Aspects de la Propagande Religieuse*, Geneva, 1957, 258-75. Famous Geneva printer of religious materials and his less successful brother.

14.312 **Klaits**, J., *Printed propaganda under Louis XIV. Absolute Monarchy and Public Opinion*, Princeton, N.J., 1976. Principally on foreign policy propaganda of Colbert de Torcy, but contains some interesting discussion of changing attitudes to public debate.

14.313 **Lough**, J., *Writer and Public in France from the Middle Ages to the Present Day*, 1978. Of considerable interest and depth despite its ambitious range.

14.314 **Mandrou**, R., *De la Culture Populaire au 17e et 18e Siècles. La Bibliothèque Bleue de Troyes*, Paris, 1964. 2nd ed., 1975. Analyses popular pamphlet literature designed for sale by peddlars; Troyes collection of this material is celebrated. See also next entry and 14.292.

14.315 **Martin**, H.-J., 'The *bibliothèque bleue*. Literature for the masses in the ancien régime', *Publishing Hist.*, 3, 1978, 70-102. Article based on A. Morin's *Catalogue Descriptif de la Bibliothèque Bleue de Troyes*, Geneva, 1974.

14.316 —— *Livre, Pouvoirs, et Société à Paris au 17e Siècle, 1598-1701*, 2 vols., Paris, 1969. Remarkable feat of analysis in which virtually all books produced by French-language presses are categorised, and social basis of readership ascertained from inventories and other sources.

14.317 —— *Le Livre Français sous l'Ancien Régime*, Paris, 1987. Collected essays, incl. some contributions to next entry.

14.318 —— and Chartier, R., eds., *Histoire de l'Édition Française*, Paris, 1982- . Of vols. so far publ., *Le Livre Conquérant* (1982) extends to mid-seventeenth century; *Le Livre Triomphant* (1984) covers 1660-1830. Itself a fine piece of book production, richly illustrated. Contributors incl. R. Darnton, Natalie Davis, Elizabeth Eisenstein, D. Roche, J. Quéniart.

14.319 **Parent**, Annie, *Les Métiers du Livre à Paris au 16e Siècle*, Geneva, 1974.

14.320 **Pottinger**, D. T., *The French Book Trade in the Ancien Regime, 1500-1791*, Cambridge, Mass., 1958. Covers plenty of ground: labour conditions, social background of authors, trends in popularity of subjects, censorship, etc.

14.321 **Roche**, D., 'Urban reading habits during

the French Enlightenment', *Brit. J. Eighteenth-Cent. Stud.*, 2, 1979, 138-49, 220-30. Emphasises differing function of reading matter for various social groups.

14.322 **Soman**, A., 'Press, pulpit, and censorship in France before Richelieu', *Proc. Am. Phil. Soc.*, 120, 1976, 439-63. Deals with period 1550-1620, with evidence from criminal records of Parlement and diplomatic correspondence.

14.323 **Wilkins**, Kay S., 'Children's literature in eighteenth-century France', *Stud.on Voltaire*, 176, 1979, 429-44. Analyses outlook and values inculcated by four popular writers for children.

14.324 **Bangs**, J. D., 'Book and art collection of the Low Countries in the later sixteenth century. Evidence from Leiden', *Sixteenth-Cent.J.*, 13 (i), 1982, 25-39. Compares four merchant inventories.

14.325 **Botrel**, J.-F., 'La Confrérie des Aveugles de Madrid et la vente des imprimés (1581-1836)', *Mél. Casa de Velazquez*, 9, 1973, 417-82; 10, 1974, 233-71. On monopoly of blind in distribution of news-sheets and pamphlet literature.

14.326 **Chevalier**, M., *Lectura y Lectores en la España de los Siglos 16 y 17*, Madrid, 1976. Assesses readership for various literary genres.

14.327 **Cortes**, J. B., 'The achievement motive in the Spanish economy between the thirteenth and eighteenth centuries', *Ec.Dev.& Cultural Change*, 9 (ii), 1961, 144-63. Attempts to link achievement themes in literature with economic growth.

14.328 **Lawrance**, J. N. H., 'The spread of lay literacy in late medieval Castile', *Bull.Hisp.Stud.*, 62, 1985, 79-94. Mainly concerns evidence of book possession by aristocracy and professional class (fifteenth and early sixteenth centuries).

14.329 **Pinto Crespo**, V., *Inquisición y Control Ideológico en la España del Siglo 16*, Madrid, 1983. Deals essentially with book censorship.

14.330 **Lowry**, M., *The World of Aldus Manutius. Business and Scholarship in Renaissance Venice*, 1979. Study of most celebrated humanist printer of late fifteenth century – goes well beyond bibliographical archeology.

14.331 **Machet**, Anne, 'Librairie et commerce du livre en Italie dans la deuxième moitié du 18e siècle', *Stud.on Voltaire*, 153, 1976, 1347-80.

14.332 **Noakes**, Susan, 'The development of the book market in late quattrocento Italy. Printers' failures and the role of the middleman', *J.Med.& Renaiss.Stud.*, 11, 1981, 23-55. Evidence from records of press at San Iacopo di Ripoli, a Florentine convent.

14.333 **Chrisman**, Miriam U., *Lay Culture, Learned Culture. Books and Social Change in Strasbourg, 1480-1599*, New Haven, Conn., 1982. Remarkable study of impact of printing and feedback from social structure, based on total publishing output of Strasbourg (see her companion vol., *Bibliography of Strasbourg Imprints, 1480-1599*, 1982). Review article: G. Strauss, *Hist.Educ.Q.*, 25, 1985, 507-11.

14.334 **Engelsing**, R., *Der Burger als Leser. Lesergeschichte in Deutschland, 1500-1800*, Stuttgart, 1974. Concentrates on evidence from Bremen.

14.335 **Ward**, A., *Book Production, Fiction, and the German Reading Public, 1740-1800*, 1974. Studies growth of novel-reading among middle classes, and repercussions for book trade.

14.336 **Woodmansee**, Martha, 'The genius and the copyright. Economic and legal conditions of the emergence of the "author" ', *Eighteenth-Cent.Stud.*, 17, 1984, 425-48. Traces emerging notion of "literary property" and authors' rights in eighteenth-century Germany.

14.337 **Cushing**, G. F., 'Books and readers in eighteenth-century Hungary', *Slavonic & E.Eur.Rev.*, 47, 1969, 57-77. Rather sketchy.

14.338 **Marker**, G., *Publishing, Printing, and the Origins of Intellectual Life in Russia, 1700-1800*, Princeton, N.J., 1985. Ambitious in range.

14.339 —— 'Merchandising culture. The market for books in late eighteenth-century Russia', *Eighteenth-Cent.Life*, 8 (i), 1982, 46-71.

14.340 —— 'Russia and the "printing revolution". Notes and observations', *Slavic Rev.*, 41, 1982, 266-83. Argues that Russia's experience down to late eighteenth century hardly bears out some of Eisenstein's sweeping assertions (see 14.276-80).

SCIENCE

See 9.500-19 for material on early modern technological developments. Also 10.107; 13.134,363; 14.237.

14.341 **Ben-David**, J., *The Scientist's Role in Society. A Comparative Study*, Englewood Cliffs, N.J., 1971. General history from classical times onward.

14.342 **Cardwell**, D. S. L., 'Science and technology in the eighteenth century', *Hist.Sci.*, 1, 1962, 30-43. Short essay on links.

14.343 **Clegg**, A., 'Craftsmen and the origin of science', *Sci.& Soc.*, 43, 1979, 186-201. On importance of artisans in development of experimental methods.

14.344 **Cohen**, I. B., *From Leonardo to Lavoisier, 1450-1800 (Album of Science, 2)*, 1980. Valuable for illustrations and diagrams.

14.345 **Dijksterhuis**, E. J., *The Mechanization of the World Picture*, 1981. Like Easlea (14.346) and Merchant (14.356), emphasises change from "vital" to "inert" view of nature, but without condemnatory overtones.

14.346 **Easlea**, B., *Witchhunting, Magic, and the New Philosophy. An Introduction to Debates of the Scientific Revolution, 1450-1750*, 1980. Interesting but eccentric account of rise of "mechanical philosophy" seen as replacing world of spirits by "inert" cosmos and so asserting bourgeois and male-dominant values.

14.347 **Feuer**, L. S., *The Scientific Intellectual. Psychological and Sociological Origins of Modern Science*, New York, 1963. Contrary to R. K. Merton's view of scientists as product of Puritan ethic, argues they were nurtured by climate he terms "hedonist-libertarian".

14.348 **Hall**, A. R., *The Revolution in Science, 1500-1750*, 1983. Rewriting of classic *The Scientific Revolution* (1954; 2nd ed., 1962). Note chaps. 8 (organisation and purpose of science) and 9 (technical influences).

14.349 —— 'The scholar and the craftsman in the scientific revolution', in M. Clagett, ed., *Critical Problems in the History of Science*, Madison, Wis., 1962, 3-23. With discussion by R. K. Merton and F. R. Johnson, *ib.*, 24-32. Questions how much interaction existed between university/gentry experimenters and artisan "improvers".

14.350 —— 'Scientific method and the progress of techniques', in *Cambridge Economic History of Europe*, 4 (2.15), 96-154. General sketch of intellectual and technical discovery from late medieval era to Industrial Revolution.

14.351 **Kearney**, H., *Science and Change, 1500-1700*, 1971. Good layman's introduction, with chapters on social background and impact of scientific revolution. Attacks "Whig view" of straight-line progress from Copernicus to Einstein.

14.352 **Kuhn**, T. S., *The Structure of Scientific Revolutions*, Chicago, 1962. Highly influential study in historical sociology of knowledge. Central concept of discontinuities in "paradigms" (mental habits and assumptions with which problems are approached) has become almost a cliché.

14.353 **McClellan**, J. E., *Science Reorganized. Scientific Societies in the Eighteenth Century*, New York, 1985. Deals with remarkable growth and powers of patronage of societies. On earlier period see still valuable Martha Ornstein, *The Role of Scientific Societies in the Seventeenth Century*, Chicago, 1928; and 14.359,365,373,375.

14.354 **Macleod**, R., 'Changing perspectives in the social history of science', in Ina Spiegel-Rösing and D. De S. Price, eds., *Science, Technology, and Society. A Cross-Disciplinary Perspective*, Beverley Hills, Calif., 1977, 149-95. Excellent historiographical article, with helpful bibliography.

14.355 **Mathias**, P., ed., *Science and Society, 1600-1900*, 1972. Lecture series. Mathias' essay 'Who unbound Prometheus?', and those by P. M. Rattansi and A. R. Hall on seventeenth century, deal widely with questions of social determinants and participants in scientific and technical activity.

14.356 **Merchant**, Carolyn, *The Death of Nature. Women, Ecology, and The Scientific Revolution*, New York, 1980. Tends to equate pre-Copernican world view with reverence for nature and the feminine. Cf. 14.346.

14.357 **Rabb**, T. K., 'Religion and the rise of modern science', *P.& P.*, 31, 1965, 11-26. Argues, chiefly in opposition to Hill's and Merton's association of Puritanism and scientific enquiry, that in rise of science (before 1640) religious adherence is irrelevant. Cf. 14.347.

14.358 **Rossi**, P., *Philosophy, Technology, and the Arts in the Early Modern Era*, New York, 1970. Related essays bearing on gradual convergence between technology and science.

14.359 **Schofield**, R. E., 'Histories of scientific societies. Needs and opportunities for research', *Hist.Sci.*, 2, 1963, 70-83.

14.360 **Smith**, A. G. R., *Science and Society in the Sixteenth and Seventeenth Centuries*, 1972. Well illustrated, but treatment of society fairly superficial.

14.361 **Webster**, C., 'Paracelsus and demons. Science as a synthesis of popular belief', in *Scienze, Credenze Occulte...* (13.366), 3-20. Deals esp. with his acceptance of *Geistmenschen* (dwarves, gnomes, etc.). Webster's *From Paracelsus to Newton. Magic and the Making of Modern Science*, 1982, deals at greater length with persistence of occult and neo-Platonic intellectual tradition.

14.362 **Westfall**, R., *The Construction of Modern Science. Mechanisms and Mechanics*, New York, 1971. Concentrates on seventeenth-century developments, and includes chapter on 'organisation of scientific enterprise'.

14.363 **Westman**, R. S., 'The astronomer's role in the sixteenth century. A preliminary study', *Hist.Sci.*, 18, 1980, 105-47. Starting from conservative reactions to work of Copernicus, examines how astronomy fitted into academic disciplines of period.

14.364 **Wightman**, W. P. D., *Science in a Renaissance Society*, 1972. Brief history of scientific thought, 1400-1600. Successfully avoids linear view, but historical background has little depth.

14.365 **Brown**, H., *Scientific Organizations in Seventeenth-Century France (1620-80)*, Baltimore, Md., 1934. Stresses integration of science with general cultural activity of academies.

14.366 **Gillispie**, C. C., *Science and Polity in France at the End of the Old Régime*, Princeton, N.J., 1980. Surveys state patronage of science, and social applications, esp. in fields of health care, economy, and engineering.

14.367 **Hahn**, R., *Anatomy of a Scientific Institution. The Paris Academy of Sciences, 1666-1803*, Berkeley, Calif., 1971.

Excellent study. See also his 'Scientific careers in eighteenth-century France', in M. Crosland, ed., *The Emergence of Science in Western Europe*, 1975, 127-38.

14.368 **Kiernan**, C., 'Science and the Enlightenment in eighteenth-century France', *Stud.on Voltaire*, 59, 1968, whole volume. New ed., *ib.*, 59A, 1973. Mainly intellectual history, but contains some material on social setting.

14.369 **Rappaport**, Rhoda, 'Government patronage of science in eighteenth-century France', *Hist.Sci.*, 8, 1969, 119-36. Begins as review of Bourde (7.301), but ranges much wider.

14.370 **López Piñero**, J. M., *Ciencia y Técnica en la Sociedad Española de los Siglos 16 y 17*, Barcelona, 1979. Deals both with social setting and actual lines of enquiry in scientific enterprise.

14.371 **Dooley**, B., 'Science teaching as a career at Padua in the early eighteenth century. The case of Giovanni Poleni', *Hist.Univ.*, 4, 1984, 115-51. Poleni left voluminous papers on his career, teaching methods, courses, etc.

14.372 **Ferrone**, V., 'Tecnocrati militari e scienziati nel Piemonte del'antico regime. Alle origini della Reale Accademia delle Scienze di Torino', *Riv.Stor.Ital.*, 96, 1984, 414-509. Stresses importance of artillery experts in Piedmontese enlightenment.

14.373 **Galluzzi**, P., and others, 'Accademie scientifiche del '600', *Quad.Stor.*, 48, 1981, 757-921. New look at Lincei and Cimento academies, at Naples Investiganti, and various Bologna societies.

14.374 **Micheli**, G., ed., *Scienza e Tecnica nella Cultura e nella Società dal Rinascimento a Oggi*, Turin, 1980. Vol.3 of *Annali* section of Einaudi *Storia d'Italia*.

14.375 **Rose**, P. L., 'The Academia Venetiana. Science and culture in Renaissance Venice', *Studi Veneziani*, 11, 1969, 191-215. Activities and business affairs of cultural society which ended in bankruptcy (1557-61).

14.376 **Westfall**, R. S., 'Science and patronage. Galileo and the telescope', *Isis*, 76, 1985, 11-30. Examination of Galileo's economic circumstances.

14.377 **Hufbauer**, K., *The Formation of the German Chemical Community, 1720-95*, Berkeley, Calif., 1982. Interesting account of embryonic scientific specialisation and its links with particular national culture.

14.378 **Moran**, B. T., 'German prince-practitioners. Aspects in the development of courtly science, technology, and procedures in the Renaissance', *Technol.& Culture*, 22, 1981, 253-74. Princely patronage of science and engineering.

14.379 **Thibodeau**, K. F., 'Science and the Reformation. The case of Strasbourg', *Sixteenth-Cent.J.*, 7 (i), 1976, 35-50. Finds that early phase of Reformation was marked by short-lived rise in scientific activity and publication.

14.380 **Frängsmyr**, T., 'Swedish science in the eighteenth century', *Hist.Sci.*, 12, 1974, 29-42. Brief essay on institutions which fostered Swedish eminence in this period.

14.381 **Vucinich**, A., *Science in Russian Culture. A History to 1860*, Stanford, Calif., 1963. Seeks to explain why, despite general social obstacles, Russian scientists made important contributions in eighteenth and nineteenth centuries.

THEATRES AND ENTERTAINMENTS
See also 5.628.

14.382 **Alasseur**, C., *La Comédie-Française au 18e Siècle, Étude Économique*, Paris, 1967. Based on theatre's account registers from 1680 to 1774.

14.383 **Arden**, Heather, *Fools' Plays. A Study of Satire in the "Sottie"*, 1980. Genre of popular farce, its social setting and targets.

14.384 **Isherwood**, R. M., *Farce and Fantasy. Popular Entertainment in Eighteenth-Century Paris*, New York, 1986. Surveys world of fairs, cafés, menageries, and boulevard theatres.

14.385 —— 'Entertainment in the Parisian fairs in the eighteenth century', *J.Mod.Hist.*, 53, 1981, 24-48.

14.386 —— 'Entertainments on the Parisian boulevards in the eighteenth century', *Proc.Western Soc.Fr.Hist.*, 11, 1983, 142-52. Deals mainly with repertoire of small theatre of Les Grands Danseurs, 1760-89.

14.387 **Lagrave**, H., *Le Théâtre et le Public de Paris de 1715 à 1750*, Paris, 1972. Detailed and handsomely illustrated thesis on both business and social aspects. Determined efforts at quantification. Designed to follow pioneering work of P. Melesse, *Le Théâtre et le Public à Paris sous Louis XIV*,

1659-1715, Paris, 1934.

14.388 **Lough**, J., *Paris Theatre Audiences in the Seventeenth and Eighteenth Centuries*, 1957. Easier introduction to subject than works cited in preceding entry.

14.389 **McManners**, J., *Abbés and Actresses. The Church and the Theatrical Profession in Eighteenth-Century France*, 1986. Text of Zaharoff Lecture at Oxford.

14.390 **Mongrédien**, G., *Daily Life in the French Theatre at the Time of Molière*, 1969. Transl. from French ed. of 1966. Anecdotal. Dwells mainly on Paris companies and fashionable patrons.

14.391 **Phillips**, H., *The Theatre and its Critics in Seventeenth-Century France*, 1980. Careful account of alleged ill-effects on society.

14.392 'La vie théâtrale au 17e siècle', *Dix-Septième Siècle*, 39, 1958, whole issue. Several essays deal with material problems of actors and dramatists.

14.393 **Metford**, J. C. J. 'Enemies of the theatre in the golden age', *Bull.Hisp.Stud.*, 28, 1951, 76-92. Spanish critics of immoral influence of stage. Cf.14.391.

14.394 **Varey**, J. E., 'Popular entertainments in Madrid, 1758-1859', *Renaiss.& Mod.Stud.*, 22, 1978, 26-44. Concentrates on new forms of entertainment such as magic lantern, peepshows, and puppet theatre.

14.395 **Weaver**, Elissa, 'Spiritual fun. A study of sixteenth-century Tuscan convent theatre', in Rose (5.481), 173-205. Background to performances put on in nunneries, and some of their themes.

14.396 **Burgess**, M., 'Fairs and entertainers in eighteenth-century Russia', *Slavonic & E.Eur.Rev.*, 38, 1959, 95-113.

14.397 —— 'Russian public theatre audiences of the eighteenth and early nineteenth centuries', *ib.*, 37, 1958, 160-83. Anecdotal account, confined to Moscow and Petersburg.

14.398 **Malnick**, Bertha, 'Russian serf theatres', *ib.*, 30, 1952, 393-411. Theatre groups assembled to entertain their gentry owners or for commercial exploitation.

14.399 **Zguta**, R., *Russian Minstrels. A History of the Skomorokhi*, 1978. Traces history of these popular entertainers from eleventh century to their proscription in mid-seventeenth century. See also his 'Skomorokhi. The Russian minstrel-entertainers', *Slavic Rev.*, 31, 1972, 297-313.

THE VISUAL ARTS
See also 5.628; 10.51,473; 11.265;
14.74,110-11,119,256,324.

14.400 **Burke**, P., 'Problems of the sociology of art. The work of Pierre Francastel', *Arch.Eur.Sociol.*, 12, 1971, 141-54. French art historian with strong interest in social and psychological context of art.

14.401 **Hauser**, A., *The Social History of Art*, 2 vols., 1951. Deals with art as reflection of socio-political background, rather than conditions under which artists operated. Inevitably rather superficial, given vast scope essayed. Parts 2-3 deal with period from Renaissance to early Romanticism.

14.402 **Kunzle**, D., *History of the Comic Strip. Vol.1: Narrative Strips and Picture Stories in the European Broadsheet, c.1450-1825*, Berkeley, Calif., 1973.

14.403 **Moxey**, K. P. F., 'The function of peasant imagery in German graphics of the sixteenth century. Festive peasants as instruments of repressive humor', in G. P. Tyson and Sylvia S. Wagonheim, eds., *Print and Culture in the Renaissance. Essays on the Advent of Printing in Europe*, Newark, N.J., 1986, 151-88. Points to mockery of roistering Catholic peasants in woodcuts designed for bourgeois Protestant households. See as examples of this his 'Sebald Beham's church anniversary holidays', *Simiolus*, 12, 1981-82, 107-30; controversy between Svetlana Alpers and H. Miedema over Dutch artist Bredero's representations of peasant feasts, *ib.*, 8, 1975-76, 115-44; 9, 1977, 205-19; and P. Vandenbroeck, 'Verbeeck's peasant weddings', *ib.*, 14, 1984, 79-124.

14.404 **Pevsner**, N., *Academies of Art, Past and Present*, 1940. A good deal on early modern training of artists.

14.405 **Trevor-Roper**, H., *Princes and Artists. Patronage and Ideology at Four Habsburg Courts, 1517-1633*, 1976. Discusses art and architecture at courts of Charles V, Philip II, Rudolf II, and Brussels governors.

14.406 **Wittkower**, R., and Wittkower, Margot, *Born under Saturn. The Character and Conduct of Artists...from Antiquity to the French Revolution*, 1963. Despite title, concentrates on artists of early modern period, seeking to document why they so often displayed social alienation.

14.407 **Crow**, T. E., *Painters and Public Life in Eighteenth-Century Paris*, New Haven, Conn., 1986. Deals esp. with role of Royal Academy and development of Salon exhibitions.

14.408 **Crozet**, R., *La Vie Artistique en France au 17e Siècle, 1598-1661. Les Artistes et la Société*, Paris, 1954. Narrowly conceived, but useful reference work on who patronised whom.

14.409 **Montias**, J. M., *Artists and Artisans in Delft. A Socio-Economic Study of the Seventeenth Century*, Princeton, N.J., 1982. Looks at social origins and professional rewards of painters, and market for their art.

14.410 —— 'The guild of St. Luke in seventeenth-century Delft, and the economic status of artists and artisans', *Simiolus*, 9, 1977, 93-105. Further article, 'Painters in Delft, 1613-80', *ib.*, 11, 1978-79, 84-114. For narrower study of another painters' guild see E. Taverne, 'Salomon de Bray and the reorganization of the Haarlem Guild of St. Luke in 1631', *ib.*, 6, 1972-73, 50-69.

14.411 **Gállego**, J., *El Pinto de Artesano a Artista*, Granada, 1976. Centres on question whether artists' sales should be subject (as "manufactures") to *alcabala* tax.

14.412 **Baxandall**, M., *Painting and Experience in Fifteenth-Century Italy. A Primer in the Social History of Pictorial Style*, 1972. Entertaining and well-illustrated examination of artist's trade, and perceptual and moral categories shared with clients. Chiefly Florentine context.

14.413 **Caplow**, Harriet M., 'Sculptors' partnerships in Michelozzo's Florence', *Stud.in Renaiss.*, 21, 1974, 145-75

14.414 **Chambers**, D. S., ed., *Patrons and Artists in the Italian Renaissance*, 1971. Selection of documents with commentary, illustrating terms of service of painters, sculptors, and architects.

14.415 **Cole**, B., *The Renaissance Artist at Work. From Pisano to Titian*, 1983. Deals mainly with Northern Italy. Useful opening chapter on social place of artists.

14.416 **Edgerton**, S. Y., *Pictures and Punishment. Art and Criminal Prosecution during the Florentine Renaissance*, Ithaca, N.Y., 1986. Argues for link between realistic portrayal of martyrdom and greater sensitivity about torture and punishment in treatment of criminals.

14.417 **Haskell**, F., 'Art exhibitions in seventeenth-century Rome'. *Studi Secenteschi*, 1, 1960, 107-21. Explains that exhibitions were primarily to honour festivals and only secondarily to advertise artists.

14.418 —— 'The market for Italian art in the seventeenth century', *P.& P.*, 15, 1959, 48-59.

14.419 —— *Patrons and Painters. A Study in the Relations between Italian Art and Society in the Age of the Baroque*, 1963. Revised ed., New Haven, Conn., 1980. Deals most fully with art in Rome and Venice.

14.420 **Hughes**, Diane O., 'Representing the family. Portraits and purposes in early modern Italy', *J.Interdisc.Hist.*, 17, 1986, 7-38. On social function of portraiture.

14.421 **Kent**, F. W., and others, eds., *Patronage, Art, and Society in Renaissance Italy*, 1987. 4 papers on political and ecclesiastical patronage; 8 on patronage of painters and architects.

14.422 **Labrot**, G., 'Images, tableaux, et statuaire dans les testaments napolitains (17e-18e siècles)', *Rev.Hist.*, 268, 1982, 131-66. Investigates types of art bequeathed by Neapolitans in variety of social milieus between 1600 and 1733.

14.423 **Lewis**, D., 'Patterns of preference. Patronage of sixteenth-century architects by the Venetian patriciate', in Lytle and Orgel (10.14), 354-80.

14.424 **Brady**, T. A., 'The social place of a German Renaissance artist. Hans Baldung Grien (1484/5-1545) at Strasbourg', *Central Eur.Hist.*, 8, 1975, 295-315. Explores Baldung's family, property interests, and role in urban institutions, to demonstrate continuity of artisan tradition in painting. See 13.347 for discussion of celebrated work by this artist.

14.425 **Christensen**, C. C., *Art and the Reformation in Germany*, Athens, Ohio, 1979. Considered from number of angles: iconoclasm, artistic subject-matter, social position and market of artists.

14.426 —— 'The Reformation and the decline of German art', *Central Eur.Hist.*, 6, 1973, 207-32. Argues that Reformation brought period of diminished employment for German artists.

14.427 **Cole**, R. G., 'Pamphlet woodcuts in the communication process of Reformation Germany', in Sessions and Bebb (13.225), 103-22. Analyses use of woodcut emblems as weapon in Reformation polemics. See also Christiane Andersson, 'Popular imagery in German Reformation broadsheets' in Tyson and Wagonheim (14.403), 120-50.

14.428 **Lepovitz**, Helena W., 'Industrialization of popular art in Bavaria', *P.& P.*, 99, 1983, 88-122. On rural trade of glass-painting in eighteenth and nineteenth centuries.

14.429 **Brunvand**, J. H., 'Traditional house decoration in Romania. Survey and bibliography', *E.Eur.Q.*, 14, 1980, 255-301.

14.430 **Kiel**, M., *Art and Society of Bulgaria in the Turkish Period*, Assen, 1985. Aims to diminish Bulgarian nationalist depreciation of effects of Turkish rule on cultural vitality.

14.431 **Farrell**, Dianne E., 'The origins of Russian popular prints, and their social milieu in the early eighteenth century', *J.Popular Culture*, 17 (i), 1983, 9-47. Good illustrations.

14.432 **Netting**, A., 'Images and ideas in Russian peasant art', *Slavic Rev.*, 35, 1976, 48-68.

MUSIC

14.433 **Koenigsberger**, H. G., 'Music and religion in early modern European history', in Koenigsberger and J. H. Elliott, eds., *The Diversity of History*, 1971, 35-78. Repr. in Koenigsberger (2.75), 179-210. Argues that history of music is closely linked with phenomenon of secularisation.

14.434 **Raynor**, H., *A Social History of Music from the Middle Ages to Beethoven*, 1972. Culled largely from biographies of composers.

14.435 **Schwartz**, Judith L., 'Cultural stereotypes and music in the eighteenth century', *Stud.on Voltaire*, 155, 1976, 1989-2013. Looks at wider implications (musical and social) of such caricatures as Osmin in Mozart's *Seraglio*.

14.436 **Benoît**, Marcelle, *Versailles et les Musiciens du Roi, 1661-1733*, Paris, 1971. Institutional study.

14.437 **Cazeaux**, Isabelle, *French Music in the Fifteenth and Sixteenth Centuries*, 1975. Partly technical history, but explores also social role, teaching, and publishing.

14.438 **Isherwood**, R. M., *Music in the Service of the King. France in the Seventeenth Century*, Ithaca, N.Y., 1973. Organisation and politico-social uses of music by government of Louis XIV.

14.439 **Massip**, Catherine, *La Vie des Musiciens de Paris au Temps de Mazarin (1643-61). Essai* *d'Étude Sociale*, Paris, 1976. Describes professional life of musicians dependent on Court or Church.

14.440 **Weber**, W., 'Learned and general musical taste in eighteenth-century France', *P.& P.*, 89, 1980, 58-85. Looks at reasons why music was largely without specialist or scholarly coterie in its following.

14.441 **Becker**, Danièle, 'La vie quotidienne au collège des jeunes chanteurs de la Chapelle Royale à Madrid au 17e siècle', *Mél.Casa de Velazquez*, 21, 1985, 219-54.

14.442 **Reynaud**, F., 'Contribution à l'étude des danseurs et des musiciens des fêtes du Corpus Christi et de l'Assomption à Tolède au 16e et 17e siècles', *ib.*, 10, 1974, 133-68. Evidence gleaned from municipal accounts.

14.443 **Fenlon**, I., *Music and Patronage in Sixteenth-Century Mantua*, 2 vols., 1980-82. Emphasises political and dynastic purposes in Gonzaga family's employment of musicians.

14.444 **Lockwood**, L., *Music in Renaissance Ferrara, 1400-1505*, 1985. Excellent study of Este family as patrons, with much detail on financing and recruitment of court musicians.

14.445 **Rosand**, Ellen, 'Music in the myth of Venice', *Renaiss.Q.*, 30, 1977, 511-37. Importance of music in civic life and prestige.

14.446 **Salmen**, W., ed., *The Social Status of the Professional Musician from the Middle Ages to the Nineteenth Century*, New York, 1983. Transl. from German ed. of 1971, with additional material. Mainly on German scene. Essays on organists, *Spielmänner* (folk musicians), wind players, court orchestras, dealers in scores, and general essay on economic situation of eighteenth-century musician (by R. Petzoldt). See also two interesting illustrated works by Salmen, *Musikleben im 16.Jahrhundert*, Leipzig, 1976; and *Haus- und Kammermusik...zwischen 1600 und 1900*, Leipzig, 1969.

14.447 **Braun**, J., 'National interrelationships and conflicts in the musical life of seventeenth- and eighteenth-century Riga', *J.Baltic Stud.*, 11, 1980, 62-70. On conflict and status gap between Germans, on one hand, and Slavs and Balts on other.

TOPOGRAPHICAL INDEX

Aachen (and region), 9.584-5; 13.193
Abruzzo, 7.134
Agnone, 5.375
Aix-en-Provence, 5.274; 6.61; 10.299; 11.37, 203; 12.42; 13.109
Akershus, 5.237
Albania, 5.212
Albi (and region), 7.65; 9.550
Albiez-le-Vieux, 7.83
Alcalá, 14.178
Alençon, 3.57
Alentejo, 7.116
Aleppo, 9.551
Alicante, 9.241
Aljarafe, 7.99
Allauch, 7.76
Almadén, 10.441
Allstedt, 13.213
Alsace, 5.88, 607-8; 6.62; 13.191, 307, 372
Altopascio, 7.137
Amasya, 8.153
Amiens, 8.32; 11.202, 316, 320; 12.35; 14.53, 153, 155
Amsterdam, 5.119, 610; 6.43; 8.64-6, 182; 9.18, 43-4, 52-5, 167, 176, 184-5, 197, 346, 414; 10.162, 165, 430; 11.9, 44-5, 142; 13.309, 293; 14.238
Anatolia, 4.82; 5.208, 210; 7.222-3; 8.153; 9.604; 12.144; 13.155
Ancona, 5.621; 9.94, 247-8
Andalusia, 3.138-9; 5.536; 7.97, 99, 344; 10.431
Angers, 12.58; 13.115
Angola, 9.397-8
Anguillara, 7.132
Anhalt, 6.185
Anjou, 3.47; 5.77, 107; 10.388
Ankara, 8.150
Ansbach, 7.154; 8.7; 9.482; 10.342

Antwerp, 3.81, 67-8; 9.56-63, 72, 177, 193, 197; 14.284-5
Apennines, 7.131
Apulia, 7.134, 146
Aquitaine, 3.48; 7.337
Aragon, 10.432; 11.327
Archangel, 9.176, 180
Arezzo, 14.189
Ariège, 4.51
Armentières, 9.557
Arnay-le-Duc, 7.37
Artois, 13.61, 378
Asturias, 3.140; 4.13
Athens, 8.158
Auch, 14.159
Aude, 4.51
Auffay, 9.460-3
Auge, 10.403
Augsburg, 5.288, 291; 8.189; 9.106, 109-11, 114, 578; 13.91, 98; 13.187, 229
Aurillac, 8.33
Austria, Lower, 9.539
Austria, Upper, 7.183; 9.580; 12.104-5
Auvergne, 5.465, 528; 7.64, 308, 342; 10.389, 398; 11.204
Avallon, 14.159
Avignon, 5.348, 605, 607; 11.217; 13.131
Azereix, 7.85
Azores, 4.107
Azov, 8.176

Baden, 6.179; 10.339, 342; 14.138
Bamberg, 7.155
Barcelona, 6.117; 8.71; 9.242, 533; 10.320; 11.63
Basle (and region), 4.93; 5.176, 396, 399; 8.117; 11.250, 350; 13.190
Bassano, 11.71

Basque provinces, 3.147; 5.326; 6.126; 13.388, 390
Bavaria, 3.223, 244; 5.188, 194; 6.188; 7.176; 9.483-4, 486; 10.245, 338; 11.253; 13.88, 393; 14.87, 428
Bayeux (and region), 6.108-11; 8.34-5
Bayreuth, 9.482; 10.342
Bazas (and region), 7.31; 10.413
Béarn, 4.40; 5.335; 7.305
Beauce, 6.65; 8.41
Beaujolais, 7.334; 11.204
Beauvais, 7.46; 8.36; 9.28
Beira, 7.116
Belalcázar, 7.102
Belgorod, 10.538
Belgrade, 5.33, 407
Belluno, 9.623
Bender-Aqkerman, 10.255
Bergerac, 7.322; 12.26
Berlin, 9.436, 476-8; 11.271
Bern, 4.41-2
Besançon, 9.428; 10.291
Biberach, 11.80; 13.98
Bilbao, 5.145; 9.310; 10.509; 11.325
Bohemia, 3.285; 5.643; 6.199, 200; 7.204-7, 296; 9.115-16, 489-91, 597, 599, 600, 648; 11.87; 12.19, 139, 141, 221
Boitzenburg, 7.167
Bologna, 5.157; 7.316; 8.94; 9.93; 12.89; 14.190, 373
Bonnières-sur-Seine, 5.70
Bordeaux (and region), 5.106, 350, 359, 607; 6.257; 7.31, 335; 8.37-9; 9.271, 292-6, 394; 10.288, 306, 399; 12.68
Boston (Mass.), 12.21
Boulogne (diocese), 13.51
Bourbonnais, 7.40
Bourges, 7.61

Brabant, 5.120; 8.63; 11.50-1, 53; 11.223
Brandenburg, 3.238; 6.182; 7.162-4, 166-7; 7.348; 9.287, 436, 476-8; 10.54, 247; 12.106
Brazil, 9.266, 285
Bremen, 9.205, 540; 14.334
Brescia (and region), 10.237
Breslau, 12.114
Brest, 8.192; 9.297
Brie, 3.50; 5.76
Brittany, 3.49; 4.39; 5.77, 88, 95; 6.90; 9.291, 555; 10.388; 11.299, 301; 12.32, 36, 41
Brno, 4.94; 9.595
Brouage, 9.364
Bruges, 9.64-6; 11.322
Brunswick, 7.150; 10.143; 13.152, 202; 14.198
Brussels, 11.321
Bureba, 7.100
Burgos, 4.77; 6.123; 9.67, 415-16, 419
Burgundy, 4.49; 5.362; 6.75; 7.37, 57, 67-8; 10.39, 193
Bursa, 5.512; 9.123, 254, 603

Cáceres, 5.151; 13.68
Cadiz, 9.308-9; 11.9
Caen (and region), 3.57; 6.101; 8.40; 13.255
Cahors, 3.62
Calabria, 3.200
Calvados, 7.35
Cambrai (and region), 5.346, 353; 7.282; 13.369, 379, 384
Campan, 7.81
Campania, 7.135
Canada, 9.268, 271-2
Cantal, 7.342
Canton, 9.320
Cape Breton, 9.270
Cape Verde Islands, 4.107
Carcassonne, 7.36
Caribbean, 9.273-8, 289
Carinthia, 5.389; 7.160
Carmagnola, 11.329
Carpentras, 5.605
Carrara, 9.620
Catalonia, 3.141-3; 4.55-6; 5.148; 7.117, 313; 9.470; 10.327; 12.75, 77
Caudine Valley, 7.129
Caux region, 9.460-3
Cévennes, 7.79; 13.247
Châlons-sur-Marne, 14.253
Champagne, 13.39
Charleroi, 9.467
Charleston, 12.21
Chartres, 5.83; 6.105; 7.61; 8.41; 13.55
Châteaudun, 8.42

Châtillon-sur-Seine, 5.79
Chesapeake, 9.362
China, 9.320, 328, 330, 334, 337
Chioggia, 8.96
Città di Castello, 9.569
Ciudad Real, 5.587; 7.108, 112; 8.72
Clairac, 6.19
Clermont-de-Lodève, 9.556
Cognac, 9.295
Colmar, 4.93; 13.193
Cologne, 5.384, 478, 509; 6.191; 9.105; 11.81; 13.145, 176, 223
Comminges, 3.51
Como region, 3.173; 5.379
Comtat Venaissin, 5.605
Condom, 14.159
Constance, 5.397-8
Copenhagen, 5.292; 8.192; 11.94, 99, 163, 271
Córdoba (and region), 5.558, 570; 8.73-5; 11.324; 12.80
Corsica, 5.344
Cortaillod, 9.576
Courland, 3.391; 5.416-21
Cracow, 5.639, 642; 9.206, 368
Crimea, 5.651
Croatia, 3.330
Crulai, 5.93
Cuba, 9.270, 627
Cuenca, 5.578; 7.346
Cyprus, 3.319-20; 5.211, 644, 650

Danzig, 9.189, 207-8
Dauphiné, 6.18; 9.29, 464; 10.189, 205; 13.124-5
Delft, 14.409-10
Deventer, 13.275 Dieppe, 9.290; 11.137
Diest, 11.47
Dijon, 3.52; 5.281; 9.528; 10.297; 13.243; 14.168
Dinkelsbühl, 13.98
Dôle, 5.109
Dordogne region, 4.67
Drenthe, 7.86
Drottninghölm, 9.492
Dubrovnik, see Ragusa
Dunkirk, 9.649

Eisleben, 9.628
Ekaterinoslav, 5.546
Elbing, 9.209
Emden, 13.277
Emilia, 7.126
Erfurt, 13.215
Erzurum, 8.153
Essen, 13.193
Esslingen, 13.182
Estonia, 5.246, 327, 414. See also Courland
Extremadura, 5.554; 6.120

Famagusta, 5.644
Faroe, 3.353
Feltre (and region), 7.128
Ferrara, 14.444
Flanders, 5.121, 364; 8.62; 9.442, 468, 557; 10.427, 500, 506; 11.50, 53, 223; 12.73; 13.50, 378
Flensburg, 9.317
Florence, 3.158, 177-9, 182; 5.159, 163, 168, 285, 287, 376, 450-1, 468, 500, 503; 6.142-9, 248, 260-1; 7.139; 8.94, 189; 9.72, 96-9, 150, 228, 421, 424, 429, 471, 567-8, 571, 640-1; 10.45-6, 230-1, 331-3; 11.153, 235, 238, 246, 332, 336, 341, 346; 13.22, 81-4, 138; 14.192, 332, 412-13, 416
Florida, 5.534
Forez, 11.204
Franconia, 3.244; 6.187-8; 7.155; 8.119; 9.482; 11.253
Frankfurt-am-Main, 5.628; 8.117, 120-1; 9.102, 542; 14.198
Freiburg-im-Breisgau, 3.227; 4.93; 8.122; 11.250
Freising, 5.194
Fribourg, 5.290
Friesland, 7.88
Friuli, 13.391; 14.85

Galata, 5.658
Galicia, 3.145; 5.537; 7.106; 9.469-70; 13.327
Gap, 13.124
Garéoult, 7.80
Gascony, 13.374; 14.50
Gâtinais, 7.39
Gâtine Poitevine, 7.60
Geneva, 5.178, 196-7, 199, 290, 511; 8.123; 9.101, 413; 10.61, 253; 11.252; 13.148-9, 233-4, 377; 14.274, 284, 311
Genoa, 3.170, 183; 6.150, 267; 8.94; 9.80 249-50, 417, 428; 11.151, 239, 338
Georgia, 3.392
Gévaudan, 3.53; 11.126
Giessen, 5.179
Gisors, 14.159
Goa, 9.331
Görlitz, 8.124
Gothenburg, 8.192; 9.210
Gotland, 5.222
Göttingen, 5.192; 13.202; 14.204
Granada (city and province), 4.16; 5.573, 590-1; 8.76
Grangärde, 5.221
Grasse, 13.37
Graubünden, 10.60
Grenoble, 3.8; 5.496; 11.215-16
Groningen, 13.277
Guatemala, 10.126
Guelderland, 4.87

Guinea, 9.289
Guyenne, 5.350; 6.19; 10.389, 414;
  12.31, 45; 13.113

Haina, 11.255
Hainault, 7.90; 11.43
Hall, 5.195
Halle, 14.203
Hamburg, 5.452; 8.117, 125;
  9.211-14, 217, 318, 435; 10.144;
  11.9, 185; 13.99, 182, 206
Hannover, 6.186; 7.149; 8.117
Harz region, 9.624; 12.135
Hattula, 7.245
Havana, 9.270; 10.126
Havelland, 3.238
Heilsbronn, 7.154
Herleshausen, 6.32
Hesse, 3.245; 5.179, 394; 6.32; 7.349;
  9.647; 10.139, 252, 342; 11.255,
  260-1; 12.132; 13.226; 14.93, 217
Hohenlohe, 5.456
Holland (province), 6.114, 116;
  10.209; 13.274
Holstein, 9.151
Hormuz, 9.324
Huy, 11.323

Iceland, 5.239; 7.242, 248; 9.370
Ile de France, 5.92; 7.49, 336;
  11.127; 13.36; 14.148
Imola, 10.235
India, 9.266, 331-3, 338
Innsbruck, 5.195; 10.52
Istanbul, 3.306; 5.646, 658; 8.159-60;
  9.124, 643; 12.145

Japan, 5.46; 9.327, 329
Jihlava, 12.114
Jura region, 5.114; 13.371, 376

Karaman, 8.153
Kassa, 5.402; 8.141
Kayseri, 5.513, 653; 8.150, 153;
  9.437; 10.344-5
Kitzingen, 6.174; 8.7
Koblenz, 5.175; 8.126
Köln, see Cologne
Kongsberg, 11.271
Königsberg, 9.215
Konstanz, see Constance
Konya, 13.157
Košca, see Kassa
Krefeld, 9.585-6, 588-9

La Mancha, 5.142, 187
Languedoc, 4.47; 5.346; 7.56; 9.465,
  550, 556; 10.26, 28, 177, 391-2,
  394; 11.214; 12.27-9, 37; 13.259;
  14.44
La Rochelle (and region), 6.76;
  9.261, 271, 295, 298-9, 394, 411;
  13.49
Latium, 3.185; 10.232
Latvia, 7.260-1
Lavaur, 9.550
Lazio, see Latium
Le Havre, 9.300, 306
Leiden, 5.478; 6.112; 8.69; 9.559;
  11.45; 13.277; 14.324
Leipzig, 13.221
Le Mans, 8.43
León, 5.136; 7.98
Le Plessis-Gassot, 7.75
Libourne (and region), 10.413
Liège, 5.124, 127; 9.531, 617;
  10.504; 11.41, 224
Liguria, 7.135; 9.80
Lille, 5.279; 6.245; 8.69; 10.280
Limburg, 4.75; 7.89
Limousin, 3.54; 6.84
Lindau, 8.115
Linz (and region), 5.382
Lippe, 3.231, 246-7; 13.210
Lisbon, 8.199; 9.72, 243, 399; 11.9
Lithuania, 6.219-20; 7.230; 14.231,
  234
Livonia, 7.255, 259-60
Livorno, 9.251-2
Lodève, 12.37
Lombardy, 3.174-6; 6.48, 151;
  7.314-15; 9.92, 642; 10.224-7;
  11.150; 13.142. See also Milan
London, 9.16, 18, 54, 77-9; 11.9;
  12.21; 13.235; 14.29
Lorient, 8.192
Lorraine, 3.55; 5.607-8; 7.32, 43;
  13.368
Loudun, 13.373
Louisbourg, 9.270, 369
Louisiana, 9.269
Lourmarin, 7.84
Lübeck, 6.46, 173; 9.216-17
Lucca, 8.97-8; 9.100
Lucerne, 5.173; 6.190; 11.350
Lüneburg, 11.106; 13.202
Lusatia, 5.661; 7.175; 8.124; 9.591
Luxembourg, 11.47; 13.369
Luzern, see Lucerne
Lvov, 9.339; 11.84
Lyon (and region), 4.70; 5.489; 7.53,
  78, 334; 8.44; 9.27, 29, 37, 410,
  428, 525, 528, 545; 11.200, 204-5,
  218-19; 13.34, 40-3, 240; 14.254

Mâcon, 13.252
Madeira, 4.107
Madrid, 4.80; 5.139-41; 6.264;
  8.77-9, 183, 200; 9.420, 532;
  11.182, 225, 233; 14.184, 325, 394,
  441
Magdeburg region, 7.165
Maine, 3.56; 10.388
Mainz, 5.200; 6.180; 8.127-8; 9.542
Malaga, 9.535, 562
Malestroit, 11.301
Mallorca, 5.565; 7.287
Malmø, 5.514
Malta, 9.229-30
Mani, 3.324; 4.88
Mantes, 5.70
Mantua, 5.380, 624; 10.236; 14.443
Marburg, 11.260; 13.226
Mark, 9.479; 13.226
Marseilles, 8.45, 193, 196; 9.236-40,
  344, 551; 11.284, 319; 13.252
Mas d'Azil, 13.270
Masovia, 3.281; 7.297
Massif Central, 7.50-1
Maurienne, 7.83
Meaux, 13.253
Mecklenburg, 7.181; 14.209
Medina del Campo, 5.143; 9.72, 419
Meissen, 9.667
Memmingen, 8.115
Merindad de Estella, 7.105
Metz, 5.608
Meulan, 5.104
Meuse (river and region), 4.75; 5.125;
  10.504
Milan, 3.170, 176; 5.624, 152-3; 8.94;
  9.422-3, 642; 10.224-7; 11.65, 68
Minho, 14.113
Minot, 5.362
Modena, 7.126, 290; 11.64, 148;
  14.190
Moldavia, 7.226, 298; 10.255
Molise, 5.375
Montagnac, 9.550
Montauban, 5.113, 340
Monte Lupo, 11.335
Montes, 7.122
Montesarcho, 7.129
Montpellier, 5.278, 445; 8.46;
  11.211, 368; 12.28; 13.118; 14.60,
  299
Montplaisant, 5.334
Moravia, 4.94; 5.643; 9.116, 489;
  11.356; 13.282, 289
Moscow, 8.177-9, 203; 9.133; 11.359,
  363; 12.153; 14.237, 397
Mozambique, 9.284
Mulhouse, 8.129; 13.213
Munich, 8.117; 9.103
Münster, 11.186; 13.89, 281, 287-8,
  295, 299, 304
Murat, 5.465
Murcia (city and province), 5.370;
  8.80; 12.86

Namur, 11.47
Nantes, 5.81, 273; 9.261, 301-4,
  393-4, 528; 12.58
Naples (Kingdom and city), 3.158,
  196-204; 5.162, 374, 613, 172;
  7.138, 146; 8.94, 99; 9.95, 232,

425; 10.166, 238-40, 334; 11.73, 152, 155, 331; 12.88, 91-3; 13.72, 74, 77-8; 14.373, 422
Narva, 9.183, 196
Navarre, 7.105
Neubourg, 7.63
Neuchâtel, 9.576; 10.450; 14.298
New Castile, 8.78
Newfoundland, 9.300
Nice, 7.34
Niederlausitz, see Lusatia
Nîmes, 11.218-19, 304; 13.251, 258
Nivernais, 5.332, 347, 357
Nördlingen, 8.130; 9.579
Normandy, 3.57; 5.88, 93, 277, 346; 6.73, 86, 102; 7.30, 63, 303; 9.290, 460-3, 616; 10.175, 403, 411; 11.316, 320; 12.34; 13.261
Novara, 13.140
Novgorod, 6.256; 7.255
Nuremberg, 3.222; 4.59; 5.393; 6.253; 7.154; 8.131-3; 9.107, 113, 487, 627; 11.257, 353; 12.115; 13.224, 227, 229, 392; 14.92

Olonets, 13.325
Oppenheim, 13.100
Orihuela, 5.370
Orléans, 7.61; 10.313
Osnabrück, 7.174, 189
Oulu, 5.516; 7.234
Overijssel, 5.128

Paderborn, 7.171-2
Padua, 11.330; 14.371
Palatinate, 3.244; 13.153
Palencia, 11.229
Palermo, 7.317; 8.94; 12.90
Papal States, 3.170; 7.141; 9.619; 10.130, 231-2, 235. See also Rome, Latium, Romagna, etc.
Paris, 4.71; 5.87-8, 103-4, 270, 342, 487, 490, 527; 6.14, 16, 22, 24, 69, 70, 96, 105, 244, 257; 7.71; 8.47-56, 182-3, 194, 197; 9.22, 26, 30-1, 36, 526-7, 529, 548, 665; 10.276-8, 284, 293, 296, 298, 302, 312, 315, 373, 386, 397, 399, 401, 407-10, 415, 418-22, 491; 11.9, 19, 20-1, 23, 28, 127, 134-6, 180, 201, 212, 220-1, 290, 300, 306, 317; 12.21, 38, 47, 55-6, 59, 67; 13.44-5, 130, 265, 313; 14.29, 40, 53, 57, 68, 148, 151, 161, 304, 316, 319, 382 384-8, 390, 407, 439. For Paris region and diocese see Ile de France
Parma, 7.145; 8.100; 14.190
Pavia, 5.155; 9.642; 11.156
Peloponnese, 3.322
Pennsylvania, 13.319
Persia, 9.338
Perugia, 8.101

Pescia, 8.102
Piacenza, 6.31; 9.423
Picardy, 6.92
Piedmont, 3.184; 5.501; 6.154-5; 7.135; 10.129, 166, 228, 412, 510; 11.69; 13.80; 14.372
Pietrasanta, 9.621
Poitou, 3.58; 7.60, 66, 304-5
Pomor'e, 12.153
Poneggen, 9.580
Pont-de-Monvert, 7.79
Port en Bessin, 5.97
Porvoo, 7.245
Poznan, 5.642; 9.218
Prague, 12.114
Prato, 11.334
Provence, 3.59, 60; 5.72, 337-9, 466; 7.27, 76-7, 80, 84; 10.31, 283; 11.283; 12.42-3; 13.37-8, 58; 14.35, 64, 70, 175
Prussia, 3.210, 248-9; 4.57; 5.507, 633; 6.7, 176, 195; 7.163, 168, 180, 188, 293; 10.5, 135, 138, 144-5, 243, 337, 340-1, 517, 519-20; 11.82; 12.138; 13.85, 87; 14.202, 206, 210, 266
Puglia, see Apulia
Pyrenees, 3.61; 4.14; 5.528; 7.81, 85; 12.48; 13.270

Quercy, 3.62-3; 5.113, 116

Raahe, 7.234
Ragusa, 3.321; 6.209; 9.255-6, 347, 602; 10.256
Ravenna, 7.125
Ravenhead, 9.644
Ravensburg, 7.185, 187; 8.115; 9.480; 13.98
Regensburg, 13.229
Reims (and region), 6.81; 13.112; 14.42, 165
Rennes (Brittany), 8.195; 9.32; 12.58
Rennes (Aude), 7.36
Reval, 9.196, 219-20
Rhineland, 5.539; 9.474, 485, 585-7, 592; 12.132; 13.153
Riazan, 5.412-13
Riga, 9.196; 14.447
Rioja, 7.101
Rochefort, 8.192-3
Romagna, 7.125
Romans, 12.60; 14.58
Rome, 3.185; 6.7, 147, 156-7; 8.94, 103-7, 182-3; 9.93, 421, 427, 432, 619; 10.9, 231; 11.149, 154-5, 241; 13.141; 14.191, 417, 419
Rostock, 8.134; 9.202; 13.209
Rotterdam, 5.132; 9.185
Rouen, 5.73, 497; 8.57-9; 9.271, 290, 305-6, 554; 10.286-7, 396; 11.137, 316, 320; 12.46; 13.30

Rovigo, 7.132
Rumeli, 9.605
Ruremonde, 11.47
Ruthenia, 9.368
Ryfylke, 7.238

Sables d'Olonne, 9.369
Saideli, 7.223
Sainghin-en-Mélantois, 5.82
Saint-André-les-Alpes, 5.338
Saint-Gobain, 9.644
Saint-Malo, 9.307
Saint-Maur, 5.105
Saint Petersburg, 4.85; 8.179, 203; 14.397
Salamanca, 14.179
Salonica, 9.257
Salzburg (and region), 5.195, 387, 390
San Felice sul Panaro, 7.126, 290
San Gimignano, 8.108
Santa Maria del Monte, 7.98
Santander, 9.310
Santiago, 8.81
São Cristóvão de Rio Mau, 14.113
Saragossa, see Zaragoza
Sarlat, 10.406
Sault region, 4.51
Savoy, 3.64; 6.93; 7.82-3; 10.129, 510
Saxony, 5.171, 381, 383; 6.185; 7.184; 9.475, 580, 625; 10.247; 13.151, 203, 319, 397
Segovia, 3.144; 7.286, 289; 11.58; 12.83
Segura (River and region), 5.138
Sennely-en-Sologne, 7.74
Sète, 8.192
Seville, 5.137, 153, 283, 588; 6.265; 7.99, 288; 8.82-5; 9.149, 267, 309, 311-16; 10.436, 439
Siberia, 5.548, 550
Sicily, 3.205-7; 5.156; 6.170-1; 7.136; 9.82, 348; 10.447. See also Palermo
Siena, 5.163, 165; 5.373; 6.140-1; 8.109-10; 9.501; 14.84, 190
Sierra Morena, 5.536
Silesia, 9.587; 10.242
Skaraborg, 7.233
Slovakia, 7.296; 13.289
Slovenia, 3.329
Soluthurn, 11.350
Speyer, 9.542
Stavanger, 7.238
Stavenow, 7.163-4
Stockerau, 5.177
Stockholm, 9.193; 11.95, 98
Stralsund, 9.202; 13.209
Strasbourg (and region), 5.84; 8.18, 135-6; 11.249-50; 13.32, 181, 186, 189-90, 198, 207; 14.333, 379, 424
Suraz, 7.319

Suzdal, 13.163
Swabia, 3.244, 250; 7.185-7; 9.104, 114; 11.253; 12.129; 13.285-6

Talavera, 12.85
Tarbes, 7.85
Tavastland, 5.230; 11.166
Thessaly, 4.20
Thoissey-en-Dombes, 5.333
Thorn, 9.189
Thrace, 13.154
Thuringia, 6.185; 9.628, 647; 10.335; 13.144, 147, 203
Tibet, 9.338
Tielt, 13.60
Toledo (and region), 5.577; 7.122, 289; 8.78, 86-8; 11.230; 13.67; 14.442
Tolfa, 9.619
Toropets, 7.330
Toul region, 7.32
Toulon, 13.273
Toulouse (and region), 3.65; 6.77-8, 257; 7.28, 41; 9.24, 342; 10.273, 399; 11.24, 207; 12.27, 57; 13.236, 238, 250; 14.44, 301
Touraine, 5.88
Tourouvre-au-Perche, 5.80
Tours, 7.61; 8.59
Trabzon, 8.153
Transylvania, 3.288; 7.228; 9.224, 227, 233; 12.146; 13.158
Trentino, 13.73
Trieste, 9.253
Troyes, 6.81
Trujillo, 5.554
Turin, 5.540; 14.372
Tuscany, 3.180-1; 5.166, 378, 418, 499; 7.127, 137, 144; 9.98, 569, 631-2; 10.229; 11.67, 155, 334-7; 13.75; 14.395. See also Florence, Siena, etc.
Tyrol, 7.157; 12.122

Uberlingen, 8.115
Udine, 11.247
Uelzen, 11.354
Ukraine, 3.393-4; 9.183, 361; 11.363; 12.142, 148, 157; 13.400; 14.231
Ulm (and region), 9.582
Unterfinning, 5.288
Urach, 9.590
Urals, 5.549; 9.636, 639
Urbino, 7.291
Ussel, 3.54
Ustiuzhna, 5.422
Utrecht, 6.113-14; 11.45

Valais, 9.365
Valencia (Kingdom and city), 3.146; 5.574, 580, 584, 586; 7.114, 312; 9.244-6; 10.435; 11.147; 12.76; 13.328
Valenciennes, 9.459, 552
Valladolid, 8.89
Vallorbe, 5.114
Vallorcine, 7.82
Vannes, 8.60; 9.343
Vaucluse, 14.138
Vaudémont, 7.32
Veluwe, 4.87
Vence, 13.37
Venice, 3.156, 186-95; 4.19, 137; 5.158, 167, 286, 377, 483, 502, 614-19; 6.43, 46, 158-69; 7.124, 132, 144; 8.183; 9.15, 83-91, 122, 222, 229-30, 234, 347, 355-6, 366, 427, 431, 434, 537, 574, 623, 662-3; 10.47-51, 161, 445, 448, 511-12, 514; 11.70-2, 74-5, 184, 242-5, 344-5, 347; 13.22; 14.83, 188, 193-5, 238, 263-4, 330, 375, 419, 423, 445
Verona, 3.158; 5.167; 6.249; 8.111
Versailles, 5.110; 10.33; 14.436
Verviers, 9.558
Vexin, 5.343
Vienna (and region), 5.387; 11.355
Vivarais, 3.66; 12.49
Vizcaya, 3.148
Vosges, 13.307
Vyg, 13.325

Waldkappel, 6.32
Waldshut, 12.126
Waldstein, 9.597
Wallachia, 3.326; 7.226, 298
Wandre, 5.124
Warsaw, 11.187
Weissenburg, 8.119
Weser (river and region), 6.192
West Indies, see Caribbean
Westphalia, 9.485, 592
Windsheim, 12.114
Wismar, 9.202; 11.351
Wittenberg, 8.137; 11.254
Wlodawa, 5.642
Worms, 9.542
Wuppertal, 9.583, 585
Württemberg, 5.541; 6.179, 189; 7.153; 9.590; 10.148, 342; 13.85, 94; 14.90
Würzburg, 7.155

Yaroslavl', 5.415

Zaragoza, 5.133; 8.90-2; 9.534
Zealand (Denmark), 4.83; 8.162
Zorita, 7.104
Zurich (and region), 5.172; 6.181; 9.488; 11.350; 13.183
Zweibrücken, 13.153; 14.216
Zwickau, 5.504; 13.221

INDEX
OF AUTHORS AND EDITORS

Aalbers, J., 10.208
Abbiateci, A., 10.383, 395
Abel, W., 3.214, 221; 7.1, 148; 11.108, 157
Abrams, P., 6.251; 8.1
Abramsky, C., 5.636
Abrate, M., 11.329
Abray, Lorna J., 13.181
Achilles, W., 7.149-50
Ackerman, Evelyn B., 5.70
Adams, J. W., 1.18
Adams, N., 9.501
Adams, R. M., 10.10
Adams, T. M., 11.196, 282
Addy, G. M., 14.136, 178-9
Adler, P. J., 14.218
Ago, Renata, 7.135
Ågren, K., 3.345; 5.222; 6.210-11
Aguilar Piñal, F., 8.83
Agulhon, M., 7.38; 14.35
Aitken, H. G. J., 9.140
Ajello, R., 10.238
Åkerman, S., 5.1, 213, 523
Alanen, A. J., 9.156
Alasseur, C., 14.382
Albert, Phyllis C., 5.610
Albion, R. G., 2.1
Alcalá Zamora, J., 9.618
Aldcroft, D. H., 2.2; 9.243
Aleati, G., 5.155
Alef, G., 4.84; 6.217; 10.351, 530
Aleksandrov, V. A., 5.411
Alexander, J. T., 8.178-9; 11.359-63; 12.159-61
Allen, E. A., 4.47
Alonso Alvárez, L., 9.469
Alpers, Svetlana, 14.403
Altbauer, D., 10.352
Alter, G., 5.2, 3, 119
Amalric, J.-P., 3.91; 7.94; 8.89
Aman, J., 10.485

Amann, P., 2.101
Ambrosini, F., 4.137
Amelang, J. S., 6.117, 133; 10.320
Anchor, R., 1.60
Anderson, C. A., 6.255
Anderson, J. L., 4.28
Anderson, M., 5.295
Anderson, M. S., 2.86-7
Anderson, P., 10.1
Anderson, Pauline R., 1.68
Anderson, R. T., 2.13
Anderson, Ruth M., 11.181
Andersson, Christiane, 14.427
Andersson, I., 3.342
Andorka, R., 5.201
Andrés-Gallego, J., 7.95
Andrews, K. R., 9.278
Andries, Lise, 14.273
Andrieux, M., 8.103
Anes Alvarez, G., 3.125, 131, 140; 7.96, 286; 10.120
Angermann, E., 7.152
Anglo, S., 13.336
Ankarloo, B., 5.472
Ansimov, E., 10.260
Ansón Calvo, María, 5.133
Anstey, R., 9.388
Antoine, M., 10.167-9
Antonovics, A. V., 13.103
Appleby, A. B., 4.30; 5.39; 11.124, 262
Applewhite, Harriet B., 10.118
Aranda Doncel, J., 5.570; 8.73
Arbel, B., 5.644
Arbellot, G., 4.65
Ardant, G., 10.160
Arden, Heather, 14.383
Argan, G. C., 8.180
Ariès, P., 1.30; 5.280-1, 426, 432; 14.106-7
Armengaud, A., 3.9, 37; 5.4, 330

Armstrong, C. A. J., 10.40
Armstrong, J. A., 10.2, 264
Armstrong, T. E., 5.544
Arnheim, A., 5.626
Arnold, C. A., 14.128
Arriaza, A., 6.1
Arthur, A. G., 12.33
Artola, M., 3.126; 7.97; 10.211
Artz, F. B., 14.146
Asch, J., 6.173
Ascher, A., 6.268
Asdrachas, S. I., 7.220
Asher, E. L., 10.487
Ashtor, E., 9.221-3, 359
Aspvall, G., 7.233
Asséo, Henriette, 5.649
Assereto, G., 11.234
Aston, Margaret, 2.56
Aston, T., 2.72; 7.2, 192
Åstrom, S.-E., 3.346, 350, 354; 4.44; 9.158-60, 375-6
Atienza Hernández, I., 6.118
Atkinson, Dorothy, 5.518
Atkinson, G., 4.126
Atkinson, W. C., 3.92
Attman, A., 9.161-3, 197; 11.1, 38
Aubin, H., 3.214
Augel, J., 5.539
Augustine, W. R., 6.218
Aunola, T., 7.234
Avrich, P., 12.147
Aymard, M., 1.23, 26; 3.68, 153; 5.156; 6.170; 9.50, 347

Babelon, J.-P., 11.180
Bachi, R., 5.611-12
Backer, Julie E., 5.214
Backhouse, M. F., 10.427
Backus, O. P., 6.219-20; 10.457
Bacon, G. C., 5.635
Badalo-Dulong, Claude, 5.269, 490

Bade, K. J., 9.538
Badinter, Elisabeth, 5.439
Baechler, J., 2.108
Baehrel, R., 5.71; 7.27
Baer, G., 9.544
Baetens, R., 10.500
Bagge, S., 14.224
Bagrow, L., 4.102
Bailey, C. R., , 14.147-8
Bailyn, B., 1.28
Bairoch, P., 4.90
Bak, J. M., 10.528; 12.1, 112
Baker, A. R. H., 4.1, 2; 7.237
Baker, G. R. F., 6.140-1
Baker, K. M., 11.133; 14.252, 275
Bakewell, P., 1.44
Bakhtin, M. M., 14.36
Balazs, Eva H., 6.50; 7.18
Baldo, V., 14.188
Ball, J. N., 9.1
Ballesteros Rodríguez, J., 11.324
Bamford, P. W., 4.48; 9.21, 164, 377;
    10.384-5, 488
Banac, I., 6.196
Banaji, J., 7.3
Bang, Nina E., 2.9
Bangs, J. D., 14.324
Banks, J. A., 5.18
Baran, P., 2.46
Baratier, E., 5.72
Barbagli, M., 5.372
Barber, B., 6.2
Barber, B. R., 10.60
Barber, Elinor G., 6.2, 55
Barber, G., 14.274
Barberis, W., 10.510
Barbier, J.-M., 5.296
Barbour, Violet, 9.52
Bardet, J.-P., 1.12; 5.5; 8.57; 11.179
Barkan, O. L., 5.207; 9.643; 11.88
Barker, T. M., 10.462, 516
Barkhausen, M., 9.474
Barkun, M., 13.280
Barnard, H. C., 14.149
Barnavi, E., 12.54
Baron, S. H., 2.109; 3.357; 9.130-1
Baron, S. W., 5.592-3
Barnett-Robisheaux, T., see
    Robisheaux
Bartlett, R. P., 3.358; 5.545; 7.255
Barton, H. A., 9.492
Barton, P. F., 12.139
Basas Fernández, M., 9.67, 415-16
Basini, G. L., 11.64, 148
Bastier, J., 7.28
Bataillon, M., 9.292
Batchelder, R. W., 10.3
Bater, J. H., 4.25
Bátori, Ingrid, 1.12; 6.174; 13.182
Bauer, P. T., 2.29
Baulant, Micheline, 1.12; 4.30;
    5.331; 9.236; 11.19-20

Baum, H. P., 9.435
Bauman, Z., 1.45
Baumgartner, F. J., 13.106
Baxandall, M., 14.412
Baxter, D. C., 10.271-2, 309
Bayard, Françoise, 8.22; 9.410
Bayard, J. P., 9.523
Baykov, A., 3.362
Bazzochi, R., 13.138
Beales, D., 13.116
Bean, R., 10.463
Beard, Mary R., 5.474
Beaud, M., 2.110
Beauroy, J., 7.332; 12.26; 13.313,
    370
Bebb, P. N., 13.225
Bechhofer, F., 5.11
Bechtel, H., 3.215
Béchu, P., 10.489
Beck, R., 5.288
Becker, Danièle, 14.441
Bédarida, F., 3.1; 8.2
Beech, Beatrice, 5.487
Behar, Ruth, 7.98
Behrens, C. Betty A., 2.88; 6.56;
    10.1, 4, 5; 14.17
Beik, W. H., 10.26; 12.27-9; 14.5,
    37, 61
Beinart, H., 5.554
Bejarano Robles, F., 9.562
Béjin, A. J., 5.281
Beldiceanu, N., 3.294
Bell, R. M., 13.26, 70
Bellettini, A., 5.157
Belmont, Nicole, 14.38
Beltrami, D., 5.158; 6.158; 7.124
Benabou, Erica-M., 5.270
Benaiteau, Michèle, 7.146
Benda, K., 3.271
Ben-David, J., 14.341
Bendix, R., 10.6
Bendjebbar, A., 3.47
Benecke, G., 3.230-1, 246-7, 256;
    6.175; 10.52; 12.1, 127; 13.8
Benedict, P., 5.73; 6.243; 8.58;
    9.305; 13.30
Benevolo, L., 8.181
Bengtsson, T., 11.91
Bennassar, B., 3.111; 8.89; 11.325;
    13.326; 14.75
Bennett, H. A., 6.221
Benoît, Marcelle, 14.436
Benzoni, G., 14.258
Bercé, Y.-M., 3.48; 7.8; 12.2, 30-1,
    61; 14.39
Berdahl, R. M., 6.176; 7.151-2
Berend, I. T., 3.301
Bérenger, J., 10.241-2; 13.8
Berengo, M., 3.158, 187; 8.97
Berg, Maxine, 9.439
Berger, P., 11.125, 198
Bergeron, L., 7.56

Bergier, J.-F., 2.62; 3.251; 9.101,
    401
Bergin, J. A., 13.107-8
Berindei, M., 10.255
Berkis, A. V., 3.391
Berkner, L. K., 5.297-300, 332,
    381-3, 418
Berlanstein, L. R., 10.273-4, 386
Bernard, G., 10.321
Bernard, J., 9.292
Bernard, L., 8.47; 12.32
Bernard, P. B., 11.355
Bernard, R.-J., 11.126
Berner, S., 3.177; 6.142
Berov, L., 4.81; 11.89
Berthold, R., 7.1, 149, 173, 292
Bertin, G. Y., 9.259
Besnard, P., 2.111
Best, G., 13.116
Beutler, Corinne, 11.21
Bever, E., 5.460
Bezucha, R. J., 5.264
Bideau, A., 5.333
Bieleman, J., 7.86
Bien, D. D., 10.275, 490; 13.236-7
Bigi, Patrizia, 7.135
Bill, V. T., 9.132
Billacois, F., 6.42; 10.387, 395
Billinge, M., 7.237
Biondi, A., 14.265
Biraben, J.-N., 5.74-5, 334; 11.263,
    283-4
Birdzell, L. E., 2.45
Birn, R., 14.289-90
Birnbaum, N., 13.183
Bishko, C. J., 3.85; 7.343-4
Bissonnette, G., 14.227
Bitar Letayf, M., 10.121
Bitton, D., 6.19, 57
Bizière, J. M., 9.353; 11.109
Bizzocchi, R., 6.143
Bjørkvik, H., 7.238, 351
Bjørn, C., 7.235
Bjurling, O., 9.165-6; 11.92
Black, C. E., 3.379; 10.118
Black, D., 13.339
Black, J. L., 14.228-9
Black, R., 14.189
Blacker, J. G. C., 6.58
Blackwell, W. L., 3.362; 8.164
Blaich, F., 10.131
Blaisdell, Charmarie J., 13.165
Blanc, Simone, 10.155
Blanchard, I., 4.49; 7.340; 9.609
Blanchet, D., 5.75
Blane, A., 14.234
Blanning, T. C. W., 8.127; 14.246
Blanshei, Sarah R., 8.101
Blaschke, K., 5.171
Blasco Martínez, Rosa M., 8.90, 92
Blayo, Y., 5.76-7, 101
Blickle, P., 3.250; 6.252; 10.53;

12.96-100, 112-13, 116, 127;
13.184-5
Blickle, Renate, 3.250
Blitz, R. C., 9.319; 10.81
Bloch, M., 7.29, 73
Blockmans, W. P., 11.223
Blodgett, Linda L., 7.204
Blok, A., 8.93; 10.374
Blomquist, T. W., 1.41
Bluche, F., 3.17, 30; 6.13, 59, 64;
10.269, 276-8, 311
Blum, A., 8.57
Blum, J., 7.4-8, 193-4, 256, 328-9;
11.100
Blumenkranz, B., 5.603-4
Blussé, L., 9.225
Bodek, Evelyn G., 14.247
Boari, M., 11.365
Bodmer, W., 9.575
Boelcke, W. A., 7.153
Boesch Gajano, Sofia, 5.612
Boethius, B., 3.340
Bog, I., 3.222; 7.154-5; 8.131; 9.115;
10.132-3
Bogucka, Maria, 3.261; 4.44;
8.143-4; 9.115, 167-9, 197, 207;
11.83; 13.166
Bohanan, Donna, 6.60-1
Bois, G., 7.2, 30
Bois, J.-P., 5.464
Bois, P., 8.43
Boiteux, L. A., 9.402
Boiteux, Martine, 14.21
Boles, Susan K., 13.144
Bollème, Geneviève, 14.291, 306
Bölts, J., 7.341
Bonazzoli, Viviana, 5.613
Bonfield, L., 5.435
Bonney, R., 10.170-1, 279; 12.62-3
Bonnet, J.-C., 11.110
Boogart, E. van den, see Van den
Boogart
Borelli, G., 6.159
Borrero Fernández, Mercedes, 7.99
Bosher, J. F., 6.104; 9.22, 268, 369;
10.172-4
Boskoff, A., 14.268
Bossenga, Gail, 10.280
Bossy, J., 5.301; 10.390; 13.2-7, 17,
22
Botrel, J.-F., 14.325
Bouchard, G., 7.74
Boucher, F., 11.171
Boulle, P. H., 9.260-1, 301
Bouloiseau, M., 2.30; 10.175
Bourde, A. J., 7.301
Bourdieu, P., 5.335
Bourdin, P. M., 3.57
Bourgeon, J. L., 9.23
Bourquin, Marie-H., 10.388
Bouton, A., 3.56
Boutruche, R., 7.31; 8.37

Bouvet, M., 3.57
Bouvier, J., 9.413; 10.161
Bouvier, R., 3.197
Bouvier-Ajam, M., 9.522
Bouwsma, W. J., 1.13; 13.179; 14.1,
2
Bowen, J., 14.127
Bowman, Mary J., 6.255; 14.128
Boxer, C. R., 4.128, 130; 9.326, 331,
653-4, 659
Boyajian, J. C., 9.417
Boyce, Mary S., 9.548
Boyd-Bowman, P., 5.531-3
Boyer, Marjorie N., 9.503
Bradley, J. F. N., 3.286
Brady, T. A., 6.177; 13.182, 186;
14.424
Brambilla, Elena, 13.139
Branca, L., 11.235
Branca, Patricia, 5.436
Brandenburg, D. J., 7.302
Bratchel, M. E., 9.2, 77-8
Braude, B., 5.645; 9.118, 601
Braudel, F., 1.1, 2, 31, 36; 2.14, 57;
3.5, 6, 142, 154, 186; 5.6; 9.251,
311; 11.2, 111
Braun, H.-J., 9.504; 10.134
Braun, J., 14.447
Braun, R., 3.252; 5.172; 9.488;
10.243
Braunstein, P., 9.610
Brendler, G., 13.281
Brennan, T., 14.40
Brenner, R., 2.112; 7.2
Brésard, M., 9.410
Brettell, Caroline, 5.369
Brezzi, P., 2.8
Bricourt, M., 11.127
Bridenthal, Renate, 5.473
Briggs, A., 8.21
Briggs, R., 3.18; 8.21; 13.368
Bright, C., 10.416
Brinton, C. C., 12.69; 14.3
Brizzi, G. P., 14.190
Broadhead, P., 13.187
Brock, P., 13.318
Brockliss, L. W. B., 14.150-1
Brodrick, J., 10.90
Bromley, J. S., 6.116; 7.311; 9.237;
10.40
Brooks, P. N., 11.255
Brown, H., 14.365
Brown, Judith C., 5.499; 5.500;
8.102
Browning, J. D., 11.227, 300
Brownmiller, Susan, 5.265
Brucker, G. A., 3.178; 5.285; 10.331
Bruckmüller, E., 3.257
Bruford, W. H., 3.240
Brügelmann, J., 11.348
Bruijn, G. de, 3.67
Bruijn, J. R., 9.655; 10.501-2

Brulez, W., 9.3, 39-40, 63, 83
Brumont, F., 7.100-1
Bruneel, C., 5.120
Brunet, C., 7.75
Brunner, O., 1.38; 6.178
Brunschwig, H., 14.266
Brunvand, J. H., 14.429
Buchanan, R. H., 7.318
Buck, L. P., 12.114-15, 119
Bücking, J., 12.122
Buczko, B., 14.306
Bueno de Mesquita, D. M., 6.151;
10.224
Buisseret, D. J., 4.66; 10.101
Buist, M. G., 10.162
Bulferetti, L., 3.184; 9.80
Bulhof, Ilse N., 1.32, 60
Bullard, Melissa M., 9.421; 10.231;
11.149
Bullough, Bonnie, 5.250; 11.264
Bullough, V. L., 5.248-50, 474;
11.264
Bur, Marta, 9.119
Burch, T. K., 5.315
Burgess, M., 14.396-7
Burgess, Renate, 11.265
Burguière, A., 1.15; 5.78, 302;
13.31; 14.4, 21, 41-2
Burke, G. L., 8.198
Burke, P., 1.1, 3, 7, 26, 33; 2.39, 67;
6.43; 8.3, 182; 12.88; 13.17, 245;
14.5, 6, 81, 238, 259, 400
Burkholder, M. A.10.322
Burrell, S. A., 2.113
Burri, H.-R., 5.173
Burrows, T., 1.63
Büsch, O., 3.248; 10.517
Bush, M. L., 6.44
Bushkoff, L., 6.228, 239
Bushkovitch, P., 6.196; 8.165; 9.133;
10.261
Bustelo García, F., 5.134
Buszello, H., 12.116
Butel, P., 8.38; 9.293, 295-6
Butler, J., 13.39, 376
Butler, T., 8.157
Buza, J., 7.350
Bylebyl, J. J., 11.330
Byrnes, R. F., 5.404

Cabantous, A., 9.649-50
Cabo, A., 4.12
Cabourdin, G., 3.55; 5.7; 7.32
Cabrera Munõz, E., 7.102
Caceres, B., 14.43
Cachinero-Sánchez, B., 5.135
Cahnman, W. J., 14.268
Caiati, V., 5.373
Cairncross, A. K., 2.46
Caizzi, B., 3.173; 9.84, 92
Calhoun, D., 5.427
Callahan, W. J., 3.127; 9.146-8;

10.122; 11.225-7; 13.8; 14.76
Calmann, Marianne, 5.605
Calvi, Giulia, 11.331
Cameron, E., 13.317
Cameron, I. A., 10.389
Cameron, J. B., 7.76
Cameron, R., 3.251
Camporesi, P., 14.82, 265
Cannon, J., 1.33
Canny, N., 4.97
Cantimori, D., 13.244
Capella Martínez, M., 9.532
Caplow, Harriet M., 14.413
Capra, C., 3.170; 6.135; 10.225
Caracciolo, A., 3.170; 9.93-4, 247
Caracciolo, F., 3.196
Carande, R., 5.571; 10.212
Caravale, M., 3.170; 10.232
Cardaillac, L., 5.572
Cardwell, D. S. L., 14.342
Carlsson, S., 6.37
Carmichael, Ann G., 11.332-3
Carmichael, J., 14.270
Caro Baroja, J., 5.555, 573; 13.64, 386-8; 14.77
Caron, X., 9.142
Carosso, V. P., 1.71
Carpanetto, D., 3.155
Carr, J. L., 3.19
Carrier, H., 13.1
Carrière, C., 9.238-9, 252, 308; 11.284
Carroll, Berenice A., 5.475
Carroll, Linda L., 14.83
Carse, J. P., 14.106
Carsten, F. L., 3.223; 5.627; 6.7; 7.156; 10.54-5
Carstensen, F., 9.131
Carter, Alice C., 9.41-4
Carter, C. H., 9.60
Carter, F. W., 3.321; 4.20; 8.148; 9.255, 602
Carter, H., 8.9
Casali, Elide, 7.125
Casey, J., 2.67; 3.146; 5.574; 10.431
Caspard, P., 9.576
Casparis, J., 10.518
Cassia, P. S., 5.650
Castan, Nicole, 10.390-5; 14.21
Castan, Y., 5.346; 10.394-5; 14.44
Caster, G., 9.24
Castillo Pintado, A., 3.112; 9.244
Castro, A., 3.93
Cattini, M., 7.126, 290
Cauwenberghe, E. H. G. van, 7.285; 11.39
Cavailles, H., 4.68
Cavallo, Sandra, 5.501
Cavanaugh, G. J., 6.56; 10.281
Cavignac, J., 9.294
Cazeaux, Isabelle, 14.437
Censer, J. R., 14.275-6, 293

Cepeda Adán, J., 10.213
Certeau, M. de, 13.9
Cerutti, Simona, 5.501
Cestaro, A., 3.199
Chabert, A. R. E., 11.66
Chacón Jiménez, F., 5.370; 8.80
Chagniot, J., 10.491
Chalumeau, R. P., 11.217
Chamberlin, E. R., 2.58
Chambers, D. S., 3.188; 13.104; 14.191, 414
Chamoux, Antoinette, 5.79
Chaney, E. P. de G., 11.236
Chapman, S. D., 9.549
Charbonneau, H., 5.8, 80
Charlier, J., 11.321
Charmeil, J. P., 10.176
Chartier, R., 6.243; 8.30; 10.372; 14.108, 129, 152, 286, 294-5, 318
Chassagne, S., 9.549
Châtellier, L., 13.32
Chauchadis, C., 14.78
Chaudhuri, K. N., 4.98; 9.319
Chaunu, Huguette, 9.267, 311
Chaunu, P., 1.4, 15; 2.16, 89-90; 3.20, 113, 142; 4.32, 99; 5.583; 7.56, 63; 9.267, 283, 311; 11.20; 13.49, 375; 14.109
Chaussinand-Nogaret, G., 6.63-4; 9.264; 10.177-8
Chauvet, P., 9.671
Checkland, S. G., 10.7
Chejne, A. G., 5.575
Cherepnin, L. V., 9.170
Cherniavsky, M., 6.232, 238; 10.21, 69; 13.323
Chevalier, B., 8.29, 59; 13.167
Chevalier, M., 14.286, 326
Chiancone Isaacs, Ann K., 8.109
Chiapelli, F., 4.100
Childs, J., 10.464
Chill, E., 11.199
Chirot, D., 1.77; 3.326; 5.404; 7.195
Chisick, H., 14.153-6
Chistiakova, E. V., 12.153
Chistov, K. V., 12.154
Chittolini, G., 13.71
Chojnacki, S., 6.160; 10.47
Chorley, P., 3.197
Chrisman, Miriam U., 5.336; 6.102; 11.249; 13.168, 188-9; 14.333
Christelow, A., 9.5
Christensen, A. E., 9.171
Christensen, C. C., 13.190; 14.110, 425-6
Christian, D., 11.170
Christian, W. A., 13.65-6
Christianson, J. R., 6.212
Church, W. F., 10.21
Cieslak, E., 9.172-3
Cipolla, C. M., 1.39; 2.17, 24; 3.108, 152, 156, 302; 5.9, 159-60; 6.136;

9.505-6; 10.465; 11.65-6, 237, 334-7; 14.130
Ciriacono, S., 9.355, 545
Çizakça, M., 3.295, 603
Clagett, M., 14.349
Clark, G. N., 10.466
Clark, J. G., 9.298, 411
Clark, Marilyn, 5.407
Clark, P., 2.67
Clark, S., 13.337; 14.7
Clarke, J. A., 10.282
Clarkson, J. D., 3.363; 10.353
Clarkson, L. A., 9.440
Clasen, C.-P., 9.578; 13.282-6
Claval, P., 4.1
Claverie, Elisabeth, 3.53
Clavero, B., 7.103
Clawson, Mary A., 5.303
Clay, J. E., 13.324
Clayton, L. A., 9.660
Clegg, A., 14.343
Clendenning, P. H., 3.358; 9.134, 157
Clissold, S., 3.327
Cloet, M., 13.60
Clogg, R., 9.120; 14.95
Clouatre, D. J., 6.15
Clough, C. H., 10.224
Clough, S. B., 2.18-19; 9.510; 10.15
Clout, H. D., 4.7
Clubb, J. M., 1.5
Coats, A. W., 10.82
Cobban, A., 2.91
Cobban, A. B., 14.177
Cochrane, E. W., 3.192; 9.574; 14.260
Cocula-Vaillières, Anne M., 4.67
Coffin, D. R., 6.156
Cohen, Elizabeth S., 14.143
Cohen, Esther, 14.8
Cohen, I. B., 14.344
Cohen, J. E., 5.10
Cohen, Miriam, 5.325
Cohn, B. S., 1.18
Cohn, H. J., 12.117
Cohn, N., 13.338
Cohn, S. K., 6.248
Colas Latorre, G., 10.432
Cole, A., 9.4
Cole, B., 14.415
Cole, C. W., 2.18; 10.102
Cole, J. W., 7.157
Cole, R. G., 4.101; 13.200; 14.427
Coleman, D. C., 2.91; 9.48, 441, 546; 10.82
Coleman, W., 11.285-6
Coles, P., 3.183
Colie, Rosalie L., 10.114
Collantes de Teran, A., 8.82
Collier, R., 3.59; 7.77
Collins, J. B., 9.302; 12.33
Collomp, A., 5.315, 337-9

Columbeanu, S., 7.221
Combes, J., 9.101
Comparato, V. I., 10.334
Confino, M., 3.384; 6.222; 7.257, 329; 14.271
Coniglio, G., 3.198; 9.95
Conrad, F., 13.191
Constant, J.-M., 6.65; 7.33
Constantini, C., 9.80
Contamine, P., 10.492
Contreras, J., 13.327
Conze, W., 3.208, 214; 5.54
Cook, M. A., 3.296; 5.207-8
Cook, T. G., 14.223
Cooper, J. P., 6.45; 7.2
Cooper, Roslyn P., 6.144
Coornaert, E., 9.56, 258, 523-4
Coppola, G., 7.314
Corazzol, L., 7.128
Corbett, T. G., 5.534
Corbin, A., 11.287
Corsini, C. A., 11.238
Cortes, J. B., 14.327
Corvisier, A., 3.2; 6.3; 10.311, 467-8, 493; 14.239
Corvol, Andrée, 4.49
Coser, L. A., 5.594
Costamagna, H., 7.34
Costantini, C., 3.170; 9.80
Cottrell, P. L., 9.243
Courdurié, M., 9.239, 252
Courgeau, D., 5.527
Couturier, M., 8.42
Cova, A., 9.422
Coveney, P. J., 2.68; 3.21; 6.68
Cowan, A. F., 6.46, 161
Coward, D. A., 5.251, 271
Cowgill, U. M., 11.144
Cox, O. C., 2.114
Cozzi, G., 10.445
Cracraft, J., 3.389
Craeybeckx, J., 9.56, 354
Crafts, N. F. R., 9.457
Crew, Phyllis M., 13.271
Crisp, Olga, 3.380
Crofts, R., 13.169
Croix, A., 3.49; 5.81
Crompton, L., 5.252
Crone, G. R., 4.102
Croot, Patricia, 7.2
Crosby, A. W., 4.103-4
Crosland, M., 14.367
Cross, A. G., 3.364; 9.157
Crouzet, D., 6.66; 13.33-4; 14.45
Crouzet, F., 3.31
Crow, T. E., 14.407
Crowley, C. J., 10.126
Crowther, P. A., 3.359
Crozet, R., 14.408
Crummey, R. O., 3.376; 6.223-7; 10.70, 365; 13.325
Cuaz, M., 14.258

Cubells, Monique, 10.283
Cullen, L. M., 9.295
Cummings, M., 5.272; 10.284
Currie, E. P., 13.339
Curtin, P. D., 9.6, 389
Curtis, L. P., 1.39
Curtiss, J. S., 1.70
Cushing, G. F., 14.337
Cuvillier, J.-P., 4.55
Cvetkova, Bistra, 3.308, 363
Czap, P., 5.245, 412-13

D'Addario, A., 3.179
Dahl, S., 7.323
Dahlgren, S., 6.38
Dainville, F. de, 14.157
Dal Pane, L., 9.536; 10.229
Dalgård, S., 9.211
Damsholt, T., 11.67
Dan, M., 9.224
Daniel, W., 9.135-7
Danière, A., 11.128
Darby, H. C., 3.327
Dardel, P., 9.306
Darmon, P., 5.253
Darnton, R., 6.243, 246; 8.46; 14.9, 275, 296-300, 318
Darrow, Margaret H., 5.340, 488
Darst, D. H., 13.389
Daston, Lorraine J., 14.26
Daumard, Adeline, 6.14
Dauphin, Cécile, 5.79
David, Z. V., 3.260
Davies, A., 7.35, 303
Davies, D. W., 9.45
Davies, Joan, 13.238; 14.301
Davies, K. G., 2.91; 4.105
Davies, N., 3.277, 279
Davies, T., 6.171; 9.348
Davis, J. C., 6.162-3
Davis, Natalie Z., 1.18, 40; 2.55; 5.341, 476, 483, 489; 9.25, 525; 11.200; 13.10, 179, 239-40; 14.21, 46-8, 302-3, 318
Davis, R., 2.20
Davis, W. W., 10.119
Dawson, P., 7.79; 10.285
Day, J., 7.30
Deahl, J., 14.131
Debien, G., 5.526; 7.304-5
Dedieu, J. P., 13.67
Dedijer, V., 3.328
De Felice, R., 3.185
Defourneaux, M., 3.114
De Groot, A. H., 9.225
Dehergne, J., 3.58
Delafosse, M., 9.299, 364
Delasselle, C., 11.201
Del Hoyo, J., 11.56
Delille, G., 5.162, 374; 7.129
Della Pergola, 5.612
Del Lungo, Mariella, 11.338

Del Panta, L., 5.163-4; 11.339
Delumeau, J., 2.59; 3.16, 157; 5.107; 8.104; 9.307, 619; 13.11-13, 58; 14.10, 49
De Madariaga, Isabel, see Madariaga
De Maddalena, A., 3.174-5; 7.9, 130; 9.423; 10.163, 236; 11.68
De Maio, R., 13.72
De Marco, D., 9.425
De Mause, L., 5.427, 432
Demidowicz, G., 7.319
De Molen, R. L., 5.428
Demonet, M., 8.141
Demos, J., 5.441
Denecke, D., 11.158
Den Hollander, A. N. J., 3.272
Deniel, R., 5.82
Denieul-Cormier, Anne, 8.48
Dent, J., 10.179-81
Depauw, J., 5.273; 10.372
Deprez, P., 5.48, 121
Dermigny, L., 9.81, 320-1; 11.22
De Roover, Florence E., 9.567
De Roover, R., 9.403-4, 424, 568; 10.83-4, 94
De Rosa, G., 3.199
De Rosa, L., 6.30; 9.425; 11.340
Derouet, B., 5.83
Derry, T. K., 3.336
Desaive, J. P., 11.288
Descadeillas, R., 7.36
Descamps, P., 3.149
Descimon, R., 3.6; 9.550; 12.55
De Seta, C., 4.18; 8.94
Desplat, C., 4.40; 14.50
Dessert, D., 10.182-3
Deursen, A. T. van, 13.241
Deutscher, T., 13.140
Devèze, M., 3.115; 4.50, 106; 7.37
De Vos, Susan, 5.189
De Vries, J., 2.69; 3.69-70; 4.30, 74, 90; 5.122; 7.87-8; 8.10, 11; 11.40
Devyver, A., 6.67
Dewald, J., 10.286-7, 396
Dewey, H. W., 10.458; 14.99, 100
Deyon, P., 3.16; 6.68; 8.32; 9.442, 458; 10.370; 13.49
Deyon, Solange, 13.242
Diaz, F., 3.180
Dickens, A. G., 13.170, 310; 14.240
Dickler, R. A., 7.293
Dickson, P. G. M., 10.244
Di Corcia, J., 6.69
Diederiks, H., 10.428-9
Diefendorf, Barbara B., 5.342; 6.70; 12.56
Dietz, A., 9.102
Diffie, B. W., 4.131
Dijk, H. van, 6.28
Dijksterhuis, E. J., 14.345
Dillen, J. G. van, 3.71; 9.53, 405
Dinet, Dominique, 5.105

Dion, R., 4.9; 7.333
Disney, A. R., 9.332-3
Di Tella, G., 2.43
Di Vittorio, A., 3.253; 9.426; 10.238, 256
Djordjevic, D., 12.143
Dmytryshyn, B., 3.381; 10.156
Dobb, M. H., 2.115
Doehard, Renée, 9.57
Doerner, K., 11.366
Dolan, Claire, 13.109
Dolan, J. P., 13.14
Dollinger, H., 10.245
Dollinger, P., 8.28; 9.201
Domínguez Ortiz, A., 1.44; 3.94, 109, 116-17, 128, 138; 5.556-7, 576; 6.119; 8.83; 9.312; 10.214-15; 12.75
Domonkos, L. S., 14.219
Donati, C., 13.73
Donézar Díez, J. M., 6.29
Dooley, B., 14.371
Doorn, J. van, 10.469
Doria, G., 7.131
Doroshenko, V., 9.349
Dorpalen, A., 3.209-10
Dorwart, R. A., 7.348; 9.436; 10.135
Doucet, R., 14.304
Douglass, W. A., 5.375; 7.98
Dovring, F., 7.257, 277, 316
Doyle, W., 2.92; 6.71; 10.288-9
Drake, M., 5.11, 30, 215-17
Dressendörfer, P., 5.577
Dreyer-Roos, Suzanne, 5.84
Dreyfus, F. G., 8.128
Driesch, W. von den, 9.68
Dübeck, Inger, 10.454
Dubois, A., 9.365
Dubois, Elfrieda T., 14.158
Duby, G., 3.7; 7.38, 143; 8.30
Duffy, C., 10.519, 531
Duffy, M., 10.328
Duggan, L. G., 13.15
Duke, A. C., 10.162; 13.272-4
Dukes, P., 3.382-3; 6.228; 10.71; 14.246
Dülmen, R. van, 2.21; 5.288; 10.449; 13.287; 14.87
Dulong, C., see Badalo-Dulong
Duncan, T. B., 4.107
Dundes, A., 14.84
Dunkley, J., 14.51
Dunn, R. S., 2.70
Dunsdorfs, E., 7.260-1
Dunthorne, H., 2.4
Dupâquier, J., 2.39; 5.12, 81, 85-8, 305, 343-4; 6.25; 7.39; 11.23
Duplessis, R. S., 6.4; 8.69
Dupont-Bouchat, Marie-S., 13.369
Dupront, A., 14.306
Du Puy de Clinchamps, P., 6.72
Duran, J. A., 5.546

Durand, G., 7.334
Durand, Y., 2.22; 10.9, 184, 388
Dvornik, F., 3.258
Dyos, H. J., 8.2
Dyrvik, S., 5.218-19

Eagly, R. V., 11.93
Earle, P., 3.71; 9.248
Easlea, B., 14.346
Easterlin, R. A., 5.13
Eaton, H. L., 3.360; 8.166
Eckardt, H. W., 6.179
Eckert, E. A., 11.349-50
Eddy, J. A., 4.29
Edelstein, Marilyn M., 13.110
Edgerton, S. Y., 14.416
Edlin-Thieme, Margareta, 9.103
Edwards, J. H., 5.558; 8.74
Edwards, M. U., 14.211
Eeckaute, Denise, 10.459
Ehalt, H. C., 10.56
Ehrenberg, R., 9.109
Eichberg, H., 14.11
Eichler, Margrit, 13.288
Eiras Roel, A., 3.106
Eisenmann, E., 10.249
Eisenstadt, S. N., 2.116; 10.10
Eisenstein, Elizabeth L., 14.276-80, 318
Eitel, P., 8.115
Ekelund, R. B., 10.85
Elias, N., 10.11-12; 14.12
El Kordi, M., 8.34
Elliott, J. H., 2.71; 3.95, 118-19; 4.108; 10.55; 12.4, 5, 75; 14.433
Ellis, H. A., 6.73
Elmroth, I., 5.254; 6.213
Elsas, M. J., 11.79
Emmer, P. C., 9.274; 9.395-6
Ende, Aurel, 5.429
Endrei, W., 9.557
Endres, R., 12.116
Engel-Janosi, F., 5.390
Engelsing, R., 3.216; 6.250, 262; 14.334
Engrand, C., 11.202
Erdei, F., 7.208
Erder, Leila, 5.209-10; 8.149
Ergang, R. R., 3.232
Ergil, D., 3.297
Ericsson, Birgitta, 7.236; 9.493
Ernstberger, A., 10.246
Esmonin, E., 3.8
Esper, T., 6.229, 174; 10.72
Estèbe, Janine, see Garrisson-Estèbe
Estes, L. L., 13.340-1
Estivals, R., 14.305
Eszlary, C. d', 7.209
Etlin, R. A., 14.111
Etzold, G., 9.219
Eulen, F., 10.136

Evans, R. J. W., 3.259; 7.163; 14.94, 196, 267
Everdell, W. R., 13.35
Eversley, D. E. C., 5.22
Eyck van Heslinga, E. S. van, 9.655
Eyre, E., 2.23

Faber, J. A., 5.123; 9.350; 11.141
Faccini, L., 7.315
Faderman, Lillian, 5.255
Fairchilds, Cissie S., 5.274; 6.257; 11.203
Fanchamps, M. L., 11.41
Fann, W. R., 10.520
Farge, Arlette, 8.49-51; 10.397
Farine, A., 5.595
Faroqhi, Suraiya, 4.82; 5.210; 7.222-3, 322; 8.149-52; 9.121-2, 604-5, 631; 13.154-7
Farr, J. R., 13.243
Farrell, Dianne E., 14.431
Fasano-Guarini, Elena, 3.158
Faure, E., 10.185
Faure-Soulet, J. F., 3.61
Favier, J., 9.26, 291
Favre, R., 14.112
Fayard, Janine, 10.323; 11.182
Feather, J., 14.281
Febvre, L., 1.7; 3.22; 13.29, 244-5, 342; 14.52, 282
Fedorov, A. S., 9.157
Fedorowicz, J. K., 3.283
Fedosov, I. A., 10.73
Fel, A., 7.306
Feld, M. D., 10.503
Feldbaek, O., 9.129, 288
Felloni, G., 5.155; 9.81; 11.69
Fenlon, D., 13.246
Fenlon, I., 14.443
Fenoaltea, S., 7.200
Ferguson, A. D., 10.457
Ferguson, E. S., 9.500
Ferguson, Margaret W., 5.499
Ferguson, W. K., 2.54
Fernández, R., 3.131
Fernández Alvarez, M., 3.140
Fernández de Pinedo, E., 3.147
Fernández Izquierdo, F., 7.104
Fernández Vargas, Valentina, 5.136
Ferrante, Lucia, 12.89
Ferraro, Joanne M., 10.237
Ferrone, V., 14.372
Ferté, Jeanne, 13.36
Feuer, L. S., 14.347
Fierro-Domenech, A., 4.7
Fildes, Valerie, 5.446
Filippini, J.-P., 9.226
Finer, S. E., 10.470
Fink, Béatrice, 11.110
Finlay, R. G, 5.614; 8.23; 10.48-9
Fischer, T., 11.250
Fischer, W., 5.14; 10.266

Fischer-Galati, S., 12.143
Fisher, A., 5.651; 8.176
Fisher, H. E. S., 9.69, 243
Fisher, R. H., 9.384
Fisher, S. N., 10.526
Fitch, Nancy E., 5.63; 7.40
Fiumi, E., 8.108
Flandrin, J.-L., 5.256-60, 274-5, 345-6, 430; 11.112; 14.306
Fletcher, J. M., 14.131, 197
Fleury, M., 5.89, 90
Flinn, M. W., 5.15, 16; 11.263
Flint, J. T., 13.179
Florinsky, M. T., 3.365
Floristan Imízcoz, A., 7.105
Flynn, D. O., 10.216; 11.3, 54
Flynn, Maureen M., 11.228
Foisil, Madeleine, 12.34
Forberger, R., 9.475
Forbes, T. R., 11.266
Ford, F. L., 6.74; 8.135
Forget, Mireille, 11.217
Forster, Elborg, 2.93; 11.126
Forster, R., 1.24; 2.93; 4.86; 5.78, 256, 282, 362; 6.64, 75-8, 155; 7.41-3, 279, 335; 11.116, 126, 289; 12.5
Forsyth, P. J., 11.55
Fortea Pérez, J. I., 8.75
Foschepoth, J., 13.192
Foucault, M., 1.19; 10.371; 11.267, 367; 14.13
Foust, C. M., 9.337
Fox, E. W., 4.8
Fox, F., 9.175
Fox, T., 7.183
Fox-Genovese, Elizabeth, 10.103-4
França, J.-A., 8.199
Francastel, P., 8.183
François, E., 5.174-5; 8.116, 126
François, Martha E., 12.6; 13.179
François, M., 3.9
Frandsen, K.-E., 7.324
Frängsmyr, T., 14.380
Frank, A. G., 2.25
Franz, G., 3.233; 7.158-9; 12.124
Fraser, D., 8.3
Frêche, G., 3.65, 342; 11.24
Frêche, Geneviève, 11.24
Freeze, G. L., 13.161
French, R. A., 4.25; 7.320
Fresacher, W., 7.160
Freudenberger, H., 4.94-5; 7.1; 9.116, 443, 489, 595-8; 10.3, 137; 11.172
Frey, Linda, 5.471; 13.247
Frey, Marsha, 13.247
Frey, W., 5.628
Friberg, N., 5.220
Fridlizius, G., 5.221
Friede, J., 5.535
Friedman, J., 5.559

Friedmann, Karen J., 7.325; 11.163
Friedmann, R., 11.356; 13.289-90
Friedrichs, C. R., 6.251; 8.130; 9.579; 12.101-3; 14.198
Friesen, A., 13.171, 291
Friis, Astrid, 11.42, 94
Frijhoff, W., 11.129; 13.16, 369; 14.159, 176
Frings, Marie-L., 7.152
Fritz, P., 8.79; 12.16
Froeschlé-Chopard, Marie H., 13.37-8
Fruhauf, C., 4.51
Fuhrmann, J. T., 9.635
Fukasawa, K., 5.551
Fulbrook, Mary, 1.29; 13.85
Fundaburk, Emma L., 10.80
Furber, H., 9.322
Furet, F., 1.25; 6.14, 16; 14.160, 306-7
Fussell, G. E., 7.299

Gaastra, F., 9.225, 325; 11.48
Gabrielsson, P., 8.125
Gage, J. S., 3.159
Gagliardo, J. G., 7.161
Galasso, G., 3.158, 200; 13.74
Gállego, J., 8.183; 14.411
Gallet, J., 12.35
Gallet, M., 11.180
Galliano, P., 5.91
Galluzzi, P., 14.373
Galpern, A. N., 13.39
Ganiage, J., 5.92
García Arenal, Mercedes, 5.578-9
García-Ballester, L., 11.326
García Baquero, A., 3.131; 9.309, 313
García-Baquero López, G., 5.137
García Carcel, R., 3.141; 5.371; 12.76; 13.328
García de Cortazar, J. A., 3.148
García Fernández, J., 4.13
García Fuentes, L., 9.279
García-Lombardero, J., 7.106
García Marín, J., 10.324
García Sanz, A., 3.131, 144
Garden, M., 8.44
Garin, E., 13.343; 14.132
Garlan, J., 12.36
Garrard, J. G., 8.202
Garraty, J. A. 11.188
Garrett, C. W., 13.344, 370-1
Garrioch, D., 8.52; 9.526
Garrisson-Estèbe, Janine, 13.13, 239, 248-9
Gascon, R., 9.27, 407
Gaskin, Katharine, 5.17
Gately, M. O., 12.10
Gates-Coon, Rebecca, 7.210
Gatrell, V. A. C., 10.377
Gaudemet, J., 5.346

Gaunt, D., 1.8; 5.222-3, 261, 461
Gautier, E., 5.93
Gavazzi, M., 5.405
Gawthrop, R., 14.199
Gay, J. L., 5.347
Gechter, Marianne, 13.145
Geison, G. L., 11.293
Gelabert González, J. E., 8.81
Gelfand, T., 11.290-4
Gélis, J., 5.431; 11.295-6
Gemery, H. A., 9.396
Georgelin, J., 3.189; 7.132
Georgescu, V., 6.207
Gerber, H., 5.512; 9.123; 11.90
Gerbet, Marie-C., 6.120; 13.68
Geremek, B., 3.284; 10.372-3
Gerhard, D., 2.26
Gerhard, H.-J., 11.79
Gerschenkron, A., 3.366-7, 369
Gestrin, F., 3.329
Geyl, P., 3.72
Gibson, C., 11.145
Giesey, R. E., 6.17; 10.290
Gieysztor, A., 3.280
Gieysztorowa, Irena, 3.281; 5.202-3
Gilbert, C., 5.462
Gilbert, F., 1.9, 78; 6.183; 10.21; 14.14
Gille, B., 3.3, 367; 9.427, 507-8, 615
Gille, H., 5.224
Gillispie, C. C., 14.366
Giménez López, E., 9.241
Ginatempo, Maria, 5.165
Ginzburg, C., 1.18; 13.17, 345, 391; 14.15, 85
Gioffrè, D., 6.267; 9.428
Giorgetti, G., 7.127, 144
Giralt y Raventos, E., 5.148; 9.242
Girard, A., 9.68, 309
Girard, R., 5.348
Girouard, M., 8.12
Gismondi, M. A., 14.16
Gist, N. P., 8.6
Giuntella, V. E., 6.7; 8.13
Givens, R. D., 6.230
Glamann, K., 9.7, 8, 321, 326-7, 335; 11.94, 164
Glanz, R., 5.629
Glas-Hochstettler, T. J., 6.180
Glass, D. V., 5.18, 22
Glassman, Debra, 11.25
Glidden, Hope, 3.46
Glinski, G. von, 9.215
Gøbel, E., 9.289
Godechot, J., 2.94; 7.10
Goehrke, C., 4.89
Goertz, H. J., 13.292
Goldberg, J., 5.637
Golden, R. M., 13.126
Goldenberg, S., 4.43; 9.224, 227
Goldin, Grace, 11.280, 322
Goldman, I., 5.457

Goldmann, L., 13.314
Goldsmith, J. L., 7.44, 342
Goldstein, J., 11.297
Goldthwaite, R. A., 6.145-6; 9.429, 640-1; 14.192
Gollin, Gillian L., 13.319
Gomez-Ibañez, D. A., 4.14
Gonnet, G., 13.330
González, M. J., 11.56
González Enciso, A., 3.132; 9.470
González Jiménez, M., 7.288
Goodman, D., 13.134
Goodman, J., 5.500; 9.96
Goodwin, A., 6.48, 79, 80
Goodwin, C. D. W., 13.173
Goody, J., 5.306-7, 315, 321, 477
Gordon, B., 10.86
Gordon, Linda, 12.148
Gorer, G., 5.457
Goris, J. A., 9.56
Gossman, L., 3.32
Gottlieb, R. S., 2.117
Gottschalk, L., 3.39; 14.241
Goubert, J.-P., 11.288, 298-9
Goubert, P., 1.9, 10; 3.10-12, 23; 5.94-6, 270, 349; 7.45-6, 73; 8.36, 183; 9.28; 10.311
Gouesse, J.-M., 5.277, 346
Gouhier, P., 5.97
Gould, J. D., 2.27
Goy, J., 7.271-3
Goy, R. J., 8.96
Grab, A. I., 11.150
Graff, H. J., 14.126, 133, 225
Grafton, A. T., 14.161, 276
Grage, Elsa-B., 9.210
Graham, J. Q., 6.11
Granasztói, G., 5.402; 8.141
Grant, A., 6.108; 10.286, 294
Grassby, R. B., 9.143
Graubard, S. R., 1.9
Greaves, R. L., 13.165
Green, L., 14.200
Green, R. W., 2.118, 136
Greenbaum, L. S., 11.300
Greene, J. P., 4.110; 12.5
Greengrass, M., 3.24; 10.28; 12.55, 57; 13.250
Green-Pedersen, S. E., 9.400
Greenshields, M., 10.398
Gregory, D., 4.1
Grekov, B. D., 7.262
Grendi, E., 6.150; 7.135; 9.82, 249-50; 11.151, 239-40
Grendler, P. F., 5.615; 14.193-4
Gresset, M., 10.291
Greve, K., 6.32
Grew, R., 10.13
Greyerz, K. von, 5.301; 8.118; 13.86, 193-4
Grice-Hutchinson, Marjorie, 10.123
Grierson, P., 11.4

Griffiths, D. M., 9.155; 10.157
Griffiths, G., 12.69
Grigg, D., 5.19; 7.11
Grimm, H. J., 11.251; 13.195-6
Grimmer, C., 8.33
Griswold, W. J., 12.144
Grønseth, E., 5.409
Gross, N., 5.596
Grozdanova, Elena, 3.289
Grubb, J. S., 3.190
Gruder, Vivian R., 10.292
Grüll, G., 9.580; 12.104-5
Gründler, O., 6.102
Grussi, O., 14.53
Gschwind, F., 5.176
Guggenheim, Ann H., 13.251
Guggenheim, S. E., 12.52
Guidoni, E., 8.190
Guignet, P., 9.458-9, 552
Guilarte, A. M., 7.107
Guillaume, P., 5.20
Guillemot, A., 11.301
Guilmartin, J. F., 10.471
Guiral-Hadziiossif, Jacqueline, 9.245
Gullickson, Gay L., 9.460-3
Gundersheimer, W. L., 10.14
Gunnarsson, G., 9.370; 11.5
Gunst, P., 7.12
Guroff, G., 9.131
Gutierrez, H., 5.98
Gutiérrez Nieto, J. I., 5.138, 560; 12.81
Gutkind, E. A., 8.184
Gutmann, J., 13.190
Gutmann, M. P., 5.68, 124-6, 363; 10.504
Gutton, J.-P., 6.258; 7.78; 11.189, 204-5; 13.40; 14.54
Guyer, P., 6.181; 8.112
Gyimesi, S., 8.142

Haan, H., 3.234
Habakkuk, H. J., 5.21
Haesenne-Peremans, Nicole, 11.224
Hagen, W. W., 7.162-4
Hahn, F., 1.61
Hahn, P.-M., 6.182
Hahn, R., 14.367
Hajnal, J., 5.22
Hale, J. R., 2.60; 5.167; 10.472-5, 511-12, 514
Haley, K. H. D., 3.73
Haliczer, S. H., 5.561; 6.121; 12.82-3; 13.329
Hall, A. R., 9.510; 14.348-50, 355
Hall, B., 13.201
Halla, F. L., 5.432
Halperin, C. J., 1.74
Halperin, S. W., 1.48, 68
Halperin Donghi, T., 5.580
Hamilton, E. J., 4.100; 9.418; 10.186; 11.6, 7, 57

Hamm, M. F., 8.164
Hammarström, Ingrid, 10.257; 11.95
Hammel, E. A., 5.308, 406
Hammond, E. A., 11.302
Hampson, N., 14.17, 246
Hamscher, A. N., 10.293; 12.61; 13.315
Hanák, P., 3.270
Hanawalt, Barbara A., 5.445
Hanley, W., 14.308
Hannaway, Caroline C., 11.303
Hannemann, M., 13.197
Hans, N., 14.231
Hansen, N. M., 2.136
Hansen, S. A., 6.214
Hansen, V., 7.237
Hanson, C. A., 3.150; 9.280
Hansotte, G., 9.617
Harding, R. R., 8.36; 10.29, 294-5; 12.58; 13.252
Harding, Susan, 10.416
Hardy, J. D., 10.296
Hareven, Tamara K., 5.118, 309-11
Hargreaves-Mawdsley, W. N., 11.173
Haring, C. H., 9.281, 311
Harnisch, H., 5.171; 7.165-70, 173; 10.247; 12.106
Harris, Barbara J., 5.312
Harris, J. R., 9.502, 644-5
Harris, P. M. G., 5.315
Harris, R. D., 10.187-8
Harsin, P., 5.23; 9.269, 405; 10.105
Hart, S., 9.176
Harte, N. B., 9.79, 557
Harth, Erica, 14.309
Hartung, F., 10.15
Hartwell, R. M., 3.31
Haskell, F., 14.417-19
Hasquin, H., 9.467
Hassell, J., 6.41
Hatton, Ragnhild, 2.95; 3.16
Hauben, P. J., 5.536
Hauser, A., 14.401
Hauser, H., 10.106; 11.26
Hawke, G. R., 9.546
Hay, D., 14.261
Hayden, J. M., 13.111
Hayek, F. A. von, 2.119
Heaton, H., 2.28
Hecht, Jacqueline, 9.144
Heckenast, G., 12.140
Heckscher, E. F., 3.340; 5.225; 9.18, 405; 10.82, 100; 11.92
Heers, J., 3.183; 14.18
Heimpel, C., 11.80
Heitz, G., 7.149; 9.581
Helczmanovski, H., 5.177
Held, T., 5.469
Hélin, E., 5.23, 127
Helleiner, K. F., 5.24-5, 44

Heller, H., 13.253
Heller, R., 11.268-9
Hellie, R., 3.368, 377; 6.269-73; 7.263; 8.167
Helmreich, E. C., 14.201
Hémardinquer, J.-J., 11.113, 130
Henderson, J., 13.22
Henderson, W. O., 9.444, 476-7
Henning, F. W., 7.171-3
Henningsen, G., 13.330, 390
Henriques, F., 5.248
Henry, L., 5.18, 26, 77, 82, 89, 93, 99-103, 178, 527; 6.87
Henry, P., 10.450
Henschke, E., 9.624
Hepburn, A. C., 13.263
Hepp, E., 10.388
Herlihy, D., 1.6, 18, 42; 5.166-7, 376
Hermann, C., 13.135
Herr, R., 3.96, 133
Hersche, P., 13.146
Hertzberg, A., 5.606
Herwijnen, G. van, 8.61
Hess, A. C., 4.15; 5.581
Hess, A. G., 13.346
Hess, U., 10.335
Hexter, J. H., 1.34; 2.82; 14.134
Heyd, U., 5.646
Heydenreuter, R., 10.338
Heymann, F. G., 12.118, 141
Hickey, D., 6.18; 9.29; 10.189; 11.206
Hicks, J. R., 2.29
Higgs, D., 11.207; 13.8
Highfield, J. R. L., 6.122
Highsmith, Anne L., 14.113
Higonnet, P. L. R., 7.79
Hildebrand, K.-G., 9.632; 10.257; 11.165
Hildebrandt, R., 9.104
Hill, C., 2.120
Hill, G., 3.319
Hill, R., 5.409
Hillerbrand, H. J., 12.119; 13.172-4
Hilton, R. H., 2.120
Hiltpold, P., 6.123
Hincker, F., 10.190
Hinrichs, C., 13.87
Hinrichs, E., 7.42
Hinton, R. W. K., 9.200
Hintze, O., 6.183; 10.267-8, 476
Hippel, W., 5.541
Hirsch, R., 14.283
Hirschfelder, H., 7.174
Hirschmann, A. O., 2.121
Hirst, P. Q., 10.1
Hitchcock, W. R., 6.184
Hitchins, K., 7.210; 13.158
Hittle, J. M., 8.168-9
Hoak, D., 13.347
Hoboken, W. J. van, 9.275
Hobsbawm, E. J., 1.19, 59; 2.46, 72,

82, 122; 6.5; 7.218; 10.374
Hochstadt, S., 5.542
Hocquet, J.-C., 9.366
Hoffman, G. W., 5.652
Hoffman, P. T., 7.47; 10.191; 13.41-3
Hoffmann, T., 7.12
Hoffmeister, G., 14.91
Hogendorn, J. S., 9.396
Hogg, P. C., 9.387
Hohenberg, P. M., 8.14
Holborn, H., 3.224, 241
Holl, B., 10.248
Holley, I. B., 13.173
Hollingsworth, T. H., 5.18, 27
Hollister-Short, G. J., 9.611
Holmsen, A., 7.238-9
Holt, M. P., 10.30
Holton, R. J., 2.123; 12.7
Honegger, Claudia, 13.344
Hook, Judith A., 8.110; 10.446
Hopkins, D. R., 11.270
Hopkins, S. V., 11.14
Hoppe, G., 8.17
Hoppe, P., 6.190
Hoppen, Alison, 13.105
Hörger, H., 13.88
Hornby, O., 3.332; 9.494
Hornik, M. P., 5.557
Horsley, R. A., 13.348
Horst, I. B., 13.293
Horvath, R., 5.204
Hoselitz, B. F., 9.9
Hoszowski, S., 9.208; 11.77, 84-5
Houdaille, J., 5.98-9, 102; 14.162
Houston, R., 9.445; 14.135
Houtte, J. A. van, 3.74; 8.62; 9.58, 64-5
Hovde, B. J., 3.337
Hovland, E., 9.495
Howe, D. W., 13.232
Howell, Martha C., 5.478-9; 8.69
Hsia, R. P., 13.89
Hudson, Elizabeth K., 14.163
Hudson, H. D., 8.170; 9.636
Hudson, Patricia, 9.439
Hudson, W. S., 2.124
Huetz de Lemps, A., 7.331, 338; 9.296
Hufbauer, K., 14.377
Hufton, Olwen H., 2.14, 91, 96; 5.480, 491-3; 7.48; 8.35; 10.399; 11.132, 208-10; 12.37; 13.8
Huggett, F. E., 7.13
Hughes, Diane O., 11.183; 14.86, 420
Hughes, J. R. T., 2.29
Hugueney, Jeanne, 8.187
Huizinga, J., 3.75
Hull, A., 10.125
Hults, Linda C., 13.347
Humbert, A., 4.16

Hundert, E. J., 11.374
Hundert, G. D., 5.635, 638-9
Hunecke, V., 11.190
Hunt, D., 5.441
Hunt, L. A., 1.72; 6.81, 247
Hunt, V. F., 7.196
Huntington, S. P., 10.16
Hunyadi, I., 5.205
Huppert, G., 2.31; 6.82; 14.164
Hurstfield, J., 13.199
Hurtubise, P., 6.147
Hutchinson, E. P., 10.151, 154
Hutchinson, J. F., 11.274
Hutchinson, W. K., 10.80
Hutton, P. H., 14.19
Huxley, A., 13.373

Ianel', Z. K., 7.264
Ibarra y Rodríguez, E., 11.146
Iggers, G. G., 1.11
Imhof, A. E., 2.32; 5.28, 179-83, 226-7; 11.271-2
Inalcik, H., 1.26; 3.290, 298-9; 6.35, 268; 7.224-5, 321; 9.124, 254; 10.150, 527; 11.107
Indova, E. I., 7.258
Ingrao, C., 3.245; 10.139-40
Iradiel Murugarren, P., 9.563
Irsigler, F., 1.12; 9.105; 11.81
Irwin, D., 14.124
Irwin, Joyce, 2.55
Isacson, M., 9.496
Isherwood, R. M., 14.384-6, 438
Islamoğlu, H., 3.291; 7.322
Israel, J. I., 3.97; 5.597, 630; 9.380; 12.24, 70
Issawi, C., 3.308
Itzkowitz, N., 10.343

Jackson, M. R., 3.301
Jacob, E. F., 6.151
Jacob, F.-D., 8.124, 185
Jacobsen, Grethe, 5.514-15
Jacquart, J., 1.10; 3.16; 6.25; 7.38, 49, 307
Jadin, L., 5.344
Jago, C., 6.124-5
Jaher, F. C., 10.367
Jansen, J. C. G. M., 7.89
Jansma, L. G., 13.293
Jeannin, P., 2.9, 97; 3.68; 9.10, 56, 62, 127, 177-8, 201, 211, 216, 407, 449
Jelavich, Barbara, 3.300
Jelavich, C., 3.254, 300
Jenness, D., 3.320
Jennings, R. C., 5.513, 653; 8.153; 9.437; 10.344-5
Jennings, R. M., 10.192
Jensen, C. R., 6.19
Jespersen, K. J. V., 10.66, 529
Jespersen, L., 10.63

Johansen, H. C., 5.228-9, 470
Johansson, E., 14.225
Johansson, S. R., 5.486
Johnson, C., 7.74
Johnson, D., 6.71
Johnson, F. R., 14.349
Johnson, H. B., 11.144
Johnson, H. C., 10.336-7
Johnson, N., 14.310
Johnson, Penelope D., 5.483
Jones, C., 5.728; 10.494-5; 11.211, 304, 368
Jones, E. L., 2.33, 39; 4.44; 7.14, 88; 9.446; 10.87
Jones, M., 4.24; 6.49
Jones, P. M., 7.50-1
Jones, R. E., 4.85; 6.231, 256; 8.202
Jones, W. G.; 14.232
Jörberg, L.; 11.91, 96-7
Jörg, C. J. A., 9.328
Jørgensen, J., 8.162; 9.217
Jouanna, Arlette, 6.20, 83
Jover Zamora, J. M., 3.101
Juan Vidal, J., 7.287
Judges, A. V., 2.23
Julia, D., 11.129; 13.112; 14.159, 165-6
Jutikkala, E., 3.355; 5.230-1, 235; 6.39; 7.240-1, 252, 254; 8.201; 9.543; 11.166
Jütte, R., 5.384; 11.191
Kagan, A., 5.415
Kagan, R. L., 10.297, 325, 433-4; 14.180-2
Kahan, A., 3.384; 6.232, 255; 7.15, 197; 9.157, 498, 637-8; 11.169, 364
Kahk, J., 5.414; 7.274
Kaiser, C., 10.298
Kalas, R. J., 6.84
Kállay, I., 7.211
Kaltenstadler, W., 9.253
Kälvemark, Ann-S., 5.232
Kamen, H., 2.34, 73; 3.97-8, 134-5, 235; 10.435, 443; 12.77; 13.133, 331
Kamendrowsky, V., 9.155
Kamenka, E., 2.125
Kammen, M. L., 1.13
Kann, R. A., 3.260; 6.197; 10.141
Kantrow, Louise, 5.62
Kaplan, H. H., 9.179
Kaplan, S. L., 7.281; 9.527-8, 541, 665; 10.401; 11.133-6; 12.38; 13.44
Kaplow, J., 6.244; 11.212
Kappen, O. van, 5.654
Karant-Nunn, Susan C., 5.504; 13.147
Karidis, D. N., 8.158
Karpat, K. H., 5.655
Kashtanov, S. M., 10.262
Kato, E., 9.329

Katz, J., 5.598-9
Katz, M. B., 6.6
Katznelson, I., 8.15
Kaufmann-Rochard, Jacqueline, 9.138
Kay, C., 7.16
Kaye, H. J., 1.76
Kazmer, D. R., 3.361
Kazmer, Y., 3.361
Kearney, H., 14.351
Keckova, Antonina, 3.368
Keenan, E. L., 3.389; 10.74
Keep, J. L. H., 3.378; 10.75, 79, 460, 533-4
Kellenbenz, H., 1.65; 2.35; 3.120, 186, 214, 217; 4.134; 9.11, 106, 128, 139, 151, 180-1, 211-12, 447-8, 509, 582, 612-13; 10.163; 11.8
Kelley, D. R., 13.254
Kellner, H., 2.57
Kelly, G. A., 10.402
Kelly-Gadol, Joan, 5.473, 481
Kelso, Ruth, 5.482
Kent, C. A., 1.50
Kent, F. W., 6.148; 10.44; 14.421
Kent, H. S. K., 9.182, 378
Kerner, R. J., 4.26
Kertzer, D. I., 5.327, 369
Keswani, D. G., 9.323
Kettering, Sharon, 10.27, 31, 299; 12.64
Keyder, Ç., 3.291
Keyser, E., 5.184; 8.113
Khachikian, L., 9.338
Kieckhefer, R., 13.349
Kiel, M., 14.430
Kieniewicz, S., 7.216
Kiernan, C., 14.368
Kiernan, V. G., 2.74; 10.17, 477
Kierstead, R. F., 6.68
Kimerling, Elise, 10.535
Kindleberger, C. P., 2.43; 8.16; 9.406, 412
King, J. E., 10.107
King, Margaret L., 5.377; 14.263
Kingdon, R. M., 11.252; 13.148, 233-4; 14.284-5, 311
Kinser, S., 1.35; 2.14
Kinsman, R. S., 6.137; 11.369
Kintz, J.-P., 8.136
Király, B. K., 3.273; 10.523, 525; 13.8
Kirchhoff, K.-H., 13.295
Kirchner, W., 5.524, 547; 9.183, 361; 13.294
Kirilly, Z., 7.294
Kirk, Linda, 13.149
Kirshner, J., 3.192; 10.84
Kisch, H., 9.583-7
Kiss, I. N., 3.261, 274, 294; 9.340; 11.78, 86

Kittelson, J. M., 13.150, 198
Kjaergaard, T., 7.17
Kjaerheim, S., 9.379
Klaasen, W., 12.122, 296
Klaassen, L. H., 4.91
Klairmont, Alison, 11.305
Klaits, J., 13.350, 372; 14.312
Klang, D. M., 10.128, 226
Klapisch-Zuber, Christiane, 5.376, 378; 6.260-1; 9.620; 13.75
Klassen, P. J., 13.297
Klaveren, J. van, 3.99; 10.88
Kleiminger, R., 11.351
Kleimola, Ann M., 3.368; 6.233-4; 10.354-5, 458, 536
Klein, E., 10.250
Klein, H. S., 9.397
Klein, J., 7.347
Klein, K., 5.177
Klein, P. W., 9.46-7, 346
Klein, T., 13.321
Klep, P. M. M., 8.63
Klier, J. D., 5.647
Klíma, A., 7.205; 9.490-1, 599, 600, 648; 11.87
Kloczowski, J., 13.8
Knabe, B., 8.171
Knafla, L. A., 10.417
Knecht, R. J., 10.33; 12.65
Knight, M. M., 1.69
Knodel, J., 5.29, 185-91, 385
Knoppers, J. T., 9.184-5
Koch, A. C. F., 13.275
Koenigsberger, H. G., 2.61, 75; 3.205; 10.21; 11.43; 12.5, 8, 90; 13.199; 14.242-3, 433
Koepp, Cynthia J., 9.528
Köhler, H.-J., 13.200
Kohut, Z. E., 6.235
Kolb, R., 12.120
Kolff, D. H. A., 13.274
Kollmann, J. E., 13.162
Kollmann, Nancy S., 5.519; 10.76
Kolsky, S., 6.157
Komjáthy, A., 7.212
Komlos, J., 7.5; 10.142; 11.159
Könenkamp, W. D., 11.185
Konig, R., 5.409
Koninckx, C., 9.336
Konvitz, J. W., 8.186, 192-3
Koonz, Claudia, 5.473
Kooy, Marcelle, 9.98
Köpeczi, B., 6.50; 7.18
Kopitzsch, F., 8.125
Körner, M. H., 10.251
Kors, A. C., 13.351
Korst, K., 2.9
Kosinski, L. A., 5.245
Kossmann, E. H., 6.116; 7.311; 12.66
Koumoulides, J. T., 14.95
Kouri, E. I., 4.93

Koutaissoff, E., 9.639
Kovacsics, J., 5.206
Krahn, C., 13.298
Kramm, H., 6.185
Krantz, F., 1.66
Krantz, O., 9.497
Kranzberg, M., 9.510
Kraschewski, H.-J., 10.143
Krause, J. T., 5.30
Kreiser, B. R., 13.45, 313, 373
Kriedte, P., 2.36; 9.449-50, 588-9
Kriegel, M., 5.562
Krieger, L., 10.21
Kristeller, P. O., 5.483
Kronshage, W., 5.192
Krüger, H., 9.478
Krüger, Kersten, 6.32; 10.252
Krumbholz, J., 14.233
Kuczynski, J., 3.218; 6.242; 7.182
Kuczynski, Marguerite, 10.104
Kuhn, T. S., 14.352
Kuklinska, Krystyna, 8.138; 9.218
Kula, W., 5.403; 7.144, 217-18;
    11.102
Kunitz, S. J., 5.31
Kunstmann, H. M., 13.392
Kunt, M. I., 10.346-7
Kunze, M., 13.393
Kunzle, D., 14.402
Kuratsuka, T., 13.299
Küther, C., 10.451; 11.253
Kuuse, J., 3.333

Labalme, Patricia H., 5.483
Labatut, J. P., 6.51, 85
Labrot, G., 6.172; 8.183; 14.422
Labrousse, C. E., 2.30; 3.6, 33; 6.25;
    7.52; 11.27; 11.128
Lach, D., 4.109
Lachiver, M., 5.104; 7.336; 10.372
Ladero Quesada, M. A., 3.122, 139;
    5.582; 7.288; 10.217
Laffargue, A., 3.197
Lafon, J., 5.350
La Force, J. C., 9.70, 564-6
Lagrave, H., 14.387
Laibman, D., 2.117
Lamaison, P., 3.53
Lamb, H. H., 4.31
Lambert, Audrey M., 4.10
Lambert-Gorges, Martine, 6.126
Lambie, J. T., 1.57
Lamet, Maryélise S., 13.255
Lamet, S. A., 6.112
La Morandière, C. de, 9.371
Lampard, E., 9.510
Lampe, J., 6.186
Lampe, J. R., 3.301
Landes, D. S., 2.126, 142; 3.33;
    9.511; 11.128
Landsberger, H. A., 10.374
Lane, F. C., 1.68; 2.49; 3.191-2;

4.61; 9.85-6, 663; 10.18, 100;
    11.70, 103
Lang, D. M., 3.392
Langbein, J. H., 10.375-6
Lange, Gisela, 9.479
Langer, H., 3.236
Langer, L. N., 8.172
Langer, W. L., 5.32
Langlois, C., 13.127
Langton, J., 8.17
Lanning, J. T., 14.183
Lantzeff, G. V., 5.548
Lanzinner, M., 10.338
Lapeyre, H., 1.43; 5.583; 9.71-2, 311
Laran, M., 3.377
Larmour, Ronda, 9.30-1
Larner, Christina, 13.352; 14.20
Larner, J., 10.19
Larose, A., 5.8
Larquié, C., 5.139-41; 6.264;
    11.182; 12.78; 14.184
Larsen, Karen, 3.356
Larsen, O., 5.227
Lartigaut, J., 3.62
Lárusson, B., 7.242
Laslett, P., 5.33, 261, 304, 308,
    313-15, 407, 463
Lassen, A., 5.233-4
Lau, F., 12.121
Laurent, Jane K., 7.133
Laveau, C., 9.364
Lavedan, P., 8.187, 194
Laven, P., 3.160
La Vopa, A. J., 14.202-3
Law, J., 4.132
Lawless, R. I., 4.20
Lawrance, J. N. H., 14.328
Leboutte, R. S., 5.363
Lebras, H., 5.105
Lebrun, F., 5.106-7, 351; 11.307;
    13.13, 52; 14.21, 172
Lebrun, P., 9.558
Leclant, J., 14.57
Leclercq, Paulette, 7.80
Lecuir, J., 5.108; 10.372
Le Donne, J. P., 10.263, 356-8, 461
Lee, E., 2.8; 9.569
Lee, R. D., 5.34
Lee, R. L., 9.386
Lee, W. R., 5.193-4, 289, 386; 7.163
Lees, L. H., 8.14
Leet, D. R.3.34
Lefebvre, H., 7.81
Lefebvre, P., 10.32
Lefebvre-Teillard, Anne, 5.109
Le Flem, J. P., 7.286, 345; 11.58
Legates, Marlene J., 6.187-8
Le Goff, J., 1.14, 15; 14.21, 66
Le Goff, T. J. A., 8.60; 9.343; 14.59
Leguay, J. P., 9.32
Lehmann, H., 13.394
Lehmann, R., 7.175

Lehners, J.-P., 5.177
Lehning, J. R., 5.447
Lehoux, Françoise, 11.306
Lehtinen, E., 10.64
Leith, J. A., 14.136, 167
Leitsch, W., 6.236
Leland, Dorothy, 14.13
Lemaître, Nicole, 3.54
Lemarchand, G., 3.43; 11.137
Lemeunier, G., 7.346
Lenhart, L., 13.97
Lenman, B., 10.377
Lentin, A., 3.385
Léon, P., 2.37, 98; 7.53; 9.27, 464
Léonard, E. G., 10.496
Lepetit, B., 4.69; 5.110; 8.57
Lepovitz, Helena W., 14.428
Lepre, A., 3.201; 7.134
Le Roy Ladurie, E., 1.15, 16; 2.39;
    3.46; 4.30, 32-5, 86; 5.35-6, 111,
    352; 6.86; 7.2, 18, 19, 27, 38, 54-7,
    271-3, 280; 8.30, 57; 11.28, 115,
    273, 288; 12.39; 13.374; 14.58-9,
    114
Letiche, J. M., 10.158
Levack, B. P., 13.353
Leventer, H., 6.271
Levi, G., 5.540; 6.243; 7.135
Levin, A., 10.457
Levine, D., 10.378
Levine, H., 11.160; 13.322
Levi-Pinard, Germaine, 7.82
Levron, J., 10.33
Levy, A., 10.528
Levy, C., 5.103; 6.87
Levy, Darlene G., 10.118
Levy, Sandry, 5.520
Levy-Leboyer, M., 4.90
Lewis, B., 3.302; 5.645; 8.159
Lewis, D., 14.423
Lewis, Raphaela, 3.303
Lewitter, L. R., 5.521; 10.159
Lewy, G., 13.18
Liautey, A., 11.32
Licata, S. J., 5.252
Liebel, Helen P., 6.189; 7.213;
    10.144, 339
Liehr, R., 6.127
Ligou, D., 3.6; 7.56; 10.193; 12.44;
    13.256; 14.168
Lilley, S., 9.509
Lindberg, C., 11.254
Lindblad, J. T., 9.186-7
Lindegren, J., 10.63
Lindemann, Mary, 5.452-3
Lindqvist, S., 4.60
Lingo, Alison K., 11.308
Link, Edith M., 7.198
Link, T., 9.317
Linz, J., 3.86; 14.257
Lipinski, E., 10.149
Lis, Catharina, 10.378; 11.192

Liss, Peggy K., 4.110
Litak, S., 14.222
Litchfield, R. B., 3.158; 5.168; 6.155; 9.150; 10.332
Livet, G., 8.18
Livi Bacci, M., 5.164
Lockwood, L., 14.444
Loewe, K. von, see Von Loewe
Logan, O., 14.264
Lo Giudice, G., 7.136
Løgstrup, Birgit, 10.65
Lohmann Villena, G., 9.73
Lombardi, Daniela, 11.341
Lombardini, G., 11.71
Longworth, P., 3.330; 5.656; 12.149-51, 162-3
Loose, H.-D., 8.125
Looz-Corswarem, C. von, 13.176
Lopez, M. D., 5.433
Lopez, R. S., 3.161
López González, J.-J., 8.91
López Piñero, J. M., 14.370
López-Salazar Pérez, J., 5.142; 7.108
Lorence, B. W., 5.422
Lorenzo Sanz, E., 9.282
Lorwin, V. R., 3.86
Lösche, D., 7.177
Loschky, D. J., 5.37
Lottes, G., 14.88
Lottin, A., 5.279, 346, 353; 6.245; 13.242
Lougee, Carolyn C., 5.494-5
Lough, J., 3.25, 35; 14.313, 388
Loupès, P., 13.113
Lovett, A. W., 2.14; 3.121; 10.218-19
Lowe, K. J. P., 13.141
Lowry, M., 14.330
Lublinskaya, Aleksandra D., 10.34, 37
Lucassen, J., 5.525
Ludloff, R., 9.647
Lukacs, G., 6.5
Lukowski, G. T., 6.201
Lunden, K., 7.243
Lundgreen, P., 10.266
Lunenfeld, M., 10.326
Luria, K. P., 5.337, 393
Lütge, F., 3.219, 225-6; 7.176-8; 9.107
Luthy, H., 9.413
Lutz, E., 9.108
Lutz, R. H., 6.252
Luuko, A., 7.244
Luzatti, M., 5.612
Luzzato, G., 9.405
Lyashchenko, P. I., 3.369
Lynch, J., 3.100
Lynch, Katherine A., 5.65, 385
Lynn, J. A., 10.497
Lytle, G. F., 10.14

McAlister, L. N., 4.135
McArdle, F., 5.418; 7.137
McClellan, J. E., 14.353
McClelland, C. E., 14.136; 14.204-5
McCloskey, D., 10.194
McCloy, S. T., 5.657; 10.108; 11.213; 13.257
McCusker, J. J., 11.9, 35
Macek, J., 12.122
McGowan, B., 3.304; 11.162
McGrew, R. E., 6.237
Machet, Anne, 14.331
Mack, Phyllis, see Crew
Mackay, A., 3.87; 4.39; 5.563-4; 11.59
McKee, D., 13.112
Mackenney, R., 9.537; 13.22
McKeown, T., 5.38-9; 11.274
Mackrell, J. Q. C., 7.58
Maclean, I., 5.484
Macleod, M. J., 10.160
Macleod, R., 14.354
McManners, J., 10.40; 13.46, 114-16; 14.115, 124, 389
Macmillan, D. S., 9.157
McNeill, J. R., 9.270
McNeill, W. H., 2.38; 3.193, 305; 4.3, 111; 10.478; 11.275
Macry, P., 11.152
Maczak, A., 3.261, 284; 4.44-5; 6.202-3; 9.115, 188, 351; 10.68; 11.10
Madariaga, Isabel de, 3.386, 389; 7.259; 14.230
Made, R. van der, see Van der Made
Magalhaes Godinho, V., 9.264; 11.60
Mager, F., 4.57
Mager, W., 9.480
Magraner Rodrigo, A., 5.584
Magnusson, L., 9.496; 10.152-3
Maiso González, J., 8.92; 11.327
Major, J. R., 6.88-9; 10.27, 35
Major-Poetzl, Pamela, 1.49
Mäkelä, A., 7.245
Makkai, L., 2.14; 3.275; 7.199
Malament, Barbara C., 10.295
Maland, D., 14.248
Malanima, P., 3.181; 6.149; 9.471
Malettke, K., 10.269
Malgeri, F., 13.9
Malino, Frances, 5.610
Mallett, M. E., 9.97, 228; 10.513-14
Mallia-Milanes, V., 9.229-30
Malnick, Bertha, 14.398
Malowist, M., 3.261, 338; 9.189-91
Maltby, W. S., 13.276
Maluquer de Motes, 4.56
Mandaville, J. E., 13.159
Mandich, G., 9.430
Mandrou, R., 2.99; 3.7, 9, 13, 26; 6.21; 7.18, 73; 9.104; 11.367; 13.375; 14.244, 314

Manheim, E., 14.268
Mankov, A. G., 11.100
Mann, H. D., 1.46
Manninen, Merja, 5.516
Mansel, P., 11.174
Mansfield, B. E., 1.47
Mantelli, R., 10.239
Mantran, R., 3.306, 308; 8.160; 9.125
Maravall, J. A., 6.128; 10.43; 14.22
Marcos Martín, A., 5.143; 11.229; 12.84
Marcus, E., 6.114
Marcy, P. T., 5.40
Mardin, S., 3.307; 14.97
Marduel, Marie-L., 7.26
Margolin, J.-C., 2.62
Marino, A., 8.190
Marino, J. A., 3.202; 9.87
Marker, G., 14.338-40
Markoff, J., 14.169
Markovitch, T. J., 9.553
Marks, L. F., 10.230
Marrus, M. R., 14.38
Marshall, G., 2.127
Marshall, Sherrin, 6.113-14; 13.278-9
Martin, A. L., 13.117
Martin, H.-J., 14.282, 286, 315-18
Martin, J., 5.502
Martín Galán, M., 5.144
Martín Rodríguez, M., 10.124
Martines, L., 3.162; 5.485, 503; 6.137; 10.333
Martínez Gijón, J., 9.74
Martynova, Antonina, 14.101
Martz, Linda, 11.230
Marvick, Elizabeth W., 5.443-4
Marx, Anna V., 9.407
Masefield, G. B., 7.300
Massafra, A., 7.10, 138
Massé, P., 7.60, 71
Masselman, G., 4.129
Massip, Catherine, 14.439
Masson, P., 9.226
Mathias, P., 9.48; 10.194; 14.355
Mathis, F., 5.195
Matilla Tascón, A., 9.532
Matis, H., 3.262
Matossian, Mary K., 5.41; 14.102
Matthews, G. T., 10.195
Mattozzi, I., 9.356
Mauersberg, H., 8.117
Mauléon Isla, Mercedes, 5.145
Maurer, J., 12.123
Mauro, F., 2.63; 4.112-13; 9.283
Mavrodin, V. V., 12.152
Mayhew, A., 7.179
Maynes, Mary J., 14.137-9
Maza, Sarah C., 6.259
Mazzaoui, Maureen F., 9.570
Mazzei, Rita, 3.163; 8.98; 9.100

Mazzi, M. S., 7.139
Mead, W. R., 4.22
Meadwell, H., 7.59
Medick, H., 1.8; 2.128; 5.316, 339;
  9.451, 590; 14.89
Medlin, W. K., 14.234
Meehan-Waters, Brenda, 10.359-62,
  365
Meek, R. L., 10.109
Megill, A., 1.51, 52
Meijide Pardo, A., 3.145; 5.537
Melesse, P., 14.387
Melis, F., 9.98
Mellink, A. F., 13.293
Melton, J. van H., 10.57; 14.220
Mendels, F. F., 4.92; 5.42, 300, 317,
  327, 364; 6.9; 9.442, 452, 468
Mendes-Flohr, P. R., 2.129
Menéndez Pidal, R., 3.101
Mennell, S., 11.138
Mensch, G., 4.94
Mentink, G. J., 5.132
Mentzer, R. A., 13.258-9
Merchant, Carolyn, 14.356
Merino Navarro, J. P., 10.507
Merle, L., 7.60
Merrien, J., 9.651
Merriman, R. B., 12.3
Merrington, J., 2.120; 8.19
Merton, R. K., 14.349
Merzario, R., 5.379
Mesnard, J., 14.245
Messmer, K., 6.190
Meszaros, I., 6.5
Metford, J. C. J., 14.393
Méthivier, H., 3.14
Mettam, R., 3.15, 27
Metz, R., 11.11
Meuvret, J., 3.16; 5.112; 7.281;
  10.196; 11.20, 29, 36
Meyer, J., 2.90, 130; 3.36; 5.261;
  6.52, 90; 7.18; 8.20; 9.303; 10.110;
  11.288; 14.109
Meyer, M., 6.184
Meyn, M., 8.120
Miccoli, G., 13.71
Michaud, C., 7.61; 10.197
Michaut, C., 10.412
Micheli, G., 14.374
Michell, A. R., 9.372
Mickun, Nina, 7.347
Middelhoven, P. J., 11.44
Midelfort, H. C. E., 2.55; 11.255,
  370-2; 12.124; 13.354-6, 395-6
Miedema, H., 14.403
Milden, J. W., 5.293
Mileski, Maureen, 13.339
Millepierres, F., 11.309
Miller, D. H., 8.174; 12.153
Miller, J. C., 6.263; 9.398
Millward, R., 7.200; 9.453
Milov, L. V., 8.173

Minchinton, W., 9.12
Mioc, D., 7.226
Miquelon, D., 9.271
Mireaux, E., 3.50
Mironov, B. N., 11.101
Miskimin, H. A., 1.6; 2.64; 11.12, 30
Mitchell, A., 14.116
Mitchell, B., 8.105
Mitchell, H., 11.310-11; 13.47
Mitchell, J., 14.287
Mitler, L., 5.658
Mittenzwei, Ingrid, 10.145
Mitterauer, M., 5.318, 387-91, 415
Mitzman, A., 14.23
Moberg, V., 3.341
Moeller, B., 13.90, 186, 200-1
Mogensen, G. V., 3.332
Mogensen, N. W., 10.403
Moia, Nelly, 13.344
Mokyr, J., 9.454
Molas Ribalta, P., 3.88; 9.75, 533;
  10.327
Molénat, J.-P., 4.77; 8.86
Molenda, Danuta, 8.139; 9.629
Molho, A., 3.164; 6.148; 9.99; 10.332
Molinié-Bertrand, Annie, 5.146;
  6.129; 13.136
Molinier, A., 3.66; 11.214
Mollat, M., 4.62; 9.290, 321
Möller, H., 5.392; 10.269
Möller, H.-M., 10.521
Moller, H., 5.43; 13.19
Mols, R., 5.44-5
Mommsen, W. J., 13.186
Mongrédien, G., 3.28; 14.390
Montelius, S., 9.634
Montemayor, J., 8.87
Monter, E. W., 5.196, 290, 473, 511;
  8.123; 10.61, 253, 452; 13.20, 175,
  332-3, 357-9, 376-7
Montgomery, A., 1.57
Montias, J. M., 14.409-10
Mook, Bertha, 5.365
Moore, K., 5.565
Moote, A. L., 10.279, 300-2; 12.9
Mora, G., 11.373
Morales Padrón, F., 8.83; 9.314
Moran, B. T., 14.378
Moran, G. T., 13.118; 14.60
Morant Deusa, Isabel, 7.109
Morazé, C., 10.89
Morell Peguero, Blanca, 8.84
Morelli, Roberta, 9.571, 621
Moret, Michèle, 9.315
Mori, G., 9.622
Morin, A., 14.315
Morineau, M., 2.14; 3.37, 68; 7.62,
  275; 9.33, 197, 231, 407; 10.198;
  11.11, 13, 31, 45, 53, 116-17;
Mörke, O., 13.202
Mörner, M., 5.538; 6.215
Morrell, M., 11.167

Morris, A. E. J., 8.188
Morton, R. E., 11.227
Mosely, P., 5.404
Mosk, C., 5.46
Mosse, G. L., 2.61; 10.453
Mosse, W. E., 2.131
Mottek, H., 3.220
Moulinas, R., 5.605
Mousnier, R., 1.17; 2.30; 3.15;
  5.354; 6.7, 8, 22-4, 91; 8.53; 10.15,
  36, 110, 269, 303-5, 311; 12.5, 10,
  40-1, 67; 14.245
Moxey, K. P. F., 14.403
Moxo, S. de, 7.110-11; 10.220
Mozzarelli, C., 6.138
Muchembled, R., 1.64; 13.48, 61,
  369, 378-80; 14.21, 61
Mueller, H.-E., 10.340
Mueller, R., 9.431; 11.70, 242
Muinck, B. E. de, 6.115
Muir, E., 10.50-1
Mukerji, C., 14.288
Müller, H.-H., 7.180
Mullett, M. A., 12.11; 13.300
Multhauf, Lettie S., 8.64
Mumford, L., 8.21
Munck, T., 7.246-7
Munk, Judith, 4.19
Munk, W., 4.19
Munro, G., 8.203
Murray, J. J., 8.65, 67
Musgrave, P., 9.357
Muto, G., 10.240
Myrdal, G., 2.46
Myška, M., 9.630

Nadal, J., 3.109; 5.147-8
Nadel, G., 12.69
Nadel-Golobič, Eleonora, 9.339
Nader, Helen, 6.130
Naff, T., 3.308
Najemy, J. M., 3.182
Narweleit, G., 9.591
Nash, Carol S., 5.522
Nauert, C. G., 14.276
Nazarov, V. D., 10.77
Neal, L., 9.54
Neale, R. S., 2.125
Neamtu, V., 7.298
Nef, J. U., 2.76; 9.456; 14.24
Netanyahu, B., 5.566
Netting, A., 14.432
Neugebauer, W., 3.248; 14.206
Neuman, R. P., 5.434
Neuschel, K. B., 6.92
Neveux, H., 7.282; 8.30; 11.117
Newitt, M, 4.133; 10.328
Newman, Karin, 9.213
Niccoli, Ottavia, 13.367
Nicholas, D. M., 1.38
Nicholas, S. J., 11.55
Nicholls, D. J., 2.34, 51; 13.260-2

Nichtweiss, J., 7.181-2
Nicolas, J., 3.64; 6.93; 12.12
Nicolas, Renée, 3.64
Nicolini, Ingrid, 6.191
Nières, C., 8.195; 12.36
Nilehn, L., 14.226
Nipperdey, T., 13.230
Noakes, Susan, 14.332
Noel, C. C., 13.69
Nol'de, B. E., 5.549
Nolte, H.-H., 3.370; 9.192
Noonan, J. T., 5.47, 319; 10.90
Nora, P., 1.15, 27
Norberg, Kathryn, 5.496; 11.215-16
Nordmann, C. J., 3.347
North, D. C., 2.40-2
North, M., 9.209
Nussbaum, F. L., 2.54

Oakley, S. P., 3.334, 342, 352; 4.23;
  7.248
Obelkovich, J., 13.30, 80
Oberlé, R., 8.129
Oberman, H. A., 5.451; 12.127;
  13.200
O'Brien, C. B., 10.537
O'Brien, P., 2.49; 10.194
O'Brien, Patricia, 10.371
Obuchowska-Pysiowa, Honorata,
  9.206
O'Dea, W. T., 9.512
Odén, Birgitta, 3.335; 9.193
Odlozilík, O., 6.199; 14.221
Oehmig, S., 13.203
Oelsner, T., 5.600
Oexle, O. G., 1.38
O'Faolain, Julia, 5.485
Ofstad, K., 5.214
Öhberg, A., 9.194
Ohlin, P. G., 5.48-9; 9.154
Okenfuss, M. J., 5.458; 14.235-7
Olechnowitz, K.-F., 9.202, 664
Olin, J. C., 13.195
Oliva, L. J., 3.387
Oliveira Marques, A. H. R. de, 3.151
Olson, R. W., 12.145
O'Neil, Mary R., 11.342
Ong, W. J., 14.140
Opalinski, E., 6.204
Orchard, G. E., 8.168
Orgel, S., 10.14
Orlovsky, D. T., 10.363
Ormrod, D., 9.48
Ornstein, Martha, 14.353
Österberg, Eva, 10.455
Osterloh, K.-H., 10.141
Østerud, Ø., 7.249
Otetea, A., 7.227
Otis, Leah L., 5.445
Otruba, G., 9.539; 10.146
Otsuka, H., 2.132
Outhwaite, R. B., 5.493

Overfield, J. H., 13.150; 14.207
Owen, R., 3.308
Owens, J. B., 6.131; 12.85-6
Ozouf, J., 14.160
Oxenbøll, E., 9.494
Ozment, S. E., 2.55; 5.393, 454;
  13.200, 204, 301

Pacey, A., 9.513
Pach, Z. P., 7.144, 214-15; 9.13, 14,
  117, 153, 233
Paci, R., 7.291
Packull, W. O., 13.205
Pagden, A., 4.97
Paglia, V., 11.241
Pahl, J., 14.25
Palacio Atard, V., 9.310
Palau García, F., 5.586
Pallach, U.-C., 9.520
Palli, H., 5.246
Palmer, R., 11.343-4
Palmer, R. R., 2.100-1; 14.170-1
Palop Ramos, J. M., 11.147
Palumbo, M., 10.126
Pamlényi, E., 3.275
Pansini, G., 7.140
Pantazopoulos, N. J., 3.309
Panova, Sneška, 9.341
Papadopoulos, T., 5.211
Papagno, G., 9.284
Pardailhé-Galabrun, Annik, 8.54
Pardo, V. F., 8.190
Parent, Annie, 14.319
Parias, L.-H., 14.172
Pariset, F. G., 8.37
Park, Katharine, 14.26
Parker, D., 7.2; 10.37; 13.263
Parker, G., 2.12, 77-8; 9.408; 10.377,
  508; 12.71-2; 13.334; 14.141
Parker, H. T., 1.69; 9.502; 10.111
Parker, J., 10.488
Parker, W. H., 4.27
Parker, W. N., 1.73; 2.43; 4.44; 7.88
Parrinder, E. G., 13.360
Parrott, D. A., 10.479
Parry, J. H., 4.63, 114-16, 136
Parry, M. L., 4.36
Parry, V. J., 10.348
Parsons, S. L., 7.263
Partner, P., 8.106; 10.233-4
Pascu, S., 3.288
Patricio Merino, J., 3.132
Paulinyi, A., 9.514
Pavan, Elisabeth, 5.286
Pavanini, Paola, 11.184
Payne, H. C., 10.112; 14.27
Payne, S. G., 1.75; 3.102
Peachey, P., 13.302-3
Pedlow, G. W., 5.394
Peeters, T., 9.20
Pelenski, J., 10.78; 12.22, 142
Peller, S., 5.50

Pelorson, J.-M., 10.329
Pennington, D. H., 2.79
Penrose, B., 4.117
Pérez, J., 12.87
Pérez Estevez, Rosa M., 11.231
Pérez Moreda, V., 3.89; 5.149-50
Perez Villanueva, J., 13.335
Peristiany, J.-G., 14.77
Peronnet, M. C., 13.119
Perouas, L., 13.49
Perrenoud, A., 5.197-9
Perrichet, M., 9.304
Perrie, Maureen, 12.154; 14.103
Perrot, J.-C., 6.25; 8.4, 31, 40;
  10.161, 493
Perry, Mary E., 5.283; 10.436
Pescatello, Ann M., 5.659
Pescosolido, G., 7.141
Peset, J. L., 7.312; 11.328; 14.185
Peset, M., 7.312; 11.328; 14.185
Pesez, J.-M., 4.86
Peter, J.-P., 11.312
Peters, Dorothea, 12.164
Peters, E., 13.21, 351
Petersen, E. L., 6.216; 7.341; 10.63,
  66, 258-9
Petersen, R. P., 5.252
Peterson, C., , 10.364
Petraccone, C., 8.99
Petrelli, R. L., 11.313
Petri, F., 13.176
Petrovich, M. B., 1.70; 3.255
Petschauer, P., 5.505-6; 14.208
Pettegree, A., 13.235
Pettengill, J. S., 10.480
Petzoldt, R., 14.446
Pevsner, N., 14.404
Pfeiffer, G., 8.132
Pfister, C., 4.30, 39, 41-2
Phelps Brown, E. H., 11.14
Phillips, Carla R., 3.103; 5.587;
  7.112; 8.72; 9.381-3, 419; 10.509
Phillips, H., 14.391
Phillips, J. A., 5.51
Phillips, R., 5.497
Phillips, W. D., 9.66, 383, 419
Philpin, C. H. E., 7.2
Pierce, R. A., 5.548
Pieri, P., 10.515
Pike, Ruth, 5.588; 6.265; 9.149, 316;
  10.43-7
Pillorget, R., 1.17; 3.16; 5.355;
  12.42-3
Pin. E., 13.1
Pinède, C., 5.113
Pinkney, D. H., 14.284
Pino, F., 6.152
Pintner, W. M., 10.365
Pinto Crespo, V., 14.329
Piper, E., 8.189
Pipes, R. E., 3.371; 5.648
Pirinen, K., 3.355

Pitcher, D. E., 4.21
Pitkänen, K., 5.235
Pitte, J.-R., 4.9
Pitz, E., 9.59
Piuz, Anne-M., 8.22; 9.101
Pizzorno, A., 10.6
Plaisse, A., 7.63; 9.297
Plakans, A., 5.416-21
Playoust-Chaussis, Arlette, 13.51
Plaza Prieto, J., 3.136
Plongeron, B., 13.52, 120
Poggi, G., 2.133
Pohl, H., 9.318
Poitrineau, A., 5.465, 528; 7.64
Poliakov, L., 5.601; 9.432
Polisensky, J. V., 6.200
Pollack, H., 5.631
Pollard, H. M., 14.142
Pollard, S., 4.92
Pollock, Linda A., 5.439
Pölnitz, G. von, 9.109-11
Pomian, K., 1.26, 27
Poni, C., 7.142, 316; 9.449, 472, 572-3
Ponsot, P., 7.94
Ponting, K. G., 9.79, 557, 559
Porchnev, B., 12.44
Portal, R., 3.264, 393; 5.550; 9.499, 639
Porter, R., 9.514; 10.1; 14.246
Posener, S., 5.607
Poshkov, A. I., 10.158
Pospiech, A., 6.205
Post, J. D., 4.31-2, 37; 11.118
Postan, M., 7.217
Postel, R., 8.125; 13.182, 206
Poster, M., 5.356
Posthumus, N. W., 11.45
Pottinger, D. T., 14.320
Pounds, N. J. G., 4.4
Poussu, J.-P., 5.20, 106, 529; 8.38-9
Poutet, Y., 11.217
Powell, J. M., 2.65
Powis, J. K., 10.306; 12.45
Prange, Ruth, 9.205
Préaud, M., 13.381
Pred, A., 7.326
Pressly, P., 14.166
Prest, W., 10.274
Preston, R. A., 10.481
Prestwich, Menna, 10.40
Preto, P., 11.345
Prevenier, W., 10.319; 11.223
Pribram, K., 10.91
Price, D. de S., 14.354
Price, J. L., 14.256
Price, J. M., 3.86; 9.362
Priestley, H. I., 4.127
Pringle, J. K., 8.196
Pris, C., 9.644-5
Pritchard, J., 9.272, 652
Procacci, G., 3.165

Prodan, D., 7.228; 12.146
Proesler, H., 9.481
Pronshtein, A. P., 12.155
Prosperi, A., 14.117, 265
Pugh, Wilma J., 11.218-19
Pullan, B., 3.156, 194; 5.616-18; 6.165-6; 11.72, 193, 242-5
Pulma, P., 11.358
Pult Quaglia, A. M., 11.153
Pursell, C. W., 9.510

Quaife, G. R., 13.361
Quataert, Jean H., 5.507
Queller, D. E., 6.167
Queniart, J., 13.53; 14.172, 249, 318
Quilliet, B., 8.30

Rabb, T. K., 1.18; 2.44, 73; 3.237; 4.30, 118; 5.33; 6.9; 11.120; 14.277, 357
Rabinovich, M. G., 5.422
Radeff, Anne, 5.114
Rader, D. L., 10.404
Radkau, J., 4.58
Raeff, M., 3.388-9; 6.238-40; 10.20, 366; 12.5
Ragin, C., 1.77
Raggio, O., 9.471
Rambaud, P., 7.83
Rambert, G., 9.240
Rammstedt, O., 13.304
Ramsay, G. D., 9.79
Ramsey, M., 11.314-15
Ramsey, P. A., 11.149
Ransel, D. L., 5.247, 412; 10.367
Ranum, O. A., 4.86; 5.78, 256, 280, 282, 362, 443; 8.55; 10.21, 38, 307; 11.116, 289; 12.31; 13.54
Ranum, Patricia, 5.280
Rapp, F., 13.13, 207
Rapp, Rayna, 5.320
Rapp, R. T., 2.19; 6.168; 9.15, 87
Rappaport, Rhoda, 14.369
Rascol, P., 7.65
Rattansi, P. M., 14.355
Rau, Virginia, 7.113
Rausch, W., 8.114, 140
Raveau, P., 7.66
Raveggi, S., 7.139
Ravid, B., 5.619
Ravitch, N., 10.199; 13.121-3
Rawley, J. A., 9.390
Rawlings, H. E., 13.137
Raynor, H., 14.434
Razzell, P. E., 5.38
Rebaudo, Danièle, 5.115
Rebel, H., 5.395; 7.183; 14.93
Rebora, G., 7.317
Rechcigl, M., 9.152
Reddy, W. M., 9.502; 12.46
Redish, Angela, 11.25
Redlich, F., 9.112, 141, 443, 625;

10.482-3, 522; 11.15, 82; 14.28
Redondo, A., 5.284, 568; 14.79
Redondo Veintemillas, G., 9.534
Reed, C. G., 2.80
Regemorter, J. L. van, 7.329
Regin, D., 8.66
Reglá, J., 3.109; 5.589
Reinhard, M., 5.52; 6.94
Reinhardt, S. G., 10.405-6
Reissmann, M., 9.214
Reitzer, L., 9.76
Remmel, M., 7.274
Remond, A., 10.113
Renouard, Y., 9.56, 424
Renouvin, P., 1.62
Reuter, O., 9.482
Revel, J., 11.154, 316; 14.62
Revel, J.-F., 11.119
Revelle, R., 5.18
Reynaud, F., 14.442
Reynolds, E., 9.391
Reynolds, T. S., 9.515
Rhodes, R. I., 3.297
Rian, Ø., 10.63
Riasonovsky, N. V., 3.372, 379
Ribeiro, Aileen, 11.175
Ribeiro, O., 7.116
Rice, E. F., 2.66; 14.250
Rich, E. E., 2.15; 9.385
Richard, G., 9.145
Richard, M., 13.264
Richard, R., 9.300
Richards, J. F., 11.16
Richarz, Irmintraut, 6.192
Richarz, Monika, 5.632
Richet, D., 3.4; 11.32-3; 13.265
Richmond, Phyllis A., 11.317
Richter, J., 14.209
Ricuperati, G., 3.155
Riemersma, J. C., 2.134; 10.41, 100; 11.46
Rigaudière, A., 7.308
Riha, T., 3.373
Riis, T., 8.163; 11.194
Riley, J. C., 3.38, 76; 5.3; 9.49; 10.165, 200; 11.34-5, 276
Riley, P. F., 10.407-10
Rimlinger, G. V., 9.626; 10.92
Ringrose, D. R., 2.42; 4.78-80; 8.77-9; 10.463
Ristelhueber, R., 3.310
Ritter, G. A., 10.353
Rivière, D., 14.63
Roach, J. P. C., 2.6
Robert, M., 7.26
Roberts, M., 3.345, 348-51; 10.67, 479
Roberts, W., 14.251
Robertson, H. M., 2.111; 10.90
Robinson, D. E., 11.177
Robisheaux, E., 10.411
Robisheaux, T., 5.456; 12.95; 14.90

Roche, D., 3.12; 6.25, 95-6, 105, 246; 7.301; 8.56; 10.412; 14.118, 252-3, 286, 292, 306, 318, 321
Rochon, A., 14.79
Rödel, W. G., 5.200
Rodenwaldt, E., 11.345
Rodger, R., 2.2
Rodriguez Díaz, Laura, 10.125; 12.79
Rodríguez Sánchez, A., 5.151
Roebroeck, E., 4.75
Roelker, Nancy L., 13.266
Roessingh, H. K., 4.87; 7.310
Rogers, J. W., 11.139
Rogger, H., 14.104
Rogič, V., 8.154
Romani, M. A., 6.31; 8.100
Romano, R., 2.78; 3.166-8, 186; 4.46; 9.251, 344, 663; 11.73
Romeo, R., 4.137
Romero de Solís, P., 5.152
Romon, C., 11.220
Roncayolo, M., 4.86
Roodenburg, H. W., 14.73
Roorda, D. J., 3.67; 6.28, 116
Roos, H., 6.206
Roos, H.-E., 2.135
Roosen, W. J., 10.22, 308
Root, H. L., 7.67; 10.39
Roover, R. de, see De Roover
Roper, L., 5.291, 508; 13.91
Ropp, T., 14.284
Rosa, M., 13.8, 76-7
Rosand, Ellen, 14.445
Rose, Mary B., 5.481
Rose, P. L., 14.375
Rosen, G., 11.277-9, 318, 352, 374-7
Rosenberg, H., 10.341
Rosenberg, N., 2.45; 9.516
Roseveare, H., 9.16
Rosovsky, H., 9.140
Ross, J. B., 5.449
Rossi, Alice S., 5.329
Rossi, P., 14.358
Rossiaud, J., 5.281-2; 8.30
Rössler, H., 6.193-4
Rostow, W. W., 2.46-8, 102
Rostworowski, E., 3.278, 280
Rotberg, R. I., 1.18; 4.30; 5.33; 6.9; 11.120
Rotelli, C., 10.235
Rotelli, E., 6.10
Roth, C., 5.567, 620
Roth, G., 1.79
Rothenberg, G. E., 3.276; 10.523-4; 11.357
Rothkrug, L., 10.114; 13.92
Roubert, Jacqueline, 4.70
Roubin, Lucienne, 14.64
Roupnel, G., 3.52
Rovitto, P. L., 10.334
Rowan, S. W., 3.227

Rowney, D. K., 6.11; 7.274; 8.168; 10.365
Rozental, A. A., 7.309
Rozman, G., 8.5, 174
Rublack, H.-C., 8.118; 13.182
Rudé, G., 1.67; 2.103; 12.13-17, 47
Rudnytsky, I. L., 5.656
Rudolph, R. L., 5.423
Ruff, J. R., 10.413-14
Ruiz Martín, F., 5.613; 9.72; 10.221
Ruiz Torres, P., 7.114
Rule, J., 10.309
Rumeu de Armas, A., 11.232
Runciman, W. G., 10.1
Runzo, Jean, 13.305
Russell, J. B., 13.362
Russell, J. C., 5.207
Russell, Jean F., 11.373
Russell, P. A., 13.208
Russell-Wood, A. J. R., 9.661
Russo, Carla, 13.74, 78
Ruwet, J., 10.505; 11.47
Rystad, G., 5.254; 10.350; 14.226

Saalfeld, D., 6.33; 7.184
Sabbe, E., 8.68
Sabean, D. W., 5.316, 321, 339; 7.185-7; 12.18, 112, 127; 13.93; 14.90
Sachsse, C., 11.256
Sadat, D. R., 6.208
Saez, E., 8.70
Safley, T. M., 5.396-9
Sagarra, Eda, 3.242
Sagnac, P., 3.39
Saint-Germain, J., 10.415
Saint-Jacob, P. de, 7.68
Sakharov, A. N., 7.264
Salas Ausens, J. A., 10.432
Salazar, A. M., 5.555
Salin, E., 1.71
Sallon, M. A., 10.201
Salmen, W., 14.446
Salmon, J. H. M., 1.2; 3.29; 6.97; 12.48-50, 59; 13.267
Salomon, N., 7.115
Salvador, Emilia, 9.246
Salvesen, H., 7.250
Samoyault, J. P., 10.310
Samsonowicz, H., 3.339; 9.115
Samuel, R., 2.128
Samuelsson, K., 2.136; 3.343; 9.438
Sandberg, L. G., 11.93, 168
Sanfaçon, A., 13.55
Santbergen, R. van, 9.531
Santosuosso, A., 3.169
Sanz Sampelayo, J., 8.76
Saperstein, M., 5.621
Sarrailh, J., 3.137
Saugnieux, J., 14.80, 186
Saunders, A. C. de C. M., 6.266
Saussay, J., 3.377

Sauzet, R., 13.167
Scammell, G. V., 4.64, 119-20
Schaeffer, R. K., 10.93
Schaeper, T. J., 3.40; 10.115
Schafer, R. J., 10.126
Schaffer, J. W., 5.332, 357
Schalk, E., 6.98-100
Schama, S., 14.74, 246
Scharfe, M., 13.94
Schelbert, L., 5.543
Scheuch, E. K., 1.5
Schick, L. L., 9.110
Schiera, P., 6.138
Schildhauer, J., 13.209
Schilling, H., 3.77; 5.530; 13.176, 210-11, 277
Schissler, Hanna, 7.188
Schleunes, K. A., 14.210
Schluchter, W., 1.79
Schlumbohm, J., 5.455; 10.58
Schmal, H., 8.11
Schmidt, H. R., 13.212
Schmidt, J., 14.91
Schmidt, Maria, 11.186
Schmitt, E., 9.287
Schmitt, H. A., 1.62
Schmitt, J.-C., 14.21
Schmitz, Edith, 5.592
Schmukler, N., 6.114
Schnapper, B., 10.202
Schnee, H., 10.254
Schneider, L., 5.400
Schneider, R. A., 10.416
Schöffer, I., 3.78; 6.7; 7.201; 11.48; 12.69
Schofield, R. E., 14.359
Schofield, R. S., 5.53-4, 65, 435
Scholz, Traute, 9.667
Schormann, G., 13.397-8
Schorsch, L. L., 2.137
Schousboe, Karen, 14.98
Schremmer, E., 2.132; 9.483-4
Schröder, Brigitte, 8.113
Schröder, K. H., 7.318
Schröer, F., 3.238
Schulte, F., 9.485
Schultz, Helga, 8.134
Schulze, W., 12.107-9; 12.116
Schumpeter, J. A., 9.4; 10.94
Schutte, Anne J., 1.55; 13.79; 14.195
Schuurman, A., 2.10
Schwartz, H., 13.306
Schwartz, Judith L., 14.435
Schwarz, K., 9.540
Schwarzmann, M., 3.105
Scott, F. D., 3.344; 5.523
Scott, H. M., 2.4
Scott, T., 4.93; 8.118, 122; 12.110, 125-6; 13.213
Scouloudi, Irene, 13.235
Scoville, W. C., 9.34, 517-18, 646, 670; 13.268-9

Scribner, R. W., 2.55; 12.112, 127-8; 13.95-6, 177-8, 182, 186, 200, 214-23
Sea, T. F., 12.129-30
Seaton, A., 5.660
Seebass, G., 13.224
Séguy, J., 13.307
Seibt, F., 3.285; 12.19
Sella, D., 3.170, 176; 9.88-9, 456, 473, 574, 612, 642
Sellin, J. T., 10.379
Senécal, Y., 1.64
Senior, Nancy, 5.446
Sennett, R., 14.29
Sentlaurens, J., 5.153
Sereni, E., 7.143-4
Sessions, K. C., 12.121, 131; 13.225
Seton-Watson, H., 3.379
Sewell, W. H., 6.26, 247
Sexauer, B., 7.283
Shafer, R. J., 10.126
Shaffer, J. W., 5.322
Shanahan, W. O., 10.126
Sharlin, A. N., 5.55-6; 8.23
Shaskolskii, I. P., 9.195
Shatz, M. S., 6.241
Shaw, D. J. B., 4.25; 8.175
Shaw, J. A., 3.34
Shaw, S. J., 3.300, 311, 318
Sheils, W. J., 13.22
Shennan, J. H., 3.41; 10.23, 312
Shephard, E. J., 9.528
Sheppard, T. F., 7.84
Sheridan, G., 6.247
Shinder, J., 10.349
Shore, M. F., 5.427
Shorter, E., 5.190, 262-5, 289, 322, 436, 486; 14.65
Shulman, N. E., 6.640
Shulvass, M. A., 5.622-3
Shumaker, W., 13.363
Shunkov, V. I., 3.357
Sica, P., 8.190
Sicroff, A., 5.569
Sieder, R., 5.318
Siegelbaum, L. H., 12.156
Silbert, A., 7.116
Silva, J. G. da, 3.104; 9.17, 72, 433; 11.74
Silverman, S., 14.84
Simonsohn, S., 5.624
Šindelář, B., 10.24
Singer, C. J., 9.519
Singerman, R., 5.553
Sivery, G., 7.90
Sjoberg, G., 8.6
Skelton, R. A., 4.102
Skendi, S., 13.101
Skocpol, Theda, 1.29
Skolnick, Arlene, 5.323
Skrubbeltrang, F., 7.251-2
Slack, P., 11.262

Slawinger, G., 9.486
Slicher van Bath, B. H., 3.68; 5.128-30; 7.20-2, 91, 276-7, 311
Sluiter, E., 9.276
Small, A. W., 10.134
Smirnov, I. I., 12.155
Smit, J. W., 12.5
Smith, A. G. R., 14.360
Smith, Catherine D., 4.11
Smith, C. T., 4.5
Smith, D., 1.45
Smith, D. G., 9.285
Smith, D. M., 3.206
Smith, D. S., 5.57
Smith, Lesley M., 2.78
Smith, R. E. F., 7.265-6, 330; 11.170; 14.105
Smith, R. S., 9.67, 311
Smith, W. D., 9.55
Smoller, Laura A., 14.92
Smolnar, F. J., 9.60
Snell, K. D. M., 9.445
Snyders, G., 14.173
Soboul, A., 2.104; 3.9, 42-3; 7.69, 70
Söderberg, J., 4.96; 11.98
Sogner, S., 5.236-7; 5.410; 7.253
Soininen, A. M., 7.327
Sol, E., 3.63
Solé, J., 5.266
Soliday, G. L., 5.294; 8.121
Solnon, J.-F., 6.13
Solomon, H. M., 11.222
Soltow, L., 6.40
Soly, H., 9.61; 10.378; 11.192
Soman, A., 10.380, 417; 13.382-3; 14.322
Sommer, J. L., 11.356
Sommer, Louise, 10.134
Sommerville, C. J., 5.437
Sonenscher, M., 9.439, 526, 529, 554, 668; 11.304
Soom, A., 9.196, 220, 352
Soriano, M., 14.66
Sothmann, Marlene, 11.257
Soubeyroux, J., 11.233
Souriac, R., 3.51
Souza, G. B., 9.334
Spading, K., 9.203
Spaggiari, P. L., 7.145
Spagnoli, P. G., 1.30
Spector, S. D., 3.310
Spencer, Barbara, 5.58
Spencer, Samia I., 5.498; 14.158
Spengler, J., 5.59
Sperling, J., 9.18
Spicciani, A., 11.246
Spiegel-Rösing, Ina, 14.354
Spierenburg, P., 5.366; 10.42, 381, 430
Spitz, L. W., 14.213
Spitzer, A. B., 5.424
Spooner, F. C., 9.414; 11.2, 36-7

Sporhan, L., 4.59
Sprinzak, E., 2.138
Sprunger, K. L., 13.62; 13.308
Spufford, P., 11.49
Spurlock, Janis, 10.116
Stadin, K., 5.517
Stahl, H. H., 7.229
Stalnaker, J. C., 13.226
Stanislawski, D., 4.17
Stankiewicz, W. J., 6.206
Stankiewicz, Z., 7.23
Stark, W., 7.206
Starobinski, J., 11.376
Stavrianos, L. S., 3.312
Stearns, Carol Z., 14.30
Stearns, P. N., 5.460; 14.30
Steckel, R. H., 11.168
Steensgaard, N., 2.78; 9.50, 234, 324; 110.18
Stein, R. L., 9.262, 360, 392-3
Steinberg, S. H., 3.239
Steinmetz, M., 3.228; 13.230
Stekl, H., 11.258
Stern, Selma, 5.627, 633-4
Stevens, Carol B., 10.538
Stevens, K. B., 14.100
Stevnsborg, H., 5.292
Stewart, Abigail, 5.438
Stewart, P., 10.222
Stinger, C. L., 8.107
Stock, Phyllis, 14.143
Stocker, C. W., 10.313-15
Stoianovich, T., 1.26, 28; 2.14; 3.313-14, 318; 5.408; 7.230; 9.126, 235
Stols, E., 9.263
Stone, B., 10.316
Stone, G., 5.661
Stone, L., 1.9, 18, 19; 5.427, 432; 14.106, 181, 204
Stoob, H., 8.113
Stow, K. R., 5.602
Strada, V., 12.151
Stradling, R. A., 3.123
Straube, M., 8.137
Strauss, G., 3.225, 229; 8.119, 133; 13.151, 227-8; 14.164, 199, 211-14, 333
Stretton, H., 1.66
Strieder, J., 9.110
Stromer, W. von, 4.59
Stroup, J., 13.152
Struck, W.-H., 12.132
Stuijvenberg, J. H. van, 2.139; 9.197
Stuke, H., 6.7
Stumpo, E., 6.139; 10.228
Sturdy, D. J., 6.101; 10.317
Sturgill, C. C., 10.203; 11.302, 319
Stürmer, M., 9.666
Subtelny, O., 6.198; 12.157
Sugar, P. F., 3.315-16; 7.231
Supple, B. E., 3.362; 9.19

Sussman, G. D., 5.447
Sutcliffe, A., 8.3; 9.451
Sutherland, D., 4.39
Sutherland, Gillian, 14.144
Svoronos, N. G., 9.257
Swain, Elizabeth, 5.380
Swanson, G. E., 13.179
Swanson, G. W., 10.453
Swart, K. W., 10.270
Swetschinski, D. M., 5.610
Symcox, G., 10.129
Szabo, F. J., 7.213
Szajkowski, Z., 5.608-9
Szeftel, M., 3.371
Szreter, R., 14.223

Tackett, T., 13.124-7
Tagliaferri, A., 6.139, 249; 8.111;
    11.247
Takahashi, K., 2.120
Talbott, J. E., 14.144
Tamse, C. A., 10.162; 13.272
Tanguy, J., 9.304, 555
Tannahill, Reay, 11.121
Tapié, V.-L., 3.265-6; 10.311
Tarrade, J., 9.273
Taveneaux, R., 13.56, 316
Taverne, E., 14.410
Tavernier, F. L., 8.45
Tawney, R. H., 2.111, 115
Taylor, Eva G. R., 4.121
Taylor, G. V., 6.27; 9.35-8
Taylor, H., 11.61
Taylor, P., 14.93
Tazbir, J., 3.280; 13.23, 399
Teall, Elizabeth, 6.102-3
Tedeschi, J. A., 10.332; 13.330
Teich, M., 9.514; 14.246
Teitler, G., 10.484
Tekeli, I., 8.156
Temple, Nora, 6.104; 10.204
Tenenti, A., 3.195; 14.119
Tenenti, Branislava, 9.434
Tennstedt, F., 10.147; 11.256
Tentler, T. N., 13.24
Thamer, H.-U., 9.541
Thane, Patricia, 9.451
Thelander, Dorothy R., 14.67
Thernstrom, S., 6.11
Thestrup, P., 5.238; 11.99
Thibodeau, K. F., 14.379
Thiriet, F., 8.183
Thirsk, Joan, 2.69; 5.324; 7.8
Thoen, E., 10.506
Thomas, K., 1.8; 14.31
Thomas, Marie A., 13.163-4
Thomas, R. P., 2.41
Thompson, D. G., 13.128-9
Thompson, I. A. A., 6.132-3; 10.330,
    443
Thompson, J. D., 11.280
Thomson, D., 8.197

Thomson, J. K. J., 9.465, 556
Thomson, S. H., 3.287
Thornton, P., 11.176
Throop, P. A., 1.48
Thrupp, Sylvia L., 13.83
Tikhonov, I. A., 7.264
Tilly, C., 1.19, 20, 26; 5.13, 61, 426;
    10.25; 11.122; 12.13, 20-1, 51-2
Tilly, Louise A., 5.267, 304, 325;
    12.21, 53
Tirat, J.-Y., 3.16; 4.71
Titone, V., 3.207
Tits-Dieuaide, Marie-J., 11.50
Toch, M., 6.253
Todorov, N., 6.36; 8.157
Tollison, R. D., 10.85
Tomasson, R. F., 5.239
Tompkins, S. R., 14.272
Tønnesson, K., 7.254
Topolski, J., 1.21; 3.261, 282-3;
    7.25, 202-3, 295
Topping, P., 3.292, 322; 12.22
Torke, H. J., 10.368
Torras, J., 7.117
Torre, A., 13.80
Toscani, X., 13.142
Touchard, H., 9.291
Toutain, J. C., 7.284
Tovrov, Jessica, 5.459
Tracy, J. D., 10.209; 11.142; 13.63
Traer, J. F., 5.358
Transue, Pamela J., 13.150
Trasselli, C., 10.447
Treadgold, D. D., 5.551
Treasure, P., 2.105
Treiman, D. J., 6.12
Tremel, F., 3.267
Trenard, L., 14.145, 254
Treue, W., 2.106; 3.249
Trevor-Roper, H. R., 1.37; 2.81-2;
    2.140; 13.364; 14.405
Trexler, Bernice J., 11.346
Trexler, R. C., 5.287, 450-1, 468;
    10.45; 11.248; 13.25, 81-2; 14.21
Tribe, K., 2.141
Trinkaus, C., 5.451
Trocmé, E., 9.299
Trout, A. P., 10.192; 11.320
Troyansky, D. G., 5.466
Truant, Cynthia M., 9.528, 530
Tucci, U., 9.90-1, 407; 11.75
Tulard, J., 6.64
Turnau, Irena, 9.607, 669; 11.177,
    187
Turner, R. S., 6.195; 14.215
Turpeinen, O., 5.240-1
Tveite, S., 5.215; 9.606
Tygielski, W., 6.205
Tyson, G. P., 14.403

Uhr, C. G., 1.58
Ulbricht, O., 11.259

Ulloa, M., 10.223; 11.62
Ultee, M., 13.130; 14.68
Unger, R. W., 4.53, 61; 9.197, 373,
    656-8
Unger, W.S., 9.198
Usher, A. P., 9.345, 510
Utterström, G., 4.38; 5.242-4;
    9.374; 10.154
Uytven, R. van, 3.79

Vacalopoulos, A. E., 3.323
Vaillé, E., 4.73
Valmary, P., 5.116
Van den Boogart, E., 9.396
Vandenbroeck, P., 14.403
Vandenbroeke, C., 9.442; 11.116,
    123, 143
Van der Made, R., 11.323
Van der Wee, H., 3.80-1; 7.285; 9.20,
    62, 197, 409, 560; 11.51
Van der Woude, A. M., 2.10;
    5.131-2, 367; 7.92
Van de Voort, J. P., 9.277
Van de Walle, E., 5.62, 117-18, 441
Van Doren, L. S., 10.205; 12.60
Vann, J. A., 3.246; 8.119; 10.148
Vann, R. T., 5.322, 426
Varela, Julia, 14.187
Varey, J. E., 14.394
Vartanian, A., 14.69
Vassberg, D. E., 5.448; 7.118-21
Vaussard, M., 3.171
Vázquez de Prada, V., 3.106; 9.72
Veinstein, G., 10.255
Veit, L. A., 13.97
Venard, M., 7.71; 11.217; 13.8, 131;
    14.172
Ventura, A., 6.169; 7.144
Venturi, F., 10.95, 130; 11.155
Verdon, M., 5.326
Vergani, R., 9.623
Verhulst, A., 7.93; 9.561
Verlinden, C., 4.122; 9.286; 11.52-3
Vernadsky, G., 3.374, 378; 7.267
Veyrassat, Béatrice, 9.577
Vicens Vives, J., 3.90, 107-9
Vickers, B., 13.368
Vidalenc, J., 9.311, 616; 10.493
Vieille, P., 8.45
Vierhaus, R., 3.243; 6.53
Vigarello, G., 11.281
Vigne, M., 9.410
Vigo, G., 10.227; 11.76
Viguerie, J. de, 13.57; 14.174
Vilar, P., 2.142; 3.124, 142-3; 7.313;
    11.18, 63
Vilar Berrogain, J., 10.127
Viles, P., 9.394
Villain, J., 10.206
Villani, P., 3.203
Villari, R., 3.158, 204; 12.91-4
Villas Tinoco, S., 9.535

Villette, P., 13.384
Vincent, B., 5.154, 590-1; 10.372
Vincent, Joan, 7.24
Viner, J., 10.96-7
Vinogradoff, E. D., 7.329
Visceglia, Maria A., 7.146
Vivanti, C., 3.168; 14.265
Vlasto, A. P., 10.159
Vogler, B., 8.18; 13.13, 153; 14.120, 216
Vogler, G., 12.133; 13.230
Vogt, J. L., 9.399
Vogt, W. P., 14.275
Volgyes, I., 7.204
Volker, R., 13.143
Voltes Bou, P., 8.71
Von Loewe, K., 7.268-9
Voort, J. P. van de, see Van de Voort
Vovelle, M., 3.60; 6.105; 8.41; 13.17, 58; 14.32, 70-1, 121-3, 175
Voyce, A., 8.177
Vries, J. de, see De Vries
Vrijhof, P. H., 13.16
Vryonis, S., 3.317
Vucinich, A., 14.381
Vucinich, W. S., 3.276, 293, 300, 318; 14.381

Waardenburg, J., 13.16
Waas, A., 12.134
Wachter, K. W., 5.63
Wagonheim, Sylvia S., 14.403
Wagstaff, J. M., 3.324; 4.88
Waite, G. K., 13.309
Wake, C. H. H., 9.358-9
Walker, D. P., 13.365-6
Walker, G. J., 9.265
Walker, M., 6.34; 8.119
Wall, R., 5.315, 327
Wallace-Hadrill, J. M., 10.40
Walle, E. van de, see Van de Walle
Wallerstein, I., 2.49, 50, 83; 3.68, 291
Wallon, A., 7.38
Walter, G., 7.72
Walters, R. G., 5.268
Wangermann, E., 3.268; 14.246
Waquet, J.-C., 10.46, 166, 318
Ward, A., 14.335
Ward, P. L., 1.11
Ward, W. R., 13.320
Waring, G. H., 12.135
Warmbrunn, P., 13.98
Warner, C. K., 7.311
Watts, S. J., 2.51
Waugh, D. C., 10.70
Wear, A., 11.326
Weary, W. A., 6.106
Weaver, Elissa, 14.395
Weaver, F. Ellen, 13.59
Webb, W. P., 4.123
Weber, E., 2.52; 14.33

Weber, W., 14.440
Weber-Kellermann, Ingeborg, 5.401
Webster, C., 11.330; 14.361
Wee, H. van der, see Van der Wee
Weeks, J., 1.53
Weenink, Hetty, 12.74
Wegert, K. H., 10.59
Wehler, H.-U., 3.211-12; 6.26; 12.136
Weickhardt, G. G., 10.369
Weinryb, B. D., 5.641-2
Weinstein, D., 13.26, 83
Weir, D. R., 5.64
Weis, E., 10.140
Weiss, Hildegard, 6.253
Weisser, M. R., 7.122, 289; 8.88; 10.382, 444
Weissman, R. F. E., 10.433, 436; 13.84
Weller, R. P., 12.52
Wells, R. V., 5.425
Wemyss, Alice, 13.270
Wensky, Margret, 5.509
Werner, E., 10.62
Werner, T. G., 9.627
Wesoly, K., 9.542
Wessely, K., 3.276
West, J. F., 3.353
Westermann, E., 7.340, 349; 9.628
Westfall, R. S., 14.362, 376
Westman, R. S., 14.363
Westrich, S. A., 12.68
Wettges, W., 13.229
Weulersse, G., 10.117
Weyrauch, E., 6.174; 8.7
Whaley, D. P., 13.99
Whaley, J., 14.124
Wheatley, P., 8.10
Wheaton, Barbara K., 11.140
Wheaton, R., 5.118, 304, 328, 359-60
White, H. V., 1.54
White, L., 14.34
Whittaker, C. R., 10.1
Whittlesey, D., 4.6
Wieczynski, J. L., 5.552
Wiener, J. M., 10.6
Wiese, H., 7.341
Wiesner, Merry E., 5.481, 510; 6.254; 9.113, 593; 11.353
Wiest, E., 9.487
Wightman, W. P. D., 14.364
Wigley, T. M. L., 4.39
Wiley, W. L., 6.107; 14.255
Wilkins, Kay S., 13.385; 14.72, 323
Wilkinson, R., 10.348
Willan, T. S., 9.199
Williams, A., 10.418-22
Williams, D., 8.79; 12.16
Williams, G., 4.124
Williams, G. H., 13.310
Williams, W. H., 13.132
Willigan, J. D., 5.65

Wills, J. E., 9.330
Wilson, A. M., 10.118
Wilson, C. H., 1.22; 2.15, 84; 3.82-3; 4.76; 5.191; 9.18, 41, 51, 547; 10.98-100, 210
Wilson, Francesca, 3.375
Wilson, S., 1.28; 5.439; 13.27; 14.125
Winchester, I., 5.66
Winius, G. D., 4.131; 9.266
Winkler, K., 7.189
Winter, J. M., 2.115; 12.72
Winter, W. L., 9.204
Winterhager, F., 12.111
Wirth, J., 13.28
Wischnitzer, M., 5.643; 9.521
Wittendorff, A., 4.83
Witthöft, H., 11.106
Wittkower, Margot, 14.406
Wittkower, R., 14.406
Wittman, T., 12.73
Woehlkens, E., 11.354
Wohlfeil, R., 12.137; 13.230
Wojcik, Z., 3.284
Wolf, E. R., 4.125; 7.157
Wolf, K., 9.594
Wolfe, M., 10.207
Wolff, I. R., 5.625
Wolff, P., 3.44-5; 8.8, 25, 28; 9.342
Woloch, I., 2.107; 3.6; 7.73
Wood, Diana, 13.22
Wood, J. B., 6.108-11; 10.498
Wood, Merry W., see Wiesner
Woodmansee, Martha, 14.336
Woolf, S. J., 3.172; 6.54, 154-5, 158; 7.14; 10.130; 11.195
Wootton, D., 13.29
Wren, M. C., 3.390
Wright, A. D., 10.448
Wright, L., 11.178
Wright, L. P., 6.134
Wright, W. E., 7.207
Wright, W. J., 11.260-1; 14.217
Wrightson, K., 5.440
Wrigley, E. A., 1.18; 5.67-9, 329; 6.251; 7.278; 8.26-7
Wrong, C. J., 10.499
Wunder, B., 10.342
Wunder, Heide, 7.190-2; 12.112, 127
Wyczanski, A., 7.25; 11.161
Wynot, E. D., 8.145
Wyntjes, Sherrin M., see Marshall
Wyrick, R., 5.126
Wyrobisz, A., 4.44; 8.146-7; 9.115, 629; 14.269

Yamey, B. S., 2.143
Yaney, G. L., 10.79
Yaresh, L., 12.158
Yinger, J. M., 13.180
Ylikangas, H., 10.456
Young, D., 14.147

Young, D. B., 4.52
Young, G. F. W., 3.110
Yun Casalilla, B., 12.80
Yver, J., 5.361

Zabinski, Z., 11.17
Zagorin, P., 12.23-5
Zak, J., 9.152
Zakythinos, D. A., 3.325
Zambelli, Paola, 1.56; 13.367
Zanetti, D. E., 6.153; 11.156
Zangheri, R., 7.147
Zaozerskaja, E. I., 9.608

Zeeuw, J. W. de, 4.54
Željazkova, Antonina L., 5.212; 13.102
Zeller, G., 9.466
Zeman, J. K., 13.311
Zguta, R., 13.400-2; 14.399
Zilfi, Madeline C., 13.160
Zimányi, Vera, 3.269
Zink, Anne, 7.85
Zins, H., 9.200; 12.138; 13.231
Zitomersky, J., 6.213
Zlatar, Z., 6.209; 9.256

Zonabend, Françoise, 5.362
Zophy, J. W., 3.213; 12.119
Zorn, J., 7.270
Zorn, W., 3.214; 9.114
Zschäbitz, G., 13.230, 312
Zschocke, A., 2.53
Zschunke, P., 13.100
Zumthor, P., 3.84
Zupko, R. E., 11.104-5
Zylberberg, M., 9.420
Zysberg, A., 10.423-6
Zytkowicz, L., 7.219, 232, 296-7